HISTORICAL TELEOLOGIES IN THE MODERN WORLD

Europe's Legacy in the Modern World

Series Editors: *Martti Koskenniemi and Bo Stråth (University of Helsinki, Finland)*

The nineteenth century is often described as Europe's century. This series aims to explore the truth of this claim. It views Europe as a global actor and offers insights into its role in ordering the world, creating community and providing welfare in the nineteenth century and beyond. Volumes in the series investigate tensions between the national and the global, welfare and warfare, property and poverty. They look at how notions like democracy, populism and totalitarianism came to be intertwined and how this legacy persists in the present-day world.

The series emphasizes the entanglements between the legal, the political and the economic and employs techniques and methodologies from the history of legal, political and economic thought, the history of events, and structural history. The result is a collection of works that shed new light on the role that Europe's intellectual history has played in the development of the modern world.

Published:
Historical Teleologies in the Modern World, edited by Henning Trüper, Dipesh Chakrabarty and Sanjay Subrahmanyam

Forthcoming:
Europe's Utopias of Peace, Bo Stråth
Political Reform in the Ottoman and Russian Empires, Adrian Brisku

HISTORICAL TELEOLOGIES IN THE MODERN WORLD

Edited by
Henning Trüper, Dipesh Chakrabarty and Sanjay Subrahmanyam

Bloomsbury Academic
An imprint of Bloomsbury Publishing Plc

B L O O M S B U R Y
LONDON • NEW DELHI • NEW YORK • SYDNEY

Bloomsbury Academic
An imprint of Bloomsbury Publishing Plc

50 Bedford Square	1385 Broadway
London	New York
WC1B 3DP	NY 10018
UK	USA

www.bloomsbury.com

BLOOMSBURY and the Diana logo are trademarks of Bloomsbury Publishing Plc

First published 2015

© Henning Trüper, Dipesh Chakrabarty, Sanjay Subrahmanyam and Contributors, 2015

All rights reserved. No part of this publication may be reproduced or transmitted in any form or by any means, electronic or mechanical, including photocopying, recording, or any information storage or retrieval system, without prior permission in writing from the publishers.

No responsibility for loss caused to any individual or organization acting on or refraining from action as a result of the material in this publication can be accepted by Bloomsbury or the authors.

British Library Cataloguing-in-Publication Data
A catalogue record for this book is available from the British Library.

ISBN: HB: 978-1-4742-2106-1
PB: 978-1-4742-2107-8
ePDF: 978-1-4742-2109-2
ePub: 978-1-4742-2108-5

Library of Congress Cataloging-in-Publication Data
Historical teleologies in the modern world / [edited by] Henning Trüper, Dipesh Chakrabarty and Sanjay Subrahmanyam.
  pages cm. — (Europe's legacy in the modern world)
  Includes bibliographical references and index.
  ISBN 978-1-4742-2106-1 (hardback) — ISBN 978-1-4742-2107-8 (paperback) — ISBN 978-1-4742-2109-2 (ePDF) — ISBN 978-1-4742-2108-5 (ePub) 1. History—Philosophy.
2. Historiography—Philosophy. 3. Teleology. 4. History, Modern—19th century.
5. History, Modern—20th century. 6. Intellectual life—History—19th century.
7. Intellectual life—History—20th century. I. Trüper, Henning. II. Chakrabarty, Dipesh.
III. Subrahmanyam, Sanjay.
  D16.9.H5325 2015
  901—dc23
  2014049151

Series: Europe's Legacy in the Modern World

Typeset by RefineCatch Limited, Bungay
Printed and bound in India

CONTENTS

List of Illustrations   vii
Notes on Contributors   viii
Preface   xi

Part I   Two Genealogies of Historical Teleology   1

1   Introduction: Teleology and History – Nineteenth-century Fortunes of an Enlightenment Project   *Henning Trüper with Dipesh Chakrabarty and Sanjay Subrahmanyam*   3

2   The Politics of Eschatology: A Short Reading of the Long View   *Sanjay Subrahmanyam*   25

Part II   Botched Vanishing Acts: On the Difficulties of Making Teleology Disappear   47

3   'The Vocation of Man' – 'Die Bestimmung des Menschen': A Teleological Concept of the German Enlightenment and its Aftermath in the Nineteenth Century   *Philip Ajouri*   49

4   Earth History and the Order of Society: William Buckland, the French Connection and the Conundrum of Teleology   *Marianne Sommer*   71

5   Against Darwin: Teleology in German Philosophical Anthropology   *Angus Nicholls*   89

Part III   Befriending Teleology: Writing Histories with Ends   115

6   Save Their Souls: Historical Teleology Goes to Sea in Nineteenth-century Europe   *Henning Trüper*   117

7   Reading History in Colonial India: Three Nineteenth-century Narratives and Their Teleologies   *Siddharth Satpathy*   143

Contents

8   A Gift of Providence: Destiny as National History in Colonial India   167
    Dipesh Chakrabarty

Part IV   Teleology in the Revolutionary *Polis*   187

9   The 'Democracy of Blood': The Colours of Racial Fusion in
    Nineteenth-century Spanish America   *Francisco A. Ortega*   189

10 Between Context and *Telos*: Reviewing the Structures of
    International Law   *Martti Koskenniemi*   213

11 Marxism and the Idea of Revolution: The Messianic Moment in Marx   235
    Etienne Balibar

Part V   Translating Futures: Eschatology, History and the Individual   251

12 Religious Teleologies, Modernity and Violence: The Case of
    John Brown   *Carola Dietze*   253

13 'But Was I Really Primed?': Gershom Scholem's Zionist Project   275
    Gabriel Piterberg

14 Catching Up With Oneself: Islam and the Representation of Humanity   301
    Faisal Devji

Part VI   Historical Futures without Direction?   321

15 Autonomy in History: Teleology in Nineteenth-century European
    Social and Political Thought   *Peter Wagner*   323

16 The Faces of Modernity: Crisis, *Kairos*, *Chronos* – Koselleck versus Hegel   339
    Bo Stråth

Index   363

ILLUSTRATIONS

9.1 Coat of arms of the Colombian Academy of History. Original design by Ricardo Moros Urbina (1904). Image reproduced with permission from the Academia Colombiana de Historia, Bogotá.   190

9.2 Emblem 'America', in Cesare Ripa, *Iconologia del cavaliere Cesare Ripa Perugino*. Originally published in 1603. Image taken from the edition published in Perugia, nella Stamperia di Piergiovanni Costantini, 1764–7. Vol. 4 out of 5 vols. Biblioteca Nacional de Colombia, RG 17066 V. 4. Image reproduced with the consent of the National Library.   191

9.3 Coat of arms, Province of Cartagena. Printed as the frontispiece to *Constitución del Estado de Cartagena de Indias: sancionada en 14 de junio de 1812, segundo de su independencia*. Cartagena de Indias: Imprenta de Diego Espinosa 1812. Biblioteca Nacional de Colombia. F. QUIJANO 153. Image reproduced with the consent of the National Library.   191

9.4 Seal accompanying the *Tratado sobre la regularización de la guerra concluído entre el Libertador Presidente de Colombia y el Jeneral en gefe del ejército español*, Angostura, Venezuela, 1820. Biblioteca Nacional de Colombia, F. PINEDA 808 FOL.9-11. Image reproduced with the consent of the National Library.   192

9.5 *Colección de Castas de Nueva España* by Mexican painter Ignacio María Barreda (1777). Oil on canvas, 77 × 49 cm (30.3 × 19.3 in). Archivo Histórico, Real Academia Española, Madrid. Image reproduced with the consent of the RAE.   194

NOTES ON CONTRIBUTORS

Philip Ajouri is currently a Fellow at the Research Association Marbach Weimar Wolfenbüttel (Deutsches Literaturarchiv Marbach). From 2005 to 2014 he worked as a lecturer at the Department of German Literature, Stuttgart University and at the Ludwig-Maximilians University Munich. His doctoral dissertation at the University of Munich (2005) was published by De Gruyter (*Erzählen nach Darwin. Die Krise der Teleologie im literarischen Realismus: Friedrich Theodor Vischer und Gottfried Keller*, 2007). He is a member of the editorial board of the *Zeitschrift für Ideengeschichte* and was a Humboldt Fellow at King's College London in 2010. His publications include *Literatur um 1900* (2009) and *Empirie in der Literaturwissenschaft* (2013), co-edited with Katja Mellmann and Christoph Rauen.

Etienne Balibar graduated at the Sorbonne in Paris, and later took his PhD at the University of Nijmegen (Netherlands). He is now Emeritus Professor of Philosophy at the University of Paris-Nanterre, and Anniversary Chair of Contemporary European Philosophy at Kingston University, London. He is author or co-author of *Reading Capital* (with Louis Althusser) (1965), *Race, Nation, Class: Ambiguous Identities* (Verso, 1991, with Immanuel Wallerstein), *Masses, Classes, Ideas* (Routledge, 1994), *The Philosophy of Marx* (Verso, 1995), *Spinoza and Politics* (Verso, 1998), *Politics and the Other Scene* (Verso, 2002), *We, the People of Europe? Reflections on Transnational Citizenship* (Princeton, 2004), *Identity and Difference: John Locke and the Invention of Consciousness* (Verso, 2013) and *Equaliberty. Political Essays* (Duke, 2014).

Dipesh Chakrabarty is the Lawrence A. Kimpton Distinguished Service Professor of History, South Asian Studies and Law at the University of Chicago, USA. He is the author of several books and articles including *Provincializing Europe: Postcolonial Thought and Historical Difference* (Princeton University Press, 2000; 2008).

Faisal Devji is Reader in Modern South Asian History and Fellow of St Antony's College at the University of Oxford. He is the author, most recently, of *Muslim Zion: Pakistan as a Political Idea* (Harvard, 2013).

Carola Dietze wrote her dissertation at the Max Planck Institute for History in Göttingen and then went on to work as a research fellow at the German Historical Institute in Washington DC and as an assistant professor at the Justus-Liebig-Universität Gießen. Currently, she is teaching as a professor of modern and contemporary history at the Ludwig-Maximilians-Universität Munich. She has published an intellectual biography on the philosopher and sociologist Helmuth Plessner under the title *Nachgeholtes Leben. Helmuth Plessner 1892–1985* (Göttingen, 2006), which received the Hedwig Hintze Award from the Association of German Historians. In her second book (forthcoming,

Hamburger Edition, 2015) she investigates the emergence of terrorism in nineteenth-century Europe, Russia and the United States.

Martti Koskenniemi is Academy Professor at the University of Helsinki and Director of the Erik Castrén Institute of International Law and Human Rights. He was a member of the Finnish diplomatic service from 1978 to 1994 and of the International Law Commission (UN) between 2002 and 2006. He is presently also teaching as Centennial Professor at the London School of Economics (LSE) and Professorial Fellow at the University of Melbourne. He is a fellow of the British Academy and has a doctorate h.c. from the Universities of Uppsala and Frankfurt. His main publications include *From Apology to Utopia: The Structure of International Legal Argument* (1989/2005), *The Gentle Civilizer of Nations: The Rise and Fall of International Law 1870–1960* (2001) and *The Politics of International Law* (2011). He is currently working on a history of international legal thought from the late medieval period to the nineteenth century.

Angus Nicholls teaches German and Comparative Literature and is Chair of the Department of Comparative Literature at Queen Mary University of London. His previous books include *Goethe's Concept of the Daemonic* (2006) and *Thinking the Unconscious: Nineteenth-Century German Thought* (2010, co-edited with Martin Liebscher). He is co-editor of *History of the Human Sciences* and of the *Publications of the English Goethe Society*.

Francisco A. Ortega is professor at the National University of Colombia and researcher with The Research Project Europe 1815–1914 at the University of Helsinki. He obtained his PhD from the University of Chicago (2001). He has been a visiting scholar at Harvard University (1995–9, 2000 and 2012), Stanford (2008) and at the Max Planck Institute, Frankfurt (2014). He has published essays focusing on social violence, history and memory and, more recently, on the political and intellectual culture of Spanish America. He is currently preparing a manuscript on the languages of social difference and the cultural, political and institutional challenges faced by early Spanish American republics during the late eighteenth and early nineteenth centuries.

Gabriel Piterberg is a professor of history and director of the G.E. von Grunebaum Center for Near East Studies at UCLA. He writes and teaches on the Ottoman Empire, settler colonialism, Zionism and Israel/Palestine. Among his publications are *An Ottoman Tragedy: History and Historiography at Play* (2003, Turkish translation 2005), *The Returns of Zionism: Myths, Politics and Scholarship in Israel* (2008) and 'The Literature of Settler Societies: Albert Camus, S. Yizhar and Amos Oz' (*Settler Colonial Studies*, 2011). He has also written for the *New Left Review* and *London Review of Books*.

Siddharth Satpathy earned a joint PhD in English Language and Literature and South Asian Languages and Civilization from the University of Chicago. He teaches in the Department of English, University of Hyderabad, India. He is presently working on a book-length study of the narratives produced by the English General Baptist Mission to Orissa in the nineteenth century. He is engaged in a second research project that aims to furnish a short history of the emergence of literature as an academic discipline in colonial Orissa. He is the author of *Bhima Bhoi: Prayers and Reflections*, an English translation of the spiritual autobiography of a nineteenth-century Oriya indigenous poet and religious leader.

Marianne Sommer is professor for *Kulturwissenschaften* at the Institute for Cultural and Science Studies of the University of Lucerne. Prior to her current position, she has been at the University of Zurich, ETH Zurich, Stanford University, Pennsylvania State University and the Max Planck Institute for the History of Science in Berlin. Her research and publications have focused on the cultural history of the life, earth and human sciences, with a particular interest in the human origins sciences. Her latest monograph represents a (pre)history of palaeoanthropology and related disciplines from c. 1800 to the present that is told along the lines of the biography of a particular fossil human skeleton (*Bones and Ochre*, Harvard University Press, 2007).

Bo Stråth was from 2007 to 2014 Finnish Academy Distinguished Professor of Nordic, European and World History and Director of Research at the University of Helsinki. Between 1997 and 2007 he was Professor of Contemporary History at the European University Institute in Florence, and from 1990 to 1996 Professor of History at the University of Gothenburg. His research has focused, often from a conceptual history perspective, on philosophy of history, and political, social and economic theory of modernity, with special attention to questions of what keeps societies together or divides them, of the ambiguities of modernity, and of how community is constructed.

Sanjay Subrahmanyam is Distinguished Professor of History and Irving & Jean Stone Chair in Social Sciences at UCLA. His recent publications include *Three Ways to be an Alien* (2011) and *Courtly Encounters* (2012).

Henning Trüper (PhD EUI Florence) is a post-doctoral researcher at the Ecole des Hautes Etudes en Sciences Sociales, Centre de Recherches Historiques, Paris and has previously been a researcher at the University of Zurich, IAS Princeton and Technische Universität Berlin. Among his recent publications are *Topography of a Method: François Louis Ganshof and the Writing of History* (Tübingen, 2014) and 'Löwith, Löwith's Heidegger, and the Unity of History', *History and Theory* 53 (2014), 45–68.

Peter Wagner is ICREA Research Professor at the University of Barcelona and currently Principal Investigator of the research project 'Trajectories of modernity: comparing non-European and European varieties', funded by the European Research Council. His recent publications include *Modernity: Understanding the Present* (Polity, 2012); *Modernity as Experience and Interpretation* (Polity, 2008) and the forthcoming *Sauver le progrès* (English version: *Progress: A Reconstruction*, 2015) as well as the co-edited volumes *The Greek Polis and the Invention of Democracy* (with Johann Arnason and Kurt Raaflaub, 2013) and *Varieties of World-making: Beyond Globalization* (with Nathalie Karagiannis, 2007).

PREFACE

This volume presents the results of a working group on historical teleologies that met on several occasions between 2010 and 2013. The theme we pursued was the simultaneous fragmentation and proliferation of teleological understandings of history – the notion that history had to be explained as a goal-directed process – in Europe and beyond throughout the nineteenth and into the twentieth century. In our understanding, historical teleologies have profoundly informed a variety of other fields, including modern philosophy, natural history, literature, philanthropism, revolutionary politics, European thought and practice in regard to colonialism and empire, the conceptualization of universal humankind, and the understanding of modernity in general. By exploring the extension and plurality of historical teleology, the essays in this volume seek to revise the history of historicity in the modern period. Our volume, *Historical Teleologies in the Modern World*, casts doubt on the idea that a single, if powerful, conception of a directional movement of peoples and societies over time could function as the unifying principle of all modern historicity; instead, the essays here seek to track the plurality of modern historicities and their underlying structures.

Our conversations took place within the framework of Bo Stråth's and Martti Koskenniemi's collaborative research project 'Europe 1815–1914: Between Restoration and Revolution, National Constitutions and Global Law, An Alternative View on the European Century'. This project, funded by the European Research Council, provided a most generous and congenial context in which to discuss our ideas, and we cannot thank Bo and Martti, as well as the participating researchers and administrative staff, enough for their prolonged engagement with and interest in our pursuits. The latter, as we moved from Berlin to Rome to Athens to Budapest to the Hambacher Schloss and to Lake Saimaa in Karelia, were often less goal-directed than the historical phenomena we discussed. The process of work on the topic for several years, however, made possible an uncommonly intense involvement with the shared themes and motifs, the subterranean linkages and subtle shades of historical teleologies, which we hope is recognizable in the volume. It was entirely through Bo's and Martti's and the ERC's generosity – and in the case of one meeting, also the generosity of the University of Zurich Research Priority Programme 'Asia and Europe' – that this sustained debate was possible. In publishing the present collection, we hope to open up this debate beyond the framework in which it has so far taken place.

Henning Trüper, Dipesh Chakrabarty, Sanjay Subrahmanyam
Berlin, Chicago, Los Angeles
November 2014

PART I
TWO GENEALOGIES OF HISTORICAL TELEOLOGY

CHAPTER 1
INTRODUCTION: TELEOLOGY AND HISTORY – NINETEENTH-CENTURY FORTUNES OF AN ENLIGHTENMENT PROJECT

Henning Trüper with Dipesh Chakrabarty and Sanjay Subrahmanyam

1. Teleology, the project

The word was a success. Invented by Christian Wolff in 1728, with Diderot's *Encyclopédie* and the philosophy of Kant as its most powerful transmitters, 'teleology' soon projected itself into the furthest corners of philosophical discourse. Wolff's placid definition held that we 'might call Teleology' that 'part of natural philosophy which explains the ends of things, and which thus far lacks a name, even if it is most ample and useful'.[1] Some two millennia after the Greek philosophers had begun to discuss the status of the explanation of something by reference to an end, goal, aim or purpose, the issue was antique. It had been overwritten by uncountable theoretical texts and traditions in various languages throughout the vast space of reception the Greek classics enjoyed. It was not, perhaps, so surprising that this palimpsest bore no definitive name when Wolff entered the scene. His seemingly minuscule intrusion into the philosophical mess of the final cause was grave in consequence, since by sleight of hand he temporalized it. As opposed to the dry technicality of the *causa finalis* or the *conatus* (inherent tendency or direction, a Leibnizian term), 'teleology' promised the *future* achievement of a well-ordered doctrine, a disciplined *logos* with a clearly and distinctly defined ambit, and a 'most ample and useful' application. In a word, teleology became a project. The very term expressed a conviction about what philosophy had so far failed to achieve but would, soon, amend. Even if the future course of the development of thought was not known in detail, the sense of direction was clear. In an oblique and imbalanced manner, Wolff coupled history and teleology. Crucially, teleology was to be self-reflective; it would ultimately include an account of itself since it was itself goal-directed. In this way, history, too, would comprise its own explanation.

Wolff's project was to have a tremendous career, but only as a project, not as an accomplishment. The promise of teleology, in combination with the obscurity that shrouded the possible paths towards its realization, generated a great variety of novel theoretical efforts that were grafted on to the older tradition of the final cause. These efforts always failed. Still, they paved one of the most important inroads for the novel conceptions of historicity that emerged in the late Enlightenment. Throughout the nineteenth century, far into the twentieth, and arguably until today, the heritage of this tradition has, if in ever more fragmented and transformed ways, continued to be passed on. Although its death certificates have piled up, teleology's demises were never more than local. Through its multiple uses in the modern European 'regime of historicity'[2] – the internally diverse and not necessarily coherent ensemble of language games and cultural practices constituting various understandings of what it meant to be historical – after 1800, teleology became a future that did not pass. It is this phenomenon that stands at the centre of the volume introduced here.

2. Bastard physics

The question of ends was a traditional component of physics, where it had been placed by Aristotle himself in his discussion of the four different kinds of causation.[3] The underlying reason for the presence of this question in physics was to be found in Greek mathematical thought. In Plato's theory of ideas, geometrical figures had acquired exemplary status for the immutable ideas or forms behind the contingent and ever-fleeting objects in perceived reality. In Aristotle's view, this left open the problem of how to account for the mutability of physical reality.[4] It was the inability of Greek mathematics to represent movement or change (*kinesis*) that constituted the distinction between mathematics and physics in Aristotle's work; it was the problem of movement that the *causa finalis* was first meant to overcome. The projection of a given object towards its form, which ultimately coincided with the object's *telos*,[5] was to be its highest-ranking explanation since it marked the transition from mere potentiality to the actualization of form. Entelechy, the immanence of the pursuit of form in nature (*phusis* – defined as 'that which can be in motion'),[6] became the foremost specialized 'teleological' doctrine in philosophy.

When Wolff entered the fray, his intention was to reconcile explanation by reference to the pursuit of ends with explanation by reference to efficient causes.[7] The protagonists of the so-called 'scientific revolution' had almost unanimously dismissed the *causa finalis* as, in Francis Bacon's words, a 'barren virgin', devoted to God in the pursuit of the inbuilt purposes of all creatures in creation, but unproductive of any such knowledge of nature that would be capable of begetting further knowledge.[8] There was no future in the knowledge of *tele*. Baconian, Hobbesian, Cartesian and Spinozist philosophies all focused on the competing notion of a comprehensive and total 'chain' of efficient, 'mechanical' causes in order to eliminate any space for teleological explanation outside – possibly – the domain of intentional human (or divine) action. Yet, the notion of the world as mechanism seemed to fall short of explaining numerous phenomena, and it laid claim to a kind of universality that was difficult to bear out. Most prominently, as Wolff believed, mechanism failed to answer the question of how mind was able to produce any effect on matter. The mechanists, he charged, had to posit a *qualitas obscura*, an inexplicable *explanans*, on at least one side of the Cartesian abyss between matter – understood as extended, inert and solid – and consciousness. More precisely, since consciousness seemed rather obviously capable of anticipation and directedness, for the anti-mechanists it was clear that the modification had to take place in the concept of matter. Wolff, for instance, proposed adding what he labelled a specific 'moving force' (*vis motrix*) to the understanding of matter.[9]

Wolff's embrace of teleology was in part motivated by English physico-theology that sought out the evidence for God's creative agency in the purposefulness of nature. That the translatability into theological concerns had to remain assured was almost taken for granted by philosophers on both sides of the divide over mechanism. Much has been made of the enlightened philosophies of history as a symptom, or a cause, of the secularization of Christian eschatology.[10] However one assesses the plausibility of this hypothesis, the marginality of classical Augustinian eschatology – be it to be opposed, be it to be corroborated as a narrative scheme – in the actual text of the philosophies of history is salient. Interferences between historical and eschatological discourse appear far more prominent and efficacious in the nineteenth and twentieth centuries; and they appear to already presuppose the vocabulary of historical teleology.

By contrast, the force of the conceptual debate in physics has often been, but ought not to be, underestimated.[11] It was this debate that provided the plot; theology was already reduced to acting as *deus ex machina* providing a forced resolution if the action otherwise failed to achieve closure. Arguably, physico-theology remained a bystander, as is illustrated by the dynamics of the Wolffian argument. Wolff's concerns were expressed through an appropriation of Leibnizian ideas, the reception of which over the course of the eighteenth century, owing to the erratic posthumous publication of several of his most important works, was a convoluted affair. It seems clear that his development of the infinitesimal calculus (simultaneous to Newton's) persuaded Leibniz to posit the existence of unextended, and therefore unqualified, atomic substances. In order to justify assuming the plurality and distinctness of such substances, and also in order to explain the possibility of movement and to legitimize perception of substances as moving, Leibniz concluded that those substances, 'monads', had to be directional. They had inherent goals that they realized in an entelechic manner.[12] Strikingly, Aristotle's mode of argument reasserted itself: the directional principle of the monad coincided with the distinction between potentiality and actualization. The multitude of the actualizations of a monadic form across time was both its movement and direction. Leibniz thus introduced a novel notion of substance into natural philosophy, a substance that was 'dynamic' and combined in itself the possibility of both mechanist and teleological explanation.[13] The momentum of creating novel conceptions of ontology fed above all on the relation between mathematics and physics, even though Leibniz's monadology also was a theological doctrine.

In the subsequent decades, cognate programmes of re-conceptualizing substance spread through European metaphysics, engendering – across emerging disciplinary fields such as chemistry and biology – a cascade of different conceptions of matter as imbued with a variety of natural forces and immanent directions.[14] At the same time, in the distant field of historical studies, the traditional *ars historica*, the moral-educational paradigm of history as life's *magistra*, was collapsing.[15] An opening emerged for new notions and approaches of historical writing. Into this opening intruded the new idiom that metaphysics and natural philosophy produced for the purpose of analysing natural reality. Still, this intrusion was not obvious and direct. Rather, it occurred by way of a bastardization that transported the ontological vocabulary of physics into the transforming field of history by way of political philosophy.

Certainly, the convergence of natural and political philosophy in the eighteenth century is not a novel discovery. Various interwar period theorists, for instance, already agreed that the mediation of nature and politics had been an indispensable driving force behind the emergence of the famed, and defamed, philosophies of history of the Enlightenment.[16] However, the eighteenth-century pioneers of philosophy of history in France, most notably Voltaire and, in his wake, Turgot, d'Alembert and Condorcet, all sided with the mechanists. As Voltaire had it, physics was to provide the epistemological model for a renewed understanding of history.[17] Until at least the 1770s, the Prussian debate, with its outright (and controversial) discussion of teleology, remained a curiosity at best. Mechanist physics, by contrast, continued priding itself for having struck down the naivety of physico-theology and conquered one of the most important bastions of religious 'prejudice'. History was to serve for the identification of the psychological laws that governed the making of human-constructed, civilizational, social and political reality. The essence of humankind, reason, was considered exempt from historical change; yet, this essence still had to realize itself over the course of history by overcoming culturally established impediments and shedding prejudice, in particular as regarding the political organization of humans *qua* social and communicative animals. History thus was conceived as a progressive process of the increasing perfection of humankind, a process over the course of which reason became transparent to itself.[18]

Among the Scottish philosopher-historians – who with the French and the Germans form the classical triangle of enlightened philosophies of history – the basic constellation was subtly different, yet led to rather similar results. Responding to a Humean understanding of causality, which undercut the epistemological trust in the recognizability of mechanist causal laws, the Scots nonetheless arrived at a conception of the new manner of writing history as 'natural history', which was both empirical and conjectural and endowed with a notion of gradual civilizational progress as its underlying principle.[19] Like the French debate, however, the Scottish one belaboured the problem of reconciling actual history with contractualist accounts of the genesis of the political commonwealth. On both sides, in spite of the overall mechanist physics, formulations of progress adopted traditional features of the self-realization of form in the inherent teleology of given entities or kinds. As political thinkers whose discourse was framed by a conceptual tradition, the power of which matched that of natural philosophy, the enlightened philosophers overwhelmingly relied on variations of the Aristotelian formulation of human nature in terms of a *zoon politikon* that as such had to be a *zoon logon echon* and realized its form or *telos* in the organization of the rationally instituted *polis*.[20] The Aristotelian heritage had been fragmented across different traditions. Into some enlightened reconceptualizations of history, teleology was inserted, not by means of an outright embrace of Aristotelian – let alone Wolffian – physics, but through a seemingly minimal opening within a specific problematic in political philosophy. Preserving the linkage between human nature and politics meant that anthropology, though part of natural reality and thus of natural philosophy, defied reduction to mechanism. Nonetheless, teleology remained a rudimentary theoretical idiom in these philosophies of history.

3. Manifold teleology

In spite of its initial marginality, it fell to the Prussian debate, and more precisely the Kantian critical project, to recognize the bastard child *de jure* and bring historical teleology into its own. Above all, this meant the multiplication of teleology as a product of the proliferation of teleological argument, especially in Kantian philosophy and its aftermath. Kant's most momentous contribution to the vocabulary of natural philosophy was arguably his explication of the meaning of 'organism' in terms of a whole as consisting of parts that were to be understood by way of their inherent purposes for the functioning of the other parts as well as the whole.[21] Organic reality thus required a set of purposive explanatory means categorically different from the efficient causes that alone were admitted in the mechanical nexus of causality. At the same time, teleology became constitutive, through the powerful vitalist metaphor of the organism, of a novel idea of self-organizing complexity. It is hardly necessary to point to the tremendously important history of 'organicist' perspectives in the nineteenth and twentieth centuries.[22]

In the *Critique of Judgment*, inherent finality was a necessary assumption in order to explain the very possibility of both theoretical and practical reason, and their unity. The decisive passage, in the introduction to the *Critique*, in which Kant stages the overarching understanding of a 'principle of purposiveness in nature' as a condition of possibility of theoretical knowledge, teems with references to mechanism and the problem of explaining change in the realm of physical bodies. Kant observes that such explanation relies on a set of principles – such as the variant of Ockham's razor Kant labelled *lex parsimoniae*: 'nature takes the shortest way' – which are underdetermined by reality as empirically given, including the production of knowledge itself, to the extent it can be empirically – psychologically – observed. Such principles indicate the unity of experience, which is a necessary prerequisite of the very notion of reason. Hence, they require a non-empirical, transcendental demonstration. Kant goes on to argue that this demonstration can only be sought in the principle that nature itself is purposively structured in such a fashion as to be amenable to our understanding. It is thus the very intelligibility of natural reality that constitutes its teleological character.[23] One might easily be tempted to conclude that it is the progressive understanding of this reality that constitutes the realization of its inherent *telos*. This would be a remarkable way of re-interpreting and nullifying the Wolffian project of teleology as a specific field. On the one hand, Kant offers a rule by the application of which any given natural object can be regarded as teleological; on the other hand, the very same rule would deprive teleology of any meaningful limits vis-à-vis other areas of knowledge. Yet Kant's barrage of carefully staked-off concepts for the distinct 'faculties' of the mind – most importantly sensibility, imagination, understanding, reason and judgement – prohibits such an escalation of teleology-as-intelligibility.[24]

At the same time, teleology-as-intelligibility might have offered Kant a most peculiar entrance into a teleological understanding of history as coinciding with the progress of understanding. Once again, the complexity of theoretical reason in the Kantian system prohibited such a move. Crucially, Kant's actual works on the philosophy of history rely on a structurally more intricate argument that draws especially on political philosophy in order to make its case. His *Idea for a Universal History with a Cosmopolitan Purpose* (1784) sets out an argument in terms of human nature and its entelechic development in the species (as opposed to the mere individual), as forming societies capable of the type of antagonism that ultimately brings forth the historical development of law-governed political systems. Kant is far from embracing an optimistic notion regarding the possibility of building something 'straight' from the 'crooked wood' of humanity. Indeed, his scepticism as to the validity of his own argument is so great that he requires history to yield merely the symptoms of a progress that will forever be too chaotic and manifold to be known in its entirety. Indeed, history is not intelligible in the same way as is nature. Its teleology requires a semiotic procedure that identifies the mere signs of the underlying 'plan of nature'. In the *Contest of Faculties* (1798), Kant developed further this notion of history as a provider of signs. In his eyes, it was the French Revolution, not in its practical realization, but in the mere impact on the way of thinking of its actors as well as its spectators, the mere *interest* it aroused in humanity, that was the privileged sign of the moral capacities of humanity as a whole, and of their progressive realization.[25]

The semiotic understanding of history ingeniously avoided the problems that beset the theory of historical knowledge, and which had been discussed, under the heading of 'Pyrrhonism', throughout post-Cartesian scholarship. Kant presented not an epistemological but an ontological argument, about the material of which history consisted. This material was none other than humanity as a whole, universally. His argument was so structured as to forbid any fragmented conception of this material, regardless of the concession that history's empirical intelligibility was limited to mere episodes. History was one and only one, it was ontologically unified, and it derived its unity from that of humanity, and more precisely human reason as constituted by 'judgement'. This unity – which might have contributed to the growing preponderance of the usage of 'history' in the singular in several European languages[26] – was achieved by means of the teleological conception of human nature. Ultimately, the basic foundations of historical ontology were laid in the complex idiom of late Enlightenment physics and anthropology, which nonetheless had undergone so many reformulations and such a degree of separation from its origins that it had become barely recognizable.

Kant's argument heavily stressed the self-reflective character of history as the prerequisite of future progress. The only way of sustaining an argument about the historical future, he claimed in the *Contest of Faculties*, was if that future was to be produced by those who made the prediction.[27] Therefore, any perspective on a historical future required notions of agency; and an optimistic perspective had to include a notion of future human self-empowerment of which the very act of thinking about the historical future had to be part. In the Kantian system, freedom and morality coincided. In this way, and in this way only, philosophy was able to have a moral-historical 'chiliasm of its own', as Kant had already put it in the *Idea for a Universal History*.[28] The idea of progress that became palpable in this context thus ultimately coincided with such visions that regarded the historical future as finite. In twentieth-century philosophies of history, much has been made, especially with reference to Darwinian evolution, of the opposition of limited progress, towards a determinate end, and unlimited progress into an open but unending future.[29] In such discussions, teleology has often been taken to reside only on the former side, the 'chiliastic' one that was built on some notion of redemption at the end of history. Yet, the Kantian argument collapsed both sides into one with the sole help of the concept of 'freedom', and by contrasting the notion of progress 'towards the better' with that of an open-ended processuality where there is no stable criterion of improvement. In Kant's eyes, the very idea of improvement required finality, even where the end can only be approximated in a process of indefinite duration.

Arguably, the most influential teleological philosophy of history of the period after 1800 was that of Hegel.[30] In his conception, which was heavily, but not perhaps obviously, indebted to the Kantian, history was progress towards, and the realization of, freedom. This progress was to take place in the form of the objectivation of reason, the workings of the 'spirit' in time, its tireless labour, in the sequence of nations, to give itself form and in this way to know itself. Hegel's teleology of history was periodic. It was conceived of as realizing forms that were then absorbed into 'higher' processes of objectivation. He, too, rejected the notion that there might be no ultimate purpose to the historical process; in his view, this purpose was constituted by the rule of law in the state, which was to mediate the individuals' claims to freedom with the idea of freedom – the universal and final *polis*. The state of law expressed the most complete self-understanding of the spirit, as a productive, self-objectivizing agency in the world; it realized freedom in the form of the maximal ability to act, the maximally attainable extent of (subjective as well as generalized) agency.

The production of knowledge about history was part of this historical process of the achievement, on the part of human reason, of self-knowledge (though the knowledge of history did not suffice for a full self-understanding of humanity). This was so because the process in question was supposed to be unified and singular; all the diverse histories one grasped when expanding the knowledge about the past formed an interconnected whole. If humanity made progress in its understanding of history, it could be certain that history as a whole progressed. Thus, the scholarly work towards the understanding of history was at least co-constitutive of the teleological character of the historical process as a whole. In a circular structure between the epistemic and the ontological side of the argument, history was always a process of making itself understood. Hegel had abandoned the finely adjusted systematic distinctions between the different kinds of understanding that had prevented, in the architecture of Kantian critique, the equalizability of the various faculties. By contrast, Hegel established a more confident and more absolute version of the Kantian argument: history was teleological progress towards freedom precisely to the extent that it understood itself; and in the very effort to understand itself, it made itself into an intelligible object.

At first glance, the Hegelian reading deprived teleology of the conceptual multiplicity that the Kantian project had borne out. Instead, it universalized history and turned it into the source of teleology. In this way, one might argue, the Hegelian argument established historical teleology autonomously, independently of the traditional debates of physics. Yet, this notion would be mistaken. Hegel embraced a philosophy of nature in which, in particular, chemistry was deployed as a field constituted not merely by mechanical causality, but also by the teleological directedness inherent in different kinds of matter as orientated towards, or against, their polar opposites.[31] Hence, the systematic place of teleology was in ontology and required physics. Yet, historical teleology derived at least in part from epistemological givens that were to be integrated with physics by Hegel's tremendous systematic apparatus. Whether or not this apparatus was functional, and thus able to keep the promise of a theoretical integration of all teleology under one principle, perhaps remains up for debate. In terms of the reception of Hegel's philosophy of history specifically, the systematic aspect was lost. Unintentionally in keeping with Kant's reservations, Hegelian philosophies corroborated the fragmentation of teleology. The mere notion of explanation by goal-directedness, the erstwhile conceptual core of the Aristotelian final cause, drastically underdetermined the theoretical variations and their incongruences as they had emerged until 1830.

4. The nature of history

Debates in the eighteenth century arrived at novel conceptions of, and about, historicity with hectic frequency. Aesthetics, as a result of the impasses incurred in the imitation of the model of idealized classical antiquity, provided a major discourse of the novelty and autonomy of modernity. Antiquarianism, expanding into ever more far-flung European and non-European funds of remnants of the past, created a vast body of empirical knowledge that subjected the cultural imagination, and the scholarly exploration, of history to constant transformation. Philology, as it deconstructed and reconstructed the ancient textual heritage, overturned everything from the trustworthiness of the sources themselves to the positive knowledge about, and the normative status of, ancient history. The philology of the Old Testament contributed considerably to purging history of the agency of the deity, thus mirroring the physical project of purging nature from the same type of agency. The political events of the period itself, above all the American, French and – as is increasingly recognized – Haitian revolutions, have often been credited with introducing a new sense of historical-political change and instability among the populaces of Europe and those under European influence abroad. Legal theories staged one of the most powerful teleological conceptions of historical change towards the perfection of national constitutions and international law. Adam Smith, in his economic work, introduced one of the key teleological tropes of the novel philosophies of history: the notion of the 'invisible hand' of the marketplace, to which Kant's

Naturabsicht and Hegel's 'cunning of reason' were mere responses. Malthusian economists invented their own genre of a socio-economic philosophy of history, often with a pessimist bent and a resulting tendency to the design of projects in the politics of population. The enlightened campaign against religious 'prejudice' discredited traditional eschatological understandings of world history, while the reception of the chronologies of Ancient China, and later Egypt, India and Babylon, and the work that historians of nature, in the wake of Buffon, conducted on the presumptive age of the planet, eroded whatever hope had been left for the preservation of biblical chronology.

There have been numerous attempts at subsuming these, and further, entrances into the plural, at most compound, regime of modern historicity under a single overriding and synthesizing principle that would ensure at least the regime's genetic unity. Some prominent attempts of this kind have been the secularization thesis; the proposal to regard modern historicity as a function of the experience of comprehensive change in the late eighteenth century;[32] and the great variety of arguments that granted primacy to aesthetics.[33] Arguably, the constructions of the history of historicity thus advanced have all proven to be empirically too narrow. Among the passages into modern historicity that have remained relatively, and unduly, neglected is the one from natural philosophy or physics. Unduly neglected, for physics supplied a foundational ontological vocabulary concerning time and space, change and duration, object and event, unity and difference, direction and repetition, agency, causation and efficaciousness.

This vocabulary has been almost self-evident for all European and Europeanized historical discourse after 1800. At the same time, due to its chequered internal history and the multiplicity of its formulations and systemic deployments, for which teleology is the most striking example, the vocabulary was in effect fragmented. It remained merely a vocabulary and did not end up forming a coherent system comparable to a theory of the components of historical reality that would have matched modern theories of physical reality. Accordingly, the passage into modern historicity from anti-mechanist eighteenth-century physics does not make any contribution to establishing the genetic unity of the regime of historicity. In general, the physical ancestry of modern historicity makes it improbable that a unified regime over such a disorderly discourse could be constructed by some sort of contractual fiat, be it in the *de facto* convention of collective practice or the *de jure* convention of a fictitious constitutional assembly of historical thought. This probably explains why the passage from physics to history has not appeared an attractive object of study to many of those scholars who sought a unified explanation of modern historicity as a unified phenomenon.

At the same time, this situation is also why it is worth dwelling on the periodic returns, and the ensuing multiplication, of that enlightened project, teleology: it provides privileged access to the physical-ontological vocabulary in question. To be sure, teleology did not constitute this vocabulary. Yet, as a result of the work philosophers invested, contingently, into the pursuit of the final cause, the project of teleology was enabled to communicate with all of the fragmentary components of the vocabulary. It was possible, for historical writing in the nineteenth century, to avoid teleology and still deploy the vocabulary commonly used for historical reality. However, owing to the dazzling multitude of ways in which teleology could figure in the overall discourse, it was *difficult* to avoid. For the same reason, the question of whether or not a specific body of textual evidence contains teleological notions is usually an intricate affair.

The teleologies of intelligibility and understanding, organicism, progress, political freedom and statehood, historical knowledge as self-knowledge, and optimistic finality provided a widely extended aggregate of low-level theoretical tools. Teleologies provided not only notions of direction and finality that were eminently usable in the construction of accounts of history. Teleologies also lent unity to the objects and events on which they were imposed. As a result of this mode of operation, historical teleologies were among the key vehicles of the formulation of universalist understandings of humankind in the eighteenth and nineteenth centuries as they offered unification in time to the species at large. Moreover, teleologies provided schemes of the ascription of intentional change effected on the part of some agency; and they provided schemes of complex organization effecting unintended change. Also, since they could be applied both to very large ranges of objects and to small-scale individual objects (including persons), teleologies constituted a highly functional resource for the movement between different scales of historical representation. Similarly, as needed, they set apart or connected the social and natural worlds. Teleologies could serve for constituting an individual object as well as for integrating such an object into a larger systematic or directional unit. Finally, teleology was constitutive of a kind of temporality apart as determined by ends and directionality. Much attention has rightly been invested in the study of historical futures as constituted by the teleologies of past project-making. However, teleology was more technical an instrument; and it did not depend on temporality as pre-given by, for instance, the phenomenal experience of time.[34] Teleological directionality was not bound to the future. Ends of history could just as well be located in the present or, in the form of the target of an envisaged return or merely a vague nostalgia, in the past. Moreover, if temporality is to be regarded as a cultural product – that is to say, at least co-constituted by practical and discursive devices as developed in and among social groups – temporality is capable of being plural. The plurality of teleology may then count among the ways in which such plural temporality is produced.

As demonstrated by this diversity of deployments, at the unravelling of the Enlightenment, the theoretical compound of teleology evolved into an indispensable component of historical writing as a *techné*. Ironically, the *nature* of history – its ontology, the range of kinds of objects and individuals it comprised, or excluded – was a technical product. The ontology of history constituted a kind of reality that was entwined with its being the target of an epistemic pursuit that, confusingly, was also named 'history'.[35] This pursuit was a matter not only of a philosophical discourse, but also of a broader practice of historical writing. Teleology was a theoretical device as well as part of the sheer craftsmanship that went into the constitution and the maintenance of the various sections, or variants, of modern historicity. A considerable part of this work was a matter of actual writing. Discussing teleology in the abstract forms of theoretical ideas is useful for a variety of purposes but tends to ignore the fact that teleologies were mostly crafted in the form of written text. Historical writing unfolded over a variety of genres and was assembled not only in the academic, but also in other societal contexts. Moreover, the limits between historical and fictional literature, while certainly present, were not impermeable. Fiction, too, comprised a discourse on teleology, which translated into far-reaching changes in the patterns of narration. The requirements of narrative closure began to appear as a burden in specific ways, in the nineteenth century, and found themselves transformed, perverted or rejected, in multiple ways.[36] Teleology constituted a poetics, and this poetics, however indirectly, also communicated with other than fictional forms and genres of writing.

Historicity and narrative schemes, as marked by the technical device of teleology, were also intimately connected to the sphere of the political as it was reconfigured throughout the tremendous processes of political mobilization that swept Europe and its colonial universe over the course of the nineteenth century. It is hardly surprising that several of those of the era's philosophers who put forward teleological conceptions of history, notably Saint-Simon and Comte, and Marx and Engels, but also somewhat lesser known figures such as Henry Maine, pursued wide-ranging and ambitious political projects. The intimacy between historicity and the political field can be observed across the constitutionalisms, the state and society-building projects, the emancipatory movements, and the imperial and anti-imperial struggles of the period, Hobsbawm's *Age of Revolution* and its aftermath. Historicization – the assignment, to some carrier, of a specific meaning within the framework of history as established through historical writing, practical commemoration and other media of representation – was and remains one of the most important resources for deciding whether something was, or was not, political. The historicization of the present developed into an ongoing and ubiquitous practice. This practice involved an ever-expanding application of inclusion and exclusion, of historicity granted and historicity denied. Yet, if historicity was plural, it was also capable of informing the political in multiple ways. This is one of the furthest-reaching issues at stake in the examination the volume intends to carry out.

5. Revisiting the history of historicity

To recap, the volume this chapter announces seeks to explore that enlightened project, teleology in its complicated combination with history, across its fragmentation and multiplication in the nineteenth century. This exploration requires coverage of multiple concrete contexts (completeness is, needless to say, unattainable) as located in a variety of broader areas – especially theoretical discourse, textuality, ontology and epistemic *techné*, and political thought and practice – in which historical teleologies manifested themselves. Neither purely a history of ideas, nor purely a history of literary or political culture, the methodological make-up of the volume will be hybrid, and by necessity so.

The broader aim is to advance a revision of the history of historicity in the nineteenth century. In Walter Benjamin's view, in the period after 1800, the philosophies of history and the practice of historical writing colluded in the creation of a 'homogenous and empty time'[37] as coinciding with linear and secular physical time, to be understood as a unified and universal frame of meaning for the experience of the world and the determination of the politically possible. This and cognate views of historical time, for the most part dating from the interwar period, continue to exert great influence on the understanding of European modernity as achieved in the nineteenth century. The correlated assumption that the modern regime of historicity possessed genealogical as well as constitutional unity continues to be widely held. Benjamin's formulation is easily recognizable as alluding to a conception of time and space usually addressed as Newtonian in the philosophy of the period. However, as sketched out in the preceding pages, the history of philosophical physics and its impact on the reconfiguration of historical writing in the late eighteenth century suggests that an equation of modern notions of historical time with Newtonian physics is imprecise. To be sure, much late-nineteenth and twentieth-century historical writing reproduced the 'homogenous and empty' temporality Benjamin attacked. Still, as a result of the considerations pursued in this introduction, the very idea that a single, however powerful, conception of time could function as the unifying principle of all modern historicity is cast in doubt. Our volume intends to expand on this doubt.

Some indispensable resources for this pursuit derive from the philosophy of history of the interwar period, which has in many respects been foundational for much of the discussion in the decades following the Second World War. Interwar period attacks on the unity of historicity – as in particular represented by nineteenth-century beliefs in progress and continuous betterment – appear remarkably concerted from today's perspective. In Heidegger's *Sein und Zeit*, for instance, a primary, existential historicity is derived from the anticipation of death and opposed to a second, mindless and dissipated historicity of the many. Thus, at least a duality of historicities is entailed.[38] Benjamin saw in 'historicism' the key to understanding the self-defeating embrace of progressivism by social democracy; the destruction of this vacuous historical time, as prefigured in earlier notions of messianic advent, was the *sine qua non* of revolution. Heidegger's and Benjamin's philosophies marked extremes of the political as well as the philosophical spectrum; and yet, their conceptions of historicity shared decisive features. The emphasis on 'historicism' as an agent of alienation required historicity in the nineteenth century to have constituted, or at least reconfigured, the modern historical consciousness in the singular. Characteristically, in both conceptions, the unity of history was to be exploded by an intervention that was envisaged in teleological terms, even if it did not theorize itself in this traditional philosophical vocabulary.

In Benjamin's conception, it is clear that the revolutionary moment, which he also described as a 'tiger's leap', was meant to be goal-directed at least in its destructive intention that targeted the all-unifying teleology of civilizational progress. If this reading is correct, Benjamin deployed one teleology against another. The references to messianic time scattered over the first half of *On the Concept of History* and the much-cited parable of the enlightened fake chess automaton also point in this direction: the insufficiency of mechanism and 'Newtonian' time. The chess automaton only worked because it was controlled by an undersized human player hidden inside. In the same way, in the reformed historical materialism Benjamin sought to formulate, historicity would secretly be governed by a concealed theology. Only intentional, directed disruption promised an escape from the historical future of modernity.

In *Sein und Zeit*, too, diluted teleological motives configured the duality of historicities. The distinction of primary and secondary historicity mirrored that between the 'ontological' and the 'ontic' ways of inquiry. Ontic inquiry comprised the domain of objects of science and bore a certain similarity with the world as conceived by the twentieth-century successors to mechanist physics. The ontological question, by contrast, concerned the essence of 'being' itself, as accessible to humans in the guise of the essence of being human. Such being was withdrawn from the domain of *physis* not merely by dint of the possession of phenomenological experience as irreducible to scientific description. Rather, being-human was un-physical through its practical and purposive interrelatedness with an irreducibly local life-world: being-there, or *Dasein*. Historicity meant to achieve an understanding of the temporal structure of *Dasein*. Heidegger claimed that secondary historicity, the history 'of the many', was always directed at submerging *Dasein* by imposing on it an ultimately fragmenting temporal structure from outside. *Dasein* had to affirm its primacy by an act of anticipation of its own finality that alone made it intelligible to itself as a unified temporal whole. At a distance, which is enhanced by Heidegger's choice of terminology, this conception reflects several aspects of teleology as refashioned in the Kantian and Hegelian discourse, not least in the form of a concern with self-observation, intelligibility and the unity of understanding, by way of a consideration of finality.

Both Heidegger and Benjamin challenged the unity of history; and both, as they were driven by a concern with contestation, posited a duality of teleologies as rending historicity apart. In their respective antagonisms, both thinkers took a radically partisan stance. For both, modern historicity was an all-engulfing structure of falsehood that had, or would, become uninhabitable. Plurality, and the actual problems of establishing it by way of argument, was not their concern. Antagonism was the chief argumentative tool they deployed. Such antagonism had just emerged in the immediate past, or only would in the near future, as a result of the epochal rupture of the twentieth with the nineteenth century both authors diagnosed. Antagonistic historicities, however, had already emerged significantly earlier, and not as an abstract philosophical project, but in historical concretion.

For much of the nineteenth and twentieth centuries, the most important context for such conflict was the ensemble of European colonial and imperial projects. Monotonously, the colonizers had legitimized their rule through the vocabulary of civilization and modernization, progress, backwardness and catching up. This vocabulary deployed the device of placement in history to work out a wealth of distinctions which often went so far as to refuse a colonized population a share in historicity altogether. Local, previously established models of staging historical time, and their respective histories,[39] were often marginalized or submerged; and other such models, as based on objects, practices and notions otherwise excluded, appeared in response.[40] On the colonial scene, the transition from the nineteenth to the twentieth century, supposedly effected by the caesura of the First World War, seems far less obvious. On the contrary, in many non-European contexts the obstinacy of teleologies of history appears only to have increased in the twentieth century, be it in alliance with anti-colonialist or anti-imperial nationalisms or emancipatory Marxisms, the critique of modernization theory, or that of 'development'.[41] In all these constellations a dual antagonism was inserted into the understanding of historicity at hand.

Yet, the application of the conceptual apparatus provided by interwar-period philosophers of history poses problems of its own, in spite of its seeming usefulness for analysing antagonist historicities. For, in the ambit of historical concretion, the dualism becomes merely relational; that is to say, it states the interrelatedness of two different orders of historical time, yet it fails to limit their absolute number to two. Conflicts proliferate and plurality is inadvertently introduced. This is a complication, not merely of history, but also of the conceptual apparatus deployed for the purpose of understanding history. This complication has been brought about by the heuristic tool of shifting perspective away from Europe; and in this way (and similar ones) debates on colonial and post-colonial histories have become, in the last few decades, one of the most important and innovative sites for discussing historicity.

Nonetheless, it remains challenging to try to trace an actual and efficacious reception of non-European political constellations into the conflictual European philosophies of history of the first half of the twentieth century.[42] As is the case elsewhere in modern history – in full awareness of the norms and values with which 'modern' as a term of periodization remains inadvertently charged[43] – a level field of equal global agency in the history of historicity since 1800 cannot be revealed by simply drawing aside a curtain. Nonetheless, when one broadens the perspective, it becomes conceivable that the uneven field at hand has never been sealed off or historically self-sufficient. Even if more recent 'western' recurrences of historical teleologies, such as the perfectibility of the 'ever closer union' pursued by the EU, or, possibly, the reassertion of autonomous historical agency in the US presidential election slogan 'Yes we can' seem in part designed precisely to avoid reckoning with the imperial past, nonetheless they only confirm the plurality of available formulations of historicity. The history of modern historicity, in the plural, cannot be written as if it had remained confined to the continental container of Europe.

To be sure, in the past, and perhaps also still in the present, European historical writing has continued to entertain more or less secret hopes precisely for such containment. This has been one of the most formidable hindrances to a revisionary understanding of modernity in general, and nineteenth-century historicity in particular. Eurocentrism today is, among many other things, also a function of the still widespread intuition that twentieth-century European history is to be regarded as determined by the historical futures of the nineteenth century, more precisely the unkept promises and failed projects of that epoch. Yet, if twentieth-century Europe is the aggregate *telos* of the nineteenth century, the nineteenth century is organized as an epoch in terms of its direction towards its future failure. It is the literature on 'futures past', in Koselleck's phrase, that has done most to explore the variations of historical teleology in the past, especially in the form of the grand projects that were pursued within a discourse of goal-directed historicity. Yet, ultimately, this literature has often drawn on a tragic emplotment of history as commented on in the final discourse of the choir, of Europe-as-choir, after the denouement, in full catharsis.[44] The problematization of historical teleology has thus often been part of another teleological arrangement – yet another dualist confrontation of historical teleologies.

As one of their mottoes, the curators of the *documenta 12* art exhibition posed the question: 'Is modernity our antiquity?'[45] The 'we' in this question is that of Europe as its own tragic choir. The question posits modernity – not merely modernism, as a period of the history of art – as an epoch of universal reference, insurmountable in its determining force for the present: the very function classical antiquity had once performed in occidental aesthetics and politics. The question also suggests that modernity is finished, a self-enclosed whole that cannot now change or, more precisely, yield itself to substantial revision. This closure of modernity reflects the need of its aftermath to see itself as teleologically determined. In the same way, classical antiquity, over the centuries, had become ever more self-enclosed and stabilized, until piecemeal, through the historical and philological work of the eighteenth and nineteenth centuries, it was interwoven with a broader context of Mediterranean and Middle Eastern ancient history. The modern notion of the unity of history as applied to the ancient world ultimately meant cancelling the historical self-enclosure of the classical, Greek or Graeco-Roman world. By subjecting modernity to a similar procedure as the one that had once created classical antiquity as a particular unit of historical meaning, it might even be that 'we' are still taking revenge, by enthroning a surrogate, for having been deprived of classical antiquity as 'our' privileged epoch of reference: choir in search of a tragedy. Since such an epoch is defined as a self-enclosed whole that excludes 'us' while it determines 'us', modernity becomes uninhabitable. The intervention this volume seeks to carry out, in retrieving the plurality – and not merely the duality – of modern historicity, also aims to counter the antiquization of modernity.

This introductory chapter does not mean to argue that it is possible, or impossible, to eliminate teleology, or even just tragedy, from history. Neither does it insist that, normatively speaking, teleology, historicity or temporality *ought* to be plural. It does, however, suggest that historically they have been and that the present-day tendency to overlook this plurality is at least in part a product of this very plurality. Ultimately, the questions of how to describe and how to explain the plurality at hand also point to the larger question of the habitability of the modern European regime of historicity. We propose a change of perspective taking into account that its inhabitants and modes of habitation have been and are multiple and change in multiple ways; that the *polis* subjected to the regime has been and continues to be rather larger than smaller, and the regime itself much less consistent and comprehensive than has often been assumed.

6. Structure of the volume

The volume is organized into six sections, in which the chapters – all of which pursue different variants of teleological understandings of history – exhibit a degree of thematic coherence. Overall, the volume also seeks to follow a rough chronological order as it moves from focal points in the late eighteenth and early nineteenth centuries into the late nineteenth and early twentieth. One of the results of the volume as a whole is that teleological discourse slowly migrated from philosophy and science into the historicity enclosed in the pursuit of political projects; the arrangement of chapters seeks to make this process visible. The closing pieces of the volume also address broader twentieth-century concerns and the current situation of historicity.

The opening section, 'Two genealogies of historical teleology', comprises the present introduction to the volume as a whole and Sanjay Subrahmanyam's contribution, which explores the history of messianism as a result of global connections. By exploring the political undergrowth of messianic conceptions of historical time, Subrahmanyam's argument enhances the understanding of the genealogy of teleological patterns of thought and strengthens the volume's overall argument for understanding the conditions that caused the deep resonance of teleological notions of history, in the plural, in European history as well as in the emerging theatres of European imperialism in Asia.

The second section, which we have entitled 'Botched vanishing acts: on the difficulties of making teleology disappear', comprises a set of chapters that discuss the nineteenth-century history of outright teleological thought in different contexts of literature and scholarship. To begin with, Philip Ajouri also pursues a genealogical argument. His chapter focuses on the trope of the 'vocation of man', that is to say, the application of teleology to humanity in general, and to the individual. Instead of an intellectual history, however, he provides a history of the uses of this trope in (mostly German) literature in the late eighteenth and across the entire nineteenth century. The integration of teleology into narrative form is another prime condition for both the pluralization and the proliferation of teleology in the modern period. Ajouri further studies the way in which resistance to the trope of the 'vocation of man' continued to organize literary plots into the twentieth century. Marianne Sommer's contribution discusses the deployments and the slow decline of teleological argument in the study of natural history, particularly in Britain, in the period before Darwin. She demonstrates that the lingering teleological idiom was drained from the empirical sciences only in a subtle and piecemeal manner, which has much to do with imaginations of the social and political world that inevitably continued to haunt scientists' perception of natural reality. Angus Nicholls, by contrast, focuses on teleology after Darwin, with particular attention on philosophical and social anthropology in the late nineteenth and early twentieth centuries. His analysis is centred on the interconnections of British and German anthropologies in particular, and shows that the field was unable, regardless of the impact of Darwinism, to abandon teleological patterns of argument and notions of humanity. Equally, it proved unable to insulate itself from normative political thought and the pursuit of political projects.

The third section, 'Befriending teleology: writing histories with ends', discusses variants of historical writing in the nineteenth century, and varying accommodations of teleology therein. Henning Trüper's contribution provides a model case for how, in the nineteenth century, a local and rather self-enclosed teleological understanding of history with a limited scope was instituted. His chapter discusses the history of philanthropic sea rescue and lifeboat organizations across Northern and Western Europe since the 1820s. The organizations were founded with the aim of departing from an age-old history of impassivity and moral neglect; the misfortune of distant strangers became engaging instead of detaching. The chapter pursues a set of surprising connections of tropes of rescue and departing from the past in modern philosophies of history. Siddharth Satpathy then discusses an early- and mid-nineteenth century set of emerging historical teleologies in missionary writings on the history of Cuttack by authors of European as well as of Oriya provenance. His case study (like Trüper's and Ajouri's) emphasizes the importance of narrative teleologies and of the appeal to readerships in the context of a goal-directed project of community formation. The chapter discusses the ways in which European and Indian traditions of historical writing, in the context of Christian mission, were combined through teleological orientation. Dipesh Chakrabarty's essay pursues these themes into the history of scholarly historical writing. His chapter tracks the afterlife of the originally Christian and Augustinian idea of divine providence that, long after scholars thought it had been put to rest by the Cartesian revolution in thinking and the consequent rise of the idea of progress, continued to play a creative role in how many nationalist historians and intellectuals in colonial India imagined the destiny of their nation.

The chapters in the fourth section, 'Teleology in the revolutionary *polis*', explore the ways in which political project-making in the century of revolutions deployed teleological patterns of discourse. Francisco Ortega provides a case study of Colombian history, and specifically the emergence of the grand political project, in the aftermath of the Bolivarian revolution, of achieving a racially mixed commonwealth. His contribution shows that the history of racism in South America was profoundly informed by a teleological understanding of post-revolutionary nation-building. Martti Koskenniemi's chapter anatomizes four different, mutually exhausting positions, which were all generated by the presence of historical teleology in the modern project of the formation of international law. The analysis lays open how international law revolved, and continues to revolve, around a set of notions it seemingly cannot escape. The revolutionary impetus of a teleological view on past, present and future as subject to comprehensive legal regulation, is here turned into a circular structure. Etienne Balibar discusses messianic motives in Karl Marx's early writings. He shows the presence of teleological thought in Marx's early understanding of revolution and the interlinking of these motives with Hegel's philosophy of history. This discussion serves to demonstrate, with great clarity, the way in which political and religious languages and the idiom of teleology intersected at the very centre of nineteenth- and twentieth-century European revolutionary politics.

The fifth section, 'Translating futures: eschatology, history and the individual', discusses interferences between eschatology, the political and nineteenth-century teleological understandings of selfhood. Carola Dietze pursues North American revolutionary messianism in the project and movement of the radical abolitionist John Brown, in the run-up to the Civil War. Dietze explores in depth the eschatological idiom in which Brown was able to generate a secular historical-political project; and she reveals the extent to which this idiom integrated also teleological motives beyond the eschatological vocabulary at its rhetorical forefront. Gabriel Piterberg's and Faisal Devji's chapters track the nineteenth-century question of the intersections of teleological political projects with eschatologies into the twentieth century. Piterberg analyses the historical writings of Gershom Scholem in correlation with his both messianic and autobiographical interpretation of Zionism and the foundation of the state of Israel. He shows how intimately Scholem's understanding of Jewish history was geared to a highly specific and at the same time extremely consequential secular interpretation of Zionism. This is a model case for the ways in which the syndrome of nineteenth-century historical teleologies informed core areas of twentieth-century global politics. Faisal Devji then analyses, in a similar vein, a discourse of universalism and humanity that became highly influential in the Muslim world in the twentieth century. The starting point of the analysis is Indian Muslim poet-philosopher Muhammad Iqbal and his blending of European and Islamic traditions in search of a political thought that would be Islamic, anti-colonial, modern, universal and addressed to the (*telos* of the) individual life. Devji shows the correlations that persist between this and cognate understandings of universality as based in nineteenth-century anti-imperial thought, and contemporary forms of a Muslim universalism as informing the ideology of global jihad.

In the concluding sixth section, 'Historical futures without direction?' two contributions explore the heritage of historical teleology in social and political thought today. Peter Wagner discusses the place of teleological notions of history in the tradition of Germanophone social thought, focusing in particular on Kant, Marx and Weber. He emphasizes the degree to which historical teleology was bound up with projects of political domination; and the resulting degree of caution with which teleological positions were formulated, critiqued, but also preserved, in one of its main traditions of thought. He also describes the emergence, within this tradition, of a withdrawal of plausible teleologies and an ensuing weakening of political critique and autonomy, leading to a profoundly ambivalent situation that, he suggests, persists in the present. Bo Stråth undertakes a confrontation of the works of Hegel and Reinhart Koselleck in order to investigate the possibility of imagining, from the tradition of European philosophy of history, historical futures without recourse to notions of directedness. In particular, he discusses the question as to the notions of temporality that are enmeshed with different conceptions of such futures. Here, the complications introduced into the understanding of historical time by Koselleck provide possibilities for thinking futures without recourse to the utopias that marked older philosophies of history; yet Hegel's reckoning with the political realities of his time (especially the Haitian Revolution) turns out to have been more global than Koselleck's, and the Eurocentrism of the regime of historicity does not seem diminished. Perhaps a re-opening of the imagination of the future would have to start at this point.

Notes

1. Christian Wolff, *Philosophia rationalis sive Logica* [1728], 3rd edn, Verona: Typographia Dionysii Ramanzini, 1735, ch. III, § 85, p. 25: 'Datur . . . philosophiae naturalis pars, quae fines

rerum explicat, nomine adhuc destituta, etsi amplissima sit et utilissima. Dici posset Teleologia.' For the history of the word, see the somewhat summary article 'Teleologie, teleologisch' (Horst Busche), in *Historisches Wörterbuch der Philosophie*, eds Joachim Ritter, Karlfried Gründer, 10, Basel: Schwabe, 1998, col. 970–7.

2. François Hartog, *Régimes d'historicité*, Paris: Seuil, 2003.
3. Aristotle, *Physica*, trans. R. P. Hardie and R. K. Gaye, Oxford: Clarendon, 1930, Book II, 3.
4. See *De motu animalium*, trans. A. S. L. Farquharson, Oxford: Clarendon, 1912, 698a26–28, where Aristotle points out the lack of movement in mathematics.
5. Aristotle, *Physica*, Book II, 8, 199a30: 'And since "nature" means two things, the matter and the form, of which the latter is the end, and since all the rest is for the sake of the end, the form must be the cause in the sense of "that for the sake which".'
6. As in *Physica*, Book II, 1, 193b4–5.
7. See Monte Ransome Johnson, *Aristotle on Teleology*, Oxford: Clarendon, 2005, p. 30f. for useful remarks on the way in which Wolff sought to reconcile efficient and final causes in the passage quoted above.
8. Francis Bacon, *De augmentis scientiarium*, Liber III, cap. 5, *The Works of Francis Bacon*, eds J. Spedding et al., New York: Hurd & Houghton and Boston: Taggard & Thompson, 1864, p. 298.
9. See the instructive discussion in William Clark, 'The Death of Metaphysics in Enlightened Prussia', in William Clark, Jan Golinski and Simon Schaffer, eds, *The Sciences in Enlightened Europe*, Chicago: University of Chicago Press, 1999, pp. 423–73, here 429–35.
10. The classical formulation of the secularization thesis is in Karl Löwith, *Meaning in History*, Chicago: University of Chicago Press, 1949; it was most famously rejected by Hans Blumenberg, *Legitimität der Neuzeit* [1966], Frankfurt a.M.: Suhrkamp, 1996; and from the standpoint of theology by Walter Jaeschke, *Die Suche nach den eschatologischen Wurzeln der Geschichtsphilosophie: Eine historische Kritik der Säkularisierungsthese*, Munich: Kaiser, 1976; see also Jean-Claude Monod, *La quérelle de la secularization. Théologie politique et philosophie de l'histoire de Hegel à Blumenberg*, Paris: Vrin, 2002.
11. A less recklessly incomplete sketch of the philosophical genealogy of historicity would also include the terrain of traditional epistemologies, psychologies and conceptions of memory, which has been analysed in great detail by Janet Coleman, *Ancient and Medieval Memories: Studies in the Reconstruction of the Past*, Cambridge: Cambridge University Press, 1992.
12. Following the discussion in Robert Spaemann and Reinhard Löw, *Die Frage Wozu? Geschichte und Wiederentdeckung des teleologischen Denkens*, Munich: Piper, 1981, pp. 114–21.
13. Ernst Cassirer, *Die Philosophie der Aufklärung*, Tübingen: Mohr, 1932, ch. 5.
14. See especially Timothy Lenoir, *The Strategy of Life: Teleology and Mechanics in Nineteenth-Century German Biology*, Dordrecht: Reidel, 1982; Peter Hanns Reill, *Vitalizing Nature in the Enlightenment*, Berkeley: University of California Press, 2005.
15. See Anthony Grafton, *What Was History?*, Cambridge: Cambridge University Press, 2007, ch. 4.
16. See e.g. Max Horkheimer, *Anfänge der bürgerlichen Geschichtsphilosophie*, Stuttgart: Kohlhammer, 1930; also Friedrich Meinecke, *Die Entstehung des Historismus*, I, Munich, Berlin: Oldenbourg, 1936, p. 2 defined 'Historismus' as the 'application' of the newly developed principles of life in German natural philosophy since Leibniz.
17. As Voltaire stresses in the 'Avant-Propos' of the *Essai sur les mœurs*, written for the Madame du Châtelet in 1740, in *Œuvres complètes*, vol. 22, Oxford: Voltaire Foundation, 2009,

pp. 1–16, here 16; similarly in 'Nouvelles considérations sur l'histoire' [1744], in *Œuvres complètes*, vol. 28B, ed. Voltaire Foundation, Oxford: Alden Press, 2008, pp. 177–85, here 177. The question as to the presence of teleological motives in Voltaire's notions of natural history is complex in spite of his partisanship for Newton.

18. See Cassirer, *Aufklärung*, pp. 288–95.
19. See Bertrand Binoche, *Les trois sources des philosophies de l'histoire (1764–1798)*, Québec: Presses de l'Université Laval, ²2008, part II.
20. As famously defined at the beginning of Aristotle, *Politics* I, I, 8–11, 1252b28–1253a18.
21. Immannuel Kant, *Kritik der Urteilskraft* [1790], Akademie-Ausgabe I, 5, Berlin: Georg Reimer, 1913, §65f., pp. 372–7.
22. Let alone more recent attempts to grapple with the problems at hand, as for instance in the literature around the concept of 'teleonomy' that emerged in the life sciences from the 1950s; see e.g. Jacques Monod, *Chance and Necessity: An Essay on the Natural Philosophy of Modern Biology*, New York: Knopf, 1971; Ernst Mayr, 'Teleological and Teleonomic, a New Analysis', in *Boston Studies in the Philosophy of Science* 14 (1974), pp. 91–117; Ernest Nagel, 'Teleology Revisited: Goal-Directed Processes in Biology', in *Journal of Philosophy* 74 (1977), no. 4, pp. 261–79. An application of the respective notion to human history and social lives has not been undertaken; unlike teleology, the concept of teleonomy has not been deployed to cover intentionality.
23. Kant, *KdU*, Einleitung, xxix–xxxviii, A A I, 5, pp. 181–6.
24. See also *KdU* §79, A A I, 5, p. 416f., where Kant places teleology, as a 'Wissenschaft' in the way envisaged by Wolff, in the mere context of the critique of judgement, denying it any applicability outside this sphere.
25. Heinz Dieter Kittsteiner, 'Kants Theorie des Geschichtszeichens. Vorläufer und Nachfahren', in id., ed., *Geschichtszeichen*, Cologne: Böhlau, 1999, pp. 81–115.
26. See Reinhart Koselleck's analysis of the 'collective singular' 'Geschichte' (as replacing the widespread use of the plural 'Geschichten' in the preceding period) in his entry 'Geschichte', in *Geschichtliche Grundbegriffe*, 2, Stuttgart: Klett-Cotta, 1975, pp. 593–717.
27. Immanuel Kant, *Der Streit der Facultäten* [1798], Akademie-Ausgabe I, 7, Berlin: Georg Reimer, 1917, Zweiter Abschnitt, pp. 77–94, here p. 79f.
28. Immanuel Kant, *Idee zu einer allgemeinen Geschichte in weltbürgerlicher Absicht* [1784], Akademie-Ausgabe I, 8, Berlin: Georg Reimer, 1923, pp. 15–31, here §8.
29. Though the model for posing the problem thus may well have been supplied by Condorcet, who put much emphasis on the openness and the absence of determinate limits on the perfectibility of the human species, though at the same time he defined progress as a march towards truth and happiness, as resulting from a perfected grasp of reality; and clearly, his ideas concerning the perfectibility of the political system envisaged a finite constitution; see Condorcet, *Esquisse d'un tableau historique des progrès de l'esprit humain* [1795], ed. Alain Pons, Paris: Flammarion, 1988, here p. 80f. and p. 294f. for a discussion of the meaning of 'indefinite' progress.
30. See Georg Wilhelm Friedrich Hegel, *Vorlesung über die Philosophie der Weltgeschichte, Berlin 1822/23*, eds Karl Heinz Ilting, Karl Brehmer and Hoo Nam Seelmann, Hamburg: F. Meiner, 1996. The history of the editions of Hegel's lectures on the philosophy of history is complex and was marked, until recently, by an almost proverbial lack of philological method.
31. Following the remarks on 'Chemismus' and teleology in the section on 'the object' in Georg Wilhelm Friedrich Hegel, *Enzyklopädie der philosophischen Wissenschaften im Grundrisse* [1830], eds Wolfgang Bonsiepen, Hans-Christian Lucas, Hamburg: Meiner, 1992, pp. 204–14.

32. As suggested influentially by Blumenberg, *Legitimität der Neuzeit*, and in a different vein Reinhart Koselleck, 'Historia Magistra Vitae: Über die Auflösung des Topos im Horizont neuzeitlich bewegter Geschichte', in id., *Vergangene Zukunft: Zur Semantik geschichtlicher Zeiten*, Frankfurt a.M.: Suhrkamp, 1979, pp. 38–66, and id., '"Erfahrungsraum" und "Erwartungshorizont" – zwei historische Kategorien', in ibid., pp. 349–75.

33. See esp. Peter Szondi, *Poetik und Geschichtsphilosophie I: Antike und Moderne in der Ästhetik der Goethezeit*, Frankfurt a.M.: Suhrkamp, 1974.

34. For much of the literature on historical time, under the influence of Husserlian phenomenology, the concern with phenomenal time, temporal experience as foundational for the understanding of time, has remained paramount; see Paul Ricœur, *Temps et récit*, 3 vols, Paris: Seuil, 1983–5.

35. As influentially reflected in Martin Heidegger's distinction between 'Geschichte' and 'Historie', *Sein und Zeit* [1927], Tübingen: Niemeyer, 2001, part II, ch. 5, here esp. §76.

36. For a discussion of this problematic see Philip Ajouri, *Erzählen nach Darwin. Die Krise der Teleologie im literarischen Realismus: Friedrich Theodor Vischer und Gottfried Keller*, Berlin, New York: de Gruyter, 2007.

37. Walter Benjamin, *Über den Begriff der Geschichte*, ed. Gérard Raulet, Kritische Gesamtausgabe 19, Berlin: Suhrkamp, 2010.

38. Heidegger, *Sein und Zeit*, part II, ch. 5.

39. See for instance Velcheru Narayana Rao, David Shulman and Sanjay Subrahmanyam, *Textures of Time: Writing History in South India 1600–1800*, Delhi: Permanent Black, 2001.

40. See Dipesh Chakrabarty, *Provincializing Europe: Postcolonial Thought and Historical Difference*, 2nd edn, Princeton: Princeton University Press, 2007.

41. See for instance Stefan Tanaka, *New Times in Modern Japan*, Princeton: Princeton University Press, 2004; Arturo Escobar, *Encountering Development: The Making and Unmaking of the Third World*, Princeton: Princeton University Press, 2011.

42. The challenges are instructively revealed in Susan Buck-Morss's endeavour, for an earlier era, to retrieve the Haitian Revolution in Hegel's philosophy: *Hegel, Haiti, and Universal History*, Pittsburgh: University of Pittsburgh Press, 2009.

43. Dipesh Chakrabarty, 'The Muddle of Modernity', in *American Historical Review* 116 (2011), no. 3, pp. 663–75.

44. Philippe Lacoue-Labarthe, in his *Poétique de l'histoire,* Paris: Galilée, 2002, ch. 1, went so far as to suggest that Hegel's notion of 'Aufhebung', the dialectical sublation so important also to his philosophy of history, derives from a specific debate on the nature of tragedy and coincides with catharsis. If this analysis is acceptable, the roots of the dominant twentieth-century mode of critique of the philosophies of history reach back far beyond Nietzsche, who is often credited as its originator.

45. See Mark Lewis, 'Is Modernity our Antiquity?' in *Documenta Magazine No.1, 2007: Modernity?*, ed. Georg Schöllhammer, Cologne: Taschen, 2007, pp. 28–53, with reference to T. J. Clark, *Farewell to an Idea. Episodes from a History of Modernism*, New Haven, London: Yale University Press, 1999 as the original inspiration for the question.

CHAPTER 2
THE POLITICS OF ESCHATOLOGY: A SHORT READING OF THE LONG VIEW*

Sanjay Subrahmanyam

I

In a volume devoted to examining teleologies in the modern world, an engagement with the career of political eschatology seems somewhat necessary, if not wholly inevitable. Itself a late and archaizing coinage, probably dating to the middle decades of the nineteenth century, and deriving from the Greek *eskhatos*, the term 'eschatology' refers to the systematic reflection on endings and End-Times, including most notably ideas such as a Day of Judgement for humankind, both present and past. In turn, it is often related to notions such as an 'apocalypse', meaning an uncovering or revelation that already in medieval Christian usages marked the closure of Time with the definitive victory of good over evil. Eschatology can of course be emplotted in any one of a diverse set of ways, and even as comedy and satire. Perhaps the most notable twentieth-century example of this last tendency is Stanley Kubrick's film *Dr Strangelove* (1964), which appeared in the same year that the American presidential race between the Democratic incumbent Lyndon Johnson and the Republican challenger Barry Goldwater placed the idea of an imminent 'nuclear apocalypse' at the centre of public debate.[1] A notorious television advertisement for Johnson implicitly portrayed his opponent as a lunatic warmonger, in a sequence where a small girl picking off daisy petals was succeeded by images of a sinister countdown to the mushroom cloud. A voice-over by Johnson intoned: 'These are the stakes. To make a world in which all of God's children can live, or to go into the dark. We must either love each other, or we must die.'[2] In Kubrick's vision, deriving from but extensively subverting an earlier novel entitled *Red Alert*, both the Americans and their Soviet counterparts are petty-minded bunglers, whose pompous (and sometimes drunken) bluster barely conceals a fundamental inability to understand the gravity of nuclear weapons and their consequences. While the Soviets strive to build a Doomsday Machine in the Arctic, which once set in motion cannot be reversed and will destroy all human and animal life, the American military is shown as having demented high officers obsessed with the purity of their 'precious bodily fluids', which they fear are in imminent danger of contamination by communist-driven modern innovations such as 'water fluoridation'. Central to the plot is a crazed messianic figure, namely a German-turned-American scientist called Dr Strangelove (originally 'Dr Merkwürdigliebe'), whose crypto-Nazi fantasies include a post-nuclear world where colonies of supermen will eventually re-emerge onto the earth's surface after having spent nearly a hundred years breeding at the bottom of deep mine shafts in order to avoid radiation fallout. The effectiveness of Kubrick's black comedy, which ends with what one presumes is a total nuclear war, is in its parade of irrational characters, who all paradoxically speak what appears to be a twisted version of the language of strategic rationality that had come into vogue in the 1950s. The only timid voice of sanity is of a British Air Force officer, Group Captain Mandrake (himself named as it happens for a hallucinogenic plant), on loan to the Americans, but whose best efforts eventually come to nothing. Kubrick's version of eschatology is one then where the Cold War is nothing other than the extension and further development of the Nazi cult of destruction, taken to a higher and more devastating technological plane. End-Times here are the consequence of collective irrationality masquerading as sophisticated rationality.

Kubrick's is a fiction, even if one based on an uncomfortable relationship with reality. We may consider a more historical set of instances, especially from the nineteenth century, which encapsulate some of the difficulties for an understanding of the longer-term trajectory of eschatology. An obvious place to start is Canudos, a small settlement in the interior of the north-eastern state of Bahia in Brazil in the last decade of the nineteenth century. This was the site of one of the most celebrated insurrections of modern times based on political eschatology, one that has had major echoes both in history-writing and literature down to recent times. Here in brief outline is what seems to have happened in Canudos. After the abolition of first slavery (1888), and then the imperial monarchy (1889), Brazil had entered into a phase of considerable political difficulty, marked at the highest levels by conflicts between the first president Deodoro da Fonseca and his deputy and eventual successor Floriano Peixoto. Both men came from a military background, but the context was one where intellectual currents such as Comtian positivism had a major role to play, as we see from the early adoption of the national motto: *Ordem e progresso* ('Order and progress'), which continues today to appear on the Brazilian flag. The first president elected by direct popular ballot followed these two, and was Prudente de Morais, who took office in late 1894. Morais had won by a handsome margin, and represented what was often described as the *café-com-leite* oligarchy based in São Paulo. But he nevertheless remained insecure, and indecisive in the face of considerable opposition. An early revolt against the republic, of the so-called *maragatos*, had already broken out in Rio Grande do Sul between 1893 and 1895, and then been suppressed militarily at some human cost. The Canudos revolt was, however, a quite different affair. Its leader was a strange and messianic figure who called himself Antônio Conselheiro, and he spoke in a deliberately religious language against what he saw as the evil projects of the emergent republic.[3] Conselheiro, whose real name was Antônio Vicente Mendes Maciel, came from a cattle-rearing background in the province of Ceará in the north-east, and had had an undistinguished early career as a salesman and rural teacher. After several minor and major personal crises, he turned in the 1860s (when he was well into his thirties) to an eclectic brand of mysticism, and began an itinerant life. In this process, however, he attracted the hostile attention of state authorities, who suspected him of stirring up trouble amongst the poor and disaffected peasants of the area. Eventually, after a brief imprisonment, Conselheiro returned to the Brazilian north-east, on the occasion of a major drought and famine in the late 1870s, where he attracted a growing group of followers by playing a significant role in relief actions.

The area in which he operated was one marked by extreme poverty and economic insecurity, as well as racial tensions in a population that included African, European and indigenous elements. Social banditry was common here, and the figures of the *cangaceiro* (or bandit) and the *jagunço* (or strongarm man) were prominent. Conselheiro's following seems to have included a high proportion of freed slaves, and his preachings were a curious mix, including both strong elements of anti-slavery and a conservative defence of the monarchy. The early 1890s were thus a moment of great discontent for this group, for they saw the new republican regime as a threat to their beliefs and values. Perhaps drawing on the colonial tradition of *quilombos*, or Maroon settlements of escaped slaves, that had already existed in the seventeenth century, Conselheiro chose to settle in the area of Canudos, which was rechristened by him as Belo Monte.[4] Making claims of radical autonomy from the state, the settlers resisted its fiscal and other demands, resulting in a series of violent actions that began in 1896, and continued through most of the following year. Initially, the Brazilian state underestimated the extent of support that Conselheiro had, and sent limited detachments that were roundly defeated, despite the primitive set of weapons that the Canudos rebels possessed. The military stakes were then progressively raised: the attacking force of November 1896 was followed by a larger one in January 1897, and then by a quite sizeable expedition in March, led by a certain Colonel Moreira César. The surprising defeat of this last force, and the death of César, meant that all moderation was now abandoned. The last expeditionary force, sent against Canudos in the second half of the year, was not only very sizeable, but armed with howitzers, mortars and machine guns. What ensued was ghastly: after deadly bombardments, almost the entire population of rebels, perhaps 15,000 or more, was massacred, including many prisoners who were beheaded after their surrender. Others, mainly women, were carried off, in order to be sold into prostitution in neighbouring cities. Antônio Conselheiro himself died in late September, possibly of disease and starvation, but his followers held out for another ten days after his death, with the resistance eventually ending on 2 October 1897.

The Canudos War, as it came to be called, attracted wide public attention almost immediately. The main account that emerged of it was by an engineer and journalist, Euclides da Cunha, who came to the area not long after the end of the resistance, as a correspondent for the newspaper *O Estado de São Paulo*. In 1902, Cunha eventually published a long and powerful account entitled *Os sertões* (*The Backlands*), where he attempted both to describe and to explain what had transpired.[5] In turn, this account – though it has been much criticized and contested – has been the basis of a large number of retellings, both fictional and non-fictional.[6] The former include a celebrated novel in Spanish by Mario Vargas Llosa, *La guerra del fin del mundo* (*The War of the End of the World*, 1981), a suitably eschatological title indeed. Cunha was very much an intellectual of his times, whom Stuart Schwartz has described as 'a positivist engineer with military training and greatly influenced by the racialist and social determinist ideas of the era'.[7] He was obviously moved by the brutality of what had transpired, even if in the final analysis he favoured the ostensible progress of the republic over the 'backward members of the nation' that he believed the Canudos community represented. For Cunha, the physical and social environment of the *sertão* was the determining factor in producing a society the values of which were naturally opposed to progress and change. Some authors have seen in this analysis a desire to produce a white Brazil, rather than the awkward mixture of races and cultures that can be found amongst the humble followers of Antônio Conselheiro. Vargas Llosa, in his late-twentieth-century novel (which is, incidentally, dedicated to Cunha), reproduces much of this ambiguity; if, on the one hand, he crafts a narrative that is deeply sympathetic to the tragic nature of the events and the actors, there is nevertheless an undercurrent that suggests that movements such as Canudos (or, for that matter, the Shining Path in Llosa's native Peru) represent a bizarre hindrance to a narrative of the progress of the properly western values of the Enlightenment.[8]

Of some importance in Cunha's account – as well as that of Vargas Llosa – is his insistence on a particular ideological influence at Canudos, namely that of 'Sebastianism'. The reference here is to a current that, since the late sixteenth century, had found a significant place in the Portuguese world, both of the Iberian Peninsula itself and of the overseas empire.[9] The reference was to the tragic and ambiguous figure of the king Dom Sebastião, who at the age of twenty-one had embarked on an ill-advised expedition in Morocco, ignoring the advice of his own advisers and other monarchs such as his own cousin Philip II of Spain. On 4 August 1578, he engaged in battle with Sultan Abd al-Malik Sa'di, was roundly defeated and disappeared in the heat of battle. Though it was quite obvious that he had been killed, rumours soon surfaced to the effect that Dom Sebastião was in reality alive and in hiding, and merely waiting for an appropriate moment to reappear. When Portugal passed under the rule of the Spanish Habsburgs between 1580 and 1640, these rumours were revived time and again. A number of pretenders came forward claiming to be the 'missing' ruler: many of these were in fact of quite humble background, such as the so-called 'pastry-cook of Madrigal', Gabriel de Espinosa in the 1590s, but nevertheless managed to stir up a certain amount of popular excitement. By the early seventeenth century, these popular movements came to be reworked around a textual corpus of enigmatic rhymes, called the *Trovas*, that had been written by or at least attributed to a shoemaker from Trancoso called Gonçalo Annes Bandarra (1500–56).[10] The tradition of Sebastianism which was consolidated at this point would be revived much later in the seventeenth century, in an ever more complex and mystical vein. What is of particular interest is that, more than three centuries after the battle of 1578, they still found a popular echo in the 'backlands' of the Brazilian north-east amongst the followers of Conselheiro.

One possible reading of the Canudos War then is in its Iberian context. But we might equally seek to compare it with other peasant rebellions with an eschatological colouring in the nineteenth century. Arguably the most prolonged and bloodiest of these would be the so-called Taiping Rebellion, which originated in the early 1850s in the southern Guangxi province (bordering on Vietnam), and then spread to overtake most of Jiangxi and Zhejiang, as well as parts of some neighbouring provinces. Eventually suppressed after almost a decade and a half, in the second half of 1864, this peasant war may have directly and indirectly claimed as many as twenty million lives, though many of these were from famine and related effects.[11] Still, it is clear that this was perhaps the most bloody of the wars of the nineteenth century, dwarfing the casualties of the American Civil War by some measure. It is obviously impossible to reduce the Taiping Rebellion to a single cause, or even to a small set of causes. We may note for example that the area of south-eastern China where it occurred had, even in the mid-nineteenth century, not entirely accepted the legitimacy of the rule of the Qing (or Manchu) dynasty who had conquered China in the 1640s, and that many southerners remained nostalgic for the rule of the earlier Ming dynasty. Further, a large proportion of participants in the rebellion belonged either to impoverished peasant groups or to distinctive minorities (such as the Hakka), an aspect that likens it to the Canudos War to some extent. But it is equally striking that at the ideological core of the affair was an eschatological issue, centring on the enigmatic person of a certain Hong Xiuquan, a failed civil service aspirant. Together with his close associate, a certain Yang Xiuqing, Hong appears to have been influenced by readings of Christian missionary tracts and materials. Whether these readings are treated as simple misunderstandings or as creative interpretations, Hong and his supporters came to the view that he himself was Jesus's younger brother, and thus 'God's Chinese son', and that his destiny was to establish a 'Heavenly Kingdom [*tianguo*]' on earth in place of the unjust rule of the Manchus.[12] Despite numerous ups and downs, and a host of internecine struggles, this enterprise remained broadly expansive through much of the 1850s, until unsuccessful attempts were made to capture Shanghai in 1860–61 by the Taiping general Li Xiucheng. Eventually, the Qing rulers accepted the help of European forces in the suppression of the rebellion, though defiant elements remained present in various pockets until even the early 1870s. In the first half of the twentieth century the Taiping Rebellion was often evoked to various political ends in China, both by the first president of the republic, Sun Yat-sen, and thereafter by Mao Zedong. In the two instances, the allegedly 'progressive' character of the movement was stressed, as was its opposition to a decadent order, that of the imperial Qing dynasty. In the case of Sun, his sympathies for Taiping may even have been linked to his own Christian background and proximity to various missionary groups.

Neither Canudos nor Taiping features in more than a passing way in what is perhaps the best and most ambitious general account of popular millenarian movements in modern times, namely Michael Adas's *Prophets of Rebellion* (1979).[13] This is because Adas chose to focus on those rebellions that occurred in the context of European colonialism, though even there he decided to pay scant attention to some conspicuous instances, such as that of Muhammad Ahmad ibn 'Abdullah, who declared himself the Mahdi in the Sudan in the 1880s.[14] Rather, Adas's work employed as its focus five examples: the revolt of Prince Diponegoro in the Dutch East Indies in the 1820s; the Hau Hau movement of the Maoris in New Zealand in the 1860s; the rebellion of Birsa Munda in Central India in the 1890s; the Maji Maji disturbances in German East Africa in the early twentieth century; and finally the Saya San uprisings in Burma between 1930 and 1932. Treating all of these within the broad category of 'revitalization movements' with a marked prophetic content, he argued that their support 'was primarily drawn from groups that had lost political support and social status and had experienced a worsening of their economic condition because of the advance of the European colonial order'. Adas insisted that an 'emphasis on or exclusive attention to groups of low social standing may obscure important sources of this form of social protest'; it was his view that, in most of these movements, a complex mix of popular and elite elements had had a significant role to play. He thus insisted not only on rejecting any form of glorification of the violence of these episodes but also that 'a class-based analysis is inappropriate for movements of the prophetic-revitalization type'.

In Adas's portrayal, the eschatologically motivated movements of the colonial epoch could be located within a broader panorama of protest and social movements. On the one hand, there were the 'Western-educated nationalist leaders' and their movements, who were usually not in the least sensitive to the 'grievances felt by displaced indigenous leaders or politically powerless peasants'. Then, on the other hand, there were the more general phenomena of 'social banditry, avoidance migration, sectarian movements, and violent resistance to colonial conquest', all of which generally proved ineffective.[15] But this failure in turn could be used, in Adas's view, to explain the success of 'the prophets' millenarian visions, which combined key elements of the belief systems and traditions of the cultures in which each leader arose, [and] provided a means of dramatically articulating the grievances of the groups to whom the prophets hoped to appeal'. Yet, he also underlined that this was no simple appeal to 'tradition', as opposed to colonial 'modernity'; rather, he writes, while they rejected the colonial order as such, 'each of the prophets sought to salvage some elements of the existing order that were European in origin'. What this might mean in the case of a figure like the Mataram prince Diponegoro would be that while he drew on Islamic eschatology, as well as appeals to the Javanese figure of the *ratu adil* (or 'just king'), he was not located in a cultural universe that was entirely alien to that of the Europeans whose rule he opposed.[16]

From the outset of his work, Adas insists that 'specific historical causes have little meaning in and of themselves', and that the historian's task is one of creating (or reconstructing) what he terms a 'sequential framework'. This raises an essential question which, however, remains unanswered. The context of the entire discussion is provided by an overarching framework given by the 'European colonial order' of the nineteenth and twentieth centuries. But it remains unclear what the sequential relationship was between the 'belief systems and traditions of the cultures' as they existed at the time of these anti-colonial movements, and their historical pasts. Were these beliefs and traditions that had always been there somehow, or did they too have a recoverable history, one moreover that went considerably beyond the time-frame of the colonial order? If this were indeed the case, how was one to treat this longer history? There are some passages in which Adas does touch on this problem, and it is largely in the context of an evaluation of the 'rationality' or 'irrationality' of these prophetic movements. We have noted above that a writer like Euclides da Cunha, while sympathetic to the tragic end of the Canudos rebels, nevertheless placed them within a narrative where it was the Republican state that represented rational progress, while the rebels stood for a form of irrationality that was explicable in social determinist vocabulary. In most of the colonial instances mentioned above (including that of the Mahdi of the Sudan), the millenarian resistance movements were treated by their opponents as 'irrational', precisely because they allegedly depended on magical materials and talismans, drew on astrology and heavenly symbols, and the like. Very often, the prophets in question were explicitly termed 'madmen'; certainly the case with Hong Xiuquan or Antônio Conselheiro, whose skull was actually exhumed and 'examined for congenital abnormalities' by medical doctors. The terms 'irrational', 'magical' and 'traditional' come to be very nearly interchangeable in these usages. An alternative, common amongst Marxist scholars at a certain time, would have been to use the terminology of 'residues' and 'leftovers', implying that the eschatological content of such movements was more or less the undissolved cultural sediment of a deeper historical past.[17] Yet what precisely was that past, beyond its residual status, and what was its version (or versions) of eschatology? Can we make some sense of it in a manner that is not in itself a teleological straitjacketing? It is to these questions that the second part of this chapter now turns.

II

The long history of eschatology before the nineteenth century is a subject that several recent authors have struggled with, amongst whom we may count Norman Cohn, Eugen Weber and Richard Landes.[18] An initial debate concerned the question of whether the term should be confined to its use in the context of the three Abrahamic religions – Judaism, Christianity and Islam – or whether it could be extended beyond this ambit. The view that is now broadly accepted admits freely that powerful forms of eschatology existed, for example, amongst Zoroastrians, and that these exercised a powerful influence on Jewish views of the question. The battle between Ohrmazd and Ahriman thus marks a form of End-Time combat, with the former being able to gain a victory for the powers of good.[19] In a similar vein, it can be argued that a number of beliefs amongst 'Hindus', and notably the powerful if controversial figure of Kalki (ostensibly the last *avatāra* of Vishnu), carry a strong eschatological odour about them.[20] To be sure, there would be little purpose to seeking out eschatological patterns in every culture and society of the pre-1800 period; and there is surely something to J. R. R. Tolkien's view that the early medieval northern European society that produced the epic *Beowulf* had a quite different conception of life, its course and its ending, despite its perfunctory genuflection in the direction of Christian themes.

Setting aside these various and diverse episodes, which would both take us into many distinct societies and also oblige us to traverse many centuries, let us focus here on the political dimension of the eschatological question as it emerged afresh in the fifteenth century of the Common Era. My broad argument here, which returns to several essays that I have published on the theme in the late 1990s and thereafter, is as follows: the particularity of the 'eschatological moment' that emerges from the latter half of the fifteenth century is that it is conjunctural and very widely connected, embracing a number of different and quite dispersed polities and societies.[21] In this respect, it differs both from far earlier episodic eschatological events that have been carefully enumerated and described by other historians, and from the phenomena that Adas and others have studied for the nineteenth and early twentieth centuries. Further, I will argue that in respect of this earlier moment, it is not in the least necessary to present eschatology as antinomian in character, or representing some form of 'popular resistance' to the dominant, and progressist, rationality of a modernizing state. On the contrary, the very social location of the most powerful eschatological currents was itself a source of deep struggle and continued controversy.

Indeed, looking to the latter half of the fifteenth century, the historian has an embarrassment of points of departure, especially from the perspective of politics. One of these is 1494–95 CE, the beginning of the tenth century of the lunar Hegiran calendar observed by most Muslims. Amongst a host of important figures who were seized by the importance of this moment was the northern Indian personage of Sayyid Muhammad Jaunpuri (1443–1505), who after a broad religious and spiritual education amongst the Chishti Sufis and extensive travels (perhaps as far as the Hijaz) eventually declared himself at Barli (in Gujarat) to be the Mahdi, or long-announced redeemer of Islam. By the time of his death a decade later in Farah (in Khurasan), Sayyid Muhammad had gathered a significant following, especially amongst elites and to a more limited extent amongst popular groups. These groups were largely to be found in regions such as Gujarat and Sind, and also in the Deccan; the extent of his following in northern India remained more limited but not entirely insignificant. As has been shown in recent studies by Derryl Maclean, Sayyid Muhammad took a number of significant and concrete steps in terms of consolidating his disciples into a movement, the Mahdawiyya.[22] He instituted a succession, and the first of his *khalīfas* was a certain Sayyid Khwandmir, followed by Shah Ni'mat. Further, the Mahdawis grouped themselves in armed encampments (or *dā'iras*), where egalitarian social practices were combined with particular and distinctive forms of religious observance. Sayyid Muhammad also threw the gauntlet down to other Muslims, accusing them of being infidels (*kuffār* or *harbī*) if they did not recognize his exalted and prophetic status. In a celebrated letter addressed to the Sultan of Gujarat, Mahmud Begarha (r. 1458–1511), he stated:

> I say by the command of Almighty God that I am the promised Mahdi of the end of time … It is obligatory (*lāzim*) for all – sultans, nobles (*umarā'*), officers (*khawānīn*), viziers, the wealthy, the *faqīrs*, the *'ulamā*, the pious and all people – to investigate, verify the truth, and accept it. If you allege that I impute slander and lies to God, and disavow me, then it is incumbent on you to prove my lie and execute me. If you do not [and you are right], everywhere I go I will proclaim my mission to the people and lead them astray, inflicting harm on them. It is incumbent on the authorities of the time (*hākimān-i zamān*) to select one of the two options [convert or execute]. If they do not, their faces will be blackened in both the worlds.[23]

The growing popularity of the movement amongst religious elites (or *'ulamā*) on the one hand, and groups of Afghan warriors on the other, seems to have caused considerable alarm at the court of the succeeding Gujarat Sultan, Muzaffar Shah (r. 1511–26). This resulted in a series of armed confrontations, culminating at Sudrasan (west of Patan) in 1524, in which the Mahdawis were defeated by the Sultan's army, and Sayyid Khwandmir himself was killed, beheaded and parts of his body dispersed in three spots. Despite this setback, the movement continued to claim many adherents in the middle decades of the sixteenth century, including in the secondary commercial centre of Bayana (west of Agra). During the reign of the Afghan ruler, Islam (or Salim) Shah Sur (r. 1545–54), in northern India, this resulted in further debates and violent clashes, which set some Afghans against others, and resulted in the castigation and execution of several prominent Mahdawi figures such as Shaikh 'Ala'i Bayanwi.

A myth has long been sustained in the historiography, according to which the Mahdawis of the sixteenth century essentially represented a popular movement of disenfranchised peasants and artisans. However, the prosopography of the early generations of converts proposed by Maclean places us on guard against such a facile view. Rather, he suggests that many converts belonged to the elite (or *ashrāf*), and included not only men of extensive religious training, but also administrators and military commanders working for various Sultanates. It was the fact that the Mahdawis gained important adherents within the state itself, he argues, that caused such a level of disquiet in the period. However, it would seem that after the 1570s, the militancy of the movement largely subsided with one or two exceptions, such as the brief *coup d'état* in the Nizam Shahi state of Ahmadnagar (in the Deccan) by a certain Jamal Khan Mahdawi in the late 1580s. It would appear that this new turn, which saw the Mahdawis becoming 'quietist' in their orientation, and accepting a place within the expanding Mughal state, followed an attempt on the part of the prominent figure of Miyan Mustafa Gujarati, a prominent Mahdawi, to openly challenge the leading Mughal '*ulamā* in debate at Fatehpur Sikri.[24] In the seventeenth and early eighteenth centuries, we find several Mahdawis in high Mughal posts, amongst whom we may count Da'ud Khan Panni (d. 1715) – governor of Gujarat and the Karnatak.

How does one account for such a turn, especially given the fact that Mahdawis continued in the late sixteenth century to enjoy prestige and support, as we learn from one of their sympathizers, the formidable intellectual and chronicler Mulla 'Abdul Qadir Badayuni? The most plausible explanation lies in the fact that the viewpoint of the Mahdawis was appropriated and transformed by the Mughal dynasty itself. In the course of the 1580s, the *Tārīkh-i Alfī*, or 'Thousand-Year History', was commissioned by the emperor Akbar, to mark the upcoming and ominous millennium of the Hegiran calendar in 1591–2.[25] This project eventually became the work of many hands, and somewhat lost its coherence as a consequence; it was also later forced to cede pride of place to what became the definitive official chronicle of the reign, namely Shaikh Abu'l Fazl's *Akbar Nāma*. It is, however, clear that, for a time, millenarian and eschatological vocabulary came to assume a primary place in the Mughal court, triumphing over the simple appeal to Timurid genealogy. Akbar thus made efforts to pose himself as a 'millennial sovereign', though the apocalyptic elements prominent elsewhere were attenuated in favour of a language of 'renewal' by a 'perfect Man (*insān-i kāmil*)'. One can see why observers like

Badayuni would feel indignant at such a move, which they felt was the usurpation by royal power of the claims of high-minded men of great spiritual accomplishments such as Sayyid Muhammad Jaunpuri.[26]

Badayuni also makes an interesting claim, namely that around 1581 Akbar was already being encouraged by some 'shameless and ill-starred wretches' amongst his courtiers to follow in the footsteps of the Safavid ruler Shah Isma'il (d. 1524). By this time, we are aware that a considerable number of Iranians had gathered at the Mughal court, and it follows that the history of the Safavid dynasty over the previous century or so was perfectly accessible to the Mughals. Akbar thus certainly knew that the Safavids had had a long and troubled flirtation with millenarianism, albeit a version that combined Shi'ism with forms of Muslim heterodoxy (*ghuluww*) prevalent in eastern Anatolia. When the young Shah Isma'il was first propelled to power at the turn of the sixteenth century, his red-capped (*qizilbāsh*) followers, who were largely drawn from Turkoman tribes, attributed messianic powers to him, while also treating him as their spiritual master (*pīr-o-murshīd*).[27] While the Safavid ruler's initial successes seemed to justify this confidence, the last decade of his career was spent under a cloud, as his invincibility was cast in serious doubt on the battlefield. Nevertheless, his successor Tahmasp (r. 1524–76) continued to maintain a link to the figure of the Imam Mahdi, and even when the sixteenth century was drawing to a close, the court of the Safavid ruler Shah 'Abbas was periodically rocked by millenarian rumours, fuelled by heterodox sects like the Nuqtawis and powerful astrologers such as Jalal-ud-Din Munajjim al-Yazdi.[28]

It would appear therefore that political eschatology took a powerful and significant form in the Islamic world in the sixteenth century, transcending the divide between Sunnis (like the Mughals) and Shi'as (like the Safavids), and also drawing on support across both elite and popular sections of society. The Mughal poet-laureate Faizi, who visited Ahmadnagar not long after the uprising of Jamal Khan Mahdawi in the early 1590s, implicitly reproached him for having created mischief and commotion (*shor-o-sharr*) and surrounding himself with 'sedition-mongers and ruffians (*fitnasāzān wa aubāshān*)', surely a reflection of the popular support the Mahdawis may have enjoyed in this instance.[29] In a similar vein, a popular millenarian revolt briefly arose in Safavid Iran in 1580–81, when a pretender claiming to be the short-lived Sultan Isma'il II managed to raise a following in excess of twenty thousand men, and challenged the Safavid regional governors of the time before being crushed by main force.[30] But for the most part, the tenor of the eschatology was such that it either engaged with and tried to influence state power (as we have seen with the Mahdawis in their first phase, prior to about 1570) or was itself directly an element of state ideology. Its antinomian dimensions in the period were strictly circumscribed.

The same broad portrayal remains true as we move westwards. Extensive research has accumulated in the past decades on the place of political eschatology in the Ottoman Empire, which – like its Mughal counterpart – was also a Sunni polity. It would now seem that from the time of the conquest of Constantinople in 1453 by Sultan Fatih Mehmed, this eschatological dimension had grown and come to occupy a place of importance in the reflections of a good number of Ottoman intellectuals. Of particular significance was the reign of Süleyman the Lawgiver (1520–66), who was seen by many – both within his own realm and to the west – as locked in a form of final combat with the Habsburg ruler Charles V, whose reign largely coincided with his. A decade into Süleyman's reign, in 1531, Erasmus wrote to one of his correspondents that it was widely thought that 'the Turk will invade Germany with all his forces, in a contest for the greatest of prizes, to see whether Charles will be the monarch of the whole world, or the Turk. For the world can no longer bear two suns in the sky'.[31] In the same decade, the figure of Alvise Gritti – the illegitimate son of a Venetian Doge, and a refugee in the Ottoman domains – emerged at the centre of a number of speculations and predictions, to the effect that the destruction of the Ottomans would be brought about by 'the son of some prince'.[32] A porous polity like that of the Ottomans, which had a marked presence of Jewish and Christian refugees, as well as converts and renegades, could very easily become a hotbed of such open-ended and disturbing notions. The prominent place in the urban culture of centres such as Delhi, Agra, Tabriz, Isfahan, Cairo or Istanbul of figures of astrologers (*rammāl*, or *munajjim*) cannot be discounted, and we know that the sixteenth century was a prolific moment for the production and circulation of such almanacs and books of omens (or *fāl-nāmas*).[33]

The work of Ottomanists over the past decades has also demonstrated time and again that it is essential to see these eschatological materials in a trans-imperial context.[34] This is for at least two reasons: first, the ideological construction of End-Time often called upon the presence of another rival empire to play an oppositional and complementary role, similar to that of the pairing of Christ (*'Īsa*) and the Anti-Christ (or *Dajjāl*) in much Muslim eschatology; and second, the place in the matter of mobile minorities (such as the Jews who had been expelled from Iberia in the late fifteenth century) who moved across imperial spaces was not negligible. Many regions of the Mediterranean were thus affected by variants of the same currents: the Ottoman domains, the Sultanates of the Maghreb, Italy, parts of France, Castile and Andalucia, and Portugal. The Iberian case in particular deserves attention, because it was through the institutions of the Iberian empires that many of the eschatological beliefs and practices of the period also managed to traverse the Atlantic, and eventually strike roots in places as diverse as Mexico and Brazil. The Catholic Monarch, Ferdinand of Aragon, was associated with messianic expectations much before his projects for the reconquest of Granada, and the expulsion of Jews and Muslims from his realms. These expectations came in part from the readings and interpretations of the medieval Italian monk and mystic visionary, Joachim of Fiore, in the late twelfth century. But late medieval Spain also saw the wide circulation of what Alain Milhou has described as 'prophecies by Pseudo-Methodius and the Pseudo-Joachim, introduced in the Catalan provinces as early as the thirteenth century, and [works] by Franciscan visionaries linked to the House of Aragon, such as Arnold of Villanova (c. 1240–1311) and Francesc Eiximenis (1340–1409)'.[35] Though less prolific perhaps than its eastern Iberian counterparts in the production of original textual materials, the Portuguese royal court from the latter part of the fourteenth century was also marked by powerful messianic currents surrounding the newly arisen Avis Dynasty, and its founder-ruler Dom João I (r. 1385–1433). The victory of João over the Castilians and their allies at Aljubarrota in August 1385 set the stage for a twofold expansion by Portugal, into the Atlantic islands on the one hand, and into the Maghreb on the other. Again, at the end of the fifteenth century, the ruler Dom Manuel – who was confronted with difficult choices concerning whether to send fleets into the Indian Ocean, or abandon the project – was encouraged to continue in his plans by ideologues such as Duarte Galvão, who helped convince the king of his own exalted and messianic role in uniting the divided world of Christianity, and striking a decisive blow against the great Muslim powers of the eastern Mediterranean, especially the Mamluk Sultanate of Egypt.[36] The official chronicler João de Barros, writing a half-century after these events, nevertheless recalled that when, in 1496, the king summoned a general council, 'the majority was that India should not be discovered'; however, Dom Manuel overruled this view, insisting that 'God, in whose hands he put the affair, would provide the means that were needed for the welfare of this Kingdom [Portugal]'.[37] The first phase of Portuguese expansion and empire-building in the Indian Ocean was thus sustained by many royal agents of the same temper, such as the governor Afonso de Albuquerque, seeking the means to destroy the 'house of Muhammad' at Mecca, and periodically reassured by heavenly signs and portents of the soundness of their projects.

The Spanish case bears some similarities to this, but also differs in some crucial respects. Columbus's own dependence on prophetic texts for inspiration is no mystery to scholars of the period; Milhou has written of how his 'mad project of reaching India by the western route' could hardly have succeeded had he not found in Spain a 'propitious atmosphere that enabled him to present his glimmering project of a planetary struggle against Islam, thanks to the alliance with the Great Khan of Cathay as well as the hidden Christendoms'. Further, he notes, Columbus's initial success lay in placing 'his own messianism within the official messianism inspired by the Catholic monarchs', and suggesting that all mankind – Christians, Muslims, Jews and Gentiles – would thus be gathered together as predicted (in John 10.16): 'and there will be one flock, with one shepherd.' However, the eventual implementation of this sort of vision depended not on Columbus or his close circle, but rather on Franciscan monks who accompanied the conquest of first the Caribbean islands and then the American mainland, and who were probably the most powerful institutional and ideological force in establishing a Spanish American empire before about 1550. If this form of royal messianism associated with Ferdinand appears to have weakened for a time in the following generation, Geoffrey Parker has made a strong case for its revival in the last third of the sixteenth century, at the court of the Habsburg ruler of Spain and the Spanish empire, Philip II. He notes that at first sight Philip's messianic vision 'seems relatively modest when compared with the claims advanced by some adherents of other creeds' at roughly the same moment. But, significantly, he goes on to add:

> Nevertheless, his messianic vision possessed two unique features. First, no other Christian ruler so openly equated his or her service with God's service – they were, as Philip memorably stated, 'the same thing'. Moreover, although many sycophants, propagandists and apologists made extravagant claims for their patrons, and

although many advisers (especially clerics) believed that God fought on their side, no other monarch of this period regularly framed foreign and domestic policy on the assumption that she or he had divined God's purpose. Fewer still routinely relied on miracles to bridge the gap between ends and means.[38]

That Philip took his eschatology rather seriously can be gauged from numerous examples in his private correspondence. In late 1574, on receiving news of serious military reverses, he wrote to his secretary: 'If this is not the end of the world, I think we must be very close to it; and, please God, let it be the end of the whole world, and not just the end of Christendom.'[39]

Philip thus participated fully, if willy-nilly, in the 'millenarian conjuncture' of the sixteenth century which I have suggested elsewhere ran at the very least from the banks of the Tagus to those of the Ganges. In turn, this construction has proven a hard pill to swallow for nationalist Iberian historians of even the late twentieth century, who remain determined to prove that the empires that the Portuguese and Spaniards created were not a form of *démesure*, or outrageous excess, as Serge Gruzinski has recently posited,[40] but rather 'strictly organized, without eschatological agitation, and in the context of the recruitment of soldiers and missionaries controlled by military and ecclesiastical authorities'.[41] For such authors, eschatology inevitably leads to 'panic movements', and thus to 'irrationality', itself incompatible for them with the very notion of the political ideology of a state. There is more than a fair part of anachronism, and even 'state-worship' here. But as a careful examination of the history of sixteenth-century Iberia shows abundantly, the behaviour of rulers and states was such that Dom Sebastião's foolhardy (and ultimately suicidal) plan to invade the Maghreb in the 1570s seems only somewhat odd, rather than a great deviation from some overall pattern of Machiavellian calculation. We may briefly consider the case, for example, of David Reuveni (or ha-Reuveni) in the 1520s. As retraced by Moti Benmelech and Miriam Eliav-Feldon, here was an unknown, a 'small, dark man', who in late 1523 disembarked from Alexandria in Venice, claiming to be the representative of a kingdom of lost eastern Jews.[42] His passage was quickly arranged to Rome, where he informed Pope Clement VII of his plan 'to forge an alliance with Christian monarchs in order to fight the Ishmaelites and liberate the Holy Land from the hands of the Turk'. The Pope determined that the matter was best left to the king of Portugal, Dom João III, and Reuveni was sent on to his temporary court at Almeirim by late 1525. Here, Reuveni was received with much pomp and circumstance, and also with a great deal of credulity. He met the king and his wife, as well as Dona Isabel, the king's sister and future queen of Charles V; the Portuguese monarchy promised him ships, men and arms in his mission, which he wished to begin with an ambitious attack on the Red Sea port of Jiddah. But difficulties now arose of quite a different order. Word was soon out in Portugal that a great Jewish prince had arrived there, and this began to create disturbances and turmoil in the community of converts, or *cristãos-novos*. Eventually, a prominent official named Diogo Pires converted to Judaism, and fled Portugal, becoming an adept of Reuveni under the name Solomon Molkho. Faced with these circumstances, the

Portuguese monarchy did indeed panic and sent Reuveni away expeditiously in June 1526 in a ship from the port of Lagos. Unable to find further patrons of substance, he was then obliged to roam the Mediterranean for the next few years, until he was finally captured, condemned and apparently executed in a prison of the Spanish Inquisition at Llerena in 1538.[43]

The example of Reuveni once more shows the close ties between different eschatological movements in the Mediterranean in the sixteenth century, and how they could in effect feed off one another. This notion, of a sort of 'Mediterranean apocalypse' of the sixteenth century, was first developed by the Ottomanist Cornell Fleischer, and it helps distinguish this extended moment to an extent from what came both before and after. For example, the instance of David Reuveni was not forgotten in the Sephardic Jewish community, and even if he was reviled by some, it continued to play a role in waves of messianism that can be found in Italy and Palestine in the second half of the sixteenth century. However, the major movement of the seventeenth century, that of Shabbatai Zvi in the Ottoman Empire, does not seem to have benefited from the same very broad conjunctural dimensions as those of the previous century.[44] Its Mediterranean echoes were certainly fairly powerful, and in the context of the Maghreb and the Iberian Peninsula they have been brought out clearly by several recent authors.[45] Further, despite considerable scepticism in many quarters, it did have some impact on the Sephardic community of Amsterdam through a figure such as Menasseh ben Israel, and may also have found some echoes in the Atlantic world. But the eschatological movements that emerge in the period after 1600, and especially after 1650, have their own characteristic limitations. In Mughal India, as we have seen, the Mahdawiyya had retreated into a 'quietist' phase, while emperors such as 'Alamgir-Aurangzeb (r. 1658–1707) seem largely to give up the millenarian pretensions that had once dominated, even if (as has recently been argued) historians 'must take into consideration the great price' that had to be paid in terms of popularity and legitimacy for this 'break'.[46] In Safavid Iran, the radical millenarianism and *ghuluww* of the first generations of Safavids had 'officially been silenced' by the second half of the seventeenth century, and instead gave way to a more domesticated form, that of Imami Shi'ism, which 'was accompanied by an enumeration of excesses that violated the tenets of Islam'.[47] Again, with the Ottomans, it was no longer the increasingly silent and confined sovereign inside the Topkapı Sarayı who became the prime carrier of eschatological expectations, but rather urban movements such as the Kadızadeli. Seen from this broad perspective, a project that stands out is that of Oliver Cromwell, and his 'Western Design' for Caribbean conquest of the 1650s, though debate remains over whether it can be qualified as millenarian or merely strongly providentialist.[48] It is no coincidence that it was to Cromwell that Menasseh ben Israel turned then, with his dreams of a millennial domain for the Jews in the lands of an America dominated by the nascent British Empire.[49] In turn, when Menasseh's acquaintance and sometime correspondent, the Luso-Brazilian Jesuit António Vieira, attempted for his part to revive the idea of a millennial Fifth Empire (or *quinto império*) in Portugal, the monarchy itself hardly seemed able any longer to bear the burden of such an idea.[50]

III

Theorists of politics in relation to cultural phenomena remain rather divided as to the correct portrayal of the long-term trajectory (or, if one prefers, 'fate') of political eschatology. An extreme view which must be addressed briefly is that of historians who – while usually standing on the sidelines of the discussion – insist that the existing historiography on the subject can simply be dismissed because of its 'indiscriminate and baseless use of the concepts that have circulated – ideology, idea, project, messianism, millenarianism, empire/imperialism – without defining their nature and historical contours'.[51] It would thus seem illegitimate to these writers, as a matter of principle, to treat the movements of Sayyid Muhammad Jaunpuri, Shah Isma'il, Shabbatai Zvi and Sebastianism together even if concrete connections (and not merely family resemblances) between them can be established. Yet one may wonder if the remedies suggested by them might not be worse than the malady: a recourse for example to 'a middle path between history and anthropology/mythological analysis' in each instance; or a 'contextualization' of texts and all other materials that draws on the techniques of deconstruction. The inherent absurdity of this critique is probably manifest, we may say, in its very terms: for who would ever wish to defend the 'indiscriminate and baseless use of concepts' in any intellectual situation? Indeed, simply to banish all broad words and concepts from the historian's vocabulary, which can operate across long periods and long distances, seems somewhat myopic and self-indulgent, condemning the historian only to the worship of the 'fragment'.

We can thus pass to enumerating several of the most common and more interesting positions, before attempting to draw some conclusions of our own. The enumeration below is naturally far from exhaustive in character.

1. A first view would propose that political eschatology had indeed existed in 'traditional' societies along with ideas like sacred kingship, but had then disappeared along with processes of 'modernization' and the consequent 'secularization' of politics itself. This view would then have it, as the modernizer Euclides da Cunha in fact did, that the last vestiges of eschatology that persisted into the late nineteenth century were in fact simply outdated, perhaps tragic, artefacts of a dying past. One can see the linear form of teleology in which this argument is located with little effort.

2. A second view, related no doubt to the first, would be one of a progressive social migration of political eschatology from the elites to the masses. In other words, as the state increasingly chose 'rationalization' as its preferred mode of functioning, millenarian aspirations that had once been easily imbibed by the agents of state power became the cultural support of movements of anti-state resistance, whether in the context of colonialism or not. Elements of this view can be found, for example, in James C. Scott's claim that millenarian and prophetic movements are 'techniques for thwarting state incorporation' in the highlands of Southeast Asia, and 'a protest against oppression and inequality' in the lowlands, though – as we

have seen – the work of Michael Adas was in part intended to challenge this view at its very inception.[52] Some analysts and supporters of recent movements with a strong eschatological flavour, such as the Rastafarians in Jamaica, have naturally been equally drawn to this view.[53]

3. A third view, present *in nuce* in the work of an author such as Norman Cohn, who we may recall was writing at the height of the Cold War, is that 'revolutionary messianism' and political eschatology from the world before 1700 are the direct precursors of 'totalitarian movements in the modern world', by which Cohn explicitly specified that he meant the 'two major forms of totalitarianism, Communism on the one hand, and German National Socialism on the other'. Cohn's claims immediately met with violent objections, but even in later editions of his book he persisted in stating that 'the more carefully one compares the outbreaks of militant social chiliasm during the later Middle Ages with modern totalitarian movements the more remarkable the similarities appear'.[54]

4. A fourth view would argue that eschatology and its concomitant chiliasm are simply recurrent phenomena in human history, which reappear in a more or less cyclical fashion, but with no particular 'developmental' logic. Some of the more descriptive accounts that have appeared in recent years, which largely content themselves with enumerating such events or movements, appear to partake of this view.[55] They thus see eschatology as in a way structurally embedded in the very nature of the religious complexes where they appear, and perhaps even of all religion.

5. A fifth view appears in a recent extended essay by the semiotician and philosopher Tzvetan Todorov, and offers us yet another angle of approach to the question of the long-term trajectories of what he presents under the head of *messianisme politique*. Todorov argues that the 'political messianism' of the past two centuries or more, while ostensibly distinct from older forms because 'it has no place for God', nevertheless 'preserves other traits of ancient religion, such as a blind faith in the new dogmas, a fervour in the acts that serve it as in the proselytism of its faithful, or the transformation of its partisans who have fallen in combat into martyrs, as figures to be adored like saints'.[56] He goes on to distinguish three 'waves' of this political messianism: that of the revolutionary and colonial wars that begin immediately after 1789; the Communist project of the later nineteenth and twentieth centuries; and the post-1989 wave of 'imposing democracy through bombs' and upheld by utopian ideologies like those of universal human rights. The target here is thus as much the neo-liberal utopia of the 'end of history' as the totalitarian movements deplored by Norman Cohn and others. Yet, have we not moved here from a literal eschatology to a largely metaphorical one, and thus to a different view and emplotment of teleology as well?

Part of the debate concerns what place we are willing to attribute to the more literal versions of political eschatology in today's world. Can we argue with conviction that it has now effectively been banished into the space of tiny sects and cults, or panicky but passing rumours, such as that 'planes would fall out of the sky', and all computers crash, on the night of 31 December 1999 (or Y2K)? Alternatively, some would argue that there is place for a discussion of End-Times, but that this is essentially a scientific discussion on subjects such as, let us say, large asteroid collisions. Yet, as we see elsewhere in this volume, notably in relation to questions of climate change, the mere intervention of 'science' does not guarantee that questions of politics are rendered moot or even irrelevant.

An interesting matter that remains open for debate is how the global evolution of political forms may itself have had an effect on political eschatology. As our survey of early modern materials shows, in the sixteenth and seventeenth centuries much eschatological debate centred on monarchy and the royal personage.[57] The figure of the messiah was usually male, and often depicted as a 'king', ruling over a millennial kingdom – as was even the case of Taiping in the mid-nineteenth century. However, as monarchical forms have progressively declined from the eighteenth into the twenty-first centuries, to be replaced by broadly 'republican' ones, can we see a concomitant shift in political eschatology? The instance of political discourse in the United States of America suggests that it is indeed possible to have a mitigated form of 'republican messianism', wherein a sublimated version of the state is wedded to a utopian vision such as that of Ronald Reagan's celebrated 'Shining City on a Hill'. Another perspective, that of a Richard Landes, for example, would point to phenomena like the 'global *jihād*' of the 1990s and early 2000s in order to argue that the extent of secularization has in fact been vastly overestimated by social scientists, and that millennial religion continues to have a strong hold in many parts of the world even today.

To return to our point of departure then, we can see that even in a film such as *Dr Strangelove*, the problem of eschatology remains an inescapably political one. In that world, monarchy and the royal personage have notionally disappeared and been replaced by republican forms, whether democratic or not. But the implication is that the nature of military power in the nuclear age is such as to create new messiahs, endowed with the power to precipitate an apocalypse by pressing a single button, and thus show up the empty character of republican sovereignty. There is no 'fail-safe' system, and only good luck prevents such an event from happening sooner rather than later. Further, since Kubrick's is a satire, it deliberately inverts the usual relationship between justice and injustice; where the older eschatology presents the messianic figure as a return to justice from tyranny (whether with the *ratu adil*, or Dom Sebastião), General Ripper incarnates the arbitrary, the unjust and the deluded. One is left then with a Swiftian paradox, that those who live in a political dystopia are usually incapable of even recognizing its existence.

Notes

* I am grateful to Cornell Fleischer, Maurice Kriegel, Geoffrey Parker and José Alberto Tavim for bibliographical references, and other aid, over the years that we have discussed issues of political eschatology; and to Henning Trüper for helpful remarks.
1. From a large bibliography on the subject, see for example Charles Maland, '*Dr. Strangelove* (1964): Nightmare Comedy and the Ideology of Liberal Consensus', in *American Quarterly* 31 (1979), no. 5, pp. 697–717.

2. See the analysis in Robert Mann, *Daisy Petals and Mushroom Clouds: LBJ, Barry Goldwater, and the Ad That Changed American Politics*, Baton Rouge: Louisiana State University Press, 2011.
3. Robert M. Levine, *Vale of Tears: Revisiting the Canudos Massacre in Northeastern Brazil, 1893–1897*, Berkeley: University of California Press, 1995.
4. For the case of the *quilombo* of Palmares in the late seventeenth century, see the documentation in Stuart B. Schwartz, ed., *Early Brazil: A Documentary Collection to 1700*, New York: Cambridge University Press, 2010, pp. 264–7.
5. Euclides da Cunha, *Rebellion in the Backlands (Os Sertões)*, trans. Samuel Putnam, Chicago: University of Chicago Press, 1944.
6. For a recent study of Cunha, see Susanna B. Hecht, *The Scramble for the Amazon and the 'Lost Paradise' of Euclides da Cunha*, Chicago: University of Chicago Press, 2013.
7. Stuart Schwartz, 'Review of Hecht, *The Scramble for the Amazon*', in *American Historical Review* 119 (2014), no. 3, pp. 835–7.
8. Renata R. Mautner Wasserman, 'Mario Vargas Llosa, Euclides da Cunha, and the Strategy of Intertextuality', in *PMLA* 108 (1993), no. 3, pp. 460–73.
9. See Jacqueline Hermann, *No Reino do Desejado: A construção do Sebastianismo em Portugal, séculos XVI e XVII*, São Paulo: Companhia das Letras, 1998.
10. Elias Lipiner, *O Sapateiro de Trancoso e o Alfaiate de Setúbal*, Rio de Janeiro: Imago Editora, 1993.
11. See Tobie Meyer-Fong, *What Remains: Coming to Terms with Civil War in 19th Century China*, Stanford: Stanford University Press, 2013.
12. Jonathan D. Spence, *God's Chinese Son: The Taiping Heavenly Kingdom of Hong Xiuquan*, London: Flamingo, 1996.
13. Michael Adas, *Prophets of Rebellion: Millenarian Protest Movements against the European Colonial Order*, Chapel Hill: University of North Carolina Press, 1979.
14. See Peter M. Holt, *The Mahdist State in the Sudan, 1881–1898: A Study of its Origins, Development and Overthrow*, 2nd edn, New York: Oxford University Press, 1977.
15. Adas, *Prophets of Rebellion*, pp. 185–7.
16. Peter Carey, *The Power of Prophecy: Prince Dipanagara and the End of an Old Order in Java, 1785–1855*, Leiden: KITLV, 2007.
17. For these usages, see Dipesh Chakrabarty, 'Subaltern Studies in Retrospect and Reminiscence', in *Economic & Political Weekly* 48 (2013), no. 12, pp. 23–7.
18. Norman Cohn, *The Pursuit of the Millennium: Revolutionary Messianism in Medieval and Reformation Europe and its Bearing on Modern Totalitarian Movements*, 2nd edn, New York: Harper & Row, 1961; Eugen Weber, *Apocalypses: Prophecies, Cults, and Millennial Beliefs through the Ages*, Cambridge, Mass.: Harvard University Press, 1999; Richard Landes, *Heaven on Earth: The Varieties of the Millennial Experience*, New York: Oxford University Press, 2011.
19. See Shaul Shaked, *From Zoroastrian Iran to Islam: Studies in Religious History and Intercultural Contacts*, Aldershot: Variorum, 1995; Norman Cohn, *Cosmos, Chaos and the World to Come: The Ancient Roots of Apocalyptic Faith*, New Haven: Yale University Press, 1993, pp. 77–104.
20. See Dominique Sila-Khan, 'The Coming of the Nikalank Avatar: A Messianic Theme in Some Sectarian Traditions of North-Western India', in *Journal of Indian Philosophy* 25 (1997), no. 4, pp. 401–26.

21. Sanjay Subrahmanyam, 'Du Tage au Gange au XVIe siècle: Une conjoncture millénariste à l'échelle eurasiatique', in *Annales HSS* 56 (2001), no. 1, pp. 51–84; revised English version published as Subrahmanyam, 'Turning the Stones Over: Sixteenth-Century Millenarianism from the Tagus to the Ganges', in *Indian Economic and Social History Review* 40 (2003), no. 4, pp. 131–63.

22. Derryl N. Maclean, 'The Sociology of Political Engagement: the Mahdawiyah and the State', in Richard M. Eaton, ed., *India's Islamic Traditions, 711–1750*, Delhi: Oxford University Press, 2003, pp. 150–68, originally published as Maclean, 'La sociologie de l'engagement politique: Le Mahdawîya indien et l'État', in *Revue des mondes musulmans et de la Méditerranée* (2000), nos. 91–94, pp. 239–56. For an earlier account, see A.S. Bazmee Ansari, 'Sayyid Muhammad Jawnpuri and His Movement', in *Islamic Studies* 2 (1963), no. 1, pp. 41–74.

23. The text is quoted by Maclean, 'The Sociology of Political Engagement', pp. 156–7, from the early seventeenth-century hagiographical text, the *Matla' al-wilāyat*, by Miyan Sayyid Yusuf, Hyderabad, 1954.

24. Derryl N. Maclean, 'Real Men and False Men at the Court of Akbar: The *Majalis* of Shaykh Mustafa Gujarati', in David Gilmartin and Bruce B. Lawrence, eds, *Beyond Turk and Hindu: Rethinking Religious Identities in Islamicate South Asia*, Gainesville: University Press of Florida, 2000, pp. 199–215.

25. For an analysis of this text, see Ali Anooshahr, 'Dialogue and Territoriality in a Mughal History of the Millennium', in *Journal of the Economic and Social History of the Orient* 55 (2012), nos. 2–3, pp. 220–54.

26. See A. Azfar Moin, *The Millennial Sovereign: Sacred Kingship and Sainthood in Islam*, New York: Columbia University Press, 2012; also Ali Anooshahr, 'Mughal Historians and the Memory of the Islamic Conquest of India', in *Indian Economic and Social History Review* 43 (2006), no. 3, pp. 275–300.

27. Jean Aubin, 'L'avènement des Safavides reconsideré', in *Moyen Orient et Océan Indien* 5 (1988), pp. 1–130.

28. Kathryn Babayan, *Mystics, Monarchs and Messiahs: Cultural Landscapes of Early Modern Iran*, Cambridge, Mass.: Harvard University Press, 2002, pp. 105–8.

29. See Muzaffar Alam and Sanjay Subrahmanyam, 'A Place in the Sun: Travels with Faizî in the Deccan, 1591–93', in François Grimal, ed., *Les sources et le temps/ Sources and Time: A Colloquium*, Pondicherry: Ecole Française d'Extrême-Orient, 2001, pp. 265–307, especially pp. 285–6.

30. Roger M. Savory, 'A Curious Episode in Safavid History', in C. E. Bosworth, ed., *Iran and Islam: In Memory of the Late Vladimir Minorsky*, Edinburgh: Edinburgh University Press, 1971, pp. 461–73; compare Suraiya Faroqhi, *Subjects of the Sultan: Culture and Daily Life in the Ottoman Empire*, London: I.B. Tauris, 2000, pp. 76–9.

31. Cited in James D. Tracy, *Erasmus of the Low Countries*, Berkeley: University of California Press, 1996, p. 195.

32. Robert Finlay, 'Prophecy and Politics in Istanbul: Charles V, Sultan Süleyman, and the Habsburg Embassy of 1533–34', in *Journal of Early Modern History* 2 (1998), no. 1, pp. 1–31.

33. Serpil Bağcı and Massumeh Farhad, eds, *Falnama: The Book of Omens*, Washington DC: Smithsonian Institution, 2009.

34. Cornell Fleischer, 'Shadows of Shadows: Prophecy and Politics in 1530s Istanbul', in *International Journal of Turkish Studies* 13 (2007), nos. 1–2, pp. 51–62; Gülru Necipoğlu, 'Süleyman the Magnificent and the Representation of Power in the Context of Ottoman-Habsburg-Papal Rivalry', in *The Art Bulletin* 71 (1989), no. 3, pp. 401–27; Kaya Şahin, *Empire*

and Power in the Reign of Süleyman: Narrating the Sixteenth Century Ottoman World, New York: Cambridge University Press, 2013.

35. Alain Milhou, 'Apocalypticism in Central and South American Colonialism', in Bernard McGinn, John J. Collins and Stephen J. Stein, eds, *The Continuum History of Apocalypticism*, New York: Continuum Books, 2003, pp. 417–40.
36. See Luís Filipe F. R. Thomaz, 'L'idée impériale manueline', in Jean Aubin, ed., *La Découverte, le Portugal, et l'Europe*, Paris: Centre Culturel Calouste Gulbenkian, 1990, pp. 35–103.
37. João de Barros, *Da Ásia*, Lisbon: Livraria Sam Carlos, 1973, Década I/1, Book 4, pp. 268–70; also the discussion in Sanjay Subrahmanyam, *The Career and Legend of Vasco da Gama*, Cambridge: Cambridge University Press, 1997, pp. 51–4.
38. Geoffrey Parker, 'The Place of Tudor England in the Messianic Vision of Philip II of Spain', in *Transactions of the Royal Historical Society* 12 (2002), pp. 167–221.
39. Cited in Geoffrey Parker, *Philip II*, 3rd edn, Chicago: Open Court, 1995, p. xvi.
40. Serge Gruzinski, *L'Aigle et le Dragon: Démesure européenne et mondialisation au XVIe siècle*, Paris: Fayard, 2012; also see the earlier essay by Gruzinski, *A Passagem do Século, 1480–1520: As origens da globalização*, trans. Rosa Freire D'Aguiar, São Paulo: Companhia das Letras, 1999.
41. Francisco Bethencourt, 'Le Millénarisme: Idéologie de l'impérialisme eurasiatique?', in *Annales HSS* 57 (2002), no. 1, pp. 189–94.
42. Moti Benmelech, 'History, Politics, and Messianism: David ha-Reuveni's Origin and Mission', in *AJS Review* 35 (2011), no. 1, pp. 35–60; Miriam Eliav-Feldon, 'Invented Identities: Credulity in an Age of Prophecy and Exploration', in *Journal of Early Modern History* 3 (1999), no. 3, pp. 203–32.
43. There remain some doubts concerning his end; see José Alberto Rodrigues da Silva Tavim, 'David Reubeni: Um "embaixador" inusitado', in Roberto Carneiro and Artur Teodoro de Matos, eds, *D. João III e o Império: Actas do Congresso Internacional comemorativo do seu nascimento*, Lisbon: CHAM, 2004, pp. 683–715.
44. Matt Goldish, *The Sabbatean Prophets*, Cambridge, Mass.: Harvard University Press, 2004.
45. José Alberto Rodrigues da Silva Tavim, 'Revisitando uma carta em português sobre Sabbatai Zvi', in *Sefarad* 67 (2007), no. 1, pp. 155–90; Mercedes García-Arenal, 'Expectativas mesiánicas en el Magreb y la peninsula Ibérica: Entre David Reubeni y Sabbatai Sevi', in Carmen Ballesteros and Mery Ruah, eds, *Os Judeus Sefarditas entre Portugal, Espanha e Marrocos*, Lisbon: Edições Colibri, 2004, pp. 53–85.
46. Moin, *The Millennial Sovereign*, p. 234.
47. Babayan, *Mystics, Monarchs and Messiahs*, pp. 484–5.
48. David Armitage, 'The Cromwellian Protectorate and the Languages of Empire', in *The Historical Journal* 35 (1992), no. 3, pp. 531–55.
49. For details see Yosef Kaplan, Henry Méchoulan and Richard H. Popkin, eds, *Menasseh ben Israel and His World*, Leiden: E.J. Brill, 1989.
50. Maria Ana Travassos Valdez, *Historical Interpretations of the 'Fifth Empire': The Dynamics of Periodization from Daniel to António Vieira, S.J.*, Leiden: E.J. Brill, 2011.
51. Maria de Lurdes Rosa, 'Velhos, novos e mutáveis sagrados. . . Um olhar antropológico sobre formas "religiosas" de percepção e interpretação da conquista africana (1415–1521)', in *Lusitana Sacra* 18 (2006), pp. 14–18. The author of this erudite essay does not seem quite so concerned, on the other hand, with the difficulty of many other loaded terms such as 'sacred'.

52. James C. Scott, *The Art of Not Being Governed: An Anarchist History of Upland Southeast Asia*, New Haven: Yale University Press, 2009, pp. 302–4, *passim*.
53. Monique Bedasse, 'Rasta Evolution: The Theology of the Twelve Tribes of Israel', in *Journal of Black Studies* 40 (2010), no. 5, pp. 960–73.
54. Cohn, *The Pursuit of the Millennium*, pp. xiv–xv.
55. See the critical review of some recent literature in Paul A. Cohen, 'Time, Culture and Christian Eschatology: The Year 2000 in the West and the World', in *American Historical Review* 104 (1999), no. 5, pp. 1615–28.
56. Tzvetan Todorov, *Les ennemis intimes de la démocratie*, Paris: Robert Laffont, 2012, pp. 47–8.
57. I have found the broad, and comparative, reflections in David Cannadine and Simon Price, eds, *Rituals of Royalty: Power and Ceremonial in Traditional Societies*, Cambridge: Cambridge University Press, 1987, useful for this discussion.

PART II
BOTCHED VANISHING ACTS: ON THE DIFFICULTIES OF MAKING TELEOLOGY DISAPPEAR

CHAPTER 3
'THE VOCATION OF MAN' – 'DIE BESTIMMUNG DES MENSCHEN': A TELEOLOGICAL CONCEPT OF THE GERMAN ENLIGHTENMENT AND ITS AFTERMATH IN THE NINETEENTH CENTURY[*]

Philip Ajouri

In the last two decades the concept of the 'Bestimmung des Menschen'[1] has attracted considerable interest, and continues to do so. Scholars researching the philosophy, theology and literature of the German Enlightenment now reckon this question to be one of the key issues in the philosophical and theological debates of the second half of the eighteenth century.[2] For the people of the eighteenth century the problem of man's vocation was of utmost importance and had an aura of great significance. The ability to discuss this issue, that is, to answer the question of to what end man existed, was even regarded as a hallmark of mankind.[3] Despite this importance, the debate about the 'Bestimmung des Menschen' has only been partly reviewed by scholars.[4] This is especially true of its aftermath. As far as I am aware, no research has been done on the usage of this formula in later nineteenth-century philosophy and literature.[5] Although I will give some examples, this omission cannot of course be made fully good in the following essay.

This chapter starts with the idea that vocation ('Bestimmung') is one of several important teleological concepts which were used to understand man and his life. Different answers were given to the question of to what end man existed, with the perfection of virtues during this and the future life and individual self-cultivation ('Bildung') being two important ones. The chapter argues that vocation also played a crucial role in contemporaneous literature, notably in the 'Bildungsroman'. Although the vocation of man was never undisputed by philosophers and poets, answers to this question became even more contested in the course of the nineteenth century, as were other teleological concepts. Literature adapted once again to this new intellectual context. Some initial brief remarks on teleology and its relationship to narration might be helpful.[6]

1. Teleology and narration

It is useful to distinguish between teleological assumptions about reality and the teleology of narrative. The former is normally conceived as an explanation of things by referring to their functions or goals, even though by our standards they do not have intentions and were not produced by someone with intentions (e.g. objects of nature, history, mankind, man's life as a whole, etc.). To ascribe a 'Bestimmung' to mankind or an individual is an instance of teleology in this sense, as long as people thought (as they sometimes still do) that some higher power (God, nature, reason, etc.) had a *telos* ('end, purpose') in creating mankind or a certain individual. In this case teleology provides explanations that are not valid.[7] I consider that teleological concepts of reality are an essential component of many philosophies, religions or ideologies.[8] 'Bestimmung' is of course only one among many historically and culturally diverse teleological concepts, such as providence, destiny or progress (to humanity, to a classless society or whatever).

In contrast, parts of a story can be rightfully explained by teleology as long as we think that the story has been intentionally created by an author.[9] Thus, it is a valid (though perhaps not very sophisticated) explanation to say that Agathon, the protagonist of a novel of the same name by Christoph Martin Wieland (1733–1813), encounters Hippias *in order to* contrast and relativize his Platonic and idealistic world view with Hippias' materialism. This proposition can be explained by referring to authorial intention. It is the author who affiliates Hippias to Agathon *because* he thinks that Agathon's Platonism should be contrasted and relativized and that contrasting and relativizing Platonism is a good thing. A teleological explanation is thus rendered as a causal one by referring to the author.[10]

The Agathon/Hippias example is taken from a fictional text, and the elaborate explanation should be applied only to texts which deal with fictional characters and events. But historical writing is probably not free from teleological thinking. Arthur C. Danto has pointed out that historiographical texts do not describe the past as it happened, but necessarily imply knowledge of the future. He argues, for example, that a complete description of the year 1715 would have to contain a 'narrative sentence' such as 'The author of *Rameau's Nephew* was born in 1715', even though Denis Diderot worked on this book only decades later.[11] An adequate account of the past therefore implies knowledge of the future.[12] It is not the aim of this essay to explore the question of teleology and historical writing, but it should be noted that changes in teleological thinking can affect not only literature, but also historical writing.

Teleology on a compositional level is not the only way teleology can occur in fictional literature. There can also be final relations between events and characters in the narrated world. Story narration relies on presuppositions about reality just like teleology. For storytelling it makes a big difference, for example, to assume that man is a rational and self-conscious being or to assume that he is motivated by unconscious drives that are beyond control and reasoning. And so teleological assertions about the world make a difference to storytelling. Does God work wonders against natural laws? Does divine providence operate through them in a way that results in direct causal chains? Theological and philosophical reasoning of how God's final causes and causality go together, so that the former direct the latter somehow, are historically diverse and often very sophisticated. Storytelling (and probably history writing) is not independent of those ideas, and they can affect both the narrated world and the manner of narration. I will speak of strong narrative teleology when the reader is made to believe that the protagonist(s) or the whole narrated world has a goal or serves a function that depends on some higher power.

There are certain strategies that tend to enhance narrative teleology. I will now suggest an ideal prototype of strong narrative teleology which applies probably only to a certain kind of fictional western literature from the eighteenth century onwards. A book like this has never been written (and it would be rather boring if it had been): at the end of the story the protagonist is in a state which is generally accepted as good and desirable, and he is aware of this. All events and characters are obviously means to this end. The reader knows this because an omniscient narrator comments explicitly on the storyline. The story is told chronologically; or at least in a way that allows the reader to gain an overview of the narrated world. The protagonist comments on teleological concepts like providence, progress or 'Bestimmung', and the narrator underpins his view. Motives, events and characters are designed and arranged in such a way that the enhancement and improvement of the state of affairs becomes clear. Chance, if it is stressed at all, moves the story forward towards its end and is judged accordingly by the narrator and/or characters, etc.

Interestingly, very different levels of narrative (point of view, chronology, motifs, events, the views of characters, etc.) can produce a strong narrative teleology. On the other hand, many structural devices on different levels can weaken narrative teleology. Narrative teleology is diminished if the end cannot be regarded as unambiguously good or if there are many possible endings; if the chronological order of events does not become clear; if the same event is told again and again; if larger parts of the story are obviously and/or explicitly not functional for the end; if the knowledge of the narrator is limited to the narrow point of view of the protagonist; if the narrator and/or the protagonist doubt that there is a direction in the course of events; or if chance crosses the intentions and destroys the plans of various characters and at the same time does not serve as an agent of providence, progress or any other higher power.

My basic assumption in this chapter is that narrative teleology is dependent on contemporary teleological concepts of reality. These ideas can be reconstructed by examining the relevant contexts of a particular text.[13] The eighteenth-century question of man's vocation provoked answers that ascribed a goal to mankind or to an individual life. I will try to demonstrate how those answers became intertwined with literature. Although already contested in the eighteenth century, those concepts became less widely accepted in the second half of the nineteenth century, partly because teleological concepts were criticized by materialistic philosophers or were made superfluous by the success of the natural sciences. I will therefore illustrate how literature adapts to different solutions to the problem of man's vocation. Although it may seem as though my argument itself is teleological (teleological assumptions of reality become more and more implausible and therefore narrative teleology becomes ever weaker), this is not the case. Although I believe that materialism and scientific progress are significant problems for teleological thinking in the nineteenth century, periods which rely to a greater extent on teleology may come and go. Finally, different individual authors, literary movements and different genres may have differing affinities in relying on teleological concepts or in treating them as a problem.

2. Spalding, Blanckenburg, Wieland: 'Bestimmung des Menschen' in the eighteenth century

The expression 'Bestimmung des Menschen' goes back to a text by the Enlightenment theologian Johann Joachim Spalding (1714–1804). In 1748 he published a book with the title *Betrachtung über die Bestimmung des Menschen*. The importance ascribed to this small brochure has risen steadily over the last two decades. It has recently been argued that it marks the turning point of German Enlightenment philosophy, because it did not presuppose the existence of God but derived him from insights into human nature.[14] Spalding's essay had eleven legal editions by 1794 (and at least seven illegal ones before 1789),[15] and was widely read. Scholars have pointed out that Gottfried Wilhelm Leibniz and Anthony Ashley Cooper, third Earl of Shaftesbury, were two main sources for Spalding's essay.[16] I will not consider these sources any further, but I will focus instead on the different forms of teleology that occur in Spalding's essay.

The essay is written in the first person. The speaker wishes to discover man's purpose. This, he continues, is not possible by observing others.[17] Furthermore, he does not try to discover the purpose of man by reading the Bible, which would be the most natural thing to do for a theologian in the middle of the eighteenth century. He instead looks into himself and tries to discover what inclinations, feelings and dispositions he has and what practices or mental activities they are likely to be designed for. The question of the vocation of man is not a matter of what determines man, but of the purpose for which he was made. Spalding does not draw a distinction between himself and man as a species.[18] Every individual represents mankind to a full extent. The vocation of man can thus be deduced from any individual without any differences.

Spalding examines three different fields of action and of mental activities: sensuality, intellectual reasoning and virtue. His question as well as his answer reveals the teleological background of his own thoughts.[19] Teleological argumentation can be found on two different levels: functions and goals.

1. Functions

Firstly, Spalding regards man and the beautifully ordered universe as the creation of God. Man has a certain 'composition',[20] very much like a complicated machine which serves different purposes. He has the facility of enjoyment with his senses, he is furthermore designed to find pleasure in theoretical reasoning, and he is delighted by being virtuous. All of these three activities are rewarded by positive feelings, and therefore it is good to carry them out (sensuality, of course, involves certain limitations which hint at a Stoic background for Spalding's thinking). Happiness is the reward for following those inclinations. The reader is almost surprised when Spalding finds that the highest degree of happiness is in acting virtuously.

Spalding does not expect that something he discovers in his inner self would have no purpose or that it would serve a primordial bad purpose. On the contrary, the 'mind which governs everything'[21] has put everything on earth in its proper place.

If one follows the analytical explanation of teleology produced by Andrew Woodfield in 1976, one can say that man is regarded here as having artificial functions very much in a way that a machine has: the purposes of human nature are traced back to a divine reason which is capable of designing man and equipping him with those purposes. The positive feelings of doing good to others can be explained in the following way: man has this positive feeling because his designer thinks that this feeling contributes to doing good to others and thinks that doing good to others is a good thing.[22] In Spalding's words,

> here I perceive without doubt that this mind which governs everything could not have any other intention than that all things should be good in their way and in the whole. To this end all laws are designed which he has laid upon them. To this end all movements of bodies aim, as well as the original drives of beings with understanding.[23]

2. Goals

Secondly, in Spalding's essay life has a goal (though not an endpoint). Most importantly, Spalding's speaker discovers in himself skills which are capable of endless development.[24] Due to this quality and due to the fact that being virtuous isn't always rewarded in this life on earth,[25] Spalding assumes that the soul must be eternal and live after death. Only in an infinite span of time is it possible for the capabilities of man to be perfected and for justice to be established: 'Therefore I was made for another life.'[26] From this point of view the three other realms of human action are insufficient. Even virtue, though human dispositions point to it, cannot be the ultimate goal due to the fact that the virtuous person may die unhappy and the villain may die unpunished. The fact that life has a goal is expressed with metaphors of movement and journeying: the speaker has to follow a 'path',[27] he has to 'ascend'[28] to greater perfection and he has to 'reach the great destination'.[29]

It is important to see that Spalding's notion of 'Bestimmung des Menschen' associates teleology with self-reference.[30] It is only because Spalding's speaker pays close attention to himself that he can explore his 'Bestimmung'.[31] And in order to fulfil his goal, life produces a task for him: he has to tell himself how to lead his future life.[32] Without using the word, Spalding basically describes the self-determination of man according to his function in nature. This presupposes, of course, that man is able to act independently of sensual needs and all external hindrances. This dominant self-reference is the reason why Spalding chose the soliloquy as a literary genre, a text type which he knew from English moral sense philosophy, notably from Shaftesbury.[33]

Spalding's *Bestimmung des Menschen* was a tremendous success. Although it was not undisputed it remained the basis for numerous debates, remarks and conceptual innovations.[34] I pass over the important and comparably well-researched debate of Moses Mendelssohn and Thomas Abbt over the question of whether man really is able to discover his 'Bestimmung' by introspection.[35]

The concept of 'Bestimmung des Menschen' played a crucial role in Friedrich von Blanckenburg's (1744–96) *Theorie des Romans* (1774), one of the most sophisticated Enlightenment German theories of the novel. Blanckenburg, who recommended learning Spalding's writings by heart,[36] placed the individual at the centre of his ideal novel. He laid emphasis on the development of the protagonist's inner self, moving away from older heroic novels which placed events and perfect heroes at the centre of the story. Blanckenburg held that the world was designed by God in order to ensure the human 'Bestimmung' of perfecting oneself.[37] He was convinced that providence was behind all causal chains and gave them their direction. This was the basis for his theory of the novel. The poet had to be like God to his narrated universe. In order to match reality, the poet had to arrange all events of the narrated world in such a way that they had a (positive) effect on the protagonist's inner self and contributed to his perfection. At the same time, the author had to establish fully both the causality of action and its relationship to the protagonist's state of mind. Therefore, the teleology of narrative was very pronounced, and it was legitimized by the teleology of the real world.

Interestingly, Blanckenburg's main example for this type of novel was Christoph Martin Wieland's *Agathon* (1766/7). Although Blanckenburg misconceived Wieland's novel by leaving out the role of the narrator and by neglecting aspects of its scepticism and irony,[38] he did realize that the question of how a character alters and possibly perfects under certain circumstances was a central issue in the book. But he did not observe how fragile and disputed the concept of a human 'Bestimmung' was. The young Wieland certainly must have read Spalding's essay in 1754 and approved of it.[39] In his novel the protagonist Agathon believes in his enthusiastic youth that he has a 'Bestimmung' which fits into a higher divine plan, and even the narrator clings to this concept in an important chapter which sums up the mental state of Agathon.[40] In sharp contrast to Agathon's very modern enthusiasm, the novel unfolds in lengthy speeches by Hippias the position of French materialism. In this view man has no higher 'Bestimmung' in the very precise sense that his only realm is what Spalding declared to be the lowest field of action: sensuality. According to Hippias, all pleasures of man are sensual. Beyond those he cannot know or feel anything. Virtue, so highly appreciated by Spalding as a means to propel man's 'Bestimmung', seems to Hippias to be conventional and arbitrary. Interestingly, the book does not reconcile the conflicting positions of Agathon and Hippias. Hippias' arguments are very consistent and hard to contradict on a theoretical level, but Agathon's idealism is necessary from an ethical point of view.[41] It is thus clear that on a discursive level Agathon's 'Bestimmung' is open to dispute. Therefore, it is with ironic reservations that the author leads Agathon to a utopian republic at the end of the book where he lives in ideal circumstances. The irony springs from the fictional editor of the book apologizing for the plot's improbability. He gives the following formal reason for why the original Greek author might have chosen to end the novel in a utopian state: the end of a story should match its beginning, and a hero who started with ambitious plans and who aroused the reader's greatest expectations should end as a wise and virtuous man.[42] The same is true for Agathon's reunion with Danae, a beloved woman he once left due to Hippias' treachery. The narrator reflects that he is still longing for her and then tells the reader, tongue in cheek, that she was brought to him by an 'eager' storm.[43] What is happening here? Obviously, Wieland wanted to give his book a positive ending in the very sense that Blanckenburg demanded a happy ending. But he could not produce this desired ending within the frame of probability, an Enlightenment concept of narration which Wieland felt obliged to follow. This would have involved narrating probable, causally motivated events and their necessary relationship to the protagonist's mind. Thus he changes the 'level' of narration by implying that a narrator is not relating things which really happened, but that the story has been invented by an author who guides the course of things in whatever direction he wishes. As the narrator puts it, the Greek author 'jumped out of the window'.[44] This ironic ending correlates to the problem that Wieland did not reconcile Agathon's enthusiasm with Hippias' materialism so as to provide a plausible and morally acceptable concept of man's 'Bestimmung'.[45] Nevertheless, the narrative teleology remains quite strong, because Wieland provides a positive ending and gives closure to the story by having Danae return.[46]

3. Johann Wolfgang von Goethe: 'Bildung' as a solution to the problem of 'Bestimmung'

A few years later the concept of 'Bestimmung' was adapted in such a way that it enabled a new appreciation of the individual's uniqueness: every human being had his own 'Bestimmung' and this, in contrast to Spalding's views, differed among individuals. To develop one's own unique dispositions in confrontation with the world became the task of the individual.[47] This process was called 'Bildung' and it was described with organic metaphors. The concept of 'Bildung' was for Johann Gottfried Herder (1744–1803), Wilhelm von Humboldt (1767–1835) and Johann Wolfgang von Goethe (1749–1832), among others, a solution to the problem of why man existed, for what end.[48] 'Bildung' as a concept was successful because it inherited the teleological component of Spalding's answer to man's 'Bestimmung'. It implied that the changes which an individual undergoes during his life are not contingent and undirected, but lead towards an end that was already included as a disposition at the beginning of one's life. As with Spalding, this process had a direction but not an endpoint. In accordance with the Enlightenment idea of perfectibility, every individual was thought to be capable of never-ending perfection. Strangely enough, it was not assumed that an accumulation of self-cultivated unique individuals might lead to social chaos. On the contrary, fully developed individuals fitted perfectly into society, and it was assumed that the dispositions of different individuals would balance each other and create social harmony.[49] It is not difficult to detect this harmony as an echo of Spalding's functional universe. Of course, in Goethe it is not a personal God and providence that establish this functional harmony as in Spalding, but nature itself. Finally, the process of perfection is an active one. It relies on the individual's fundamental capability of free self-direction. Having said this, it is important to note that Goethe of course realized that there might be detours in a person's life and that he/she might even go astray for a time.⁵⁰ It shows the great power of the concept of 'Bildung' that even such misspent times could be accepted as somehow necessary detours that contributed, in a more or less visible way, to the process of 'Bildung'.

Although Goethe was very critical of certain kinds of external teleological functionality,⁵¹ Fotis Jannidis has argued that both forms of teleology also occur in a very subtle form in Goethe's concept of 'Bildung'.⁵² The individual has his own prescribed goal towards which he should strive. At the same time it is ensured that a society of self-cultivated individuals will operate in functional harmony. Even if Goethe realized that these ideas were not at all enacted in practice, it seemed necessary to believe in them as ideas to guide our actions.

It has been demonstrated that this concept of 'Bildung' shaped Goethe's autobiography, *Dichtung und Wahrheit*.⁵³ But it is more difficult to show that it is also a leading idea in Goethe's so-called 'Bildungsroman', *Wilhelm Meisters Lehrjahre* (1795/6). Although it is not possible to discuss this intricate problem in detail here, it is clear that the question of Wilhelm's 'Bestimmung' lies at the heart of this novel. At the start Wilhelm believes that his 'Bestimmung'⁵⁴ is to become an actor, although the narrator presents his wish with mild irony. On the stage he hopes that he will cultivate himself ('auszubilden'). Wilhelm writes in his important letter to Werner: 'To speak it in a word; the cultivation of my individual self, here as I am, has from my youth upwards been constantly though dimly my wish and my purpose'.⁵⁵ In the very same letter, he takes the final decision to become an actor. And this step does not prove to be part of a straightforward progress towards his final goal of becoming a member of the Tower Society. This scene is characteristic of Wilhelm. He is a very passive hero and hardly acts. And when he does, he often takes the wrong decision. So how is he able to declare at the very end of the novel (and this is the final sentence): '. . . but I know I have attained a happiness which I have not deserved, and which I would not change with anything in life'?⁵⁶ A possible answer might be that members and agents of the Tower Society have secretly directed Wilhelm to his end. Friedrich Schiller suggested in a letter to Goethe that the Tower Society is to Goethe's novel what the gods were to the epic.⁵⁷ Schiller conceived of the Tower Society as a 'secretly acting higher reason'.⁵⁸ But it is difficult for an analysis of the novel to detect any important influence of the Tower Society on Wilhelm,⁵⁹ and the same applies for any other higher power such as fate. But if there is no higher reason in the narrated world of *Wilhelm Meister*, if the Tower Society is insufficient to explain Wilhelm's luck at the end of the book, and if even his own actions are not adequate to reach this end, how does he achieve a happy end? The answer is probably so problematic because the novel places less importance on giving sufficient causal motivations in the narrated world than does Wieland's *Agathon*. At the same time, the philosophical problems are not elaborated independently of the limited views of the novel's characters. Manfred Engel has emphasized that the novel is structured by symbolic and typological motifs, and has suggested that final causation does not appear on the level of the narrated world but on the level of this 'poetic nexus'.⁶⁰ Indeed, typology in the theological meaning of prefiguration and fulfilment implies teleology. On the level of narration it is well able to constitute a strong narrative teleology as soon as the reader realizes these relationships.

The clearest examples of this foreshadowing are situated in Wilhelm's youth: in the puppet show, in his first readings, and in the painting of the sick king's son that he saw when he was a child. One of his first impressions at the puppet show is of Saul entering the stage, and in the second last sentence of the novel he is compared to him. Wilhelm finally becomes engaged to the most important female character in the book, Natalia. She is the antitype of Chlorinda, a female character of Tasso's *Gerusalemme liberata*, a book that Wilhelm read when he was a child.[61] And the painting of the sick king's son, as the young Wilhelm conceived, shows 'the history of that king's son dying of a secret love for his father's bride'.[62] At the end of the book, Wilhelm is unhappily in love with Natalia, and is declared to be ill because of this. The whole art collection of Wilhelm's father has been sold years ago, but happens now to be in the very house where Wilhelm is staying at the end of the book. And this is how another character, Friedrich, is able to describe the same painting again. But this time it becomes clear that the painting shows a very decisive moment; and not a moment of despair, but of cure: a doctor has recognized the cause of the son's illness.[63] And describing the picture in this way prompts the happy ending of the story, Wilhelm's union with Natalia: 'Nature has performed her part',[64] as Lothario explains. Reality has somehow answered the needs of Wilhelm; it fits to his inner self in a way that is not fully explained. This harmony between the individual and his environment, *despite* the intentions of the protagonist and other characters, hints at a teleological background of Goethe's thinking, even if in the narrated world no final causes motivate the course of events. Wilhelm's 'Bestimmung' is visible largely in the symbolic structure of the book.

4. Aftermath in the nineteenth century

As noted above, the aftermath of the debate about the vocation of man has not been extensively researched until recently. The aura surrounding the formula obviously still existed, but the debates usually did not reach the intellectual level of 1800. Jannidis has recorded books with 'vocation of man' or the like in the title up to the 1850s.[65] These are quite numerous, and the concept will have played a crucial role in many more books and articles than those that mentioned it explicitly in their titles. Reinhard Brandt, who closely connected the debate about man's 'Bestimmung' with neo-stoicism, argued that the interest in this issue diminished after 1800, as the influence of Christianity and Platonism strengthened. From a philosophical perspective this may very well be the case, but the concept of man's 'Bestimmung' remained an important means of cultural self-understanding. It spread, for example, into protestant dogma. Karl Gottlieb Bretschneider refers to it in his *Handbuch der Dogmatik der evangelisch-lutherischen Kirche* (1814). Like Herder, Bretschneider proposed that the vocation of man lay in actualizing his Godlikeness ('Gottesebenbildlichkeit'). He argued against the notion that after man's fall from grace Godlikeness was no longer achievable.[66] Therefore Bretschneider's notion of the vocation of man is not so very different from Herder's, even though he did not use the term 'humanity'.

In the 1840s the Catholic theologian and philosopher Johann Nepomuk Ehrlich (1810–64), who was influenced by Anton Günther (1783–1863), wrote two volumes on the *Lehre von der Bestimmung des Menschen als rationale Teleologie* (1842/45).[67] His attempt to establish Christian ethics was in line with Spalding and even more with Kant, and was shaped by an ambivalent attitude towards Hegel. According to him, it is through an analysis of self-consciousness that man is able to discern the idea which God had in producing man. This idea is his 'Bestimmung'. In order to fulfil this idea it has to be put into practice on the basis of free self-determination. Ultimately, this idea is based on the unity of spirit and nature,[68] and duty, morality and happiness are three aspects of it.[69] Moral action and happiness are, with some restrictions, linked in Ehrlich's book.[70] To say that man's 'Bestimmung' is moral action implies the proposition that his 'Bestimmung' is happiness.[71] In contrast to Spalding, the idea of afterlife does not play any significant role in this work.

His highly sophisticated and lengthy account of man's 'Bestimmung' certainly did not reach a broad public. For an impression of a more popular Catholic conception of man's 'Bestimmung' we can turn to a sermon that was given on this topic in Munich on New Year's Eve 1854. The preacher, Daniel Bonifacius Haneberg (1816–76), mentions nature and human dispositions, which point to man's 'Bestimmung', only briefly.[72] In line with Spalding, he argues that man's soul is too rich to be designed to fit into this world and therefore must have been made for the afterlife.[73] But ultimately man's vocation is not derived from man's nature, but is gained from the Bible and therefore is already presupposed. Man's eternal vocation is to be near to God and to find his satisfaction in him. Not nature, but the Bible and above all the life of Jesus give us an example of a fulfilled 'Bestimmung'.[74] Interestingly, Haneberg argues against the notion that man's dispositions develop themselves naturally and without any external help. Man cannot reach his 'Bestimmung' by himself but is dependent on the grace of God.[75]

Spalding's question continued to influence nineteenth-century religious thought, but with Haneberg the insight into human nature was replaced by revelation, and self-determination by dependence on God's grace. Any assumption of an autonomous individual being able to fulfil his own 'Bestimmung' was rejected. Despite this, man still has an eternal 'Bestimmung', a direction to his life that encloses moral action and leads to an ultimate goal. Despite all these different approaches to the question of man's 'Bestimmung', and despite such major changes in intellectual history, teleology still remained in place.

In the 1840s, however, those answers became less and less generally acceptable. It is hard to say why this happened, but it is clear that materialistic philosophers were attacking the idea of man's vocation as well as other important closely related notions. And at the same time literature was referring to the vocation of man in a very different way than Goethe or Wieland had. Even after Goethe's proposed solution of 'Bildung' as the vocation of man the idea of vocation remained contested.

Ludwig Feuerbach (1804–72), for example, not only famously held that God was only a projection of man, but attacked the idea of man's supernatural vocation that theologians had elaborated. He denied that perfectibility was an essential characteristic of man or that it proved the existence of an afterlife.[76] He disputed that sensuality was only a means to 'higher' activities like morality. The vocation of man was to Feuerbach simply – and quite tautologically – to be a human being.[77] The essence of man included so-called inferior activities like eating and sleeping.[78] In addition to this, man had a special vocation, but that was nothing more than an occupation somebody chose in accordance with his nature, his drives and dispositions.[79] It is crucial to see that man's nature, his dispositions and drives had nothing to do with any higher (divine or supernatural) forces and that neither were directed to them. Where Goethe relied on the Spinozian assumption that 'God is nature' ('deus sive natura'),[80] Feuerbach opposed God to nature and forced the readers and listeners of his popular lectures to choose one side of this alternative: '*Either* God *or* nature!'[81] And this is why Feuerbach insisted that the meaning of a sentence like 'God's will has determined that a being has certain dispositions' was simply that a certain being lives under circumstances that are determined by chance or necessity.[82] Thus teleology was excluded from understanding nature, mankind or the individual.

Other philosophers such as Ludwig Büchner (1824–99) had similar inclinations to destroy teleology. In his tremendously successful book *Kraft und Stoff* (1855), he denied that nature had functions and goals. He followed Immanuel Kant in assuming that teleology was only a heuristic projection of the human mind on nature. With some emphasis, he told his readers how many dysfunctional things nature produced and how many natural objects could have been made much better.[83] The idea that man should have a vocation from a higher, divine being was not an assumption that filled him with any respect and pride, but with fear. Why should it be agreeable to think of man as a plaything of higher and unknown forces?[84] In addition, he severely restricted free will and denied completely the immortality of the soul.[85] As we have seen, both of these concepts were repeatedly associated to the idea of vocation.

These remarks are perhaps sufficient to suggest that a very powerful teleological concept of structuring one's life for many people no longer seemed plausible around 1850. There were of course opponents who wrote against such materialistic notions and argued in favour of vocation. One such publication is the anonymous brochure *Kurze populäre Widerlegung der neueren materialistischen Behauptungen über Gott, Welt, Bestimmung des Menschen und angebliche Sterblichkeit des menschlichen Geistes* (1857).[86] Interestingly, the concept of vocation does not play an explicit role in this essay. It is about the human soul and its immortality, about the existence of God, and about free will. The vocation of man seems to be a mere consequence of these suppositions and not something that has to be considered in its own right. For a religious audience, as for example in Haneberg's sermon, vocation was still a formula which stood for the highest capabilities and characteristics of man in a world designed by God.

The Swiss poet Gottfried Keller (1819–90) wrote in the midst of those quarrels. Initially influenced by Idealism and Romanticism, he attended the lectures of Feuerbach in Heidelberg in 1848/9 and became acquainted with Büchner as well. His 'Bildungsroman' *Der grüne Heinrich* (1854/5) is a story about Heinrich, a young man who grows up without a father and decides to become a painter. Thanks to great sacrifices by his mother he studies abroad, but nevertheless he fails to become a successful artist. He begins with imaginative but bland landscapes and ends up painting a gigantic cobweb, a piece of abstract art *avant la lettre*. But Heinrich, like a friend and the narrator, feels uncomfortable with this astonishing result and so he starts to draw the human figure from a model. But this is also inadequate and so, having earned money by painting flag posts for a royal wedding, he travels home to his mother. On the journey back he falls in love with a girl named Dortchen. As he enters his home town, without having confessed his love to Dortchen, he encounters his mother's funeral procession and dies shortly afterwards. It is clear that a novel with a plot like this deals with the question of man's vocation in a very different way.

The novel's characters repeatedly interpret their own decisions and plans as depending on their vocation. Heinrich, for example, after having been thrown out of school, is tempted to see these unhappy events in the light of a divine plan. When he is asked to choose a profession, he thinks about his 'higher vocation'[87] and believes that his inclinations will be protected by God. So he decides to become a landscape painter. His mother also is convinced that her savings have to be sacrificed on the 'altar of my vocation'.[88] Mother and son think in terms of categories such as 'Bestimmung', and they are supported in this by their environment. 'Bestimmung' has a peculiar meaning here: it combines old and popular views about a personal God who cares for all individuals (*procuratio individualis*) with late eighteenth-century views on individual dispositions. The aim which Heinrich strives for is Romantic in a broad sense. He seeks to paint nature because that is where God reveals himself.

But all these ideas prove vain. The fact that Heinrich is obviously mistaken about his vocation is not as problematic as it may seem. Wilhelm, in Goethe's *Wilhelm Meisters Lehrjahre*, is also wrong to assert that his vocation is to become an actor, and yet he is guided to happiness. And even the fact that Heinrich himself at one point recognizes that his emphatic choice was based on arbitrary ideas and circumstances can be formulated within the frame of 'Bestimmung', as long as his awareness is characterized as limited. More importantly, the narrator himself also attacks the idea of vocation. In the scene where Heinrich paints a human figure, the narrator confirms Heinrich's fear that his choice of becoming a landscape painter was only chance and explains that Heinrich could have had thousands of different 'vocations', if arbitrary circumstances had been different.[89] This is the point where goal-directed concepts of life like 'Bestimmung' become irrelevant, simply because there is no necessary goal in his life. It is likely that this is a reflection of Feuerbach's lectures, which confronted Keller with closely similar ideas. It is therefore clear that in the narrated world of *Der grüne Heinrich* the teleological ideal of vocation exists only as an erroneous projection of some characters. And the plot confirms this view by ending with Heinrich's death.

How does Keller organize the plot and its motives so that it becomes clear that Heinrich has no vocation? I think that Keller drew upon certain narrative structures and techniques that he knew from the 'Bildungsroman' and from other traditional literary forms and gave them a negative twist. A few examples can illustrate this. In this novel, as in Goethe's, typology plays an important role,[90] but it is used in a notably different manner. Unlike in Goethe, the narrator – the older Heinrich as a first-person narrator who remembers his childhood – says explicitly that the events of his youth are worth telling because they are a prelude to incidents of his later life.[91] But from the context it is obvious that the narrator is referring to negative incidents. Indeed, events like a quarrel between Heinrich and a friend or the wasting of his money are taken up later. But they cannot be understood in the typological scheme of foreshadowing and (improved) fulfilment, because even in their second, 'fulfilled' appearance they are adverse to the protagonist. The structure of promise and fulfilment is changed to an increased reiteration of failings. Keller uses the narrative frame of journey and homecoming in a similar way. He stresses this subject by repeatedly referring to the story of Ulysses so that Heinrich appears as a sort of nineteenth-century Ulysses. But his homecoming brings no reunification or reconciliation. On the contrary, he is not only separated from Dortchen, but finds his mother dead and dies himself shortly afterwards. Again, Keller uses a traditional narrative frame and transforms the effect on the reader with a negative twist. Finally, an important motive, the title-giving colour green, is used in a highly ambivalent way. Heinrich is called the 'green Henry' because he wears the green clothing of his deceased father. In the few scenes in which Heinrich remembers him, his father's green clothes have a dominant role. Furthermore, Heinrich feels obliged to continue the successful life of his father.[92] Green is the colour of hope and stands for the possibility of success.[93] But the last sentence of the novel refers to the green grass that grows on Heinrich's grave. Once again a sequence of motifs ends with a negative twist. As a result, the narrative teleology on a compositional level can be considered to be quite strong: many narrative elements point to the end of the story. But these motifs and events do not lead to an ending in the sense of a positive *telos*, and they result in Heinrich's death.

In the second version, which Keller revised during 1879 and 1880, Heinrich does not die but instead becomes a senior clerk in the Swiss administration and therefore a useful member of society. The idea that the result of 'Bildung' should involve becoming a useful and respectable member of society obviously persists. But Keller's revised ending fails to support any claim to a successful life. Heinrich is resigned. He is alienated from his job and has considered suicide. He has finally found his place in society, but this is not the result of a directed process of self-cultivation, and the ending cannot be viewed as a happy one.

Wieland's *Agathon*, Goethe's *Wilhelm Meister* and Keller's *Der grüne Heinrich* all refer, with different narrative strategies and on different narrative levels, to the problem of man's vocation. From the perspective of a literary critic, it may seem as if literature changes because of intellectual contexts changing in time. And this may well be the case here: Keller certainly was influenced by Feuerbach's views on the essence of religion and man, including subjects like vocation, teleology, nature and free will. And it seems reasonable to draw upon those contexts to understand Keller's novel in a more precise way. But those intellectual contexts need not be the only causes of Keller's new treatment of vocation, and social factors may also be relevant. Firstly, it is also possible to ask the question why Feuerbach or Büchner rejected teleology. Perhaps they did so because they were sensitive to natural sciences that were successfully explaining the world without teleology. Perhaps they felt that the old idea of teleology no longer suited current society. And this leads to a second aspect. Keller would not have taken up these ideas if his own experiences had not supported them. Furthermore, he could not have communicated them successfully to his audience if his readers had not also experienced them to a certain degree. For example, for an author like Keller, 'Bildung' became implausible as an answer to man's vocation, not only because of changes in other fields of knowledge like philosophy, but because the middle class was now trained in publicly maintained schools in order to fill highly specialized jobs. Keller's novel shows how difficult it is to educate a child in a school with pupils from a socially weak background and with different and varied teachers. He points out that Heinrich's expulsion from school is his social death,[94] and he stresses how difficult it is to assert oneself as a painter in a highly commercial art market. The novel pays attention to all these social conditions. It discovers restraints, economic pressures and arbitrary occurrences that contribute to the implausibility of the idea of 'Bildung' as an answer to 'Bestimmung' in a modern society. The philosophical thinking of Feuerbach and Büchner had certainly contributed to the crisis of teleology, and for literary critics they remain a privileged context that can enhance our understanding of literary works. But for a full analysis of the change of ideas in literature, one must consider not only philosophy or related intellectual contexts, but also social conditions in a broader sense.

The vocation of man had lost much of its initial aura when it was once again disputed in the last third of the nineteenth century. This time the offending object was Darwin's theory of evolution. In Germany, Darwin's theory was broadly understood as a process involving progress, and so teleology was preserved even in these versions of a Darwinist world view. This idealist interpretation of Darwin was especially popularized by Ernst Haeckel (1834–1919). There was also a non-teleological understanding of Darwin's teaching, which is only now starting to be fully recognized.[95] Both teleological and non-teleological interpretations of the history of evolution presented a problem to the concept of man's vocation. Haeckel held that man's place in nature had to be re-evaluated.[96] With his strict anti-clericalism, he attacked the idea that the immortality of the soul could be proved by referring to man's higher vocation of potentially endless perfectibility.[97] This was exactly what Spalding had tried to do. In accordance with non-teleological interpretations of Darwin, the saying spread that man's vocation would have been 'won in a lottery' if Darwin's theory of evolution proved to be right.[98] There were also writings by theologians who opposed a Darwinian approach with the question of 'Bestimmung'. The churchman Paul Gerhard, for example, rejected Haeckel's notion that man's 'Bestimmung' had to be re-evaluated in the light of evolution, and he insisted on a teleological interpretation of nature, in which man's 'Bestimmung' was given by God.[99] And there were projects which interwove a Romantic philosophy of nature with Darwinism in order to draw conclusions from evolution about man's 'Bestimmung'.[100] But in general the idea of man's vocation was downgraded to a phrase that had only a limited capability in terms of defining and understanding life. A few years later, the philosopher Fritz Mauthner (1849–1923) included the lemma 'Bestimmung' in his *Wörterbuch der Philosophie* (1910), and wrote that it was then of only linguistic interest.[101]

'The Vocation of Man'

This is reflected in a short story entitled 'Der Corsetten-Fritz' (1893) by Oskar Panizza (1853–1921). In one passage of this story the protagonist Fritz (who is obsessed with an orange corset he once saw in a shop window) has to take his final secondary school examinations. The subject of the German essay which he has to write is the vocation of man. To begin with, he is helpless:

> The German essay was about 'the vocation of man'. I remember that I stared at these words for about a quarter of an hour, but I couldn't come up with anything. Now I knew that this essay would be a waste of time too. But I pondered without haste just to see if any idea would occur to me in the face of such an earth-shattering subject. And nothing came. Then I realized more clearly from minute to minute that this essay would not only be a very bad one but that there was no chance of ever treating this subject in a regular, competent or honest way. The 'vocation of man'? I didn't know that! My classmates picked on me from behind. They were used to me helping them with the German essay and they whispered: 'Hey, what's the vocation of man?' I didn't know, and they didn't know either. The answer that I'd have given in Christian religious instruction – that I was very familiar with: to lead a God-fearing life and to die blessed. But that was only fine words, a phrase that everybody mouthed in emergency but that nobody believed.[102]

This extract is highly revealing about the cultural importance of the vocation of man in the late nineteenth century. This expression was clearly still deep-seated in educational institutions. Fritz as a pupil knows what the teacher expects him to write. He recognizes that the vocation of man is a theological subject and has to do something with leading a God-fearing life. But it seems that he cannot see any relationship between this answer and *his* own life. Thus a 'regular, competent and honest' answer to this question seems impossible to him. Interestingly, he ends up answering the question by referring to his obsession with the orange corset. He is still aware that this question is about the most important things in one's life, which is why he ironically calls it 'earth-shattering'. But by answering the question in this way he draws on his own individual experiences, which are somewhat arbitrary and variable, and which certainly contradict the traditional notions of virtue or Godlikeness that were once associated with the vocation of man. In this passage we can see how the ability of a teleological concept to understand one's life and to ascribe meaning to it had come to an end for many intellectuals, poets and philosophers.

Notes

* I would like to thank Richard B. Parkinson for revising the English of my paper.
1. This term can only approximately be translated as 'vocation of man', but I will here use both the German original and the English expression 'vocation (of man)'. Please note that 'vocation' in this context does not mean 'occupation'. It is therefore misleading to think of Max Weber's essay 'Wissenschaft als Beruf' (1919), which is translated as 'Science as a Vocation'.

2. See e.g. the verdict by Norbert Hinske, 'Die tragenden Grundideen der deutschen Aufklärung: Versuch einer Typologie,' in Raffaele Ciafardone, ed., *Die Philosophie der deutschen Aufklärung: Texte und Darstellungen. Deutsche Bearbeitung von Nobert Hinske und Rainer Specht*, Stuttgart: Reclam, 1990, pp. 407–58, here 434–5. Furthermore: Norbert Hinske, ed., *Die Bestimmung des Menschen*, Hamburg: Meiner, 1999, 3 [also in *Aufklärung* 11 (1999), no. 1]; Reinhard Brandt, *Die Bestimmung des Menschen bei Kant*, Hamburg: Meiner, 2009, p. 61.

3. Cf. the Kantian Christian Friedrich Michaelis, who noted that the possibility to consider that question was already a reason for admiring and respecting mankind. See Christian F. Michaelis, *Ueber die sittliche Natur und Bestimmung des Menschen: Ein Versuch zur Erläuterung über I. Kant's Kritik der praktischen Vernunft*, Leipzig: Iohann Gottlob Beigang, 1796, III.

4. See Wolfgang Albrecht, 'Die Bestimmung(en) des Menschen: Zu einem Zentralthema des Aufklärungsdiskurses und einigen seiner Facetten im Umkreis Lessings,' in Richard E. Schade and Dieter Sevin, eds, *Practicing Progress: The Promise and Limitations of Enlightenment. Festschrift for John A. McCarthy*, Amsterdam, New York: Rodopi, 2007 (*Internationale Forschungen zur allgemeinen und vergleichenden Literaturwissenschaft* 106), pp. 21–34, here 22.

5. However, see the bibliography by Fotis Jannidis which covers titles up to 1850. Fotis Jannidis, 'Die "Bestimmung des Menschen": Kultursemiotische Beschreibung einer sprachlichen Formel,' in *Aufklärung* 14 (2002), pp. 75–95. Wolfhart Pannenberg refers to theologians of the nineteenth century, e.g. Karl Gottlieb Bretschneider (1776–1848), see Wolfhart Pannenberg, *Gottebenbildlichkeit als Bestimmung des Menschen in der neueren Theologiegeschichte*, München: Verlag der Bayerischen Akademie der Wissenschaften, 1979 (Sitzungsberichte / Bayerische Akademie der Wissenschaften. Philosophisch-Historische Klasse 1979, 8), pp. 14–15. Mark-Georg Dehrmann has discussed the concept of 'Bestimmung' in Kleist. Mark-Georg Dehrmann, 'Die problematische Bestimmung des Menschen: Kleists Auseinandersetzung mit einer Denkfigur der Aufklärung im "Aufsatz, den sichern Weg des Glücks zu finden", im "Michael Kohlhaas" und der "Hermannsschlacht"', in *Deutsche Vierteljahresschrift für Literaturwissenschaft und Geistesgeschichte* 81 (2007), pp. 193–227.

6. For more details see Philip Ajouri, *Erzählen nach Darwin: Die Krise der Teleologie im literarischen Realismus: Friedrich Theodor Vischer und Gottfried Keller*, Berlin: de Gruyter, 2007 (Quellen und Forschungen zur Literatur- und Kulturgeschichte 43 (277)), pp. 11–43.

7. I am assuming that the majority of the academic community does not consider that Nature or God are agents that created mankind or an individual to a certain end.

8. Cf. the introduction of this volume. It seems that teleological thinking is very hard to abandon. Immanuel Kant argued that teleological explanations are not valid when applied to natural objects and may only be given as a heuristic means of research and observation (see Kant, *Critique of Judgement*, §61). And Charles Darwin's theory of evolution provided a non-teleological explanation of natural functionality. However, many individuals and groups – such as the creationists – still believe that nature must be explained with reference to the intentions or plan of an almighty God.

9. I am very aware of many objections to an intentional view of authorship. Suffice it to say that I am not referring to the author's intention here in order to ascribe meaning to a certain text, but only to explain the origin of its formal characteristics.

10. For this explanation of teleology I follow Andrew Woodfield, *Teleology*, Cambridge: Cambridge University Press, 1976, pp. 111–13.

11. Diderot was in fact born in 1713, not in 1715, but this does not alter Danto's argument. *The New Encyclopaedia Britannica*, 29 vols, London, New Delhi, Paris, et al.: Encyclopaedia Britannica, 2010, vol. 4, p. 80.

12. See Arthur C. Danto, *Analytical Philosophy of History*. Cambridge: Cambridge University Press, 1968, pp. 18, 143–81. Cf., with reference to Danto, Paul Ricoeur, *Temps et récit. L'intrigue et le récit historique*, vol. 1, Paris: Seuil, 1983, here especially pp. 256–65.

13. Two short remarks may avoid misunderstanding. Firstly, I do not of course hold that literature stands in a causal relationship to its contexts in the way we think of causality in natural sciences. Having said this, it is important to see that texts are not independent of relevant contexts. Karl Eibl suggested that literature adapts to its environment (i.e. its contexts in a broad sense including social conditions) in the way that people adapt their clothes to the weather. If it rains it is more likely that people will wear raincoats or umbrellas, but nobody is forced to do so. For a more sophisticated discussion of causality, see Karl Eibl: 'Literaturgeschichte, Ideengeschichte, Gesellschaftsgeschichte – und "Das Warum der Entwicklung"', in *Internationales Archiv für Sozialgeschichte der deutschen Literatur* 21 (1996), no. 2, pp. 1–26, here 11–14. Secondly, from a theoretical point of view it is perfectly possible to interchange text and context so that literature itself is regarded as a context in order to explain changes in other fields of knowledge. This is, however, not my intention here.

14. See Brandt, *Bestimmung*, p. 63f.

15. See the introduction by Albrecht Beutel in Johann Joachim Spalding: *Die Bestimmung des Menschen* [^{1}1748, ^{2}1748, ^{3}1749, ^{4}1752, ^{5}1754, ^{6}1759, ^{7}1763, ^{8}1764, ^{9}1768, ^{10}1774, ^{11}1794], eds Albrecht Beutel, Daniela Kirschkowski and Dennis Prause, in Johann Joachim Spalding: *Kritische Ausgabe*, ed. Albrecht Beutel, Tübingen: Mohr Siebeck, 2006, I/1, XXI–XLIX, here XXV–XXVI.

16. See Clemens Schwaiger, 'Zur Frage nach den Quellen von Spaldings "Bestimmung des Menschen": Ein ungelöstes Rätsel der Aufklärungsforschung', in Hinske (ed.), *Bestimmung*, pp. 7–19.

17. Spalding, p. 1. (I refer to the first edition, 1748).

18. See Fotis Jannidis, ' "Bildung" als "Bestimmung des Menschen", Zum teleologischen Aspekt in Goethes Bildungsbegriff', in *Pädagogische Rundschau* 53 (1999), pp. 441–51, here 445.

19. I do not discuss the question whether this world view can be traced back to Stoic nature-philosophy or if it is rooted in a more Christian tradition. Brandt, *Bestimmung*, p. 69f. argues in favour of the Stoic tradition.

20. 'Einrichtung meiner Natur' (Spalding, p. 17) (translation P.A.).

21. 'Dieser alles regierende Verstand' (ibid., p. 16) (translation P.A.).

22. Andrew Woodfield gives this explanation for artificial objects. See Woodfield, *Teleology*, p. 210.

23. 'Hiebey erkenne ich denn nun auch ungezweifelt, daß dieser alles regierende Verstand keine andere Absicht haben könne, als daß alle Dinge in ihrer Art und im Ganzen gut seyn mögen. Dahin sind alle Gesetze eingerichtet, die er in sie gelegt hat. Dahin zielen die Bewegungen der Körper, und die ursprünglichen Triebe der verständigen Wesen' (Spalding, pp. 16–17) (translation P.A.).

24. 'Ich spüre Fähigkeiten in mir, die eines Wachsthums ins Unendliche fähig sind' (ibid., pp. 20–1) (translation P.A.).

25. See ibid., p. 19.

26. 'Ich bin also für ein anderes Leben gemacht' (ibid., p. 22) (translation P.A.).

27. 'Weg[ ]' (ibid., p. 23) (translation P.A.).
28. 'Hinan zu steigen' (ibid., p. 21) (translation P.A.).
29. 'Das grosse Ziel … erreichen' (ibid., p. 24) (translation P.A.).
30. See Brandt, *Bestimmung*, 72.
31. A typical expression is 'wenn ich auf mich Acht gebe …' (Spalding, p. 21) ('if I pay attention to myself') (translation P.A.).
32. See ibid., p. 23f. and Joseph Schollmeier, *Johann Joachim Spalding: Ein Beitrag zur Theologie der Aufklärung*, Gütersloh: Gütersloher Verlagshaus Gerd Mohn, 1967, p. 56.
33. See notes 17, 11 and Cornel Zwierlein, 'Das Glück des Bürgers: Der aufklärerische Eudämonismus als Formationselement von Bürgerlichkeit und seine Charakteristika,' in Hans-Edwin Friedrich, Fotis Jannidis and Marianne Willems, eds, *Bürgerlichkeit im 18. Jahrhundert*, Tübingen: Niemeyer, 2006 (Studien und Texte zur Sozialgeschichte der Literatur 105), pp. 71–113, here 100f.
34. As an overview cf. e.g. Giuseppe D'Allessandro, 'Die Wiederkehr eines Leitworts: Die "Bestimmung des Menschen" als theologische, anthropologische und geschichtsphilosophische Frage der deutschen Spätaufklärung,' in *Die Bestimmung des Menschen: Zugleich Aufklärung* 11 (1999), no. 1, ed. Norbert Hinske, pp. 21–47. Laura Anna Macor, *Die Bestimmung des Menschen (1748–1800): Eine Begriffsgeschichte*, Stuttgart-Bad Cannstatt: Frommann-Holzboog, 2013 (Forschungen und Materialien zur deutschen Aufklärung, Abteilung 2, 25).
35. Cf. Stefan Lorenz, 'Skeptizismus und natürliche Religion: Thomas Abbt und Moses Mendelssohn in ihrer Debatte über Johann Joachim Spaldings Bestimmung des Menschen,' in Michael Albrecht, Eva J. Engel and Norbert Hinske, eds, *Moses Mendelssohn und die Kreise seiner Wirksamkeit*, Tübingen: Niemeyer, 1994 (Wolfenbütteler Studien zur Aufklärung 19), pp. 113–33; see note 5, p. 28f.; Raffaele Ciafardone, 'Der Mensch und seine Bestimmung', in: idem (ed.), *Philosophie der deutschen Aufklärung*, 1990, pp. 39–44; John H. Zammito, *Kant, Herder, and the Birth of Anthropology*, Chicago: University of Chicago Press, 2002, pp. 167–71.
36. See Friedrich v. Blanckenburg, *Versuch über den Roman: Faksimiledruck der Originalausgabe von 1774*, mit einem Nachwort von Eberhard Lämmert, Stuttgart: Metzler, 1965, p. 43, footnote.
37. 'Der Urheber der Natur hat uns gewiß nichts versagt, das, auf irgend eine Art, unsrer Bestimmung uns näher bringen kann' (ibid., p. 31f.). 'The creator of nature surely did not refuse us anything which is in one way or another necessary to a better fulfilment of our vocation' (translation P.A.).
38. See Jürgen Jacobs, 'Die Theorie und ihr Exempel: Zur Deutung von Wielands "Agathon" in Blanckenburgs "Versuch über den Roman"', in *Germanisch-Romanische Monatsschrift* new series 31 (1981), pp. 32–42.
39. See Dehrmann, 'Die problematische Bestimmung', p. 200 (footnote 28).
40. See Christoph Martin Wieland, *Geschichte des Agathon*, in Klaus Manger and Jan P. Reemtsma, eds, *Wielands Werke: Historisch-kritische Ausgabe*, Berlin and New York: de Gruyter, 2008ff., 8.1, pp. 1–455, here 173 (part 1, book 7, ch. 2) and ibid., p. 413f. (part 2, book 10, ch. 5). Walter Erhart assumes that Spalding's essay presents basically the same arguments as Agathon in his discussion with Hippias. Walter Erhart, *Entzweiung und Selbstaufklärung: Christoph Martin Wielands 'Agathon'-Projekt*, Tübingen: Niemeyer, 1991, p. 110.
41. Cf. as a summary Manfred Engel, *Der Roman der Goethezeit: Anfänge in Klassik und Frühromantik: Transzendentale Geschichten*. Germanistische Abhandlungen 71, Stuttgart and Weimar: Metzler, 1993, p. 144f.

42. See Wieland, *Agathon*, p. 418, note 41 (part 2, book 11, ch. 1).
43. 'dienstwilligen Sturmwind' (ibid., p. 433, part 2, book 11, ch. 3) (translation P.A.).
44. 'Sprung aus dem Fenster' (ibid., p. 420, part 2, book 11, ch. 2) (translation P.A.).
45. It was Engel who explained the ironic ending with the missing reconciliation of Agathon's and Hippias' views. Cf. Engel, *Roman der Goethezeit*, p. 145.
46. Cf. Dehrmann, *Die problematische Bestimmung*, p. 202, note 41, who stated that the concept of 'Bestimmung' in Wieland's *Agathon* has not become irrelevant but aporetic.
47. See Jannidis, ' "Bildung" als "Bestimmung des Menschen" ', p. 446. Against this background it becomes clear that older attempts to call Wieland's *Agathon* a 'Bildungsroman' were misconceived. The main reason why Wieland's *Agathon* is not a 'Bildungsroman' lies in the fact that the hero's inner development cannot be conceived as a unique and individualistic development and is not described by using organic metaphors.
48. See Fotis Jannidis, *Das Individuum und sein Jahrhundert. Eine Komponenten- und Funktionsanalyse des Begriffs 'Bildung' am Beispiel von Goethes 'Dichtung und Wahrheit'*, Tübingen: Niemeyer, 1996, p. 42.
49. See ibid., pp. 144–6.
50. 'Zerstreuung' ('distraction') und 'falsche Tendenzen' ('wrong ambitions') are the words Goethe uses for these ill-spent lifespans. Cf. ibid., pp. 134–9.
51. See ibid. Jannidis discusses the latter aspect on pp. 130–2 and in Jannidis, ' "Bildung" als "Bestimmung des Menschen" ', pp. 449–51.
52. See ibid.
53. See Jannidis, *Das Individuum und sein Jahrhundert*.
54. Johann Wolfgang Goethe, *Wilhelm Meisters Lehrjahre: Ein Roman*, ed. Hans-Jürgen Schings, in *Sämtliche Werke nach Epochen seines Schaffens: Münchner Ausgabe*, ed. Karl Richter, München: Hanser, 1988, 5, pp. 6–610, here 35 (book I, ch. 9).
55. 'Daß ich dir's mit Einem Worte sage, mich selbst, ganz wie ich da bin, auszubilden, das war dunkel von Jugend auf mein Wunsch und meine Absicht' (ibid., p. 288, book V, chap. 3; translation: Thomas Carlyle).
56. '. . . aber ich weiß, daß ich ein Glück erlangt habe, das ich nicht verdiene, und das ich mit nichts in der Welt vertauschen möchte' (ibid., p. 610, book 8, ch. 10; translation: Thomas Carlyle).
57. See Schiller's letter to Goethe (8.7.1796). Cf. Johann Wolfgang Goethe and Friedrich Schiller, *Briefwechsel zwischen Schiller und Goethe in den Jahre 1794 bis 1805*, ed. Manfred Beetz, in *Sämtliche Werke nach Epochen seines Schaffens: Münchner Ausgabe*, ed. Karl Richter, München: Hanser, 1990, 8.1, here p. 203.
58. 'verborgen wirkender höherer Verstand' (ibid.) (translation P.A.).
59. See Engel, *Roman der Goethezeit*, p. 277.
60. See ibid., pp. 279 and 282f., note 107.
61. See ibid., pp. 285–9.
62. '. . . es stellte die Geschichte vor, wie der kranke Königssohn sich über die Braut seines Vaters in Liebe verzehrt' (Goethe; *Wilhelm Meisters Lehrjahre*, p. 69, book I, ch. 17; translation: Thomas Carlyle).
63. See Engel, *Roman der Goethezeit*, pp. 280–9.

64. 'Die Natur hat gewirkt …' (Goethe; *Wilhelm Meisters Lehrjahre*, p. 608, book VIII, ch. 10; translation: Thomas Carlyle).
65. Jannidis, 'Die "Bestimmung des Menschen"'.
66. Karl G. Bretschneider, *Handbuch der Dogmatik der evangelisch-lutherischen Kirche oder Versuch einer beurtheilenden Darstellung der Grundsaetze, welche diese Kirche in ihren symbolischen Schriften ueber die christliche Glaubenslehre ausgesprochen hat*, Leipzig: Johann Ambrosius Barth, 1828, vol.1, pp. 747–53. Cf. Pannenberg, *Gottebenbildlichkeit*, pp. 14–15.
67. Clemens Engling, *Die Bedeutung der Theologie für die philosophische Theoriebildung und gesellschaftliche Praxis: Historisch-systematische Untersuchungen. Zum Werk Johann Nepomuk Ehrlichs (1810–1864)*, Göttingen: Vandenhoeck & Ruprecht, 1977 (Studien zur Theologie und Geistesgeschichte des Neunzehnten Jahrhunderts 20), pp. 192–203.
68. Johann N. Ehrlich, *Lehre von der Bestimmung des Menschen als rationale Teleologie*, Wien: Fr. Beck's Universitäts-Buchhandlung, 1842/1845, vol.1, p. 37.
69. Ibid., vol.1, p. 22.
70. Ibid., vol.1, pp. 167–9.
71. Ibid., vol.1, pp. 169–71.
72. Daniel B. Haneberg, *Von der Bestimmung des Menschen und dem Dank dafür*, Predigt am Sylvesterabend 1854 gehalten in der Basilika zu München, München: Matth. Rieger'sche Buch- und Kunsthandlung, 1855, p. 4.
73. Ibid., p. 5.
74. Ibid., p. 4.
75. Ibid., p. 11f., 14.
76. Ludwig Feuerbach, *Gedanken über Tod und Unsterblichkeit*, Leipzig: Otto Wigand, 1847, p. 358.
77. Ibid., p. 330.
78. Ibid., pp. 332–4.
79. Ibid., pp. 335–9. See the *Vorlesungen über das Wesen der Religion*, where Feuerbach says that chance or necessity are the cause of the dispositions of a certain human being (Ludwig Feuerbach, 'Vorlesungen über das Wesen der Religion: Nebst Zusätzen und Anmerkungen,' 2nd edn, in *Gesammelte Werke*, ed. Werner Schuffenhauer, Berlin: Akademie, 1967ff., vol. 6, here p. 184).
80. See Alfred Schmidt, 'Natur,' in Bernd Witte, Theo Buck, Hans-Dietrich Dahnke, Regine Otto and Peter Schmidt, eds, *Goethe-Handbuch*, 4 vols, Stuttgart, Weimar: Metzler, 1996–2012, vol. 4/2, pp. 755–76, here 769–72.
81. '*Entweder* Gott *oder* Natur!' (Ludwig Feuerbach, 'Vorlesungen über das Wesen der Religion', p. 183) (translation P.A.).
82. Ibid., p. 184.
83. See the chapter 'Die Zweckmäßigkeit der Natur' ('The Purposefulness of Nature') in Ludwig Büchner, *Kraft und Stoff: Empirisch-naturphilosophische Studien. In allgemeinverständlicher Darstellung*, Frankfurt am Main: Meidinger Sohn und Cie., 1856, pp. 90–106.
84. See ibid., p. 36.
85. See the chapter 'Der freie Wille' ('Free Will') in ibid., pp. 244–57.

86. Anonymous, *Kurze populäre Widerlegung der neueren materialistischen Behauptungen über Gott, Welt, Bestimmung des Menschen und angebliche Sterblichkeit des menschlichen Geistes: Für Jedermann. Auch als Leitfaden beim Unterict, Von einem Freunde der Menschen und der Religion*, Berlin: W. Weber & Comp., 1857.
87. 'höhere Bestimmung' (Gottfried Keller, *Der grüne Heinrich* [1854/5], in *Sämtliche Werke: Historisch-kritische Ausgabe*, ed. Walter Morgenthaler, Basel: Stroemfeld, 1996ff., 11–12, here vol.11, p. 263) (vol. 2, ch. 2).
88. 'Altar meiner Bestimmung' (ibid., vol.11, p. 313) (vol. 2, ch.4).
89. This is no isolated comment of the narrator but is enacted in the scenes of Heinrich's school years. Here arbitrary occurrences more than once hinder the development of any coherent knowledge that could serve as a basis for a future choice of occupation.
90. See Ajouri, *Erzählen*, pp. 271–3.
91. Keller, *Der grüne Heinrich*, p. 216 (vol.1, ch. 9).
92. Ibid., p. 81.
93. The colour green is charged during the novel with additional meanings such as 'premature'. It stands also for a certain concept of a comforting and ensouled nature, so that the green grass on Heinrich's grave might provide an element of comfort also.
94. Ibid., p. 218f.
95. Cf. Ajouri, *Erzählen*, pp. 90–142.
96. See Ernst Haeckel, *Natürliche Schöpfungsgeschichte: Gemeinverständliche wissenschaftliche Vorträge über die Entwickelungslehre im Allgemeinen und diejenige von Darwin, Goethe und Lamarck im Besonderen, über die Anwendung derselben auf den Ursprung des Menschen und andere damit zusammenhängende Grundfragen der Naturwissenschaft*, Berlin: Georg Reimer, 1870, p. 6.
97. See Ernst Haeckel, *Die Welträthsel: Gemeinverständliche Studien über monistische Philosophie*, Bonn: Emil Strauß, 1899, p. 235.
98. Friedrich Theodor Vischer probably picked up this expression from a review. In 1872 he used it in a letter to his friend David Friedrich Strauß. Friedrich Theodor Vischer, 'Ein Manuskript von Friedrich Theodor Vischer über das Buch: "Der alte und der neue Glaube": Mitgeteilt von Robert Vischer,' in *Deutsche Vierteljahresschrift für Literaturwissenschaft und Geistesgeschichte* 5 (1927), pp. 583–608, here 597. I have tried to find the review from which Vischer took this quotation, but so far without success.
99. Cf. e.g. Paul Gerhard, *Der erste Mensch, seine Entstehung, Beschaffenheit und Bestimmung oder die monistische Weltanschauung der Darwininianer im Gegensatz zur culturhistorischen christlichen*, Breslau: F. Willkomm, 1875, 2, p. 34.
100. E.g. the social democrat Albert Dulk. He found man's 'Bestimmung' in the idea of a peaceful future which united mankind and contributed to its moral and intellectual refinement. See Albert Dulk, *Thier oder Mensch?: Ein Wort über Wesen und Bestimmung der Menschheit*, Leipzig: Otto Wigand, 1872, pp. 226–7.
101. Fritz Mauthner, *Wörterbuch der Philosophie: Neue Beiträge zu einer Kritik der Sprache*, München, Leipzig: Georg Müller, 1910, vol.1, p. 102.
102. 'Als deutsches Thema erhielten wir "die Bestimmung des Menschen". Ich weiß noch, ich starrte diese Worte wohl eine Viertelstunde an, aber es fiel mir nichts ein. Ich wußte nun, daß auch der Aufsatz verlorene Arbeit sei. Aber ich grübelte ruhig weiter, um zu sehen, ob sich gar keine Gedanken angesichts dieses weltbewegenden Themas einstellen würden. Und es kam nichts. Ich merkte jetzt, von Minute zu Minute deutlicher, daß nicht nur der Aufsatz

eine schlechte Arbeit werden würde, sondern daß auch gar keine Aussicht für eine regelrechte, tüchtige, ehrliche Behandlung des Themas sei. Die "Bestimmung des Menschen?" – Ich wußte sie nicht! Hinter mir zupften mich meine Mitschüler, die gewohnt waren, im deutschen Aufsatz von mir Hülfe zu bekommen, und flüsterten: "Du, was ist die Bestimmung des Menschen?" – Ich wußte es nicht; und sie wußten es auch nicht. – Die Antwort, die ich in der Christenlehre vor zehn Jahren gegeben hätte: gottesfürchtig zu leben, und selig zu sterben, – die war mir wohl geläufig; aber das war ja nur eine schöne Rede, eine Phrase, die Jeder im Nothfall im Mund führt, und Keiner glaubt' (Oskar Panizza, 'Der Corsetten-Fritz', in *Der Korsettenfritz: Gesammelte Erzählungen*. Mit einem Beitrag von Bernd Mattheus, München: Matthes & Seitz, 1981, pp. 203–22, here 219) (translation P.A.).

CHAPTER 4
EARTH HISTORY AND THE ORDER OF SOCIETY: WILLIAM BUCKLAND, THE FRENCH CONNECTION AND THE CONUNDRUM OF TELEOLOGY

*Marianne Sommer**

The early nineteenth century is often referred to as the Golden Age of Geology, a time of sensational discoveries, of identifications and reconstructions of an antediluvian (pre-Flood) fauna. Besides exotic mammals such as mammoth, rhinoceros, cave bear and hyena, much older 'terrible lizards' – or dinosaurs – were unearthed. Growing insights into geology had led to an expansion of the history of the globe. At the same time, even though the concept of a great human antiquity was beginning to dawn on the scientific horizon, since there were reports of crude stone tools and human bones found in close association with fossil bones of extinct animals, human history was still largely dictated by the chronology of the Bible. Furthermore, the new insights into the history of life on earth did not necessarily lead to evolutionary thinking. Nonetheless, historical geology implied diverse aspects of progress and teleology that resonated with societal changes and understandings of the social order. In this contribution, I approach these aspects through the work of the British geologist William Buckland and through his local circle and connections, especially to the French savants.[1]

Advances in geological knowledge in Britain were linked to the processes of industrialization. The drilling of holes into the bowels of the earth in search of coal and other riches not only brought to light stratification and fossil content, but also allowed insights into geological mechanisms such as erosion, marine sedimentation and the folding of strata. Generally speaking, the so-called age of improvement provided many opportunities to those interested in geology. The rapid growth of the domestic agrarian and industrial productions and of the associated national and international markets necessitated and allowed the building of roads, bridges and canals that facilitated the travel of persons and the transport of goods as the basis of international networks of exchange of information and specimens. With the age of the railways – in 1830 a railway connection was established between Manchester and Liverpool – modern industry became the dominant sector of the entire national economy, and a period of prosperity set in that would last without any major setbacks until the 1870s. At the time of the Great Exhibition of 1851, Britain was the leading economic and financial power.[2]

Furthermore, after the Napoleonic wars the second peace of Paris (1815) facilitated travel within Europe, so that historical geology from Germany and France was increasingly introduced into Britain – albeit British geology did not integrate the secular

German philosophy of history. Particularly influential was the French naturalist George Cuvier, who was a great expert on vertebrate palaeontology and comparative anatomy, which he institutionalized at the Muséum d'Histoire Naturelle in Paris. His knowledge of the functional whole of the organism became so thorough that he boasted of being able to reconstruct an entire animal from a single fossil bone. Where the history of vertebrates was concerned, Cuvier worked with geological revolutions and with the concept of extinction. The bones found in caves and open sites of fossil animals such as hippopotamus, elephant, hyena and lion that no longer inhabited Europe were thought to be the remains of species that had been extinguished in the region through a violent geological upheaval.[3] To Cuvier, the Scriptures were one among several historical texts that could be used in the reconstruction of the history of humankind. Significantly, Cuvier restricted the chronological authority of the Bible to the human realm, and conceptualized the geological processes that led to the current shape of the earth's crust as of much longer duration. Equally significantly, for a number of reasons, Cuvier rejected supposed evidence of the coexistence of humans with the extinct European fauna throughout his life. But Cuvier's geology and palaeontology were also adjusted to a peculiarly English taste when Cuvier's last geologically significant revolution – the *déluge* – was identified with the biblical Flood.[4]

Regency England provided a different environment to what French society was to its savants after the assaults on the power of the Church in the French Revolution. State, Church and society were still closely intertwined, and a powerful Church was considered to be the backbone of a stable and well-ordered society. Throughout the seventeenth and eighteenth centuries and well into the nineteenth, sacred chronology, which reconstructed earth and ancient human history by means of the Scriptures and other historical sources, and increasingly by means of geology, remained an important tradition with varying degrees of literalism. The adherence to an age of the earth of approximately 6,000 years stayed in place until well into the Enlightenment. Towards the end of the eighteenth century, the days of Creation came to be interpreted allegorically, so that the possibility of a very long history of the earth arose. Growing knowledge of the primary and also secondary rock formations, the latter of which often contained marine shells, demanded a timescale far transcending a literal interpretation of Genesis. Furthermore, the argument from design in natural theology, which went back to classical and medieval philosophy, in which the order of nature was indicative of the existence of a supreme designer or creator, had been taken up in early modern times. A new wave of physico-theology began with William Paley's (1743–1805) *Natural Theology* (1802), which was a centrepiece of the Oxford University curriculum, and culminated in the 1830s in the Bridgewater Treatises on the 'Power, Wisdom, and Goodness of God, as manifested in the Creation'. These tracts, instigated by the Earl of Bridgewater, were widely circulated and represented the scientific elite's reconciliation between science and religion as dominant in the liberal Anglican stance of the members of the British Association for the Advancement of Science (BAAS, founded 1831).[5]

Buckland, who had succeeded to the readership of mineralogy at Oxford University in 1813, wrote the last Bridgewater volume on geology as a kind of climax of the belief in the divine design of each organism for its environment. He also demonstrated the overall increase of organic complexity throughout the geological layers – a concept that guided palaeontological reconstruction and theory in the 1820s and 1830s.[6] Nonetheless, geology did have subversive potential. With regard to the new readership in geology that Buckland was given in 1818, he wrote to the Prince Regent

> [t]hat Geology is a Branch of Knowledge at this time so much cultivated, of so much National importance, and so liable to be perverted to Purposes of a tendency dangerous to the Interests of Revealed Religion, that it is considered by persons of the highest Authority in the University to be a proper and desirable Subject for a Course of Public Lectures in Oxford.[7]

With its great utilitarian potential, geology represented a branch of knowledge a nation should not disregard. The dangers to the status quo would best be met by making geology the subject of the establishment, thereby securing its services. The universities of Oxford and Cambridge were institutions for the education of the Anglican clergy, and they therefore valued geology according to its synergies with their classical traditions and its ecclesiastical relevance.

Buckland also made a career in the Church. The Prime Minister Lord Liverpool appointed him to the canonry of Christ Church Cathedral, Oxford, in 1825, and Tory Prime Minister Robert Peel, who was connected to Buckland through a long friendship, recommended him to the Queen as Dean of Westminster in 1845. Nonetheless, even though the Scottish University of Edinburgh criticized the universities of Oxford and Cambridge for their mingling of science and belief, the new geology of the 1820s was an important factor in at least forcing biblical literalism out of English academe.[8]

1. Man as a 'Crocodile Superior'?

British geology, and in particular the interpretations by Buckland and others of human artefacts and bones found among extinct animal species, took place within this complex situation and has to be viewed in relation to further characteristics of the time. In Britain, the first half of the nineteenth century saw an increasing number among the industrial working classes turning away from Christianity. And in the aftermath of the French Revolution and in a climate of exploitation in an industrialization built on laissez-faire liberalism, science could work as a weapon against oppression through the ruling classes in Church and state. Freethinkers tried to reach the working and middle classes through articles on science in the secular press and public lecture series. British libertarians and French materialist radicals embraced Fossil Man as evidence for human descent from the animal world and organic transmutation in general as a way of rethinking the social body.[9] For revolutionary potential, they could draw among other sources on Jean-Baptiste Lamarck and Etienne Geoffroy Saint-Hilaire's theories of the transmutation of species. Lamarck's notion of the inevitability of progress 'from the bottom' through individual effort and improvement of circumstances inspired atheists and socialists in France and Britain alike.

Lamarck, professor of invertebrates, and Geoffroy Saint-Hilaire, the much younger professor of vertebrates, were both direct opponents of Cuvier at the Muséum National d'Histoire Naturelle in Paris. As the disputes around transmutationism in the Académie des Sciences and inside the museum walls were carried outside and taken up by materialist republicans and the socialist press, who attacked the authority of the Church as well as the privileges of the upper classes, it was also the social order that was under attack. As Adrian Desmond has shown, in Britain, anti-clerical and anti-aristocratic ideas were promoted on the basis of transmutationism in the illegal penny press, and transmutation mixed with political radicalism was discussed in secular anatomy rooms and Nonconformist colleges, first and foremost at the secular universities of London and Edinburgh. The challenge of social hierarchies was therefore also aimed at what were perceived to be the petty privileges of the Anglican gentlemen at the English centres of education.[10]

For Lamarck – no doubt influenced by his teacher and predecessor at the Jardin des Plantes, Comte de Buffon, particularly his *Histoire naturelle* (1749–1804) – animate nature was ordered according to a chain of organisms of increasing complexity from infusoria to humans. In his *Philosophie zoologique* (1809), ongoing spontaneous creation from inanimate into animate matter guaranteed the simultaneity of organisms at all grades of the chain of beings. A strong incentive for teleological thought was the analogy to the predetermined process of ontogeny, and Lamarck envisioned organisms to be driven up the ladder through an internal mechanism. If the series of increasingly higher beings was somewhat irregular, it was therefore due to a second mechanism of transmutation, the so-called use-inheritance, through which the organisms actively adjusted to gradually changing environments by developing new habits that eventually altered their structure inheritably. For organisms lower down the scale that did not show active adjustment to environments through new behaviours, the changed conditions in temperature, humidity, air and light could still shape their form durably through the inheritance of acquired characteristics. Like Charles Darwin after him, Lamarck used domestication as an analogy to the workings of natural transmutation. The keeping of plants and animals in artificial environments and their hybridization transformed their organs and structures much faster than would occur under natural conditions. Humans could further tamper with the linear and complete chain of beings by causing the extinction of a species, for example through over-hunting. Generally speaking, however, Lamarck worked with the concept of plenitude and uninterrupted lines of transmutations rather than with the Cuvierian mechanisms of extinction and novel creation.[11]

In contrast to Lamarck, Cuvier abandoned the linear gradation in the eighteenth-century notion of a scale of beings, while retaining its fixism. Geoffroy Saint-Hilaire, on the other hand, shared Lamarck's belief in the transmutation of organisms. His attempt to build a natural classification system on the basis of the analogy of organs and structures between groups of animals was inspired by the German *Naturphilosophie*. He explained the transmutation of the animals whose fossil remains were now being discovered into their recent kin through the direct influence of the environment, building strongly on the principle of an underlying unity of plan of organic composition, and on the analogy to individual embryonic development. He eventually tried to reduce the anatomy of all animal species to one plan (*Bauplan*). When he claimed to thus bridge the gap between vertebrate and invertebrate anatomy, the disputes between 'transmutationists' and 'fixists' in the Parisian Academy of Science flared up with unprecedented violence in the aftermath of Lamarck's death in 1829.[12]

Buckland dealt with the problem by means of ridicule. Referring to Geoffroy Saint-Hilaire's work on reptiles, he taunted that the doctrine of the transmutation of species reduced man to a 'Crocodile Superior'. In the mid-1820s Cuvier had identified a fossil from near Caen as an extinct species of gavial. Geoffroy Saint-Hilaire, who re-examined the specimen, instead announced it to be an intermediary between reptile and mammal, a *Teleosaurus*, supporting Lamarck's tree of vertebrate genealogy at the end of the *Philosophie zoologique* (1809). In the early 1830s, Geoffroy Saint-Hilaire expanded his work on the saurians, which led him to believe that the *Teleosaurus*, which had evolved from the *Ichthyosaurus*, was the ancestor of the Tertiary crocodile.[13] In notes dating from the 1830s, Buckland objected that there were no intermediate states, and that a change in circumstances did not alter a species. The *Ichthyosaurus* had not existed before the Lias epoch, and then had not changed up to the Chalk – the proportion of its bones had remained consistent. Then, at the end of the Chalk, the saurians had suddenly become extinct, while the crocodile, which had already lived with the *Ichthyosaurus*, was still a crocodile in the present day. Buckland also rejected the *Ichthyosaurus* – *Plesiosaurus* – *Pterodactylus* sequence, which was rendered impossible by stratigraphic knowledge. No saurian had thus changed into the *Plesiosaurus* or the crocodile, and it seemed even more illogical to claim that the saurians had become mammals. Rather, the mammals had simply been added. After all, the *Ichthyosaurus*, *Plesiosaurus*, *Pterodactylus* and crocodile had been contemporaries and part of an intricate system of interdependences.

Buckland deconstructed the ontogeny–phylogeny analogy and the associated linear progressionism that he saw as a prerequisite for Geoffroy Saint-Hilaire's and Lamarck's 'Absurd Doctrines'. Although he granted that both individual development and the succession of animal species throughout earth history showed an overall increase in complexity, there had been no transmutation of fish into reptile and into bird or mammal. Buckland quipped that if new organs were the effect of appetency, and fish had once turned into reptiles when tired of swimming, just as reptiles had begun to fly through intensive wishing, then surely these days one would witness schoolboys producing wings to escape from school.[14] On a more serious note, he reasoned that there were cases where the ancient animals were more complex in structure than the recent ones, such as in the example of ammonites and nautili. This was no major problem for Buckland, who saw no imperfection in any work of God. Although humankind was God's special creation, for whom he had prepared the earth through a series of dramatic events as well as by steady changes under forces still at work, animals were proof of the Creator's existence and attributes in their own right. On the contrary, for Lamarck, perfection was achieved only in humans. Though both worked with a hierarchical chain of beings, for Buckland every creature was absolutely perfect with regard to the sphere for which it was created; progress in his sense referred to the overall advance of the organic and inorganic systems towards modern conditions throughout the stratigraphic layers. Thus, Buckland's 'Chain of organized Beings' as designed by the Creator was flawless, hierarchical and fixed: 'I am not quarrelling or finding fault with a Crocodile / a Crocodile is a very respectable Person in his way / but I quarrel with the calling a Man a Crocodile Superior'.[15]

In agreement with Cuvier, Buckland identified the mechanisms of change not as those of transmutation, but as extinction and novel creation. Materialist transmutationism was a most unwelcome theory for Buckland, and Lamarck's conjecture of a race of apes developing into humans by inheritance of acquired characteristics was no more attractive to him than accepting a crocodile as cousin: 'We shall not be degraded from our high Estate to say to that Reptile Crocodile trust & greet you well right loving Cousin'.[16] To prevent man's 'degradation', Buckland, again similarly to Cuvier, maintained that breeding and nurture could modify the individuals within a species, but not transform one species into another: 'all Monsters professing to be Unions of Diff[erent] Species [were] morbid unions of Parts of individuals of the same Species'. Buckland's moral objection to Geoffroy Saint-Hilaire, in whose argument for organic transmutation through geological epochs deviations from the default path of embryonic development played a central role, was thus not restricted to the theoretical realm. Geoffroy Saint-Hilaire's experiments with the embryos of chickens were morbid actions producing monstrous results: 'all monstrosities [were] the effect of morbid action'.[17]

By this time, Buckland was working on his Bridgewater Treatise (*Geology and Mineralogy*, 1836) and had come to separate the last geological flood and the Deluge. He hid this check on the authority of the Scriptures in a footnote, explaining that the change was due to the preponderance of extinct animal species in the diluvium as well as the absence of accepted human remains. In other words, while according to the Scriptures humans had been killed in the biblical Flood, but no species had suffered extinction, the opposite seemed to have been the case in the last geologically formative inundation. The necessity of allowing enormous stretches of time for geological changes, as well as the insight that the diluvium was not a universally uniform deposit, added to the problems Buckland encountered with the diluvial theory. In the adapted version of catastrophism, the flood that extinguished the animal species, which may have existed over more than one geological period, was thus one in a series of such geological cataclysms, and did not correspond to the rather tranquil and recent event of the biblical Deluge.[18]

This non-biblical catastrophism still satisfied his obligation to reconcile geology and the Bible at a place like Oxford University. At the same time, it allowed Buckland to define the pre-human world as the realm of science, while the human world, beginning after the last geologically significant inundation, but before the Mosaic Flood, would be left to the account of the Scriptures. In his inaugural lecture, Buckland had already argued that the word *beginning* in the first verse of the book of Genesis referred to an undefined primeval period antecedent to the last great change affecting the surface of the earth (then equivalent to the Flood) and to the creation of the present plants and animals. Into the long series of geological changes that preceded the story of concern to the human race, geology might make investigations. Within the new scheme, the Bible had lost nothing of its moral authority, but the 'primeval period' now included all of the history of the earth to its present state. The Bible contained no history of geological phenomena, which one might with justification expect to find in an encyclopedia of science, 'but are foreign to the objects of a volume intended only to be a guide of religious belief and moral conduct'.[19]

Within the new model in which the last geological cataclysm was dissociated from the Mosaic Flood, and which was associated with millions and millions of years of earth history, there was therefore no need to find human fossils associated with the fossil fauna any more. One may even argue that, given the new situation, it would have been highly disturbing to find human bones that preceded the last geological turmoil, since at that stage the earth was not yet ready for human arrival, and humans – as the Bible states – are a recent creation. If anything, fossil humans would have supported the transmutationists' case. In *Geology and Mineralogy*, Buckland was thus quite firm on the point:

> no conclusion is more fully established, than the important fact of the total absence of any vestiges of the human species throughout the entire series of geological formations. Had the case been otherwise, there would indeed have been great difficulty in reconciling the early and extended periods which have been assigned to the extinct races of animals with our received chronology. On the other hand, the fact of no human remains having as yet been found in conjunction with those of extinct animals, may be alleged in confirmation of the hypothesis that these animals lived and died before the creation of man.[20]

This verdict was most controversial where the discoveries made by the physician and natural historian Philippe-Charles Schmerling in Liège were concerned. Schmerling began to explore the caves on the banks of the Meuse and its tributaries in 1829. He discovered human bones of at least six individuals, worked bone, and flint flakes in the caves of Engis, Engihoul, Chokier and Fond-de-Forêt (among them the Neanderthal child skull, Engis 2). Schmerling was confident that the sediments had not been disturbed, and that the human remains had been brought into their present situations at the same time and by the same means as the bones of the now extinct animals with which they were associated. In his *Recherches sur les ossemens fossiles* (1833–4), he therefore concluded that these were the traces of an antediluvian race:

> As I dare guarantee that none of these pieces [artefacts] has been introduced at a later time, I attach great importance to their presence in the caverns; since even if we had not found human bones, in conditions entirely favouring the consideration that they belong to the antediluvian époque, these proofs would have been provided to us by the worked bones and flints.[21]

The decomposition, the often broken and rounded state, the colour and relatively slight weight of both the animal and human bones further strengthened Schmerling's conviction. Well aware of the rejection of fossil human bones by such authorities as Buckland and the by then deceased Cuvier, whose verdict haunted science even after his death, Schmerling expounded the reasonableness of assuming antediluvians: it must have taken a long time to people the earth from a single original couple in India; the voyages of discovery had shown that humans indeed inhabited all the corners of the world; these geographical varieties exhibited huge differences in culture; to reach even the lowest rungs of civilization must have taken a very long time in view of the slow pace at which humans progressed.[22]

At the meeting of the natural historians in Bonn in 1835, Schmerling confronted the international audience with his spectacular discoveries. Among the gentleman naturalists was Buckland, who had inspected Schmerling's collection prior to the meeting. Buckland challenged the claim for contemporaneity of the human with the animal remains, humorously referring to Schmerling as 'the doctor of the antediluvian hyenas'.[23] He rejected Schmerling's estimate that the human bones were in the same state as those of extinct animals and claimed them to be less decayed. Buckland presented his argument very figuratively. Although the proceedings of the meeting only report Buckland's doubt about the contemporaneity of the human skull and the animal fossils, eyewitnesses told of other happenings. Buckland demonstrated to the assembly that while the human bones did not stick to his tongue, he could deliver his entire address with a bear bone from the same cave sticking to the inside of his lower lip, or his tongue.

The French geologist Élie de Beaumont (1798–1874), who had replaced Cuvier at the Collège de France in 1832, and held the chair of geology at the École des Mines, remembered Buckland's 'tongue-test' to determine the mineralization of the bones many years later in the context of a discussion on the means of determining the age of osseous remains:

> Mr Buckland immediately took a bear's bone, attached it to the end of his tongue, from which it remained suspended, which did not prevent the savant professor in the least from talking, and, while turning towards the different parties of the assembly, Mr Buckland repeated at several occasions with a slightly guttural voice: *You say it does not stick to the tongue!*'[24]

After what must have been a most hilarious spectacle, Schmerling had to accept the challenge. He could but try to achieve the same with one of the human bones – in vain. Amused by the show, the audience might have forgotten to think about whether the competition was suited to decide the matter at hand, or whether it was not rather a mere question of who was the better performer. As we have also seen in his dealings with transmutationism, Buckland used humour as a form of attack. Paradoxically, as a socially accepted and attenuated form of aggression, humour at the same time functioned as a stress-releaser and unleashed its cathartic quality to satisfy Buckland's desire for harmony. It could be used to avoid controversy. As I have shown elsewhere, humour was Buckland's means to distract from inconsistencies in the defence of orthodox ideas as well as to advance unorthodox interpretations. In the latter case, humour may serve to introduce an unorthodox theory while maintaining the possibility of retraction. It is up to the audience whether to transpose the content from the realm of the jest to the serious.[25]

Buckland left the arena victorious, and he published his verdict on the Schmerling discoveries in an authoritative style in the new theoretical context of his Bridgewater Treatise. In confirmation of influential figures such as Charles Lyell, Buckland supported the persistent scepticism towards the contemporaneity of humans and the extinct mammals found in Europe: 'M. Schmerling, in his Recherches sur les Ossemens Fossiles des Cavernes de Liège, expresses his opinion that these human bones are coeval with those of the quadrupeds, of extinct species, found with them; an opinion from which the Author, after a careful examination of M. Schmerling's collection, entirely dissents.'[26] This despite the fact that in the case of the caves explored by Schmerling the standard arguments against the contemporaneity of human and animal remains from caves do not seem to have applied: the human bones were not arranged in a burial, and no humans, animals or water currents seemed to have disturbed the floor. Unfortunately, Buckland – as usual when writing about human bones – did not specify the nature of his 'careful examination', or what it brought to light, so that his verdict has to be taken at face value.

Buckland was also troubled by the discovery of fossil monkeys in the Tertiary of the Siwalik Hills in 1836. In a kind of self-fulfilling prophecy he acknowledged that '[t]here is no escape from the facts', but at this point could still reassure himself: 'But monkeys are not men, though the reverse is not always true.'[27] Buckland and his fellow geologists felt justified in their cautious treatment of the human antiquity question when confronted with support for fossil humans in association with the doctrine of transmutation from the politically radical stratum of society. Indeed, 'Fossil Man' captured the imagination of popular writers, in the hands of whom he became a subversive tool for the 'perversion' of geology, a danger to revealed religion and to the interests of the class to whose advantage the current system worked.[28] One particular instance in Buckland's role as a priest will serve to illustrate his understanding of the social and the natural spheres as structured by the same holy principles, and governed by the same divine laws. In Buckland's cosmology, the social realm was deeply affected by changes in the way one thought about the natural realm, both of which were of the same making. Of course, this does not come as a surprise considering Buckland's natural theology background. But the consequences this perception had for his thinking about the order of society still need spelling out in the attempt to uncover the 'interests' under threat through the 'perversion' of geology discussed above.

2. The holy order of nature and society

The production and reception of Buckland's Bridgewater Treatise is illustrative of the area of tension occupied by the gentleman scientists of Buckland's *couleur*. It represented a manifesto of the British Association for the Advancement of Science's stance towards science and its relation to religion. As such, it was very successful, because it was widely read and discussed. However, it was also wildly attacked by biblical literalists on the one hand and appropriated by radical circles on the other. Buckland's demonstration of the overall increase in complexity in the fossil record especially lent itself to an argument in favour of the transmutation of species in the secular press. As Jonathan Topham reconstructs, among the gentlemen of science and in fashionable society the book could be read as a specialist tract and a synthesis between science and religion. In the public arena of the BAAS it was welcomed as representative of the liberal Anglican conciliation. In middle-class homes it could function as a morally uplifting text suited to reading aloud. In the newspapers, in factional periodicals and pamphlets and from the pulpit it was also attacked as blasphemy. And, at the other end of the scale, in radical artisan circles it could be appropriated for materialist purposes.[29]

In the hungry forties, the real social unease was again linked to the heresies of transmutationism, when the hideous subject of the transmutation of species was brought into English parlours with the anonymous *Vestiges of the Natural History of Creation* (1844). The development of organic forms on the basis of a uniformitarian natural law introduced by the author, who forty years later was officially pronounced to be the Scottish publisher and journalist Robert Chambers, was understood as a challenge to the existing social order, suggesting the potential of each individual organism for improvement. As James Secord shows in his cultural history of the production and reception of *Vestiges*, like Buckland's Bridgewater Treatise, it was read in different local and social settings, interpreted in various ways and adapted to diverse purposes. With its avoidance of direct divine intervention and the rather marginal and apologetic allusions to the Divinity in general, it could certainly be seen as undermining the authority of the Church, and, although after some delay, the Cambridge professor of geology, Adam Sedgwick, finally protested in revolt that 'the world cannot bear to be turned upside down; and we are ready to wage an internecine war with any violation of our modest principles and social manners.'[30]

Chambers's combination of transmutationism with the argument from design was particularly unpalatable for natural theologians, who had relied on divine providence as an alternative exactly to the principle of transmutation to explain the progressive complexity exemplified in the fossil record throughout the rock series. In addition, natural theology as advocated by the members of the BAAS in the 1830s and 1840s was increasingly aiming at a secularization of science, while maintaining the claim that religion and science would not be at odds. *Vestiges* now seemed to prove the Scriptural Geologists' accusation that instead natural science would lead to materialism and atheism – a fear addressed in Buckland's early letter to the Prince Regent – to have been well founded. As we have seen, Buckland had deconstructed an exact progressionism throughout the fossil record in connection with the theories of transmutation advocated by Lamarck and Geoffroy Saint-Hilaire. He felt the impetus to do so even more strongly with the appearance of *Vestiges*, and in lectures he warned his students against the dangerous theory promoted by the book.[31]

Later in the decade, the Continent was unsettled by revolutions, and in England the discontent grew. On 10 April 1848, London was in great alarm, with 150,000 volunteers sworn in as constables due to the great Chartist meeting. The Chartists, who were socialist but not irreligious like the more radical freethinkers, demanded universal suffrage for males, equal electoral districts, annual parliaments, the payment of members of parliament, vote by secret ballot and abolition of property qualifications for the franchise. Even though the People's Charter was presented to the House of Commons in 1839, 1842 and 1848, it was merely ridiculed, despite a large number of bourgeois signatures. Now, to hold back the tides of unrest, the Duke of Wellington had placed his troops in the houses and gardens of Bridge Street and Parliament Street, to be ready in case of emergency.[32] On Easter Day, 23 April 1848, in the choir of Westminster Abbey, newly reopened after a restoration, Buckland gave a sermon that was clearly meant to remind his congregation of the true order of the world. This order, installed by the only God, was expanding its dominion with the British Empire. The congregation had reason to be proud since 'colonial bishops ... have gone forth under the national sanction of the Government of this country to preach the gospel in many of the extreme regions of the world ... Never before did the compass of Christianity circumscribe so vast a circle.'[33] The hierarchy ordained by God structured the natural as well as the social realms also in 'the dark and savage regions of the world', and here as there it was a fixed order.

Just as there was no transmutation from one species into another in nature, every man and woman had his and her proper place in society:

> The God of Nature has determined that moral and physical inequalities shall not only be inseparable from our humanity, but coextensive with His whole creation. He has also given compensations co-ordinate with these inequalities, working together for the conversation of all orders and degrees in that graduated scale of being which is the great law of God's providence on earth. From the mammoth to the mouse, from the eagle to the humming-bird, from the minnow to the whale, from the monarch to the man, the inhabitants of the earth and air and water form but one vast series of infinite gradations in an endless chain of inequalities of organic structure and of physical perfections ... Equality of mind or body, or of worldly condition, is as inconsistent with the order of Nature as with the moral laws of God ... There may be equality in poverty: equality of riches is impossible. Equality of poverty is the condition of the negro, the bushman, and the Esquimaux. Equality of wealth and property never has and never can exist, except in the imagination of wild transcendental theorists.

The chain of beings appears as a tripartite structure ordering the inorganic cosmos, the natural world of animal species and human 'races', and finally the social world of human classes. This inflexible and all-pervasive order was seen to provide society with security and stability. The wild imagination of transcendental theorists had to be kept at bay if peace was to be maintained. Thus, Buckland warned the people of Britain of Continental threats and reminded them of their due and happy place in a society organized according to the sacred principles of Crown and Church: 'In the years of peril and perturbation which agitated Europe half a century ago, it was the personal character of the king of this country [King George III] which, under Providence, was mainly instrumental to preserve us from the sanguinary revolutions which then overran the fairest part of the Continent.' The Queen would once again, with God's blessing, preserve Britain from 'the returning hurricanes of European political revolution'. Each British subject was called upon to do his service to the beloved Queen, to protect 'that great united kingdom and justly balanced constitution at the head of which a gracious Providence has placed her'.

Within a system where the natural and social were of one and the same making, terms from one realm, such as *hurricanes*, smoothly entered the other. Britain did not and was not going to have a history marked by *revolutions*, a term used for both geological and social upheavals. Whereas many radical transmutationists had no need for cataclysms in their science, they regarded them as a social necessity. Buckland, on the contrary, preferred smooth and gradual progress in political matters, the traditional recipe of British stability and success. However, he saw no such way leading either from peasant to monarch, or from mouse to mammoth (who would speak of elephants knowing of mammoths!). What we have seen with regard to his belief in the bounded variability within the natural entity of species was true also for social entities; change of station could only happen within certain limits without disrupting the entire system. Otherwise, what might seem like social advance could prove to be a monstrosity.

The utilitarianism of the early industrial Britain taught its followers to take advantage of nature, while the duty of the gentleman scientist was also to employ science for the general good as well as to educate the public, to spread and maintain the belief in a social and natural order that represented God's will. According to the same logic, the British Empire had a responsibility for the distribution of Victorian ethics beyond the Isles. Buckland lived up to the expectation in both his role as scientist, as illustrated for example in the Bridgewater Treatise, and in his role as clergyman. To that purpose, a sermon was an effective means in Victorian England, since, as George Young puts it, 'the sermon was the standard vehicle of serious truth, and to the expositions and injunctions of their writers and statesmen the Victorian public brought the same hopeful determination to be instructed, and to be elevated, which held them attentive to the pleadings, denunciations, and commonplaces of their preachers.'[34]

Especially in the advanced stage of his career, Buckland increasingly regarded science as something also meant for practical application. He worked on the draining of marshes and bogs, and he was a member of the Royal Agricultural Society as well as an honorary member of the Institution of Civil Engineers. He even bought some clay land near Oxford and turned it into a model sanitary village. He personally instructed farmers and circulated papers on agriculture, such as one on the problem of potato disease. He further experimented on different sorts of wheat and barley and pioneered the use of coprolites as fertilizer. As a firm believer in progress, he trusted in the ability of science to provide remedies for hunger and disease, which he recognized as side effects of industrialization and population growth.[35]

A foreshadowing of Buckland's taste for the utilitarian potential of mineralogy and geology had been given in the Bridgewater Treatise, and also when members of the BAAS, accompanied by a large crowd, visited the Dudley Caverns in 1839. The owner of the limestone quarries had made a fortune from iron-smelting. The company travelled in boats on the canal; rockets of red and blue light were lit – 'the effect of which was striking and magnificent in the extreme' and opened to the eye 'scenes of *indescribable* grandeur' of 'the immeasurable sea of light and flame,' of 'the fairy-like spectacle'.[36] Buckland lectured for over an hour, pulling all the strings of his great oratorical talent and humour. He declared to his large audience in this artificial subterranean dome that the richness of Britain's soil in iron, coal and limestone was no coincidence, but a sure sign of divine providence, and of God's intention to make Britain the most powerful and the richest nation on earth. After all, Buckland argued, it was due to iron that humans rose to dominion over the earth, and to the high culture they currently enjoyed. He reminded his audience of the inexhaustible source of power iron possessed through its magnetism, and of how it guided the pioneers' way across the waters to explore new land. Continuing on this note, the crowd left the caverns singing 'God Save the Queen'.[37] This is the image Buckland wanted for his geology and his scientific persona, not the 'perversions' and dangers to the status quo that lay in the concepts of human antiquity and transmutationism. Symbolized by the fireworks at Dudley Caverns, the knowledge his researches brought forward would be used for the best interests of Empire, Crown and Church. Geology meant welfare tied to a social stability based on a hierarchy that was increasingly in need of protection through education and entertainment.

Around the time of the Dudley Caverns excursion, the last major threat to Buckland's negation of human antiquity took shape. In France, Jacques Boucher de Crèvecoeur de Perthes published the first of his three volumes of *Antiquités celtiques et antédiluviennes* (1847–9). In 1837, he had begun his work in the quarries of the Somme Valley, where he discovered different kinds of flint instruments, which he classified as antediluvian and Celtic, pottery and fossil animal bones. The combination of typology, stratigraphy and palaeontology allowed the reconstruction of a sequence of human inhabitants of the valley from the antediluvians to the (pre-)Celts, Gallo-Celts, Gallo-Romans and Romans and to the people of the Middle Ages and modern times. However, far from postulating such a long pedigree for modern humans, Boucher de Perthes regarded his antediluvian stone axes as the products of an extinct human race, exterminated by a geological catastrophe. Following this, as well as earlier cataclysms of total annihilation, there had been a special creation of modified and well-adapted animal species and humans alike. Yet, from the catastrophes that followed there had always been survivors, as was recorded in historical documents. Boucher de Perthes linked the antediluvians with Adam's clan, the postdiluvians with that of Noah (or the antediluvians with a pre-Adamite creation and the postdiluvians with Adamite creation). Noah's three sons Sem, Cham and Japhet had given rise to the three main human races: Mongolian (yellow), African (black) and Caucasian (white).[38]

In 1844, the Académie des Sciences in Paris reacted negatively to his findings: some of the discoveries, they said, were mere tricks of nature, while the genuine ones were not as old as Boucher de Perthes claimed. In addition to his outdated geological views, and the inconsistencies within the text, Boucher de Perthes had also identified unworked flints as tools, animals and humans cut out of stone, as well as religious totems. He even claimed to have found evidence for early hieroglyphs. He had furthermore been the victim of frauds by his workers, who had fabricated some of the flint tools.[39] Therefore, if Buckland was aware of the new discoveries made by Boucher de Perthes, he was reassured in his stance towards the question of human antiquity by the scientific community's reaction one last time. Buckland was effectively removed from the scientific arena by the close of the 1840s, and died in August 1856. However, three years later consensus was reached on the contemporaneity of humans and the fossil mammals of Quaternary Europe. Charles Lyell gave a speech at the BAAS in Aberdeen, accepting the Somme Valley evidence for prehistoric humans. At the same meeting Lyell, whose *Principles of Geology* (1830–3) had been a great inspiration to Darwin, announced the forthcoming *On the Origin of Species* (1859). With evolutionism added to uniformitarianism as the new frameworks for geology and biology, Buckland would have turned into a living fossil.

At the same time, Buckland might have been positively surprised to learn that, even despite the initial tide of indignation, once taken up by members of the scientific elite who were themselves prime examples of the Victorian lifestyle, evolutionism turned out to be less socially explosive than anticipated.[40] Buckland's system of parallel natural and social hierarchies did not simply crumble, although it was increasingly grounded on other than divine authority. Teleological underpinnings were not removed once and for all from theories of evolution. The 'Lamarckian' mechanisms of orthogenesis and the inheritance of acquired characters, as well as the analogy between ontogeny and phylogeny, continued to influence notions of biological and social advance well into the twentieth century.

Notes

* Parts of this chapter are reprinted by permission of the publisher from *Bones and Ochre: The Curious Afterlife of the Red Lady of Paviland* by Marianne Sommer, pp. 21, 25, 26–7, 36, 91–101, 106–112, Cambridge, Mass.: Harvard University Press, Copyright © 2007 by the President and Fellows of Harvard College.

1. For a more extensive treatment and more detailed references, in particular to the archival material consulted for this text, see Marianne Sommer, *Bones and Ochre: The Curious Afterlife of the Red Lady of Paviland*, Cambridge, Mass.: Harvard University Press, 2007, particularly pp. 91–104, on which this chapter is based.

2. Asa Briggs, *The Age of Improvement, 1783–1867*, 2nd edn, Harlow: Longman, 2000 (1959); Gottfried Niedhart, *Geschichte Englands im 19. und 20. Jahrhundert*, München: C. H. Beck, 1987, pp. 15–39 (Geschichte Englands in drei Bänden, 3); on the contributions of mining engineers, mineral surveyors and inventors to the knowledge of stratigraphy in the context of the developing industrial economy see Hugh Torrens, *The Practice of British Geology, 1750–1850*, Aldershot: Ashgate, 2002 (Variorum Collected Studies).

3. Georges Cuvier, *Recherches sur les ossemens fossiles de quadrupèdes, où l'on rétablit les caractères de plusieurs espèces d'animaux que les révolutions du globe paroissent avoir détruites*, 4 vols, Paris: Deterville, 1812; Jean André de Luc, *Lettres physiques et morales sur l'histoire de la terre et de l'homme*, 5 vols, La Haye, 1779; for a comprehensive history of the development of a historical geology in the late eighteenth and early nineteenth century see Martin J. S. Rudwick, *Bursting the Limits of Time: The Reconstruction of Geohistory in the Age of Revolution*, Chicago: The University of Chicago Press, 2005.

4. Georges Cuvier, *Essay on the Theory of the Earth, with Mineralogical Notes by Professor Jameson*, translated by Robert Kerr, Edinburgh: William Blackwood, 1813; William Buckland, *Vindiciae Geologicae; or, the Connexion of Geology with Religion: Explained in an Inaugural Lecture Delivered Before the University of Oxford, May 15, 1819*, Oxford: Oxford University Press, 1820.

5. On the BAAS see Jack Morrell and Arnold Thackray, *Gentlemen of Science: Early Years of the British Association for the Advancement of Science*, Oxford: Clarendon, 1981.

6. Nicolaas A. Rupke, *The Great Chain of History: William Buckland and the English School of Geology (1814–1849)*, Oxford: Clarendon, 1983, pp. 51–7, 233–40.

7. 9 November 1818, reproduced in J. M. Edmonds, 'The Founding of the Oxford Readership in Geology, 1818,' in *Notes and Records of the Royal Society of London* 34 (1979), pp. 33–51, here 39–41.

8. On the peculiarities of the universities of Oxford and Cambridge in contrast to the Scottish universities of the Enlightenment tradition, the French reformed institutions and the Humboldtian German university model in the first half of the nineteenth century see L. W. B. Brockliss, 'The European University in the Age of Revolution, 1789–1850', in M. G. Brock and M. C. Curthoys, eds, *The History of the University of Oxford. VI: Nineteenth-Century Oxford, Part I*, Oxford: Clarendon, 1997; on criticism levelled at Oxford see Asa Briggs, 'Oxford and Its Critics, 1800–1835', in M. G. Brock and M. C. Curthoys, eds, *The History of the University of Oxford*; on Oxford and geology in particular see Rupke, *The Great Chain of History*; 'Oxford's Scientific Awakening and the Role of Geology', in M. G. Brock and M. C. Curthoys, eds, *The History of the University of Oxford*; on the Oxford of Buckland's time see also M. G. Brock, 'The Oxford of Peel and Gladstone, 1800–1833', in M. G. Brock and M. C. Curthoys, eds, *The History of the University of Oxford*; on the wider impact of the early geology see for example H. Hamshaw Thomas, 'The Rise of Geology and Its Influence on Contemporary Thought', in *Annals of Science* 5 (1947), no. 4, pp. 325–41.

9. James Secord, *Victorian Sensation: The Extraordinary Publication, Reception, and Secret Authorship of Vestiges of the Natural History of Creation*, Chicago: The University of Chicago Press, 2000, pp. 299–320; on radical evolutionism see also Peter J. Bowler, *Charles Darwin: The Man and His Influence*, Oxford: Basil Blackwell, 1990, pp. 20–7 (Blackwell Science Biographies, ed. David Knight).

10. Adrian Desmond, 'Artisan Resistance and Evolution in Britain, 1819–1848,' in *Osiris* (1987), no. 3, pp. 77–110; id., *The Politics of Evolution. Morphology, Medicine, and Reform in Radical London*, Chicago: The University of Chicago Press, 1989 (Science and Its Conceptual Foundations Series, ed. David L. Hull).

11. Jean-Baptiste de Lamarck, *Zoologische Philosophie*, translated by Arnold Lang, *Ostwalds Klassiker der exakten Wissenschaften* 277 [1809], repr. vols 277, 278, 279, Frankfurt am Main: Harri Deutsch, 2002, chs 6–7 in particular; on Lamarck's transmutationism see also Pietro Corsi, *The Age of Lamarck: Evolutionary Theories in France, 1790–1830*, translated by Jonathan Mandelbaum, 2nd edn, Berkeley: The University of California Press, 1988 [1983]; Wolfgang Lefèvre, *Die Entstehung der biologischen Evolutionstheorie*, Frankfurt am Main: Ullstein, 1984, ch. 2.

12. See also Donald K. Grayson, *The Establishment of Human Antiquity*, New York: Academic Press, 1983, ch. 4. The classical study on the history of the *scala naturae* concept is Arthur O. Lovejoy, *The Great Chain of Being: A Study of the History of an Idea, The William James Lectures Delivered at Harvard University, 1933* [1936], Cambridge, Mass.: Harvard University Press, 1964.

13. On Geoffroy Saint-Hilaire see Corsi, *The Age of Lamarck*, pp. 230–68.

14. Oxford University Museum of Natural History, Buckland Papers (OUMNH, Bu P), Notes for the Bridgewater Treatise/Notes by Subject (box 2), 'Species change of Lamarck' (folder 6ii, p. 26).
15. Ibid. (folder 6ii, p. 29; see also 6i, pp. 6, 7, 11). That Buckland regarded every creature as perfect becomes wonderfully obvious from his defence of the sloth, which, too, was perfectly fitted for its niche (William Buckland, 'On the Adaptation of the Structure of the Sloths to their peculiar Mode of Life', in *Transactions of the Linnean Society* 17 (1837), pp. 17–27).
16. OUMNH, Bu P, Notes for the Bridgewater Treatise/Notes by Subject (box 2), 'Species change of Lamarck' (folder 6ii, p. 26).
17. Ibid. (folder 6ii, p. 29); see also Rupke, *The Great Chain of History*, pp. 174–6.
18. William Buckland, *Geology and Mineralogy Considered with Reference to Natural Theology*, 2 vols, *The Bridgewater Treatises VI, On the Power, Wisdom, and Goodness of God, as Manifested in the Creation*, London: William Pickering, 1836, vol. I, pp. 21, 94–5, footnote.
19. Buckland, *Geology and Mineralogy*, vol. I, p. 15.
20. Buckland, *Geology and Mineralogy*, vol. I, p. 103; for a synopsis of Buckland's stance towards human antiquity in relation to his theoretical development see Grayson, *The Establishment of Human Antiquity*, pp. 63–72, and Rupke, *The Great Chain of History*, pp. 91–5.
21. Philippe-Charles Schmerling, *Recherches sur les ossemens fossiles découverts dans les cavernes de la province de Liège*, Liège: Collardin, 1833–4, vol. 2, p. 179, my translation; on the flint tools and worked bone in general see ch. 10.
22. Schmerling, *Recherches sur les ossemens fossiles*, on human bones see vol. 1, ch. 3. The last edition of Cuvier's *Recherches sur les ossemens fossiles*, which appeared posthumously in 1834, maintained the claim that none of the human bones so far discovered were fossil (Georges Cuvier, 'Discours sur les révolutions de la surface du globe, et sur les changements qu'elles ont produit dans le règne animal,' in id., *Recherches sur les ossemens fossiles, où l'on rétablit les caractères de plusieurs animaux dont les révolutions du globe ont détruit les espèces*, Paris: Dufour and d'Ocagne, 1834, p. 216).
23. C. Morren, 'Notice sur la vie et les travaux de Philippe-Charles Schmerling', *Annuaire* 4 (1838), pp. 130–50, p. 147, my translation. As a physician, Schmerling had been interested in deformed fossil bones to determine from what kind of diseases the antediluvian animals might have suffered.
24. Élie de Beaumont, 'Mémoires et communications,' in *Compte rendu des séances de l'Académie des Sciences 69 (séance du lundi, 6 décembre)* 69 (1869), Juillet–Décembre, pp. 1211–13, here 1213 (my translation); the report of the meeting is given in 'Erste Sitzung am 19. September', 1836.
25. Marianne Sommer, '"An Amusing Account of a Cave in Wales": William Buckland (1784–1856) and the Red Lady of Paviland,' in *British Journal for the History of Science* 37 (2004), no. 1, pp. 53–74; id., *Bones and Ochre*, part I; on Buckland's abhorrence of controversy see OUMNH, Bu P, Lecture Notes (box 1), 'Lecture notes on the Mosaic Deluge' (folder 5, p. 9).
26. Buckland, *Geology and Mineralogy*, vol. I, p. 598, note to p. 106.
27. Buckland to Henry Brougham, 26 November 1838, reproduced in Rupke, *The Great Chain of History*, p. 164.
28. The radical French popular writer, botanist and geologist Pierre Boitard took the side of Fossil Man and organic transmutation as early as 1838, the year of the coronation of Queen Victoria, in his article 'L'Homme fossile' in the *Magasin universel* (Pierre Boitard, 'L'Homme fossile, étude paléontologique', in *Magasin universel* 5 (1838), avril, pp. 209–40). The article that drew on human remains claimed to be fossils such as those discovered by Schmerling was accompanied by a visualization of an ape-'Negro' chimera representing Fossil Man. He swings a hand-axe modelled on Schmerling's finds. Boitard made fun of the orthodox

geologist who was immune to evidence, explicitly mocking the deceased Cuvier and his conservative ghost still haunting the Academy of Sciences. To herald the English paper *Oracle of Reason*'s use of science to undermine religion, the image opened the 'Theory of Regular Gradation' series in 1841 (see Secord, *Victorian Sensation*, pp. 312–13).

29. Morrell and Thackray, *Gentlemen of Science*, pp. 226–7; Jonathan R. Topham, 'Beyond "Common Context": The Production and Reading of the Bridgewater Treatises,' in *Isis* 89 (1998), no. 2, pp. 233–62, here 250–61.

30. Adam Sedgwick, 'Natural History of Creation,' in *Edinburgh Review* 82 (1845), pp. 1–85, on p. 3; Secord, *Victorian Sensation*, on Whewell's and Sedgwick's responses see pp. 227–47, on responses from exponents of Oxford University see pp. 253–60. Among the latter, the strategies of coping with the claims brought forward in *Vestiges* varied from straightforward attack and defence of natural theology, to an agnostic stance towards its scientific claims with an emphasis on religion's independence from science, to attempts at rendering transmutationism compatible with Christian doctrine.

31. John Hedley Brooke, 'The Natural Theology of the Geologists: Some Theological Strata,' in Ludmilla J. Jordanova and Roy S. Porter, eds, *Images of the Earth: Essays in the History of the Environmental Sciences*, Aberdeen: Rainbow, 1979, p. 50; Morrell and Thackray, *Gentlemen of Science*, p. 245. Brooke, 'Natural Theology', argues that the design argument of the natural theology of the time had a mediating function between different religious traditions. It was thus advantageous in the unification of men of different Christian sects under the roof of the BAAS. On Buckland's reactions see Rupke, *The Great Chain of History*, p. 179; Secord, *Victorian Sensation*, pp. 209, 226.

32. Elizabeth Oke Gordon, *The Life and Correspondence of William Buckland, D.D., F.R.S., Sometime Dean of Westminster, Twice President of the Geological Society, and First President of the British Association*, London: Murray, 1894, pp. 241–6.

33. The sermon is reproduced in Gordon, *Life and Correspondence of William Buckland*, pp. 242–4; see also Charles Coulston Gillispie, *Genesis and Geology. A Study in the Relations of Scientific Thought, Natural Theology, and Social Opinion in Great Britain, 1790–1850* [1951], 2nd edn, Cambridge, Mass.: Harvard University Press, 1996, pp. 201–2 (Harvard Social Studies, 58).

34. George Malcolm Young, *Victorian England: Portrait of an Age*, New York: Doubleday, 1954, p. 30.

35. Gordon, *Life and Correspondence of William Buckland*, pp. 150–72.

36. *Illustrated London News*, 22 September 1849, p. 89, in Rosalind Williams, *Notes on the Underground: An Essay on Technology, Society, and the Imagination*, Cambridge, Mass.: MIT Press, 1990, p. 106.

37. On the happenings in the Dudley Caverns see Gordon, *Life and Correspondence of William Buckland*, pp. 79–83.

38. Jacques Boucher de Perthes, *Antiquités celtiques et antédiluviennes: Mémoire sur l'industrie primitive et les arts à leur origine*, 3 vols, Paris: Treuttel et Wurtz, 1847–9, vol. 1, chs 3, 12, 23, note 38. On Boucher de Perthes see Claudine Cohen and Jean-Jacques Hublin, *Boucher de Perthes (1788–1868): Les origines romantiques de la préhistoire, un Savant, une Époque Series*, Paris: Belin, 1989, particularly chs 6 and 7. His later editions were more in line with the current scientific views and were better received (Jacques Boucher de Perthes, *Antiquités celtiques et antédiluviennes: Mémoire sur l'industrie primitive et les arts a leur origine*, vol. 2, Paris: Treuttel et Wurtz, 1857; id., *Antiquités celtiques et antédiluviennes. Mémoire sur l'industrie primitive et les arts a leur origine*, vol. 3, Paris: Jung-Treuttel, 1864).

39. Boucher de Perthes, *Antiquités celtiques et antédiluviennes,* vol. 1, chs 21, 23.

40. Michael Ruse, *The Darwinian Revolution: Science Red in Tooth and Claw* [1979], Chicago: Chicago University Press, 2nd edn, 1999, pp. 250–63.

CHAPTER 5
AGAINST DARWIN: TELEOLOGY IN GERMAN PHILOSOPHICAL ANTHROPOLOGY*
Angus Nicholls

1. Introduction: the problem of the human being

The human sciences are faced with an ontological and a definitional problem because human nature is not an empirical thing. This is the argument with which Roger Smith begins a recent study on the history of the human sciences.[1] Smith's opening premise is not an exercise in mystification. Human 'nature' is not a stable empirical object precisely because human beings have continually to decide – from within the limitations of their own historical and cultural standpoints – what it means to be human. And it is precisely here where the problems begin: when I attempt to understand other human beings, I must necessarily do so on the basis of my own self-understanding; yet because my consciousness is conditioned by a history and by a culture that can never be completely external objects for me, precisely because I am *in* them, I can never achieve full self-transparency when it comes to understanding myself and my relation to other human beings. Writing in the early 1970s, in a late contribution to the German tradition of philosophical anthropology, Hans Blumenberg described this epistemological situation as follows:

> Man has no immediate, no purely 'internal' relation to himself. His self-understanding has the structure of 'self-externality'. Kant was the first to deny that inner experience has any precedence over outer experience; we are appearance to ourselves, the secondary synthesis of a primary multiplicity, not the reverse. The substantialism of identity is destroyed; identity must be realized, it becomes a kind of accomplishment, and accordingly there is a pathology of identity. What remains as the subject matter of anthropology is a 'human nature' that has never been 'nature' and never will be.[2]

One possible way to resolve the situation described here by Blumenberg might be to objectify the human being by way of what Smith terms biological reductionism.[3] Humans would in these terms be seen as nothing more than organisms that have evolved through natural selection, and whose thinking and cultures might be explained via recourse to the biological sciences of the brain. Such a view would also hold that Darwin's discoveries concerning human evolution began a process that will one day resolve the central problem of the human sciences as it had been identified by Kant – that of teleology or the distorting use of overarching reflective judgements, perhaps even of 'values' or 'ideologies'

– in scientific method. This human tendency to take recourse to bigger orienting judgements, world-pictures, narratives or organizing metaphors has seen humans understanding themselves according to a range of divine and human purposes that could not empirically be measured by the methods of the natural sciences,[4] and which therefore came to be seen, during the second half of the nineteenth century, as unscientific.

The question as to whether such biological reductionism could escape these nineteenth-century problems concerning teleology and values is one that cannot be answered in any detail here. But my strong suspicion, which follows the analysis of Smith, is that any narrative that would see the history of the human sciences as progressively overcoming teleology, presumably through the increasing deployment of empirically testable scientific methods as they are applied to human beings, would itself be teleological in its orientation. To be human, my view would hold, means to tell stories to oneself and about oneself in which the present and past are seen in terms of an always already posited future. Only in this way can the human being acquire a fundamental orientation in its world. In this sense, the human condition would have to be seen as a *narrative condition* in the ways described not only by nineteenth-century historians like Johnann Gustav von Droysen but also by those, like Blumenberg, who belong to the tradition of phenomenology.[5] According to this view, teleology is not necessarily a 'bad' thing, so long as it does not remain unconscious and unquestioned, and so long as it is susceptible to being made into an object of critical reflection. The notion that teleology can and should be 'overcome' would then have to be seen as an unrealistic expectation for a species which, in having at some point developed the capacity for self-reflection and deliberation, is no longer automatically or instinctually able to know what the best course of action is within any given situation. In other words: making decisions requires us to formulate some kind of narrative about how we got here and where we want to go, and at any one point in time there may be multiple such narratives in play.

The phraseology that I am using in this introduction – for example, the notion that humans need a 'fundamental orientation' because they lack 'instinctive' or 'automatic' behaviours designed to respond to certain situations – is self-consciously suggestive of a tradition. The tradition that I am invoking – that of German philosophical anthropology – is a contested tradition. This is partly because it is possible to speak of philosophical anthropology in both the broad and narrow senses. One could argue, as Max Scheler has done, that if philosophical anthropology simply undertakes the activity of defining the essence of the human being in philosophical terms, then it has existed at least since Aristotle.[6] One could, however, equally claim that the inaugural moment of modern philosophical anthropology occurs in 1800, when Kant proposes that the first three of his four questions – 'What can I know? What should I do? What may I hope for?' – can only be answered by way of his fourth and final question: 'What is the human being?'[7] Kant's answer to this question had already been delivered in his *Anthropology from a Pragmatic Point of View* (1798): the human being is subject to a range of physiological inclinations (the needs for food, shelter and sex), which we should come to recognize so that they can be transcended via the exercise of reason in ethics. This position led Kant sharply to differentiate *physiological* anthropology from *practical* anthropology, while also making it perfectly clear that the former variant amounted only to a mundane and empirical preparation for the latter.[8]

The most commonly accepted and narrow view of philosophical anthropology sees it not so much as a school, but only as a mere 'direction of thought' (*Denkrichtung*) in German philosophy which had its heyday in the interwar period,[9] and which can now be likened to a 'field of ruins' in need of a total reconstruction.[10] If anything united the members of this tendency in early twentieth-century German thought, then it was dissatisfaction with the way in which Kant, and after him the entire tradition of German idealism, had answered Kant's fourth question. In his essay 'On the Idea of the Human' (1914), Max Scheler both answers and does not answer Kant's fourth question by claiming that the essence of the human being inheres precisely in its indefinability.[11] Paul Alsberg, in his *Puzzle of Humanity* (1922), addresses Kant's question by claiming that our pre-human ancestors only became human when they began to use stone projectiles as a means of self-defence – a form of mediation that presaged later technologies of distance, along with language and conceptual thought, and which sees human beings as animals who need cultural compensations in order to survive.[12] In *The Stages of the Organic and the Human Being* (1928), Helmuth Plessner claims that to be human means to be 'eccentric' in the sense of being only weakly predetermined by instincts and therefore open to making artificial and self-reflexive adaptations.[13] While in *Man: His Nature and Place in the World* (1940), Arnold Gehlen argues that the human being is a 'creature of deficiencies' (*Mängelwesen*), which compensates for its lack of biological adaptations through the development of technology, culture and institutions.[14]

The other reason why this narrower tradition of philosophical anthropology is contested is because one of its foremost exponents – namely Arnold Gehlen – was implicated within National Socialism.[15] In the editions of *Man* published during the 1940s, Gehlen proposed that precisely because humans are only weakly predetermined by instincts, they require strong 'command systems' (*Führungssysteme*) in order to provide them with orientation.[16] In post-war Germany, such arguments were seen to be situated within a tradition of conservative political thought that goes back to Thomas Hobbes's *Leviathan*, and which found its more explicitly political analogue in the early twentieth-century writings of Carl Schmitt, for whom the Sovereign must always make crucial orienting decisions – most crucially the supposedly 'primordial' distinction friend and enemy – in exceptional circumstances or states of emergency (*Ausnahmezustände*).[17]

In an important article on philosophical anthropology written in 1958, the young Jürgen Habermas pointed to these dangers when he accused the proponents of philosophical anthropology – and particularly Gehlen – of engaging in reductive and ahistorical statements about the so-called 'essence' of the human being. Any discussion of what the human being essentially *is* would, implied Habermas, potentially circumscribe what the human being *could and should be* in the future, a position that is later echoed by Theodor W. Adorno in *Negative Dialectics* (1966) when he observes: 'We cannot say what man is … To decipher the human essence by the way it is now would sabotage its possibility.'[18] This is why Habermas, at that time still Adorno's assistant, ended his article by stating that philosophical anthropology could only become truly 'critical' (*kritisch*: arguably *the* keyword of the Frankfurt School) by entering into a dialogue with a 'theory of society'.[19] Implicit in Habermas's critique is the notion that any story told about the human being, and particularly about the original conditions out of which the human beings and societies *came to be*, will have political implications. Furthermore: the necessity of incorporating historicity into such stories might also suggest that they can never be 'told' once and for all, but will always need to be retold and agreed upon in ways that presuppose an open and relatively free dialogue about what it means to be human at any given point in history. And even from a strictly natural scientific point of view, such stories about the human being might also need to be told and retold precisely because the natural sciences might never be able to provide a definitive account of the evolutionary processes that originally brought human beings into existence, which would mean that narrative will always be an indispensable component of palaeoanthropology.[20]

Rather than attempting to address these enormous issues, or, for that matter, to answer the difficult question as to when philosophical anthropology began and what its essential or dominant characteristics are, my approach here will be to consider certain less well-known aspects of this intellectual tradition as providing innovative responses to the problem of teleology in the human sciences. The innovative and potentially useful – but, for the reasons mentioned above, also potentially dangerous – aspects of this philosophical tradition can only be grasped when one considers what these thinkers were writing *against*: namely, biological reductionism in general and Darwinism in particular. What ensures the ongoing relevance of philosophical anthropology – notwithstanding its failure to establish itself as a 'school' in German philosophy, and despite its politically conservative manifestation in the work of Gehlen – is its attempt to deal with the problem of teleology in a way that fundamentally departed from the Darwinian route that dominated the Anglophone human sciences during the late nineteenth century. Philosophical anthropology did not oppose evolution by natural selection in general, but it did – in stark contradistinction to Darwin – insist upon seeing human development as an exceptional case that required a different theoretical approach. And although Darwin did not explicitly authorize a teleological view of human cultures and of human history in the *Descent of Man*, both the general tenor of his arguments and the colonial context in which they were made tended to bolster teleological narratives concerning the relation between so-called 'primitive' and 'advanced' cultures.

The point here will not be retrospectively to hold Darwin directly responsible for the prevalence of a colonially slanted social Darwinism at the origins of British anthropology, but to examine the pitfalls of an exclusively empirical approach to questions of human development and culture. I will propose that the indirect consequence of Darwin's scientific attempt to *avoid* recourse to teleology in his theory of natural selection was precisely to make teleology *rampant* – because largely unconscious and unquestioned – at the origins of British anthropology. Here my main case in point will be the first Professor of Anthropology in Britain, Edward Burnett Tylor (1832–1917) and his major theoretical work, *Primitive Culture* (1871). As a counterpoint to Tylor, I will then examine the different approach taken to questions of human development by a thinker who can safely be described as the 'forgotten hero' of German philosophical anthropology: Paul Alsberg (1883–1965).[21]

Alsberg is now enjoying a minor renaissance in German philosophy, due to his apparently having been 'rediscovered' by Dieter Claessens, by Hans Blumenberg and more recently by Peter Sloterdijk.[22] An examination of Alsberg's only book – *The Puzzle of Humanity* (1922) – will show the extent to which certain strains of German philosophy took a different approach to the question of teleology, by seeing it as something essential and unavoidable within human thinking, rather than as something that should be overcome for methodological reasons and in the name of a so-called 'scientific method'. Moreover, the roots of Alsberg's approach to questions about the human being can be found in a source that was roughly contemporaneous with Tylor: the writings of Friedrich Nietzsche. But before turning to Tylor, to Alsberg, and to Nietzsche, it will be necessary to examine why teleology came to be seen as a problem for scientific method at all.

2. 'Science' and teleology in late nineteenth-century German thought

Before the middle of the nineteenth century, and especially before Darwin, science and *Wissenschaft* were used very generally in English and in German to refer to any field of inquiry with a systematic structure. The English philosopher who coined the term 'scientist' in 1833 – William Whewell (1794–1866) – pointed out that science refers not only to knowledge concerning the material world, but also to any systematic area of study:

> The views respecting the nature and progress of knowledge, towards which we shall be directed by such a course of inquiry as I have pointed out, though derived from those portions of which are more peculiarly and technically termed Sciences, will by no means be confined, in their bearing, to the domain of such Sciences as deal with the material world, nor even to the whole range of Sciences now existing. On the contrary, we shall be led to believe that the nature of truth is in all subjects the same, and that its discovery involves, in all cases, the like conditions. On one subject of human speculation after another, man's knowledge assumes the exact and substantial character which leads us to term it Science; and in all these cases, whether inert matter or living bodies, whether permanent relations or successive occurrences, be the subject of our attention, we can point out certain universal characters that belong to truth.[23]

Whewell's general assumption was that one essential truth underlay the various different fields of knowledge, including, for example, theology. Whewell was influenced by the writings of Immanuel Kant,[24] and in Germany it was Kant and his German idealist successors who had dominated the ways in which the term *Wissenschaft* was used, at least up until around the middle of the nineteenth century. Kant's key move, undertaken in the *Metaphysical Foundations of Natural Science* in 1786, was to associate scientific knowledge with necessary or apodictic knowledge. 'What can be called proper science,' he wrote,

> is only that whose certainty is apodictic; cognition that can contain mere empirical certainty is only knowledge improperly so-called. Any whole of cognition that is systematic can, for this reason, already be called science, and, if the connection of cognition in this system is an interconnection of grounds and consequences, even rational science. If, however, the grounds or principles themselves are still in the end merely empirical, as in chemistry … then they carry with them no consciousness of their necessity … chemistry should therefore be called a systematic art rather than a science.[25]

Kant thought that science must show how empirical observations correspond with the a priori categories of the Understanding. This is why, for example, Kant sees physics as being *wissenschaftlich*, since it corresponds with the a priori category of causality. By contrast, chemistry – which Kant sees as relying upon empirical observation alone – is described only as a 'systematic art'.

But the real problem case for Kant was biology, which he tackled in the second part of the *Critique of Judgement* (1790). For Kant, biological organisms cannot be understood only in the mechanistic terms of Newtonian physics. The scales, gills and fins of a fish, for example, work together in such a way as to suggest that there is a design or purpose in nature (§61). Since this conception of the organism is a reflective judgement that cannot be proven by way of scientific experiment, it is, strictly speaking, unscientific (§75). In this way, Kant describes teleology as being a device to which one needs to resort, especially in biology, in order to explain how organisms work. But in such cases we must be aware that these reflective judgements, even if they seem highly plausible, are in the end not provable in scientific terms. And the idea that there are purposes in nature will eventually lead us to the theological consideration of final causes, as Kant suggests in §72 of the third *Critique*:

> It must therefore be a certain presentiment of our reason, or a hint as it were given to us by nature, that we could by means of that concept of final causes step beyond nature and even connect it to the highest point in the series of causes if we were to abandon research into nature (even though we have not gotten very far in that), or at least set it aside for a while, and attempt to discover where that stranger [*Fremdling*] in natural science, namely the concept of natural ends, leads.[26]

Teleology, we are told here, is a stranger or *Fremdling* in the context of scientific method, something that is unavoidable and that arises necessarily as a result of inherent tendencies of reason, but which at the same time does not really belong in science, because it posits hypotheses that can neither be proven nor disproven within the restrictive apodictic confines of scientific knowledge as Kant had defined them.

Now to cut a very long and complicated story short, the *Fremdling* of teleology mentioned here by Kant wandered off into the fully blown versions of German idealism found in the thought-systems of Fichte, Schelling and Hegel. These three thinkers ignored the necessary limitations of reflective judgements and therefore also of teleology. For them, teleology or purposiveness did not exist only as a regulative idea as it did for Kant. Rather, it existed objectively: either as self-consciousness realizing itself in the world through its own activity (in Fichte's *Wissenschaftslehre* of 1794–5); as the indwelling unity between the individual soul and the world-soul or nature (as in Schelling's *Ideas Towards a Philosophy of Nature*, 1797); or as the progressive unfolding of spirit (*Geist*) in human history (according to Hegel in the *Phenomenology of Spirit*, 1807). However misleading their usages of this term may be from our present-day point of view, all three thinkers associated their respective philosophical systems with a general and speculative concept of *Wissenschaft* or science as a form of universal knowledge.[27] That these teleologies were roughly contemporaneous with one another points to a problem already highlighted in the introduction to this volume: namely that in German philosophy since the age of Christian Wolff there have been multiple, and even mutually exclusive, teleologies.

But by the middle of the nineteenth century, when academic disciplines as we know them today were taking shape, these thought-systems experienced a decline that has been described as nothing less than the so-called 'collapse' of German idealism.[28] This 'collapse', according to Herbert Schnädelbach in his authoritative history of philosophy in Germany between 1831 and 1933, 'plunged philosophy into a profound identity crisis',[29] and this crisis was accompanied by a change in the meaning of the term 'science' (*Wissenschaft*). This was especially so after Darwinian natural selection demonstrated that non-human biology was certainly possible, and that the human sciences might also be possible, without the aid of teleological arguments. The 'hard' natural scientific interpretation of Darwin holds that because genetic variations in organisms are random, and because 'selection' is simply a process according to which these random variations are either more or less conducive to survival and reproduction, natural selection dispenses completely with the idea that there is a purpose in nature. In response to this development, natural scientists in Germany such as Hermann von Helmholtz attempted to remove all traces of idealism from their methodologies. This also meant that a bifurcation took place within the sciences.[30] For Helmholtz – writing in 1862, just three years after the publication of Darwin's *Origin of Species* – speculative arguments like those found in the thought of Hegel were perfectly acceptable in human sciences or *Geisteswissenschaften* such as history or law, but they could never find a place in the *Naturwissenschaften*. This is because, according to Helmholtz,

> the natural sciences are normally in a position to derive sharply defined general rules and laws from their inductions; the human sciences are, by contrast, overwhelmingly concerned with judgements according to psychological tact.[31]

Within German philosophy towards the end of the nineteenth century, what Helmholtz refers to as 'judgements according to psychological tact' became associated with the philosophical problem of 'values' (*Werte*) in Southwestern or 'Baden' Neo-Kantianism.

Before we turn our attention to Tylor – who was writing some twenty years before the two chief protagonists of Southwestern Neo-Kantianism, Wilhelm Windelband and Heinrich Rickert – it will be instructive briefly to examine why Windelband and Rickert perceived 'values' to be a problem for philosophy, and what this problem has to do with the question of teleology.

In his Strasbourg rectorial address of 1894, Windelband makes the important distinction between the so-called *nomothetic* and *idiographic* modes of research. The nomothetic method is associated with the natural sciences, which seek to establish general laws or principles such as those found in physics, whereas the human sciences are idiographic, seeking to understand unique events or individuals in history.[32] While the natural sciences are said to select their objects of research objectively, in relation to how they coincide with or contradict general laws or principles, the selection of facts in the human sciences, and especially in the historical sciences, is never neutral: it is always informed by human values and interests. For Windelband, historical facts only ever come to be selected and analysed when they are seen to constitute a 'significant component' (*bedeutsamer Bestandteil*) of a 'total organic conception' (*lebendige Gesamtanschauung*). The implicit suggestion here is that the problems relating to teleology that Kant had found in biology are even more prominent in history; just as the parts of an organism can be seen to express that organism's presumed overall purpose, so too are historical facts always already laden with teleology, since they will inevitably be embedded within historical narratives that might suggest ultimate human purposes or ends.[33] As an assiduous reader of Kant, Windelband is highly conscious of Kant's reservations about the uses of teleological judgements in science. The first step towards 'controlling' such teleological judgements, he argues, would therefore consist in making them into conscious objects of reflection.

Heinrich Rickert addresses similar issues in his conception of the cultural sciences (*Kulturwissenschaften*) as outlined in *Cultural Science and Natural Science* (1898).[34] Here he undertakes a stringent distinction between nature and culture. 'Nature' refers to physical events, laws and processes that are not subject to human intervention. Culture exists where humans have modified, shaped or harnessed nature (such as through agriculture), or where they have developed institutions (political bodies, religious beliefs, social practices) that are connected with values. Natural objects are subjected to processes of perception (*Wahrnehmung*) that are allegedly not distorted by values, whereas cultural objects are objects of understanding (*Verstehen*) that become worthy of attention within a grander set of values or narratives which endow them with meaning or significance (*Bedeutung*). Natural science is thus said to be value-free (*wertfrei*), whereas the cultural sciences are taken to be value-laden (*wertbehaftet*).[35]

These distinctions made by Windelband and Rickert offer an important counterpoint to the views of Tylor because they display the recognition that human beings are always historically situated observers who view history and culture in terms of grander 'big pictures' – or, in Windelband's words, 'total organic conceptions' – that may be either conscious or unconscious. The advance made by German philosophy of the late nineteenth century was to have attempted, insofar as this is possible at all, to make such teleological narratives or perceptual frames into objects of conscious methodological reflection. And similar efforts were also made by Wilhelm Dilthey, in his attempts to found a separate and non-positivist methodology for the human sciences (*Geisteswissenschaften*) from the early 1880s onwards, and especially in his *Introduction to the Human Sciences* of 1883.[36]

In Dilthey's late formulation, expressed in his *Construction of the Historical World in the Human Sciences* of 1910, the task of the human sciences is to understand the 'life-expressions' (*Lebensäußerungen*) of human beings who lived in different epochs from our own. These life-expressions – poems, novels, historical documents, and so on – are inevitably marked by the historically contingent cultures in which they were produced, and the researcher's perception of them will also be influenced by the values peculiar to his or her own historical and cultural contexts. This historical gap is to be bridged through a meticulous historical contextualization of the cultural artefact under investigation, combined with the empathetic ability to enter into (*Hineinversetzen*) the culture and values of another age.[37] Again, the point here is that to be a human being means to be situated within a cultural context that is marked by value-judgements concerning what is culturally noteworthy and what ends human life should achieve. In both Windelband and Dilthey, this feature of human consciousness is also given explicit anthropological expression: just as for Windelband 'the human being ... is the animal that has history',[38] so too for the late Dilthey it is 'anthropology' that must outline a 'science of the human being' by endeavouring to 'understand the totality of experiences according to a structural context'.[39] Thus, although the grandiose thought-systems of German idealism had given teleology a bad name, teleology was able to make its way back into German philosophy at the end of the nineteenth century, only this time as an object of reflexive methodological awareness. But as we shall see, Tylor's approach to anthropology was a rather different one.

3. Rampant teleology: Tylor and Darwin

Edward Burnett Tylor was appointed to the first Chair of Anthropology in the world at Oxford in 1896. Although the main part of his career coincided with the rise to prominence of Darwin, his essential intellectual orientation was pre-Darwinian. Darwin's *Descent of Man* appeared in the same year (1871) as Tylor's *Primitive Culture*. Tylor's and Darwin's contemporaneity – combined with the fact that they both propounded theories of evolution – might be the cause of some confusion. It is certainly the case that there are some passages in Tylor's works in which it sounds as though he is applying natural selection to human culture. Tylor does refer to some of the 'ethnographic' observations in Darwin's *Journal of Researches* (that is, his account of the *Beagle* voyage, first published in 1839) in his *Researches into the Early History of Mankind* (1865),[40] but Darwin's *Journal* pre-dates the theory of natural selection by some twenty years. In fact, Tylor himself felt the need, in the Preface to the second (1873) edition of *Primitive Culture*, to explain to readers why he had not mentioned Darwin within its pages:

> It may have struck some readers as an omission that in a work on civilization insisting so strenuously on a theory of development or evolution, mention should scarcely have been made of Mr. Darwin and Mr. Herbert Spencer, whose influence on the whole course of modern thought on such subjects should not be left without formal recognition. This absence of particular reference is accounted for by the present work, arranged on its own lines, coming scarcely into contact of detail with the previous works of these eminent philosophers.[41]

While it is certainly hard to believe that Tylor would have come 'scarcely into contact' with Darwin's ideas after 1859 (they even shared the same publisher, John Murray), when one looks at his *Researches* and his *Primitive Culture*, it is plausible to claim that these texts were, in theoretical terms, conceived along their own pre-Darwinian lines. The same cannot, however, be said of Darwin: as we shall see, Darwin invoked the ideas of Tylor in relation to one of the most crucial arguments within the *Descent of Man*: that concerning the continuity between animal and human mentality.

George Stocking and Joan Leopold have shown the extent to which Tylor's intellectual roots belong in the notion of comparative method associated with German linguistics of the mid-nineteenth century; for example, in the works of Franz Bopp and Max Müller. The essential idea was to see linguistics as being akin to an empirical natural science or 'linguistic palaeontology', in which one collects a variety of specimens together (in this case languages, primarily ancient Greek and Sanskrit) and undertakes comparisons between them.[42] Tylor's innovation was to take this comparative method and to apply it to the differences between 'primitive' and 'modern' cultures. Tylor uses the term 'culture' more or less interchangeably with civilization:

> Culture or Civilization, taken in its wide or ethnographic sense, is that complex whole which includes knowledge, belief, art, morals, custom and any other capabilities and habits acquired by man as a member of society.[43]

Tylor has a purely empirical conception of culture. 'A first step in the study of civilization', he argues, 'is to dissect it into details, and to classify these under their proper groups.' Just as the 'naturalist' studies 'the species of plants and animals', so too can culture be studied as a collection of material objects organized according to an overarching theoretical schema.[44] Of particular interest to Tylor are tools, technology, mythology and religious beliefs. Since most of the relevant information could apparently be gleaned from the examination of material objects and relics alone, Tylor does not consider knowledge of languages to be of overriding importance for the understanding of culture.

Tylor saw culture in materialist terms, as a field of knowledge functioning in accordance with 'laws as definite as those which govern the motion of the waves, the combination of acids and bases, and the growth of plants and animals'.[45] He argues that all human cultures are characterized by a 'general likeness' that transcends ethnic, racial and linguistic boundaries. For this reason Tylor proposes that it would be possible to map the development of a universal human culture 'stage by stage, in a probable order of evolution'.⁴⁶ Within the context of the British Empire, Tylor was interested in what he regarded as 'primitive' cultures. Tylor associated primitivism with animism, which he saw as a misconceived forerunner to science. By attributing certain events to supernatural causes, animism is said to display a pre-scientific causal logic. This animistic stage is later replaced by monotheism and finally by science, and all cultures pass through these stages at various points in their history, with some progressing faster than others. Tylor was influenced by Auguste Comte's eminently teleological three-stage model of culture outlined in the *Course of Positive Philosophy* (*Cours de philosophie positive*, 1830–42), according to which human cultures progressively pass through stages described as being 'theological', 'metaphysical' and finally 'positive' (in the sense of empiricist-scientific 'positivism').⁴⁷

Tylor's explanation for the coexistence of various developmental stages of culture across the globe is evolutionist, but also pre-Darwinian, and it corresponds with what J. W. Burrow has called 'the central idea of evolutionary anthropology – that contemporary primitive societies can be used as evidence for reconstructing the past of our own'.⁴⁸ Tylor had already outlined this theory in 1865, in his *Researches into the Early History of Mankind*, and it runs as follows:

> The facts collected seem to favour the view that the wide differences in the civilization and mental state of various races of mankind are rather differences of development than of origin … [these] … similar stages of development recur in different times and places … there is reason to suppose that our ancestors in remote times made fire with a machine much like that of the modern Esquimaux [Eskimos].⁴⁹

When Tylor rejects the notion that there are differences of origin in human races he is favouring *monogenesis* (the notion of one human ancestor) over *polygenesis* (the notion of different species of human being with separate biological origins). In this he sides with Darwin. When it comes to questions of development, Tylor simply assumes that some human cultures (namely European cultures) have evolved at a faster rate than so-called 'primitive' cultures, which represent the childhood of the human race. This view was of course perfectly fitted to the purposes of Empire, in that it assumed that those cultures considered as childlike or primitive could then be 'reformed' within the colonial context.

We can see, then, that Tylor's basic notion of human progress is an Enlightenment notion that is rampantly value-laden and teleological, tacitly assuming that European civilization is the *terminus ad quem*, the endpoint towards which all human civilization necessarily progresses. For Tylor,

> The educated world of Europe and America practically settles a standard by simply placing its own nations at one end of the social series and savage tribes at the other, arranging the rest of mankind between these limits according as they correspond more closely to savage or to cultured life.⁵⁰

The appearance of Darwin's *Descent of Man* in the same year as Tylor's *Primitive Culture* served not only to endow such evolutionism with natural scientific prestige; it also broadened its context, by positing a developmental continuity between higher animal mentality on the one hand and so-called 'primitive' human mentality on the other. Here it is noteworthy that Darwin relied upon Tylor's references, within the *Researches into the Early History of Mankind*, to 'gesture languages' as a primitive form of articulate language, used by different so-called 'savage' peoples to communicate with one another. But while Tylor did not posit a continuity between animal and human language, Darwin did, claiming that such gesture languages are common to humans and animals.[51]

Darwin was especially keen to demonstrate this continuity between animal and human mentality, so that he could explain how language had developed by way of natural selection. Countering Kantian theorists like Max Müller, who had openly opposed Darwin by claiming that language is based on a priori concepts and that therefore only humans can have conceptual language,[52] Darwin claimed that animals also have abstract or conceptual mentality. This debate, which originated in the 1860s, forms the context for a passage in which Darwin compares the mental capacities of a domestic dog to those of a female Australian Aborigine:

> It may be freely admitted that no animal is self-conscious, if by this term it is implied, that he reflects on such points, as whence he comes and whither he will go, or what is life and death, and so forth. But how can we feel sure that an old dog with an excellent memory and some power of imagination, as shewn by his dreams, never reflects on the pleasures and pains of the chase? And this would be a form of self-consciousness. On the other hand ... how little can the hard-worked wife of a degraded Australian savage, who uses very few abstract words, and cannot count above four, exert her self-consciousness, or reflect on the nature of her own existence.[53]

Although Darwin did not directly adopt Tylor's teleology concerning the relation between so-called 'primitive' and 'advanced' cultures, it is relatively easy to see the extent to which these pre-Darwinian ideas concerning evolution were part of the background to Darwin's theory concerning the relation between animal and human mentality, the implication here being that 'higher' forms of animal life might, in their level of development, be compared with purportedly 'lower' or 'primitive' forms of human life. And here it is perhaps no coincidence that Darwin singles out the Australian Aborigines, whom Tylor thought to be the least evolved people on the face of the earth.[54]

What is the significance, then, of Tylor for our consideration of teleology? The relation between Tylor and Darwin shows that when it came to early British anthropology, there was a kind of blending of pre-Darwinian Enlightenment teleology on the one hand with Darwinian natural selection on the other. When considering human subject matter, and especially in the colonial context, it was very easy indeed to conflate natural selection with pre-Darwinian Enlightenment narratives concerning civilization and human progress. And as the last quotation from Darwin shows, Darwin seems tacitly, if not explicitly, to have agreed with these narratives. In fact, when it came to questions of culture Darwin was, like Tylor, an implicitly teleological thinker. Within the colonial context, this teleology became rampant not only because of the economic and political interests that it served, but also because it was taken to have a decisive scientific underpinning in theories of evolution, however different these theories may have been from one another. Far from being seen in Kantian terms as a mere regulative idea, far from being regarded as *contingent*, this teleology was regarded as an incontrovertible fact.

4. Contingent teleology: Nietzsche, Alsberg, Blumenberg

One of the reasons why German philosophical anthropology ended up offering a conspicuously different reception of Darwin to that found in the Anglophone world lies in the simple fact that it is not really 'anthropology' at all in the Anglophone sense of that term. Indeed, the main proponents of philosophical anthropology did not undertake fieldwork research at all. In being a sub-discipline of twentieth-century German philosophy, philosophical anthropology simply re-posed Kant's fourth question – 'What is the human being?' – within a new, post-Darwinian historical context. It is precisely because philosophical anthropology was in dialogue with the preoccupations of German idealism that it was, in the words of Herbert Schnädelbach, a 'German peculiarity'.[55] And in being a sub-discipline of philosophy, philosophical anthropology also inherited the anxieties relating to teleology and to values that had so exercised not only Windelband and Rickert but also Edmund Husserl.

Husserl's famous solution to the distorting effects exercised by teleology and values in philosophy was the dubious claim that such prejudices or pre-understandings could methodologically be bracketed out or suspended by way of what he called the phenomenological reduction. The phenomenologist, he thought, would outline a science of pure consciousness as such, independently of the positive sciences and in strict opposition to the empiricist science of psychology. In offering such a foundational account of human consciousness, it would become the science of sciences, 'an *a priori*, or, as we also say, eidetic science'.[56] The late Husserl was, of course, forced to admit that this early conception of phenomenology had failed. The so-called *Krisis-Schrift* of 1936 scaled down these early ambitions by reconceptualizing phenomenology as a science of the *Lebenswelt* or life-world: the 'realm of original self-evidences' or presuppositions that shape the horizon of all the sciences.[57] No longer could these presuppositions be completely bracketed out; becoming aware of them *at all* would now be the primary task of phenomenology.

What is of interest here is not the ultimate failure of Husserl's initial vision for phenomenology; it is much more the mechanism through which Husserl tried to secure its results: that of the reduction. The phenomenological reduction was a renewed expression of German philosophy's 'will to science', and this 'will to science' is something that philosophical anthropology shared with early phenomenology. If we accept Herbert Schnädelbach's claim that the history of German philosophy between 1831 and 1933 was 'in essence a history of philosophical reactions to what was happening in science and in connexion with science in a changed culture',[58] then we can see why the method of the reduction became particularly attractive. That which needed to be 'reduced', or in Husserl's initial vision bracketed out altogether, was the unspoken teleologies and value-judgements concerning human history that had destroyed the reputation of German idealism during the second half of the nineteenth century.

The form of reduction favoured by twentieth-century philosophical anthropology can then fittingly be called the 'anthropological reduction', and the anthropological reduction consists in attempting to answer Kant's fourth question in a rigorously non-teleological way. The only way to answer this question is not to ask what is the goal or purpose of human life; it is to rephrase the question as follows: how was it possible for human beings to survive at all? The tenor of this new question assumes that prior to posing the question concerning purposes or ends, the question of bare existence must first be answered. This explicit re-posing of Kant's fourth question only occurs quite late in the history of philosophical anthropology, in the works of Arnold Gehlen.

Writing in 1940, Gehlen observes: 'If any approach can be called biological, then it is the following one: to ask by what means a given being is able to exist. By adopting this approach, the ground work is laid for a new science – a universal science of man.'[59] Some thirty-six years after Gehlen, Hans Blumenberg would then repeat this reformulation of Kant's fourth question, adding to it his own assessment of Gehlen's notion that the human being was originally a poorly adapted 'creature of deficiencies' that only survived by way of culture and institutions. To express a methodological (and not an ontological) preference for the idea of the human being as maladapted or 'poor' is, writes Blumenberg,

> not a value-judgement, and not even predominantly a deciphering of the empirical material; it is much more based on the tendency towards rationalisation of the anthropological question, in order to be freed from its substantialist presuppositions. It did not emerge directly from the question 'What is the human being?', but rather via the intermediate stage of the genetic question of evolutionary theory: 'How did the human being come to be?'[60]

The text from which this quotation is taken – *Beschreibung des Menschen* (*Description of Man*) – is, alongside an essay published in 1971 and quoted at the beginning of this chapter,[61] Blumenberg's most direct contribution to the tradition of philosophical anthropology. It is therefore significant that, in both of these texts, Blumenberg regards the most compelling answer to Kant's fourth question as having been provided by an obscure German book published in 1922: Paul Alsberg's *Das Menschheitsrätsel: Versuch einer prinzipiellen Lösung* (*The Puzzle of Humanity: An Attempt at an In Principle Solution*). Already in the 1971 essay, Blumenberg's view on this is quite unequivocal: 'I see no other scientific course for an anthropology except ... to destroy what is supposedly "natural" and convict it of its "artificiality" in the functional system of the elementary human accomplishment called "life". A first attempt of this kind was made by Paul Alsberg in 1922.'[62]

What, then, was Alsberg's view concerning the apparent 'artificiality' of the human being? Its main feature was to object, on philosophical grounds, to the strong continuity between human beings and animals posited by Darwin. Darwin and Ernst Haeckel, according to Alsberg, were the main 'champions' (*Vorkämpfer*) of the view that there is an 'essential sameness' (*Wesensgleichheit*) between humans and animals, seeing the differences between them as being only those of developmental grade and not of fundamental type. But for Alsberg this natural scientific view simply fails to explain what it means to be human. Alsberg makes it clear that he agrees with Darwin's theory of human descent, while at the same time arguing that it cannot be regarded as a sufficient basis upon which to claim a thoroughgoing continuity between humans and animals. The differentiating factor for Alsberg is culture: 'the cultural human being (*Kulturmensch*) demonstrates itself to be so different from the animal in every respect' that the 'notion of a mere intensification of animal life processes' within human beings becomes impossible to accept. In fact it is 'precisely the conceptual differentiation of the human being from the animal that is the *conditio sine qua non* for an essential determination of the human being'.[63]

Alsberg outlines this conceptual differentiation by attributing entirely different developmental principles to animals and human beings. 'In the case of the human being,' he writes,

> an adjustment, a turning away from the body and towards artificial tools, has taken place within adaptation. This compensatory adjustment makes the special mode of development of the human being, at least at its beginnings, immediately comprehensible. The artificial means stepped into the place of natural bodily equipment. That which was gained in the case of artificial means of adaptation was in the same measure lost in the case of bodily qualities, as a consequence of lower demands being made upon the body.[64]

The similarities between the position of Alsberg and those of later writers in the tradition of philosophical anthropology – especially Plessner and Gehlen – become immediately clear upon reading this passage. Alsberg seems to agree with the view that humans were either 'eccentric' and open in their instinctual orientation, thereby requiring artificial compensations in order to survive (as in Plessner); or that they were 'weak' or insufficiently adapted, requiring compensatory technologies and institutions in order to make life possible (Gehlen). Alsberg's 'will to science' is expressed in his vehement rejection of the category of *Geist* (mind or spirit) as the differentiating factor between humans and animals. This, according to Alsberg, is 'a completely unproven claim' that is based upon the 'presupposition that all humans partake of the capacity for reason'. Alsberg's mode of the anthropological reduction consists precisely in claiming that human survival was not the *necessary* outcome for a being that was supposedly endowed with reason; it was much more the *contingent* outcome of a primordial evolutionary event. Alsberg's account of this primordial scene of anthropogenesis is openly speculative; it is, he argues, a story that requires 'the strongest usage of fantasy', but which could nonetheless enable a theoretical (if not an empirical) resolution to the puzzle of humanity.[65]

This is the story: our pre-human ancestor, having been forced by climatic changes to leave the rainforest and enter the open savannah, was increasingly confronted by predators upon open ground. Whereas this ancestor had previously been a 'fleeing creature' (*Fluchttier*) that took refuge in the trees, its new environmental situation forced it to become a *Kampftier* or 'creature of combat'. Because this pre-human ancestor lacked bodily weapons with which to fight off its predators, it was forced to survive via non-bodily means. Its ability to throw stones in the direction of its predators allowed it to emerge victorious from these confrontations, and over time it also began to hoard these projectile weapons in preparation for future battles. The necessity of carrying these weapons around gradually led to upright gait, since the hands could no longer be used to assist with walking or crawling.[66]

This story is forced by Alsberg to bear a huge theoretical burden, since he describes the use of projectile weapons as *the* decisive and originary event in anthropogenesis. The human hand, with its ability to pick up and throw weapons (and later to make them into tools), is what set humans upon their special technological path of development. It was this exclusively 'human track' (*Menschenbahn*) that enabled human beings to bypass, or at least to put at a distance, the pressures of natural selection. It is, therefore, *technological and cultural selection*, or non-bodily adaptation, that constitutes the essence of what it means to be human. And this also means that as technology came to play a more dominant role in human survival, the selection and adaptation of human bodily features and instincts were accordingly reduced. In short: in the human sphere, biological evolution was displaced by cultural evolution. The key issue for Alsberg lies in the mediating and prosthetic features of technology, which are not only physical but also conceptual, and which allow the pressures of natural selection to be ameliorated by putting them at a distance. The use of stone projectiles is thus merely the beginning of other, more abstract technologies of distance, and in this way the 'human principle' (*Menschheitsprinzip*) coincides with what Alsberg refers to as the 'cultural principle' (*Kulturprinzip*). Seen in these terms, the use of language and concepts is simply a further development of the human capacity for mediation. Words and concepts, like projectile weapons, are tools of distance, allowing humans to speak of things that are not immediately at hand. For Alsberg 'technology, language and reason' are the tools (*Werkzeuge*) that helped human beings to survive an initial biological crisis situation, and which later enabled them to prosper.[67]

Here one cannot avoid alluding to the aspects of this story that are – albeit perhaps unintentionally – political. Despite its scientific framing, Alsberg's tale concerning the initial situation of the human being – his account of the human *Ausgangssituation* – is at the same time the delineation of an *Ausnahmezustand*: a state of exception, of crisis, or of emergency. According to this story, the human being only came to be because its predators forced it to create its own technological path of development. Alsberg's imagined primordial situation therefore necessarily involves something resembling the distinction between friend and enemy. Writing in 1927, only five years after the appearance of Alsberg's *Puzzle of Humanity*, Carl Schmitt would famously come to locate this allegedly irreducible distinction or 'decision' at the heart of the political.[68] And it is here that we also need to note one important historical fact: that Paul Alsberg himself experienced the terror and violence that can arise from such purportedly 'primordial' distinctions. Having studied medicine and worked as a bacteriologist and later as a practising doctor in Berlin, Alsberg suffered the indignity of seeing his only book burned in 1933, on account of his Jewish descent. He was also interned in the Oranienburg concentration camp during 1933 and 1934, before being released (via American assistance) in 1934, upon which he emigrated to England.[69] Yet in 1922, Alsberg could not have known what resonances the notion of the human being as a *Kampftier* might come to have in Germany between 1933 and 1945. Alsberg's aim was expressly *not* to elaborate a political description of the human being, but only to posit an alternative account of anthropogenesis to that offered by Darwin and Haeckel.

With respect to the subject of teleology, the key aspect of Alsberg's story of anthropogenesis is its inherent contingency. Both Alfred Russel Wallace and Darwin also make the claim that the use of tools and other technologies would have reduced the selective pressures placed upon human beings by their environments.[70] But the standard Darwinian explanation for tool use is that it arose necessarily and gradually from mental capacities already present within animals that had evolved through natural selection.[71] This is not Alsberg's explanation, precisely because his human primordial scene is a contingent event: there is, in his implicit view, *no sufficient reason* for explaining why our ancestor picked up the first stone, but the adaptive advantages that arose from its doing so led to a fork in the developmental road that gave rise to anthropogenesis. Alsberg openly admits that this story of contingency is not susceptible of being proven; but it also cannot be disproven, since the primordial scene that it invokes is so far behind us.

For Blumenberg – writing over fifty years after Alsberg and having himself been persecuted under National Socialism[72] – the usefulness of Alsberg's story lies in its explaining 'wherein the decisive advance can have consisted', namely in the human capacity for '*actio per distans*'.[73] This refers not only to the avoidance of direct body-on-body combat alluded to in Alsberg's imagined primordial scene of anthropogenesis, but also to the processes of mediation offered by language and culture in general. The crucial point is that Blumenberg no longer thinks it is possible to deliver a definition of the human being that can be afforded the status of objective truth. And he also recognizes that 'primordial' anthropological claims can quickly become political ones. In a late text that addresses Carl Schmitt's distinction between friend and enemy, Blumenberg observes that 'the primordial scene [*Urszene*], abstractly construed as the beginning of all other scenes, is absolutely political'. Here Blumenberg concedes that 'enmity' (*Feindschaft*) is a political category, because a being under threat from potential predators must make a very quick decision as to whether that which approaches over the horizon is a friend or an enemy, and in cases of doubt the latter assumption will usually be the safer one. Yet Blumenberg also claims that 'friendship' (*Freundschaft*) is an anthropological category, in that the presumed enemy

> can only refute this presumption through being 'recognized' or 'proving himself to be' one who has already gone through the long term process of becoming friends.

> Because of this possible history, which may reach into the scene of recognition (*Erkenntnisszene*), the anthropological category [i.e. friendship] can set the political one [i.e. enmity] out of play.⁷⁴

The danger to which Blumenberg alludes here is that of endowing so-called 'primordial' scenarios with universal or ahistorical validity – which means denying their inherent historicity and contingency. Even if the human situation 'in the beginning' may have been one in which the presumption of enmity had to override that of friendship, the very purpose of culture is to create the distance – and thereby the time – in which humans can make more considered decisions under conditions of greater safety.

This also holds for the 'decision' concerning the status of the human being. Precisely because human nature is not an empirical thing, and precisely because human beings are at once natural and artificial beings that are susceptible of cultural alteration over time, no anthropological claim could ever answer Kant's fourth question once and for all, and any answer would need to be defended rhetorically, which for Blumenberg means politically. We are therefore forced to make use of the best and most productive answer that is available at any given time: 'in a field in which we know almost nothing and in which we will perhaps also know almost nothing in the future,' argues Blumenberg, 'it must be permitted to choose the most effective (*leistungsfähigste*) model.'⁷⁵ All of this is entirely in the spirit of Alsberg, who wisely gave his book the following subtitle: *an attempt at an in principle solution* (*Versuch einer prinzipiellen Lösung*).

Here a further contextualization of Alsberg's contingent position is necessary, since something resembling his brand of speculative anti-Darwinism can already be found in the writings of Friedrich Nietzsche. In Nietzsche's *Nachlass* fragment of 1873, 'On Truth and Lie in an Extra-Moral Sense', the contingent and even the ephemeral aspects of human existence are given a heavy rhetorical emphasis. 'In some remote corner of the universe,' writes Nietzsche,

> there once was a star on which the cleverest animals invented knowledge. That was the haughtiest and most mendacious minute of 'world history' – yet only a minute. After nature had drawn a few breaths the star grew cold, and the clever animals had to die. One might invent such a fable and still not have illustrated sufficiently how wretched, how shadowy and flighty, how aimless and arbitrary, the human intellect appears in nature. There have been eternities in which it did not exist; and when it is done for again, nothing will have happened.⁷⁶

In underlining the contingency of the human intellect, Nietzsche strikes some of the chords that will later resound in philosophical anthropology and especially in Alsberg. It is only because humans were 'weaker' and 'less robust' than animals – and because they were 'denied the chance of waging the struggle for existence with horns or the fangs of beasts of prey' – that they were forced to develop the intellect as a means of survival. This in turn gave rise to the human tools of sophistry and rhetoric, which describe 'the relations of things to man' through the 'boldest metaphors'. In a similar way to Alsberg,

Nietzsche claims that 'everything that sets the human being apart from the animal' depends upon this capacity for mediation through language. It is the human tendency to assemble in 'herd-like' groups – not to mention their related need to resolve arguments by making purportedly objective truth claims – that requires these metaphors to set themselves up as universal truths rather than as merely instrumental appearances. Nietzsche's aim here is undermine the correspondence theory of truth, arguing that *nothing* secures the veracity of human truth claims other than their functionality and their usefulness for life.[77] In other words: all truths, narratives and stories are instrumental and therefore contingent.

Nietzsche's anti-Darwinism then becomes more pronounced and explicit in his *Twilight of the Idols* (1889). The outcome of Darwin's 'struggle for existence' is *not* that the strong prevail over the weak; rather

> the weaker dominate the strong again and again – the reason being that they are the great majority, and they are also *cleverer*. Darwin forgot the mind (– that is English!): *the weak possess more mind* ... One will see that under mind [i.e. *Geist*] I include foresight, patience, dissimulation, great self-control, and all that is mimicry.[78]

It is likely that Nietzsche, despite his own critique of metaphysics, undertook a metaphysical interpretation of Darwin insofar as he tends to conflate natural selection or the so-called 'struggle for life' with the will to power, as he does here. Despite all of Nietzsche's contempt for Socratism and Christian morality, he does have a grudging respect for these interpretations of life, as successful examples of exercising the will to power via the intellect. In Nietzsche's account, intellect, as an expression of will, is always the most important human adaptation. This interpretation of Darwin tends to suggest that Darwin neglected to consider that human culture, as opposed to human nature, is the primary object of selection. Interpretations of life, which in Nietzsche's account compete with one another under the auspices of the will to power, may be selected, not naturally, but culturally; that is: in terms of how convincing they are and depending upon their capacity to enhance power.

5. Concluding remarks

In Nietzsche, Alsberg and Blumenberg we have three examples of *contingent teleology*. All three thinkers claim that the human being might just as well not have existed as have existed. There are, they argue, no objective grounds upon which to claim that human life is necessary for the world, just as there is no necessary reason to believe that human life has an inherent purpose or destination. Even to attempt to define what 'human nature' is would be implicitly to prescribe its purpose in a reductive way. The only way out of this conundrum is to say that human nature is *both* nature and culture, and since culture is itself protean, artificial and subject to selection, no description of 'human nature' could ever meet the expectations of the 'will to science'. This means that teleology can never be overcome or dispensed with, no matter how fragile and contingent it may be. Human beings need teleology because it provides them with an always-only-provisional orientation within the world. Or, to rephrase Windelband: *the human being is the animal that has teleology*. The only normative moment, indeed the only consolation of contingent teleology might be that it is able to recognize itself as such. And by charting this middle and essentially sceptical path, it may be able to avoid the two chief dangers identified by Nicolai Hartmann in his critical reckoning with teleology: 'the mistake of materialistic simplification' on the one hand, and of unchecked 'teleological speculation' on the other.[79] Unlike the rampant teleology of Tylor and Darwin, contingent teleology would at least appear to know what it is doing.

Or maybe not always, since it is precisely here that a difficult coda to our own story about contingent teleology emerges. The example of Alsberg demonstrates very clearly that any tale about how the human being *came to be* can also – perhaps even unwittingly – be a tale about what the human being *is*, and implicitly what it *should do* in a given situation. In other words, 'state of nature' anthropological theories can quickly take on political dimensions. As Blumenberg's remarks on the friend/enemy distinction demonstrate, the mere fact that such tales are contingent and potentially self-reflexive does not prevent them from having political implications, however different these implications may be from those that emerged from Tylor's colonial teleology, which was in some respects specific to the aims of British imperialism. This is not to conflate the ideas of Alsberg with those of Carl Schmitt, but simply to note their contemporaneity and their affinity, which underlines the complexity of German-language culture during the period of the Weimar Republic. If the human being is the *animal that has teleology*, and even if such teleology is only contingent, we would still also need to examine how this coincides with another well-known conception of the human being: namely, as the *political animal*.

Notes

*   Aspects of this chapter appear in different argumentative contexts in Angus Nicholls, 'The *Fremdling* of Teleology, or: On Roger Smith's *Being Human*,' in *History of the Human Sciences* 23 (2010), no. 5, pp. 194–201; Angus Nicholls, 'A Germanic Reception in England: Friedrich Max Müller's Critique of Darwin's *Descent of Man*,' in Thomas F. Glick and Elinor Shaffer, eds, *The Literary and Cultural Reception of Charles Darwin in Europe*, London: Bloomsbury, 2014, pp. 78–100; and in Angus Nicholls, *Myth and the Human Sciences: Hans Blumenberg's Theory of Myth*, London and New York: Routledge, 2015. I wish to thank Henning Trüper and the other participants at the Hambach and Helsinki meetings of the *Teleology and History* working group for their helpful comments on earlier drafts of this chapter.

1. Roger Smith, *Being Human: Historical Knowledge and the Creation of Human Nature*, New York: Columbia University Press, 2007, p. 1.

2. Hans Blumenberg, 'An Anthropological Approach to the Contemporary Significance of Rhetoric,' trans. Robert M. Wallace, in Kenneth Baynes, James Bohman and Thomas McCarthy, eds, *After Philosophy: End or Transformation*, Cambridge, MA: MIT Press, 1987, pp. 429–58; here 456; 'Anthropologische Annäherung an die Aktualität der Rhetorik' (1971), in

Wirklichkeiten, in denen wir Leben. Aufsätze und eine Rede, Stuttgart: Reclam, 1986, pp. 104–36, here 134.

3. Smith, *Being Human*, p. 6.
4. See Hans Blumenberg's discussion of this human tendency in his *Paradigms for a Metaphorology*, trans. Robert Savage, Ithaca, NY: Cornell University Press, 2010; *Paradigmen zu einer Metaphorologie*, 1960, Frankfurt am Main: Suhrkamp, 1997.
5. See, for example, Wilhelm Schapp, *In Geschichten verstrickt: Zum Sein von Ding und Mensch*, Hamburg: Meiner, 1953; and more recently, Hermann Lübbe, *Bewußtsein in Geschichten. Studien zur Phänomenologie der Subjektivität. Mach – Husserl – Schapp – Wittgenstein*, Freiburg: Rombach, 1972, pp. 103–14. Blumenberg's own extended meditation on storytelling as an irreducible aspect of being human is to be found in his *Work on Myth*, trans. Robert M. Wallace, Cambridge, Mass.: MIT Press, 1985; *Arbeit am Mythos*, Frankfurt am Main: Suhrkamp, 1979.
6. Max Scheler, *Philosophische Weltanschauung*, in *Gesammelte Werke*, eds Maria Scheler and Manfred S. Frings, 15 vols, Basel: Francke; Bonn: Bouvier, 1971–97), 9, pp. 73–182; here 126.
7. Immanuel Kant, *Logik* (A 25), in *Werke in sechs Bänden*, ed. Wilhelm Weischedel, 7th edn, 6 vols, Darmstadt: Wissenschaftliche Buchgesellschaft, 2011, 3, pp. 447–8. (All translations of German texts are my own unless otherwise noted).
8. Immanuel Kant, *Anthropology from a Pragmatic Point of View*, ed. and trans. Robert B. Louden, Cambridge: Cambridge University Press, 2006, p. 3; *Anthropologie in pragmatischer Hinsicht,* in *Werke in sechs Bänden,* 6, p. 399.
9. Joachim Fischer, *Philosophische Anthropologie. Eine Denkrichtung des 20. Jahrhunderts*, Freiburg: Alber, 2008, p. 14.
10. Christian Thies, *Einführung in die philosophische Anthropologie*, Darmstadt: Wissenschaftliche Buchgesellschaft, 2004, p. 7.
11. Max Scheler, 'Zur Idee des Menschen,' in *Gesammelte Werke*, 3, pp. 170–95.
12. Paul Alsberg, *Das Menschheitsrätsel, Versuch einer prinzipiellen Lösung*, Dresden: Sibylle Verlag, 1922. A revised version of this book later appeared in English as *In Quest of Man: A Biological Approach to the Problem of Man's Place in Nature*, Oxford: Pergamon Press, 1970.
13. Helmuth Plessner, *Die Stufen des Organischen und der Mensch*, Berlin: Walter De Gruyter, 1928.
14. Arnold Gehlen, *Der Mensch: Seine Natur und seine Stellung in der Welt*, Berlin: Junker und Dünnhaupt, 1940; *Man: His Nature and Place in the World*, trans. Clare McMillan and Karl Pillemer, New York: Columbia University Press, 1988.
15. See Christian Thies, *Gehlen zur Einführung*, Hamburg: Junius, 2000, pp. 12, 15–19; Ernst Klee, *Das Personenlexikon zum Dritten Reich*, 4th edn, Frankfurt am Main: S. Fischer, 2013, pp. 176–7; Christian Tilitzki, *Die deutsche Universitätsphilosophie in der Weimarer Republik und im Dritten Reich*, 2 vols with continuous pagination, Berlin: Akademie Verlag, 2002, 1, pp. 633–5.
16. See Arnold Gehlen, *Der Mensch: Seine Natur und seine Stellung in der Welt* [1940], 2nd edn, Berlin: Junker und Dünnhaupt, 1941, p. 448. This section of *Der Mensch*, entitled 'Oberste Führungssysteme' (the highest command systems), was removed from post-war editions, and therefore does not appear in the English translation, which is based on the third edition (published in 1950).
17. See Carl Schmitt, *Political Theology: Four Chapters on the Concept of Sovereignty*, trans. and introd. George Schwab, Chicago: University of Chicago Press, 2005; *Politische Theologie. Vier*

Kapitel zur Lehre von der Souveranität [1922], 2nd edn, Munich: Duncker and Humblot, 1934; Carl Schmitt, *The Concept of the Political*, trans. and introd. George Schwab, Chicago: University of Chicago Press, 1996; *Der Begriff des Politischen* [1927], Berlin: Duncker and Humblot, 1979.

18. See Theodor W. Adorno, *Negative Dialectics*, trans. E. B. Ashton, London: Routledge, 2004, p. 124; *Negative Dialektik*, Frankfurt am Main: Suhrkamp, 1966, p. 128. Also quoted by Blumenberg in *Beschreibung des Menschen*, ed. Manfred Sommer, Frankfurt am Main: Suhrkamp, 2006, pp. 487–8.

19. Jürgen Habermas, 'Anthropologie', in Alwin Diemer and Ivo Frenzel, eds, *Das Fischer Lexikon Philosophie*, Frankfurt am Main: Fischer, 1958, pp. 18–35; here 33–4.

20. See Nils Eldredge and Ian Tattersall, *The Myths of Human Evolution*, New York: Columbia University Press, 1982; and Misia Landau, *Narratives of Human Evolution*, New Haven, CT: Yale University Press, 1994.

21. Despite being little known, Alsberg turns out to have been an important point of reference for many key thinkers in the tradition of philosophical anthropology, having been prominently mentioned by Scheler, Plesser and Gehlen. See Scheler, *Die Stellung des Menschen im Kosmos*, in *Gesammelte Werke*, 9, pp. 7–72; Plessner, 'Vorwort zur zweiten Auflage,' in *Die Stufen des Organischen und der Mensch* [1928], 3rd edn, Berlin: Walter De Gruyter, 1975, pp. vii–xxiii; here xvi; and Gehlen, 'Philosophische Anthropologie', in *Gesamtausgabe*, vol. 4, Frankfurt am Main: Vittorio Klostermann, 1983, pp. 236–46; here 238. See also Fischer, *Philosophische Anthropologie*, pp. 47–8, 271.

22. See Dieter Claessens, *Instinkt, Psyche, Geltung. Bestimmungsfaktoren menschlichen Verhaltens*, Cologne: Westdeutscher Verlag, 1968, pp. 81–94 and *Das Konkrete und das Abstrakte. Soziologische Skizzen zur Anthropologie*, Frankfurt am Main: Suhrkamp, 1980. Blumenberg's main treatment of Alsberg appears in his *Beschreibung des Menschen*, ed. Manfred Sommer, Frankfurt am Main: Suhrkamp, 2006, and is discussed below. Sloterdijk's chief deployment of Alsberg appears in his *Sphären III, Schäume*, Frankfurt am Main: Suhrkamp, 2004. For further context, see Kasper Lysemose, 'The Being, the Origin and the Becoming of Man: A Presentation of Philosophical Anthropogenealogy and Some Ensuing Methodological Considerations', in *Human Studies* 35 (2012), no. 1, pp. 115–30. For a consideration of these questions in relation to teleology, see also Pieter Lemmens, 'The Detached Animal – On the Technical Nature of Being Human', in Martin Drenthen, Jozef Keulartz and James Proctor, eds, *New Visions of Nature*, Dordrecht: Springer, 2009, pp. 117–27.

23. William Whewell, *The Philosophy of the Inductive Sciences, Founded Upon Their History*, 2nd edn, 2 vols, 1840, London: John W. Parker, 1847, 1, p. 3.

24. On Whewell's use of something resembling Kant's transcendental deduction, see Menachem Fisch, 'A Philosopher's Coming of Age: A Study in Erotetic Intellectual History,' in Menachem Fisch and Simon Schaffer, eds, *William Whewell: A Composite Portrait*, Oxford: Oxford University Press, 1991, pp. 31–66, here 62–3.

25. Immanuel Kant, *Metaphysical Foundations of Natural Science* (1786), ed. and trans. Michael Friedman, Cambridge: Cambridge University Press, 2004, p. 4; *Metaphysische Anfangsgründe der Naturwissenschaft*, in *Werke in sechs Bänden*, 5, p. 12.

26. Immanuel Kant, *Critique of the Power of Judgment*, ed. Paul Guyer, trans. Paul Guyer and Eric Matthews, Cambridge: Cambridge University Press, 2000, pp. 261–2; *Kritik der Urteilskraft*, in *Werke in sechs Bänden*, 5, p. 504.

27. H. Hühn, S. Meier Oeser and H. Pulte, 'Wissenschaft', in *Historisches Wörterbuch der Philosophie*, 12 vols, Basel: Schwabe, 1971–2004, 12, pp. 902–47, here 915–20.

28. See Hans Vaihinger, *Hartmann, Dühring und Lange. Zur Geschichte der deutschen Philosophie im XIX. Jahrhundert. Ein kritischer Essay*, Iserlohn: Baedecker, 1876, p. 1.

29. Herbert Schnädelbach, *Philosophy in Germany, 1831–1933*, trans. Eric Matthews, Cambridge: Cambridge University Press, 1984, p. 5.
30. Alwin Diemer, 'Die Differenzierung der Wissenschaften in die Natur- und die Geisteswissenschaften', in *Beiträge zur Entwicklung der Wissenschaftstheorie im 19. Jahrhundert*, Meisenheim am Glan: Verlag Anton Hain, 1968, pp. 174–221.
31. Hermann von Helmholtz, 'Über das Verhältnis der Naturwissenschaften zur Gesammtheit der Wissenschaft in (1862)', in *Vorträge und Reden*, 4th edn, vol. 1, Braunschweig: Viehweg, 1896, p. 172.
32. Wilhelm Windelband, 'Natural History and Science', trans. Guy Oakes, in *History and Theory* 19 (1980), no. 2, pp. 165–84, here 175; 'Geschichte und Naturwissenschaft (Staßburger Rektoratsrede 1894)', in *Präludien. Aufsätze und Reden zur Einleitung in die Philosophie*, 3rd edn, Tübingen: Mohr, 1907, pp. 355–79; here 364.
33. Windelband, 'Natural History and Science,' p. 181; 'Geschichte und Naturwissenschaft,' pp. 372–3.
34. See Heinrich Rickert, *Kulturwissenschaft und Naturwissenschaft* [1898], 6th edn, Tübingen: Mohr, 1926.
35. Rickert, *Kulturwissenschaft und Naturwissenschaft*, pp. 18–19.
36. Wilhelm Dilthey, *Introduction to the Human Sciences*, eds and trans. Rudolf A. Makkreel and Frithjof Rodi, Princeton, NJ: Princeton University Press, 1989; *Einleitung in die Geisteswissenschaften*, in *Gesammelte Schriften*, 26 vols., eds Karlfried Gründer et al., Göttingen: Vandenhoeck und Ruprecht, 1959–2005, vol. 1.
37. See Dilthey, 'The Understanding of Other Persons and Their Life Expressions', trans. Kurt Mueller-Vollmer, in *The Hermeneutics Reader: Texts of the German Tradition from the Enlightenment to the Present*, New York: Continuum, 1985, pp. 152–64; here 153–6; 'Das Verstehen anderer Personen und ihrer Lebensäußerungen', in *Der Aufbau der geschichtlichen Welt in den Geisteswissenschaften*, in *Gesammelte Schriften*, 7, pp. 205–27.
38. Windelband, 'Natural History and Science', p. 180 (translation altered); 'Geschichte und Naturwissenschaft,' p. 371.
39. Dilthey, *Der Aufbau*, in *Gesammelte Schriften*, 7, pp. 278–9.
40. See Edward Burnett Tylor, *Researches into the Early History of Mankind and the Development of Civilization*, 2nd edn, London: John Murray, 1865, pp. 51, 162, 236, 240, 310.
41. Preface to the second edition, reprinted in *Primitive Culture: Researches into the Development of Mythology, Philosophy, Religion, Art and Custom* [1871], 2 vols, 3rd edn, London: John Murray, 1891, 1, p. vii.
42. George Stocking, *Victorian Anthropology*, New York: The Free Press, 1987, pp. 56–62; Joan Leopold, *Culture in Comparative and Evolutionary Perspective: E.B. Tylor and the Making of Primitive Culture*, Berlin: Dietrich Reimer, 1980, p. 31.
43. Tylor, *Primitive Culture*, 1, p. 1.
44. Tylor, *Primitive Culture*, 1, pp. 7–8.
45. Tylor, *Primitive Culture*, 1, p. 2.
46. Tylor, *Primitive Culture*, 1, p. 5.
47. Tylor, *Primitive Culture*, 1, pp. 17–18.
48. J. W. Burrow, *Evolution and Society: A Study in Victorian Social Theory*, Cambridge: Cambridge University Press, 1970, p. 18.
49. Tylor, *Researches into the Early History*, pp. 361–2.

50. Tylor, *Primitive Culture*, 1, p. 26.
51. Tylor, *Researches into the Early History*, chapters ii–iv, pp. 14–82; cited in Darwin, *Descent of Man*, 2 vols, London: John Murray, 1871, 1, p. 54.
52. See Friedrich Max Müller's 'Lectures on Mr Darwin's Philosophy of Language,' published in *Fraser's Magazine* during 1873: first lecture, May, pp. 525–41; second lecture, June, pp. 659–79; third lecture, July, pp. 1–24. See also Nicholls, 'A Germanic Reception in England'.
53. Darwin, *The Descent of Man*, 1, p. 62.
54. See Tylor's remarks in *Primitive Culture*, 1, p. 27.
55. Schnädelbach, *Philosophy in Germany*, p. 219.
56. Edmund Husserl, *Ideas: General Introduction to Pure Phenomenology* [1931], trans. W. R. Boyce Gibson, Abingdon: Routledge, 2012, pp. 1, 5; *Allgemeine Einführung in die reine Phänomenologie*, in *Gesammelte Werke (Husserliana)*, vol. 3/1, *Ideen zu einer reinen Phänomenologie und phänomenologischen Philosophie*, ed. Karl Schuhmann, The Hague: Martinus Nijhoff, 1976, pp. 3, 8.
57. Edmund Husserl, *The Crisis of European Sciences and Transcendental Phenomenology*, trans. David Carr, Evanston, Ill.: Northwestern University Press, 1970, p. 127; Husserl, *Gesammelte Werke (Husserliana)*, vol. 6, *Die Krisis der europäischen Wissenschaften und die transzendentale Phänomenologie*, ed. Walter Biemel, The Hague: Martinus Nijhoff, 1954, p. 130.
58. Schnädelbach, *Philosophy in Germany*, p. 92.
59. Gehlen, *Man*, p. 10; *Der Mensch*, p. 10.
60. Hans Blumenberg, *Beschreibung des Menschen*, ed. Manfred Sommer, Frankfurt am Main: Suhrkamp, 2006, p. 523. This quote is taken from part two of *Beschreibung des Menschen*, which is based on lectures delivered in the winter semester of 1976–7.
61. Blumenberg, 'An Anthropological Approach,' pp. 429–58; 'Anthropologische Annäherung', pp. 104–36.
62. Blumenberg, 'An Anthropological Approach,' pp. 438–39; 'Anthropologische Annäherung', p. 115.
63. Alsberg, *Das Menschheitsrätsel*, pp. 25, 32, 38, 67–8.
64. Alsberg, *Das Menschheitsrätsel*, p. 101.
65. Alsberg, *Das Menschheitsrätsel*, pp. 84, 277, 363.
66. Alsberg, *Das Menschheitsrätsel*, pp. 309–12, 356, 350, 361–2.
67. Alsberg, *Das Menschheitsrätsel*, pp. 377–9, 431, 448–9.
68. See Schmitt, *The Concept of the Political*; *Der Begriff des Politischen*.
69. See Dieter Claessens, 'Vorwort zur Neuauflage,' in Paul Alsberg, *Der Ausbruch aus dem Gefängnis. Zu den Entstehungsbedingungen des Menschen*, ed. Dieter Claessens, commentary by Hartmut and Ingrid Rötting, Gießen: Focus, 1975, pp. 5–7. This is a republished and retitled version of *Das Menschheitsrätsel*.
70. See Alfred Russel Wallace, 'The Origin of Human Races and the Antiquity of Man Deduced from the Theory of Natural Selection,' in *Anthropological Review* 2 (1864), pp. clvii–clxxxvii; here clxiii; Darwin, *Descent of Man*, 1, p. 53.
71. See Kathy D. Schick and Nicholas Toth, *Making Silent Stones Speak: Human Evolution and the Dawn of Technology*, New York: Simon and Schuster, 1994, p. 18; Ian Tattersall, *Becoming Human: Evolution and Human Uniqueness*, Oxford: Oxford University Press, 1988, pp. 128–9.

72. See the section entitled 'One Life, One Identity?' in chapter 1 of Angus Nicholls, *Myth and the Human Sciences: Hans Blumenberg's Theory of Myth*, London and New York: Routledge, 2015.
73. Blumenberg, *Beschreibung des Menschen*, p. 575.
74. Hans Blumenberg, 'Die Heterogonie von "Feind" und "Freund"', in id., *Die Vollzähligkeit der Sterne*, Frankfurt am Main: Suhrkamp, 1997, pp. 345–8; additions in square brackets are my own.
75. Blumenberg, *Beschreibung des Menschen*, p. 575.
76. Friedrich Nietzsche, 'On Truth and Lie in an Extra-Moral Sense,' trans. Walter Kaufmann, in *The Portable Nietzsche*, ed. Walter Kaufmann, New York: Penguin, 1976, pp. 42–6; here 42; 'Über Wahrheit und Lüge im aussermoralischen Sinne,' in Giorgio Colli and Mazzino Montinari, eds, *Kritische Studienausgabe* (hereafter cited as *KSA*), 15 vols, Berlin: De Gruyter, 1967–77, 1, pp. 873–90; here 875.
77. Nietzsche, 'On Truth and Lie in an Extra-Moral Sense,' pp. 43, 45–6, 44; 'Über Wahrheit und Lüge im aussermoralischen Sinne,' in *KSA*, 1, pp. 876, 879, 881, 877 (the quote from p. 881 of the German edition is my own translation, since Kaufmann translates only part of Nietzsche's text).
78. Friedrich Nietzsche, *Twilight of the Idols*, *The Anti-Christ*, trans. R. J. Hollingdale, Harmondsworth: Penguin, 1968, pp. 75–6; *Götzen-Dämmerung*, in *KSA*, 6, pp. 120–1.
79. Nicolai Hartmann, *Teleologisches Denken*, Berlin: De Gruyter, 1951, p. 2.

PART III
BEFRIENDING TELEOLOGY: WRITING HISTORIES WITH ENDS

CHAPTER 6
SAVE THEIR SOULS: HISTORICAL TELELOGY GOES TO SEA IN NINETEENTH-CENTURY EUROPE*

Henning Trüper

> Perhaps genius is by no means so rare: but rather the five hundred *hands* which it requires in order to tyrannize over the καιρός, 'the right time' – in order to take chance by the forelock![1]

1. A veil withdrawn

In 1808 Sir William Hillary, an upstart Quaker courtier who had retained only debt and a baronetcy from recent ventures as a military entrepreneur for the British crown, outflew his creditors to Douglas on the Isle of Man and settled to a life of provincial withdrawal. Over the next fifteen years, he came to witness a multitude of nautical accidents in Douglas Bay. Having personally assisted in the rescue of a navy cutter's crew in October 1822, he re-emerged on the national scene the following spring as the author of a single-minded and surprising appeal for the creation of a system of lifeboat stations that was to cover the entire national coastline.[2] The Admiralty snubbed his pamphlet, but after a few months' delay, London society, under the sway of local Member of Parliament Thomas Wilson, embraced the proposal with the characteristic philanthropic zeal of the period and took to celebrating its author. In March 1824, the donation-funded National Institution for the Preservation of Life from Shipwreck was established. The institution was to provide lifeboats and other means of rescue to designated localities along the coast and organize volunteer crews. In Douglas, Hillary himself, in spite of his 53 years, would serve as coxswain. In 1830, during a particularly dramatic rescue operation, together with several other crew and passengers, he survived being washed off the Douglas lifeboat.[3] His charisma as founder of the Institution was such that Wordsworth glorified him in a sonnet, 'On Entering Douglas Bay', in 1833.[4]

The charisma of the Institution radiated abroad. By December 1824, two rescue societies for servicing the Dutch coastline had been set up in Amsterdam and Rotterdam,[5] and in 1825 at Boulogne-sur-Mer on the southern Channel coast a humanitarian association was instituted for the same purpose. Other French cities in the Manche and Normandy regions followed suit over the next couple of years. The United States reorganized already existing local initiatives into nationwide sea rescue as a service of the federal government from 1848.[6] Denmark instituted national sea rescue in 1852. France took until 1865 to create a national service, the Société Centrale de Sauvetage des

Naufragés (SCSN); and, dissatisfied with its slow expansion, in 1873, a separate organization, the Hospitaliers Sauveteurs Bretons, was founded in Brittany, where it was to occupy itself also with other humanitarian projects and the general betterment of Breton society.[7] The year 1865 was an *annus mirabilis* for sea rescue. With the Swedish–Norwegian and German organizations emerging next to the French, philanthropic lifeboat associations achieved coverage of almost the entire North Sea coastline and significant parts of the Northern Atlantic and Baltic seaboards. France also serviced parts of the Mediterranean, and the new national society installed a first lifeboat in Algeria as early as 1866.[8]

Over the course of four decades, the previously widespread impassivity regarding coastal shipwreck had become inadmissible, and the imperative of the rescue of the shipwrecked had become an institutional and biographical reality for coastal populations across Europe. Much like the Red Cross and other aid organizations – most of which came into existence later – sea rescue carried a notion of humanitarian universalism; it was to bring relief to the distressed wherever possible and regardless of whatever marks of distinction were commonly placed on them as human beings. In the state of nautical emergency that was shipwreck, humanity was established as one. The rescue society of Boulogne-sur-Mer expressed the radical novelty, the transformative force to which the movement aspired by electing as their motto: *Je sauve donc je suis*, 'I save, therefore I am'.[9] Echoing Descartes's pronouncement on the certainty of the *cogito*, this assertion expressed the idea that life-saving amounted to an irrefutable justification, and thus foundation, of one's own being.

On the surface, the Boulogne device was conceived *sub specie aeternitatis* and set in a present tense that suppressed connotations of temporal change. Yet, if read in context, the sense of foundation the phrase expressed entailed a notion of departure from a past in which such a foundation had been lacking. This past had been governed by passive acceptance of disaster. Hillary motivated his intervention by reference to an inhumanity of age-old historical standing:

> From the most early periods, and in every state of society, shipwreck has been one of those never ceasing evils which has excited the commiseration of mankind; but, until recently, scarcely ever to have called forth their humane efforts to mitigate its deplorable consequences. For centuries, our mariners have been left, unassisted, to endure every peril of the sea, as if shipwreck were a calamity in every instance utterly beyond all reach of mortal succour.[10]

In other words, this was a past defined by what it had failed to accomplish; its coherence, as a history, was constituted by the moment of departure, the acquisition of agency in spite of, and in moral compensation for, the impassivity of old:

> I am firmly convinced that these appalling facts have never yet reached the great majority of the nation; but the veil once withdrawn, the honour, the justice, and the humanity of Britain will be deeply compromised, if the evil is not promptly and

effectually redressed; – not any human means should be spared to atone for the past, and to alleviate the future.[11]

The moment of foundation was the *telos* both of a particular history that was directed at its own undoing; and, in an inverse fashion, of a future that was defined by its ability to uphold a previously achieved moral agency.

The account Hillary sketched in his pamphlet rested on a number of contemporary changes in the notions that more generally underpinned the representation of the past in the form of history. To a certain extent, the representation of the past of nautical disaster was simply drawn into this process. One of the most persistent campaigners for the foundation of the SCSN had been Théodore Gudin, official *Peintre de la marine* (Painter of the Fleet), and a renowned and successful specialist in the depiction of shipwreck, a familiar and highly popular genre in the salon since Géricault's *Raft of the Medusa*. In the early nineteenth century, the meanings of pictorial shipwreck had shifted.[12] In the seventeenth century, the genre had emerged as such, and come to occupy a position of middling prestige, in the Dutch art market. Paintings were marked by a realism of detail that was meant to attract marvel and affective involvement by symbolic appeal to an intricate iconography of moral commonplaces of purportedly eternal validity.[13] Gudin, whose own brother had perished in a boating accident,[14] was representative of the jettisoning of this iconography. After 1800, pictorial realism began to serve the representation of the historical specificity, the then-and-there, of a given disaster. Historical individuality undermined the traditional symbolic order. The new historical realism discharged the unfortunate mariner from representing the overwhelming misfortune that was the world at large. This was a precondition for the moral scandal Hillary discerned, as if by sudden epiphany, in the needless smothering of individual lives. In the traditional competition of genres, the inability to comprehend, and make visible, the general meaning behind the lowly individuality of a drowning sailor would have entailed a reduction of the potential for the representation of eternal values and Christian dogma, and thus a lowering of status. Yet, by 1800, the meaning-giving standards of evaluation that governed the competition of art forms and genres had been comprehensively transformed. Gradually, the aesthetic undertaking was invested with autonomy over its choice of object and mode of representation. This change in itself entailed a sense of rupture that pertained to the very understanding of historical significance. The ascription of historicity (the quality of being historical) did not any longer depend on the relations of some past event to a super-historical set of eternal meanings; rather, historical significance came to reside in the interconnections that bound one past event to others. The very understanding of historical reality was shifting. Hillary's trope of the withdrawal of a veil referred to nothing less than such a shift.

Gudin's engagement in the philanthropic campaign indicates that the historical-realist model of recognizing and representing events and its accompanying sense of modernity were present in the actual foundation and institutionalization of sea rescue. As I will argue, the explanation of this process requires accounting for the history of a particular, small-scale 'regime'[15] of ascribing historicity that mingled features of a more general nature with others that were peculiar to the perception of nautical accidents. In the first part of the present chapter I will explore in some detail the emergence and the features of this regime, which was constituted, and set apart from other forms of historicity, by way of its uses of historical teleology. In the second part, I will then discuss a number of textual sources that emanate from, or problematize, wider intellectual contexts of the phenomenon at hand. These texts provide a commentary on the meanings that informed the historical teleologies scrutinized in the first part. Yet, in turn, if indirectly, the textual production around sea rescue historicity itself also provides a commentary in a reverse direction, as the Boulogne motto in its mock Cartesian phrasing already indicates: philosophy had been on board all along, and it had also received instruction in the procedures of rescue.

2. The five hundred hands, a history

In order to persuade the potential bourgeois donors in coastal and inland cities as well as the local coastal populations that were to render the actual service, the nascent sea rescue organizations relied on a specific scheme for concretizing the plotline of departure from the past that had only been sketched in Hillary's pamphlet. Unfailingly setting up a system of annual reports to their donors, the organizations legitimized themselves by reference to a small set of specific shipping disasters. These disasters were annunciatory events; they marked the impending end of the monotonous history of centuries of neglect and the arrival of a decisive moment, an opportunity for disrupting the continuous perpetuation of the old and the foundation of a new order. In short, it was *kairos* that was imminent, a counter-time, teleological inasmuch as it was determined by its direction towards an aim, in contrast with the course – or more precisely, the rudderless drift – of tradition. This direction was not simply a product of intention and agency on the part of the founders of sea rescue; it was part of a temporal and passing situation not entirely subject to human control, of a history that was not simply made teleological by subjection to human design, but that was also itself directional. Organizing sea rescue was not merely a project, but expressive of a historical conjuncture. Remarkably, foundation narratives never drew on only a single shipwreck. They usually highlighted at least two specific cases, both in order to indicate the plurality of the phenomenon – which had indeed increased drastically in proportion in the wake of the massive expansion of colonial empires and sea traffic in the period – and in order to infuse the narration of *kairos* with the sense of complexity and contingency required by a proper conjuncture. Organized sea rescue emerged, thus the implication, because its time had come.

The German campaign was typical. Initiated in 1860 by Adolph Bermpohl, a teacher of navigation in the small Weser estuary port of Vegesack, it highlighted in particular two shipwrecks that had occurred in recent years off the islands of Eastern Friesland. The first case was the stranding of a New York-bound emigrant carrier, a short distance from Spiekeroog, in 1854, in which more than eighty passengers and crew were drowned while a still larger number of survivors managed to scramble to the beach. The islanders aided those who attained the shore but did not make the slightest attempt to reach the wreck. The second case was that of a much smaller vessel, the brig *Alliance* (from Newcastle), which ran aground in a windstorm within sight of the beaches of the island of Borkum in the summer of 1860. While the billows destroyed the ship piecemeal, the islanders once again merely stood by and watched. Some busied themselves with the inspection of the incoming wreckage from the *Alliance*. The crew of a mere nine sailors, who had climbed into the rigging of their ship and continued desperately to signal to the shore for help, finally perished when the masts came down, almost a full day after the vessel had grounded. However, this time the islanders were not the only spectators. The emergence of bathing tourism had begun to bring city people to the islands. The shipwreck was publicized by one such holidaymaker, who mailed an outraged report to the *Preußische Nationalzeitung*, a paper of national significance, in which he described the visitors' futile attempts at organizing a boat and crew for the rescue.[16]

Bermpohl, who had begun his seafaring career as a cabin boy in the short-lived fleet of the German revolutionary government of 1848 and had himself experienced a collision of ships at sea, took up the cause. In particular, he attacked the customary law according to which all flotsam on a beach belonged to the finder. The impassivity of the islanders was ultimately, Bermpohl argued, a result of their poverty; but this poverty also included the moral shortcoming of profiting from wreckage. Both material and moral impoverishment had pressed on the coastal populations for centuries. The time had come for this pressure to be eased. Nonetheless, the purpose of rescuing the shipwrecked did not go along with any scheme of ameliorating the economic situation of the population.[17] Rather, the new association merely aimed to expose, and then remove, the moral taint, by encouraging the inhabitants of the coastlines to correct their moral shortcomings and catch up with the values of the new times as embodied by British sea rescue and embraced by the bourgeois campaigners. The teleological understanding of the historical process of the emergence of organized sea rescue comprised a specific kind of aim: for others to catch up with a more advanced state of morality that had already been accomplished by some. Yet, once again, this envisaged accomplishment was not only a matter of human intention, but also one of opportunity, of conjuncture, of *kairos*.

The histories that emerged from this constellation were strongly selective. The problem of wrecks and flotsam was of considerable concern to nascent sea rescue organizations since it was capable of mobilizing the commercial element so essential for fundraising. Under customary law, shipwreck was not only sailors' misfortune but also shipwrights' expropriation, and property was a central preoccupation, next to, and at times above, life-saving. Thus, there was a competition of concerns; but in the foundation histories, life-saving prevailed as the tendency to downplay the economics of shipwreck carried the day. The SCSN, too, was founded with reference to two disasters in previous years: the sinking, during the Crimean War, of the frigate *Sémillante* on the Corsican coast, in which more than 700 French soldiers were drowned; and the 1833 stranding and perishing, off Boulogne-sur Mer, of the British vessel *Amphitrite*, a particularly remarkable disaster because it involved a gruelling moral lesson. The *Amphitrite* had carried a group of over a hundred female convicts to be deported to Australia. Her captain, or so the story was told in the literature, rejected the rescuers of Boulogne because he was concerned that rescued prisoners might escape, and possibly for fear of being charged a compensation fee. All passengers were drowned, and of the crew, only three men survived; the inhabitants of Boulogne were left to bury the corpses that washed up on the beach.[18] The message was clear: life-saving had to override economic motives, and morality was to be sovereign, the supreme source of commandment that defined the nature of the situation. Yet the story of the *Amphitrite* also demonstrates that even where institutions of sea rescue were already present, matters remained intricate. Accounting for the emergence of organized sea rescue in terms of historical departure and *kairos* meant suppressing rather a lot of information.

This is best illustrated by the British case, the local complexity of which appears hard to match. Hillary's lifeboat institution was founded on a stock of dozens of independent lifeboats already in existence in 1823. Following a much-publicized 1785 shipwreck in the Tyne estuary in front of an extraordinarily sizeable crowd of onlookers, there had been a national competition for the construction of an unsinkable lifeboat, which was won by local shipwright Henry Greathead. A boat built to the design was eventually installed, in the framework of a local volunteer association, at the site of the disaster. Greathead sold lifeboats to numerous similar organizations both in Britain and abroad, as far as the southern Baltic.[19] The contexts of deployment these boats encountered are not always entirely clear. In the small Norfolk community of Caister-on-Sea, a short distance north of Great Yarmouth, around the same time, a number of local labourers pulled their resources together and purchased two ordinary boats. With these they went out to freshly stranded ships in the hope of salvaging some of the cargo, or even, when possible, the entire ship, and selling it back to the owner, or collecting rewards. The revenue was split according to investment. The co-operative operated in a sort of moral economy: they also saved people, but that was not their primary purpose; on the other hand, there seem to have been cases in which the shareholders agreed that people did have priority to the extent that there was a choice. Apparently, a moral balance needed to be struck between self-interest and rescue. The co-operative continued to exist into the twentieth century. From 1845, it added and manned an actual lifeboat, which was incorporated into the national rescue organization only in 1857. In subsequent years, the boat twice became the subject of disaster, and the lives of more than thirty Caister crewmen were lost.[20] Such coexistence of sea rescue, and specifically its moral standards, with the exploitation of wrecks usually features neither in the historical argument with which the organizations were originally promoted, nor in the organizational histories derivative of this argument. Yet, local economic conditions may help understanding the success of the organizations. If the presence of shipwrecked sailors was an impediment to the exploitation of wrecks, the lifeboats and accompanying institutional frame for rescue could be a welcome resource. Similarly, the founders of the novel organizations were sometimes economically interested, as for instance in the case of the South Holland Association, whose decisive initiator, Rotterdam merchant Willem van Houten, was an outfitter of ships and profited directly from the establishment of lifeboat stations.[21] A further-reaching argument might also draw on the growth of the shipping insurance business as the prime context for the bourgeois sponsorship of sea rescue.[22]

Perhaps more surprising than the exclusion of the economy of shipwreck from the ambit of historicity in which sea rescue organizations situated their foundation was the almost total suppression of religious motives. Only the case of the explicitly Catholic-orientated Hospitaliers Bretons appears to have been exceptional in this respect. It is generally remarkable that the early- and mid-nineteenth-century spread of seamen's missions in various countries, both Protestant and Catholic, seems to have unfolded in almost total separation from that of organized sea rescue.[23] Although the scandal of the neglect of rescue might easily have been phrased in terms of a neglect of Christian duty, and although the religious fervour of the period was considerable,[24] the moral discourse of Christian improvement remained absent from the foundation campaigns. Arguably, Christian values were too strongly associated with tradition – and the traditional high stratum of aesthetic value from which the new historical-realist aesthetics of representing shipwreck sought to depart – to be deemed of use in the set-up of the organizations. The sovereignty of the morality of universal life-saving was to be unrivalled. The Christian tradition had coupled salvation with damnation, thus conceding that rescue did not disregard merit. Sea rescue, however, offered such disregard, which was disregard of the past. Hence, sea rescue foundation histories do not appear to present yet another case of a model of historicity as emerging from a secularization of Christian eschatology, if by that one means a process of filtering religious content from a structural scheme that is otherwise sustained.

All sea rescue organization histories were, and continue to be, written in strictly national frameworks, even though the pioneering role of the British association has usually been acknowledged. This national orientation entailed the exclusion, from sea rescue historicity, of a third aspect; namely the installation of means of salvage along colonial coastlines, a theme which hardly ever figured in the organizations' historical publications. It appears as if already in the nineteenth century the Europe of nations constituted itself by forgetting about its colonies. Small-scale regimes of historicity, such as that of organized sea rescue, to the extent that they served as symbols of the national, may have set a quite important precedent for the withdrawal of historical consciousness from the far-flung domination over other parts of the world that marked modern Europe. Hillary's actual innovation had been to conceive of the rescue of the shipwrecked as a national task that required standardization and geographically consistent coverage in the British Isles, but not the British Empire. The excitement of nation-building, not that of empire-building, was to drive the philanthropic undertaking. Boats and crews were furnished with uniform equipment and apparel. Although privately organized, the design of sea rescue was that of a state service. Similar to the military profession – which had itself been transforming rapidly in the aftermath of the French Revolution – rescue work required a reservoir of sacrificial connotations as well as a system of honour and recognition that centrally involved historical narrative.

The peculiar character of sea rescue historicity can only be made visible by recourse to a different understanding of the historical, one that is more akin to the customs of historical scholarship as practised in academic contexts. This kind of scholarship is based on an imperative of expansive historicization; it seeks to extend its reach and to include novel entities by means of the positing of explanatory relations. The very gesture of including an aspect hitherto ignored in the explanation of, say, the foundation of national lifeboat organizations, is emblematic of the dominant scholarly understanding of historical writing. Yet, the understanding of the history of sea rescue informing the textual production that has been part of this very history since its beginnings was and remains different in kind. The historicity instituted through this tradition of writing remains stable in its exclusion of certain kinds of entities, such as practices of wrecking or religious belief. Although the explanations sea rescue historicity implies may appear feeble from the point of view of academic historical writing, they do not seem to be deprived of their functionality merely because they lack the impulse of criticizing and expanding the ontology, the range of kinds of objects and individual entities, on which they are based. The opposite impulse, towards the exclusion even of proximate realities, was, on the contrary, most effectually at work in the foundation of the organizations. Only, this analysis – according to which the particular regime of historicity contributed to the foundation process of the organizations – is itself part of a scholarly mode of historical explanation and not part of sea rescue historicity. This latter discursive regime did not count itself among the objects to which it pertained or which it purported to explain.

The functional core of the particular historicity that emerged in the foundation of sea rescue organizations appears to have been twofold: on the one hand, the organizations laid out the genesis of their project for the purpose of fundraising; on the other, the provision of historical meaning was a prime tool of volunteer mobilization. The *Annales du sauvetage maritime*, in their initial statement of purpose, described the goal of moral development as follows:

> Finally, we will relate the outlines of our mariners' courage, the dangers to which they will have voluntarily exposed themselves, the sang-froid, the skill of which they will have given proof, and we will strive thus to develop among their comrades the reckless devotion [*folie de dévouement*] of which every single one of them possesses the seed, and which, after the English expression, will bring forth, along the coastlines, populations of heroes.[25]

Strikingly, the anonymous author presented the heroic efforts of individual lifeboatmen in the tense of future perfect; their exploits were thus historicized – inserted into a larger nexus of historical meaning – before they had even taken place. From the foundation onwards, sea rescue organizations promised historical significance in return for the excessive self-abnegation required for an extremely dangerous service in which, over the course of the nineteenth century, hundreds of volunteers lost their lives, and which even in favourable conditions involved tremendous physical hardship and next to no material reward. Historicity – and more precisely, the assurance that the exploits of the lifeboatmen were not meaningless from the perspective of a future looking back on the present as a historical past – was the least, and at the same time all, the organizations could offer. Historical significance, in some sense or other, had to translate into recognition.

Recognition was granted not only by the literature with which sea rescue accounted for itself, but also by recourse to outside sources of symbolic value. One of the most important instances of recognition was, as one might say, the downward gaze of the monarch. All private-initiative national sea rescue organizations of the nineteenth century were founded in monarchies where inadvertently they solicited royal patronage.[26] Such patronage was decisive for the funding structure of the organizations, which excluded the state but typically included the monarch. In the 1840s, when the enthusiasm of the opening period had receded, the British association, lacking in central steering and systematic fundraising, floundered; its funds were reduced to vanishing point and most of its boats lay in disrepair. Hillary had died in 1847 amid a new ocean of debt, into which he had plunged himself by means of yet another series of catastrophic investments. The credit of the organization was only restored when, in 1849, Prince Albert became involved, both as figurehead and large-scale donor. A few years later, the name was changed to the Royal National Lifeboat Institution (RNLI). In the imagination of the organizations, the monarchy represented an idealization of the financial support structure that was mapped onto the hierarchical structure of the society of the monarchical state and was connected with a socially upward gaze, the correlate of which was the bestowal of royal recognition on royal subjects. It is crucial that this foremost source of recognition from outside the organizations was bound up with the act of donation. Recognition was granted as a privilege, at the discrimination of the sovereign. Historical significance in terms of sea rescue did not automatically entail historical significance on a national scale; national historical significance was contingent upon a recognition that could also be withheld. Rescue organizations used frameworks of national history from the start, but, nonetheless, their historicity remained a domain apart.

An exemplary case for the workings of recognition is that of Den Helder coxswain Dorus Rijkers who, at a count of almost 500 individuals saved with his assistance, ranked as the most effective rescuer in the Netherlands and was, from the late 1880s, singled out as an embodiment of lifeboat heroism. A motorized lifeboat was named after him in 1923. His funeral in 1928 attracted tremendous crowds and was exhaustively covered by the national media. Like Hillary on the Isle of Man, Rijkers remains multiply monumentalized. Nonetheless, he spent his life in difficult material circumstances, which his diverse meetings with the monarch and unrivalled collection of rescue medals did little to amend. The most meaningful use he seems to have found in the national significance bestowed on him was to speak out, if coyly, in favour of creating social security for lifeboatmen when, in the 1920s, he mentioned to a newspaper that he had had to sell one of his gold medals so as to be able to purchase a bicycle.[27] On Rijkers's part, this was a signal that the recognitions he had received, in terms of national historicity, had only little to do with his self-image as a lifeboatman, with the actual significance of his commitment. This was a common gesture; the much-celebrated and monotonous modesty of the rescuers indicated a certain degree of pride in the maintenance of a sphere of significance that was not requiring of monarchical medals. In this way, the recognition of the lifeboatman as a national hero also served to demarcate the particularity of sea rescue historicity.

The founding figures of organized sea rescue, by contrast, acquired their historical status by operating not only within the limits of sea rescue historicity, but also on an unequivocally national scene. Hillary for instance, after the striking success of his first pamphlet, published a variety of other, completely ineffectual appeals in search of national significance.[28] In the histories of their own organizations, perhaps surprisingly, the founders were frequently treated as only marginal subject matter.[29] In the exclusionary workings of sea rescue historicity, this treatment equalled a sort of quarantining of that which was too clearly national-historical. With Hillary, who was also a lifeboatman, as an exception, the actual founders have consistently played a secondary role in the self-histories of sea rescue organizations, although the notion that these histories had to comprise biographical accounts was universally accepted from the moment of foundational *kairos* onwards.

Arguably, the heroization of the founders would also have counteracted the kind of teleology *kairos* entailed, in that it would have emphasized individual initiative over historical conjuncture. The heroization of individual lifeboatmen such as Rijkers, by contrast, was less problematic since it did not belong to the foundational moment of sea rescue but was part of post-foundational maintenance. It was crucial for the reliability and the organizational stability of rescue that lifeboatmen were active and available in the long term. By increasingly highlighting exemplary rescuers, sea rescue histories disseminated a biographical model. This model incited a covert competition for duration of service, number of rescues and medals. The nautical expertise required for the operation of lifeboats was a further aspect to turn rescue into an agonal, competitive activity that was a source of pride and recognition. However, the foundation of sea rescue by means of a historical narrative that emphasized compensation for a moral taint contributed to ensuring the preponderance of the pathos of self-abnegation. The commitment of coastal populations was always to be re-demonstrated whenever a ship was in distress. This imperative pervaded coastal Europe to considerable depth.[30] To an astonishing extent, sea rescue became a matter of family commitment, ostentatious performance of genealogical stability confirming that the deficiency of old had been compensated for. As lifeboatmen's sons succeeded their fathers, they arranged themselves with a durable imperative that was never entirely satisfied.

Since the foundational histories drew on a strong emphasis of conjuncture and the opportune moment, they faced a problem of permanence, to which their authors reacted with an implicit conception of permanent re-foundation. Re-foundation was represented in two ways. On the one hand, it manifested itself in episodes of rescue which often made for gripping stories and unfailingly carried the sign of a 'yet again'. On the other hand, re-foundation was also entailed in a history of the technology that enabled rescue and at the same time constituted a renewal of the conditions of the underlying unchanging morality.[31] Of particular interest in the mid-nineteenth century were, firstly, lifeboat construction and, secondly, rope-gun devices with which a connection could be established between shore and stranded ship. Towards the end of the century, the motorization of lifeboats became the predominant concern.³² Twentieth-century histories of sea rescue organizations usually comprise large sections on the development of motor lifeboat technology. The effects of this development were profound. Lifeboat stationing systems became hierarchical with larger and smaller boats, the larger ones with much greater operating ranges than the old rowing boats, and staffed with much smaller, but increasingly professional crews. While nautical skill had always been necessary for the operation of the boats, twentieth-century lifeboat heroism became much more integrated with the technical ability required for handling the ever more sophisticated machinery. In general, the progress of lifeboat technology appears to have transformed and expanded the modes of the production of *personae* in sea rescue histories.

After the Second World War, motorized lifeboats were increasingly built to be virtually unsinkable and self-righting. Many of the nineteenth-century rowing boat designs had possessed these qualities, which, however, proved difficult to replicate in motor boats since the engines had to be protected against the impact of capsizing. Even the size of the new boats was a problem, for they took longer to right than the open boats of old. When the Helgoland-based *Adolph Bermpohl*, in a particularly heavy storm in the winter of 1967, capsized and righted, all four crew and three previously rescued Dutch fishermen were drowned in the process, and only the empty boat was recovered, days later, damaged only in the super-structural parts, and with its machines still running.³³ Thus, the faultless functioning of the technology had not done anything to save the men. Nonetheless, this and similar results did not pose a challenge to the technological self-understanding of lifeboat organizations. The aim of a fully controlled lifeboat environment was not the point of the technological narrative. The point was the continuous improvement of the equipment. The *Bermpohl*, a pioneering experiment in German lifeboat construction, was deemed a success after the 1967 accident, and the technology was applied to subsequent vessels and even retroactively built into other boats already in service.³⁴ Four new lifeboats were named after the perished crewmen. The quasi-perfectibilist understanding of technology incorporated sacrifice. Technological progress would absorb disaster as a sign of its own continuation.

This understanding was already present at the foundation of sea rescue. The projection of technological development was the historical future written into the foundational histories of sea rescue. This historical future was a model case of technological progressivism, judging improvement by the measure of the reduction and elimination of individual elements of risk in the complex danger rescue situations posed. This understanding of history was quietly teleological in that it was constituted by its being directed, if only approximately, at a distinct target. This aim, however, was not easily reconciled with the compound teleological structure of opportune conjuncture and the moral imperative of catching up, on which foundation histories of sea rescue organizations were built. These foundation histories were enthusiastic about the irrational embracing of risk, the *folie de dévouement* the SCSN glorified. In the translation of foundation into re-foundation, however, the technological reduction of risk was established as a distinct structure of historical teleology in its own right.

Hence, the historicization of sea rescue, as accomplished in the foundation process of national lifeboat organizations, comprised two distinct patterns of teleological organization: departure, because the right time had come, from past moral negligence; and intentional genealogical and technological maintenance paired with perfectibilism. These patterns were not antagonistic; on the contrary, they collaborated in the production of the particular historicity of sea rescue. Although they were so closely aligned, however, they were not generated by one another, but were in principle independent. Technological perfectibilism did not follow by necessity from the *folie de dévouement* that was central to the notion of moral departure from the past. Maintenance of the foundation could also have been effected by continued irrational sacrifice.

The foundation of sea rescue, which went along with an instantaneous and peculiar self-historicization, thus relied, not on a dualist, but on a dual (and potentially plural) historical teleology to generate its particular regime of historicity. This regime, although its description requires a theoretical terminology, emerged from a non-overtly philosophical historical discourse. Nonetheless, the discursive labour that went into the setting up of sea rescue historicity was subtly connected, and responsive, to overt philosophies of history; and even where such connections are difficult to trace, the philosophies in question help in elucidating the particular historicity at hand. This is the theme of the second part of the present chapter.

3. Tyrannizing over *kairos*, a commentary

Shipwreck, as a type of event overburdened with multiple traditions of tropical deployment, an 'existential metaphor', as Hans Blumenberg had it, has been a carrier of philosophical cargo since classical antiquity. In his essay *Shipwreck with Spectator*,[35] Blumenberg dissected the fortunes of the *topos*, classically formulated in Lucretius' *De rerum natura*, through which classical antiquity celebrated the sensations of unconcern, detachment and joy at one's own security that were to be experienced by the true philosopher as a spectator of shipwreck from the safety of the coast. In Greek antiquity, the ocean represented a sphere of disorder and incalculability, and seafaring was transgressive. Zeno of Citium, the founder of the Stoa, in an aphorism ascribed to him by Diogenes Laertius, had argued for the necessity of accepting shipwreck – failure – as a precondition for happiness: 'Only when I produced shipwreck, I navigated well.'[36] With the Epicurean Lucretius, the sea came to represent the world at large, the atomic chaos of the universe. Only philosophy was able to yield firm ground, a position of self-consciousness that was above the world. Over the centuries, the *topos* was appropriated by a host of Christian theological as well as classicist readings. Detachment from the world, 'that universal shipwreck', as Montaigne had it, was expressive of a highly normative ethical stance. *Schadenfreude* at the calamities of the un-detached was compatible with this stance, which in a Christian perspective also comprised acceptance of the salvation of some and the damnation of others. The *topos* invaded political language, especially in the tragic representation of kingship. The oceanic chaos came to mirror the chaos and failure, not merely of the cosmos, but also of history.

Yet, over the course of the eighteenth and early nineteenth centuries, according to Blumenberg, the trope became at first contentious and then unintelligible. From this period on, shipwreck directed an imperative at the spectator, who felt morally compelled to engage and bring relief to the suffering. Piecemeal, the spectatorial position, the firm standpoint ashore, disappeared from metaphorical uses of shipwreck until everybody was always already at sea and involvement was a universal reality that ethics simply was to mirror. Each shipwreck was everyone else's, and whoever tried to rescue others tried to rescue themselves: *Je sauve donc je suis*. Blumenberg's entire discussion was directed at the problematic of the modern understanding of history. History, shipwreck, concerned everyone and comprised all attempts of humans to salvage themselves. In this way, Blumenberg identified the *unity* of history as the notion that condemned to oblivion the *topos* of shipwreck and spectator: there was only one history in which humanity was adrift together. The very idea of detachment, the shore, became incomprehensible. In this development, Blumenberg detected the workings of an imperative of self-empowerment. He stressed the importance of technological change as providing prosthetic instruments with the help of which the natural boundaries of human agency could be expanded. He identified modernity, if cautiously, with a development of anthropological status so as to enhance the human ability to take an ever greater, but only ever relative, distance from nature. The way in which the *topos* of shipwreck with spectator lost its meaning was meant to illustrate what he labelled, elsewhere, 'the legitimacy of the modern age'.

Curiously, although in passing Blumenberg remarks that the nineteenth century was 'the century of shipwreck',[37] he does not make any attempt to connect his analysis of the trope with the history of actual nautical distress. This is all the more astounding since the history of instituted sea rescue appears, at first glance, closely to match his account. Sea rescue organizations emerged in order to respond to coastal shipwreck, which frequently took place in front of witnesses ashore. By the 1820s, a remarkable shift had occurred in attitudes towards this scenario, and with the aid of technological and institutional means, the witnesses, in the form of a social movement, without notable state or religious interference, reached an accord to abandon their position of security in order to bring relief to the unfortunate. This accord was carried out through a gradually increasing technological self-empowerment, and with stunning success. The number of lives saved by the organizations added up into the tens and even hundreds of thousands even before 1900. Sea rescue was the nineteenth century at its best; European modernity at its most legitimate. In their scope, the organizations introduced, and applied, rigid standards of moral universalism. During the Second World War, on all sides, lifeboatmen unflinchingly salvaged enemy combatants, many of these bomber pilots who had parachuted from their crashing aeroplanes.

Nevertheless, the transfer of the Blumenbergian scheme from the sphere of learned literature into practice is problematic. As the history of the German foundation campaign suggests, the matter could not be reduced to the relationship between subject and world (or history). At first glance, to be sure, it seems as if the campaign almost exactly replicated the *topos* of shipwreck with spectator. Only, the spectatorial reaction was plural. At least some of the islanders were ultimately more interested in the debris than in the spectacle of the destruction of the *Alliance*; and the bourgeois holidaymakers were second-order witnesses, spectators of the spectators. The imperative that resulted from their testimony was also split: it aimed at the financial engagement of the newspaper's readership, and the practical engagement of the islanders. This was a deployment of moral discourse for the demarcation of distinctions between different social groups. To be sure, such distinctions were also, but not exclusively, the outcome of the new uncomprehending rejection of the *topos*, on the part of the holidaymakers, as meeting with its old self-evidence, on the part of the islanders. 'Yes, what is a human life?' an islander was quoted as musing before taking off with a bundle of driftwood.[38] The new imperative was universal in that it pertained to all spectators; but at the same time, it was not universal inasmuch as it pertained to spectators of different orders unevenly. It entailed a speaker's position, for it was to be expressed by the second-order spectator.

The *Annales du sauvetage maritime*, in their first issue, published the eyewitness report of a shipwrecked passenger whose vessel had run onto a reef and sunk near its destination, Oran:

> Never have I seen, never have I read so horrible, so affecting a scene. Being there, full of life, of health, and facing a death one believed certain, and so dreadful a death . . .!
>
> In this supreme and indescribable moment, the Reverend Vicar Mr Moisset issued the benediction to all of us. The tearful voice of this pitiable priest, trusting into God's care 150 unfortunates whom the sea was going to swallow, churned one's innermost.[. . .]
>
> A *contrôleur* sees his wife taken away by a wave; she had her eighteen-month-old child in her arms; unable to retain her, he jumps into the sea, saying: 'We will die together!' The Vicar Mr Moisset perished next to me; I extended my hand towards him, but he missed it and clasped the end of my trouser leg instead; a piece of it remained in his hand as the wave took him away.[39]

Even the victim of shipwreck, then, was a spectator. The author seems remarkably determined to present himself as his own audience in the 'scene' he is witnessing. Shipwreck is at once life-threatening and theatre. Even in its victims it seems to merge with a notion of the theatrical that aims for overwhelming affect and has difficulty disentangling reality and text, since the disaster is both *vu* and *lu*, seen and read; and although, if the latter, it must be textual in some sense, it is also ineffable and purely visceral. The scene, as giving space to a spate of figurations, is productive of *personae*;[40] and also of spectatorial positions which are subject to multiplication, as scenes within scenes.

It was precisely within the framework of a theatrical understanding of seafaring emergency that the novel organizations created a number of new *personae*, such as the founder, the lifeboatman and the commiserating spectator-donor. Theatre was literally a means of generating donations.[41] Piecemeal, this genre of representation eliminated the personification of exemplary suffering and death, as given by the *contrôleur* and the Vicar Moisset: where coastal sea rescue was involved, shipwreck was primarily misfortune, and dying was not a social or religious act with significance for others, but belonged to the dead. Rescuers were not generally concerned with the salvage of corpses; only survivors counted.[42] To be sure, following Peter Szondi, it is only living human beings that figure in modern drama; the scene becomes social and humanist as the interference with the divine world that marked ancient drama is relinquished.[43] Nonetheless, the Oran account suggests that the theatrical frame retained the possibility of admitting religious sentiment to the scene. Blumenberg's account is, if implicitly, one of the onset of a secular age. Although Christianity was denied any agency in the foundation histories of sea rescue organizations, it found its abode in the plurality of spectatorial positions coastal shipwreck provided even to its victims. When the Morse code distress signal SOS was instituted, first in Germany in 1905, then internationally in 1906, it had been selected for the simplicity and recognizability of its constituent signs. In the midst of this most sober and technical question of dots and dashes, Christian semantics soon made themselves at home when the letters were re-interpreted as an acronym for 'save our souls'.

From this point of view, the Borkum scene some forty years before may be read, not as the imploration the distress signal entails, but as the imperative: save *their* souls! The *epoché* made by the advent of sea rescue organizations – that is to say, the disruption of the monotonous temporal continuity their novel historicity meant to effect – was operated by this imperative. If this *epoché* was constitutive of modernity, within the circumscribed ambit of sea rescue historicity, then modernity, the 'tyranny' of the 'five hundred hands' over *kairos*, was the commandment to others to catch up. It was not the result of a blind, non-teleological passage into a state of relative and provisional technological mastery of nature; and it did not pertain to humanity as a whole but was marked by subtle and precise divisions between speakers and addressees. Even if the imperative, like Wordsworth's 'noble Hillary', sat as it were in the same boat: Hillary's status was meant to be that of a moral model. Naturally, he took at least the nominal command of the boat, even though his navigational skills were inferior to those of some of the fishermen who served with him.

Wordsworth's sonnet captures some of the strangeness of the entire construction. In 'On entering Douglas Bay', the poet describes the seascape as marked by Hillary's new 'tower of refuge', a shelter for the shipwrecked built on an outlying reef. Wordsworth appears taken aback by the mock mediaeval architecture Hillary, a connoisseur and collector of art, had selected, and which presided over a set of dark associations: 'The feudal Keep', 'Tides of aggressive war', 'Greedy ambition, armed to treat with scorn / Just limits; but yon tower, whose smiles adorn / This perilous bay, stands clear of all offence; / Blest work it is of love and innocence, / A tower of refuge built for the else forlorn.' The poem conveys a sense of the structure of rescue as being a mere exception from a much broader architecture of tyranny. Wordsworth does not express a sense that this architecture is solely a matter of the past, nor that Hillary's construction represents an overall departure from a history of political oppression.[44] The tower of refuge represents, more precisely, a benign tyranny.

Wordsworth's poetical interest in Hillary's rescue organization seems to have been occasioned precisely by its surplus of allegorical meaning in terms of such a notion of the political that allowed for the exception to the rule. The emphatic 'but' with which the 'tower of refuge' is introduced in the second quartet of the sonnet announces the antithesis to the dark images of the political as evoked in the first quartet. The following tercets present the conclusion in the form of an apostrophe of the ocean: 'Spare it, ye waves, and lift the mariner / Struggling for life, into its saving arms! / Spare too the human helpers! Do they stir / 'Mid your fierce shook like men afraid to die? / No; their dread service nerves the heart it warms, / And they are led by noble Hillary.' The context is thus one of an all-overwhelming oceanic disorder – with a nod to Blumenberg's Lucretius – in which human consciousness is represented by a 'nerved' hope for the sparing of the architecture of a benign tyranny, and of individual courage in the face of death. Wordsworth's access to rescue work was through the reservoir of the tragic. Douglas Bay is a scene for the action of rescue; the contrary emotional reactions the latter elicits are fear and compassion, thus cathartic in the traditional Aristotelian sense. The catastrophe is avoided; yet not because its raging onslaught, its 'fierce shook', might be durably withheld, but rather because of the sense of solidarity with the rescuers the poem exudes. However, this solidarity remains ambiguous since it subscribes to the exceptional character of the tyranny of rescue; and since this tyranny itself is constituted through tragic motives. Catastrophe is merely postponed.

At the close of the very same summer in which Wordsworth visited the Isle of Man, Heinrich Heine – who wrote at the other, the revolutionary end of the political spectrum – witnessed the wreck of the *Amphitrite* off Boulogne. He never turned this experience into poetry, but vividly described it in a letter to a Parisian journalist.[45] In this description, which experiments with a variety of strategies for the poetical processing of the event, Heine is preoccupied with the 'inexorable' violence of the sea, which he likens to the British legal system that had prevented the women convicts from being saved. Unlike Wordsworth, he is drawn to a mixture of sentiment and irony. Accordingly, he ends his account by decrying – as the theatre critic of this *triste spectacle* – the lack of gallantry that lies in the senseless destruction of so much female beauty. With a sure instinct for the subversion of classicism – in which he colludes with the tyrannous sea and British law – he describes the stranding of one particularly attractive corpse as the emergence, 'from the foam of the sea, of a true Aphrodite, but a dead Aphrodite'. The scene of historical reality trumped the aesthetic cliché of myth. The mixture of the tragic and the comical is peculiar to Heine, yet the politicization of oceanic chaos in terms of tyranny – which was especially heightened when it victimized women – was a *topos* he shared with Wordsworth. In the case of the *Amphitrite*, Heine insisted, like most observers, that the rescue could have been most easily effected. The conspiring of law and sea in the needless creation of a malign tyranny was the source both of the melancholy and the ridiculous aspects of the scene.

Walter Benjamin, in his study of baroque tragedy, noted the orientation of the genre towards the *mise-en-scène* of the tyrant as martyr, as failing in history and against history.[46] The underlying theory of sovereignty, Benjamin argues with reference to Carl

Schmitt, was based on the idea of countering the chaotic 'state of exception' through the instalment of a permanent constitutional order. This political project, always utopian to a certain extent, was correlated with a stoic technology for reining in the state of exception of the soul, the rule of the affects, in a 'counter-historical' (*widerhistorische*) initiative.[47] Arguably, it was in the context of this tradition of political aesthetics, and more specifically its reflections in the romantic era, that sea rescue organizations achieved their understanding of the historical process of which they were to be the benign tyrant.

Benjamin also suggests that the philosophy of history of the baroque period idealized, not the finality of history, nor the end of times, but 'the acme: a golden age of peace and the arts'.[48] Thus, the aim of the historical activity that constituted the plot of baroque tragedy was not necessarily located at the end of the historical process. It rather lay in a notion of taking the process to insurmountable heights. Acme indicated a temporal arrangement that allowed for a pre-history and, as it were, a post-history. This is a structural model that was, it seems, of great interest to Benjamin. It is mirrored in the transformative historical perspective he describes in the preface to his study on tragedy, as a study of the 'origin' of an 'idea'. The origin, situated 'in the flow of becoming as a whirlpool', effects a forceful disturbance of linear time. The idea – understood in an idiosyncratically Platonist fashion – unfolds in 'the historical world' in a specific form and scope, which are defined by, and provide evidence of, an origin. The unfolding in question takes place until a totality of the idea's historical potential, in the form of the possible 'extremes' contained in it, has been realized. This gives rise to the possibility of a 'philosophical history as the science of origins', which is, ultimately, a virtual history, that is to say, concerned with history as a content, as a material to traverse, but not with history as continuous sequence. More precisely, the coming-to-being of the idea structures the historical into a pre- and a post-history. In this way, 'the idea is monad'. It commands its history in the sense that it determines its own historical ontology; it is ontologically self-sufficient and independent, hence the status of its history as 'natural', as unmarred by the distortions of human intentionality, of the phenomenality of the idea in the form of historical experience.[49]

Benjamin's recourse to Platonism and Leibniz indicates that he aimed for a divergence of ontologies within, or by way of, the problematic of historical times. He was interested in the possibility of a particular historicity as comprising the unfolding of an idea. Teleology remained remarkably absent from his discussion, and yet it was implicitly omnipresent in the vocabulary he deployed, derived as it was from the ancient and early modern metaphysics on which he drew. Hence the suggestion to see, in sea rescue's pursuit of *kairos*, something that is structurally remarkably similar to Benjamin's historical monadology. In the particular historicity of organized sea rescue, the centuries of spectatorial detachment from shipwreck plausibly figured as a pre-history, as a mostly undocumented state of darkness from which a decisive departure had occurred. The history of technological refinement and episodic heroism, on the other hand, as depending on a conception of re-foundation, has the bearings of an aftermath, a *post-histoire* proper, as marked by infinitesimal progress and repetition. The actual history of organized sea rescue thus collapses into the moment of foundation. It is this moment of departure from, of rupture with, the past that integrates the distinct modes of directedness that constitutes the pre- and post-histories. The *telos* of the former consisted precisely in achieving foundation. The *telos* of the latter, by contrast, was negative in nature in that it consisted in edging away from a risk that was, for the lifeboatmen, created only in the moment of foundation. This moment was thus a condensed *acme*, the result of the retention and making durable of a fleeting stretch of time, an act of *epoché*. Historicity, and therefore also the teleologies on which historicity was built, enjoyed primacy over temporality since they were presumed at liberty to manipulate time.

Benjamin remarked in his preface that the aim of his method – method understood as 'detour' by way of *Darstellung*, that is to say, *mimesis* or 'presentation'[50] – was 'to save the phenomena' (τὰ φαινόμενα σώζειν), by an operation that would salvage them into the realm of ideas.[51] The crypto-Platonic phrase had been brought to the forefront of philosophical debate by Pierre Duhem in the years before the First World War.[52] In Hellenist philosophy, and in various reincarnations until the age of Galileo, thus Duhem, the formula had served as the shorthand version of a methodological prescript for astronomical hypotheses. By no means were such hypotheses to be formed from physical theories as pertaining to the sublunar sphere; and by all means were they to be made up in such a way as to account for all observed phenomena of stellar movement, and not to discount any of them. As Duhem points out, ultimately, this was a formula of caution in the construction of theory. The knowledge of the movement of the stars was deemed transparent only to divine intelligence; human astronomers' hypotheses were at best feeble approximations that always under-determined the phenomena.

Benjamin, too, emphasized the fragmentary nature of *Wissenschaft* and the 'discontinuous structure' of the monadic world of ideas. This world was constituted by the absence of intentionality, the utopian exercise of a non-instrumental, non-communicative original language symbolized by Adam's invention of original names in Paradise as reported in Genesis. The preservation of the appearances was meant to be achieved through their connection with this discontinuous structure of names. Benjamin provides, as examples for such names, the epochs of literary and art history with which his study is concerned, such as 'the baroque', whose function was not to achieve, in inductive or deductive fashion, the assimilation of the phenomena comprised in them; but a dialectical 'synthesis' of their extremes.[53] In Benjamin's perspective, then, the salvaging of the phenomena coincided with their preservation within an epoch.

The epoch was also related to *epoché* as a methodological concept of nineteenth-century philology, the continuous self-interruption of textual scholarship, its sense of preserving the singular phenomenon, its abstention from speculation and judgement, and from the temptations of easy historical narrative and continuity.[54] In nineteenth-century Germany, philology could not fail to connect with even as remote an activity as organized sea rescue. After Bermpohl's initial campaign in 1860, the first regional rescue society was founded in 1861 in Eastern Friesland, at the initiative of Georg Breusing, a customs inspector in Emden. Bermpohl began to work at the nautical school in Emden in 1867, where he was certainly in touch with Breusing. He transferred to the navigational college of Bremen in 1870, where he became a colleague, collaborator and friend of

Breusing's older brother Arthur. Arthur Breusing had studied mathematics (under Gauss) and philology in Göttingen in the 1840s. Much involved with the activities of student corporations, he had been a local protagonist of the revolution of 1848, after which he had taken to sea, then specialized in navigational theory, soon becoming one of the most prestigious teachers of the field in Germany. After retirement in the 1880s, he returned to the historical and philological studies that had occupied him in his youth. In his *Nautik der Alten* ('Nautics of the Ancient') he included a lengthy chapter on the shipwreck of St Paul (Acts 27), which he retranslated and commented on verse by verse.[55] Breusing undertook to solve the extraordinary linguistic difficulties of the Greek original by reference to the natural characteristics of the Mediterranean and the technical characteristics of ancient navigation. He stubbornly abstained from discussing the theological import of the passage, the soteriological symbolism of which was, to be sure, not subtle: after the ship in which the prisoner Paul is being carried to Italy has been drifting in an unceasing storm for two weeks, the crew, under the guidance of the apostle, runs it aground on a sandbank in sight of the coast of Malta; all passengers attain the beach while the ship is wrecked by the surf. As a philologist, Breusing was only concerned with the precise meanings of the nautical terms the terse narrative contained. Meaning here was strictly a matter of tangible objects. Breusing was an enthusiastic adherent of *Realphilologie*, an approach pioneered by the Graecist August Boeckh, which sought to elucidate linguistic meaning by reference to archaeological finds and technical and natural givens and necessities. Text and reality were to converge. A heavy bias in favour of referential and against metaphorical semantics ensued, a specific aesthetics of denotation and names that unsettlingly cohered with the methodological ethos of *epoché*.

Unsettlingly, because while the aesthetics in question defined the targets of abstention in some respects, for instance with regard to theological content, it created licence for indulgence and transgression in others. Repeatedly, Breusing conjectured that the conditions on Paul's ship were, in some aspect or other, similar to those on nineteenth-century transatlantic emigrant carriers.[56] Similarly, he included a lengthy digression on seasickness, of which no mention is made in Acts, but which, Breusing suggested, is in accordance with 'the image as it is, not created by imagination, but gathered from experience. It would have to be completed by the cries and lamentations of women and children if such had been aboard.'[57] The nineteenth-century psychological common sense at work in this passage also affected Breusing's reading of Paul's intentions, when for instance he ascribed to the apostle a 'moral principle that the preservation of a human life at risk was worth more than great amounts of gold'.[58] Here, the ethical universalism of nineteenth-century organized sea rescue, and the supremacy of life-saving over economic reasoning, shone through; almost it seemed as if Paul had had in mind the misfortune of the *Amphitrite*. The Blumenbergian notion that ancient shipwreck topically disposed of a clear distribution of participant and spectator positions was alien to Breusing; hence he overlooked that Acts may have departed from this distribution pattern deliberately so as to change the focus to the shipwrecked. It was only in a matter-of-fact aside that Breusing mentioned the Maltese population, of which the first verses of Acts 28 recount that they supported the shipwrecked in various ways;[59] their supportive attitude was taken for granted. While an organized infrastructure of salvage did not exist ashore, certainly, the ancient mariners disposed of a large variety of technical skills that were conducive to the rescue and deftly employed, according to Breusing, in the episode. Paul, himself a seasoned traveller, contributed by soothing a commotion that otherwise would have led to

> one of those atrocious scenes [*Auftritte*] in which everyone, for fear of death, only thinks of their own rescue and struggles for their own lives, as they are amply known from reports by the shipwrecked in recent times.[60]

Unquestioningly, such a shipwreck, too, was a scene. Breusing's philology of Acts 27, in short, drew on an understanding of the reality of nautical disaster that derived from the regime of historicity of organized sea rescue. Thus, there was dialogue between the practice of rescue and its representation in scholarly texts.

Breusing's discussion of Paul, but also the motives of tyranny and tragedy in Wordsworth's poem and Heine's letter, as well as the theatrical motives in the anonymous report on the shipwreck outside Oran, all indicate the *Eigensinn*, the semantic obstinacy and efficaciousness, of the regime of historicity of organized sea rescue vis-à-vis the philosophical and literary discourse Blumenberg dissected. The authority over historicity was not located in this discourse as a central, one might say gubernatorial, agency. Neither did this discourse function as the overwhelming architecture of tyranny as which 'historicism' – the notion that *everything* had to be subsumed under a single and unified history – has so often been described, not least by Walter Benjamin. Nonetheless, sea rescue historicity was by no means an antagonist of such a totalizing understanding of historical time. It was progressive, seemingly secular, national, humanitarian-universalist, focused on heroic individuals, both dismissive and discriminating of social and economic distinctions, and perfectly aligned with a bourgeois monarchist liberalism. Yet, it was also teleological in a plural (non-singular and non-dualist) sense; and it was by dint of this feature that it insulated itself from other types of historicity and enclosed itself in a specific tragic scene, the acme of a benign tyranny. The historicity of organized sea rescue was based on a teleologically constituted 'epoch' in terms of dramatic acme; in terms of the grasping of *kairos* in order to escape from a linear temporal drift; and in terms of a philologized epistemology that was based on the 'saving of the phenomena'. In all these senses, epoch was narrowly circumscribed. It never pertained to the world at large, and it did not propose a universal structure of rescue to function as a *salvator mundi*. For Breusing, it did not matter that Paul's ship signified the world soon to be unmade, and that the promise of rescue was universal, provided one complied with certain conditions. The historicity of sea rescue, with which Breusing's philological work subtly communicated, was, once again, not a product of a process of secularization that would have maintained all the functions and categories of a previous discourse and merely charged them with non-theological content.

The unresponsiveness to secularization might be an indicator that the motive of rescue as epoch-making, which emerged pell-mell in the sea rescue movement from around the time of Hillary's pamphlet, was not itself the merely provincial product of an overarching process of modernization befalling a putative comprehensive history of historicity in nineteenth-century Europe. Rather, sea rescue historicity was epoch-making in its own right. If so, historicity in nineteenth-century Europe was not only structurally but also genetically de-central. This de-centrality, however, does not invalidate the notion that the historicity in question was marked by the setting of epochs. Arguably, because of the importance of periodization for the understanding of 'modernity' – which no matter how else it is determined must be an epoch – these findings have considerable consequences. A peripheral phenomenon such as organized sea rescue is thus enabled to make its own modernity. The lack of an all-encompassing regime of historicity with gubernatorial agency then allows for a pluralization of modernity that seems difficult to track other than by a small-scale historical census of historicities, in the full mess of their diversity. Only to the extent that such historicities were limited to specific spatial and temporal containers would modernities still be classifiable in the traditional fashion. Modernity might transform, or lapse, between here and over there, between one storm and the next. No doubt this is an unnerving prospect. Yet, it might well be an inevitable one.

In 1937, in an interview with the Austrian Nazi journalist Roland Strunk, Gandhi noted:

> But the West attaches an exaggerated importance to prolonging man's earthly existence. Until the man's last moment on earth you go on drugging him even by injecting. That, I think, is inconsistent with the recklessness with which they will shed their lives in war.[61]

This inconsistency was not merely that of European medical practice, but pertained to humanitarian rescue of all varieties. Everywhere it coexisted with, and even integrated, a sacrificial discourse that could not be reconciled with the elevation, the central, epochal importance ascribed to life-saving. If associated with the latter, modernity was neither able to perpetuate itself nor was it, in spite of all pretence, quite capable of being universal. It may well be that in this kind of predicament, the stubborn self-enclosure organized sea rescue achieved by means of its twofold teleological historicity provides the most workable, the relatively most stable position.

Notes

* In the writing of this paper, I have received support from the Gerda Henkel Foundation. For helpful comments and discussion I am indebted and grateful to the Working Group History and Teleology, to Danielle Allen and the unthematic working group at the Institute for Advanced Study, 2013–14, and to Joan W. Scott.

1. Friedrich Nietzsche, *Beyond Good and Evil: Prelude to a Philosophy of the Future*, trans. Helen Zimmern, Edinburgh: Foulis, 1911 (Complete Works, 12), § 274.
2. William Hillary, *An Appeal to the British Nation on the Humanity and Policy of Forming a National Institution on the Preservation of Lives and Property from Shipwreck*, London, 1823.

On Hillary see Robert Kelly, *For Those in Peril: The Life and Times of Sir William Hillary, the Founder of the RNLI*, Douglas: Shearwater Press, 1979.

3. On the history of the RNLI, see Richard Lewis, *History of the Life-Boat and Its Work*, London: Macmilllan & Co., 1874; John Cameron Lamb, *The Life-Boat and Its Work*, London: RNLI, 1911; and as more recent popularizing accounts: Alec Beilby, *Heroes All! Story of the RNLI*, Sparkford: P. Stephens, 1992; Ian Cameron, *Riders of the Storm: The Story of the Royal National Lifeboat Institution*, London: Orion, ²2009; Karen Farrington and Nick Constable: *Mayday! Mayday! The History of Sea Rescue Around Britain's Coastal Waters*, London: Collins, 2011.

4. William Wordsworth, 'Itinerary Poems of 1833', in *The Poetical Works of Wordsworth*, ed. Thomas Hutchinson, London: Oxford University Press, 1932, here p. 469.

5. The confusingly named Noord- en Zuid-Hollandsche Redding-Maatschappij (North and South Holland Rescue Association, Amsterdam) and the Zuid-Hollandsche Maatschappij tot Redding van Schipbreukelingen (South Holland Association for the Rescue of the Shipwrecked, Rotterdam); see Bram Oosterwijk, *De zee was onstuimig . . . Fragmenten uit de historie van de Konikilijke Zuid-Hollandsche Maatschappij tot Redding van Schipbreukelingen 1824–1991*, Amsterdam: De Bataafsche Leeuw, 1994.

6. See Ralph Shanks and Wick York, with Lisa Woo Shanks, *The U.S. Life-Saving Service: Heroes, Rescues and Architecture of the Early Coast Guard*, Petaluma: Costaño Books, 1996.

7. See Michel Giard, *S.O.S. Sauveteurs en mer*, Paris: Editions Glénati, 1997.

8. As recounted in *Annales du sauvetage maritime* 1 (1866), pp. 33–7.

9. Giard, *S.O.S.*, p. 70.

10. Hillary, *An Appeal*, London: G. B. Whittaker, ⁵1825, Appendix, p. 54.

11. Ibid., p. 15.

12. On the wider cultural significance of shipwreck in the nineteenth century, see Alain Corbin, *Le Territoire du vide: l'Occident et le désir du rivage (1750–1840)*, Paris: Ed. Aubier, 1988, pp. 274–81.

13. Following Lawrence Otto Goedde, *Tempest and Shipwreck in Dutch and Flemish Art: Convention, Rhetoric and Interpretation*, University Park: Penn State University Press, 1989.

14. Michèle Battesti, 'Le sauvetage maritime en France au XIXe siècle ou la mer apprivoisée?', in Christian Buchet and Claude Thomasset, eds, *Le naufrage: Actes du colloque tenu à l'Institut Catholique de Paris (28–30 janvier 1998)*, Paris: Honoré Champion Ed., 1999, pp. 111–37, here p. 114.

15. With reference to François Hartog, *Régimes d'historicité*, Paris: Seuil, 2003.

16. The article was taken over by the *Weser-Zeitung* of Bremen on Sunday 30 September 1860, p. 1f.; the shipwreck itself had already been reported on 12 and 13 September. See also the account in Hans Berber-Credner, *Retter an der Küste: Die Entstehung des Seenot-Rettungswerkes an der deutschen Küste*, p. l.: Deutsche Gesellschaft zur Rettung Schiffbrüchiger, n.d. See further Hermann Neuber, Hans Peter Jürgens, *Schiffbruch und Strandung: Vom selbstlosen Einsatz deutscher Ruderrettungsboote*, Herford: Koehler, 1979.

17. Structurally similar accounts of wreckage and moral neglect also shaped British campaign literature; see for instance Anon., *On the Means of Assistance in Cases of Shipwreck*, Norwich: S. Wilkin, 1825, p. 3f.

18. See e.g. Giard, *S.O.S.*, p. 20.

19. See the account of eighteenth-century developments in Cameron, *Riders*, pp. 15–19. It is worth mentioning that Dutch sea rescue, too, has a complex pre-history with a first

campaign for consistent coverage of the coastline through lifeboats around 1802 by East India Company official A. Titsingh; see Oosterwijk, *Zee*, p. 10; another life-saving organization, the Maatschappij tot Redding van Drenkelingen (Association for the Rescue of Drowning People) was founded in Amsterdam as early as 1767; see H. M. Brokken and W. T. M. Frijhoff, *Idealen op leven en dood: Gedenkboek van de Maatschappij tot Redding van Drenkelingen 1767–1992*, Den Haag: Stichting Hollandse Historische Reeks, 1992. The London-based Royal Humane Society was founded after the Dutch model in 1774. The historical precedence of British initiative might thus appear doubtful.

20. Colin S. Tooke, *The Beachcompany: A History of the 'Caister company of Beachmen'*, Caister: the author, 1981; id., *Caister: Beach Boats and Boatmen*, North Walsham: Poppyland, 1986; David Higgins, *The Beachmen: The Story of the Salvagers of the East Anglian Coast*, Lavenham: Terence Dalton, 1987.

21. Oosterwijk, *Zee*, p. 14.

22. Following an argument proposed by Burkhardt Wolf, 'Schiffbrüche wider den Kult der Sicherheit: Paulus, Mallarmé und das Ereignis nach Alain Badiou', in Gernot Kamecke and Henning Teschke, eds, *Ereignis und Institution: Anknüpfungen an Alain Badiou*, Tübingen: Gunther Narr, 2008, pp. 115–34, here esp. 130–2; see also Burkhardt Wolf, *Fortuna di mare: Literatur und Seefahrt*, Zürich, Berlin: Diaphanes, 2013, ch. 2.

23. To be sure, the life-saving associations did regard mission work with benevolent appreciation, but did not see it as an integral part of their own work; see the account of a seamen's church in London in *The Life-Boat, or Journal of the National Shipwreck Institution*, no. 6, 1 September 1852, pp. 93–5. For the history of the British and American variations of the mission movement, see Roald Kverndal, *Seamen's Missions: Their Origin and Early Growth*, Pasadena: William Carey Library, 1986.

24. For England, see Boyd Hilton, *The Age of Atonement: The Influence of Evangelicalism on Social and Economic Thought, ca. 1795–1865*, Oxford: Oxford University Press, 1988.

25. 'Avant-propos', in *Annales du sauvetage maritime* 1 (1866), p. 2. Translations are my own unless otherwise indicated.

26. See e.g. Lewis, *History*, p. 14 and Oosterwijk, *Zee*, p. 14f. for Britain and the Netherlands respectively. The outlying case is Germany, which sought royal patronage only after the unification of the Second Empire; conversely, the French organization had to replace its royal patron, Empress Eugénie, after the advent of the Third Republic.

27. See Tjeerd N. Adema, *De koning der menschenredders*, Alkmaar: Kluit, 1927; for the wider context also Jan T. Bremer, *Roeiredders aan het Marsdiep, 1824–1923*, Den Helder: Nationaal Reddingmuseum 'Dorus Rijkers', 1998.

28. For instance: William Hillary, *A Plan for the Construction of a Steam Life Boat, Also for the Extinguishment of Fire at Sea etc.*, 2nd edn, London: s.n., 1825; id., *A Sketch of Ireland in 1824: The Sources of Her Evils Considered and Their Remedies Suggested*, London: W. Simpkin & R. Marshall, 1825; id., *Suggestions for the Improvement and the Embellishment of the Metropolis*, London: W. Simpkin & R. Marshall, 1825; and id., *Suggestions for the Christian Occupation of the Holy Land as a Sovereign State by the Order of St. John of Jerusalem*, London: John Mortimer, 1841; this last intervention is perhaps the most remarkable one and has to do with Hillary's long-standing involvement with the Maltese Knights.

29. See for instance the accounts in *Annales du sauvetage maritime* 1 (1866), pp. 11–14 and 152f. respectively.

30. See the careful anthropological fieldwork in a contemporary lifeboat station conducted by Patricia Thibaudeau, *Sauver des vies: La Société nationale de sauvetage en mer*, Paris: Editions Textuel, 2001.

31. Blueprints for the technological component in the self-historicization of sea rescue organizations are provided by Lewis, *History*; and Lamb, *Life-boat*; in both books, the discussion of technological progress makes for somewhat more than half of the content.
32. Hillary's 1824 pamphlet (*A Plan*) was an astoundingly early outlier.
33. Following the account in Berber-Credner, *Retter*, pp. 35–47.
34. Wilhelm Esmann, *Die Rettungsboote der DGzRS von 1865–2009*, 2nd edn, Bremen: Hauschild, 2009.
35. Hans Blumenberg, *Schiffbruch mit Zuschauer: Paradigma einer Daseinsmetapher*, Frankfurt a.M.: Suhrkamp, 1979.
36. Diogenes Laertius' version: 'Naufragium feci, bene navigavi', was also taken up by Nietzsche, *Der Fall Wagner*, Sämtliche Werke, KSA, 6, 2nd edn, Berlin, New York: de Gruyter, 1988, p. 20, in the form 'Bene navigavi cum naufragium feci', in which it occurs in Schopenhauer, 'Transscendente Spekulation über die anscheinende Absichtlichkeit im Schicksale des Einzelnen', in *Parerga und Paralipomena* 1, ed. Hans Henning, Leipzig: Insel, s.d., p. 244 (as *tunc bene navigagi . . .*) and appears to derive from Erasmus, *Adagia* 2.9.78. Erasmus took the quotation to be in praise of fortune, which often, against hope, turns the adverse into the advantageous; Schopenhauer still uses it in this sense, while Nietzsche takes it to glorify failure as such. Blumenberg follows this reading. See also Manfred Riedel, 'Der Doppelblick des Exilanten: Karl Löwith, Martin Heidegger und die Deutschen', in Stefanie Rosenmüller, ed., *Hannah Arendt: Verborgene Tradition – Unzeitgemäße Aktualität? Deutsche Zeitschrift für Philosophie*, Sonderband 16 (2007), pp. 123–43, here p. 142 for the fine grain of the reception of the phrase by Löwith, which may have been a context for Blumenberg's use.
37. Blumenberg, *Schiffbruch*, p. 64.
38. *Weser-Zeitung*, 30 September 1860. The phrase: 'Ja, wat is en minskenleven?', was rendered in Low German dialect so as to further mark the backwardness of the Borkumers.
39. 'Chronique', in *Annales du sauvetage maritime* 1 (1866), pp. 50–60, here p. 52f.
40. Following Philippe Lacoue-Labarthe and Jean-Luc Nancy, *Scène* [1992], Paris: Christian Bourgois, 2013.
41. A striking example is Louis Napoleon Parker, *Their Business in Great Waters: A Play in One Act, written for and presented to The Ladies' Life-Boat Guild of the RNLI*, London: RNLI, 1929.
42. Nineteenth-century lifeboats brought corpses ashore on occasion, but the respective episodes usually seem to pertain to lifeboatmen or to sailors who had expired aboard during rescue missions. The fieldwork in Thibaudeau, *Sauver* includes a mission in which a lifeboat takes on the corpse of a fisherman killed in a work accident; the episode indicates that the status of the dead has changed in sea rescue, and possibly in seafaring more generally, in recent decades.
43. Peter Szondi, *Theorie des modernen Dramas*, Frankfurt a.M.: Suhrkamp, 1956.
44. See John Douglas Kneale, *Romantic Aversions: Aftermaths of Classicism in Wordsworth and Coleridge*, Québec: McGill-Queen's University Press, 1999, here esp. ch. 6 ('Wordsworth in the Isle of Man').
45. Heine to Jacques Coste, 7 September 1833, in Stuart Atkins, 'Heine and the Wreck of the "Amphitrite"', *Harvard Library Bulletin* 14 (1960), no. 3, pp. 395–9.
46. Walter Benjamin, *Ursprung des deutschen Trauerspiels* [1928], ed. Rolf Tiedemann, Frankfurt a.M.: Suhrkamp, 1978, pp. 46–57.
47. Ibid., p. 55.
48. Ibid., p. 61.

49. Ibid., pp. 28–30; translations of quotes are mine.
50. Ibid., p. 10. In translating the term, I follow Lacoue-Labarthe's remarks in id. and Nancy, *Scène*, p. 47.
51. Benjamin, *Ursprung*, p. 16.
52. Pierre Duhem, S*auver les apparences – Σωζειν τα φαινομενα: Essai sur la notion de théorique physique de Platon à Galilée* [1908], 2nd edn, ed. Paul Brouzeng, Paris: Librairie philosophique J. Vrin, 2003. Benjamin only references Emile Meyerson, *De l'explication dans les sciences*, 2 vols, Paris: Payot, 1921, through which he likely picked up Duhem's discussion.
53. Benjamin, *Ursprung*, pp. 15–20.
54. See Christian Benne, 'Philologie und Skepsis', in Jürgen Paul Schwindt, ed., *Was ist eine philologische Frage?*, Frankfurt a.M.: Suhrkamp, 2009, pp. 192–210.
55. Arthur Breusing, *Nautik der Alten*, Bremen: Carl Schünemann, 1886, here ch. 9, pp. 142–205. See also the short discussion in Wolf, 'Schiffbrüche'.
56. Thus Breusing, *Nautik*, pp. 161f., 195f., 198.
57. Ibid., p. 198.
58. Ibid., p. 162.
59. Ibid., p. 197.
60. Ibid., p. 193f.
61. M. K. Gandhi, 'Interview to Capt. Strunk: Harijan, 3 July 1937', in *The Collected Works of Mahatma Gandhi*, vol. 65, New Delhi: Publications Division Government of India, 1976, p. 361. See also the discussion in Faisal Devji, *The Impossible Indian: Gandhi and the Temptation of Violence*, Cambridge, Mass.: Harvard University Press, 2012, pp. 185–8, to which I owe knowledge of the passage.

CHAPTER 7
READING HISTORY IN COLONIAL INDIA: THREE NINETEENTH-CENTURY NARRATIVES AND THEIR TELEOLOGIES*

Siddharth Satpathy

Prologue: two historians from Cuttack

This chapter offers a reading of two nineteenth-century historians from Cuttack, Amos Sutton and Pyarimohan Acharya. A Baptist missionary by profession, Sutton resided at Cuttack, the principal town and seat of English colonial administration in Orissa – a province on the east coast of India, in the first half of the century. Pyarimohan, a Brahmo public intellectual and educationist, lived in the same town in the second half of the century. Sutton was a pioneer of European-style history writing in the province. Pyarimohan was one of the first Oriya practitioners of the trade in the town. Pyarimohan did not know Sutton personally, but he had read the Baptist missionary's works. Both wrote histories of Orissa.

This chapter reads three such histories of the province, two by Sutton and one by Pyarimohan. As a Christian historian, Sutton wrote an account of the work of the Baptist mission in the province, *Narrative of the Mission to Orissa* (1833). Written in English, this was primarily meant for metropolitan readers in England and America. But it also had a limited circulation in the colony. He also wrote, in Oriya, *A History of Urissa: Itihasa Sarasangraha* (1846) for the school textbook society of the colonial government. The first ever European-style history written in Oriya, the text had a long run in the schools across the province, and played a pivotal role in shaping a new historical sensibility among Oriyas.

Pyarimohan wrote *Odisara Itihasa* (1879) in response to an advertisement by the local colonial government that sought, again, a school textbook on the subject, and promised financial reward for such a volume. Pyarimohan's work passed through governmental scrutiny, and won the prize money. However, its publication gave birth to a heated controversy that eventually led the government to refrain from inducting it into school syllabuses. The first history textbook to be written by a native author, *Odisara Itihasa*, however, acquired a canonical status in the Oriya public sphere.

From an analysis of these three histories of Orissa, written in both English and Oriya, and roughly between 1830 and 1880, will emerge, I hope, a short history of the European genre of writing known as *history* as it played out in the town of Cuttack, in Orissa, India. In keeping with the spirit of the edited volume, the history I reconstruct pays particular attention to the kinds of teleologies that animate these narratives.

Historical Teleologies in the Modern World

1. Birth of the reader as a teleological event

As I tell the story of these two nineteenth-century historians, Sutton and Pyarimohan, I work with a particular conception of teleology. In his reflections on the European literary genre of *bildungsroman*, Franco Moretti identifies two different ways in which the plot of a narrative generates meaning.[1] On one hand there is a teleological rhetoric; narrative events have meaning in so far as they lead to one definitive ending. The English domestic romance of Jane Austen, for instance, acquires its meaning in the definitive final event of marriage. On the other hand, a plot may not present the ending as a privileged narrative moment. Meaning is the result not of a fulfilled teleology, but rather of the rejection of such a solution. Moretti would cite Stendhal's arbitrary closures or the *Comédie Humaine*'s perennially postponed endings as instances of narrative logic according to which a story's meaning resides precisely in the impossibility of *fixing* it. Both the principles, Moretti suggests, are present simultaneously in any narrative work. But they carry an uneven weight. I use this Morettian framework to read these colonial histories.

On the one hand, all the three texts under consideration – *Narrative of the Mission to Orissa*, *History of Urissa: Itihasa Sarasangraha*, and *Odisara Itihasa* – have a teleological rhetoric. The final narrative event, which gives meaning to their historical explanation, I suggest, is the act of imagining into being a particular type of reader. These historical narratives produce different kinds of readers as their final narrative events. On the other hand, to different degrees, these histories are also animated by a narrative logic where meaning resides in the impossibility of *fixing* this final event. My analyses of these historical narratives from colonial Cuttack intend to show the different kinds of readers they postulate as their definitive final events, and how meaning, at times, exceeds these final events. Between the postulation and the impossibility of *fixing* the reader emerges insight into the practice of historiography in the town.

2. *Narrative of the Mission to Orissa*: pastoral historiography and its sympathetic reader

The English General Baptist Missionary Society began its work in Orissa in 1822. It established its principal station at Cuttack. Within a short span of two decades between 1830 and 1850, it produced multiple histories of its work in the colony. Apart from *A Narrative of the Mission to Orissa*, Sutton wrote two more accounts: *History of the Mission to Orissa* (1835) and *Orissa and its Evangelization* (1850). James Peggs, a fellow missionary of Sutton's, was also a prolific writer devoted to the pious cause. He wrote *A History of the General Baptist Mission* (1846).[2] Despite all their differences, what unites these histories as a genre – I shall soon explain why I call it pastoral historiography – is their conformity to certain textual markers and procedures.[3]

First, these are histories written from the perspective of a particular position, or identity. That is, Sutton and others write their histories as Christians, and specifically for a partisan community of believer-readers. They seek to narrate the heroic struggles of a small group of Baptists who are determined to evangelize in the hostile and difficult climate of Orissa. Thus, in the 'Introductory Remarks' to *A Narrative of the Mission to Orissa*, Sutton writes that his purpose is to '[preserve] an account of the efforts of a body of Christians engaged in attacking one of the strongest holds of the prince of darkness'.[4] Such histories, he comments, impart 'instruction' and encourage people to lead a moral life as supporters of 'the cause of God and man'. They also help in eventually creating an evangelical public sphere where 'missions established in various parts of the heathen world' can share news of their 'progress'. 'Hence,' Sutton concludes, 'the history of attempts to spread among the benighted nations of the earth the light of the glorious gospel, has always been acceptable to the Christian reader.'[5] We will shortly return to the notion of the reader in these narratives.

Second, I call this historiography *pastoral* because, as a generic procedure, it forges close alliances with diverse forms of life writing, and thus with certain procedures, as it were, of taking care of the self. Sutton includes in the text proper elaborate quotes from letters and diaries written by his fellow missionaries, their wives, visitors and some of the early Oriya converts to Christianity. These autobiographical materials lend the narrative its density, and help to create a vivid sense of everyday Christian life and work in the colony. They serve as eyewitness evidence of evangelical heroism. In the 'Advertisement' to *A Narrative of the Mission to Orissa*, Sutton dwells on the delicate problem of proof: since he is himself closely associated with the mission, how credible are his words? The author finds a solution to the 'difficulty', Sutton says, by compiling and arranging 'such materials as he could obtain from printed documents or private memorandums' and then connecting these materials 'by remarks of his own'.[6] The Baptist historian from the colony is thus not interested in producing an eloquent prose narrative but rather a mosaic of texts that wears its evidentiary value on its sleeves. This reliance on genres of life writing is of crucial importance to the evangelical notion of the reader.

Third, pastoral historiography pays specific attention to the construction of the locale where the mission is stationed. It presents Orissa as a particularly challenging field of evangelical labour. Set against the difficult and hostile climate of the environment, the everyday struggles of the evangelical soldiers appear even more heroic. The significance they attach to the locale justifies reading these narratives as histories not only of the mission but also of Orissa. Thus, *History of the Mission to Orissa* (1835) includes an elaborate chapter on Orissa, its geography, population, religion, manners and customs, principal towns and language. *Orissa and its Evangelization* (1850) includes a section devoted to the history of Orissa. James Peggs even goes a step further and attaches a separate history of the province written by a colonial bureaucrat as a sort of long preface to his own narrative on the Baptist mission. All this ethnographic, historical and geographical information on the region was collected in aid of depicting the inner resolve and struggle of the evangelist.

3. Sentimental histories of colonial life

Pastoral historiography's reliance on genres of life writing to construct credible portraits of heroic everyday life in the colony had an immediate precursor in the tradition of sentimental history writing in eighteenth-century England. In its attempt to expand the scope of traditional historiography, which typically focused on public life, sentimental history forged collaborations with diverse genres of life writing.[7] Life writing, unlike history, was concerned with the domain of the private life. Eighteenth-century traditions of life writing conceptualized private life on two registers. On the one hand, it referred to the quotidian, what happened every day. On the other, it gestured towards the intimate, the interior world of the emotions and passions. Private life was considered worth studying since it could produce knowledge about the common condition of mankind, the sentimental life of the human being. This concern with the common life, human life in its quotidian and sentimental aspects, animated the genre of sentimental history. By including the quotidian and the sentimental in its narrative economy, this particular genre tried to furnish a fuller account of the past as a lived experience. It sought to bring the past alive to the reader.

An insistence on a particular mode of reading accompanied this emphasis on the sentimental experience of the everyday life. If traditional conceptions of historiography expected the reader to emulate the ideal representations of public life history offered, the new genre of sentimental history presented sympathy as the ideal way of engaging and experiencing a narrative text. A sympathetic reading would help the reader to cultivate his or her moral capacities. Lively historical portraits of characters and experiences, even though more ordinary than ideal, could foster habits of benevolence in the sentimental reader.

To turn to the issue of teleology, the meaning of the myriad sentimental and quotidian experiences the colonial pastoral histories narrate lies in their endings, in their final events. This event is the invoking of the figure of the sympathetic reader. Consider, for instance, the concluding remarks in Sutton's *A Narrative of the Mission to Orissa*:

> And now beloved reader if thou hast been taught to feel the value of those privileges which a Christian land affords, pause I beseech you. Yes, look at dark, awfully dark, benighted Orissa! Gaze on its awful desolation and sin. Behold its impure temples, its bloody sacrifices, its shasters. . . Unhappy land! Can we be Christians and not lament its sorrows![8]

A sympathetic perusal of Sutton's history would help the metropolitan reader to cultivate his moral virtues of being a Christian. Sutton returns to the figure of the sympathetic reader at the conclusion of his *Orissa and its Evangelization*. Admonishing his American reader for a weakening of resolve and support, Sutton wonders if the sympathy he had shown earlier was a temporary one: 'What mean those strong expressions of interest, those flowing tears, those hands uplifted in solemn pledge to pray for and support the mission? Must I conclude that all this was the mere sympathy of excitement, a feeling akin to that produced by the novel or the drama – the interest of an hour?'[9] The metropolitan evangelical reader Sutton postulates is animated by a sympathy that differs from the literary conceptualizations of the sentiment in degree but not in kind. The conclusion in Peggs' *A History of the General Baptist Mission* is an elaborate exercise in intertextuality. It quotes from Sutton's conclusion in *A Narrative of the Mission to Orissa* at length and redeploys the figure of the sympathetic reader as the final event of his historical narrative.

4. Beyond the sympathetic reader

If pastoral historiography derives its meaning from a teleological rhetoric, it also gestures towards the opposite principle through which a plot generates meaning. As Moretti suggests, both principles are present in a narrative work though they carry uneven weight. These pastoral histories privilege the final event of the birth of the sympathetic metropolitan reader. But they also postulate a more open-ended conclusion. They do so by introducing yet another teleology, a theological one, and by constantly deferring its fulfilment. This theological teleology posits universal conversion to Christianity as its final event. Sutton's *A Narrative of the Mission to Orissa* presents a portrait of this finality that is pretty much representative of the other histories in the genre. In his Introductory Remarks, the historian writes with some passion: 'Jugurnath, the great, the obscene, the bloody Jugurnath, must fall; long, perhaps, will be the struggle, and fierce the conflict, but he must fall; and the place which knows him now will know him no more for ever.'[10] In his narrative, Sutton constructs Orissa as a stronghold of Hindu worship: the Jagannatha temple at Puri, a town some sixty miles to the east of Cuttack, draws thousands of pilgrims from all over India every year for its famous festivals. Set against it, the evangelical resolve to bring about Jagannatha's fall looks even more heroic. For the Baptist missionary who writes history as a Christian, the final event of this theological teleology, universal conversion to Christianity, is a certainty. But it poses a historico-temporal problem. Concerned as they are with finite periods of time, pastoral historiography cannot accommodate the final event within the narratives it produces. Consequently, this particular ending is always suggested and its fulfilment is always deferred. The meaning of these histories is the result not of a fulfilled teleology, but of the continuous deferral of the final event.

The presence of the two teleologies – the narratological one that finds resolution in the positing of the sympathetic metropolitan reader and the theological one that has its resolution continuously deferred – result in a historiographical anxiety. The missionary historian is concerned if the deferral of the theological final event would effect a similar deferral, if not the disappearance, of the moment of arrival of the sympathetic metropolitan reader. This anxiety is a constant feature of pastoral historiography and it surfaces more frequently in the later narratives. It arises through a sentimental admonition issued to the metropolitan reader. We have already seen the one issued to Sutton's American reader who is not adequately sympathetic to the cause of the Orissa mission. Consider his appeal to the English readers:

> We as your missionaries, share with you in the solemn responsibilities of this vast undertaking, and groan under the task of urging you to duty in this matter. I had

thought I had discharged my share of this duty by my many letters and personal appeals; but as my thoughts rest on the still hapless condition of that dark land, the burden rolls afresh upon my conscience, and I feel that I must again and again plead with you and continue to do so till I die. And, then, if I were permitted, I would on my dying day visit your Committee room, and placing myself at your feet, plead with my last breath for Orissa.[11]

I will conclude this section by making a reference to Michel de Certeau's analysis of religious history in the seventeenth and eighteenth centuries. His larger point would be familiar: Christianity loses its medieval role of providing the totalizing frame of reference for European society. State and politics begin to provide the new conception of order. As it unfolds, 'Christian organizations are put to renewed use, in relation to an order which they no longer have the power of directing ... Political institutions use religious institutions, infusing them with their own criteria, dominating them with their protection, aiming them towards their goals.'[12] De Certeau traces the consequences on several registers: one is of primary importance to our story. With this change of order, religion begins to be perceived from the outside. It is classified as a particular social custom, one among many. In the eighteenth century, de Certeau writes, 'it [is] seen from an already ethnographical bias from the stand point of the "students of man".'[13] I draw two quick conclusions: first, the Christian pastorate takes recourse to sentimental histories to overcome this European practice of perceiving it from the outside. It mobilizes a sentimental language of the common condition of mankind to clothe and counterbalance its practice of identity-based historiography. Second, colonialism plays an important role in this sentimental mobilization. Through the nineteenth century, heroic colonial lives constitute the sentimental archive on which pastoral historiography rests its architecture.

5. *Itihasa Sarasangraha*: colonial historiography and its judicious reader

Colonial government had immense confidence in Sutton's command of the Oriya language. One contemporary inspector of schools even considered him 'almost as its creator as a written language'. The opinion is hardly justified. Rather, it would be more historically accurate to speak of Sutton as one of the creators of modern, standardized Oriya prose. As a translator, he rendered into Oriya classics of English Protestant literature such as John Bunyan's *Pilgrim's Progress*. As an editor, he supervised the compilation and publication of popular Oriya *translations* of medieval Sanskrit verse narratives such as the *Battrish Simhasana* and the *Gitagovinda*. As a lexicographer, along with his pundit Bhobanananda Niayalankar, Sutton compiled a three-volume dictionary of Oriya. As a school textbook writer, he produced volumes on a range of subjects such as Geography, Natural Philosophy and Ethics. Besides, as the first, and, for a long time, the only printer in the town, Sutton monitored the publication of a vast body of literature in Oriya, mostly evangelical tracts and pamphlets, but also some government laws and regulations.[14]

Sutton's interest and competence in the local vernacular rested on a Baptist philosophy of pedagogy at Cuttack. Instead of English, the mission employed Oriya and Sanskrit as the medium of instruction in its schools. Education through English, the missionaries felt, would hinder the growth of a Protestant theology in the local language. It would also render native Christian ministers and preachers of the gospel ineffective in their engagement with the vast local populace, which had hardly any English. Colonial government did not endorse the cause of evangelization. But it saw no harm in giving Sutton a commission to write the first history of Orissa in Oriya.[15]

Itihasa Sarasangraha was published by the Calcutta School-Book Society Press.[16] Of its three volumes, the first relates the history of Orissa proper, from the earliest times to the arrival of the English in the region. The two companion volumes relate a brief history of India and of some of its prominent cities. The author feels that the companion volumes contribute to a better understanding of the local history of Orissa. It is the slim first volume, however, that is of particular interest to our discussion. It includes an elaborate self-reflexive chapter on historiography where Sutton talks about his procedures, and, sets out to construct an ideal Oriya reader for his history. Sutton's procedures in *Itihasa Sarasangraha* are not the procedures of sentimental history writing. In it, Sutton introduces a different genre of European historiography to the town. The school textbook does not invite the reader to cultivate his capacity for sympathy. Rather it calls upon him to cultivate his capacity for disinterestedness and act like a judge.

6. Judgement and comparison: *bibechana* and *taula*

Sutton's reflections on historiography emphasize two procedures in particular, *bibechana* and *taula*. On the one hand, derived from the Sanskrit root verb *bich*, literally 'to separate, judge', *bibechana* has a range of meanings: 'discriminating between good and bad', 'investigation', 'judgement', 'ascertainment after consideration'.[17] The procedure that Sutton calls *bibechana* has two components: first, it is an ethical project of cultivating a disinterested self, one that is above the narrow sentiments of national chauvinism. Second, it is an empirical project of distinguishing fact from fiction and arriving at what is true or probable.

People of all nations, Sutton writes, usually succumb to chauvinism (*ahankari hoi*), and out of a desire to acquire fame as a very ancient race, they write imaginary histories (*kalpana itihasa*), especially if they do not have proper histories (*jathartha charita*) written about them. Real history (*satya itihasa*), Sutton declares it as a rule (*bidhana*), begins precisely where the wonderful statements of imaginary history (*kalpita itihasa*) come to an end. He invites his reader (*ehi samkshepa brutantara padhua*) to judge dispassionately (*bibechana karibaku*) as to whether what is written in many traditional Oriya narratives (*pothi*) about the past is acceptable (*grahya*). They have, for instance, inflated calendars: thirteen kings of ancient Orissa have allegedly ruled for three thousand years between them. And this is something, he submits, a reasonable man (*subuddhimanta loka*) will of course find improbable (*asambhaba jnana karibe*).[18]

On the other hand, *taula* is derived from the Sanskrit root verb *tul*, that is, 'to compare' and 'to weigh'.[19] The procedure that Sutton designates as *taula* is one of comparing and weighing diverse source texts in more than one language. It is thus a philological project of comparative textual criticism, which furnishes historical evidence. Sutton explicitly addresses the reader on how he uses his sources to write history: 'This short history is available only after we compare (*tauli*) the account given in these books [Oriya narratives about the past] with the account found in books in other languages. Only what is considered truth or probable (*satya kiaba sambhaba mani*) is written here.'[20] The compound word *sarasangraha* in the title of Sutton's history refers precisely to this process of research, comparison and collection of the truth or the probable.

Between *bibechana* and *taula*, then, emerge the central tenets of Sutton's historiography: both the historian and his reader are thus to cultivate a disinterested self, an empirical inclination to separate fact from fiction, and the expertise to sift through evidence in multiple languages. In short, both the historian and his reader are expected to act like a judge. The birth of this judge-like disinterested reader is the final event that lends Sutton's *Itihasa Sarasangraha* its meaning.

7. Decline and fall of an empire

Itihasa Sarasangraha is built around a central question and its explanation. The question Sutton asks is this: Orissa was once a powerful Hindu empire in the early centuries of the millennium, spread across a vast swathe of land on the east coast of India. In the course of time, however, the empire lost its pre-eminence, and its geographical boundaries were reduced considerably. So much so that by the time Sutton writes his history, a large number of Oriya-speaking peoples inhabited large tracts of land beyond the nineteenth-century boundaries of the colonial province. How, then, to account for this decline in the imperial fortunes of Orissa?

Sutton, the historian, goes on to furnish several reasons for the decline: the emergence of powerful external enemies, internal conflicts within the empire and natural calamities. He writes, 'After the death of Prataparudra in 1525 AD, the Ganga dynasty lost its pre-eminence. The throne of the Gajapatis was shaken in the midst of constant attacks from both sides of Orissa by the powerful Muslim rulers of Bengal and the Telenga armies. Moreover, famine and internal conflicts made the process of decline easy.'[21] This process of decline, which began with the fall of Prataparudra, continued unabated through the subsequent centuries and eventually culminated in the advent of the English colonial regime in 1804. The last autonomous successor of the imperial Gajapatis, Sutton writes, 'rebelled quite unnecessarily' against the newly established government of the East India Company. He was summarily defeated and imprisoned. Since then, the successors of the Gajapatis were counted as mere *zamindars*. Only through the benevolence of the colonial government, Sutton concludes, they still lead an aristocratic life within the township of Puri.[22]

The plot of Sutton's history, then, is that of the decline and fall of a glorious empire. Students of English historiography would be only too aware that Edward Gibbon's majestic *Decline and Fall of the Roman Empire* had a wide circulation in the late eighteenth and early nineteenth centuries. It is tempting to speculate as to whether or not Amos Sutton was emulating the model in the colonial context. Nevertheless, Sutton's *emplotment* of Oriya history as a story of decline and fall of a glorious empire remained influential in subsequent vernacular historiography on Orissa.[23]

Sutton's historical explanation, however, is meaningful only for a nineteenth-century Oriya reader who is proficient in *taula* and *bibechana*. The judicious reader is expected to do, for instance, a comparative reading of Muslim and Hindu sources on the death of Kalapahad, a particularly notorious Muslim army general from Bengal whose invasion of Orissa in the late sixteenth century was a considerable blow to Gajapati power. Sutton writes, 'Moreover, on Kalapahad, the Musalmans say that he went towards Sambalpur and there received capital punishment. The Hindus say that once, as he was passing by the temple at Bhubaneswar, a swarm of bees came out of the temple and stung him to death.'[24] The judicious Oriya reader is also expected, for instance, to relate to his own past with enough cultivated disinterestedness so as to have a better understanding of Kalapahad's supposed attempt to burn the wooden images of Jagannatha, and the subsequent recovery of the half-burnt substance by a valiant Oriya believer. Sutton describes the episode as it is given in Hindu sources and concludes, 'There are several inconsistencies in this account. So, the reader should believe only those parts of it that he can think of as facts.'[25] The production of meaning in *Itihasa Sarasangraha* thus coheres around the figure of the discriminating reader capable of making a disinterested judgement. The lesson in disinterestedness is delivered where it is most required for an Oriya reader; that is, when he peruses his own history.

8. *Bibechana* in eighteenth-century Oriya literary discourse

Was the disinterested reader, capable of discriminating between texts, a new phenomenon in the Oriya discursive world? In other words, did the acts of engaging in *bibechana* and *taula* have any significant role to play in the history of Oriya reading practices prior to the publication of *Itihasa Sarasangraha*? If yes, what sort of roles were they essaying? And how do these precolonial roles relate to the ones that Sutton assigns each of them in the mid-nineteenth century?

A perusal of the history of Oriya *kavya* – that is, high poetry – suggests that the late seventeenth and early eighteenth centuries witnessed the birth of a well-trained and discriminating reader, one who could be expected to do *bibechana*. That is, poets of this era self-consciously wrote for a specialized audience. Most literary histories describe this phase as *riti yuga*. Poetry was highly ornate: it scrupulously followed stylized conventions of composition, indulged in elaborate word play, and mostly mobilized the erotic sentiment.

Oriya poetry, prior to the *riti yuga*, does not seem to have been particularly fussy about the discriminating abilities of its readers. It is content to address pretty much anyone who is interested in reading it. Jagannatha Dasa's sixteenth-century *Bhagabata* is meant for all who seek salvation: the poet frequently addresses his readers as *jiva* and *sujana*, literally *living beings* and *good human beings*.[26] *Riti* poetry, however, grows more particular about its readership. The poet now demanded superior and specialized skills in hermeneutics from his reader. A reader will be able to derive pleasure only if his skills of *bibechana* match the erudition of the poet.

Dinakrusna, a popular poet of the era, addresses his reader as '*kobide*'; that is, a learned man, a skilled man: 'O learned readers, spring left soon. And Cupid, humbled in the absence of his friend, spring, lay dormant in people's heart.'[27] Dinakrusna is quite particular that poets should not address the ignorant: 'nothing is more perilous than a poet addressing a dunce!'[28] Upendra Bhanja, the most representative voice of the era, articulates a similar hope that his compositions are read by the experienced and learned and not the dunce: '[O Lord,] have mercy, may this book of mine fall in the hands of the erudite, / may it never enter the ears of the ignorant.'[29]

Both Dinakrusna's and Bhanja's anxiety over the kind of reader their work should or should not address suggests that, in the *riti yuga*, Oriya high poetry developed a self-consciously literary status, and this status cohered around the figure of an erudite and sophisticated reader who is skilled in *bibechana*. Consider the following usage of the word from Upendra Bhanja's *Koti Brahmanda Sundari*: 'One who has a facility with words and their meanings, one who knows all about poetic ornaments, he should judge (*bibechana*) the merits of this canto, of the poet's description of her childhood, teenage and youth.'[30] The reader who is expected to do *bibechana* in Bhanja or Dinakrusna's poetry, then, cultivates an expertise in lexicons (*sabdakosa*) and formal treatises on poetic ornamentation (*alankara sastra*), and applies standardized rules to particular compositions. This remains the dominant model of a secular and erudite reading in Oriya literary circles in the immediately precolonial period. The task of *bibechana* here, unless future research suggests otherwise, does not seem to involve a cultivation of disinterestedness, which Sutton invests in it in the nineteenth century.

9. Beyond the judicious reader

The judge-like reader who cultivates disinterestedness was, then, quite possibly, a new phenomenon in the Oriya discursive world of the early nineteenth century. The birth of this reader is the final event that lends *Itihasa Sarasangraha* its meaning. Does the narrative also gesture towards the opposite principle through which a plot generates meaning, that is, not through a fulfilled teleology but through a continuous deferral of the final event? In other words, is there a narrative logic in the history textbook where meaning resides in the impossibility of 'fixing' the final event? I suggest that it exists. And it is visible in certain awkward moments in the narrative.

As we saw, Sutton constructs a normative schema of two kinds of histories, real/proper (*satya, jathartha*) and imaginary (*kalpana, kalpita*). The judicious reader is trained to judge all kinds of narratives about the past through this binary schema. Sutton impresses on him the following conclusion: though Hindus have long-established expertise in diverse fields of intellectual inquiry such as grammar, lexicography, astrology, poetry and medicine, it is a surprise that they have written no real history (*satya itihasa*) of their own origins and progress: 'If we consider *Ramayana* or *Mahabharata* as accounts of the origins of the Hindus, then, we get scant information on their origins, arrival in Hindustan and their gradual expansion through the land from them.'[31]

This leads to an awkward moment where Sutton must comment on the precolonial Oriya tradition of historiography that he relies on to write *Itihasa Sarasangraha*. It is this tradition which Narayana Rao, Shulman and Subrahmanyam would call *karanam* historiography: *Madalapanji* is the narrative maintained by the *deula-karana* or the accountants of the temple of Jagannatha at Puri.[32] Here is what Sutton has to say on it: 'Thus, though all Hindus have neglected to write the history of the country, and of their own, still then, the Brahmins of Orissa are least culpable as they have, for the last fourteen hundred years, written about their past in the *Madalapanji Rajacaritra* and other *vamsavalipothis*.'[33]

Sutton's history offers a judicious reading of the *Madalapanji* corpus. However, his reading ultimately remains indecisive on the normative status of the precolonial corpus. On the one hand, he does not discredit or delegitimize it as imaginary history. He does not place it in the same category as the *Ramayana* and *Mahabharata*. Rather, he makes a case for Oriya historiographers and their age-old practice of recording their past. On the other hand, he does not quite recognize it as real history because it does not meet the criteria he sets up. Sutton seems less sure of where to place the precolonial corpus in the normative binary schema he sets up in the first place.

Sutton then resorts to an empirical way out of the normative impasse: he declares that, prior to a particular period in time, the precolonial narrative is not reliable: 'It seems, since no real account was available till the advent of the *kesharivamsa* kings, poets began to fill the gaps in the history (*charita*) by these events of their own creations (*kalpana kari*) or wrote what was handed down through the tradition (*paramparagata katha dhari rachile*). The *kesharivamsa* began counting its royal years from 473 AD; prior to this, a reliable history of Orissa is not available at present.'[34]

This empirical approach prompts Sutton not exactly to see the *Madalapanji* corpus as a *document* that needs to be preserved in an archive. Rather he sees it as a tradition of writing that has continued over the centuries. He makes no predictions on the fate of this tradition of historiography in the colonial times: we find no pompous declaration that the kind of real history he writes would or should replace the kind of history that Oriyas have been writing and reading in the *Madalapanji* corpus.

What comes through Sutton's comments is a deliberate slip from normative declarations to an acknowledgement of empirical particularities. This slide is what exceeds the position of the judge-like reader who is supposed to see all narratives of the past through the normative binary of real and imaginary histories. It is the barely acknowledged presence of the writer and reader of this precolonial tradition of historiography in the *Itihasa Sarasangraha* that shadows the final figure of the reader who is meant to judge in a decisive manner.

10. *Odisara Itihasa*: sentimental reception of a disciplinary reader

Sympathetic and judicious readers thus indicate the two principal genres of European history writing that Amos Sutton introduced to the reading public at Cuttack. He was not the only European scholar to write histories of Orissa. Several other names suggest themselves. Andrew Sterling wrote his in 1825. Nearly fifty years later, William Hunter published his work in 1872, and George Toynbee followed it up with his volume in 1873.[35] However, it was only Sutton who worked with multiple genres of European historiography, and wrote in both English and Oriya. Shifting between genres or languages while writing history does not seem to have been a problem for him: Sutton has not written anything that self-consciously reflects on the issue. Cultivation of disinterestedness, separation of facts from fiction and comparison of multiple sources in diverse languages – these criteria of what he calls *real* or *proper* history do not seem to preoccupy him while he writes histories of Christian life and work in the town. But these play a significant role when he writes for Oriya students of history in colonial schools across the province. This duality does not seem to bother Sutton, perhaps because he understands the genres and their audiences to be mutually exclusive. This understanding seems to rest on an unstated consensus among European lovers of history in the nineteenth century.

This distinction between the genres and their audiences, however, appears less tightly marked when we trace a history of how European historiography takes root in the colonial soil at Cuttack towards the end of the century. For this we need to turn to Pyarimohan's *Odisara Itihasa*.[36] In the preface to his work, Pyarimohan acknowledges his debts to Sutton, Sterling, Hunter, Toynbee and other Indian historians whose works he has perused. In the Oriya public sphere of the time, however, *Odisara Itihasa* was most frequently compared with Sutton's *Itihasa Sarasangraha*. In a review of the book, the editor of the *Utkal Dipika*, the most prominent Oriya newspaper in the town, compared Pyarimohan favourably with Sutton: 'It will not be an exaggeration to say that there was no history of Orissa in Oriya language [prior to the publication of *Odisara Itihasa*]. The work compiled by Sutton sahib is history only in its name.'[37] The reviewer does not say why he considers Sutton's work to be only a nominal history. But it seems that since Sutton wrote his slim volume, a history reading and reviewing public had emerged at Cuttack, and it had grown habituated with perusing much fuller histories of Orissa, albeit in English. Besides, by the 1870s, history seems to have established itself more securely as an academic discipline at Cuttack schools, and the reading public had as such grown more discerning.

11. Between history and literature: the question of discipline

The tension between history and literature which finds mention in Sutton's reading of the *Madalapanji* corpus seems to have acquired a larger profile in the Oriya public sphere by the time Pyarimohan writes *Odisara Itihasa*. His preface takes trouble to distinguish the work it introduces from literature. Historical truth (*aitihasika satya*) is presented as the object of the author's labours (*chesta*). The historical mode of investigation and method (*aitihasika anusandhana / aitihasika sutra*) is differentiated from literary explorations (*sahitya charcha*). Commenting upon a primary source – *Karana Kundala*, a recent compilation of older *pauranic* verses on the origins of a particular prominent caste of the region – Pyarimohan observes: 'we rarely find in our province such scrupulous scholarly exertion in the realm of literary explorations. Still then, it is but a pity that the author has not tried to gather together an account of the *karanas* in the historical mode.'[38] The historical mode is held as a higher epistemological order than literary forms of explorations. The author writes a long paragraph on the subject of the *karanas* in the preface to give readers a glimpse of what a proper historical form of enquiry looks like. He even promises to write a monograph on the history of the caste at a future date.

Pyarimohan's desire to set history apart from and above literature leads us to enquire more into the contemporary Oriya literati's epistemological conceptions. Two unusual texts, both published in the same year as Pyarimohan's history, throw some light on how the Oriya public sphere understood the relationship between the two disciplines in the 1870s. *Model Questions on Oriya Literature* and *Model Questions: History of India* were meant for teachers and students in the schools run by the colonial government across the province. The writers of these volumes, Bhuvaneswar Datta for Literature, and Bhola Nath De and Haris Chundra Sarkar for History, all acknowledge in the prefaces their intellectual debts to one man, Radhanatha Ray. The most famous Oriya poet of the era, Ray was also a high-ranking colonial official in the education department; it seems these volumes were conceived by him as companion projects. These compilations of questions aimed to train scholars and pupils to think about the disciplines, and the relationship between the two.[39]

The first questions from the volume on history are theoretical in their orientation: some of them are of particular interest to our discussion. These are, maintaining the order in which they appear: 'What is the purpose of history'; 'Whether or not reading history generates a tendency in the reader to desire and do good of his nation?'; 'History is chiefly divided into how many categories?'; 'What differentiates old from modern history?' and 'What are the differences between history and biography?' A chronological reading of these questions leads one to make several preliminary observations on the status of history as discipline. First, Oriya literati learnt to associate history with the nation: reading history inspires the reader to work for national well-being. Second, they learnt that history is written in different forms: some of these forms are more modern than others. Third, they learnt that history needs to differentiate itself from literature; importantly from certain genres of literature, which might look suspiciously like history, such as biography. In other words, sentimental histories of the kind that Amos Sutton wrote about the Baptist mission and its work in Orissa, the ones that forged close alliances with several genres of life writing, have come to occupy a marginalized space, and are now considered less than modern. History now seems to be sure of its disciplinary moorings in what Pyarimohan calls investigation (*anusandhan*) and method (*sutra*) – notions that have a close affinity to Sutton's thoughts on judgement (*bibechana*) and comparison (*taula*).

155

Literature, on the other hand, seems to be engaged in a status struggle. The volume on Oriya literature has a long preface addressed to the teachers of the subject. The preface has the primary responsibility of carving out a defined space for the discipline. First, it tries to impress on the reading public that literature is not merely a teaching of grammar. Rather, it aims at creating an internal experience, an understanding of the diverse subjects that one reads about in a literature textbook. These subjects could range from history to *puranas*, to geography and so on. Second, it argues that composition is an integral aspect, if not the primary purpose, of history as a discipline.[40] And it is literature pedagogy that aims at teaching students the art of composition (*rachana*). To this effect, literary education should encourage students to write narrative essays on historical events as well as on other subjects. The volume, for instance, includes the following composition questions: 'Write an essay on the origins and uses of camphor'; 'Describe the funeral rites and related notions of pollution among the Hindus'; ' "Enthused with hope, Clive, the warrior, fought on the battlefields of Palasi" – Describe in brief, the historical subjects alluded to in the aforementioned quotation. Write what you know about [Robert] Clive.' Two observations need to be made: vernacular literature, as an emerging discipline in the 1870s, is yet to establish a direct association with the nation: it operates at the level of an individual's inner experience and understanding. Second, it forces on history an awareness of its narrative aspect, something that its practitioners in the town forget, caught up as they are in the normative charms of investigation, method, judgement and comparison.

By taking the trouble to distinguish history from literature in his preface, Pyarimohan helps us to conceptualize the reader he writes for: it is a disciplinary reader, that is, one who is reading history as an academic discipline.[41] This reader is seemingly less interested in the literary or narrative (*rachana*) aspects of the pleasure of history writing and reading. Rather, he is more concerned with investigation (*anusandhana*) and method (*sutra*). This disciplinary reader bears a close affinity to the judicious reader: both Sutton and Pyarimohan are writing versions of colonial historiography that espouse the ideal of a disinterested pursuit of truth. The disciplinary reader, however, is more preoccupied with questions of his own identity: he self-consciously sees himself in relation to disciplines other than his own. How history as a disinterested pursuit of knowledge differs from literature is a question, for instance, that animates the disciplinary reader more than it perhaps would a judicious reader. Consequently, the former lays a more detailed emphasis on modes and methods of enquiry.

Of all the history texts considered in this paper, Pyarimohan's *Odisara Itihasa* uses the disciplinary method of footnotes most scrupulously. Anthony Grafton has persuasively argued that the appearance of critical devices such as the footnote and documentary appendices lent history its modern double form: the narrative in the text proper runs parallel to the author's identification of sources and reflection on his methods either at the bottom of the page or at the end of the text. These devices separated historical modernity from tradition; they transformed history from eloquent narratives into a critical discipline which relied on systematic scrutiny of original evidence and evaluation of sources.[42] Pyarimohan and the authors of the model questions were engaged in establishing history as a critical discipline in vernacular Oriya. Here is a footnote from *Odisara Itihasa*: 'Sterling sahib writes that the kingdom of the Odras spread from the river Rusikulya, that flows to the south of Khorda, up to the river Kansabansa in the north. But, there is no evidence of such an expansive realm. Rather, a copper plate suggests ...'[43] The anticipation of a disciplinary reader who is proficient in reading footnotes, one who recognizes history through its double form is the final event that lends *Odisara Itihasa* its meaning.

12. Beyond the disciplinary reader

What exceeds the invocation of the figure of the disciplinary reader as the final event in *Odisara Itihasa* is precisely the association that history as a discipline forges with nationalist sentiments in the contemporary Oriya public sphere: perusal of history, it was widely believed, inspired the reader to work for national well-being. Pyarimohan writes not only as a historian but also as an active member of an emerging Oriya civil society that worked to achieve the twin goals of progress (*unnati*) and civilization (*sabhyata*) for Orissa. As a historian, he sees humankind on a continuous path of progress (*manaba samajara kramonnatishilata*), and from the perspective of a nationalist, he is immensely hopeful of the bright future that awaits Orissa in particular and India in general. This nationalist perspective is most strongly articulated in the epilogue (*upasamhara*) to *Odisara Itihasa*. The epilogue postulates a flourishing and progressive Oriya civil society as the final event of the historical process of progress that *Odisara Itihasa* charts:

> Now, under English rule, the people of Orissa are moving towards progress and civilization. Once more, construction of national literature has begun. Intellectual inquiries and erudite debates are on the rise ... Whether literate or illiterate, people are reflecting on purer forms of religion ... Printing presses have been established. Newspapers are brought out, societies are formed: debates are being held on political, social and religious issues. All these contribute to a gradual refinement of taste. Besides, people are more concerned with the generation and accumulation of wealth; consequently, trade and agriculture are receiving more attention. These are all auspicious signs. In brief, if we look around these days, we find only the signs of hope.[44]

Writing from the particular perspective of an Oriya nationalist, Pyarimohan sees the colonial regime as a benevolent ally who will help the fledgling civil society to flourish and progress. An unstated goal of the epilogue is to furnish a portrait of colonial rule, which will serve as a foundation for a close alliance between the English and the people of Orissa. This portrait, as such, does not abandon the critical methods and ideals of historiography as a discipline. Pyarimohan strives to remain disinterested in his judgement on the colonial regime: it levies oppressive taxes, and does not allow native participation in the process of governance. In the final analysis though, it is beneficial (*hitabaha*) for people as it has brought justice (*nyaya*), rule of law (*bichara*) and peace (*shanti*) to the land. However, what exceeds the disciplinary reader in this portrait of colonial rule is a certain moment of sentimental attachment to the colonizers who are described as brothers: 'If God bestows mercy,' the historian writes, 'with the help of the English, our advanced Aryan brothers, the face of our nation will glow radiant.'[45] This nationalist language of sentiment and affect is the excess that accompanies the figure of the disciplinary reader and his critical, disinterested pursuit of truth in *Odisara Itihasa*.

13. A sentimental reception

Odisara Itihasa received a rousing sentimental response in the Oriya public sphere: a sympathetic perusal of the history helped the reader to cultivate his Oriya nationalist identity. Thus, the reviewer of the *Utkal Dipika* caught on to the value of the history text beyond the classroom and urged the general reading public to read it: 'In the end, I appeal to the general public (*sarbasadharana*) in Orissa, especially the kings and *zamindars*, to read this book and reflect on the subjects mentioned in it. It will help them to keep the past glory [of Orissa] alive in their minds, make them eager to resurrect it, and will enthuse them to work towards progress.'[46] Another contemporary review in the *Baleswar Samvad Bahika*, another Oriya newspaper, is even more emphatic in its sympathetic reading:

> Especially, if we take a look at the beautiful way in which it [*Odisara Itihasa*] treats the subject of ancient Orissa, we can say without any hesitation that such a history is rare even in the comparatively refined and advanced language of Bengali. A perusal of this book will enhance the self-esteem of the inhabitants of Orissa and with honest pride they will consider themselves fortunate to be the children of Utkal.[47]

In subsequent years, Pyarimohan's membership of Oriya civil society and contribution to language-based nationalism overshadows his claim to critical historical scholarship. Writing the preface to the second edition, published nearly half a century later in 1925, Viswanatha Kara admires Pyarimohan's scrupulous (*sabadhanata*), truthful (*satyanishtha*) and often physically demanding (*kathor parishrama*) pursuit of historical investigation (*aitihasika tathyanusandhana*). But what endears *Odisara Itihasa* to Kara's generation is the literary value (*sahityika mulya*) the text has accrued over the years. Written during the formative years of modern Oriya language, *Odisara Itihasa* has a special value for a literary historian. The language it deploys has a primitive and natural sweetness (*aadima, akrutrima madhuri*) about it, which is lost in the subsequent processes of refinement and development.[48] The irony of Kara's literary appreciation of *Odisara Itihasa* would not have been lost on Pyarimohan, who took pains to distinguish the historical from the literary modes of enquiry.

14. Inadequately disinterested: the case of a public controversy

Publication of *Odisara Itihasa* also gave birth to a heated public controversy in the town of Cuttack. The controversy revolved around the issue of writing genuine history that is critical and disinterested in its pursuit of truth. Pyarimohan was born into a Bengali-speaking family long settled in Orissa. Scholars have suggested that his commitment to Oriya language nationalism flowed from his Brahma leanings. Brahma Dharma was a socio-religious reformist movement that originated in Calcutta. Under the leadership of Kesabchandra Sen, it developed an intimate relationship with Bengali language nationalism. Pyarimohan was a member of the Orissa chapter of the movement, Utkala Brahma Samaj. Following the Brahma model of social and religious reformation that put an emphasis on vernacular language, Pyarimohan devoted his energies to the Oriya language movement.[49]

Pyarimohan's Oriya nationalist and reformist Brahma leanings led his enemies at Cuttack – conservative Bengali Hindu service class men who had moved into town to work for the colonial administration – to accuse the work of being partisan. They wrote to newspapers, published and distributed pamphlets in the town, and appealed to local colonial authorities suggesting that *Odisara Itihasa* had hurt Hindu sentiments. Allegedly, the history entailed an inaccurate episode – made up by the author (*swakapolakalpita*) – of Muslim maltreatment of the Hindu deity Jagannatha in medieval times.[50] Public intellectuals in support of Pyarimohan dismissed the controversy as an unnecessary fracas (*gandagol*). They pointed out that the episode concerned was not a fabrication: it was drawn from several reliable histories including Sutton's *Itihasa Sarasangraha*.[51]

The colonial regime's response to this public controversy is revealing. Pyarimohan, as mentioned earlier, wrote *Odisara Itihasa* in response to an advertisement by the government to write a textbook on history. Prior to its publication in 1879, it had passed through elaborate official scrutiny, and had even won prize money from the government. After the controversy broke out, the government set up a committee to specifically look into the charges levelled against the work. Apparently, the committee dismissed the allegations. However, even then, an apprehensive colonial government refused to endorse *Odisara Itihasa* and decided not to induct the text in the school curriculum. Public intellectuals at Cuttack found the colonial decision incomprehensible. Here is a letter to the editor of the *Utkal Dipika*, the most prominent newspaper in the town:

> The education committee has decided that the allegations levelled against the history are baseless. Then why do not concerned authority induct it into school curriculum? We do not understand who might have what secret and godforsaken objections (*gupta srustichhada apatti*) to a book being inducted into school syllabuses that received prize money of three hundred rupees from the government, and that is widely appreciated as excellent in its accomplishments . . . ?[52]

The incomprehensibility of the decision to forsake *Odisara Itihasa* rested on an irony: the colonial regime promoted a genre of historiography that prized critical and disinterested pursuit truth as an ideal, but in practice, when pushed to pass a judgement, it was unable to endorse any pursuit of truth as adequately critical and disinterested.

Epilogue: of history and pedagogy

Students of George Eliot would know that this chapter has tried to comment on some of the 'Dear Reader' moments in three nineteenth-century history texts from the colonial town of Cuttack. It suggests that each narrative generates its meaning through a fulfilled teleology, which is the birth of a particular type of reader. At the same time, each of the texts is animated by a narrative logic where meaning lies in the impossibility of fixing the final events. Between the postulation and the impossibility of fixing the reader emerges insight into, I submit as a conclusion, the pedagogic nature of the practice of historiography in the town.

A pedagogic discourse operates, Roland Barthes suggests, under two constraints.[53] Barthes begins with the basic premise that teaching is fundamentally tied to speech: in a teaching situation, speech proceeds under two alternative constraints. On the one hand, the speaker may choose a role of authority and speak in compliance with the law, to serve the law. A good pedagogic speech is thus marked with clarity: *polysemy* is banished from the discourse. On the other hand, the speaker may precisely choose to undermine the task of laying out the law. He may choose the irreversibility of speech to disturb its legality. Speech is irreversible in the sense that a spoken word cannot be retracted, except precisely by saying that one retracts it. Thus, to cross out a speech is to add and supplement what has already been said. This correcting, improving and adding movement of speech is what the speaker may rely on to disturb the clear and authoritative legal message he is expected to deliver. Every speaker – not in what he says, but in the very fact of speech – essays the role of a policeman and lawgiver. This role is then rendered less disagreeable by a resort to the irreversibility of speech, into the infinitude of language. 'The teacher escapes', Barthes submits, 'neither the theatre of speech nor the Law played out on its stage.' That is, a pedagogic discourse, by its nature, operates under both the constraints: it lays out the law, and also proceeds to disturb it.

The practice of historiography at Cuttack is marked by these constraints of the pedagogic discourse: it lays out the law, and also proceeds, in a supplementary move reminiscent of speech as it were, to subvert the law. The narratives under discussion authoritatively lay out the image of the intended reader. The clarity of such declarations is also compromised by the supplement, and the excess that accompanies the images. Thus, the sympathetic reader is accompanied by an anxiety over its disappearance; the judicious reader is accompanied by an inability to reflect decisively on a precolonial tradition of Oriya historiography; and the disciplinary reader is accompanied by a sentimental reception. Not only the authoritative construction of the image of the intended reader but also the subverting supplement – both constitute the history of the European genre known as *history* in the colony.

In a teaching relationship, Barthes observes as he draws out a comparison with psychoanalysis, the teacher is the person who is analysed, not the student audience. As he puts out a discourse never knowing how that discourse is being received, the teacher is thus forever forbidden the reassurance of a definitive image that would constitute him. If he receives a response, he grows distrustful of it, dismissing it as a manifestation of complicity coming from imbeciles or flatterers. If he does not receive a response, he continues to glory in the solitude of his speech.

The discourse of historiography puts the colonial and evangelical regimes at Cuttack under analysis. What acquires clarity through the process is precisely the need these regimes experienced to indulge in pedagogy. Of the diverse genres of pedagogy these regimes produced and deployed in the town, given the serious patronage invested in it, historiography was the most relied upon. As pedagogues, the regimes are, however, forbidden the reassurance of definitive images that would constitute them. Pastoral historiography discourses on sympathy as the ideal mode of engaging with its narrative. However, it also displays remarkable anxiety over the deferral and possible disappearance of the sympathetic audience. In the teaching relationship he institutes, Amos Sutton, the evangelical historian, is caught up in the pedagogic position from where he would always find any response inadequately sympathetic. Colonial historiography discourses on a critical and disinterested pursuit of truth. However, the colonial regime is inevitably caught up in a pedagogic position where it finds no pursuit of truth adequately disinterested. It hesitates to arbitrate over the public controversy surrounding Pyarimohan's alleged partisanship, and chooses to dismiss the work *tout court*.

As a project of pedagogy, nineteenth-century historiography refers to certain ethical practices that the evangelical and colonial regimes cherished as *telos*. Cultivation of sympathy as an ideal way of experiencing the present and disinterested pursuit of truth as an ideal mode of engaging the past: these are some of the ethical practices that historiography promoted in the town of Cuttack. I have chosen the birth of the reader as a metaphor to describe what historiography aimed at. *Birth* is admittedly a late twentieth-century metaphor. Though both anticipate particular sorts of audience for their narratives, the two historians the paper discusses, Sutton and Pyarimohan, may not see their narratives as *giving birth* to specific types of readers. *Cultivation* or *education* might be the tropes more familiar to these Victorian authors: they may agree that their narratives contribute to the cultivation or education of certain types of readership. However, the *birth* metaphor, as opposed to the alternative tropes of *cultivation*, or *education*, serves to underscore, as it were, the messiness of the projects of pedagogy, the excesses that accompany the *telos*.

Notes

*   Siddharth Satpathy is grateful to Gaganendranath Dash and the members of the Working Group, History and Teleology: A Critical Assessment of an Enlightenment Thought for their comments on the chapter.
1. Franco Moretti, *The Way of the World: The Bildungsroman in European Culture*, London: Verso, 1987, pp. 7–8.

2. Amos Sutton, *Narrative of the Mission to Orissa, the Site of the Temple of Jugurnath*, Boston: David Marks, 1833; Amos Sutton, *History of the Mission to Orissa: The Site of the Temple of Juggernaut*, Philadelphia: American Sunday-School Union, 1835; Amos Sutton, *Orissa and its Evangelization Interspaced with Suggestions Respecting the More Efficient Conducting of Indian Missions*. Boston: W. Heath, 1850; James Peggs, *A History of the General Baptist Mission*, London: John Snow, 1846.

3. These markers and procedures often have older roots in Ecclesiastical Histories. For a discussion of these histories, see Anthony Grafton, *The Footnote: A Curious History*, Cambridge, Mass.: Harvard University Press, 1999; A. Momigliano, *The Classical Foundations of Modern Historiography*, Berkeley: University of California Press, 1990.

4. Sutton, *Narrative*, 'Introductory Remarks', p. viii.

5. Sutton, *Narrative*, 'Introductory Remarks', p. v.

6. Sutton, *Narrative*, 'Advertisement', pp. iii–iv.

7. Mark Salber Phillips, *Society and Sentiment: Genres of Historical Writing in Britain, 1740–1820*, Princeton: Princeton University Press, 2000. Especially see the chapters titled 'History, the Novel and the Sentimental Reader' and 'Biography and the History of Private Life,' pp. 102–28, 131–46.

8. Sutton, *Narrative*, pp. 419–20. The passage is reproduced in the *History of the Mission to Orissa*, p. 190.

9. Sutton, *Orissa and its Evangelization*, p. 395.

10. Sutton, *Narrative*, 'Introductory Remarks', p. viii.

11. Sutton, *Orissa and its Evangelization*, p. 393.

12. Michel de Certeau, *The Writing of History*, trans. Tom Conley, New York: Columbia University Press, 1988, p. 156.

13. De Certeau, *The Writing of History*, p. 152.

14. The inspector of schools was one Dr E. Roer, who also compiled a list of Sutton's works. For his comment on Sutton and the list of the latter's works see Smarana Kumara Nayaka, *Unabinsha Satabdira Odishaku Missionary Dr. Amos Suttonka Dana*, Cuttack: Jagannatha Ratha, 2011, pp. 72–3.

15. For the General Baptist philosophy of pedagogy see Sutton, *Orissa and its Evangelization*, pp. 271–89.

16. Rev. A. Sutton, *History of Urissa, with brief notices of Bengal, Upper India: Itihasa Sarasangraha, arthat Odishara Adi-bibarana-Samkshepa*, Calcutta: Calcutta School-Book Society Press [1846], 4th edn, 1866.

17. Gopal Chandra Praharaj, comp., *PurnachandraOrdia Bhashakosha*, Cuttack: Utkal Sahitya Press, 1936, vol. V, p. 5691.

18. See the chapter '*Odisa Desara Prachina Itihasa*' in *Itihasa Sarasangraha*. Consider the following passages: '*kalpita itihasara ascharya bakya jeunthare samapta huai, se sthanare satya itihasara arambha huai. Ehi nitanta bidhana janiba. Sabu desiya loka ahankari hoi, apanamananku ati prachina jati kari bikhyata hebaku banchha karanti matra semanankara jathartha charita lekha nathibaru semane nana prakara kalpana itihasa karanti*' ('Real history begins precisely where the wonderful statements of imaginary history comes to an end. Consider it as a necessary rule. People of all nations succumb to chauvinism, and desire to acquire fame as very ancient races. However, since they do not have proper histories written on them, they indulge in writing all sorts of imaginary history') (Sutton, *Itihasa Sarasangraha*, p. 3); '*ehi samkshepa brutantara padhua jebe ehipari bodha nakari odisara pothire lekhita*

bibaranaku grahya manai, tebe bibechana karibaku uchita jeun raja manankara nama odisha deshara rajavalire lekha hela, sehi nama sabu hindustan jaka praya sabu kshudra bada raja charitrare lekha achhi' ('If the reader of this short account [Sutton's *Itihasa*] does not think like this, and is inclined to accept what is written in the palm leaf chronicles of Orissa as plausible, then he must [take the following into careful consideration and] judge dispassionately. The names of the kings mentioned in the royal chronicles of Orissa also find mention in almost all the royal chronicles, high and low, slim and voluminous, all over Hindustan' (ibid., p. 6).

19. Praharaj, Comp., *PurnachandraOrdia Bhashakosha*, Vol III, p. 3308.
20. '*ehi sabu pustakara bibarana ana bhasare lekhita charitra sangare tauli ehi samkshepa brutanta prapta huai. Enu kebala jeun kathaku satya ki aba sambhaba mani taha ethire lekha jae*' (Sutton, *Itihasa Sarasangraha*, p. 7).
21. Sutton, *Itihasa Sarasangraha*, p. 17.
22. Sutton, *Itihasa Sarasangraha*, p. 23.
23. Writing in the third decade of the twentieth century, historian Krupasindhu Mishra retains the framework of decline: 'It will be written, in due course, how this vast empire of Utkal got gradually reduced and became the present day Orissa.' Krupasindhu Mishra, *Utkala Itihasa*, Kataka: Granthamandira, 2010, p. 3. The original in Oriya reads, '*ehi bishala Utkala rajya chidi chidi kipari bartamana Odisare parinata hela taha prasanga krame lekha jiba*.'
24. Sutton, *Itihasa Sarasangraha*, p. 20.
25. Sutton, *Itihasa Sarasangraha*, p. 21.
26. A typical appeal would read, '*Nirmala Visnura charita, Krusna bisaya Bhagabata / Sujanankara hite, kahai dasa Jagannathe*'; '*Suna sakala muni jana, sadhu e tumbhara bachana / parama mangala e bani, jiva nistare jaha suni.*' Jagannatha Dasa, *Shrimadbhagavata*, Nilamani Mishra, comp., Bhubaneswar: Odisha Sahitya Akademi, 2006, First–Second Canto, pp. 6–7.
27. Dinakrusna Dasa, *Rasakallola*, ed. Bansidhar Mohanty, Cuttack: Friends Publishers, 2013, Sixth Edition. The original in Oriya reads, '*Kobide, kale se antara hoila / kandarpa darpa rahita hoi sakha abhabe hrudare soila*' (Canto 15, Quatrain 7) (author's translation).
28. Dinakrusna, *Rasakallola*. The original in Oriya reads, '*Kabi ja kare murkhaku stuti, ethiru bali nahin bipatti*' (Canto 16, Verse 29) (author's translation).
29. Upendra Bhanja, *Rasika Harabali*. Quoted in Surendra Mohanty, *Odiya Sahityara Madhyaparva O Uttara Madhyaparva*, Cuttack: Cuttack Students' Store, p. 282. The original in Oriya reads, '*Kara e karuna bijna hastagate, e pustaka mora hoiba / ajna samuhara kuharaku, kebehen prabesha nohiba*' (author's translation).
30. I am indebted to Prof. Gaganendranath Dash for pointing out the couplet to me. Upendra Bhanja, *Koti Brahmanda Sundari*, Cuttack: Dharmagrantha Store, [n.d.]. The Original in Oriya reads, '*nana sabadare je bichakshana, jehu jane alankara lakshana / sehi karu e chhanda bibechana, balya pauganda jaubana rachana*' (Canto 3, Quatrain 1) (author's translation).
31. Sutton, *Itihasa Sarasangraha*, '*Mahabharat, Ramayana jebe Hindumanankara nija mula bibarana pothi janiba, tebe tahinre Hindujatira mula puni Hindustanre adya prabesibara, puni krame krame desaku jayakari sarbatra byapibara ityadi brutanta bibarana ati alpa katha prapta huai*' (pp. 6–7).
32. Velcheru Narayana Rao, David Shulman and Sanjay Subrahmanyam, *Textures of Time: Writing History in South India 1600–1800*, Delhi: Permanent Black, 2001, pp. 120–30. For the tradition of historiography associated with the temple of Jagannatha at Puri, see Gaganendranath Dash and Ranjan Kumar Das, *Jagannatha and the Gajapati Kings of Orissa: A Compendium of Late Medieval Texts*, New Delhi: Manohar Publishers and Distributors, 2010.

33. Sutton, *Itihasa Sarasangraha*, 'Ehipari jadyapi sabu Hindumane desara charitra puni nijara brutanta lekhibara hela kari achhanti tebehen Odisha brahmana mane sabutharu una dosi atanti jehetu praya chaudasa barasabadhi semane madalapanji rajacharitra boli pustakare nana bansavali pothire nanabidha prachina bibarana katha lekhichanti' (p. 7).

34. Sutton, *Itihasa Sarasangraha*, 'Anamana huai satya brutanta nathibaru kesharivamsa rajamanankara upasthita heba jaen charitrare jeun phanka thae taha purna kariba pain kavimane esabu kathaku kalpana kari aba paramparagata katha dhari rachile. Masihara 473 barasare kesharivamsa Ankara arambha huai puni taha age odisa desara biswasa jogya charitra bartamana samayare prapta na huai' (p. 6).

35. Andrew Sterling, *Orissa: Its Geography, Statistics, History, Religion, and Antiquities*, London: John Snow, 1846; W. W. Hunter, *Orissa: or the Vicissitudes of an Indian Province under Native and British Rule*, London: Smith, Elder & Co., 1872; George Toynbee, *A Sketch of the History of Orissa from 1803 to 1828*, Prafulla: Jagatsinghpur, Orissa, [1873] 2005. Sterling's history was first serialized in *Asiatic Researches* XV (1825). See Gourangacharana Dasha, 'Odishara Itihasa Charcha: Pyarimohan Acharya,' in Vijayananda Simha, ed., *Konarka: Aitihasika Pyarimohan Acharya Bisesanka*, Bhubaneswar: Odisha Sahitya Akademi, vol. 131, November–January 2004, p. 54.

36. Pyarimohan Acharya, *Odisara Itihasa*, comp. Sk. Matlub Ali, Cuttack: Orissa Book Store, 3rd edn, 1991.

37. 'Odisara Itihasa', *Utkal Dipika*, 20 September 1879. Quoted in full in Gourangacharana Dasha, 'Odishara Itihasa Charcha: Pyarimohan Acharya,' pp. 67–8. The original in Oriya reads, 'Odia bhasare odisara itihasa adau nathila kahile atyukti heba nahi. Karana Sutton sahebanka sankalita pustaka kebala namamatra itihasa atai.'

38. Pyarimohan Acharya, *Odisara Itihasa*, 'Bhumika', pp. kha–ga (2–3).

39. Bhuvaneswar Datta, *Model Questions on Oriya Literature: Sahitya Bisayaka Adarshaprasnavali*, Cuttack: Cuttack Printing Company, 1879. Bhola Nath De, Haris Chundra Sarkar, *Model Questions, History of India: Adarsha Prasnavali, Bharatavarshara Itihasa*. Balasore: Dwarka Nath De, 1879. Especially see the 'Bhumika' and 'Bijnapana' sections in the respective volumes.

40. Bhuvaneswar Datta, *Model Questions on Oriya Literature*, 'Sikshakamananka prati katipaya upadesha.'

41. Dipesh Chakrabarty locates the emergence of history as an academic discipline in India in the early twentieth century: it began to be taught as a university subject at postgraduate level only after the First World War. However, history seems to have had a robust life in colonial pre-university education through the last quarter of the nineteenth century. I would argue that as a subject taught in schools it had already acquired a remarkable degree of self-consciousness precisely about its disciplinary status that hinged on methods of enquiry by the turn of the century. See Dipesh Chakrabarty, 'The Public Life of History: An Argument out of India,' in *Postcolonial Studies* 11 (2008), no. 2, pp. 169–90.

42. Grafton, *Footnote*; see the chapter 'Footnotes: The Origin of a Species', pp. 22–4.

43. Pyarimohan Acharya, *Odisara Itihasa*, p. 24.

44. Pyarimohan, *Odisara Itihasa*, 'bartamana inrejanka sasanare odisa basie unnati o sabhyata digaku gati bistara karunchanti. Jatia sahityara gathana punaraya aarambha hoichi. Bidyalochana or jnanacharcha dinaku dina bruddhi ki prapta hoichi . . . ki sikshita ki asikshita dui sampradaya madhyare bartaman bisuddhatara dharmara aalochana arabdha hoichi . . . mudrajantramana sthapita hoiachhi. Sambadpatramana prakashita hoi o sabhamana sthapita hoi ki rajaniti, ki samajika, ki dharmaniti sabu bisayare alochana heuachhi. Se sabu dwara ruchi Madhya dinaku dina parimarjita heuachhi. Loke artha samchaya o dhanabruddhi prati sutaram krusi o banijya prati adhika drusti nikshepa kariachhanti. E samasta subha lakshana. Samkshepatah chari adaku anaile bartaman kebala ashara chinha dekha jaae' (p. 179).

45. Pyarimohan, *Odisara Itihasa*, 'Iswaranka krupa hele ambhamananankara unnata aryabhrata inrejanka sahajyare ambhamananka deshara mukhashri samujvala heba' (p. 179).

46. 'Odisara Itihasa', *Utkal Dipika*, 20 September 1879. Quoted in full in Gourangacharana Dasha, 'Odishara Itihasa Charcha: Pyarimohan Acharya'.

47. 'Prapta granthara samalochana: Odisara Itihasa babu Pyarimohan Acharyanka pranita,' *Baleswar Samvad Bahika*, 9 February 1880. Quoted in full in Gourangacharana Dasha, 'Odishara Itihasa Charcha: Pyarimohan Acharya', pp. 76–7. The original in Oriya reads: '*bisesatah prachina odisara bisayamana ethire emanta sundara rupe bibruta hoiachhi sethiprati drustipata kale mukta kanthare swikara karibaku heba je, unnata ebam apekshakruta marjita bangala bhasare suddha epari itihasa birala lakshita hue. Samsita pustaka patha dwara odisabasira atma gauraba bardhita heba ebam saadhu ahamkara sahita semane utkala santana boli aapanaku bhagyabaan boli manibe.*'

48. Pyarimohan Acharya, *Odisara Itihasa*, ed. Viswanatha Kara, 'Dvitiya Sanskarana Bhumika,' p. cha (6). Quoted in full by Sk. Matlub Ali in edition cited (n. 36 above).

49. Devendra Kumara Dasha, 'Charoti Patra: Brahma Dharma O Pyarimohan,' in Vijayananda Simha, ed., *Konarka: Aitihasika Pyarimohan Acharya Bisesanka*, Bhubaneswar: Odisha Sahitya Akademi, vol. 131, November–January 2004, p. 146.

50. 'Kalibabunka Gandagol', *Utkal Dipika*, 10 April 1880. 'Prerita Patra', *Utkal Dipika*, 8 May 1880. Quoted in full in Gourangacharana Dasha, 'Odishara Itihasa Charcha: Pyarimohan Acharya,' pp. 71–2, 75–6.

51. See Sutton's comments on the *kalapahad* episode in section 7 of this chapter.

52. 'Prerita Patra', *Utkal Dipika*, 8 May 1880. Quoted in full length in Gourangacharana Dasha, 'Odishara Itihasa Charcha: Pyarimohan Acharya', p. 75. The original in Oriya reads: '*Itihasa prati jeu sabu apatti hoithila taha amulaka boli siksha kamitire sthira hoiachi. Tebe kartrupakhiyamane kahinki e pustakaku skulre chalau nahanti? Jeun pustaka pranayana nimante gabarnment tini saha tanka puraskara dele o jahaku utkrusta grantha boli samaste mata dele . . . se pustakaku pathya pustaka karibare kahara ki gupta srustichada apatti achhi taha ambhemane bujhiparu nahun.*'

53. Roland Barthes, *Image Music Text: Essays selected and translated by Stephen Heath*, London: Fontana Press, 1977. I refer to the essay 'Writers, Intellectuals, Teachers', pp. 190–215.

CHAPTER 8
A GIFT OF PROVIDENCE: DESTINY AS NATIONAL HISTORY IN COLONIAL INDIA
Dipesh Chakrabarty

'On this occasion of your 86th birthday,' wrote Sir Jadunath Sarkar (1870–1958), the pre-eminent historian of Mughal India in the first half of the twentieth century, addressing his life-long friend, Govindrao Sakharam Sardesai (1865–1959), a historian based in Pune, Maharashtra, 'I have given the finishing touches to the last chapter of my *Fall of the Mughal Empire* and sent it to the press.' This was written on the night of 15 May 1950. The letter is well known to Sarkar scholars but is worth quoting at some length for it expresses the tragic passion of a particular variety of nationalist historical thought that I will characterize here as 'providentialism'. Sarkar continued in his letter:

> I can say that I have written it, not with ink, but with my heart's blood. In saying so, I am not thinking of personal sorrows and anxieties – which have clouded the evening of my day, nor of the minute study and exhausting labour that had to be devoted to the subject in this terrible summer heat, – but of the subject-matter of the last chapters, – the imbecility and vices of our rulers, the cowardice of their generals, and the selfish treachery of their ministers. It is a tale which makes every true son of India hang his head in shame. . . .[1]

The 1932 foreword to the first edition of the first volume of Sarkar's *Fall of the Mughal Empire* provides a clue to understanding what it was about India's Mughal past that made Sarkar feel so sad. In that volume Sarkar described that empire of the Mughals as having 'broke[n] down the isolation of the provinces and the barrier between India and the outer world, and [having] thus [taken] . . . the first step necessary for the modernization of India and the growth of an Indian nationality in some distant future'.[2] But this future was not to be. True, the Mughals had united a fragmented polity. 'It must be admitted', he wrote as he brought his multi-volume *Fall* to a conclusion, 'that the Mughal Emperors united many provinces of India into one political unit, with uniformity of official language, administrative machinery, coinage and public service, and indeed a common type of civilization for the higher classes. They also recognized it as a duty to preserve peace and the reign of law throughout their dominions.'[3] What was remarkable for Sarkar about the Mughals was that it was their rule that initially prepared the country for a movement in this direction:

> Administrative and cultural uniformity was given to nearly the whole of this continent of a country; the artery roads were made safe for the trader and the

traveler; the economic resources of the land were developed; and a profitable intercourse was opened with the outer world. With peace, wealth, and enlightened Court patronage, came a new cultivation of the Indian mind and advance of Indian literature, painting, architecture and handicrafts, which raised this land once again to the front rank of the civilized world. Even the formation of an Indian nation did not seem an impossible dream.[4]

Yet, Sarkar wrote at the end of his study of Aurangzeb, 'Aurangzib did not attempt such an ideal [of nation-making], even though his subjects formed a very composite population . . . and he had no European rivals hungrily watching to destroy his kingdom. On the contrary, he deliberately undid the beginnings of . . . a national and rational policy which Akbar had set on foot.'[5]

At first sight, statements lamenting the alleged failure of the Mughals to build a nation-state in India could appear anachronistic to the modern reader, for there is no indication that the Mughals actually ever wanted to transform India into a nation or that the word 'nation' in its nineteenth- or twentieth-century sense would have even meant anything to them. But such a judgement would be too hasty. What I want to bring out in this essay is a particular form of *telos*-thinking that actually undergirded Sarkar's position. This was the idea of providence. It had a very significant impact on the historical imagination of Indian nationalists during British rule. It did not make for any inexorable sense of teleology and yet could make the idea of the 'nation' the end point of their historical vision without making the vision in any sense inevitable. Central to the idea of providence, I will also try to show, was another European idea, that of character.

1. Providence and Indian history

Rooted in Christian thought, the idea of Providence and its importance to human history was championed in the nineteenth century by none other than Leopold von Ranke.[6] 'History when rightly read', Sarkar also wrote, opening the concluding paragraph of his five-volume study of Aurangzeb in 1924, 'is a justification of Providence, the revelation of a great purpose fulfilled in time.'[7] What was this purpose? It was for India to become a self-governing modern nation. Ideally, Sarkar would have liked it if the process had completed itself *before* British rule – in the seventeenth and eighteenth centuries. His wish for the eighteenth century was that Indians had been rational, nationalistic and united enough to learn from Europeans (in areas where the latter were genuinely superior), so as to foil their attempt to take control of India. It was a matter of profound and lasting sorrow to him that 'a union of hearts between Sindhia and Holkar [two leading Maratha leaders], which alone could threaten danger to British Power . . . was an impossibility.'[8] The charge of helping India realize her destiny then fell to the British. Sarkar returned to this thought in 1950 while composing the last few sentences of the fourth and final volume of his *Fall*:

Modern India has become an independent, fully sovereign state. That political evolution has been made possible only by British imperialism. This is the reason why the noblest sons of India, like Bankim Chandra Chatterji, Dr. Prafulla Chandra Roy, and Gopal Krishna Gokhalé, have recognised a divine dispensation in the fall of the Mughal Empire, as looked at from before and behind.[9]

But India had a long way to go before it could meet with its destiny. As late as 1928, Sarkar was of the opinion that the process for creating the 'necessary basis for nationality' had 'just begun' in India and 'its completion [was] yet far off.'[10]

Sarkar was by no means alone in taking a providentialist view of British rule. The tradition of providentialist thinking by Indians goes back at least to the early part of the nineteenth century. Rammohun Roy (1772/4–1833), the putative 'father of modern India', expressed his hope that 'through Divine Providence and human exertions' the 'advocates of idolatry' would one day 'avail themselves' of a 'true [and non-idolatrous] system of religion.'[11] Decades later, Rabindranath Tagore, writing at the height of the Swadeshi (nationalist) movement (c.1905) in Bengal, underlined the idea again by referring to the greater purpose that revealed itself through the British domination of India:

Like the ambassador of the lord of all ceremonies [*jaggeshvar*], England has forced herself right into our homes by breaking down our old and creaking doors in order to stir up in us a spirit of initiative that [would make us realize] that we also were needed in the world . . .

Tagore did not think independence was even possible until this destiny had been fulfilled: 'We will not have the strength to expel the English by force until we have responded to their invitation, until our union with them has achieved its results. England has been sent for the sake of the India that, having germinated in the past, is now sprouting towards the future.'[12]

Or consider the point that the twentieth-century nationalist leader and writer Chittranjan Das made as part of his presidential address to the Indian National Congress's annual session held in Gaya in December 1922. Das spoke on 'Non-Co-Operation and Council Entry'. 'Throughout the pages of Indian history,' he said, 'I see a great purpose unfolding itself. Movement after movement has swept over this vast country, apparently creating hostile forces, but in reality stimulating the vitality and moulding the life of the people into one great nationality.'[13]

In the secular form in which the originally Christian idea of divine providence circulated among Hindu-Indian nationalist thinkers, it became deeply tied to another originally European idea: that of civilization, the idea that there was a specific, Indian civilization and that India's historic destiny was to give it the form of the nation.[14] Listen, again, to Chittaranjan Das:

Now what is nationalism? It is, I believe, a process through which a nation expresses itself and finds itself, not in isolation from other nations, not in opposition to other nations, but as part of a great scheme by which, in seeking its own expression and therefore its own identity, it materially assists the self-expression and self-realization of other nations as well … [E]ach nationality constitutes a stream of the great unity, but no nation can fulfill itself unless and until it becomes itself and at the same time realizes its identity with Humanity. The whole problem of nationalism is therefore to find that stream and to face that destiny.

Since destiny was civilizational, a nation's 'becoming itself' was also a matter of being able to infuse the process of modernization with its own distinct sense of a being a civilization. Das therefore concluded: 'If you find the current and establish a continuity with the past, then the process of self-expression has begun, and nothing can stop the growth of nationality.'[15] Tagore made a very similar point in the essay cited above, invoking Rammohun Roy:

The main reason why Rammohun Roy was able to absorb Western thoughts was that he was never overwhelmed by the West. There was no weakness on his side. He stood on a firm ground of his own in order to acquire from the outside [world]. He knew where Indian treasures lay and had made them his own. He therefore possessed the measures and the balancing instrument with which to judge whatever he found.[16]

Sarkar's providentialist position, then, was that India was destined to become a nation, for that was the way peoples in the world had been moving since the seventeenth century. Nationalism, properly constituted, could act as the vehicle that took the nation to its tryst with destiny. The later Mughals failed in this mission in spite of their forebears' having laid down the basis of nationhood. They were either incurious about the scientific spirit of modern Europe, or their interest in this new knowledge was superficial. 'The mere copying of the externals of European civilisation, without undergoing a new birth of spirit, cannot produce a renaissance,' wrote Sarkar:

It only led to the growth of the Anglo-Muslim culture of the Oudh Nawab's Court, which was a bastard sprout producing no flowers or fruit. In it the inner spirit of modern civilization was wanting … No modern literature took its birth at the Lucknow royal court; the picture and poetry it produced were mostly pornographic; Asaf-ud-daula used to eat 64 grains of the strongest Turkish opium every day. His successor, Sadat Ali, knew English and a little French too, but turned out on the throne to be a drunkard …[17]

'The Indian Renaissance' of the nineteenth century under British rule was possible 'only because a principle was discovered' that had not been discovered in Mughal times. It was one by which 'India could throw herself into the full current of modern civilization in the outer world without totally discarding her past'. True, she was an 'impoverished cousin of Europe', but 'India was not called upon to plume herself in the borrowed feathers of European civilization' – all she had to do was 'to assimilate modern thought and modern arts into her inner life without any loss of what she had long possessed'.[18] The Mughals, Sarkar would often say, had no curiosity about print, modern science or institutions such as the academy or the university.

2. Not anachronism

Providential thinking was not the same as anachronistic thinking; nor was it deterministically teleological. There was no provision in it, for example, for something like the Hegelian 'cunning of reason' that triumphed over human folly and ignorance and set the world right in the end. While the 'great purpose' of national history revealed itself through historical events, the purpose depended on self-conscious human action for its realization. The Mughals, the Rajputs and the Marathas and their likes in the seventeenth and eighteenth centuries needed to be more curious about the sciences and the institutions of Europe, but they lacked the requisite character, both collectively and in their individual leaders. 'India had ceased to produce leaders, with the sole exception of Mahadji Sindhia.' The task was unfinished even in 1947, when India became a sovereign nation-state but – to Sarkar's mind – not yet a nation. For a 'necessary condition' of 'democratic government or true nationhood' was 'a long course of preparation or practical education and a surging up of the masses in search of a new political ideal'. This process, interrupted since Aurangzeb, was restarted by the British, but even England 'failed to form a nation in India' while unwittingly putting in place much of the basic framework needed to make it successful. 'When the British resigned their trusteeship for India in 1947,' writes Sarkar, using the tell-tale word 'trusteeship', 'they had failed to give the Indian people a political education which would enable them to stand on their own feet', for 'two successive deluges of world-wars within 30 years of each other upset all former political speculations and prophecies, and forced the hands of the rulers and the ruled in India'.[19] The British left India before India could be fully prepared to assume the responsibilities of nationhood, something Sarkar thought was at the root of the problems the country faced at independence: partition, corruption and other evils. 'But all this', he consoled himself, 'will pass away, if only we are vouchsafed by the kind heaven fifty years of peace and strong and wise hands at the helm of India's government. Then England's marvelous achievement in India will be appraised in a just balance, in peace of mind, all passion spent.'[20]

3. Character mediates destiny

What mediated between the 'destiny' of a people and the contingency of their empirical reality, in Sarkar's view, was 'character', the sheer capacity in humans for leadership, discipline, effort, reason, mastering passions and self-cultivation. It was what separated destiny from fate and left the former open to multiple possibilities. Take away the question of character, and the revealed greater purpose in human history remains unfulfilled.

'Character' was a keystone concept in the architecture of Sarkar's political thought. It determined a country or kingdom's success or failure at embracing the modern world created by the expansion of Europe. Character was thus both a moral and a political word, signifying a zone of human freedom within the structure of providence, creating space for human drama and action. It was therefore also a literary device. The centrality of 'character' to Sarkar's texts takes us back to the question of his intimate relationship to the imperial literary canon, for he was, after all, a teacher of English literature.[21]

'Shah Alam's character *alone* was responsible for the fate that now overwhelmed him and his house,' wrote Sarkar, referring to the situation in Delhi months before the Afghan Ghulam Qadir invaded the royal residence in Delhi in 1788 to torture and blind Emperor Shah Alam II, violate women of the royal family, and loot their wealth. The emperor, in Sarkar's judgement, 'had no strength of character, energy or even personal courage, [and] was bound to pass his life under the tutelage of some cleverer brain or stronger will.'[22] Later Sarkar said, in a more nuanced voice, that while

> the Padishah was extremely weak and inconstant . . . [he] was not treacherous nor incapable of right thinking. He only lacked firmness of purpose and the capacity for action. . . . Hence with all his intelligence, his daily study of scripture and history, . . . he only proved another example of how cowards die many times before their death.[23]

That quotation from Shakespeare in the last sentence of this quote – obviously too familiar to be acknowledged – is a key to Sarkar's thinking on character. It is true that he borrowed much from contemporary sources when it came to describing individuals. But 'character' for Sarkar belonged to a liberal form of thought the British Empire in India had encouraged. In that, it was probably different from what historians of Mughal times may have understood by corresponding words in Persian that European scholars translated as 'character'. Potentially, anybody could acquire strength of character, for 'character' implied sovereignty over self. It was like virtue: it needed to be cultivated. It was a measure of sovereignty because in it lay one's destiny; one became the maker of one's own fate by imbibing character. As Sarkar said – again, of Shah Alam – and with further unacknowledged but obvious debt to Shakespeare: 'No man can rise above his destiny as the wise of the ancient days have truly said. Destiny is only another name for character, and Shah Alam's character alone was responsible for the fate that now overwhelmed him and his house.'[24] One source for the idea that character was destiny was the philosophy of Heraclitus, who said, in the much discussed 119th of his *Fragments*, 'Man's character is his daimon [sometimes translated 'destiny'].'[25] Heraclitus may not have been unknown to Sarkar and other Indian thinkers, for the nationalist 'sage' Aurobindo published six commentaries on Heraclitus in the journal *Arya* between 1916 and 1917, responding not only to Nietzsche's discussion of the philosopher but also to a 'small treatise' that an Indian professor, R. D. Ranade, had published in India on the ancient Greek philosopher.[26] But it is more likely that Sarkar, being a teacher of English literature, got the idea more immediately from his readings of Shakespeare – from famous lines such as 'The fault, dear Brutus, is not in our stars but in ourselves' that Indian students were often expected to commit to memory.²⁷ Sarkar's own expectation that his reader would be familiar with the Bard comes through even in the way he explained the expression '*domni-bachcha*' – 'son of the lowest caste dancing girl' – with which Ghulam Qadir abused Prince Akbar Shah, 'the heir to Shah Alam's throne'. Sarkar described the invective to his reader as something similar to 'Falstaff's favourite epithet'.²⁸

As readers make their way through the first volume of Sarkar's *Fall*, 'character' – or the lack of it in late-Mughal India – dominates the props with which Sarkar sets the scene for his larger narrative to unfold. The book opens with a short note that mentions that while Sarkar's narrative begins in 1738, the 'unperceived origin and gradual spread of the moral decay' and a 'step by step' account of 'how the poison worked in the body politic of the Delhi empire' had been detailed in Sarkar's earlier multi-volume work on Aurangzeb and elsewhere. But the 'dry rot' that destroyed the empire from within in the eighteenth century clearly had something to do with the run of 'weaklings and imbeciles' on the throne of Delhi. At the root of this 'moral canker' was the question of the character of the ruler: 'A nemesis worked itself out inexorably on the destiny of the Empire from the character of the Emperor and his leading ministers'.²⁹

Sarkar's indictment of Muhammad Shah, for example, who ascended the throne in Delhi in 1719 at the age of 17, is all about the emperor's lack of a statesmanlike character:

> He possessed natural intelligence and a good deal of foresight; but ... [events] crushed any desire that he might have once had to rule for himself and to keep his nobles under control. He ... plunged into a life of pleasure and amusement ... of inactivity and sexual excess [that] soon impaired his constitution and he became a confirmed invalid by the time he was only forty.³⁰

Sarkar's 'facts' about, say, the slothfulness or diligence of particular rulers came, naturally, from the sources he used. For instance, while writing of the 'nemesis that worked itself ... on the destiny of the Empire', Sarkar referred, though only just, to a text by Muhammad Bakhsh, a foster brother of the emperor – *Tarikh-i-Shahadat-i-Farrukhsiyar wa Jalus-i-Muhammad* – preserved at the India Office Library.³¹ Even the image of the 'dry rot' through which Sarkar attempted to convey something of his assessment of Mughal rulers in the eighteenth century did not originate with him. For example, *Seir Mutaqherin*, the well-known Persian history written in the early 1780s by a Syed Gholam Hossein Khan, 'a Moslem Nobleman' belonging to 'the Court of the Nawabs of Bengal, Behar and Orissa', used exactly this image to describe the weakening of 'foundations of the Delhi monarchy' under the rule of the emperor Muhammad Shah (1702–48; r. 1719–20; 1720–48). Gholam Hossein's expression (at least in translation) was 'really rotten'.³²

It was not only Sarkar who owed his damning facts about weaknesses in the ruler's character to his Persian sources; so did his mentor and predecessor, the colonial administrator-historian William Irvine, in his book *Later Mughals*, edited and published by Sarkar after Irvine's death.³³ Could one argue, then, that more than being influenced by European ideas about character, Sarkar and Irvine derived their judgement from the very Persian sources they used? There is no question that they sometimes did so. Thus, Gholam Hossein's criticism of Farrukhsiyar – Aurangzeb's grandson (1683–1719), who occupied the throne between 1713 and 1719 – was scathing; it could easily have found a place in Sarkar's narrative (if Sarkar had covered the period) or in Irvine's. 'Feroh-syur had neither the extent of genius, nor the firmness of temper, nor the keenness of penetration, requisite in an Emperor ... He was low-spirited, and homely-minded, as well as sordidly inclined,' wrote Hossein. Irvine's judgement was not much different: 'He was strong neither for evil nor for good ... feeble, false, cowardly, contemptible.'[34]

4. Character as a historiographical category

The category of 'character' in Sarkar or Irvine had the nature of a palimpsest.[35] There was no question that Sarkar or Irvine often shared the mood and sometimes even the biases of their sources. But, historiographically speaking, they were also heirs to an English tradition of historical narratives that included separate sections on the 'character' of particular kings and queens, a tradition that appears to go back to the seventeenth century. Sir Richard Baker's *Chronicle of the Kings of England* (1643), which combined 'native chronicle traditions' with 'the newer politically oriented approach that reached England through Machiavelli and continental historians and ultimately through Tacitus', is said to have followed Suetonius in including discussions of the kind under sections like 'Of his personage and condition' or 'Of men of note in his time'.[36] By the end of the eighteenth century, an author named John Holt had published a large compendium of sketches of royal 'characters' culled from a variety of historical narratives for use in schools for the benefit of youth.[37] This tradition was overlaid by a Victorian sense of character as something one could acquire through sheer dedication and effort. The layers in the composite category 'character' did not always sit easily with one another, for the early-modern preference for 'birth and nobility' did not jibe with the Victorian idea of 'self-help'. But even after taking all these different qualifications into account, one can identify at least four features that distinguished Sarkar's use of the word 'character' in his narratives from the way early-modern Indian historians used it.

i. A motive force of history

For Sarkar or Irvine or others writing in the traditions of European historiography, 'character' was an abstract but determinate motive force of history. What I mean is something like this: Sarkar and Irvine would have held that that the character of rulers and of members of the ruling households determined, causally, the course of their histories. India's precolonial historians would not have held this kind of sociological and abstract view of character. This is not to say that precolonial Muslim historians did not see individuals as characters. They did, and they sometimes even saw a particular person's character as contributing to the person's rise or downfall. They sometimes even saw, with reason, particular administrative or strategic gains or lapses as emanating from the strengths or weaknesses of an individual king's character; and modern historians such as Irvine and Sarkar occasionally borrow those earlier historians' opinions and observations. Sarkar, for example, consciously echoes Gholam Hossein, the author of *Seir* (also called the *Siyar*), when he writes of Nasir Khan, the *subahdar* (provincial governor) of Kabul around 1709/10, that he was a 'simple-minded and indolent man' whose 'chief business was hunting' and who was therefore unfit to defend Kabul against Nadir Shah's aggression.[38] Or Irvine himself would mix his language with that of late-Mughal historians to write: 'Contemporaries concur in asserting that, although Muhammad Murad had liberality (*sakhawat*) and kindliness (*maruvvat*), he had not the talent (*hausla*) required in a *Wazir*, or even a great noble. Nor was he valorous.'[39] So the point is not that Mughal historians did not work with ideas about character. But their comments were embedded in discussions of particular individuals and situations; they did not see character itself as an abstract and motive force of history in general.

ii. An analytical category

Character, then, was also an independent analytical category for colonial historians of Sarkar's or Irvine's ilk. Irvine would actually set aside a section in nearly every chapter under the heading 'character' and thus abstract characterological comments from the flow of particular narratives. *Later Mughals* has sections explicitly devoted to the discussion of the 'characters' of different emperors and nobles of Delhi: Bahadur Shah, Jahandar Shah, Farrukhsiyar, the Sayyid brothers, and so on.[40] Sarkar would do the same. He would say of the Rajput rajas of Jaipur and Marwar: 'A study of the characters of the chief actors in this tragic drama will help us to understand the course of events better.'[41] Chapter 7 of the first volume of his *Fall of the Mughal Empire* began with a section entitled 'Emperor Ahmad Shah: His Character'.[42] His *History of Aurangzib* had pages devoted to discussing the character of Dara Shikoh, Murad Baksh and others. Sarkar said in writing about the *Wazir* Intizam-ud-daulah's conflict with the Bakshi Safdar Jang that ultimately undid the rule of Emperor Ahmad Shah (r. 1748–54): '[t]he character of these two chiefs made such a catastrophe as inevitable as the working of destiny.'[43]

In completing William Irvine's *Later Mughals* and writing the final few chapters, Sarkar stated the point as a general principle. He asked: 'Why did the seemingly flourishing State of Aurangzeb fall down like a house of cards only 31 years after his death?'[44] His answer, firstly, was 'a startling decline in the character of the nobility', but this decline 'of the Mughal nobility' was 'mainly due to the decline in the character of the Emperor.' Sarkar does not rest there. The idea of character, taken in abstraction, was such an important category in Sarkar's histories of Mughal India: it was a shorthand for a certain theory of sovereignty that provided the mainstay of Sarkar's narrative.

Consider how the connection between 'character' and 'sovereignty' works itself out in Sarkar's logic. The character of the nobility in late Mughal times suffered because of a decline in the quality of the character of the emperors. Why? 'Because', Sarkar explains, 'it is *the first duty of a sovereign*, to choose the right sort of servants and give them opportunities for developing their talent and acquiring experience by instructing and supervising them during administrative apprenticeship.' The very crisis of the late Mughal empire lay in the nobles' finding that 'career was not open to talent, that loyal and useful service was no security against capricious dismissal and degradation'.[45] The theme of character in Sarkar thus leads back to some general ideas about modernity. Throughout his entire writing career, Sarkar judged the Indian kings he wrote about – Aurangzeb, Shivaji, the later Mughals, Maratha leaders like Mahadji Sindhia – by this standard of sovereignty. A good sovereign ran a government open to talents and did not cater to the prejudices of any single religious group or caste or an ethnic collectivity. Sarkar considered this particularly important in the case of a country as diverse internally as India.

iii. As indicator of social status

Another major difference between Sarkar's or Irvine's use of the word 'character' and its use by earlier historians was that 'character' signified a high/low distinction of social status in what Mughal or precolonial Muslim historians wrote about political rule. However pragmatic and 'liberal' Akbar or Jahangir or Muslim emperors before them may have been in their recruitment of nobles, they lived and ruled in a society where all Muslim theorists of sovereignty emphasized the difference between the low-born and the high-born and claimed the capacity to rule for the high-born only. This is not to say that in reality only the high-born ruled, but the distinction between the high and the low remained of critical importance to the theorists of rule in precolonial Muslim India. Thus, Ziauddin Barani's *Fatawa-i Jahandari* (c.1358–9) claimed:

> As excellences have been put into those who have adopted the nobler professions, they alone are capable of virtues ... *These groups alone are worthy of offices and posts in the government* ... On the other hand, the low-born, who have been enrolled for practicing the baser arts and meaner professions, are capable only of vices ... The promotion of the low and the low-born brings no advantage in this world, for it is impudent to act against the wisdom of Creation.[46]

Muhammad Baqir Najm-i Sani's *Mauaizah-i Jahangiri*, a book of advice for kings, produced in Jahangir's time – around 1612/13 – expressed similar sentiments: 'Rulers should not place incompetent and low-born (*bad-gauhar*) people on the same footing with a high-born [person] (*asil*) and prudent persons of pure extraction.'[47] In fact, in much of the mourning that accompanied the eclipse of Mughal power in the eighteenth century, the lament had to do precisely with the breakdown of this hierarchy between the high and the low.

In writing about the eighteenth century, Sarkar undoubtedly sometimes sympathized with the 'hereditary nobility' – for he also saw the fall of Mughals as having been caused in major part by the incompetence of rulers who did not have the requisite training and background. It is also true that for such information Sarkar was dependent upon chronicles that echoed the points of view of the nobility. More than that, he sometimes even shared the sentiments of contemporary historians who had decidedly partisan sympathies. Witness his reference – in the course of his discussion of the all-powerful eunuch Javid Khan, who for a while exercised a stranglehold on the mind of the emperor Ahmad Shah – to a passage from *Chahar Gulzar-i-Shujai*, a 1784 manuscript by a Harcharan Das, found in Patna: 'Well might a Delhi historian of the time reflect with sadness,' wrote Sarkar in introducing the following lines from Harcharan Das's manuscript: 'Never since Timur's time has a eunuch exercised such power in the state; hence the Government became unsettled. The hereditary peers felt humiliated by having to make their petitions through a slave and to pay court to him before any affairs of the state could be transacted.'[48]

But what Harcharan Das wrote was a contemporary complaint. Sarkar, while sometimes sharing these sentiments, had nevertheless a distinct though implicit theory about why character remained a main guiding factor in the history of the rise and fall of empires. We will come back to this point later.

iv. A gendered and heroic category

The category of 'character' also worked as a modern, liberal, but imperial and 'manly' (i.e. gendered) category in Sarkar's prose.[49] The point relating to gender is not hard to prove. Sarkar described eighteenth-century battles as 'the manly game of war' in which the Holkar queen Ahalya Bai's virtues, for instance, 'counted for nothing', because 'she could not command in the field'.[50] Of Shah Jahan's loss of Qandahar to the Persians in 1649, he wrote (mimicking Napoleon): 'In war it is not men but *the man* that counts.'[51] When Aurangzeb's forces invaded Golkonda in 1656, Sarkar described the local king, Qutb-ul-mulk or Qutb Shah, as 'more helpless than a child and more unnerved than a woman'. When the Maratha captain Santa Ghorparé was killed in 1697 by some machinations on the part of the wife of Nagoji Mane – for Ghorparé had killed her brother – Sarkar saw her behaviour as marked by 'a woman's unquenchable vindictiveness'. And he thus described Begum Samroo's dismissal of the Irish mercenary George Thomas from her service on charges of 'wenching': 'The Irish youth must have wearied of the faded charms of the old hag and consoled himself among the younger beauties of her large mestizo household. So, she dismissed him.'[52]

Some elements that went into the making of Sarkar's ideas on gender and manliness definitely appear Victorian and prudish when looked at today. 'It was a most painful surprise for me', he wrote in a footnote to the fourth volume of the *Fall*, 'to learn from the Marathi despatches that many of the Rajput Rajas, nobles and ministers were infected by the filthy unmentionable disease which is Nature's punishment for gross licentiousness.' There are several places where he writes with severe moral disapproval of anybody's love of 'wine and women'. Even of his favourite Najaf Khan in 1780, he said: 'Excess in wine and women quickly sapped Najaf Khan's vitality.' Or consider his harsh judgement of the character of the Kachhwa (Rajput) Raja Sawai Pratap Singh, who, as Sarkar put it, had 'no brains, but was not harmless and quiescent like most other imbeciles ... Anticipating the decadent Nawabs of Oudh, he used to dress himself like a female, tie bells to his ankles and dance within the harem.'[53]

Sarkar's anathema of 'amorousness and epicureanism' may have owed something – but only something, for one cannot imagine the Mughals to have been very strongly anti-epicurean – to the misogyny of his sources.[54] Muhammad Qasim, who worked for the sons of Shah Alam (Bahadur Shah) and eventually became *Bakshi* in the army of the Nizam-ul-Mulk, wrote excoriatingly of the emperor:

> The king is sitting like a woman within the four walls [of the palace]. If the king follows the manners of women and acts on what the effeminate say, then it is the more necessary that the Muslims should take up the path leading to Mecca and Madina, . . . [or] commit suicide by taking poison.[55]

Long before him, there was Khusrau, who commented in his *Tughlaq-Nama*:

> It does not behoove the ruler to become immersed in love and lust. A king is the constant protector of God's creatures. It would be wrong for such a guardian to remain intoxicated . . . for the enemies [would then take over].[56]

But Sarkar's misogyny also had a strong code of modern military honour attached to it, and this becomes evident in his choice of the kind of violence he took pleasure in relating. He exulted in describing regular battles, paying detailed attention to military formations, weapons used and strategies executed. This was moral violence of a sort, for military discipline had to do with character. But he would desist from taking any pleasure in describing the violent cruelties that marked life in the royal circles of late-Mughal India, often reducing pages-long accounts in his sources into a few, sometimes colourful, sentences. Thus, in describing the 'torture and dishonour' inflicted by Ghulam Qadir Khan on Shah Alam II and his family, including women, children, 'servant-girls, eunuchs, petty store-keepers and humble valets', Sarkar mentions that the account in his 'manuscript of Khairuddin's Persian history [*Ibratnamah*]' filled up '33 foolscap folio pages with 20 lines to the page, and drags on from day to day for two months'.[57] Now *Ibratnamah*s were meant to do just that, for, rhetorically speaking, they belonged to a 'poetic genre of lamenting social and political chaos (*shahr ashobs*) or books of warning (*ibrat namahs*)'.[58] But Sarkar would include none of that in his description:

> A modern historian [can]not conduct his reader through all the agonized circles of this *Inferno* of the living; he must pass over the horrid details of suffering borne by the Timurid royal house, not a hundredth part of which was endured by the house of Capet, whose misery too found a mercifully speedy end on the guillotine, four years later.[59]

At work was not only Sarkar's reluctance to describe these gory and 'unmanly' cruelties that speaks of his modern military relation to violence, and thus of his chivalry (to use a Burkean term); it is also his brief references to European literature and history, to Dante and the French revolution that do the same.

Though an English word of fourteenth-century vintage, 'character' in the sense of 'a person in a play or novel,' says the *Online Etymology Dictionary*, dates from the 1660s 'in reference to the "defining qualities" he or she is given by the author.'[60] The word was obviously in popular use in what European observers wrote of the late Mughal world. Francklin's well-known account of the rule of Shah Alam that was published in 1798 described the Rohillas and Afghans as a 'hardy warlike race, equally capable of arms and husbandry', 'Shuja o Dowla' as 'active and vigorous in his mind', the 'Raja of Jynaghur', 'Pertaub Singh', as of 'weak capacity' and as 'enervated by a long interval of effeminate pleasures'. Shah Alam himself, the 'nominal emperor of Hindustaun' who was 'now in his 75th year', appeared 'irresolute and indecisive in his measures'. 'His excessive love of pleasure, and infatuated attachment to unworthy favourites, ... degrade[d] him in the eyes of his neighbours and allies.' Long before Francklin, the Jesuit priest Francis Catrou's 1708 description of Aurangzeb was also fundamentally a description of the emperor's character: 'Nature seemed ... to combine, in the person of this prince, the perfection of mind and body.... Though affecting in his discourse the most retired sentiments, Aurengzebe concealed an ambitious mind.'[61]

But Catrou's history clearly belonged to the 'universal history' of the Enlightenment tradition. His aim was to give 'the Public a General History of the Mogul Empire' based on Manucci's Portuguese manuscript (1697), for 'the History of the Mogul Dynasty was wanting [a] universal history' that would show 'that the human passions ... are the same in Asia as in Europe; that the people of France might acquire instruction from the example of Indian virtues....'.[62]

I do not know exactly when 'character' ceased to be a gift from nature and became something that one could inculcate in oneself through discipline and effort. Henry George Keene, the colonial historian of Mughal India, cites [Harry] Verelst, the governor of Fort William in Bengal from 1767 to 1769, who wrote to the Court of Directors of the East India Company on 28 March 1768 about the Afghan 'premier [Mughal] noble' Najib-ud-Daulah in the following terms: 'He is the only example in Hindostan of, at once, a great and good character.' Verelst's description suggests that the idea of 'character' had already achieved a degree of democratization; for one did not have to be born into a noble family in order to have a noble character. Verelst again: 'He [Najib] raised himself from the command of fifty horses to his present grandeur entirely by his superior valour, integrity, and strength of mind. Experience and ability ... and the native nobleness and goodness of his heart have amply made amends for the defect of his birth and family.'[63] The fact that Holt's 1789 collection, mentioned above, of sketches of 'royal characters' was compiled for the 'instruction of youth' suggests a further movement toward the view that character was something one could acquire through disciplined effort; one did not have to be born to it.

5. Character and the cultivation of discipline

Very closely tied to Sarkar's idea of character, then, was the idea of discipline, both self-discipline and military discipline as we will see. This is also what made this particular strand of thinking fundamentally *liberal* – in that anyone, even a low-born person, could aspire to be disciplined – and national, for a nation's future depended on a disciplined citizenry. Discipline, statesmanship, military heroism and valour are what Sarkar admired in the likes of General Lake of the East India Company, the European mercenary Benoît de Boigne, Mahadji Sindhia and the army minister of Shah Alam, Mirza Najaf Khan.[64] De Boigne and Pierre Cuillier-Perron act as each other's foil in Sarkar's narrative, but they embody, in the first place, the discipline and character Sarkar considered integral to statesmanship: 'The aim of these two French officers was to do their duty of collecting money smoothly, and they took care to save the peasantry from plunder or molestation by their soldiery.'[65]

There was a special aspect to Sarkar's emphasis on military discipline. Sarkar was convinced that the increasing introduction of European battle practices in eighteenth-century India through European mercenaries fundamentally put more premium on disciplined military training and this in time would lead to a more general adoption of scientific reasoning.[66] 'True discipline in the army', Sarkar wrote once, 'is impossible without discipline at home and regular habits in daily life.'[67] He made a similar point in his obituary of the Maratha historian Viswanath Kashinath Rajwade (1823–1926):

> Rajwade, with an insane hatred of modern Europe, could not realise, in spite of his omnivorous reading, that behind a modern European army there are years of self-control, hard training, exact co-ordination of individual effort, and the brain power of the General Staff – that discipline is a moral product and not a matter of long-range guns – that an honest law court implies something different from a knowledge of physical science or even of jurisprudence.[68]

Mirza Najaf Khan, the Persian *mir bakshi* (army minister) of the Emperor Shah Alam we have met before, was admirable to Sarkar because 'he possessed that cool leadership, that power of co-ordination and that skill in the choice of fitting instruments which were indispensable for success in the new system of war that the Europeans had introduced into India.'[69] Sarkar also admired Najaf Khan's ability to make use of European mercenaries – Rene Madec, Walter Reinhard and the Comte de Modave – without becoming, unlike the Maratha Daulat Rao Sindhia, 'the helpless slave of his foreign mercenaries'. Indeed, in a section on the 'Character of Mirza Najaf Khan' Sarkar remarked: 'When we contemplate the career of Najaf Khan we do not know what to admire most – his military capacity, his political insight, or his humanity.'[70]

6. Character as the mediator of providence and history

Later historians have mostly missed the intellectual significance of the category of character in the historiographical tradition that Sarkar both drew on and enriched. It has recently been said, partly in criticism of Sarkar, that those who 'look for causes of decline in the character of the reigning emperor and the alleged moral degeneration of Mughal aristocracy' end up 'over simplifying ... the complex issues and factors involved in the discussion of the collapse of Mughal empire.'[71] I hope I have shown that character was no simple matter in Sarkar's thinking.

Character was what made the logic of providence open to the historical foibles of human beings. By the same token, the imperial-liberal idea of character helped to open up an imaginary and utopian space for a politics of will: as in the case of the individual, a nation also could enjoy its tryst with destiny, provided it had the will to develop character. What was the nature of this will? It was the capacity to face up to one's defects and not allow the temptation to glorify an identity – be it of the individual, a caste, a region, an ethnic group, a religious community, or a nation – to stand in the way. This is where Sarkar found a moral place for the historian. As he said about his researches on Maratha history:

> At the end, it is the impartial historian's duty not to conceal the defects of the Maratha racial character. They have been strong, they have been free, but they have not been united. Like the Afghan tribes or the clans of the Scottish highlands, Maratha family has fought Maratha family, clan has fought clan, in selfish personal feuds. The result has been disastrous to the interests of the nation as a whole.[72]

Or again: 'The Maratha failure to create a nation even among their own race and in their small corner of India, requires a searching analysis on the part of the Indian patriot and the earnest student of Indian history alike.' For 'we cannot blink at the truth that the dominant factor in Indian life – even to-day, no less than in the 17th century – is caste, and neither religion nor country.' He stated the principle again at the very beginning of his *Fall*:

> The headlong decay of the age-old Muslim rule in India and the utter failure of the last Hindu attempt at empire-building by the new-sprung Marathas, are intimately linked together, and must be studied with accuracy of detail as to facts and ... causes if we wish to find out the true solutions to the problems of modern India and avoid the pitfalls of the past.[73]

And the point was reinforced famously in a letter Sarkar wrote on 19 November 1957, about a year before his death, to his former student and the then president of the Republic of India, Dr Rajendra Prasad, who had written to him about the idea of a 'national' history of the country. Sarkar insisted on this quality of truthfulness as something absolutely essential to the function of a truly national historian, and we may let his words stand as testimony to the idea that 'character' opened up the logic of providence to the contingencies of history:

> National history must be comprehensive, true, accurate and impartial ... [The historian] will not suppress any defects of the national character but add to his portraiture those higher qualities which, taken together with the former ... constitute the entire individual.[74]

Notes

1. National Library, Calcutta, Jadunath Sarkar Papers, letter no. 1034, Sarkar to Sardesai, Calcutta, 15 May 1950, 'night'.
2. Jadunath Sarkar, *Fall of the Mughal Empire*, vol. 1, Delhi: Orient Longman, 1971; first pub. 1932, 'Foreword,' p. iii.
3. Sarkar, *Fall*, vol. 4, p. 338.
4. Sarkar, *Fall*, vol. 1, p. 2.
5. Jadunath Sarkar, *History of Aurangzib: Based on Original Sources*, vol. 5, New Delhi: Orient Longman, 1974; first pub. 1924, p. 378.
6. It is well known that Ranke's ideas on Providence and world history evolved. See Leonard Krieger, *Ranke: The Meaning of History*, Chicago: University of Chicago Press, 1977, p. 136. See also Leopold von Ranke, 'On Progress in History', and in particular his dialogue with King Maximilian II of Bavaria (1854) in his *The Theory and Practice of History*, ed. Georg Iggers, trans. Wilma A. Iggers, London: Routledge, 2011, pp. 20–3; and the discussion in Frederick C. Beiser, *The German Historicist Tradition*, Oxford: Oxford University Press, 2011, p. 264. Hegel famously argued (against the likes of Niebuhr and Ranke) that 'world history is governed by an ultimate design, that it is a rational process, whose rationality is . . . but a divine and absolute reason' and hence could be accessed 'from a knowledge of reason itself'; Georg Wilhelm Friedrich Hegel, *Lectures on the Philosophy of World History: Introduction: Reason in History*, trans. H. B. Nisbet, with an introduction by Duncan Forbes, 1975, Cambridge: Cambridge University Press, 1996, p. 28. See also pp. 19, 22, 26, 30. This Christian theological disputation about the accessibility or obscurity of God's intent with respect to human history is totally absent from Sarkar's thoughts.
7. Sarkar, *Aurangzib*, vol. 5, p. 378.
8. Sarkar, *Fall*, vol. 4, p. 261.
9. Ibid., vol. 4, p. 350.
10. Jadunath Sarkar, *India through the Ages* [1928], Calcutta: Orient Longman, 1993, p. 58.
11. Roy said this in his introduction to his English rendering of the *Kathoponishad*. See Stephen Hay, ed., *Sources of Indian Tradition*, New York: Columbia University Press, 1988, p. 23. Also see C. A. Bayly, *Recovering Liberties: Indian Thought in the Age of Liberalism and Empire*, Cambridge: Cambridge University Press, 2012, chs 2 and 3.
12. Rabindranath Tagore, 'Purba o poshchim', 1315; c. 1908–9, in *Samaj* collected in *Rabindrarachanabali*, centenary edn, Calcutta: Government of West Bengal, 1368 [1962], pp. 53–4.
13. Rajen Sen and B. K. Sen, comps, *Deshbandhu Chitta Ranjan Das: Brief Survey of Life and Work[,] Provincial Conference Speeches, Congress Speeches*, Calcutta: Karim Bux, [1926?], pp. 190–1.
14. My essay 'From Civilization to Globalization: The West as a Signifier in Indian Modernity,' in *Inter-Asian Cultural Studies* (Taiwan) 13 (2012), no. 1, pp. 138–52.
15. Sen and Sen, *Deshbandhu*, pp. 189–90.
16. Tagore, 'Purba o poshchim', p. 56. See also the discussion in C. A. Bayly's *Recovering Liberties*.
17. Sarkar, *Fall*, vol. 4, p. 349.
18. Ibid., vol. 4, p. 348.

19. Ibid., vol. 4, pp. 344, 342–3.
20. Sarkar, *India through the Ages,* pp. 99–100.
21. Sarkar was not alone in thinking of character as something that determined the destiny of an individual. In a letter he wrote in 1908 the poet Rabindranath Tagore spoke of character in the same vein: 'You have read in [*The*?] *Creed of Buddha* that Buddhadev said that "conduct moulds character and character in [is?] destiny". Whether it is an individual or a nation, destroying one's own character to achieve a short-term objective dissipates one's capital and leads to bankruptcy.' See *Rabindra biksha,* no. 40, 23 December 2001, p. 7. Edmond Holmes's *The Creed of Buddha* was a favourite book of Tagore's. See Prabhatkumar Mukhopadhyay, 'Tukro tukro chhobi' [vignettes], in Bishnu Bose and Ashokkumar Mitra, eds, *Nanajoner Rabindranath* [Rabindranath as he appeared to many], Calcutta: Punashcho, 2003, p. 110.
22. Sarkar, *Fall*, vol. 3, pp. 305, 60.
23. Ibid., vol. 3, p. 305. See also vol. 3, p. 117.
24. Ibid., vol. 3, pp. 304–5.
25. Heraclitus, *Fragments*, Fragment B119: 'A man's character is his guardian divinity', cited in Friedrich Nietzsche, *The Pre-Platonic Philosophers*, trans. and ed. Greg Whitlock, Urbana: University of Illinois Press, 2001, p. 73. See also the discussion in Shirley Darcus, ' "Daimon" as a Force Shaping "Ethos" in Heraclitus', in *Phoenix* 28 (Winter 1974), no. 4, pp. 390–407. For a modern and fascinating discussion that traces connections between the idea of 'ethos' and 'dwelling' and etymologically connects 'daimon' to 'that which lacerates', see Giorgio Agamben, ' *Se: Hegel's Absolute and Heidegger's *Ereignis*', in his *Potentialities: Collected Essays in Philosophy*, trans. and ed. Daniel Heller-Roazen, Stanford, CA: Stanford University Press, 1999, pp. 117–18.
26. Aurobindo's essays, reprinted in his *Essays in Philosophy and Yoga*, are available at www.aurobindo.ru/workings/sa/16/0033_e.htm (accessed 9 March 2015).
27. *Julius Caesar*, 1.2.140–41; also 2.2.32–33. Sarkar was not aware of the distinction Nietzsche made in his discussion of Heraclitus between 'destiny' and 'fate', destiny being what happens to man from within, and fate from without. Nietzsche, *Pre-Platonic Philosophers*, p. 73.
28. Sarkar, *Fall*, vol. 3, p. 312.
29. Sarkar, *Fall*, vol. 1, pp. xvii, 2, 4.
30. Ibid., vol. 1, p. 5.
31. Ibid., vol. 1, p. 4.
32. Preface (1902) to 'Nota-Manus', in *A Translation of the Seir Mutaqherin or View of Modern Times . . . by Seid-Gholam-Hossein-Khan . . .*, Lahore: Sheikh Mubarak Ali, 1975; first published in Calcutta in 1789, vol. 1. (hereafter *Seir*). Sarkar cites *Seir*, vol. 3, p. 25, in his *Fall*, vol. 1, pp. 6–7.
33. William Irvine, *Later Mughals*, edited and augmented with the History of Nadir Shah's Invasion by Jadunath Sarkar, vols 1–2, New Delhi: Munshiram Mahorlal, 1996.
34. Hossein, *Seir*, vol. 1, p. 65; Irvine, *Later Mughals*, vol. 2, p. 397. But see pp. 392–3 for Irvine's critique of the biases visible in his Mughal 'sources'.
35. I owe to Daniel Woolf the metaphor of the palimpsest and leads to some of the references I have used here.
36. Martine Watson Brownley, 'Sir Richard Baker's *Chronicle* and Later Seventeenth-Century English Historiography', in *Huntington Library Quarterly* 52 (Autumn 1989), no. 4, pp. 481–500.

37. J[ohn] Holt, *Characters of Kings and Queens of England, selected from different histories; with observations and reflections chiefly adapted to common life; and particularly intended for the instruction of youth. To which are added, notes historical*, Dublin: J. Moore, 1789.

38. Jadunath Sarkar, chap. 11, in Irvine, *Later Mughals*, vol. 2, p. 323.

39. Irvine, *Later Mughals*, vol. 1, p. 345.

40. Irvine, *Later Mughals*, vol. 1, pp. 133, 240, 394; vol. 2, pp. 95–8.

41. Sarkar, *Fall*, vol. 1, p. 150.

42. Ibid., vol. 1, pp. 205–6; but also vol. 1, p. 69 on Bengali character; vol. 1, p. 146 on Rajput character; vol. 1, p. 251 for Sarkar's characterization of Naga *sannyasi*s – 'utterly naked savages'.

43. Sarkar, *History of Aurangzib: Mainly Based on Persian Sources*, vols 1 and 2, New Delhi: Orient Longman, 1973; first edition 1912, vol. 1, pp. 170–2, 182–3; Sarkar, *Fall*, vol. 1, p. 332. The original title of vol. 2 of *History of Aurangzib* (1920 edition) had this for its subtitle: 'Based on Original Sources'. Longmans, Green and Co., London, published this edition. A copy of this edition held by the University of California Library can be consulted on the Internet at the Hathi Trust (http://babel.hathitrust.org/cgi/pt?id=uc1.b3850580, accessed 27 March 2015).

44. Sarkar's chap. 11 in Irvine, *Later Mughals*, p. 307. The word 'seemingly' in Sarkar's prose was deliberately used, for he went on to argue in his five-volume *History of Aurangzib* that the roots of this decline go back to some of the bigoted policies of Aurangzeb.

45. Sarkar, chap. 11, in Irvine, *Later Mughals*, vol. 2, pp. 311, 312, emphasis added.

46. Mohammad Habib and Afsar Umar Salim Khan, *The Political Theory of the Delhi Sultanate (Including a Translation of Ziauddin Barani's 'Fatwa-i Jahandari,' Circa 1358–9 A.D.)*, Allahabad: Kitab Mahal, [1960], pp. 97–8.

47. *Advice on the Art of Governance, Mau'izah-i Jahangiri of Muhammad Baqir Najm-i Sani, an Indo-Islamic Mirror for Princes*, trans. and intr. by Sajida Sultana Alvi, Albany: SUNY Press, 1989, p. 65.

48. Sarkar, *Fall*, vol. 1, pp. ix, 212.

49. One of the best recent discussions of liberal imperialism is in Karuna Mantena's book *Alibis of Empire: Henry Maine and the Ends of Liberal Imperialism*, Princeton, NJ: Princeton University Press, 2010.

50. Sarkar, *Fall*, vol. 4, p. 76.

51. Sarkar, *Aurangzib*, vol. 1, p. 76.

52. Sarkar, *Aurangzib*, vols 1 and 2, p. 128 (vol.1); vol. 5, p. 98; Sarkar, *Fall*, vol. 4, pp. 232–3.

53. Sarkar, *Fall*, vol. 4, p. 72n.; Sarkar, *Fall*, vol. 3, pp. 133, 230.

54. The quoted phrase is from Alan McNairn's *Behold the Hero: General Wolfe and the Arts in the Eighteenth Century*, Montreal: McGill–Queen's University Press, 1997, p. 5.

55. Muhammad Umar, 'A Comparative Study of the Historical Approach of Muhammad Qasim and Khafi Khan', in Mohibbul Hasan, ed., *Historians of Medieval India*, Meerut: Meenakshi Prakashan, 1968, pp. 156, 158.

56. Amir Khusrau, *Tughlaq-Nama*, ed. Syed Hashim Faridabadi, Aurangabad, 1933, p. 16, cited by Mohibbul Hasan, ed., in *Historians of Medieval India*, Meerut: Meenakshi Prakashan, 1968, p. 30.

57. Sarkar, *Fall*, vol. 3, p. 308.

58. *Advice on the Art of Governance*, p. 2. See also Alvi's comment on p. 104, n. 7: 'The tradition of historiography changed in eighteenth-century India. The historians, unlike their predecessors, criticized the shortcomings of the government and named their works *Ibrat Namahs*. Notable

among these historians are: Muhammad b. Muhammad Khan, Sayyid Muhammad Qasim Husayni, and Maulawi Khayr al-Din.'

59. Sarkar, *Fall*, vol. 3, p. 308, emphasis added.
60. See http://www.etymonline.com (accessed on 23 September 2014).
61. W. Francklin, *The History of the Reign of Shah-Aulum, the Present Emperor of Hindustaun*, 1798; Allahabad: Dr L. M. Basu, M.B., Panini Office, Bahadurganj, 1934, pp. 61, 67, 147, 201; Father Francis Catrou, S.J., *History of the Mogul Dynasty in India from Its Foundation by Tamerlane, in the Year 1399, to the Accession of Aurengzebe, in the Year 1657*, trans. from French, The Hague, 1708; London: J. M. Richardson, 1826, pp. 200–1.
62. Catrou, *History*, author's preface, pp. ix–xi. Sarkar, in editing Irvine's book, suggested that Catrou had plagiarized from Manucci. Catrou's cavalier treatment of Manucci's text receives detailed commentary in Irvine's 'Introduction' to his translation of Manucci. See William Irvine, *Mogul India 1653–1708 or Storia do Mogor by Niccolao Manucci, Venetian*, vols 1–4, New Delhi: Atlantic, 1989; first published from London in 1906–7, vol. 1, pp. xviii–xxxii, xxxviii–xl.
63. Henry George Keene, *The Fall of the Moghul Empire – An Historical Essay*, London: Wm. H. Allen; Calcutta: Brown, 1876, p. 93.
64. Sarkar, *Fall*, vol. 4, has extensive and admiring discussion of the character of de Boigne; see pp. 33, 82, 84, 88, 90, 92–4, 107, 134, 145, 146, 149, 187. On General Lake's heroism, see pp. 308–9.
65. Ibid., vol. 4, p. 52.
66. This theme is ubiquitous in Sarkar, *Fall*, vol. 4.
67. Jadunath Sarkar, 'India's Military Discipline: What It Implies', in *Modern Review* (October 1929), p. 374.
68. Jadunath Sarkar, *House of Shivaji: Studies and Documents on Maratha History – Royal Period*, 'greatly enlarged third edition', Calcutta: M. C. Sarkar, 1955, p. 288.
69. Sarkar, *Fall*, vol. 3, pp. 155–6.
70. Ibid., vol. 3, p. 30.
71. Zahir Uddin Malik, *The Reign of Muhammad Shah 1719–1748*, New Delhi: Icon, 2006, preface, p. x.
72. Sarkar, *House of Shivaji*, 3rd edn, p. 339.
73. Ibid., pp. 106–7; Sarkar, *Fall*, foreword, vol. 1, p. iii.
74. Sarkar's letter of 1957 cited in Mani Bagchi, *Acharya Jadunath: Jibon o sadhana*, Calcutta: Jijnasa, 1975, pp. 192–193. The context for, and the substance of, the historical writings by Jadunath Sarkar receive a larger elaboration in my book, *The Calling of History: Sir Jadunath Sarkar and His Empire of Truth*, Chicago: The University of Chicago Press, forthcoming.

PART IV
TELEOLOGY IN THE REVOLUTIONARY *POLIS*

CHAPTER 9
THE 'DEMOCRACY OF BLOOD': THE COLOURS OF RACIAL FUSION IN NINETEENTH-CENTURY SPANISH AMERICA
Francisco A. Ortega

1. Veritas ante omnia

On 9 May 1902, as Colombia painfully inched towards the end of the War of the Thousand Days (1899–1902), the Ministry of Education created the Colombian Academy of History to commemorate the independence centennial from Spain (1810–1910) and to preserve American antiquities. Founded at the end of the most devastating civil war since independence, the Academy's creation date is highly significant as political instability and a beleaguered economy allowed for the involvement of the United States in the region of Panama, then a part of Colombia, instigating its separation and independence in 1903.

The Academy's founding was part of a collective moment of taking stock. José Manuel Marroquín's government sought to promote reconciliation through the centennial celebration and the revival of old revolutionary glories after a century of disappointments concluded by the Thousand Days' War. The well-known engraver and painter Ricardo Moros Urbina designed the Academy's coat of arms adorned with an indigenous man crowned with a feathered hairpiece, a Spaniard conquistador with a basinet and a female republican allegory of freedom modelled after the French Marianne (Figure 9.1).

What sort of consolation could this contrived staging of conviviality offer to a country exhausted by war and dismembered by the US intervention in Panama? Did the coat of arms have anything to say to a nation that began the nineteenth century with enthusiasm and ended it with nothing but disappointment?

The three superimposed figures placidly stare towards the left, away from the viewer, as if removed from the immediate wreckage, contemplating the nation's past glories. Each figure represents a major epoch of national history – the indigenous or pre-conquest, the Hispanic or colonial and the republic – chronologically staged but without entirely effacing each other. Marianne and her bright Phrygian cap appear closest to the viewer, indicating that she represents the historical present of the nation, the natural repository of pre-national history. The figures also represent recognizable local iconographic traditions: Marianne, the republic, which enjoyed some pre-eminence during the early years of independence but only occasionally resurfaced, especially during official ceremonies; the popular gallery of prominent Spanish conquistadors, favoured by Hispanicized local elites; and the American Indian, which draws on previous iconography, such as the 1811 coat of arms of the Province of Cartagena with a young

Figure 9.1 Coat of arms of the Colombian Academy of History. Original design by Ricardo Moros Urbina (1904).

Indian maiden or the 1821 seal accompanying the printing of the Armistice between the American republican armies of Bolívar and the Spanish forces commanded by Pablo Morillo (see Figures 9.3 and 9.4).

In each of these cases, the images do not constitute sites of identity or cultural recognition. Thus, the American Indian is a highly coded allegorical inscription after the manner of Cesare Ripa's emblem *America* (1593) (Figure 9.2), which simultaneously inscribed and muted cultural difference.[1] Whereas previous representations displayed the full image of the Indian woman for the spectator's avid consumption, the masculine Indian of the Academy's coat of arms is partly concealed and is presented as partaking with the two other figures in a collective enterprise.

The masculine Indian, alongside the conquistador, re-inscribes fierce historical antagonisms but Marianne's dominant position dissolves their ethnically marked presences into a shared destiny of republican conviviality. The figuration of the republic as the feminine mediator of two masculine historical antagonisms evinces the centrality of gendered civility for the republic. Their evident engagement in a shared destiny and unity of purpose in the republic, turning a colony of enemies into a country of fellow

The 'Democracy of Blood'

Figure 9.2 Emblem 'America', Cesare Ripa, *Iconologia del cavaliere Cesare Ripa Perugino*. Originally published in 1603. Image taken from the edition published in Perugia, nella Stamperia di Piergiovanni Costantini, 1764–67. Vol. 4.

Figure 9.3 Coat of Arms, Province of Cartagena. Printed as the frontispiece to *Constitución del Estado de Cartagena de Indias: sancionada en 14 de junio de 1812, segundo de su independencia*. Cartagena de Indias: Imprenta de Diego Espinosa 1812.

Figure 9.4 Seal accompanying the *Tratado sobre la regularización de la guerra concluído entre el Libertador Presidente de Colombia y el Jeneral en gefe del ejército español*, Angostura, Venezuela, 1820.

citizens, speaks of the political possibilities of reconciliation. In that sense, the coat of arms is a source of pride and a call for action and national regeneration.

The convivial scene is all the more intriguing – and brutally commanding – as we realize the radical disavowal of Afro-Colombians. The coat of arms' displacement of a social group that figured abundantly in the polemical literature of the period indicates that what matters in this image is not the integrity of the independent parts but the collective effect of the image; not the individual statements but the narrative. Contrary to appearance, the coat of arms does not recognize the differences of those individuals who make the nation; rather, it is the denial of these differences in the union that is the nation to come.

The three figures are bounded by a double circle with the name of the Academy in the upper section and the words *Veritas ante omnia*, 'truth before all things', at the bottom. The circle sits on a blazing star, the Masonic symbol for knowledge and truth which indicates a representation beyond debate, opinion and politics, certified by the National Academy of History: the willingness of the republic to accommodate differences and generate collective unity.

The coat of arms was mounted on the Academy's entrance as an opening message that relied heavily on its teleological nature. It staged what Russian literary critic Mikhail Bakhtin called a *chronotope*, the fusion of time and space into a socially recognizable account which, in this case, constituted the minimal unit of a teleological project.[2] The chronotope pointed to a unity to come, the transit of a troubled past into a shared future; it promised reconciliation for a fragile and torn republic while providing a positive distinction from European culture and a contribution to world civilization. If, as Henning Trüper indicates in the opening chapter to this volume, teleology 'promised the future achievement of a well-ordered doctrine, a disciplined *logos* with a clearly and distinctly defined ambit, and a "most ample and useful" application', in this case we might say that the coat of arms works as a point of condensation of a widely shared, future-oriented and socially effective flexible narrative structure.[3] This teleological project of recent invention was central to a collective self-understanding that became prevalent at the end of the nineteenth century.

2. Of ancient and modern constitutions

Like the Academy's coat of arms, *casta* paintings were not a popular genre, nor were they produced in order to recognize diverse cultural identities. *Casta* paintings were a late eighteenth-century bureaucratic genre that offered a taxonomic gaze classifying passive, non-political subjects in a hierarchical organization. They start with the clear identification of Europeans, natives and blacks and their immediate offspring, and descend by means of a strange racial alchemy on to murkier regions inhabited by the offspring of *mestizos* and mulattoes, to finally enter the very heart of darkness, peopled by diffuse hybrids such as the *lobo* (wolf), *tente en el aire* (floating in the air) and the *salta-atrás* (jump-back).[4]

Casta paintings offered a vastly different narrative of social cohesion (Figure 9.5). They did not stage the 'empty homogenous time' of modern nations, as Walter Benjamin put it, but the multiplicity of heterogeneous concrete temporalities and experiences of the various people and vassals of the monarchy.[5] The representation of contiguous domestic scenes neatly contained in their own cells and individualized by rich chromatic elaboration and attention to detail shows the multitude of peoples that comprised the empire. Albeit

Historical Teleologies in the Modern World

Figure 9.5 *Colección de Castas de Nueva España* by Mexican painter Ignacio María Barreda (1777). Oil on canvas, 77 × 49 cm (30.3 × 19.3 in). Archivo Histórico, Real Academia Española, Madrid.

the events represented might have been simultaneous – and they depict the complementary roles assigned to the different *castas* – they remain intractably discrete and do not flow or aggregate into a single historicity. *Casta* paintings figured a corporate model in which diverse political bodies offer partial and fragmented representations, and which only the king could resolve by embodying the entire monarchy.

Casta paintings visually represent the ancient constitutions of Spanish America in their rigid moral and social hierarchical ordering within which Creoles (white Spanish

Americans) benefited from the labour of Indians and blacks in exchange for caring for their spiritual and material instruction. The 1687 Constitution of Caracas' Diocesan Synod tersely expressed this view when it addressed Creoles as 'parents' and warned that 'God has not given them children, servants, slaves and estates ... to live idly in the Republic ... He has made them parents so that by love and in accordance with the rules of justice, they correspond to the honour, service, obedience and reverence bestowed upon them, with good parenting, teaching, support and care of their people ...'.[6] The social and moral hierarchies, undergirded by the legal separation between Indians, Europeans and slaves, constituted the foundation of the early colonial system. Despite the effect produced by the familial metaphor, the Spanish American provinces were inhabited by individuals who viewed themselves as participants in discrete groups with multiple conflicting interests whose final if benevolent arbiter was the king. Calling on the kingdom's constitution constructed a political community where difference was reaffirmed as the means to guarantee a hierarchical ordering.

The moral and political boundaries of such constitutions were fiercely defended. By the end of the colonial period the demographic emergence of a broad stratum of racially mixed and acculturated people, imprecisely known as *castas* or free men of colour, threatened the old constitution. The threat became explicit in 1795 when the king granted wealthier members of the *castas* the right to seek white status. The Creole elite spiritedly fought the decree with an argument that gives insight into colonial assumptions of worth and honour which informed the moral conception of the old constitution. According to the elite, the decree ignored that *castas* were

> men possessing a perverse inclination ... marked with all the ignominy of barbarism and the infamy of slavery. Stupid, rude, naked men, without signs of rationality ... Men who were victims of the ferocity of their brothers, who took their freedom away. Men in whom the coarsest passions rule to such an extent that almost deny them of their being. Men prone to theft, bloodthirsty, suicidal, covered by the common confusion of the most barbarous customs ...[7]

A collection of unsavoury images drawn from biblical hermeneutics, natural and criminal law, moral theory and natural history converged in an unsettling portrayal. Clearly, granting dispensation to such subjects would 'cause an extraordinarily dangerous disruption'.[8] They urged the king to prevent the subversion of the social order by 'keeping them in dependence and subservience to Whites as hitherto; otherwise they will become unbearable and will want to dominate those who have been their Lords'.[9] If the king did not take energetic actions, *pardos* (mulattoes) would turn 'this beautiful portion of the universe into a filthy and reeking compilation of sins, crimes and evils of all kinds: the social machine will be dissolved: corruption will arrive'.[10]

Spanish colonial administrators viewed the opposition of class interests as the means to guarantee imperial governance. In 1808, on the eve of the political revolutions, the prosecutor of Caracas' Royal Court dismissed the possibility of local revolts against the metropolis by arguing that:

The multitude classes that constitute these provinces ... offer ... insurmountable obstacles for their reunion in a political body. Rivals of each other, the nobles would never admit commoners among themselves, and these would never admit *pardos*, and none of them would admit the other *castas*, and much less that of the slaves. These differences in colour and condition produce a violent shock that would destroy the parts among themselves. All of this will always present insurmountable difficulties for them to come together and reconcile their opposing wills and interests.[11]

Two years later Spanish American Creoles initiated the political process that resulted in formal independence. As anticipated by the prosecutor, the ensuing wars often turned into civil conflicts with a strong racial component that threatened to override the push for independence. Social antagonism reached such intensity that it produced a dislocation in the structure of internal power and planted the seeds for hotly contested legal, ideological, political and sociocultural debates. These debates constituted the grounds upon which much of Spanish American intellectual life turned during the nineteenth and early twentieth century.[12] Although the intensity of the conflict was not the same everywhere, colonial certainties had been weakened and social expectations about equality had been generalized so that the ancient constitutions lost their aura. Consequently, the Spanish American nineteenth century may be understood as an agonizing attempt to regain social equilibrium.

Spanish American elites believed that the republic faced three major threats. First, independence leaders' commitment to the republican system was at odds with their view of the people. The republican system required a virtuous people for political stability; an educated people to engage in deliberation and reach the common good; and an industrious people to secure prosperity. For independence leaders, on the other hand, it was quite evident that the Spanish American people were not virtuous: they lived under the 'triple yoke of ignorance, tyranny and vice' and did not have the 'noble passions, which constitute the springs of civic virtues.'[13] Most authors agreed on the long list of vices and they similarly attributed them to a limited number of causes: the lack of education, the colonial legacy and the natural inclinations of diverse peoples and races. 'Therefore,' wrote a Peruvian republican, 'the national spirit remains unknown to our people and the name of Peru scarcely has a vague and indifferent meaning among the multitudes.'[14]

Second, republican leaders were concerned about the diversity of classes and the resulting proliferation of heterogeneous interests. Venezuelan philosopher and pedagogue Simón Rodríguez (1771–1854) denounced such fragmentation in the wake of political independence. The colonial experience, claimed Rodríguez in 1828, produced a variegated populace, a mob composed of:

Rustics, Chinese and Barbarians
Gauchos, Half breeds and Huachinangos
Negroes, Blackish and Gentiles
Highlanders, Coastals, Indians

> People of Color and of Ponchos
> Browns, Mulattoes and Knock-kneeds
> Stubborn Whites and Yellow Feet
> and a CREW of Crossbreds
> Terceroons, Quadroons, Quintroons
> and Throwbacks
> that make, like in botany,
> a family of CRYPTOGAMS.[15]

Rodríguez' page appeared fragmented, like a *casta* painting, an excess of aggregates: rustics, Chinese, Barbarians / Gauchos, half-breed and Huachinangos etc. For Rodríguez, as for his contemporaries, the problem was not simply the degree of ethnic diversity, but the assumption that such heterogeneity atomized public life and rendered unfeasible the idea of a shared general interest as the proliferation of diverse and divergent, if not outright antagonistic groups competed for resources and pre-eminence. It is no accident that this collection of differences culminated in the cryptogam: a figure of sterility that symbolized the impossibility of social and political reproduction.[16] The *excess* of *peoples* produced a *lack of peoplehood* that nullified the republic. As Gran Colombian diplomat Juan García del Río put it in 1829, 'heterogeneity [is] a harmful principle' to the viability of the republic.[17]

Third, republican leaders understood that the threat did not derive from heterogeneity alone. Diverse races possessed, according to these authors, contrasting degrees of civilization. Alexis de Tocqueville made it clear such a predicament was not exclusively Spanish American. Towards the end of Volume I of *Democracy in America* he shifted from the description of North American democratic institutional forms to the dangers facing the new republic. The fact that 'human beings who are scattered over this space do not form, as in Europe, so many branches of the same stock' is among the most pressing problems.[18] These 'three races', continued Tocqueville, '[are] naturally distinct, and I might almost say hostile to each other' (I: 313). There were 'Almost insurmountable barriers ... raised between them by education and by law, as well as by their origin and outward characteristics' and though 'fortune has brought them together on the same soil ... each race fulfils its destiny apart' (I: 313). Two alternatives remained for the future: the different races 'must either wholly part or wholly mingle' (I: 353). For Tocqueville mixed races formed 'the true bond of union', but given the above-mentioned 'insurmountable obstacles' and as 'mulattoes are by no means numerous in the United States' (I: 354), he concluded by forecasting the inexorability of civil war 'and perhaps ... the extirpation of one or other of the ... races' (I: 359).[19]

If Tocqueville was sceptical about the possibility of *castas* being the affective bond for Anglo-American society, Spanish American leaders harboured their own doubts. Bolívar wrote about the 'Natural enmity of the *colours*' and progressively feared the day *castas* 'will rise and put an end to everything'.[20] Not only, according to their assessment, were they ill-prepared for liberal politics and the exercise of popular sovereignty, the broad democratization of the language of liberty and equality during the wars of independence had opened the possibility of contentious subaltern participation in post-independence politics. *Pardos* in Venezuela and Colombia, for instance, mobilized legal and institutional resources in order to sustain their claims to be treated as equals in the republic but they were often accused of being anti-republicans and inciting racial wars.[21]

The political thought of Simón Bolívar offers an impassioned meditation on the dissolving effects of racial diversity and conflict. He first addressed the issue in two extraordinary letters written during his Jamaican exile in 1815, at the height of the Spanish reconquest. In the first letter, Bolívar presented the case for American independence. He drew on anti-Spanish propaganda to depict a long list of abuses and oppressions but he grounded the reason for independence on the disregard colonial authorities had shown for the ancient constitution:

> Emperor Charles V made a pact with the discoverers, conquerors, and settlers of America, and this ... is our social contract. ... In return, they were made the lords of the land, entitled to organize the public administration and act as the court of last appeal, together with many other exemptions and privileges that are too numerous to mention ... Yet there are explicit laws respecting employment in civil, ecclesiastical, and tax-raising establishments. These laws favour, almost exclusively, the natives of the country who are of Spanish extraction.

Despite the existence of this time-honoured constitution, 'by an outright violation of the laws and the existing agreements, those born in America have been despoiled of their constitutional rights as embodied in the code'.[22]

The argument must not have been entirely convincing because Bolívar wrote a second letter in which he sought to refute those who insisted that 'the main obstacle to [the] attainment [of independence] lies in the difference between the races that make up the people of this immense country'.[23] Bolívar countered that Spanish America's 'domestic disputes have never stemmed from differences of race: rather, they were born of divergent political opinions, and the personal ambition of a few men, like all those that afflict other nations' (121). Instead, he painted a picture of racial harmony. Even if whites constituted the smallest portion of the population

> it is also certain that [they] possess intellectual qualities which confer on them relative equality and an influence which may seem excessive to those who have not been able to judge for themselves of the moral situation and material circumstances ... Understanding of these could not fail to foster a desire for unity and harmony among all the inhabitants, regardless of the numerical disproportion between one colour and another. (118)

Thus, other races regarded Creoles with awe and admiration: natives worshipped them; they were rustic, indifferent and content with their peace, land and family.[24] As offspring of whites and Indians, *mestizos* were mild-mannered and devotees of whites. As for the African, elsewhere the most oppressed of all races, in America he vegetated in complacent inertia on his master's estate, enjoying all the benefits that accrue from being part of such an establishment, as well as a considerable degree of freedom. Since religion has taught him that to serve is a sacred duty, and since all his life he has lived in this state of domestic dependence, he feels that he is leading a natural life, as a member of his master's family, whom he loves and respects. (120)

Slaves only mobilized against Creoles because Spaniards compelled them but, once given their freedom again, they 'have gone over to the revolutionary side, even though the latter had not offered them absolute freedom as the Spanish partisans had' (120). Bolívar concluded that 'we feel justified in believing that all the sons of Spanish America, of whatever colour or condition, hold one another in a reciprocal brotherly affection which no amount of scheming can ever alter' (121). Such a gullible picture is nothing else than the old constitution as expressed by the 1687 Synod of Caracas.

In the opening address to the Congress of Angostura, the constitutional convention that created the Republic of Colombia in 1819, Bolívar abandoned the language of ancient constitutions. Henceforth, the people do not appear in his writings as harmonious or virtuous; they 'have been able to acquire neither knowledge nor power, nor virtue ... [They] have been degraded more by vice than by superstition ... a blind instrument of its own destruction'.[25] Furthermore, ignorance is not the only problem. Bolívar called on legislators to keep in mind that:

> our people is not European, nor North American ... it is more a composite of Africa and America than an emanation of Europe, because even Spain itself is not quite European because of its African blood, its institutions, and its character. It is impossible to determine with complete precision to which human family we belong. The majority of the indigenous has been annihilated, the European has mixed with the American and the African, and the African has mixed with the Indian and the European. All born of the womb of the same mother, our fathers, different in origin and in blood, are foreigners, and all of them differ visibly in their epidermis; this dissimilarity carries an obligation of atonement of the greatest significance. (9)

The political institutions designed by Bolívar sought to conduct with a 'steady hand and an infinitely delicate touch to guide this heterogeneous society, whose complex contrivance is dislocated, is divided, is dissolved at the slightest disturbance' (10).

It might seem paradoxical that Bolívar's fundamental political principle is equality before the law (alongside the division of powers and the representative system) and thus he repeatedly offered an explanation: 'We need equality in order to recast as a whole ... the race of men, political opinions and public practices' (10). The levelling effect produced the salutatory 'merging of all classes into one state – in which diversity used to increase by virtue of the propagation of the species ... By this single step, cruel disharmony has been pulled up by the roots.'[26] Furthermore, formal equality does not preclude 'physical and moral inequality' and thus his institutional proposals might be best understood as an attempt to combine the democratic nature of American societies with the aristocratic principle of a hereditary senate and a strong executive elected for life. These institutions, together with a fourth moral power in charge of overseeing public behaviour, are designed to 'provide our existence with a basis of guarantees'.[27]

Bolívar's ultimate objective was not only to safeguard stability and order but to set in motion a nation to come:

> All our moral strengths will not be enough to extract our nascent republic from this chaos if we do not fuse the mass of people into a whole, the makeup of the government into a whole, the legislation into a whole, and the national spirit into a whole. Our slogan must be 'unity, unity, unity'. The blood of our citizens is various, let us mix it to unify it . . .[28]

The new constitutional language, an extraordinary formula with remarkable endurance, did not turn Bolívar's injunction into a teleological project but it furnished the ingredients that would be picked up by the next generation of Spanish American intellectuals. They continued Bolívar's musings on the delicate art of governing heterogeneous societies and offered a wide array of formulas that sought to provide the institutional basis of which he spoke. In the process the continent was often understood as destined for a grandiose mission.

3. Diversity, miscegenation and democracy

In the mid-nineteenth century, Domingo Faustino Sarmiento complained that 'South America lacked a Tocqueville'. The Argentine writer viewed the need for someone who 'penetrated the interior of our political life as a vast field still unexplored and undescribed to science and revealed . . . this new way of being that has not well known mark or precedent'.[29] Sarmiento's biographical essay *Facundo: Civilization and Barbarism* purported to fill such a role by analysing Argentinian history since its independence in 1810. According to Sarmiento the past three decades did not provide a stable institutional design and left the country in the hands of *caudillos*, local warlords who ruled by force. These *caudillos* were the true 'manifestation of [American] life as it has been made by colonization and the peculiarities of the land' (38); examining their lives and deeds would allow observers to penetrate the barbarous constitution of the country (128). Spanish American countries, continued Sarmiento, were engaged in an 'obstinate struggle tearing [the] republic to pieces . . . an ingenuous, open, and primitive struggle between the latest progress of the human spirit and the rudiments of savagery, between the populous cities and the gloomy forests' (33); in short, between European ideas and American brute force, between, as he famously and enduringly termed it, civilization and barbarism. The dilemma facing Americans was succinctly put: 'to be or not to be *savages*' (35).

Sarmiento set the issue in teleological terms: 'Is there nothing providential in these struggles among people?' (35). Of course, he replied, the promising future of the republic will not be surrendered so easily:

It will not be surrendered because an army of twenty thousand men may guard our homeland's borders … It will not be surrendered because fortune may have favoured a tyrant through long and hard years … No! a future so unlimited, a mission so exalted, will not be surrendered because of this accumulation of contradictions and difficulties. Difficulties can be vanquished, and contradictions are ended by contradicting them! (36)

Civilization was destined to triumph over savagery and the question remained how. Promoting European immigration was a favoured policy. On the other hand, Sarmiento did not have Bolívar's faith in miscegenation. For him 'the fusion of these three families [whites, blacks and Indians] has resulted in a homogenous whole, distinguished by its love for idleness and incapacity for industry, except when education and the exigencies of social position put the spurs to it and pull it out of its customary pace' (51). More decisively, if barbarism was the exercise of power through sheer force, civilization could only achieve dominion through persuasion, deliberation and ideas. Therefore, the mandate to civilize America must be realized through the spread of public, massive, popular education. Not surprisingly, Sarmiento implemented during his presidency (1868–74) Spanish America's largest and most successful educational system.[30]

However, educational policies had a natural limit. 'Indians', according to Sarmiento, did not seem conquerable by education. These 'savages lurk, waiting for moonlit nights to descend, like a pack of hyenas, on the herds that graze the countryside, and on defenseless settlements' (46) and are naturally inclined to idleness, passively resist civilizing policies and threatening civilization by staging raids (51). Consequently, for Sarmiento, extermination was a legitimate government policy:

Will we be able to exterminate the Indians? I feel invincible repugnance for the savages of America and cannot help it … Unable to progress, their extermination is providential and useful, sublime and great. They should be exterminated without even forgiving the young one, who already has the instinctive hatred for the civilized man.[31]

Sarmiento was already conversant with US historical literature and his solution resonated with Anglo-American classical anthropology.[32] For many Spanish American elites, Sarmiento's *Facundo* captured the kernel of the region's troubles and set up the enduring terms – civilization and barbarism – within which any solution had to tread in years to come. Despite this formulation's popularity, there were many others who were critical of its extremism and inherent pessimism.

Colombian publicist José María Samper, for instance, offered a more appealing and viable alternative proposal in which diversity was simultaneously an obstacle and a resource. Like Sarmiento, Samper evinced his disappointment with the progress made since independence. In *An Essay on the Political Revolutions and Social Conditions of Spanish American Republics* (1861), portions of which he presented to British and French scientific societies, he provided an ethnographic characterization that sought to uncover the social logic behind the civil wars and anarchy, the *caudillos* and the rule by force, and the chronic poverty in the midst of plenty. Samper's conclusion was not very different from his predecessors: the multitude of 'races and *castas*' holds 'the secret or key to the most important social phenomena and to the causes of almost all of the revolutions that have stirred the republics'.[33] In this 'most incongruous composition' (201) European civilization and law, 'the essential base of all property, social force and progress' (298), was in a permanent struggle with other races and cultures that remained antagonistic to the work of civilization.[34]

On the other hand, Samper marvelled at the 'incredible . . . variety of types that occurs in the country, the providential combination of permanent cold and heat, of high mountains and deep valleys, of four or five great races divided in many kinds, and of the many types of food production and greatly diversified industries' (327). He regarded this diversity as mutually complementary and not a threat. Its initial complementarity was economic but its ultimate effect was political as it grounded the democratic nature of the continent: 'This society – composed of many antagonistic races and *castas* – comprises the germ of democracy . . .' (201). Where no race, continued Samper, 'might claim purity, none can claim supremacy; all interests are to be complex, and the system of equality is also the only possible form of organization' (292). Thus, it is a law of nature that wherever 'black, white, yellow and brown citizens are destined to coexist the democratic republic can be the only rational form' (174). In other words, the 'democracy of blood' – as Samper called it – was the required foundation for a political system that could carry out the full realization of citizens' equal rights and ideas (292).

From the concept of a 'democracy of blood' a more optimistic teleological narrative emerged: Spanish America was intensely dynamic, an 'ongoing search towards progress and order' (288). The changes brought about by the rise of *castas* during the late colonial period rendered the political revolutions of 1810 inevitable: 'a mixed people would not tolerate dynasties and aristocracies' (174). Local histories are turbulent because the coexistence of privileges and inequalities in the republic 'is a social contradiction, something impossible,' which created the conditions for 'social war and permanent insurrection' (174). But conditions were gradually changing. Legal equality finally brought the country's social and racial groups to the same level (282); increased commerce provided an irresistible impetus to fraternize; greater sociability furthered the advancement of civilization (339). Even such an unfortunate event as slavery had prepared the advent of this major democratic process:

> Surely . . . those counsellors to Charles I did not imagine that introducing the blood of blacks . . . in the form of goods, prepared for the near future not only the advent of a very courageous and completely Christian democracy but also the solution to the great problem of racial fusion of all different human races. (292)

The innate tendency towards racial fusion had already produced 'a population of excellent qualities' (328) and had contributed to the spread of civic culture while readying the country for democratic political participation.[35]

Samper's optimism reached all social groups. Given the proper conditions, even the lowest of the *castas*, the Zambo (an individual of African and Native descent), 'a race of animals before whom Humanity is disgusted when discovering its own image or a part of it in their forms and faculties …' (95–6), could be redeemed. But the phrase already suggests that, in all cases, the mixture of races 'allows for the domination of the European element' (337). Samper's goal was to create a '*mestizo* but Caucasian' (80) by 'the development of commerce, navigation, roads, agriculture … in short time these lower *castas* … will receive instruction … until they rise themselves, thanks to the benefits of freedom and equality, by contact and fusion with other *castas*' (98–9).[36] Racial fusion guaranteed vigorous and free democracy (338); the white race's superior intelligence advanced civilization. The teleological thrust was so vigorous that government was not a matter of policy but of comprehending the scientific tendencies of these societies and deftly allowing them to unfold.

Like Bolívar and Simón Rodríguez, Samper embraced monogenism and observed a diffused sense of racial boundaries which undermined rigid systems of racial classification. Such commitments arose out of two very different circumstances. On the one hand, their Catholic intellectual milieu sanctioned a pre-Darwinian Catholic anthropology which upheld the unity of all races and their equality before God. On the other, as statesmen and public intellectuals these men's experience indicated the persistence of variations and nuances over starkly defined ethnic groups. Clear-cut categories did not produce useful instruments to understand and transform their immediate surroundings. Instead, they found resonance with Lamarckian theories of evolution – the idea that racial diversity was the result of environmental adaptation passed on to future generations, thereby causing the organism's progressive modification or functional adaptation – and developed their ideas along these lines.[37] Thus, Samper attributed racial and cultural differences to climate and social conditions. In particular, he regarded the legacy of colonial practices – the *encomienda* and the Indian tribute; slavery and the importation of Spanish criminals to settle the New World – as deep-seated habits that with the lack of education, opportunities, institutional support and freedom created 'a radically vitiated society' that held back the 'lower races' (291). If this view sometimes encouraged environmental determinism it also allowed for a fairly flexible sense of racial identity that did not lead to the idea of racial mixing as degeneration, as had recently been developed by Gobineau.[38] Instead, miscegenation was decoupled from illegitimacy, moral turpitude and turbulent behaviour and became associated with the nation's social harmony and moral improvement.

4. Imagining desire

Teleological projects are not just about the availability of arguments. They also require the means by which localized and technical discourses become attractive to a broad population. For a 'democracy of blood' project to become a successful politically and emotionally viable vernacular it required diverse people to accept it and be willing to mix with others. In the course of less than a century, Bolívar's injunction to mix had become an official national ideology in several countries, as the Academy's coat of arms testifies. The question remains how such a highly intellectualized discourse acquired the emotional texture of a national project.

In colonial Spanish Americans even elite members had no problem loving racialized difference, a practice that had respectable precedents in the many Indian and black virgins and saints. The famous *Virgin of Guadalupe* in Mexico powerfully exemplifies this devotion.

However, the point here is that worshipping native, black or *mestizo* saints and virgins sublimated social difference and did not preclude the hierarchical ordering of the ancient constitutions. The language of the 'democracy of blood' demanded that Spanish Americans learned to recognize others as social equals and desire them; it required that citizens integrate this sensual desire as a social value that was acceptable and desirable. Teleology constitutes a poetics[39] and we must turn our attention to the cultural forms being produced in order to fashion a new civic and national sensibility. As other authors have previously remarked, the narrative form gives us a glimpse of how this learning to desire was accomplished during the nineteenth century.[40] The Cuban novel *Sab* (1841), by Gertrudis Gómez de Avellaneda, is a good example of the kinds of narratives that taught readers how to fall in love with a teleological political project.[41]

Sab takes place in mid-nineteenth-century colonial Cuba in a context of harsh repression and great control over slaves. The background is the 1791 massive slave uprising on Saint Domingue that led to the destruction of the plantation system and the establishment of Haiti as an independent black republic in 1804, as well as uprisings in Cuba including the one led in 1812 by José Antonio Aponte which spread throughout the island.[42] These events created a climate of fear and hysteria in the Antilles. The main character, Sab, is a noble slave, son of a Congo Princess, who is brought up in the house of Carlota, daughter of an insolvent landowner from Camaguey, Cuba. Though Sab and Carlota spent their youth together, Carlota falls in love with Enrique Otway, the son of a wealthy merchant from La Habana, who cares mostly about money and leisure. Sab, in the meantime, is madly in love with Carlota and dies burdened by his secret love. When Sab dies, Carlota, already disappointed with Enrique, realizes the mulatto was truly her great love. The novel closes with her melancholic visit to Sab's grave.

The novel is peopled with confusing identities: Enrique Otway is a wealthy handsome man who fulfils social expectations but is a great disappointment as it becomes evident he and his father are only interested in Carlota's hacienda and her social status. Sab has a semblance that is neither black nor white; his colour is yellowish; his condition does not correspond to his clothes; he is both docile and threatening. Soon we discover he is a noble soul within an enslaved body. Furthermore, Sab is adopted by Martina, an indigenous woman descended from Chief Camaguey, the last of the original natives in the island. As a sum of black, white and Native American, Sab is truly Cuban, as opposed to Enrique Otway, whose foreign name betrays him.

Carlota's inability to see through appearances dooms her to unhappiness. Her melancholic state corresponds to her incapacity to recognize actual historical possibilities.

Doubly gendered, she is at once the object of desire (the *telos* of the narrative) and the rectified subject. The novel does its best to teach the reader to navigate amidst such confusions and discern true character from pretence. The narrative point of view remains close to Sab, producing intense identification: we occupy Sab's space, his desires become ours, his tragedy is ours. While readers are masculinized – and thus properly set on the learning track – their object of lust is thoroughly feminized. Hopefully, we learn the lesson and will not incur in denying conviviality and allow ourselves to fall in love with Sab. Though the novel was banned in Cuba and was only reprinted in 1937, well after independence, *Sab* – like other similar novels across the continent – became foundational fictions, to use the expression deftly coined by Doris Sommer, that offered new modes of public and domestic conviviality.[43]

Such learning to desire had become a 'natural instinct' by the end of the nineteenth century. Cuban José Martí, a major intellectual and political figure at the turn of the century, could claim that 'There is no racial hatred, because there are no races' (1891).[44] And a quarter of a century later, in the aftermath of the Mexican revolution, José Vasconcelos triumphantly announced that a new race 'made of the treasury of all the previous races, the final race, the cosmic race' had finally come into being in Latin America.[45] By then, *mestizaje* – as the language of the 'democracy of blood' became known – had successfully challenged the exclusive association of modernity with European whiteness and created its own alternative teleology.

5. Conclusion: redemptive violence

Bolívar's desperate injunction to mixture acquired a teleological dimension when Samper reformulated it and turned it into a natural process that simultaneously revealed the unfolding democratic character of the region while fating 'the New World to be the stage of the fusion and reconciliation of the races, inaugurating the basis for a new civilization' (79). The 'wonderful work of the mixing of races . . . gives the New World its particular character' and will give democracy its final universal character (299). Spanish America was now republican and 'destined to regenerate the world through the practice of the fundamental Christian principle of fraternity' (79). The formulation vastly compensated for any feelings of inadequacy. The fact that Europeans did not share this teleological narrative rendered mysterious what should have been obvious and made explanations futile: namely, that the state of institutional and social disarray was necessary and temporary.

The nineteenth-century language of the 'democracy of blood' emerged as a critical response to the generalized assumption that the coexistence of racial and cultural groups created difficulties to the viability of the political community. But it became truly compelling when broad and contentious popular participation during the wars of independence created the need for a new kind of social narrative of cohesion. Thus, earlier republican elites appealed to the idea of racial mixture as a way to appease the social unrest that beleaguered the nascent republics. If Bolívar issued the mandate to mix in the wake of flourishing *pardo* activism in Venezuela and Colombia, Mexican liberal Jose María Luis Mora urged 'the fusion of all races and colours' as a means of curbing Indian rebellions in Yucatán during the 1830s.[46] In both cases the language of racial mixing emerged to counter social antagonism and not as a reflection of racial harmony. Consequently the 'democracy of blood' was understood to be a 'process of racial eugenization ... a way of elevating the Indian and other "inferior" types to the "superior" standards of the Europeanized mestizo',[47] of creating, as Samper wrote, a '*mestizo* but Caucasian' (80). Mora expressed it succinctly in 1836: 'The white population is far too dominant in the day, their numbers, their enlightenment and wealth, their unique influence on public affairs, and their advantageous position in relation to others: it is here that we must seek the Mexican character, and it is such race the one called on to keep the reputation of the republic.'[48] It was an 'all inclusive ideology of exclusion' (like the Academy's coat of arms), as a contemporary scholar has aptly summarized it.[49]

However, because it was structurally harmonious with early American republican aspirations for universal citizenship, the language of the 'democracy of blood' became a field of contention and negotiation and served to address a myriad of contending issues, such as the nature of the community, the limits of citizenship and freedom, the possibility or desirability of equality, the roots of American democracy, the role of civic participation and the pursuance of morality, progress and public happiness. The 'democracy of blood' discourse addressed these themes by engaging in deliberation on how to properly construe a political community out of the cultural and social diversity that comprised it. It was conceived as the civilizing work of masculine desire, mediated by a gendered republic which is at once the object of lust and of pedagogics. The starting point was that cohering a diverse racial and ethnographic composition into a moralized nation was fundamental in order to effect good government.[50]

Not entirely a colonial project, it bears recognizable colonial traits. The intellectual and political elite 'legitimized their rule through the vocabulary of civilization and modernization, progress, backwardness, and catching up'; yet, the teleological project did not refuse the colonized its 'share in historicity'.[51] Rather, as the Colombian Academy of History's coat of arms efficiently heralded it, it staged a new kind of national historicity – one that it believed to be redemptive of all the fragmented histories of the world. After all, this teleological project might have been nothing more than the 'obligation of atonement' Bolívar had already announced in the Angostura speech.

Finally, the language of the 'democracy of blood' assumed the mixture was never completed. It emerged, therefore, as a narrative *in permanent transit*, from a colonial aggregation of races into a collective national will; from the *casta* painting into the coat of arms; from colonial taxonomies to the national novel; from Indians and blacks into the 'Caucasian *mestizo*'. With time, antagonism was understood to be necessary, even beneficial, but a definite resolution was permanently deferred. Such a narrative of transit redefined democracy as a natural – not political – process and gave way to the idea that society should be administered, not governed by elected representatives.[52]

Teleological projects, such as the one studied in this chapter, attempt to suture the social and arrest indetermination. On the one hand, foreclosure enables collective projects by cohering fragmented identities, strengthening belonging and lending a sense of mission. But, on the other, the uncontested consolidation and hegemony of teleological projects impoverishes our political imagination by excluding other possible futures and often resulting in forms of authoritarianism. The need to critically engage this teleological project derives from its existence as a fantasy of unity veiling social antagonisms that created a nation where there was none.

Notes

1. Ripa provided a detailed explanatory description of the image: 'AMERICA: A naked woman of dusky complexion, with a yellowish terrible face, and a colorful veil draped from one shoulder across the body, covering her shameful parts. It is best her hair be spread and around her body be a vague and artificial adornment of feathers of various colors. It is important she be holding a bow with her left hand and an arrow with the right; the quiver be by her side, full of arrows. Under one foot a human head pierced by an arrow; and on the ground, by her side, there could be a lizard or an alligator of excessive size.' Ripa goes on to explain the reasons for each of these iconographic decisions. Cesare Ripa, *Iconologia*, 4 vols, Perugia: Pergiovanni Constantini, 1766, vol. 4, p. 166.

2. Mikhail Bakhtin, 'Forms of Time and of the Chronotope in the Novel', in Michael Holquist, ed., *The Dialogic Imagination*, trans. Aryl Emerson, Austin: University of Texas, 1981, pp. 84–258.

3. It is widely shared because diverse sectors of the population find it useful to organize their lives around its narrative structure; it is future oriented because the narrative sequence posits an end result as the latent and natural consequence of past and present conditions; and they are socially effective because they mobilize symbolic and institutional resources in order to bring about the end result. In all cases, social efficacy is related to values and, thus, to social reproduction. Teleological projects formalize meaning and provide the scripts for social action through their narrative structure because they are structurally flexible and able to harbour different meanings such as inclusion *and* exclusion, inscription *and* disavowing, etc.

4. The term *castas*, as used by eighteenth- and nineteenth-century Spanish Americans, does not denote the closed, rigid and inheritable system of stratification defined by Louis Dumont in *Homo Hierarchicus*, Paris: Gallimard, 1967. Originally the term referred to lineage (see Sebastián de Covarrubias, *Tesoro de la Lengua Castellana o Española*, Barcelona: Editorial Alta Fulla, 1998, originally published in 1611) but in Spanish America it soon designated the strata of so-called 'mixed bloods' that made up an important segment of plebeian society. See Douglas Cope, *The Limits of Racial Domination: Plebeian Society in Colonial Mexico City, 1660–1720*, Madison: The University of Wisconsin Press, 1994.

5. Walter Benjamin, *Selected Writings*, eds Howard Eiland and Michael W. Jennings, vol. 2: 1927–1934, Cambridge, Mass.: Harvard University Press, 1999, Thesis XIII, p. 395. It was Benedict Anderson who explicitly connected Benjamin's reflection on historicism with the emergence of nationalism. See Benedict Anderson, *Imagined Communities: Reflections on the Origins and Spread of Nationalism*, 2nd revised edn, London: Verso, 1991.

6. See 'Título IX', article 346–68, Manuel Gutiérrez de Arce, *El Sínodo diocesano de Santiago de León de Caracas de 1687*, 2 vols, Caracas: Academia Nacional de la Historia, 1975, vol. 2, p. 144 and ff. See also Elías Pino Iturrieta, *Contra lujuria, castidad. Historias de pecado en el siglo XVIII venezolano*, Caracas: Alfadil Ediciones, 1992, specifically pp. 28–34.

7. 'Representación from the University of Caracas to the King on October 20, 1803', reproduced in Ildefonso Castro, ed., *Cedulario de la Universidad de Caracas*, Caracas: Universidad Central de Venezuela, 1965, p. 36.
8. Ayuntamiento de Caracas, 'Informe que el Ayuntamiento de Caracas hace al Rey de España referente a la real cédula del 10 de febrero de 1795', in José Félix Blanco, ed., *Documentos para la historia de la vida pública del Libertador*, Caracas: Imprenta de la Opinión Nacional, 1875, p. 290.
9. 'Acta del Cabildo de Caracas de 21 de noviembre de 1796', reproduced in Santos Rodulfo Cortés, *El régimen de 'las gracias al sacar' en Venezuela durante el período hispánico*, 2 vols, Caracas: Academia Nacional de la Historia, 1978, vol. 2, pp. 46–7. The second passage appears in José Hernández Palomo and Lila Mago de Chopite, *El Cabildo de Caracas, 1750–1821*, Caracas–Sevilla: CSIC-Escuela de Estudios Hispano-Americanos-UPEL-Cabildo Metropolitano de Caracas, 2002, p. 507.
10. In Ayuntamiento de Caracas, 'Informe', p. 291.
11. 'Representación fiscal de Francisco Berrío y Francisco Espejo (20 de abril de 1808)', in Angel Francisco Brice, ed., *Conjuración de 1808 en Caracas para formar una junta suprema gubernativa. Documentos completos*, 2 vols, Caracas: Academia Nacional de la Historia, 1969, vol. 1, p. 323.
12. See Germán Carrera Damas, 'República monárquica o monarquía republicana', in *Historia de América Andina*, vol. 4, Quito: Universidad Andina Simón Bolívar, 2003, p. 359 and ff.
13. Simón Bolívar, 'Address to the Angostura Congress, 15 February 1819, the Day of the Installation', in Janet Burke and Ted Humphrey, eds, *Nineteenth-Century Nation Building and the Latin American Intellectual Tradition. A Reader*, Indianapolis: Hackett Publishing Company, 2007, p. 5. Benito Laso, *Exposición que hace el Diputado al Congreso por la provincia de Puno*, Lima: Imprenta Republicana Administrada, 1826, p. 13.
14. Laso, *Exposición*, p. 14.
15. Simón Rodríguez, *Sociedades americanas*, Valparaiso, 1842, p. 24. For a definition of these terms, see Thomas M. Stephens, *Dictionary of Latin American Racial and Ethnic Terminology*, 2nd edn, Gainesville: University Press of Florida, 1999.
16. In botany the cryptogam designated species such as fungus and moss that do not reproduce by seeds. Though it is no longer used as a category for classifying, it was then – and still is – associated with sterility.
17. In Juan García del Río, *Meditaciones colombianas*, Bogotá: J. A. Cualla, 1829, p. 45.
18. Alexis de Tocqueville, *Democracy in America*, trans. Henry Reeve, 2 vols, New York: George Dearborn & Co., 1838, vol. I, p. 313. Henceforth page numbers will be provided within parentheses in the main text.
19. For an exploration of the place of miscegenation in the United States, see Elise Lemire, *Miscegenation: Making Race in America*, Philadelphia: University of Pensylvannia Press, 2002.
20. First part of the quote from a letter to General Pedro Briceño Mendes, 7 May 1828; the second from a letter to Colombia's Vice-president Francisco de Paula Santander, 7 June 1826. In Simón Bolívar, *Obras completas*, eds Vicente Lecuna and Esthel Barrel, 2nd edn, 2 vols, La Habana: Editorial Lex, 1950, vol. II, pp. 849, 403.
21. 'Talk of a race war became a recurrent element in conflicts between *pardos* and local elites over the meaning of revolutionary change during the early decades of the republican era.' Marixa Lasso, *Myths of Harmony: Race and Republicanism during the Age of Revolution, Colombia 1795–1831*, Pitt Latin American Series, Pittsburgh: University of Pittsburgh Press, 2007, p. 114.

22. Simón Bolívar, *Selected Writings*, ed. Harold A. Bierck, trans. Lewis Bertrand, 2nd edn, 2 vols, compiled by Vicente Lecuna, New York: Colonial Press, 1951, vol. 1, p. 112.

23. Simón Bolívar, *The Hope of the Universe*, ed. José Luis Salcedo-Bastardo, Mayenne, France: UNESCO, 1983, p. 118. The letter was written barely two years after Spanish officers Boves and Morales instigated a racial war to annihilate all 'white' Americans in Venezuela. See Germán Carrera Damas, *Boves. Aspectos socioeconómicos de la guerra de la independencia*, Caracas: Ediciones de la Biblioteca de la Univsidad Central de Venezuela, 1972; Miguel Izard, *El miedo a la revolución: La lucha por la libertad en Venezuela (1777–1830)*, Madrid, 1979; and Winthrop Wright, *Café con leche: Race, Class, and National Image in Venezuela*, Austin: University of Texas Press, 1990. Henceforth page numbers will be provided within parentheses in the main text.

24. What follows is from Bolívar, *Hope of the Universe*, pp. 118–21.

25. I quote from the more recent translation found in Bolívar, 'Angostura', pp. 5–6. Henceforth page numbers will be provided within parentheses in the main text.

26. Ibid., p. 10. I have corrected the translation.

27. 'Letter to General Santander', 6 January 1825, in Simón Bolívar, *Doctrina del Libertador*, 3rd revised and expanded edn, ed. Manuel Pérez Vila, Caracas: Biblioteca Ayacucho, 2009, p. 216.

28. Bolívar, 'Angostura', p. 17.

29. Domingo Faustino Sarmiento, *Facundo: Civilization and Barbarism*, trans. Kathleen Ross, Berkeley: University of California Press, 2003, pp. 32–3. Henceforth page numbers will be provided within parentheses in the main text.

30. His book *Educación Popular* (1849) became a classic and strongly influenced educational systems all over the continent.

31. *El Progreso*. Buenos Aires, 27 September 1844.

32. For an extended discussion of anthropological debates in the English-speaking world, see George Stocking, *Victorian Anthropology*, New York: Macmillan, 1987. For a useful description of anthropological debates in the US, see Stephen Jay Gould, 'American Polygeny and Craniometry before Darwin: Blacks and Indians as Separate, Inferior Species', in *The Mismeasure of Man*, New York: Penguin Books, 1996, pp. 62–104. I thank Marianne Sommer for her clarifying remarks on this and other points.

33. José María Samper, *Ensayo sobre las revoluciones políticas y la condición social de las Repúblicas colombianoas (Hispano-americanas); con un apéndice sobre la orografía y la población de la Confederación Granadina*, Paris: Imprenta de Thunot y C., 1861, p. 108. Henceforth page numbers will be provided within parentheses in the main text.

34. For an approach to Samper's writings as bearing a Creole legal consciousness which turned law into a civilizatory project, see Liliana Obregón, 'Completing Civilization: Creole Consciousness and International Law in Nineteenth-century Latin America', in Anne Orford, ed., *International Law and its Others*, Cambridge: Cambridge University Press, 2006.

35. According to Samper, as miscegenation became more intense 'civilization ameliorated among the masses, showing signs of more vitality, spontaneity, initiative, spirit of independence and equality; they exhibited stronger aspirations for improvement and welfare; more courage, intelligence and passion, less superstition and religious fanaticism, and a stronger tendency to participate in democratic institutions and in public affairs' (336–7). Racial fusion was also credited with fomenting the sentiments of right and duty, the art of deliberation, the need for freedom, respect for the family, the striving for property and the spirit of business, industry and commerce (328).

36. Nancy Leys Stepan, 'The Hour of Eugenics.' Race, Gender and Nation in Latin America, Ithaca, NY: Cornell University Press, 1991, p. 151. For a summarized position of the eugenic movement in Latin America, see pp. 147–70. Also Marisol de la Cadena, Indigenous Mestizos: The Politics of Race and Culture in Cuzco, Peru, 1919–1991, Durham, NC: Duke University Press, 2000.

37. Jean Baptiste Lamarck's Recherches sur l'organisation des corps vivants (1802), Philosophie zoologique (1809) and System of Invertebrate animals (1815–22) were out of print by the early 1830s and had remained out of the limelight until 1859 when Darwin engaged them in sustained criticism. However, his ideas were familiar – even summarized and widely refuted in Charles Lyell's celebrated Principles of Geology (1831–3) – and in many ways the broad outlines of his arguments had become shared assumptions. See Goulven Laurent, La Naissance du transformisme. Lamarck, entre Linné et Darwin, Paris: Vuibert, 2001, pp. 123–8. Carrera Damas ascertains that Lamarck's ideas were discussed in Caracas during the late colonial period. See Germán Carrera Damas, Historia de la historiografía venezolana: textos para su estudio, Caracas: Universidad Central de Venezuela, 1961, p. 66. For the Colombian case, see Alfonso Múnera Cavadía, Fronteras imaginadas: la construcción de las razas y de la geografía en el siglo XIX colombiano, Bogotá: Planeta, 2005.

38. Joseph Comte de Gobineau published his Essay on the Inequality of the Human Races between 1853 and 1855, six years before Samper's Ensayo. Gregor Johann Mendel's theory of inheritance was not published until 1866 and remained largely ignored until the twentieth century, when it was rediscovered by early genetic researchers.

39. See Henning Trüper with Dipesh Chakrabarty and Sanjay Subrahmanyam, Chapter 1 in this volume.

40. For a sample of these arguments, see the collection of essays in Homi Bhabha, ed., Nation and Narration, New York: Routledge, 1990.

41. I rely heavily on Doris Sommer's canonical account as put forth in her Foundational Fictions: The National Romances of Latin America, Berkeley: University of California Press, 1991.

42. In 1843, two years after the publication of the novel, there was a large black revolt that resulted in massive repression. See Robert L Paquette, Sugar is Made With Blood: The Conspiracy of La Escalera and the Conflict between Empires over Slavery in Cuba, Middletown, Conn.: Wesleyan University Press, 1990. For a history of black resistance in Cuba during the nineteenth century, see Ada Ferrer, Insurgent Cuba: Race, Nation, and Revolution, 1868–1898, Chapel Hill: University of North Carolina Press, 1999.

43. Doris Sommer devotes Chapter 4, 'Sab c'est moi', to a reading of this novel. See Sommer, Foundational Fictions, pp. 114–37.

44. 'Idea de nuestra América', in José Martí, Nuestra América, Caracas: Biblioteca Ayacucho, 2005, p. 38.

45. José Vasconcelos, 'El movimiento intelectual contemporáneo de México' (1916), in Antonio Caso et al., eds, Conferencias del Ateneo de la Juventud, México City: Universidad Nacional Autónoma de México, 2000, p. 120. See also his hugely influential Cosmic Race. La raza cósmica, ed. Didier T. Jaén, Baltimore: Johns Hopkins University Press, 1997.

46. Jose María Luis Mora, 'Letter to the Ministry of Foreign Relations', 31 July 1849, in Luis Chávez Orozco, ed., La gestión diplomática del doctor Mora, México: Editorial Porrúa, 1970, pp. 151–2.

47. Stepan, 'Hour of Eugenics', p. 151.

48. José María Luis Mora, Ensayos, ideas y retratos, Mexico City: Universidad Nacional Autónoma de México, 1991, p. 133.

49. Ronald Stutzman, 'Mestizaje: An All Inclusive Ideology of Exclusion', in Norman E. Whitten, ed., *Cultural Transformations and Ethnicity in Modern Ecuador*, Urbana-Champagne: University of Illinois Press, 1981.

50. Saint-Simonian Victor Courtet de L'Isle presented the argument that ethnographic data was central to the understanding of human history and meaning and the study of politics. See Victor Courtet de l'Isle, *La science politique fondée sur la science de l'homme, ou Étude des races humaines sous le rapport philosophique, historique et social*, Paris: A. Bertrand, 1838, pp. vi–xiii. For more on Courtet, see Jean Boissel, *Victor Courtet, 1813–1867: premier théoricien de la hiérarchie des races*, Paris: Presses Universitaires de France, 1972; Loïc Rignol and Philippe Régnier, 'Races et politique dans l'Histoire de France chez Victor Courtet de l'Isle (1813–1867). Enjeux de savoirs et luttes de pouvoir au XIX siècle', in Philippe Régnier, ed., *Études saint-simoniennes*, Lyon: Presses Universitaires Lyon, 2002; and the more recent Martin S. Staum, *Labeling People: French Scholars on Society, Race, and Empire, 1815–1848*, Montreal, Canada: McGill-Queen's Press, 2003. Jaime Urueña demonstrated the structural affinity of Samper's and Courtet's arguments. See Jaime Urueña Cervera, 'Idea de heterogeneidad racial en el pensamiento politico colombiano: una mirada historica', in *Análisis Político* 22 (1994).

51. Trüper, Chakrabarty and Subrahmanyam in Chapter 1 of this volume.

52. Charles Hale, 'Political and social ideas in Latin America, 1870–1930', in Leslie Bethell, ed., *The Cambridge History of Latin America*, New York: Cambridge University Press, 1985, p. 387.

CHAPTER 10
BETWEEN CONTEXT AND *TELOS*: REVIEWING THE STRUCTURES OF INTERNATIONAL LAW
Martti Koskenniemi

The law of nations – 'international law' – is the last refuge of political idealism. Throughout the last century diplomats, politicians and European intelligentsias vested their hopes of a more peaceful and a more just world in international institutions and rule-systems directed by international law. In the post-Cold War world of the 1990s, faith in law's ability to point beyond the mundane antics of contextual power was manifested in the stream of new institutions such as the World Trade Organization, set up in 1995 with a powerful system of dispute settlement, the International Criminal Court, established in 1998, and the complex mechanisms that arose for the protection of human rights across the world. Legal theorists may still puzzle over the meaning of the 'rule of law' but that vocabulary is nowadays deeply enshrined in the work of international institutions. A few years ago the UN even set up a special 'rule of law unit' and in 2012 a high-level meeting of the heads of state and government in the UN declared that the world's 'complex political, social and economic transformations ... must be guided by the rule of law, as it is the foundation of friendly and equitable relations between states and the basis on which just and fair societies are built'.[1]

That declaration, as well as countless other UN documents, takes it as given that law itself must guide social development, that the 'challenges and opportunities' in 'international peace and security, human rights and development' cannot be adequately met without law. This suggests an image of international law as more than just another governmental technique, that in acting as the 'foundation ... on which just and fair societies are built' law *itself* embodies a vision of a better world. In a massive recent collection of writings significantly titled *Realizing Utopia* (2012), edited by the late Antonio Cassese, an influential legal academic and activist, leading jurists speculate about the teleology of international law, the way it may lead from a world of conflicting sovereignties to a united 'international community'.[2] It is very difficult to think about international legal principles, treaty-making, just war and human rights protection without situating them within a historical trajectory of efforts to bring about the unity of humankind. International law's intrinsic virtue seems inextricable from its teleological character.

But as long as international law has been teleological, its relative distance from the present world of power has been the target of vigorous critiques. In one of the first works of 'modern' law of nations, *De jure belli ac pacis* of 1625, the Dutchman Hugo Grotius already sought to refute the claim attributed to the sceptic Carneades that 'right' was only a fancy name for 'interest', that it was a 'folly' to obey it on the ground that it might stand for some higher norm or purpose.³ Grotius operated with a vocabulary of natural sociability that his forerunners, the Spanish scholastics of the sixteenth century, had envisaged in terms of the supernatural beatitude to which all creation was oriented. Since then, 'sociability' has offered a predominant platform over which sceptical minds have been challenged by reading the facts of the present in view of their orientation to an ideal future. Anthropology, political theory and economics have each been enlisted to give scientific assistance to this process. When international law arose as a 'modern' profession in the late nineteenth century within the institutions of Western academy and diplomacy it was underwritten by a liberal cosmopolitanism that posited free individuals as the objective of a supranational law that, although it arose from a world divided in nation-states, would in due course transgress the conditions of its emergence.

In the twentieth and twenty-first centuries, international law's moral pull received expression in increasingly complex technical institutions whose orientation towards a future world in the image of the European state was seldom questioned. Activist lawyers read the Covenant of the League of Nations in the 1930s as 'Higher Law' and it is quite common today to address the UN Charter of international law itself as a kind of a world 'constitution'.⁴ The rapid, uncoordinated emergence of universal and regional legal regimes in the recent decades has often been read as 'resumption' of a historical process that had been only temporarily arrested by the Cold War. If lawyers today express some anxiety about the resulting 'fragmentation of international law', this reflects the assumption that humanity's *telos* was political unity within a single, coherent system of international law.⁵

However, since Grotius's quarrel with Carneades, for every effort to articulate the objective of international law in universal terms there have been those who have insisted on the local, particular and materially limited ambitions of a 'realistic' international law. Grotius formed his views about intrinsic sociability during a religious crisis in Europe that would be temporarily settled in the Peace of Westphalia (1648). The peace became a symbol of the political-legal order of modernity, built on the sovereignty of states, that has since then been endlessly interpreted both as an early milestone in a continuous progression towards world peace and justice and a *realpolitik* arrangement about the momentary balance of power between Europe's warring factions. The 'myth' of Westphalia continues to give expression to the opposition between 'believers' and 'sceptics' – those to whom international law does have an inherent objective in a morally united humankind and those to whom it is at best simply an instrument of political states for the realization of their divergent objectives.

In this chapter I aim to discuss the ways in which teleology animates and structures views on how legal rules and institutions govern the world. The distinction between 'believers' and 'sceptics' or 'idealists' and 'realists', although not wrong, is too crude to give a reliable orientation to the debates. Teleology can and does take different forms and I will identify four of them. I will start out by sketching the emergence of what could be called 'internal teleology' that sees law *itself*, the very form and way of operation of legal rules and institutions, as embedded with a moral ethos. In this view, commitment to law (in its various forms) is not only necessary but sufficient to bring about the gradual unification of the world. I will contrast this with 'external teleology', the view that law is above all a neutral and 'empty' instrument for the realization of a purposefulness to be found in an external world of ideas or facts. A third view – 'anti-teleology' – denies any significant identity or purpose to law. International law is simply what international actors make of it, a more or less (often less) useful tool to enable them to pursue their conflicting agendas. A final view – 'hyper-teleology' – understands international law as *both* a carrier of an autonomous moral objectivity *and* responsive to the 'needs' or 'interests' that exist in the deep structure of the international society. In this view, international conflict results from international actors' misunderstanding of their interests that, rightly seen, lie in scrupulous respect of legal rules.

The four positions capture, with a different focus, an argument that I have made earlier about the structure of international legal argument.[6] In that work, my intention was to illustrate the way prima facie plausible arguments are created and operate in professional international practice so as to create disputes and help to resolve them. My interest was to account for the argument's formally repetitive and substantively indeterminate character. In this chapter I would like to link familiar ideas about international law's role in the world to their historical and ideological contexts so as to demonstrate the reasons both for their persistence and for their inconclusiveness.

1. Internal teleology

The most important aspect of the development of the academic discipline of 'law of nature and of nations' (*ius naturae et gentium*) in Germany during the eighteenth century had to do with efforts to develop the notion of 'sociability' that Grotius once situated at its core. In the tradition inaugurated by Samuel Pufendorf, 'sociability' was understood as a rational conclusion that self-loving but rational individuals drew from their existential situation. Owing to their pathetic weakness, humans could only survive and flourish by cooperating with each other. Natural law was the name for those forms of collaboration that reason taught that humans had an interest to adopt.[7] It provided for the establishment of private property and that contracts should be binding. And it suggested that humans should join together in political states so as to be able to enforce the legal relations formed spontaneously in civil society. Moreover, because humans were weak and unreliable, they needed a strong executive power – an absolutist sovereign – to coerce them. '*Salus populi suprema lex esto*' – let the good of the people be the supreme law, Pufendorf wrote, but insisted that the happiness of the nation had to be imposed on an ignorant and fickle population by a political superior.[8]

The rules concerning the relations between states were analogous to the rules that had applied in the state of nature between individuals. They were what reason suggested was in the interests of the states themselves. This mostly meant collaboration through traditional forms of diplomacy and treaty-making. War for punishment of breach of natural law was prohibited; only a universal sovereign could engage in such. The only legitimate reason for violence was to react to injury – that is to say, for self-preservation and self-defence.⁹ For Pufendorf and the tradition that followed him in the German law faculties, the law of nations was part of the utilitarian pursuit of the happiness ('*Glückseligkeit*') of the nation. It had no independent objective beyond what was good for each state. Therefore, it could also not be enforced by any higher power. This led some eighteenth-century natural lawyers, such as Christian Thomasius, to believe that the law of nations was not really a part of what he called '*iustum*', strict law, but instead '*decorum*', rules of behaviour based on diplomatic tradition and prudence.[10]

Much of the eighteenth-century debate on the law of nations concentrated on demonstrating the balance of power as a principle of European public law. This view was based on the well-founded suspicion among the jurists that even if the sovereigns did not have a rational interest to engage in war with one another, they were unreliable and egoistic, always ready to run after short-term gratification. They could only be withheld from aggression by the conviction that violence would be immediately met by overwhelming force. Famously, Emer de Vattel in his 1758 classic *The Law of Nations* consecrated the right of European nations to take pre-emptive action against ambitious sovereigns whose power had increased and who had a reputation for aggressive behaviour as a principle of the law of nations.[11]

It was against all this that Immanuel Kant developed his view of the law of nations as in itself a carrier of the ideal constitution of a cosmopolitan world. When Kant's *Critique of Pure Reason* (1781) descended upon German intellectual life, natural law's philosophical support to the already fragile theory of monarchic absolutism collapsed and 'the categorical imperative was immediately taken as providing a new foundation of natural law theory'.[12] *The Critique of Pure Reason* completely undermined the effort to find from nature the principles of just government. Either it manifested excessive faith in abstract reason – or then it assumed that empirical nature itself might give norms to human behaviour. Both views were mistaken. The hubris of abstract reason led into contradictions and 'antinomies' with which anything could be proven. And pure empiricism unthinkingly bound itself in conventional concepts and categories that would always maintain what already existed. Hence Kant concluded:

> Unfortunately for speculation – but perhaps fortunately for the practical interests of humanity – reason, in the midst of its highest anticipations, finds itself jostled by claims and counterclaims, from which neither its honour nor its safety will permit it to draw back.[13]

'[P]erhaps fortunately for the practical interests of humanity'. With that Kant referred to the way the critique pointed to the primacy of practical over theoretical reason. For although people did look for happiness, their concept of what 'happiness' meant differed, and coercing humans in view of a notion of happiness they did not share was a violation of their freedom. But, he argued, the important question was not 'how to be happy but how we should become worthy of happiness' – a distinction that humans may not always honour but that they routinely made.[14] In regarding human beings as objects of happiness-inducing policies, the natural lawyers assimilated humans with passive nature.

This undermined their freedom, superimposing on them an external authority claiming to know better what it was they really needed or what was in their interest.

The only way to maintain freedom in society, Kant argued, was by governing it with universal laws, the most important of which said 'act only in accordance with that maxim which you can at the same time will that it become universal law'.[15] In order to find a legitimate basis for social constraint, humans had to abstract themselves from their particular notions of happiness and imagine what kind of rule would be rationally acceptable for all. This, Kant explained, could only be a 'republican' system of rule under law, enacted in accordance with a constitution. '[T]he ground of all practical lawgiving lies (in accordance with [the categorical imperative]) objectively in the rule and the form of universality which makes it fit to be a law.'[16]

Here now was an 'internal teleology' for which it was not the law's point to advance particular interests, agendas or notions of happiness but simply to be 'law', to have universal form. That universality would then *itself* bring about the freedom that was the immediate object of the law and enable humans to be seen as *ends in themselves*, not as instruments for others' purposes.[17] Kant then projected his 'legalism' onto the international level in the small essay on 'Perpetual Peace' (1795) where he claimed that a condition of lawfulness could only be attained internationally by reforms at three levels: state law, international law and cosmopolitan law. First, all states ought to become 'republican' – they should adopt a representative ('non-despotic') form of government operating under a constitution.[18] Second, existing states ought to join in a 'pacific federation' 'that would not aim to acquire the power of a state but merely to preserve and secure the freedom of each state in itself, along with that of other confederated states'.[19] And third, there ought to be a 'cosmopolitan law' that would consecrate the 'right of a stranger not to be treated with hostility when he arrives in someone else's territory'.[20] This did not mean a right to any particular type of treatment, merely to allow the foreigners to conduct their affairs peaceably.

Kant believed that such a three-level structure would *in itself* already bring about the most important objectives of social life, namely the autonomy of the individual and the equal respect of each. This idea sought practical expression in the proposal made in the French National Assembly in 1793 and 1795 by the Abbé Grégoire on the adoption of a *Declaration of the Rights of Nations* that in twenty-one articles sought to do to international relations what the *Déclaration de droits de l'homme et du citoyen* of 1789 had aimed to accomplish at home. This was to treat each state as a free and independent subject, equal to every other nation and entitled to follow its policies without external intervention.[21] The proposal was never adopted but its thrust was repeated by liberal spirits across the nineteenth century. For example, the Erlangen philosopher Johann Heinrich Abicht (1762–1816) explained that experience could not expound the law 'as it ought to be'. Instead he deduced a full conception of law from the absolute and conditional rights of humans derived from the nature human beings as *ends for themselves*. The absolute rights were valid everywhere and formed the foundation of all public power. Among them, autonomy was essential and it was realized in society by *Selbstverpflichtung* – voluntary submission to laws designed to organize social life in such a way as to maintain the maximal freedom of everyone.²² Abicht's law of nations was based on the 'general rights of each people' in which a 'people' was defined as any community united by virtue of language, common territory or social objective.²³ The right of self-determination would realize a world of free nations in the image of the domestic rule of law.²⁴

In the course of the nineteenth century, this view came to be expressed in a legal formalism whose concept of 'sovereignty' expressed the nature of states as both internally and externally free and equal 'subjects' of international law that could be bound only to the extent that they so willed. The Kantian principle of autonomy was respected in the (German) theory of 'autolimitation' that saw the binding force of treaties and customs explained by reference to their expressing state will.²⁵ Such 'will', adherents of this view added in the same breath, would not be what statesmen might at any moment prefer, however. 'Will' as an expression of state autonomy was derived from the conditions of the international world expressed in an objectified legal conviction ('*Rechtsüberzeugung*') that, as the public lawyer Paul Schoen put it, was 'the solid moment standing behind individual legal sources'.²⁶

Kantian agendas for federalism and cosmopolitan law in the nineteenth century remained largely confined in jurisprudence classes and peace movements. They inspired informal citizen activity across boundaries but failed to emerge as serious governmental blueprints. Legalism, however, the view that law has moral value through its constitutional form or as a representative of a 'legal consciousness', became an enormously influential aspect of liberal legislative ideology. Yet that ideology was afflicted by an internal tension between the support it gave to the absolute autonomy of the state's legal order and its pull towards a binding system of international law. Throughout the twentieth century liberal legalists walked a narrow path between loyalty to the complex system of state law and the expanding legislative work of international institutions such as the League of Nations, the United Nations and the European Union. It was true, as Hans Kelsen, the twentieth century's most important representative of Kantian 'legalism' pointed out, that domestic and international laws were often incompatible and that legalism necessitated a choice between them. Which one would be superior? In practice, judges and other actors at home tended to privilege domestic laws while international activists opted for the primacy of the international. Kelsen himself was a critic of the 'unscientific' nature of teleological views of law.²⁷ Accordingly, he also thought that the question of primacy was one of political value incapable of being resolved on legalist premises. And yet, this did not prevent him from making his own preference clear. Priority to international laws was a 'pacifist' solution while priority to domestic law led to 'imperialism'.²⁸

At the beginning of the twenty-first century, the significance of that juxtaposition has no doubt diminished. The domestic and the international legal worlds have fragmented into relatively autonomous systems (trade law, humanitarian law, security law, environmental law, etc.) that regulate disparate aspects of social behaviour for which their 'domestic' or 'international' origin is no longer decisive. They operate in a 'transnational' fashion and no longer derive their moral force from a teleology internal to law. In fact, to commit to 'law' makes little sense in a world where the important question is about *which* law (and *which* institution) one should commit to.[29] The fact that the laws of these 'regimes' are conceived in a wholly functional fashion, that is to say that their normative pull is received not from their character as 'law' (indeed, much of the new global regulation does *not* have that character) but from their ability to advance this or that technical, economic or moral imperative, marks a move from 'Kantian' – internal – teleology to one that is externally constructed.

2. External teleology

Kant's optimism about the growth of international law did not rely only on its internal teleology. In the essay on 'Universal History with a Cosmopolitan Purpose' (1784) and also later in 'Perpetual Peace', Kant laid out the principle of 'unsocial sociability', whereby nature itself, by creating problems and challenges, would ultimately induce humans to take measures to enter a 'civil state' under a binding constitution.[30] Out of the very experience of wars and devastations would gradually emerge a conviction that the dangerous state of nature among nations must be left behind and a peaceful, law-governed international order should be created. Even the separation of nations, Kant believed, might help in this by compelling nations to seek goods that are lacking in their own territories from other nations: 'the *spirit of commerce* sooner or later takes hold of every people, and it cannot exist side by side with war'.[31]

The view of nature itself as a 'guarantee of a perpetual peace' constituted a partial accommodation by Kant of ideas about natural sociability that he had earlier rejected. Kant refrained from speaking about 'providence', but regarded his teleology as a transcendental hypothesis humans needed to make in order for everything else they knew about the world to make sense. Nevertheless, it still resembled greatly the evolutionary ideas that natural lawyers at German universities had been putting forward so as to create a scientific concept of law that would attach law's normativity to an underlying – 'external' – *telos* to be found in nature itself. This was a powerful eighteenth-century idea, perhaps most famously present in Montesquieu and the comparativist tradition. It would now be the task of scientific jurists to survey the histories and living conditions of nations so as to see what kinds of law would be appropriate for each society. The view had been put forward with perhaps the greatest influence in Adam Smith's *Lectures on Jurisprudence* (1762–4), where Smith had discussed the development of property laws and contracting through a frame in which societies would move 'naturally' from hunters to shepherds and then to agricultural and finally commercial forms of organization. Each stage, Smith and a whole tradition of historical jurisprudence assumed, corresponded to a distinct system of ownership rights; the law, as it were, would 'borrow' its teleology from the society that it would help organize and govern.[32]

The historical view transformed the universal principles of *jus naturae et gentium* into a 'Public Law of Europe' or a 'modern law of nations of Europe'. If the law was a historical phenomenon, its rules and principles closely tied with the development of the social institutions that it regulated, then there was no doubt that the law that had governed contacts between European capitals was *European* law. The leading early-nineteenth-century international lawyer Georg Friedrich von Martens, the head of something like the first school of diplomats in Göttingen, for example, rejected any hypothesis of a universal ('rational') law of nations.[33] The peoples of the world were simply too different and had to be governed under different rules. Instead, a practical community had arisen among Europeans that had its origins in antiquity, and had developed through progress of religion, voyages of discovery, the rise of a system of hierarchy and equilibrium. The Peace of Westphalia (1648) and Utrecht (1713) had begun 'a new and memorable epoch of positive law of nations', allowing the development of a *pragmatic* science of international law, with consciousness of the history of the nations to which it was to be applied.[34]

> C'est donc dans l'histoire générale et particulier des Etats de l'Europe . . . qu'on doit puiser l'histoire de l'origine et du progrès du droit des gens conventionnel et coutumier; histoire qui n'a pas encore été traitée avec tout le soin qu'elle merite, quoiqu'on aïe commence à s'en occuper avec success.[35]

In a footnote to that sentence, Martens referred to the first full-scale post-naturalist history of international law, Robert Ward's *An Enquiry into the Foundation and History of the Law of Nations from the Time of the Greeks and the Romans to the Age of Grotius* (1795), which opened with a touching admission by its author that once he had collected all the treaties, cases and other materials, he found himself unable to answer the question about their universally binding force.[36] Although he could see how the practices of Christian nations might become binding to Christians, he found no basis on which to claim that they were binding everywhere. Besides, 'natural law' usually meant different things for different people, so that it was futile and misleading to treat it as if it stood for universal law. Only religion could provide certainty; where religions differed, uniformity was impossible. This meant that there must be 'a different law of nations for different parts of the globe'.[37]

During the first half of the nineteenth century, jurists were clear that international law was a product of European history and reflected the aspirations of European nations. To think otherwise was to remain imprisoned in an altogether abstract world of moral principles that could not found an objective, scientific pursuit of international law. The protest against natural law took sometimes striking forms. The English lawyer Richard Wildman, for example, who insisted that international law had emerged from customary practices among European nations, contrasted this reality with the moral concerns that had been voiced at the time he was writing (1849). There was no doubt, he observed, that 'by the law of nature, all men are born free' and that slavery and the slave trade were contrary to natural law.[38] But this did not at all mean that if a ship with slaves on board was captured at sea for one or another reason, the slaves were to be set free. Slavery had been with us 'from the earliest periods of history of mankind', he wrote, 'found existing, and as far as appears, without adimversion from the earliest and most authentic records of human race'. From such facts it followed that '[s]lavery is an institution of the law of nations, whereby one man is subject to the dominion of another, contrary to nature'.[39]

Perhaps it was precisely the objectionable character of that conclusion that moved late-nineteenth-century jurists to reject an exclusively historical orientation. A new generation of lawyers organizing themselves around the *Institut de droit international* in the 1870s and 1880s began to use international law as an instrument of liberal progress in Europe and the 'civilization' of the colonies. A leading member of this group, Johann Caspar Bluntschli, for example, who had studied under the head of the German historical school, Carl Friedrich von Savigny, and was the author of some of the most widely appreciated codifications of private law in his native Switzerland, tried expressly to find a moderate centre between purely historical and rationalist views on international law, putting the advancement of a shared universal human nature as its ultimate objective in his widely read treatise on 'modern' international law (1868).[40] Together with a number of colleagues and friends from Belgium, France, Netherlands and the United Kingdom a new generation of liberal, Protestant jurists with a cosmopolitan mindset came to see international law as an instrument to advance the cause of liberal reform.[41]

The new generation regarded as part of international law's liberal *telos* the 'civilization' of the non-European world. This meant the gradual adoption by Turkey, China, Japan, Siam, and the rest of what was addressed collectively as 'the Orient', of European legal principles, codes and procedures. Even as the jurists were not always happy with the vocabulary of 'civilization' they had no doubt about the benefits of European culture and interpreted world history through a frame that presented European modernity as its highest achievement. The jurists engaged in extensive debates about the nature of 'Oriental' cultures so as to develop a hierarchy of civilizational stages that would help in administering the eventual entry of non-European states as full subjects of international law. Nothing came of this effort, however, and the lawyers continued to have widely opposite views on the standard as well as the defensibility of the extraterritorial and consular jurisdiction under which Europeans exempted themselves from the laws of the 'Oriental' world until late in the twentieth century. It throws a dubious gloss over the workings of the *Institut* that most of its members took part in the colonial ventures of their nations, which they understood as part of the same process of modernization as the law in which they were experts.[42]

The peace conferences of 1899 and 1907, as well as increasing recourse to arbitration treaties at the turn of the century, supported by this group of jurists from their positions in the academy and diplomacy, did little to prevent Europe's descent into the Great War in 1914. But the war did induce anxious questions about what had gone wrong. Many jurists – especially non-German jurists – blamed the historical school for having supported a rather extreme form of nationalism and the consolidation of a strong concept of 'sovereignty' at the heart of international law. This view was taken, for example by Georges Scelle, the most visible international lawyer in interwar France, who was inspired by Emile Durkheim and based his notion of international legality on the biological need for social solidarity among states and international institutions, and ultimately among humans generally. In Scelle's expressly 'sociological' concept, rules of law emerged from and expressed material necessities of the 'social milieu'. The laws, conventions or customs that are recognized as the 'formal' sources of international law did not receive their binding force from any postulated 'will' of a sovereign legislator but from its conformity with what Scelle chose to call 'la necessité et l'intérêt publics ou la finalité sociale'.⁴³ Writing within the idiom of radical French public law, Scelle rejected 'sovereignty' as having any reality; on the contrary, it was the expression of frankly anti-social and egoistic policies of some national leaders, responsible for the interwar crisis. Rightly conceived, state power was simply the right of decision entrusted to domestic institutions by an overriding (public) international legal order.⁴⁴

The sociological movement responded to what it saw as the wholly mystical and retrograde principle of sovereignty by postulating objective laws of societal development to which international law was expected to 'respond'. Jurists such as the Belgian Charles de Visscher or Percy Corbett from Princeton and Virginia Law School were disappointed by the 'idealism' of the interwar jurists and sought a legal idiom more respectful of diplomacy and the political interests of states.⁴⁵ Others were interested in recent technological and economic developments that in an interdependent world might help international law to give formal articulation to the unity of humankind. In the 1950s and 1960s jurists at political science departments in the United States began to carry out studies on the 'functions' of international law in the modern world. International reform was now advocated in terms of the need to make law better 'reflect' societal transformations always already under way somewhere. '[I]mbued with a new practical spirit, an orientation to process and policy at once contextual, purposive and functional, the new international lawyer/academic for the sixties would be an ethical pluralist and technician, the consummate advisor to enlightened government or business, and the skilled architect of a new "transnational" order.'⁴⁶ The title of the most famous international law book of the 1960s, Wolfgang Friedmann's (1907–72) *The Changing Structure of International Law*, said it all: as aspects of modernity, international trade, technology, development and human rights were uniting the world, so now it was necessary to transform the legal superstructure to reflect those changes.⁴⁷

Alongside the scientific-technical there has also persisted a form of morally imbued external teleology that often looks to 'humanity' as a set of normative demands on international law. This generalizes from developments in international human rights and humanitarian law, from the rise of international criminal tribunals and the overall concern with 'victims' and 'dignity' an updated vocabulary of liberal internationalism. 'Global law, or the Law of Humanity, does not yet constitute a legal order in the strictest sense, but it is called to become one … It is the task of jurists to bring us to the point where we can accurately speak of a new global legal order.'⁴⁸ These texts pursue the anti-sovereignty ethos of twentieth-century international law in a partly new tone that mixes moral pathos with abstract sociological generalization. It is hard to know what to make of the widespread uses of words such as 'humanity' or 'human dignity' as the centre of a new law. In part operating with the most tired twentieth-century internationalist clichés, in part enlisting well-founded concerns over the possibilities of regulating 'globalization', these works resemble a kind of postmodern naturalism which presumes the presence of a unity of vision that, if it existed, would render them superfluous.

Such 'external teleologies' are poised between two familiar dangers. On the one hand they reduce international law into a 'dependent variable' of some factual constellation of effective power, an uncritical consecration of the status quo. Much of the political science-inspired work in the United States, for example, was and remains nationalistic and directed to assist US foreign policy decision-making.[49] On the other hand, in their moralist incarnation, their generality and open-endedness account for their appeal as well as their futility. During the interwar era, for example, a moral view of law as an expression of social solidarity was used both by socialist agitators and traditionalist Christians to heighten the European crisis.[50] A view of law as a carrier of a teleology adopted from the external world of social and technological progress or from large sentimental notions of 'humanity' and 'dignity' appears in the end as natural law *redivivus* that, like its eighteenth-century predecessors, produces conclusions that are either politically contested or then formulated with such abstraction that nothing definite would follow from them.

3. Anti-teleology

But the natural law tradition also produced a powerful critique of the originally scholastic view that nature itself had a purposefulness with which the law of nations was to align itself. In *Leviathan* (1651), Thomas Hobbes famously identified only one international principle – namely that of the bottomless fear and egoism that reigned between sovereigns who 'because of their Independency, are in continuall jealousies, and in the state and posture of Gladiators'.[51] In such a situation, international law could exist only as temporary strategic accommodations with no independent normative pull. Later natural lawyers such as Pufendorf and Thomasius, for example, agreed with Hobbes to the extent that they, too, thought the international world was devoid of a sovereign to enforce its commands. But they insisted that it possessed tangible reality as a cultural practice and projection of the interests of European states. Its purposefulness was inextricable from the *Staatszweck*, the purpose of the state; namely the happiness of its people. For many, this always seemed a fragile compromise. If it was the essence of modern law that it arose out of sovereign command and was backed up by the complex enforcement machine of the modern state, then international law was 'law' only in a most tenuous, metaphoric sense. In his *Province of Jurisprudence Determined* (1832) the Englishman John Austin concluded that international law was in truth just a positive morality: 'positive' inasmuch as it had to do with what states and their leaders did and wanted and 'morality' owing to the absence of centralized enforcement.[52] In itself this might not have purged international law from teleological sense – after all, as 'morality' it could well be invested with a purposefulness of its own. But when connected with the liberal principle of subjectivity of value the Austinian view led to the fragmentation of the law of nations from a single 'morality' into opinions that men in high positions held about 'moral' matters generally.

Most nineteenth-century writers engaged with the Austinian view in one way or another. Some tried to repair the situation by arguing that international public opinion operated as a unifying force behind an otherwise unenforceable law of nations. For liberal thinkers such as James Mill, for example, public opinion was an inherently progressive expression of the cultural consciousness of a well-informed, modern (European) public. Honour and shame were prime movers of politics and every nation had a lot to gain from the maintenance of a good reputation. Although popular views would not have much of an effect in autocracies, nevertheless

> in countries the rulers of which are drawn from the mass of the people, in other words, in democratic countries ... the sanction of the laws of nations can be expected to operate with any considerable effect.[53]

The late nineteenth-century liberal elites that participated in the professionalization of international law in foreign ministries and law schools largely shared this view. For them, too, public opinion represented the articulation of modern history's intrinsic goal-directness that would eventually include a more organized enforcement of the law as well. It was this view, the view that international law represented some global developmental *telos*, that was vigorously contested by especially German jurists who denied that, unlike domestic law, international law would have represented any unified, historically informed social ideal. The Hegelian Adolf Lasson, for example, writing in the aftermath of the Franco-Prussian War in 1871, identified a supranational legal system precisely as a 'Jesuit' idea that, however appealing it might seem to some liberals, nevertheless constituted an unjustifiable expansion of the concept of 'law'.[54] What we see in the international world is irreducible antagonism between states, each inspired by its history and interest, by the 'social ideal' that it has come to represent. No comparable ideal is to be found anywhere in the international world. The state, he wrote, that began as a system of external order has eventually become 'Mittel zum Schutze aller Heiligthümer des Volkes, seiner gesammten geistigen Cultur'.[55]

Lasson's work was produced during the Franco-Prussian war and although his celebration of the power of a 'free people' may have seemed understandable at the moment of the declaration of a unified German *Reich*, the point about international law lacking a social ideal of its own, and thus any independent teleology, had a persisting legacy. In 1911 Erich Kaufmann, Germany's legal counsel in many of its interwar cases with the Permanent Court of International Justice, published a notorious work arguing that every international obligation actually contained a silent reservation concerning the protection of the vital interests of the states. For both Lasson and Kaufmann, international law was possible only as a 'law of coordination' – a technique whereby they could advance their parallel interests. But its power was strictly limited by the maintenance of the harmony of those interests; once an antagonism resurfaced, the law was unable to transcend it. 'The State must, in order for the law to preserve its nature as a law of coordination law and not subordination, stand above its treaties.'[56]

Under such a view, represented today by a sizeable part of the US legal academy, international law is devoid of any independently normative teleology. It may be useful as a technical tool to organize reciprocal relations or engage in common ventures. But it could not impose any demands on states from the outside.⁵⁷ If its normative pull is exhaustively determined by the interest of the state – in practice, the perception of their interests by the leading elites – then it is devoid of autonomously binding force. What binds and compels are the interests or interest-perceptions, not the law. Among the most powerful presentations of this view in the twentieth century was E. H. Carr's attack on the legalist myth of a 'harmony of interests' supposedly bringing nations to cooperate under international law. In truth a mere 'combination of platitude and falseness', the harmony interests meant in practice whatever was dictated by the leading powers in an effort to avoid the more costly alternative of war. Law had a place in providing regularity and creating expectations. But because there was no 'international community' that would represent an ethical system, international law remained just the preferences of the stronger group and 'valid' only as long that group thinks it useful.⁵⁸ A parallel point was made by one of the founders of 'international relations', the jurist Hans Morgenthau, in a 1940 article where he called for a 'functionalist' approach to international law that would move from the 'indefatigable repetition of magic formulae' to the examination of the 'rules of law as they are actually applied'.⁵⁹ Morgenthau's 'functionalism' was a mixture of empirical analysis, mass psychology and decisionism. But he never followed up on it himself. Indeed, there was little reason why ambitious academics would waste time on an irrelevancy. To the extent that international law was merely a surface reflection of power and ideology, it offered no promise at all that its practitioners might find themselves in the avant-garde of global progress.

4. Hyper-teleology

The prior three types of teleology each postulated a gap between the law and the context in which it was to apply: indeed assuming such was nothing more than presuming that law did not just 'reflect' the world but posed demands to it. Internal teleology received that demand from the quality of law as 'law'. To the command 'obey' it gave no further explanation than 'because it is law'. External teleology received law's normative force from its hooking onto a moral or social rationality that also explained and justified its normative pull. Anti-teleology denied both, arguing that law was empty of intrinsic normative sense as well as incapable of efficiently seizing any external rationality. It was merely a formal reflection of relations produced and upheld by other forces. 'Hyper-teleology' is the most ambitious of the four concepts. While it the most difficult of law's teleologies to grasp (because it is ubiquitous), it embodies a powerful invitation to join modern law's project of constant renewal.

I call hyper-teleology that aspect of (modern) international law that has erased the gap between law and reality – where law is simply the formal articulation of a reality that *has already changed and only calls for accepting and adapting to the change.* 'The future', this type of law claims, 'is already here; we just have to open our eyes, and act accordingly.' Instead of calling for unconditional loyalty to law (internal teleology) or joining law's effort to change a present reality that is in some regards retrograde or unacceptable (external teleology), and instead of adopting a purely strategic attitude to law (anti-teleology), hyper-teleology invites a change of consciousness. The problem is not with the world but with our retrograde, confused or mistaken cognition of it. That cognition must change and the law is expected to achieve just that. Today's hyper-teleology would argue, for example, that the law of a 'fluid' globalization does not remain ('formalistically') tied to sovereign boundaries but turns into professionally organized 'regulatory networks' operating as an 'international governance mechanism' that

> offers a fast and flexible alternative to more cumbersome hierarchies of international treaties ... [and] promote[s] the distribution of best practices and allow[s] for technical standardization and enforcement assistance.[60]

Under this view, new technologies have opened unforeseen possibilities for expanding security and happiness. The only problem lies in the lack of understanding among lawyers and decision-makers of this fact.

The power of hyper-teleology lies in its scientism, the way it erases the boundary between law and technologies of expertise that claim to seize society's 'real' dynamic directly, without the mediation of slow and cumbersome political (legislative) decision-making. The same move may be witnessed in the slippage in eighteenth-century naturalism to governmental science and economics. In the 1760s the French Physiocrats suggested – as illustrated by their leader, François Quesnay's *tableau economique* – that the economy operated as an autonomous system that only needs to be liberated to produce all the 'happiness' that natural lawyers had been looking for. It did not yet immediately follow that 'law' would have been replaced by 'economy'. However, this is what was effectively suggested by the most ambitious of the group, the lawyer Paul-Pierre Le Mercier de la Rivière. There was, he wrote in *Natural and Essential Order of Political Societies* (1767), a 'natural order' for societies that 'is nothing but a branch of the physical order'.[61] By grasping this, humans could realize the principal objects of all their actions: enjoyment of pleasure and avoidance of pain. Societies were based on the search for happiness, and the greatest happiness was abundance: 'le plus grand bonheur possible consiste pour nous *dans la plus grande abondance possible d'objets propres à nos jouissances* ...'.[62]

To achieve this, production had to increase. This, again, was possible only in a regime of liberty – through the free use of our forces and our properties. As social order was part of the physical world, knowledge of its laws was knowledge of *absolute justice and absolute injustice*; like the laws of nature they operated in an absolute way.[63] Everything either pointed to increased abundance or it did not; that is, everything was either called upon or prohibited. Private vices turn into public virtues. 'In the system of nature every human being tends constantly to its best possible state of being and in this, it necessarily strives to the best state of the whole corpus of society.'[64]

That Le Mercier repeated over again the italicized expression '*absolute*' highlighted the *necessary* character of this order of relationships. Quesnay had already written that '[t]he natural laws of the social order are themselves the physical laws of perpetual reproduction of those goods necessary to the subsistence, the conservation, and the convenience of men'.[65] This led Le Mercier to propose that society was to be governed by the intrinsic laws of the social order, given by nature itself. The only task was to discover them and to 'dictate' them to society at large.[66] For this reason, there was no point in distinguishing between legislative and executive power: one was merely the extension of the other: 'Partager l'autorité, c'est l'annuller.'[67] A multitude of opinions would create chaos, while the power and correctness of legislation would be guaranteed by the proof of the laws of the social order. One needed only to read 'society' to receive its 'absolutely' binding norms.

In the German realm, too, a major part of natural law would transform itself into political economy, with the first chair of the discipline established at the University of Tübingen in 1817.[68] That had been an offshoot of the realization, in part owing to the influence of the French economists, in part the reception of Adam Smith in cameralism and policy-science (*Policey*), that state governance might also require refraining from intervention in the civil society – that is to say, to allow its intrinsic laws to operate 'naturally'. A new generation of natural lawyers now began to emphasize the freedoms of the individual, as articulated in the inalienable nature of their (freedom-) rights not only as the core of natural law and the basis of a well-functioning economy but also of a cosmopolitan world order.[69] Though written in a natural law idiom (and thus adopting an external teleology), the linking of that argument with modernity's developmental rationality tended to support a post-ethical world where among free individuals only technical questions of governing would remain. When Wilhelm von Humboldt in the 1790s made the argument for limiting the state's role to that of guardian of 'security', this opened the door for arguing that peace and progress in the *international* world, too, might best be achieved by allowing its dynamism to operate freely and without external intervention.[70] The point of the techniques of diplomacy and treaty-making would henceforth be to lift the 'artificial' boundaries that had been established to control the free movement of persons, goods and ideas.

Many international lawyers in the first part of the nineteenth century shared Cobdenite views about the pacific effects of free trade. But neither then nor in the 1870s and 1880s, when dismantling customs barriers became an official part of the international law project, was that seen in the frame of a larger effort to have the intrinsic laws of economy, science and technology rule the international world. But already at that time, the argument was increasingly heard that the world was undergoing a tremendous transformation and that the 'modernity' that was inaugurated in Europe posed a fundamental challenge to traditional political and legal authority. In the aftermath of the First World War, as we have seen, with the revolt against ideas of nationhood and sovereignty, some international lawyers began to argue that an old world had simply been destroyed and global interdependence had inaugurated a new law that struck against inherited legal thought. Many in the French sociological school did suggest precisely this, and no one more insistently than the Chilean jurist Alejandro Alvarez, who waged a breathless campaign in favour of a 'new international law' that had arisen as a result of economic, technological transformations that had made sovereignty and old diplomacy obsolete, and called for a corresponding change of legal consciousness.[71]

The distinguishing character of this argument, found in many versions during the interwar period and later, was to stress that, as a loyal reflection of modernity's developmental trends, law *had already changed* and what was needed was a corresponding change of elite and popular consciousness. As we have seen, much of the sociological school was vulnerable to the objection that its perceived 'necessities' were just an updated natural law that was as indeterminate and as politically suspect as any other rationalist abstraction. Hyper-teleology does not invite lawyers to change the law or the facts of the world. It assumes that these changes *have already taken place*: science, technology and economics inform us of the novel requirements of cosmopolitan life. The only thing left is to choose among law's various 'design alternatives' those that best serve the functions that science and technology have identified as the law's *telos*.[72]

This argument is today most visible in the literatures that address international law as so many technical or functional 'regimes' that each operate their own teleologies. Environmental law, trade law, human rights law, humanitarian law, refugee law, laws of war and so on almost ad infinitum are each defined by their specific normativity that is received from the scientific or technical 'facts' produced by the experts of those disciplines themselves. The goal of the regimes is to be 'efficient' in view of the grounding assumptions of each discipline. They are 'hyper' inasmuch as they do not at all seek a legislative debate about their conflicting priorities. Instead, they *deny* such conflict and take the problems of regulation as technical and scientific ones, problems of coordination and not about political objectives or priorities of distribution. The debate on the 'fragmentation of international law' today is one platform on which the functioning of these regimes and in particular the conflicts between their differing teleologies has been addressed. So far, however, note has merely been taken of such conflicts while the practical suggestion remains that through increased cooperation between the technical experts of each such regime (between trade and environmental experts, say, or security and human rights experts), any potential conflicts may be settled.

The weakness of international political mechanisms has no doubt provided support for hyper-teleology: the huge transformations in science, technology and economics have not been accompanied by equally significant changes in international legal or political consciousness. International legal principles such as statehood, sovereignty and self-determination, and the techniques of diplomacy, treaty-making, war and dispute-settlement have remained relatively stable through four centuries. It is understandable to try to overcome this gap by *fiat*: science, technology and economics *are themselves the law*, their modernity is the law's modernity, their requirements the novel (ordoliberal) global constitution.[73]

5. Conclusion

The idea of an international law regulating life on the globe analogously to the way domestic law regulates life at home has always been controversial and vulnerable to two types of critiques. The more powerful the challenge law poses to the 'social reality' in which it is expected to operate, the more utopian it seems and the less its principles or projects can be verified empirically, by reference to what actually exists. The *internal* teleologies discussed above, often associated with 'positivism' or 'legalism', are routinely faced with such criticisms. Why should anyone obey something merely because it is 'law', irrespective of what external purpose it appears to advance? Hence the turn of law to the world outside as a source of purposes embedded in social practices themselves. And yet, if that law's principles are *really* embedded, then its autonomy is lost. The more 'reflective' law is to predominant trends in society, the more it is just an apology for existing power. Hence the opposite turns to anti-teleology and hyper-teleology. The former is sceptical about international law *tout court*: it has neither a strongly appealing set of objectives to guide society, nor it is very reflective of what actually goes on. It is best understood as a technical instrument for coordination and, as such, of some temporary use for powerful actors. As soon as it ceases to be useful in this way, however, it loses its normative, action-guiding power. Hyper-teleology, by contrast, accepts the world, in Candide's famous image, as 'the best of all possible worlds' on the strength of what science, technology and economic expertise have told us about it. What is scientifically 'true', technically 'operative' or economically 'optimal' does not only inform legislative enterprises but is the 'real' law that consciousness must only seize in order to gain an effective grasp of its fate. Hyper-teleology avoids the charge of 'utopianism' because it is respectful of the most up-to-date scientific, technological or economic knowledge. Nor is it vulnerable to the charge of being an apology for existing power because there is no centre of 'power' anywhere that would compel or coordinate the operation of its regimes. They are each internally validated and their (internal) judgement of validity is what makes them authoritative as 'law'.

The four positions can also be graphically exposed as four ways to respond to two demands that are posed to (international) law, namely those of normativity and concreteness (see Table 10.1).

The demand of normativity expresses the law's need to be something else than just (a description of) what actually exists. This can also be expressed as law's ability to sustain an autonomous teleology. The demand of concreteness, again, reflects the wish that law not be just an abstract utopia, that it embrace a teleology operative in social life itself. Every system of law, every idea of what the law stands for must, in order to be prima facie plausible, contain an element both of normativity and of concreteness. But those elements cancel each other out. The more normative something is, the less concrete it can be. Hence they contain those two elements in different proportions: one dominates; the other exists only as a secondary position, an afterthought, and vanishes when pressed by argument. 'Internal teleology' is strongly normative, but contains a secondary argument about the way the teleology is also produced by 'the world' itself. 'External teleology' is very concrete – its teleology is embedded in the world itself. But it is also only weakly normative because it accepts the constellation of power and policy that the 'world itself' has produced. Anti-teleology and hyper-teleology emerge as reaction-formations to the weaknesses and tensions embodied in the former. Anti-teleology does not believe that the law would stand for any powerful purpose – but nor does it think the law very

Table 10.1

N= strongly normative / n= weakly normative
S= strongly social / s= weakly social

Internal teleology (N/s)	External teleology (S/n)
(International) law is enshrined in valid rules reflecting the 'will' of the legislator. It is normatively powerful but not very concrete.	(International) law is enshrined in broad 'policies' that respond to the functional needs of society; it is concrete but normatively weak.
Legal formalism. Bright-line rules. Predominance of treaty and diplomacy. Supports formal sovereignty, national self-determination, looks for a 'standard of civilization'.	Legal instrumentalism. Large 'principles' and 'policies'. Predominance of governmental coordination and functional institutions. Law as a malleable instrument of policy-makers, responding to economic interests and scientific and technological progress.
Anti-teleology (n/s)	**Hyper-teleology (N/S)**
The rules of (international) law are not really very binding – nor does the law respond to any powerful needs or interests (scepticism).	The rules of (international) law are binding *and* they reflect the changing needs and operations of society.
(Foreign) policy-makers are free to act as they see best. International law as 'positive morality' or 'external municipal law'. It does not carry any normative idea in itself.	Law is a reflection of present scientific laws that govern the global world, and as mediated by the best technical expertise. Law is (scientific) truth and binds absolutely as such.

important as an aspect of social reality, either. Hyper-teleology embraces contradiction: its law is both normatively compelling because it is 'true' – but for the same reason it is also maximally concrete: determinate and derivative simultaneously, this expresses the hubris of law in globalization.

There is no doubt that international law – like all law – contains a teleological element.[74] It is not just a description of what exists presently, or what used to be the case in the past. Law is critical of the present and uses the resources of the past in order to bring about a better future. But its future-orientation cannot be expressed in single philosophical or scientific formulas. It brings us to jurisprudential debates about the nature of law that are also about the nature of the desired future. How we understand law's teleology is thus a profoundly normative, and not a scientific or technical question. That those debates seem interminable is only a reflection of the fact that we disagree about desirable futures. This fact goes some way as a defence of the commonplace view of law as a social technique, operated by legal professionals through bureaucratic procedures in domestic or international institutions. In the absence of a consensus about the character of the 'good society', law at least offers a second best that allows peace while disagreement on matters of political value will persist. But there are also moments when those procedures turn into a burden, perpetuating privilege and hierarchy. Something like that may have happened in respect of international law's most visible institutions in the past decades – the United Nations system, the Bretton Woods institutions, aspects of formal multilateral diplomacy. Law's teleology may then be turned against its institutions to show the gap between the ideal and its realization. That might bring new actors into the debate and lead to new routines with new emphasis and novel priorities. But it would not end the work of making the future concrete; the objective does not lie still, the goalposts constantly move. And the fact that law is, after all, a politics will reassert itself, over again.

Notes

1. 'Declaration of the High-level Meeting of the General Assembly on the Rule of Law at the National and International Level' 30 November 2012 (UN Doc A/RES 67/1).
2. Antonio Cassese, ed., *Realizing Utopia: The Future of International Law*, Oxford: Oxford University Press, 2012.
3. Hugo Grotius, *The Rights of War and* Peace, edited and with an introduction by Richard Tuck, Indianapolis: Liberty Fund, 2005, Book I Prolegomena § XVII–XIX (pp. 93–5).
4. Hersch Lauterpacht, 'The Covenant as "Higher Law"', in *British Year Book of International Law* 17 (1936), pp. 54–65. See also Jan Klabbers, Anne Peters and Geir Ulfstein, *The Constitutionalization of International Law*, Oxford: Oxford University Press, 2009.
5. Out of the wealth of materials on this item, see Mario Prost, *The Concept of Unity in Public International Law*, Oxford: Hart, 2012.
6. See my *From Apology to Utopia. The Structure of International Legal Argument*, reissue with a new epilogue, Cambridge: Cambridge University Press, 2005.
7. Samuel Pufendorf, *On the Law of Nature and of Nations*, in Craig Carr and Michael Sandler, eds, *The Political Writings of Samuel Pufendorf*, Oxford: Oxford University Press, 1994, bk II, ch. 1, pp. 136–40.
8. Pufendorf, *On the Law of Nature and of Nations*, bk VII, ch. 2 § 11 (p. 214) and ch. 4 § 11 (p. 223).
9. Pufendorf, *On the Law of Nature and of Nations*, bk VIII, chs 6 & 9 (pp. 257–63). See further Simone Goyard-Fabre, *Pufendorf et le droit naturel*, Paris: PUF, 1994, pp. 211–20.
10. Christian Thomasius, *Grundlehren des Natur- und Völkerrechts*, Hildesheim: Olms, 2003 [1709], bk I, ch. 5 § 70 and generally 65–81 (pp. 105–8).
11. Emer de Vattel, *The Law of Nations*, eds B. Kapossy and R. Whatmore, Indianapolis: Liberty Fund, 2008 [1758], bk III, ch. 3 § 42–48 (pp. 491–7).
12. Knud Haakonssen, 'German Natural Law', in Mark Goldie and Robert Wokler, eds, *The Cambridge History of Eighteenth-Century Political Philosophy*, Cambridge: Cambridge University Press, 2006, p. 279.
13. Immanuel Kant, *Critique of Pure Reason*, ed. Vassilis Politis, London: Everyman, 1991 [1781], p. 342 [A463/B491].
14. Immanuel Kant, 'Theory and Practice', in *Political Writings*, ed. Hans Reiss, Cambridge: Cambridge University Press, 1991, pp. 64, 68–72.
15. Immanuel Kant, *Groundwork of the Metaphysics of* Morals, ed. Mary Gregor, intr. C. Korsgaard, Cambridge: Cambridge University Press, 1997 [1785], [4:421], p. 31.

16. Kant, *Groundwork* [4:431], p. 39.
17. Kant, *Groundwork*, [4: 428], pp. 36–7.
18. Immanuel Kant, 'Perpetual Peace', in *Political Writings*, ed. Hans Reiss, Cambridge: Cambridge University Press, 1991, p. 100.
19. Kant, 'Perpetual Peace', pp. 104–5.
20. Kant, 'Perpetual Peace', p. 105.
21. For the proposal, see Marc Bélissa, *Fraternité universelle et intérêt national (1713–1795)*, Paris: Kimé, 1998, pp. 365–71.
22. Johann Heinrich Abicht, *Neues System eines aus der Menschheit entwickelten Naturrechts*, Beyrouth: Erben, 1792, pp. 31–3.
23. Abicht, *Neues System*, p. 525.
24. Abicht, *Neues System*, pp. 526–7.
25. See especially Georg Jellinek, *Die rechtliche Natur der Staatenverträge*, Vienna: Hölder, 1880.
26. P. Schoen, 'Zur Lehre von den Grundlagen des Völkerrechts', in *Archiv für Rechtsphilosophie* VIII (1914–15), no. 293, pp. 301–2.
27. See especially Mánica García-Salmones Rovira, *The Project of Positivism in International Law*, Oxford: Oxford University Press, 2013, pp. 275–86.
28. Hans Kelsen, *Das Problem der Souveränität und die Theorie des Völkerrechts*, Tübingen: Mohr, 1922.
29. See e.g. my 'Hegemonic Regimes', in Margaret Young, ed., *Regime Interaction in International Law: Facing Fragmentation*, Cambridge: Cambridge University Press, 2012, pp. 305–24.
30. Immanuel Kant, 'Idea for a Universal History with a Cosmopolitan Purpose', in *Political Writings*, ed. Hans Reiss, Cambridge: Cambridge University Press, 1991, 'Fourth proposition', pp. 44–5.
31. Kant, 'Perpetual Peace', p. 114 (italics in original).
32. Adam Smith, *Lectures on Jurisprudence*, eds R.L. Meek et al., Indianapolis: Liberty Fund, 1978, pp. 14–16 and passim.
33. See, further, Martti Koskenniemi, 'Into Positivism: Georg Friedrich von Martens (1756–1821) and Modern International Law', in *Constellations. An International Journal of Critical and Democratic Theory* 15 (2008), pp. 189–207.
34. Georg Friedrich von Martens, *Prècis du droit des gens moderne de l'Europe fondé sur les traités et l'usage*, Dieterich: Göttingen, 1801, p. 15.
35. Ibid., pp. 16, 18.
36. Robert Ward, *An Enquiry into the Foundation and History of the Law of Nations from the Time of the Greeks and the Romans to the Age of Grotius*, 2 vols, London: Butterworth, 1795.
37. Ward, *Enquiry*, vol. I, pp. xiv, xii–xv.
38. Richard Wildman, *Institutes of International Law. Vol I: International Rights in the Time of Peace*, London: Benning, 1849, p. 7.
39. Wildman, *Institutes*, 10, pp. 7–8.
40. Johann Caspar Bluntschli, *Das moderne Völkerrecht als Rechtsbuch dargestellt*, Nördlingen: Beck, 1868.
41. See my *The Gentle Civilizer of Nations. The Rise and Fall of International Law 1870–1960*, Cambridge: Cambridge University Press, 2002, pp. 11–97.

42. Koskenniemi, *Gentle Civilizer*, pp. 160–4. For a lively case study of the colonial activities of one of these jurists, see Andrew Fitzmaurice, 'The Justification of King Leopold II's Congo Enterprise by Sir Travers Twiss', in Shaunnagh Dorsett and Ian Hunter, eds, *Law and Politics in British Colonial Thought. Transpositions of Empire*, New York: Palgrave, 2010, pp. 109–26.

43. Georges Scelle, *Cours de droit international public*, Montchrestien: Domat, 1948, p. 11.

44. Scelle, *Cours*, p. 107.

45. Charles de Visscher, *Theory and Reality in International Law*, Princeton: Princeton University Press, 1957, 3rd edn, 1970; Percy Corbett, *Law in Diplomacy*, Princeton: Princeton University Press, 1959.

46. David Kennedy, 'The International Style in Postwar Law and Policy', in *Utah Law Review* 7 (1994), p. 21.

47. Wolfgang Friedmann, *The Changing Structure of International Law*, London: Stevens & Sons, 1964.

48. Rafael Domingo, *The New Global Law*, Cambridge: Cambridge University Press, 2010, p. 121. For a more moderate statement, see also Ruti Teitel, *Humanity's Law*, Oxford: Oxford University Press, 2011.

49. For a useful new study, see Lucie Delabie, *Approches américaines du droit international: Entre unité et diversité*, Paris: Pedone, 2011, pp. 116–68.

50. For the divisions inside French 'solidarism' see Koskenniemi, *Gentle Civilizer*, pp. 309–27.

51. Thomas Hobbes, *Leviathan*, ed. C.B. Macpherson, Harmondsworth: Penguin, 1961 [1651], part I, ch. 13, p. 187.

52. John Austin, *The Province of Jurisprudence Determined*, intr. H. L. A. Hart, Cambridge: Hackett, 1998 [1836], pp. 126–7.

53. James Mill, 'Law of Nations', in *The Supplement to the Encyclopaedia Britannica*, 1825, p. 9.

54. Adolf Lasson, *Princip und Zukunft des Völkerrechts*, Berlin: Hertz, 1897, p. 4.

55. Lasson, *Princip und Zukunft*, p. 10.

56. Erich Kaufmann, *Das Wesen des Völkerrechts und die Clausula rebus sic stantibus*, Tübingen: Mohr, 1911, p. 181.

57. For a useful discussion of the many variants of this view, see Alejandro Lorite Escorihuela, 'Cultural Relativism the American Way: the Nationalist School of International Law in the United States', in *Global Jurist Frontiers* 5 (2005), pp. 1535–653.

58. E. H. Carr, *The Twenty Years' Crisis 1919–1939*, 2nd edn, London: Macmillan, 1946, pp. 153, 78–180.

59. Hans Morgenthau, 'Positivism, Functionalism and International Law', in *American Journal of International Law* 34 (1940), pp. 260, 261.

60. Abraham L. Newman and David Zaring, 'Regulatory Networks', in Jeffrey L. Dunoff and Mark A. Pollack, *Interdisciplinary Perspectives on International Law and International Relations: The State of the Art*, Cambridge: Cambridge University Press, 2013, pp. 247, 250.

61. Paul-Pierre Le Mercier de la Rivière, *L'ordre naturel et essentiel des sociétés politiques*, London: Nourse, 1767, p. 37.

62. Le Mercier, *L'ordre naturel*, p. 27 (emphasis in original).

63. Le Mercier, *L'ordre naturel*, p. 11.

64. Le Mercier, *L'ordre naturel*, p. 35.

65. François Quesnay, 'Despotisme de la Chine', quoted in David McNally, *Political Economy and the Rise of Capitalism: A Reinterpretation*, Berkeley: University of California Press, 1988, p. 123.

66. Le Mercier, *L'ordre naturel*, pp. 75–8, 105, 113.

67. Le Mercier, *L'ordre naturel*, p. 129.

68. Keith Tribe, *Governing Economy: The Reformation of German Economic Discourse 1750–1840*, Cambridge: Cambridge University Press, 1988, pp. 177–9.

69. See Diethelm Klippel, 'The True Concept of Liberty: Political Theory in Germany in the Second half of the Eighteenth Century', in Eckhart Hellmuth, ed., *The Transformation of Political Culture: England and Germany in the Late Eighteenth Century*, Oxford: Oxford University Press, 1990, pp. 456–60 and id., 'Naturrecht als politische Theorie: Zur politischen Bedeutung des deutschen Naturrechts im. 18 und 19. Jahrhundert', in Hans-Erich Bödeker and Ulrich Herrmann, eds, *Aufklärung als Politisierung: Politisierung als Aufklärung*, Hamburg: Meiner, 1987, pp. 273–7.

70. Wilhelm von Humboldt, 'Über die Sorgfalt der Staaten für die Sicherheit gegen auswärtige Feinde', in *Berlinische Monatsschrift* 20 (1797), pp. 346–54.

71. See e.g. Alejandro Alvarez, *La codification du droit international – ces tendences, ces bases*, Paris: Pedone, 1912 and discussion in Koskenniemi, *From Apology to Utopia*, pp. 209–18.

72. See e.g. Gregory Schaffer and Mark A. Pollack, 'Hard and Soft Law', in Dunoff and Pollack, *Interdisciplinary Perspectives*, pp. 202–4.

73. See especially Gunther Teubner, *Constitutional Fragments: Societal Constitutionalism and Globalization*, Oxford: Oxford University Press, 2012, pp. 30–33, 42f., 75–8 and passim. See also Martti Koskenniemi, 'The Fate of International Law. Between Technique and Politics', in *The Modern Law Review* 70 (2007), pp. 1–32.

74. I have discussed this also in my 'Law, Teleology and International Relations: An Essay in Counter-disciplinarity', in *International Relations* 26 (2012), pp. 3–34.

CHAPTER 11
MARXISM AND THE IDEA OF REVOLUTION: THE MESSIANIC MOMENT IN MARX
Etienne Balibar

Quite intentionally, this chapter will cover only part of the huge problem concerning the function of teleological arguments in Marx, or the tension of causality, teleology and eschatology in Marx's philosophy of history. My aim is to address a controversial issue: that of the affinities of Marx's concept of politics with a religious or theological discourse.[1] More precisely, I will focus on the founding moment when different possibilities associated with the Marxian concept of the communist revolution and the emancipatory role of the 'proletariat' are enunciated for the first time, in the framework of Marx's critique of the Hegelian philosophy of Right. This novelty took place in his essay published in 1844 in *Deutsch-Französische Jahrbücher* (German-French Annals) with the title 'Zur Kritik der Hegelschen Rechtsphilosophie. Einleitung' ('Critique of Hegel's Philosophy of Right: An Introduction').[2] I will submit that it was associated with a typically 'messianic moment' in his philosophy, which never entirely disappeared in his later writings. I choose this expression – 'messianic moment' – to evoke the idea later developed by Jacques Derrida in his 1992 *Specters of Marx*: the 'messianic without messianism',[3] but also to introduce a symmetry with another expression: 'the Machiavellian moment in Marx', that was used by Miguel Abensour in a seminal essay.[4] Abensour focuses on a companion piece, the '1843 Manuscript' (also known as 'Critique of the Hegelian Philosophy of the State'), which was left unfinished by Marx. Note that the two writings bear a quasi-identical title, and were probably intended to be part of a common project which was never completed, but their style and content is strikingly different. In fact, they propose different conceptions of politics and use different names for its ends. Whereas the 'Machiavellian moment' illustrates a radically democratic concept of the political that is essentially a-theological (I completely follow Abensour on this point), the 'messianic moment' focuses on the redemptory function of the proletariat, which rather leads to introducing what Roberto Esposito would call the 'impolitical' element – or the element of radical negativity and excess – at the heart of the definition of revolutionary politics.[5] Accordingly, the tension between the two moments delineates a symbolic structure that will keep offering a choice to later Marxists. I will also submit that they can be used to understand a more general tension between a *teleological* and an *eschatological* discourse on the 'end(s) of history', for which Marxism is a privileged illustration, although by no means the only possible one. *Telos* (the orientation, the goal or ideal aim of an action or a process) and *eskhaton* (the final point or termination, or the vanishing moment, beyond which one may imagine either nothingness or a new birth), which are also often represented in modern philosophy as infinity and finitude, can be either wholly separated, or merged, or tentatively articulated in the definitions of what Reinhart Koselleck has called the 'past futures' of our culture.[6]

1. 'Le monde va changer de base'[7]

I begin with a quick description of the 1844 *Einleitung*. It is advisable to read first the conclusion of the text: 'When all the inner conditions are met, the *day of the German resurrection* [*der deutsche Auferstehungstag*] will be heralded by the *crowing of the cock of Gaul*'. The inner conditions mentioned here refer to the 'alliance' of German philosophy and the proletariat, which are like 'the social head and the social heart' of human emancipation. To my knowledge, among the many commentators, none has indicated the precise origin of this formulation, which I think is decisive.[8] With only a minor change (*schmettern*, which more explicitly indicates the eschatological Trumpet of the Judgement, instead of the original *krähen*), it comes from a famous essay written by the poet Heinrich Heine to greet the French Revolution in July 1830, which also contained the typical analogy between Lutheran Reform, French Revolution and German post-Kantian Philosophy adopted by Marx.[9] This phrase was obviously very influential on Marx: he used it again in his articles of 12 November 1848 and 1 January 1949 in the *Neue Rheinische Zeitung*, to qualify the cycle of revolutions in Europe which started in France: 'Von Paris aus wird der gallische Hahn noch einmal Europa wachkrähen' ('From Paris the sound of the cock of Gaul crowing will once again wake up Europe').[10] The 'crowing of the cock of Gaul' is thus associated with an interpretation of modern revolutions as a *pan-European* historical and intellectual cycle whose imminent 'resolution' through the arrival of a saviour of the world (namely the proletariat) is prophesied by Marx (as he will do again in more 'secular' terms in the *Communist Manifesto* from 1847). The 'Gallic cock' is still a French national (and nationalist) symbol today, which traces back to the French Revolution. Its messianic connotations are associated, in the Christian tradition, with the episode of 'Saint Peter's denial' (reported by Matthew and Luke), and, in the Jewish tradition, with the exile in Babylon.[11] This is a fascinating moment in the development of Marx's work, where his personal 'voice' merges with that of his close friend, the poet Heine. To show how it illuminates the general meaning of the text, I offer now some philological clues.

First, we must discuss the relationship in the text between the 'trumpeting' closure and the better known opening formulas about *religion* as 'opium of the people':

> For Germany, the *criticism of religion* has been essentially completed, and the criticism of religion is the prerequisite of all criticism … the foundation of irreligious criticism is: *Man makes religion*, religion does not make man … but *man* is no abstract being squatting outside the world. Man is *the world of man* – state, society. This state and this society produce religion, which is an *inverted consciousness of the world*, because they are an *inverted world* … The struggle against religion is, therefore, indirectly the struggle *against that world* whose

spiritual *aroma* is religion. *Religious* suffering is, at one and the same time, the *expression* of real suffering and a *protest* against real suffering ... The criticism of religion is, therefore, *in embryo, the criticism of that vale of tears* of which religion is the *halo*.[12]

The Feuerbachian sources of these formulas which convey the idea of the 'anthropological reversal of theology' are well known. They are also indebted to an 'atheist' discourse of the Radical Enlightenment which Marx largely endorsed in his critique of the monarchic and clerical Restoration in post-revolutionary Europe. But more relevant for our purpose is the kind of 'political theology' arising from the clash of the text's opening, where religion is declared dead, and its conclusion, where the proletariat is clearly endowed with a messianic role. It cannot only illustrate an ironic style, although Marx was a great ironist, but it expresses the core of the political problem that preoccupies him in the pre-1848 conjuncture (*Vormärz*): in order to overcome the alienation of the real world which has produced a religious illusion or mystification, a practical force or an agent is needed, that is still invisible or missing.

The longest part of the essay offers a complex historical and theoretical elaboration, which includes in particular a remarkable 'teleological' combination of the notions of *pre-history* and *post-history*, to describe Germany's paradoxical situation as a political space, when compared to the more 'advanced' parts of Europe: this dialectical unity of opposites (*Vorgeschichte* and *Nachgeschichte*) will certainly influence later 'Marxist' analyses of historical and social situations characterized as 'uneven development', but it was not before the (otherwise very different) works of Walter Benjamin, Ernst Bloch and Louis Althusser that it became an object of philosophical elaboration. I will return to this in a moment. In the final developments, however, the missing force is identified with the material figure of the proletariat, on the condition of its own 'alliance' with philosophy. Philosophy arises as an agency of freedom out of a long struggle with religion in the element of thought. The proletariat on the other hand appears as the *antithesis* of religion, but also as the *expression* of its internal contradiction, a 'protest' against human suffering, now manifesting in the open a latent secret that religion had long contained. This is indeed a scheme of thought that largely pre-dated Marx and continued after him: the eschatological promise of emancipation that religion would have betrayed or perverted will be retrieved and imposed against her by the Messiah (or, better, the 'messianic force'). It does not so much indicate a dialectical or teleological *Aufhebung* of religion than its interruption, in order to return to the authentic source of redemption that religion no longer represents in the world.

We recognize here a traditional movement that was already inspiring the Protestant Reform, when it denounced the 'visible Church' as a corrupted institution, a 'new Babylon' which had prostituted the Revelation to serve worldly powers.[13] Marxists from Engels to Ernst Bloch will consider the shift from criticizing the Church to creating a new ('evangelical') one and the conflict between Luther and Thomas Munzer in the Peasants' War a paradigmatic case of the contradiction between the two faces of Christianity: revolutionary and conservative.[14] We find a similar movement in the self-identification of romantic socialism with a 'new Christianity' claiming to suppress theological superstitions in the name of an authentic 'Religion of Man'.[15] And today we observe a reiteration of this move by Liberation Theologians in their critique of the capitalist 'religion of money' as *idolatry*, which confers the eschatological function of the Redemptor to the paupers of the Third World, seen as a collective reincarnation of Christ, i.e. both a victim who is sacrificed and an incarnation of protest and rebellion against injustice.[16]

What is also crucial to an understanding of Marx's text is to relate it to an antinomian tradition, which belongs both to the Jewish Kabbalah and the Christian Millenarists, where the coming of the Messiah is read as an interruption of the written Law in the name of the Law itself.[17] Together they inspire Marx in defining the proletarian mass that is located at the centre of modern history as the paradoxical 'passive force', which is able to perform a radical transformation of the world, emerging from a history of servitude to create the new promised man. This transposition is made possible by the fact that for Marx the proletarians embody antithetic characters, instantly oscillating between *nothingness* (abandonment, absolute poverty, exclusion, precariousness of life) and the *wholeness* or the totality (the fulfilment of the human essence as community or plenitude of the *Gattungswesen* or 'species'), which indeed evokes a theological *plerôma*:

> a sphere, finally, which cannot emancipate itself without emancipating itself from all other spheres of society and thereby emancipating all other spheres of society, which, in a word, is the *complete loss* of man and hence can win itself only through the *complete re-winning of man* [*einer Sphäre endlich … welche mit einem Wort der* völlige Verlust *des Menschen ist, also nur durch die* völlige Wiedergewinnung des Menschen *sich selbst gewinnen kann*]. This dissolution of society as a particular estate is the *proletariat*.[18]

Marx uses different 'codes' or 'idioms' to express the idea that the negative side of society is manifested in the ontological 'nothingness' of the proletariat. One of them comes from the political language of the French Revolution, where the notions of equality and the sovereignty of the people were closely knit together. In a prosopopeia of the revolutionary class, Marx writes: '*I am nothing but I must be everything*': this directly echoes the phrases through which Abbé Sieyès launched the Revolution in 1789: '*Nous avons trois questions à nous faire:* 1. Qu'est-ce que le tiers état? Tout. 2. Qu'a-t-il été jusqu'à présent dans l'ordre politique? Rien. 3. Que demande-t-il? À y devenir quelque chose.'[19] They also anticipate the verses of 'L'internationale', the anthem of the socialist and communist movement composed by Eugène Pottier and Adolphe Degeyter after the Paris Commune: 'Debout! les damnés de la terre / Debout! les forçats de la faim / La raison tonne en son cratère: / C'est l'éruption de la fin / Du passé faisons table rase / Foule esclave, debout! debout! / *Le monde va changer de base:* / *Nous ne sommes rien, soyons tout!*'.[20] But they should be referred as well to a much longer signifying chain, which includes mystical poetry and negative theologies: I am thinking in particular of Juan de la Cruz's *todo y nada, nada per todo*.[21] This analogy has been acknowledged in particular by Stanislas Breton:

The strength of early Marxism, which is at the same time prophetic and critical, lies in converting the human multitude, seen as an inert mass at the time, from a 'zero class' into a transformative energy, with universal range and unrivalled intensity. If I am not mistaken, this is the hidden meaning of 'nothingness' and 'everything', reciprocally involving each other, underpinning the faith in a new elect people, arising after centuries of humiliation.[22]

And certain 'post-Marxist' philosophers in the recent period (e.g. Lyotard) have been particularly receptive to this dimension of Marx's writing, at the same time ethical and messianic.

Using these heterogeneous sources, Marx produced a phenomenology of the crisis of the civil-bourgeois society (*bürgerliche Gesellschaft*) whose terminology resonates both on the historical and the eschatological plane. The key category is *Auflösung* (dissolution), which means that the conditions of existence of the proletariat annihilate every institutional form of recognition through which a 'class' (or a *status*: *Stand,* the key category in Hegel's 'organic' construction of the bourgeois State as historical objective of a teleology of reason) can become integrated in the social order. It communicates etymologically with *Lösung* (the 'solution' or 'resolution' of the political problem of emancipation, left unresolved both by the religious reformation and by the mere 'political' bourgeois revolution), but also with *Erlösung* (the redemption). In Marx's text the two aspects are combined though the expression *die Rolle des Emanzipators*, or the task of the emancipator, referring to the proletariat.

Having described the proletariat as a radically oppressed class which is reduced to a bare human condition at the same time elementary and generic, with no *property/propriety* of its own (*Eigentumslos*), Marx can retrieve the biblical myth of an 'elect people' bringing emancipation, not only to itself, but also to humankind as such: extreme enslavement becomes reversed into a redemptory mission for the *remainder* which forms a 'people of the people'. This mission is rooted in suffering and humiliation: this is the analogy with Christ, which was duly identified by contemporary theologians (mainly Protestant) and prepared for the fusion of Marxism and Catholicism in 'Liberation Theology'. The theologico-political trajectory which identifies the proletariat with a Christic figure incarnating the universal human suffering passed from Ernst Bloch to the invention of the 'theology of the cross' by Moltmann and to Liberation Theology.[23] This is the Christian genealogy. But in a more subtle manner it can be referred also to models which trace back to Jewish messianism: this is the idea of 'absolute injustice' which puts a limit on historicity and opens the possibility for a realization of the human as such: 'Where, then, is the *positive* possibility of a German emancipation? *Answer*: In the formation of a class with *radical chains*, a class of civil society which is not a class of civil society, an estate which is the dissolution of all estates, a sphere which has a universal character by its universal suffering and claims no *particular right* because no *particular wrong*, but *wrong generally*, is perpetuated against it; which can invoke no *historical*, but only *human*, title' ('kein besondres Unrecht, sondern *das Unrecht schlechthin* … welche nicht mehr auf einen *historischen*, sondern nur noch auf den *menschlichen* Titel provozieren kann.').[24] As in the Kabbalah and especially the 'revolutionary' tendencies of Jewish messianism, according to Gershom Scholem, the redemption of historical injustice is not so much conceived as a move into the transcendent other world than as a *new creation of the world*, which involves the destruction of the old world ('Auflösung der bisherigen Weltordnung').[25] For a certain Jewish tradition, the people of Israel which has been 'exiled' from the community of nations has become itself a 'Messiah' bringing redemption to humankind as a whole. It could be called therefore a 'people of the peoples', just as Marx's proletariat which resolves the aporia of revolution can be seen as 'the people's people'.

Crucially important from this point of view is the continuous repetition in Marx's text of the name *World*: in the language of a Christian theology which opposes the worldly/secular to the 'heaven' or 'beyond', it proposes a radical critique of *religion*, whose dualism also *permeates* the secularized forms of bourgeois politics, insisting by contrast on the *materiality* or 'worldliness' of the Promised Land where the 'human emancipation' will lead. And thus, while continuously borrowing from eschatological traditions concerning 'resurrection' and 'redemption' which are mutually exclusive, even if they are historically articulated, what Marx is offering here is a *new messianism*, essentially the same as that, in the following years, in the *Theses on Feuerbach*:

> The coincidence of the changing of circumstances and of human activity or self-changing can be conceived and rationally understood only as *revolutionary practice* ... The philosophers have only interpreted the world, in various ways; the point is to change it. ('Das Zusammenfallen des Änderns der Umstände und der menschlichen Tätigkeit kann nur als umwälzende Praxis gefaßt und rationell verstanden werden ... Die Philosophen haben die Welt nur verschieden interpretiert; es kommt aber darauf an, sie zu verändern.')[26]

The *Communist Manifesto* will then renew this in the form of a prophetic warning for all 'dominant classes': 'Let the ruling classes tremble at a Communistic revolution. The proletarians have nothing to lose but their chains. They have a world to win.' This is not only a 'militant' messianism, but a statement that the transformation of the world is already under way because a certain social order has 'manufactured' unbearable forms of exploitation, equivalent to a modern slavery, that are ultimately incompatible with its own survival. Before our eyes, *in the present*, radical 'passivity' becomes 'activity', and dissolution amounts to creation.

But the question is also: to what extent does Marx really master the implications of the language game that he is using and recreating? It is here that the comparison between contemporary writings becomes truly illuminating.

2. *Demos*, or the revolutionary subject as a 'full subject'

What I have just described, in fact, could be more a matter of rhetoric and style than theory and concept. It is not enough to characterize a problematic. But it is also not simply a starting point for a general description of the 'theological metaphors in Marx'.[27] What is required in order to understand it is a double inquiry, comparing Marx's formulas with others in the same historical context, and comparing his 'messianic' discourse with other dimensions of his critique of bourgeois society and capitalism.

To begin with, we may recall the frequency of the prophetic and apocalyptic vocabulary in Europe between the French Revolution and the 1848 revolutions – the period known in Germany as the *Vormärz*. This is indeed the case in the writings of 'utopian' socialism and communism, particularly with the Saint-Simonian idea of 'New Christianity'. At the other end of the spectrum, it is also illustrated by the 'theocratic' discourses of counter-revolutionary writers (from De Maistre to Donoso Cortes), but above all by romantic *nationalism*. The key ideological issue, it seems to me, is the symmetry between the 'messianism of class' and the 'messianism of nation', because it indicates a correlation between opposite reactions to bourgeois 'individualism' and 'liberalism'. In an important essay published only in 1975, Eric Voegelin (who coined the category of 'political religion') has submitted that in his 1844 *Einleitung* Marx 'comes closest to the preoccupations of a German national thinker'.[28] It is true that Marx in 1844 was actively confronting the idea of national redemption and a universal mission for Germany. To the common idea that the European Restoration and the conservative turn of Prussian monarchy had blocked the revolution against feudalism and clericalism, he would add that the German bourgeoisie was wholly unable to become a 'universal class' that would represent the interests and vindicate the rights of the whole society (as the French bourgeoisie did in 1789). It is this contradiction that, in his view, opened the possibility that Europe as a whole be pushed beyond the bourgeois political regime through a German social revolution. There are indeed striking analogies here with the patriotic scheme adopted by Fichte in his 1807 *Addresses to the German Nation* (where the defeated and divided German nation is described as a meta-political spiritual force, which through liberating itself from foreign rule will also liberate mankind from egoism), and with the more recent theory of August Cieszkowski (who conferred upon the 'dismembered' Polish nation a redemptory function in world history, overcoming the antithesis of theory and praxis). It was Cieszkowski who, in his 1841 *Prolegomena zur Historiosophie*, invented the 'philosophy of action' so influential on Moses Hess and the young Marx, then closely associated.[29]

However, these analogies cannot lead, in my opinion, to simply *equating* the discourses of national messianism and proletarian messianism, exchanging one 'subject of history' (the class) for another (the nation) as it were. This is too quick a conclusion of Voegelin. I prefer to admit that, in the context of a *discursive conflict*, the messianisms of class and nation were constructed one against the other. In this respect an essential argument can be derived from the proximity between Marx and Heinrich Heine, as studied in particular by Kouvelakis. As Marx was writing *Zur Kritik der Hegelschen Rechtsphilosophie*, Heine wrote his great poetic cycle *Deutschland: ein Wintermärchen*, where (against the 'Teutomaniacs') he tries to transform patriotism into cosmopolitanism. Hence derives the Marxian idea (in the *Communist Manifesto*) that 'proletarians are nationless', which is the result of a generalized negation of all 'properties' and memberships, making the proletariat 'a class that is not a class' in society, and the internationalist motto endowing the communist revolution with its universalistic meaning.

Even more decisive is the comparison with other writings in the same extraordinary year, 1843–4. A remarkable feature of this textual ensemble, where all the major Marxian concepts – *communism,* human or 'social' *emancipation,* the *proletariat* as 'universal class', the 'end of the political State', the *alienation* and the *externalization* (*Entfremdung-Entäusserung*) of the generic essence of man, revolutionary *praxis* – now considered typical of the 'young Marx' are developed, is the fact that they never use all concepts simultaneously in any single piece of writing. There is a sort of circulation which also testifies for a permanent tension between the different points of view brought together in a problematic unity. We must try to unfold this complexity, in order to understand the antithetic orientations which resulted from there in the continuation of Marx's thinking, and the various 'Marxist' discourses up to today.

I shall single out the most striking comparison: between the two successive 'Critiques of the Hegelian Philosophy of Right', each being centred on a specific way of articulating the issue of *agency* or *praxis* with the idea of a 'collective subject'. In the first case this subject is called *demos*, in the second it is called *proletariat*, with completely opposite relations to the problem of subjectivity and sovereignty. I see no reason to decide that one is more 'materialist' than the other, although the first one leads quite naturally to emphasizing the political importance of empirical conflicts within the bourgeois society, whereas the other leads to emphasizing the 'encounter' between a social subject and a radical theoretical critique which is performed by intellectuals or philosophers as the decisive condition of revolutions.

In his excellent commentary of the 1843 *Critique,* Miguel Abensour has insisted that Marx's intention was to perform a 'symptomatic' reading of the Hegelian theory of the constitutional State, in order to demonstrate that it would never achieve its proclaimed goal of solving the conflicts of the 'civil society' (*bürgerliche Gesellschaft*), thus accomplishing the idea of liberty (or *right*) and making it a political realization of the absolute.[30] Marx's materialist reversal of the sovereignty of the constitutional State denounced an *abstract* character of the institutions of the Modern State, which for that stake remains essentially a political representation of the interests of property-owning individuals. To this pragmatic objective, Hegel would only add a teleological justification, or a speculative attire which provides the illusion of dialectical necessity and reconciliation. However in this early critique Marx did not exactly substitute an inverted abstraction, a theory of 'society' as real economic subject of the political process, as 'historical materialism' would later insist. On the contrary, according to Abensour, he would focus on a *political subject* which at the same time generates the modern secular universal State and pushes it towards its own dissolution, by radicalizing its internal contradictions. For Abensour the typical name of this constituent subject emerges when Marx attacks Hegel for identifying the political sovereignty with the monarchic 'power of decision' (or, more generally, the executive power of the State), contrasting with it the constituent democratic element:

> Democracy is the truth of monarchy, monarchy is not the truth of democracy. Monarchy is necessarily democracy in contradiction with itself, whereas the

monarchial moment is no contradiction within democracy. Monarchy cannot, while democracy can be understood in terms of itself. In democracy none of the moments obtains a significance other than that which befits it. Each is really only a moment of the whole *demos*. In monarchy one part determines the character of the whole; the entire constitution must be modified according to the immutable head. Democracy is the generic constitution; monarchy is a species, and indeed a poor one. Democracy is content and form; monarchy *should* be only form, but it adulterates the content.[31]

This notion of the 'complete *demos*' must be related to the Marxian idea that it is the 'legislative power' which 'has created the great organic revolutions in history'; therefore *de jure* and *de facto* precedes the legal constitutions. It also leads to the idea that the possibility of a *true democracy* is contained in the internal conflicts of the civil society, arising from the 'religion of private property' and receiving from the State only a formal, bureaucratic solution. This would be *a democracy without the State*, in which (in the words of the *Communist Manifesto*) the 'legislative power' has become an *association* of the producers, or is abolished as a separated institution in its own realization. This is exactly what Abensour calls the 'Machiavellian moment' (or the moment of the full realization of the political) in Marx: since the very power which, through democratic revolutions, had created the Modern State now takes the people beyond a mere juridical formalization of social conflicts by the State. 'Sovereignty' is thus overcome as an institutional figure, whether monarchic or republican. It is replaced by an 'institution of the social' which is immanent to its own conflicts. In other terms, Marx is looking for a difficult *third way* between Proudhonian anarchism and Saint-Simonian 'administration of things'. And he is trying to understand an emancipation of the popular subject as a public process of the constitution of the community (or the 'common'), which gives a concrete historical figure to the 'generic' dimension of man. This would be again, in particular, his interpretation of the Paris Commune.

There are difficulties, however, in this idea of the 'true democracy' and the possibility of a *political institution* located beyond the State, which Abensour perfectly perceives. This probably explains why, in the conclusion of his essay, he suggested that Marx had missed (or lacked) an understanding of the *element of finitude* of the political which, on the contrary, was there in Machiavelli himself, in the form of *civil conflict* as a permanent character of the political. This, according to Abensour, came from the fact that for Marx to think of the people (or *demos*) as a *totality* ('das ganze *demos*') was also to think of it as a substantial *unity*:

Force est de relever que Marx pense la vraie démocratie sous le signe de l'unité, c'est-à-dire travaillée en permanence par une volonté de coïncidence avec elle-même, donc à l'écart d'une pensée de la démocratie comme forme de société qui se constitue de faire accueil à la division sociale, qui se distingue de reconnaître la légitimité du conflit dans la société. Contrairement à Machiavel . . . Marx voit dans l'unité un bien tout uniment positif, sans soupçonner, semble-t-il, qu'il puisse exister un lien entre certaines formes d'unité et le despotisme, et inversement des liens entre la division sociale et la liberté ...[32]

Another way of indicating the difficulty, it seems to me, is to suggest that the *demos* presented by Marx in 1843 as the constituent subject of the political institution through a reversal of the Hegelian idea of the political State was indeed a 'full' or 'effective' subject, or a *subjectum*. Abensour says as much. It was permanently exposed, however, to symmetric dangers. On the one side, it remained *virtual*, a projection or anticipation of what the contradictions inherent in the political State should produce, or a development of the divisions of the society arising from the domination of private property, whose practical modalities remained enigmatic. As a consequence, the 'time of revolution' also remained a speculative idea, linked with the perspective of a continuation of the historical 'movement of revolution' from 'below', a movement which the *Critique*, unsurprisingly, identifies with 'progress':

> In order not only that the constitution be altered, thus that this illusory appearance not be in the end forcefully shattered, but also that man do consciously what he is otherwise forced to do unconsciously by the nature of the thing, it is necessary that the movement of the constitution, that progress, be made the principle of the constitution, thus that the real corner stone of the constitution, the people, be made the principle of the constitution. Progress itself is then the constitution.[33]

But on the other side the very same 'popular' subject tends to emerge in front of the State not so much as its dissolution than as its inverted image, at least an inverted 'sovereignty', because Marx here claims to continue the tradition of the 'constituent power', or the revolutionary people which 'rises from particularity to hegemony' ('wo sie in ihrer Besonderheit als das Herrsschende auftrat'),[34] and because the people or *demos* is endowed with the immediate 'self-consciousness' of its historical function, albeit emancipated from the bureaucratic mechanisms of representation.

3. Proletarians: the empty subject

Now what I want to suggest is that, in what I called the messianic moment, Marx did not resolve these aporias, but he displaced them from one extreme to the other of the philosophical spectrum. The 'proletariat' that he introduced for the first time in the 1844 *Einleitung* is characterized ontologically and historically in a manner wholly opposed to the *demos* that Abensour perfectly recognized in the 1843 *Critique*: not a 'full subject' but an 'empty subject', or even emptiness or *void* (absolute negativity) *as subject*. This is what the notion of a 'dissolution of bourgeois society' coinciding with the material existence of the proletariat amounts to. The subject is ontologically empty, but it is not deprived of *practical* capacities. On the contrary, this very negativity makes it possible to intensify the disruptive character of the proletariat and to think the 'impolitical' dimensions of political practice, as a 'revolutionary transformation' of existing social conditions that leaves nothing untouched. The opposition could not be stronger with the 'radical democratic' perspective of the 1843 *Critique*. This can be seen in at least two respects, on which I want to conclude.

First, the opposition is very visible in the understanding of the *time of the revolution*. What first emerged as a contingent exception, namely the fact that Germany was essentially 'anachronistic' in European history, because it was *politically backward* with respect to France (and socially backward with respect to England), now becomes a general structure. It is transformed into the very essence of *historicity*, allowing it to understand that a force tied to the past (or the *pre-history*) now becomes able to push humankind into the future (or the *post-history*). This is where Marx's description clearly jumps from teleology into eschatology, becoming irreducible to a representation of linear progress, even in a dialectical form. Just as the proletariat is seen as 'a class in the society that does not belong to the society', Germany appears as 'a nation in history which does not belong to history', and these two characters precisely merge in the singular figure of the German proletariat. In a sense, Germany does not live 'in the present'; it is a contradictory crystallization of the past and the future, *Vorgeschichte* and *Nachgeschichte*. Already (re)presenting the future within the past, it can re-enter the movement of history only if blowing up the limits within which every previous evolution remained enclosed, which are also limits of a politics of progress:

> *Germany, as the deficiency of the political present constituted a world of its own*, will not be able to throw down the specific German limitations without throwing down the general limitation of the political present. ('*Deutschland als der zu einer eigenen Welt konstituierte Mangel der politischen Gegenwart* wird die spezifisch deutschen Schranken nicht niederwerfen können, ohne die allgemeine Schranke der politischen Gegenwart niederzuwerfen.')[35]

As I mentioned earlier, this notion of a 'condensation' of backward and forward positions within the structure of the revolutionary event will be periodically retrieved in the history of Marxist theory. It will be asserted either as a 'strategic' scheme (e.g. by Lenin about the possibility of an anti-capitalist revolution in Russia, or by 'third world' Marxists, especially in Latin America in the twentieth century), or philosophically, as a foundation for a non-linear, non-deterministic, non-homogeneous 'concept of historical time' whose key category is the 'non-contemporaneity' of the present, and especially it will powerfully re-emerge in Benjamin's 'Theses on the Concept of History' from 1941.[36]

Second, we must return to the relationship between the proletariat and 'philosophy' (today we would probably say theory). It is presented in the famous metaphor of the 'head' and the 'heart', which is supposed to solve the 'main difficulty' (*Hauptschwierigkeit*) facing the idea of a 'radical German revolution', namely its lack of a 'material basis' that could be 'seized' by philosophy, for it to become a historical force after it had transformed the critique of religion into a critique of human alienation:

> Wie die Philosophie im Proletariat ihre *materiellen*, so findet das Proletariat in der Philosophie seine *geistigen* Waffen, und sobald der Blitz des Gedankens gründlich in diesen naiven Volksboden eingeschlagen ist, wird sich die Emanzipation der *Deutschen* zu *Menschen* vollziehn. ('As philosophy finds its material weapon in the proletariat, so the proletariat finds its *spiritual* weapon in philosophy. And once the lightning of thought has squarely struck this ingenuous soil of the people, the emancipation of the *Germans* into *men* will be accomplished.')[37]

Again, several historical contexts are relevant here. A comparison with Auguste Comte's notion of the 'alliance of the proletarians and the philosophers', in the *Discours sur l'esprit positif* published in the same year (1844), appears quite natural, and it is important to understand what kind of pedagogic function later Marxists granted to the institutional figure of *the party*.[38] Comte elaborated a project of social 'alliance' based on his programme of popular scientific education in order to overcome a gap which threatened a progress conceived as 'development of order', and he wanted to create a new 'spiritual power' to put an end to the succession of popular revolutions and aristocratic counter-revolutions by combining the modern forces of science and industry which oppose the traditional forces of religion and metaphysics. In that sense, it was just the opposite of Marx's perspective, albeit composed of homonymous elements (and they had a common starting point in the Saint-Simonian evolutionary theory).

An equally interesting formal analogy can be found with the Kantian 'scheme' of transcendental synthesis. It is indirectly quoted in the phrase 'Die Philosophie kann sich nicht verwirklichen ohne die Aufhebung des Proletariats, das Proletariat kann sich nicht aufheben ohne die Verwirklichung der Philosophie' ('Philosophy cannot realize itself without the transcendence of the proletariat, and the proletariat cannot transcend itself without the realization of philosophy').[39] This typical *double negation* is an old philosophical scheme, once invented to represent the articulation of mind and body, later transferred to the intelligible and the sensible, concept and intuition, theory and praxis. But Marx displaced its subjects. He speaks of the 'head' (or the brain) and the 'heart', which is not exactly the same as 'body'. It involves a different, non-substantialist, ontology. What he tried to present allegorically was not so much the constitution of a collective subject or a historical *individuality*, composed of form and matter, or spirit and body, it was *the event of a historical initiative*, arising from the imminent conjunction of 'consciousness' and 'suffering' on a world scale. When passivity becomes reversed into activity, forming the 'heart' of the messianic moment, what we should call *praxis* is not so much one side of the synthesis, as the revolutionary *effect* of the conjunction of two conditions itself, each of which remained defective when taken alone. The event, compared by Marx to a 'lightning of thought', is not really a representation; it is taking place on the limit, where the forms of representation are dissolved politically and ontologically ('die faktische Auflösung dieser Weltordnung': 'the practical dissolution of this universal order'). And so the historical 'subject' is but a contingent combination of two 'non-subjects'. Revolution is not thought of as the *telos* of a long historical progress (as will again be the case in later summaries of 'historical materialism' – such as the famous 1859 Preface of the *Critique of Political Economy*, where a 'maturity' of the material conditions of revolution generates its own 'ideological superstructure' as a form of 'social consciousness'); it is thought of as an interruption and an encounter of the negative (or critical) parts of society.

My conclusion is the following: the messianic moment really forms the reverse side of the Machiavellian moment, emerging as soon as an aporia had become manifest, which concerned the possibility of defining the 'political' beyond the State (and against it), but also the representation of a collective political subject which should be at the same time *a given totality* (the 'people'), and *a missing figure* in the historical present, still virtual or 'to come' (the people of the people, the 'emancipator'). Certainly it would be insufficient to consider that Marx's formulas as they were enunciated in the breaking moment of 1843–5 are his final formulations. Breaks and reversals are going to take place, as Marx proceeds towards an effective critique of political economy and reflects the consequences of actual revolutionary events (which in practice were *failed* revolutionary events). Nevertheless, I submit that the 'differential' which they contain did not wither away. On the contrary, it would become continuously reiterated, because of the difficulty faced by Marx and Marxists to define the 'class struggle' as either *political* or *impolitical*. The 'messianic' vocabulary used by Marx to introduce the notion of the proletariat receded before a more 'positive' and 'positivist' definition of the 'class of workers' (*Arbeiterklasse*), linked to the analysis of the exploitation of the labour force and the organization of surplus labour, but it would periodically return in the apocalyptic representation of a final confrontation between revolution and counter-revolution, prompted by the violence of the repression of popular and proletarian insurrections in the nineteenth century, or the intensification of capitalist exploitation itself.[40] This complex pattern indicates both the interest and the narrow limits of an understanding of Marx's theory as a variety of modern teleology of history as 'secularized' versions of the 'history of redemption'.[41]

Notes

1. This chapter is adapted from 'Le moment messianique de Marx', now Chapter 6 of my book *Citoyen Sujet et autres essais d'anthropologie philosophique*, Paris: Presses Universitaires de France, 2011. In this new version, I have benefited, in particular, from critiques and suggestions by Adrian Brisku, Bo Stråth and Francisco Ortega. I have already touched upon the issue of teleology in Marx in an earlier book, *The Philosophy of Marx*, London: Verso, 1995 (particularly Chapter 4, 'Time and Progress: Another Philosophy of History'). See also my contribution to the volume *Derrida and the Time of the Political*, eds Pheng Cheah and Suzanne Guerlac, Durham, NC: Duke University Press, 2008: 'Eschatology versus Teleology: The Suspended Dialogue between Derrida and Althusser'.

2. English translations of this famous essay can be found in most editions of Marx's Philosophical writings, or separately in *Marx's Critique of Hegel's Philosophy of Right (1843)*, ed. Joseph O'Malley, trans. Annette Jolin and Joseph O'Malley, Cambridge: Cambridge University Press, 1970.

3. Jacques Derrida, *Specters of Marx: The State of the Debt, the Work of Mourning, and the New International*, New York: Routledge, 1994.

4. 'Marx et le moment machiavélien', first published in 1989, later expanded and revised. See Miguel Abensour, *La démocratie contre l'Etat*, Paris: Editions du Félin, 2004. The title bears an obvious reference to J. G. A. Pocock's famous book, *The Machiavellian Moment: Florentine Political Thought and the Atlantic Political Tradition*, Princeton: Princeton University Press, 1975.
5. I borrow the category 'impolitical' from the work of Roberto Esposito (see 'Preface to *Categories of the Impolitical*', trans. Connal Parsley, in *diacritics* 39 (Summer 2009), no. 2, pp. 99–115).
6. See Bo Stråth's essay in Chapter 16 of this volume.
7. 'The world is about to change its foundation' (from *L'internationale*: see below).
8. With the partial exception of Stathis Kouvelakis, *Philosophy and Revolution from Kant to Marx*, London: Verso, 2003, from which I draw precious indications.
9. Introduction to *Kahldorf über den Adel, in Briefen an den Grafen M. von Moltke*, 1831, in Heinrich Heine, *Historisch-Kritische Gesamtausgabe der Werke*, Hamburg: Hoffmann und Campe, 1979, Bd. XI, p. 174. Indeed in 1841 Bruno Bauer had published the pamphlet *The Trumpet of the Last Judgment against Hegel, the Atheists, and the Antichrist: an Ultimatum* (*Die Posaune des jüngsten Gerichts über Hegel, den Atheisten, und den Antichristen: ein Ultimatum*), considered the manifesto of the 'Young Hegelian' school.
10. Karl Marx, *Zur Kritik der Hegelschen Rechtsphilosophie: Einleitung*, in Marx-Engels Werke ('M.E.W.'), Berlin: Dietz Verlag Berlin, 1961, vol. 1, p. 391; 'Die Kontrerevolution in Berlin', 12 November 1848, M.E.W., vol. 6, p. 10; 'Die revolutionäre Bewegung', 1 January 1949, M.E.W., vol. 6, p. 149.
11. See jewishencyclopedia.com, 'Cock' (accessed 10 March 2015).
12. M.E.W., vol. 1, p. 378.
13. As in John Napier's 1593 pamphlet 'A Plain Discovery of the Whole Revelation of St John'.
14. See John Lewis, 'The Jesus o History', in John Lewis, Karl Polanyi and Donald K. Kitchin, eds, *Christianity and the Social Revolution*, New York: C. Scribner's & Sons, 1936.
15. Pierre Leroux, *De l'Humanité. De son principe et de son avenir* [1840], in *Corpus des Œuvres de philosophie en langue française*, Paris: Fayard, 1985.
16. H. Assmann and F.J. Hinkelammert, *L'idolâtrie du marché*, Paris: Éditions du Cerf, 1993; Michaël Löwy, *La guerre des dieux: Religion et politique en Amérique latine*, Paris: Éditions du Félin, 1998.
17. See the classical studies by Gershom Scholem, in particular *Major Trends in Jewish Mysticism*, New York: Schocken Books, 1941; *The Messianic Idea in Judaism and Other Essays*, New York: Schocken Books, 1971; *Sabbatei Sevi: The Mystical Messiah 1626–1676*, Princeton: Princeton University Press, 1973.
18. M.E.W., vol. 1, p. 390.
19. Abbé Sieyès, *Qu'est-ce que le tiers-état?* 1789. I translate literally: 'The three questions we must ask are: 1) What is the third estate? Everything [or: the whole]; 2) What was it until now in the political order? Nothing; 3) What does it demand? To become something.'
20. Eugène Pottier, 1871. Literal English translation (Wikisource): 'Stand up, damned of the Earth / Stand up, prisoners of starvation / Reason thunders in its volcano / This is the eruption of the end. / Of the past let us make a clean slate / Enslaved masses, stand up, stand up / The world is about to change its foundation / We are nothing, let us be all.'
21. Cf. *Subida del Monte Carmelo*, t. II, chap 4 (http://www.portalcarmelitano.org/component/k2/item/118-subida-al-monte-carmelo- -pdf.html, accessed 10 March 2015).
22. Stanislas Breton, *Esquisses du politique*, Paris: Messidor, 1991, pp. 37–8.

23. Cf. Richard J. Baukham, *Moltmann: Messianic Theology in the Making*, London: Marshall Pickering, 1987. On the key theological category of *kenosis*, literally 'emptiness' or 'emptying', translated by Luther as *Entäusserung*, see Georges G. M. Cottier, *L'athéisme du jeune Marx: Ses origines hégéliennes*, Paris: Vrin, 1959, p. 176.

24. M.E.W., vol. 1, p. 390.

25. See Gershom Scholem, *The Messianic Idea in Judaism: And Other Essays on Jewish Spirituality*, New York: Schocken Books, 1971.

26. Karl Marx, *Thesen über Feuerbach*, 3, 11, M.E.W. vol. 3, pp. 5–7.

27. Enrique Dussel, *Las metaforas teologicas de Marx*, Estella: El Verbo Divino, 1993.

28. Eric Voegelin, 'Marx: The Genesis of Gnostic Socialism', in id., *From Enlightenment to Revolution*, Durham, NC: Duke University Press, 1975.

29. See my essay 'Fichte and the Internal Border: On Addresses to the German Nation', in *Masses, Classes, Ideas. Studies on Politics and Philosophy before and after Marx*, London: Routledge, 1994, pp. 61–84; *Selected Writings of August Cieszkowski*, ed. and trans. with an introductory essay by André Liebich, Cambridge: Cambridge University Press, 1979.

30. Abensour, *La démocratie.*

31. 'Die Demokratie ist die Wahrheit der Monarchie, die Monarchie ist nicht die Wahrheit der Demokratie . . . In der Demokratie erlangt keines der Momente eine andere Bedeutung, als ihm zukommt. Jedes ist wirklich nur Moment des ganzen Demos. In der Monarchie bestimmt ein Teil den Charakter des Ganzen.' M.E.W., vol. 1, p. 230.

32. 'We must admit that it is under the sign of unity that Marx conceives true democracy, which therefore is permanently subjected to a will to coincide with itself. He stands apart from a conception of democracy as a form of society constituted through its acceptance of social division, and whose distinctive mark lies in the recognition of the legitimacy of conflict within society . . . In social unity Marx sees a completely positive value: he does not seem to understand that there could exist a correlation between despotism and certain forms of unity, just as there are, conversely, linkages between social divide and liberty . . .' Abensour, *La démocratie*, pp. 124, 127 (my translation).

33. 'Damit der Verfassung nicht nur die Veränderung angetan wird, damit also dieser illusorische Schein nicht zuletzt gewaltsam zertrümmert wird, damit der Mensch mit Bewusstsein tut, was er sonst ohne Bewusstsein durch die Natur der Sache gezwungen wird zu tun, ist es notwendig, dass die Bewegung der Verfassung, dass der *Fortschritt zum Prinzip der Verfassung* gemacht wird, dass also der wirkliche Träger der Verfassung, das Volk, zum Prinzip der Verfassung gemacht wird', M.E.W., vol. 1, p. 259.

34. M.E.W., vol. 1, p. 260.

35. M.E.W., vol. 1, p. 387f.

36. See Walter Benjamin, 'Theses on the Concept of History', in *Illuminations,* ed. Hannah Arendt, trans. Harry Zohn, 2nd edn, New York: Schocken Books, 1986. Interestingly, the idea of the essential 'non-contemporaneity of the present' was developed independently by Ernst Bloch in 1935 (*Erbschaft dieser Zeit*) and Louis Althusser in 1965 (*Pour Marx*). We should also add to this Derrida's considerations on the relationship between the 'messianic element' in Marx and the Shakespearian motto: 'Time is Out of Joint' (in *Specters of Marx*).

37. M.E.W., vol. 1, p. 391.

38. Auguste Comte, *Discours sur l'esprit positif*, intr. Annie Petit, Paris: Vrin, 1995, troisième partie.

39. M.E.W., vol. 1, p. 390.

40. On competing uses of 'proletariat' and 'working class' in Marx's *Capital*, see my essay 'La vacillation de l'idéologie dans le marxisme, III. Le prolétariat insaisissable', in *La crainte des masses*, Paris: Galilée, 1997, p. 231f.

41. A perfect example is Karl Löwith, *Weltgeschichte und Heilgeschehen: Die theologischen Voraussetzungen der Geschichtsphilosophie*, in id., *Sämtliche Schriften*, Stuttgart: Metzler, 1983, vol. 2, ch. 2: Marx, here p. 61.

PART V
TRANSLATING FUTURES: ESCHATOLOGY, HISTORY AND THE INDIVIDUAL

CHAPTER 12
RELIGIOUS TELEOLOGIES, MODERNITY AND VIOLENCE: THE CASE OF JOHN BROWN*

Carola Dietze

On Sunday 16 October 1859, at around eight o'clock in the evening, the elderly abolitionist John Brown said: 'Men, get on your arms; we will proceed to the Ferry.' His band of twenty-one men – five Afro-Americans and sixteen Euro-Americans – reacted promptly: they took their rifles and started out on the road to Harpers Ferry in Virginia (now West Virginia).[1] This little town at the confluence of the Shenandoah and Potomac rivers, enclosed by the Blue Ridge Mountains, housed the only arsenal of the US military in the southern states: thousands of cannon, muskets and rifles were stored here. For this reason, Brown had decided that it was the best place to start his uprising to free the South's four million slaves. Initially, everything went according to plan: John Brown and his men seized the nightwatchmen and occupied the armoury yard. This was all they needed to bring the weapons under their control. Then some of the volunteers went out to neighbouring plantations to free the slaves and take their masters hostage. They took the enslaved men with them, so that they could guard their former masters, and asked the slave women to spread the word that their liberators had come. On Monday morning, a fair number of hostages were assembled in the fire-engine house and about a dozen former slaves had cooperated with the group. Now would have been the time to leave Harpers Ferry, ascend into the mountains and start the guerrilla war. But John Brown hesitated. He waited for more slaves to come and join them. He had anticipated, correctly, that word of the raid would spread quickly in the region, but, contrary to his expectation, rather than slaves or sympathetic whites, the militiamen of the neighbouring communities arrived in order to squash the rebellion. On Monday, around noon, they opened fire and forced Brown and his volunteers to retreat into the fire-engine house. In the evening, US marines arrived from Washington DC. Early the next morning, they started an assault and quickly overpowered the small group. Brown and his men were taken into custody, interrogated, tried before a Virginia court and hanged.[2]

John Brown's raid on Harpers Ferry is one of the iconic events in American history.[3] It was a decisive step in the run-up to the election of the first Republican president, Abraham Lincoln, which led to the secession of the southern states and helped to provoke the Civil War.[4] As the recent literature has shown, the raid cannot be understood without reference to religion. John Brown was an orthodox Calvinist, a descendant of the Puritans in the proper sense of the word. Moreover, this raid cannot be understood without reference to religious teleological concepts of history. Brown's views about his own place in history, as well as the role of the United States in God's plan for the history of mankind, are crucial in this respect.[5] What we have here, is an incidence of Calvinist teleological thinking with major historical consequences in the middle of the nineteenth century in the United States. The article explores the consequences of this incidence for the history of teleological thinking and – as they are intricately linked – the concepts of modernization and modernity.

Narratives of the history of teleological thinking, which have been prominent since the Second World War, typically run roughly as follows. In the beginning, there are traditional, religious concepts about world history and its end. In Christian contexts, such pre-modern concepts refer to biblical visions and divisions of history as well as to messianic expectations about the return of Christ and God's eternal kingdom. Beginning in eighteenth-century Europe, a twofold secularization of such eschatological concepts of history can be observed: in the field of ideas, they turn into teleological philosophies of history and historicist historiography.[6] There is a parallel politicization of eschatology, that is: in the field of politics, eschatology and apocalyptic beliefs are transformed into utopian political ideas (such as Jacobinism, Communism and National Socialism), which – if put into practice – turn into totalitarian regimes.[7] The twofold transformation in the intellectual and political fields – according to these narratives – marks the advent of modernity. From now on, instead of God, nature and humans are perceived as making history.[8]

In recent scholarship, such histories of teleological thinking and modernity, which were widely accepted during the Cold War, have been challenged from different sides. While, for example, John Gray added modernization theories and neo-liberal economic theories to the list of secularized eschatologies, Martin Riesebrodt, in 2000, stated an end to secularization and the return of religion in modern societies; Jürgen Habermas, since 2001, has spoken of 'post-secular' society.[9] And while Sanjay Subrahmanyam has shown the impact of political eschatology for early modern kings and their empires, not just in Christian Europe, but also for Muslim and Jewish societies in Asia and Latin America, Hartmut Lehmann has pointed out that secularization has been a European *Sonderweg* ('special path') and that developments in other regions of the world (such as the United States) contradict the standard narratives of modernity. Moreover, he critically notes that narratives of teleological thinking and modernity tend to create the impression of irreversible progress.[10]

In this chapter, I build on such objections to counter the standard narratives of modernization and modernity from two directions. On the one hand, I argue that religious teleological concepts were political from their very beginning. Just as philosophical or ideological concepts of time, history and the future, they shape believers' ideas about their society's place in history, their expectations about its future and the way they act in politically significant ways.[11] On the other hand I use the case of John Brown and his conception of history to underline the fact that religious teleological concepts are also what one generally calls modern: the case study taken from American history can show that, in the nineteenth century, Christian concepts of history and teleology underwent changes and adaptations (just as they had done before), but continued to exert great influence.[12] In this way, I attempt to challenge the idea of a twofold secularization of eschatological concepts by arguing that – according to the standard criteria – modernity, so to speak, already existed in so-called pre-modern times while pre-modernity is still strongly present in European and American modernity.

From a methodological point of view, the arguments that eschatological thinking is political and that it is modern, do not mean, however, that we can assume one single continuous history of political eschatology. On the contrary, I would suggest conceiving of eschatological conceptions of history as connecting to and aligning with the specific political language(s) prevalent in different political contexts at various places and points in time. What would merit further investigation in a systematic, comparative manner are the precise forms and functions of the connections and alignments of eschatological conceptions of history with political language(s).[13] The example of John Brown stresses the potential of a social and cultural history of salvation history and eschatology: in order to understand the full range of teleological thinking in the nineteenth century, we need to study not only the *Höhenkammliteratur* (literally 'mountain ridge-literature') of philosophical or theological giants, but also the concepts of history, which different groups of society shared and on the basis of which they acted.

In the following section, first, I will consider the relationship of the terms 'salvation history', 'eschatology' and 'teleology'. In a second step, I will look at some sources crucial for the history of Christian teleological thinking in the European context as well as their reception, transformation and usage. This part serves to substantiate my argument that religious teleological thinking has always been political and to outline how eschatological conceptions of history were connecting to different intellectual and political contexts in Europe over time. In this way, this chapter attempts to sketch the history of teleological thinking and its political impact in order to indicate an alternative to the Cold War narrative of modernization and modernity. In the third part, I focus on the case of John Brown's raid on Harpers Ferry in order to point to teleological thinking and its political impact inherent in New England Puritanism and American abolitionism. What interests me among other things is the role of violence and its specific political-secular as well as religious function here.[14]

A caveat has to be introduced: eschatological thought-patterns have a long history; they can be traced back to Babylonian cosmogony, and they have been the subject of extensive scholarship since the nineteenth century.[15] I am neither a theologian nor a historian of religion, but a historian of modern and contemporary history, who – as a student – was lucky to have the chance to delve into medieval and early modern studies. The following remarks therefore have a hypothetical character, attempting to gain plausibility for a new way to think the relationship between eschatology, teleology, politics and modernity, in order to further provincialize Europe and work towards a history on equal terms.[16]

1. Terms and definitions: salvation history and eschatology as religious teleology

Teleology in the context of religious beliefs is usually called *Heilsgeschichte* ('salvation history'). It ends in eschatology. As the editors have pointed out in their introductory article, Christian Wolff in 1728 defined teleology as that 'part of natural philosophy which explains the ends of things' and thus temporalized philosophical thought about the final cause, coupling history and teleology. Analogous, since the mid-nineteenth century, according to the *Oxford English Dictionary*, eschatology is defined as that 'part of theology concerned with death, judgment, and the final destiny of the soul and of humankind'. The *Merriam-Webster* defines eschatology as the 'branch of theology concerned with the final events in the history of the world or of humankind'.[17] The term summarizes 'all those views and beliefs, relating to the "last things" (τὰ ἔσχατα)' in different religions all over the world concerning the individual or the universal or both in their interrelationship.[18] Salvation history and eschatology explain the ways and the ends of things (the individual, the soul, the history of the world and of humankind) in relation to the metaphysical realm, based on religious texts, coupling the individual, history and religion. Therefore, salvation history and teleology can be regarded as parallel ways of thinking about history, with the principal difference that salvation history and eschatology include God(s) as driving force(s) in history while teleology refers to philosophical entities such as ideas. Salvation history ending in eschatology can be regarded as a specific version of teleology and vice versa. For this reason, the terms 'salvation history', 'eschatology' and expressions such as 'religious teleological thinking' or 'religious concepts of teleology' are used synonymously here.

Perceived through the lens of narratives of modernity and their double secularization thesis, one might be tempted to think that teleology is a secularized version of salvation history. The development of teleology in response to the long-standing tradition of natural philosophy, however, rather suggests constant interaction between religious and philosophical concepts of teleology across ages and religious traditions. Instead of a one-way road from salvation histories and eschatology to philosophical and secular teleology, we should rather expect influences in both directions.

2. Christian teleological thinking and its political impact in Europe: before and after the French Revolution

Christian religious thinking about history and 'the ends of things' has been connected to various intellectual and political languages in different contexts since biblical times. In the Jewish and Christian traditions, eschatological concepts of history emerge from the prophecies of the Old Testament. These prophecies were recorded over many centuries for more than a dozen prophets, who were already 'religious politicians' in their time.[19] Accordingly, their prophecies differ in nature and concretion. Cold War narratives of modernity typically refer to a specific type of prophecy, prophecies, namely, which explicitly outline the whole course of history as well as its end and provide a division of world history into ages.

The most important example of such an (alleged) prophecy of world history is Daniel's vision of Nebuchadnezzar's dream which forms the basis of the *Vierreichelehre* ('doctrine of four empires').[20] For Christians, Paul's letters and the Revelation of St John in the New

Testament complement the *Vierreichelehre* of the Old Testament. The Apostle Paul, in his Epistle to the Romans, divides world history into three ages subjected to *lex naturae*, *lex Mosaica* and *lex Evangelica* (AV Rom. 2.11–16). This division is no longer a prophecy, but a concept of history using as its criterion the revelation of God's Law. The Revelation of St John has the character of a prophecy, again. A passage about the great whore Babylon (Babylon being an alias for Rome) explicitly addresses world history: 'And there are seven kings: five are fallen, and one is, *and* the other is not yet come; and when he cometh, he must continue a short space.' (AV Rev. 17.10). The story continues in complex ways and defies any simple transfer into world history (AV Rev. 17.11–18).[21] Notwithstanding such difficulties of interpretation, the Apocalypse and Paul's division of history gave Christians crucial indications about world history. First, by the time the Book of Revelation was written (probably in the first century) and by the time the Western Church adopted it into the biblical canon (around 400), the world had entered into the third age and the sixth kingdom. This kingdom had to be the Roman Empire. There would be one more kingdom to come, and then history would end. Second, this end of history was imminent, as the final verses of the Apocalypse (and thus the Bible) assert: 'Seal not the sayings of the prophecy of this book: for the time is at hand' or 'He which testifieth these things saith, Surely I come quickly,' (AV Rev. 22.10 and 20).[22] Therefore Christians believed (and still believe) that they live in a late epoch of world history.

A comprehensive study of Christian traditions of thinking about history and the ends of things would have to include the return of Christ, the Millennium, Judgement Day and God's eternal kingdom, which feature prominently in the Apocalypse. But even from this selective and preliminary investigation we can conclude, first, that these prophecies and concepts of history are political from the very beginning in that they were linked to specific political entities, situations and aims; and second, that over the centuries these concepts of history reached (and still reach) enormous audiences, because they are read in private or from the pulpit every year. Concerning views of history and the ends of things in the Christian tradition, there is thus no clear distinction possible between the religious and the secular, the political and the historical sphere.

Much of later eschatological historiography in the Christian tradition is a direct and explicit variation on these biblical themes. In late antiquity, Eusebius Hieronymus (*c*. 340 to 420), the most influential Church father for medieval Europe (his Latin translation of the Bible, the *Vulgata*, became the authoritative text), filled the gaps between the prophecies of the Old and New Testaments. In his commentary on the Book of Daniel, he stated that, if the golden head of the statue in Nebuchadnezzar's dream was the Babylonian empire, the second kingdom – *Medorum videlicet atque Persarum* – was 'obviously' the Achaemenid or First Persian Empire, the third had to be the Macedonian Empire of Alexander and his successors, and – *Regnum autem quartum, quod perspicue pertinet ad Romanos, ferrum est* – the fourth kingdom from iron clearly referred to the Romans.[23] The fact that the Roman Empire split into a Western and an Eastern part towards the end of the fourth century added much plausibility to this interpretation: the description of the statue's feet had seemingly predicted the rupture. Modifying Roman historiography, another late antique church father, Aurelius Augustinus (354–430), in his

De civitate dei, extended Daniel's four kingdoms to six ages of history, which he equated with the six stages of human life from *infantia* to *senectus*. With this salvation history he aspired to embrace all of world history.[24] Thus, late antique authors adapted certain biblical teleological concepts to their current political situations and in this way created a range of anthropological, historical and political interpretations, which were linked to the biblical sources, patterns of history writing in their societies, and to each other's interpretations.

In Europe, these late-antique concepts were authoritative through the Middle Ages and well into the seventeenth century. They provided the framework for various historical and computational works – from Gregory of Tours' (538–94) *Historia Francorum* and Bede's (672/3–735) *De sex aetatibus mundi* up to Jacques-Bénigne Bossuet's (1627–1704) *Discours sur l'Histoire universelle*, to name only a few.[25] They lost their canonical function only gradually. Christoph Cellarius (1638–1707), a Lutheran professor of Rhetoric and History at the enlightened reform university of Halle was crucial to this process. With his *Historia universalis* he popularized the division into ancient, medieval and modern history, still used today.[26] In this way he modified and at the same time perpetuated Paul's tripartite division of world and salvation history.

The impact of the biblical prophecies turned historiography was not restricted to the intellectual field of history writing, however; it directly influenced politics and its legitimation. The most important concept in this respect is the idea of *translatio imperii* (literally 'transfer of empire / imperial rule'). The term and idea of *regna transferre* (the verb 'to transfer (imperial) rule') refer to Hieronymus's translation of the Old Testament into Latin: after God had disclosed Nebuchadnezzar's dream to Daniel, according to Hieronymus's translation, Daniel thanked and blessed the Lord as the one who (among other things) *transfert regna atque constituit* (in the translation of the King James Bible: 'removeth kings, and setteth up kings', literally 'transfers rule [away from somebody] and establishes it').[27] Thus, according to the version of the Bible with the widest circulation in Europe up to the reformation in the sixteenth century, God actively intervenes in history by passing rule on from one people to the next, depending on the way they use it – an eminently political concept.

Hieronymus's translation of the Bible allowed for more flexibility than the biblical prophecies of world history, but could still be combined with them. On Christmas Day in the year 800, Pope Leo III crowned the King of the Franks, Charles I (Charlemagne), as *Imperator Romanorum* ('Emperor of the Romans'). At the time, the event was not interpreted as *translatio imperii*. Fifty years later, however, we find the first note that through this act imperial rule was transferred from the Romans to the Franks, and in the tenth and eleventh centuries, when the Saxon kings of the Ottonian dynasty revived the title of *Imperator Romanorum*, chroniclers close to these 'Holy Roman Emperors' developed the political theory of *translatio imperii*. They argued that the Ottonian Empire was a continuation of the Roman Empire and in this way incorporated the kingdom they inhabited into an updated version of the teachings about the four kingdoms.[28] A strong point in favour of this interpretation was the fact that history obviously had not come to an end yet, thus the Roman Empire had to continue somewhere. Around 1200, Pope Innocent III put forth a rival theory of *translatio imperii*, which became part of Church Law. In a power struggle with the emperor, he maintained that it was he, the Bishop of Rome, who transferred imperial rule. Intense fights between the adherents of the Church's theory and those of the emperors followed, with one emperor pointing explicitly to Hieronymus's Bible, stressing that it said that God (and not the pope) transferred imperial rule.[29] Ultimately, however, both sides contributed to the consolidation of the concept of *translatio imperii* and the political entity called the *Sacrum Romanum Imperium* ('Holy Roman Empire') from the thirteenth century and *Sacrum Romanum Imperium Nationis Germanicæ* ('Holy Roman Empire of the German Nations') from the fifteenth century. It lasted until 1806.

The prophecies in the Old and New Testament in the interpretation of Hieronymus's translation and the theory of *translatio imperii* had multiple political consequences. In the competition between European rulers as well as between emperor and pope, it singled out certain dynasties by bestowing special religious and political prestige on them, and it gave extra powers to the pope. Therefore it comes as no surprise that in the later Middle Ages and since the early modern era other theories of *translatio imperii* to other European kingdoms (such as Bulgaria, France, Great Britain and Russia) followed. This pluralization correctly reflected political realities in Europe, but brought with it a dilution of the theory.[30] The concept of *translatio imperii* did not only affect the elites, however. In the Holy Roman Empire of the German Nation, the idea of living in a society that was a continuation of the Roman Empire entailed, for example, the introduction of Roman Law and for about eight centuries gave some coherence and justification to this extremely diverse, multi-ethnic and multi-lingual polity.

Not only medieval and early modern historiography, but also teleological philosophies of universal history and theories of progress predominant since the Enlightenment can be and have been interpreted as worldly continuations of eschatological concepts of history. This is readily evident for somebody like Johann Gottfried Herder (1744–1803), a theologian, philosopher and poet prominently depicted as one of the founding fathers of historicism.[31] He reactivated Augustine's six stages of human life as a framework for a universal history.[32] Karl Löwith famously maintained that important variants of nineteenth-century philosophies of universal history and theories of progress have to be read as modifications of eschatology in secular disguise. God as actor and driving force of historical change, His grace as the decisive criterion for a division of the ages and His Kingdom on Earth as the end-point of history are replaced by other agents, criteria and goals, such as the world-spirit, freedom and its self-realization (G. W. F. Hegel) or the masses, the social-economic conditions and world revolution followed by communist society (Karl Marx).[33]

Just as in the centuries before, the adaptation of eschatology in the modern era did not only concern the intellectual, but also the political field. The French Revolution is one important example in this respect. When the revolution entered its radical phase, the Jacobins transformed Catholic (mostly Jansenistic) beliefs into a civic religion and visions of the virtuous nation – a utopian idea, which (under the conditions of internal and external war) ended in excessive violence: *La terreur*.[34] In the German case, the term

Drittes Reich ('Third Reich', literally 'Third Empire') is telling: after the end of the First World War and the collapse of the German Empire established in 1871, the radical conservative nationalist Arthur Moeller van den Bruck in his book *Das Dritte Reich* suggested that, after the end of the Holy Roman Empire in 1806 and the German Empire in 1918, the combination of nationalism and socialism would lay the basis for a Third Empire.[35] The National Socialists used the term for the political entity they intended to establish and, after 1933, for the *Tausendjähriges Reich* ('millennial empire') they claimed they were creating. From the moment of its adoption the term *Drittes Reich* did not only refer to an enumeration of the German empires, but had an eschatological connotation resonating with Paul's tripartite division of history.[36]

From these equally selective and preliminary investigations into the impact of religious traditions of teleological thinking in European history, we can conclude that biblical salvation history and eschatology had a decisive influence on historical thinking and acting before and after the French Revolution, and that is on what is usually called pre-modern as well as modern historiographies, theologies, philosophies of history and politics.

Some of the meta-narratives of modernity and modernization pointed out and analysed these processes in intriguing ways. At the same time, however, they typically can be read as versions of such historical concepts themselves, replacing the agents, criteria and goals of religious teleology and nineteenth-century historical philosophy by sociological and market forces, personal freedom, wealth and democracy. In this way, they reiterate and re-establish the narrative, sharing important characteristics of it. One such characteristic is Eurocentricity. The Cold War meta-narrative of modernity and modernization based on the secularization thesis takes as its point of departure a specific interpretation of the European experience, focusing on the French Revolution as the decisive transformation point. Other revolutions, such as the English revolution or the American Revolutions – North, Central and South – are excluded from this meta-narrative of modernity, just as are the revolution on Haiti or the Taiping rebellion.[37] But as the case study of John Brown shows, Christian concepts of teleology were also of crucial importance for historical visions, politics and violence in the British colonies, which became the United States. The religion, which deeply shaped the society and the self-understanding of the first colonies especially in the North, was Protestantism in the form of Puritanism: the Calvinist, Reformed Church. After the United States had gained independence from England, Calvinism in many ways remained a formative creed.

3. Puritan teleology, politics and violence in the United States: the case of John Brown

Eurocentric Cold War narratives of modernity typically refer to prophecies depicting the whole course of world history, its stages and its end. In the reformation, Johannes Calvinus had rendered this type of prophecy unsuitable for any interpretation of real-world history for his followers. In his exegeses of the Book of Daniel called *Praelectionum in Danielem Prophetam*, Calvinus followed Hieronymus and interpreted Daniel's vision as symbolizing the Babylonian, Persian, Macedonian and Roman empires. Contrary to Hieronymus and the other church fathers of antiquity, however, he then maintained that Daniel's prophecy predicted the empires until the resurrection of Christ only, not all history until God's eternal kingdom. The fact that powerful empires still existed after Christ's resurrection, therefore, could not refute Daniel's vision. His prophecy had already been fulfilled and was of no further value for current or future history. This interpretation was a death-knell for the theory of *translatio imperii*. It implied that the Holy Roman Empire could not have anything to do with the Roman Empire, because the latter had ceased to exist with the spreading of Christ's Gospel over the planet. Instead, Calvinus interpreted *imperium transferre* in a new way. For him, *translatio imperii* was the fate of all worldly rule. Only the fifth monarchy, the *regnum Christi*, is permanent, but that is of a wholly different nature. It is invisible, because it does not comprise all subjects of a particular kingdom and does not strive for worldly power and splendour, but consists of the community of saints (that is: all righteous believers), wherever they might live, and its sole purpose is the glorification of God.[38]

As Calvinus – in the eyes of his followers – had destroyed all possibility of political interpretations of Daniel's vision and the theory of *translatio imperii*, Puritan historical concepts relied on a different type of biblical prophecy: the idea of the covenant and God's intervention in history. For example, according to the Fifth Book of Moses (AV Deut. 31.16–17 and 29) the Lord predicts to Moses: 'Behold, . . . this people will rise up . . . and break my covenant which I have made with them. Then my anger shall be kindled against them . . . and many evils and troubles shall befall them; so that they will say in that day, Are not these evils come upon us, because our God *is* not among us?' And Moses passes this prophecy on to the congregation of Israel: 'For I know that after my death ye will . . . turn aside from the way which I have commanded you; and evil will befall you . . .; because ye will do evil in the sight of the Lord'. Both these prophecies – the Lord's and Moses' – predict certain events in an uncertain future after Moses' death. They do not outline the end of all history, but describe in what way the people of Israel is going to break its covenant with God, and God's reaction: His anger and withdrawal. God's withdrawal is a punishment depicted as an educational measure: redemption is possible and history will continue. Still, the prophecies contain crucial lessons concerning politics and history. They teach that a chosen people that neglects the rules given by God and that ceases to function as a righteous polity will be punished by the Lord. Moreover, they teach that the Lord intervenes in history, and how He does that: through His presence and protection or His withdrawal, leaving His chosen people to fend for themselves against the evils of the world. A nation that has a covenant with God and disregards it has to expect destruction.

For Puritans, such biblical prophecies about God's intervention in history aligned with an additional set of beliefs determining the place of the individual in national, world and salvation history. Puritans were convinced that man is per se evil and that there is no progress in the moral realm. Only Christ – through the Covenant of Grace – can grant salvation. Puritans also believed in predestination in its most comprehensive sense: they believed that God when creating the world predestined the entire world history as well as the actions of each individual; at the beginning of time He predetermined everything that would ever happen on this planet until the end of time. Moreover, the Puritans, who founded the New England colonies, believed that every nation had a covenant with God. If a nation did not keep its part of the contract – that is: if it did not live according to God's laws – God would punish it. They had left Old England, because they thought sin was so omnipresent in their home country that God's punishment would be imminent. This is why they strove to build a model society in the New World, 'where the will of God would be observed in every detail, a kingdom of God on earth', and a 'citadel of God's chosen people', 'a Citty vpon a Hill' serving as an example to the rest of the world.[39]

For everybody living in the 'citadel of God's chosen people', these beliefs had very tangible consequences. If history and biography are predestined by God, Puritans believed, every human being has a divine commission in life, and it is every man's sacred duty to understand and embrace his or her commission and to fulfil its demands. (The contradiction between complete predetermination and the necessity to find out about God's plan for oneself has been discussed by Calvinists since the reformation, without coming to a solution.) Moreover, if only the Chosen will be saved, believers have to live a life worthy of God's salvation. Worthy of salvation are those who follow God's laws and the teachings of the Bible in every detail and without compromise in every respect. Experience of God's grace in a moment of conversion was a sign that one might be preordained for salvation, a 'saint'. Sainthood was a precondition for the Church to admit somebody as a member, and membership in a Church was the precondition for political rights. Still, nobody while living in this world could be certain if he was destined for eternal heaven or eternal hell. One could only believe in God and do good deeds, because God – according to the Covenant of Works – recognized and rewarded good deeds.[40] Moreover, it was crucial to acknowledge one's sins and repent for them through prayer, deed and the ready acceptance of just punishment. This was all the more important because unpunished sins would expose the whole of society to God's anger. Therefore, it was the duty of each head of a family to detect and punish the sins of everybody under his care: his wife, children, servants and any boarder who might live with them.

From this – again – very selective and ideal-type-like analysis of basic Puritan beliefs, we can conclude that anthropological, political, historical and religious thought and practice cannot be separated in early New England Puritanism. A well-ordered society had to be based on the Bible and its God-given laws. Thus, Puritan concepts of history and teleology were fundamentally political, shaping believers' ideas about their society's place in history, their expectations about its future and the way they acted in politically more intense ways than the usual Catholic belief in a succession of empires or in historical stages. Erecting and maintaining a model society, a 'City on the Hill', required religious dedication from every member of society and placed a high amount of responsibility on each believer: the zeal and responsibility to save his or her own soul, to fulfil the nation's covenant with God and thus give an example for the whole of mankind.

Although, by 1700, leading Puritans thought their holy experiment had failed, important aspects of their beliefs lived on through the American Revolution, which politicized, intensified and enlarged them in certain respects. The United States was still a model society. Now, it was a model not only in the keeping of God's Law, however, but in its form of government: a republic, in which basic liberties were guaranteed to all citizens. The responsibility felt by everybody who believed in the principles of the Declaration of Independence and the Constitution and therefore thought that the United States was a political model society was thus expanding: Americans had to prove that their institutions worked. Now, they had to take responsibility not only for their community and colony, but for the entire union – irrespective of the fact of whether they lived in one of the northern or one of the southern states.[41] Puritan concepts of biography, the nation and history, as well as the responsibilities connected with those concepts, were thus expanding in content and geography.

The abolitionist movement in the United States can be regarded as a consequence of the expansion of the Puritan Covenant and the responsibilities it entailed. The anti-slavery movement, as a mass phenomenon, was one important outgrowth of a broad religious movement, the Second Awakening, which in many ways ran counter to orthodox Calvinist beliefs, but generally aimed at conversion and the intensification of religious life, reform of society according to God's Law and a revival of the righteous life of the colonial beginnings. Reform societies addressing all sorts of 'social evils' were formed everywhere in the country; the American Anti-Slavery Society was one of them. The majority of the founding members of the Society were great patriots, highly valuing the American liberties and the republican form of government, and at the same time imbued with a strong awareness of their responsibilities before God.[42]

The founding document of the American Anti-Slavery Society – the 'Declaration of Sentiments' drafted by William Lloyd Garrison (editor of the anti-slavery newspaper *The Liberator*) and accepted by the sixty founding members in Philadelphia in December 1833 – is based on the Bible and the Declaration of Independence: 'We plant ourselves upon the Declaration of our Independence and the truths of Divine Revelation, as upon the Everlasting Rock.'[43] The document clearly shows the interconnection, interaction and convergence between religious and political concepts of history, emancipation and notions of progress in abolitionism at this specific point in time:

> More than fifty-seven years have elapsed since a band of patriots convened in this place to devise measures for the deliverance of this country from a foreign yoke. The cornerstone upon which they founded the Temple of Freedom was broadly this –, that all men are created equal ... We have met together for the achievement of an enterprise, without which that of our fathers is incomplete; and which, for its magnitude, solemnity, and probable results upon the destiny of the world ... far transcends theirs ...[44]

This passage expresses the notion of political progress primarily in terms of a perfection of the political and social institutions of the United States, but it also addresses the idea that the abolition of slavery in the USA would have important repercussions for the rest of the world. The inviolability of human liberty and dignity is motivated by religion: 'The right to enjoy liberty is inalienable. To invade it is to usurp the prerogative of Jehovah.'

This religious argument establishes that slavery is sin and slave-owners are man-stealers (Exodus 21.16). Such sin is especially blatant in the United States, because of the liberties the people here enjoy: 'therefore, . . . it [the nation] is bound to repent instantly . . . and to let the oppressed go free.' Emancipation is especially urgent, because the federal structure of the nation implicates the northern states in a grave crime, even though these states freed their slaves. 'We also maintain that there are, at the present time, the highest obligations resting upon the people of the free States to remove slavery by moral and political action.' The document then enumerates the different ways in which the free states support slavery through federal institutions: 'This relation to slavery is criminal, and full of danger: IT MUST BE BROKEN UP.'[45] This danger refers to God's punishment for the United States, a model society, if slavery is not abolished.

While the founding document of the American Anti-Slavery Society expresses these thoughts in a rather diplomatic language, radical abolitionists like John Brown put the same idea more bluntly. One of his close friends reports that he often said:

> I believe in the Golden Rule and the Declaration of Independence. I think they both mean the same thing; and it is better that a whole generation should pass off the face of the earth, men, women, and children, by a violent death, than that one jot of either should fail *in this country*. I mean exactly so, sir.[46]

Slavery violated the Higher Law of men's God-given liberty as well as the Golden Rule: 'And as ye would that men should do to you, do ye also to them likewise' (AV Luke 6.31). Therefore slavery was sin, the 'sum of all villanies' and its supporters diabolic, 'Satan'.[47] The fight against slavery was a fight between good and evil. When slave-owners resisted the Law of God, they endangered the United States, because they called God's anger upon the entire nation, including the free states. Emancipation was therefore both the completion of the American Revolution *and* repentance of this blatant sin, in order to escape God's punishment. In the worldview of the abolitionist movement, political and religious interpretations of emancipation, history and the future cannot be separated.

But how could one act upon these beliefs? In the 'Declaration of Sentiments' the founding members of the American Anti-Slavery Society announced that – true to the New Testament and contrary to their revolutionary forefathers – they would not use force:

> Their principles [the principles of the patriots in 1776] led them to wage war against their oppressors, and to spill human blood like water, in order to be free. Ours forbid the doing of evil that good may come, and lead us to reject . . . the use of all carnal weapons . . . relying solely upon those which are spiritual, and mighty through God . . .[48]

Members of the American Anti-Slavery Society tried to convince the slaveholders in the southern states through 'moral suasion' that slavery was wrong. But when they sent petitions to Congress, the pro-slavery majority enforced a rule, according to which it was forbidden to present or discuss any anti-slavery petitions. When Anti-Slavery Societies flooded the South with pamphlets to reach the masters' hearts, slaveholders broke into post offices at night and burnt all the material addressed to them, because they feared that it might find its way into the slave quarters. Instead of repenting, pro-slavery intellectuals went on the offensive and suggested slavery for white workers in the north. Mobs of 'gentlemen of property and standing' used violence against abolitionists and their meetings. Towards the end of the 1850s, it was obvious that the strategy of 'moral suasion' had failed.[49]

For Americans who strove to abolish slavery in order to fulfil the covenant with God there were two ways of dealing with this situation. Garrison prominently took one of them: leaning towards perfectionism (a new belief in the possibility to free oneself from sin and reach a state of moral and spiritual perfection in this world through conversion, religious life and one's own endeavour), he felt that moral reform was necessary, before slavery could be abolished. He supported all sorts of reform movements and propagandized to dissolve the Union, so that northerners would no longer be responsible for the sins committed in the southern states. In order to give emphasis to this idea, he publicly burnt the Constitution in Boston. Towards the end of the 1850s, most abolitionists agreed with him. John Brown was one of the few who did not. According to him, slavery was the problem, not the Union or the Constitution. Separation of the free states from the slave states would give northerners an unblemished conscience, but it would not abolish the sin of slavery, because it would not free the slaves. By demanding separation, Brown maintained, abolitionists did not live up to their responsibility before God. Instead, they had to engage actively with the southern states and bring down slavery.

John Brown was born in Torrington, Connecticut, in 1800 to a family of old Puritan stock. He believed that he was a descendant of one Peter Brown, who had come to New England on the *Mayflower*. Both his grandfathers had fought in the American War of Independence. Thus, he belonged to the tacit aristocracy of the northern United States. When he was five years old, his parents moved west to Hudson in the Western Reserve, Connecticut's newly opened frontier region in Northern Ohio, which became the region with the most intense anti-slavery activity in the United States. In his personal biography John Brown followed all important stages demanded by orthodox Calvinism: after a short sceptical phase in his youth, he experienced his conversion, learned the Bible by heart and embraced the religion of his parents and forefathers, Congregationalism, the variant of orthodox Calvinism prevalent in New England. Soon, he was admitted as a member of the local Congregational church and strictly fulfilled the demands of the Scripture. He prayed and read the Bible several times each day, thanked the Lord for every meal (even in the most adverse circumstances), and saw to it that he and his large family held the laws of God, such as honesty, protection of the weak, sharing with the needy, regular prayer and Sabbath on Sundays. Moreover, John Brown taught in Sunday school, founded a church on the frontier, where he acted as a lay preacher, and loved to discuss theological subtleties. He scorned the theologies of perfectibility Garrison adhered to, because to him it was blasphemous to think that human beings could raise themselves out of sin through their own intentions and actions. Instead, he conscientiously fulfilled his duty to detect and punish the sins of everybody under his care, as all his children later testified.[50] In short: John Brown was a good Calvinist and the representation of a model Puritan.

Brown (and those who supported him) had been sympathetic to the abolitionist cause all his life. As long as a political solution of the slavery question seemed possible, he propagated and used pacific means: he read abolitionist newspapers and books on slavery and slave rebellions, spoke in meetings, drafted and signed petitions to Congress, and participated in the Underground Railroad.[51] But from the end of the 1830s onwards, when pro-slavery mobs frequently attacked abolitionists and killed the editor Elijah Lovejoy, Brown began to believe that God had given him powers and faculties, which He intended him to use in order to deliver the slaves from bondage. In front of his congregation, he pledged to devote his life and everything he had to bring down slavery.[52] The longer he worked in the abolitionist movement, the more he became convinced that his divine commission was to end slavery in the United States. He saw himself as God's instrument, as a soldier of God.[53]

In the ensuing fight between free-state and pro-slavery settlers in the new territory of Kansas (where five of his sons had settled) Brown escalated the conflict into civil war and established for himself the image of a ruthless fighter for the abolitionist cause. As such, he was much admired in abolitionist circles in the north-east. After his return to New England, Brown started to lobby among abolitionists for a militant intervention in the South that would end slavery in the United States.[54] A raid on the arsenal at Harpers Ferry would be the rallying call for the slaves in the region and provide him with the weapons necessary to arm them. Together his band of well-trained abolitionists and the slaves who had come to join them would escape into the mountains, where they would use guerrilla tactics to defend themselves against the slaveholders' militias and start their journey south, gathering strength by attracting more slaves as they went. Brown was certain that the opportunity for slaves to flee into the Appalachian Mountains and to defend themselves against slaveholders or to escape to the north would be the beginning of the end of slavery in the United States.[55]

Puritan beliefs were crucial for the realization of this plan in a number of ways. Brown hatched it for almost twenty years. The fact that he regarded himself as a soldier of God let him always return to his divine commission to end slavery in the United States. It also helped him to develop the charisma necessary to entertain a group of supporters and volunteers over an extended period of time as well as the psychological tenacity and physical endurance to overcome a plethora of obstacles. The implementation of Brown's plan relied on God's intervention. If somebody expressed doubts about his chances to succeed, he usually replied: 'If God *be* for us, who *can be* against us?' (AV Rom. 8.31). If God had predestined Brown to end slavery in the United States and arranged everything accordingly from the beginning of time (for example by placing the Appalachian Mountains as a refuge for him and the slaves), God would intervene in h/His fight and help him to prevail against the mightiest foe, just as He had done, when He had helped the Israelites to fight the Amalekites in the desert during the exodus from Egypt (Exod. 17.8-10), supported Gideon in the war against the Midianites (Judg. 6–8), or given special powers to Samson (Judg. 13–16).[56]

Brown's strategy was a mixture of political and religious rationales. First, he wanted to forestall the election of a Republican candidate in the presidential race in 1860, because he feared that the Republican Party would protect slavery where it existed, and that it would be much harder to mobilize an abolitionist opposition, once a Republican candidate was elected. Second, Brown and his supporters wanted to give the slaves an opportunity for self-emancipation through violence. As they had learned from the American Revolution, true emancipation was possible through violence only, because the successful use of violence conferred a feeling for one's own individuality, manhood and power that was a necessary precondition for a successful life in a democracy and competitive market-society. Third, the slaveholders in the United States and citizens of the entire nation had to incur punishment for the sin of slavery it had supported or tolerated for so long. This sin was so enormous that it could only be purged with blood. Otherwise God's anger would annihilate the entire nation.[57]

While John Brown's plan failed militarily after 36 hours, politically it succeeded beyond everything he could have expected. This political success was mainly due to the fact that a substantial part of the population in the northern states did not ridicule Brown's politico-religious self-conception, but took him and his mission seriously. For weeks after the raid, John Brown commanded the news of the national press. Determined 'to make the most of his defeat', he embraced his trial and his execution as a means to take the fight against slavery onto a different level. Just as God had intended, His soldier had survived the army's assault and was publicly tried to turn into a saint, martyr, Moses and Christ. In the North, this self-interpretation was taken up readily and augmented through religious and political language and symbolism in newspapers, speeches, sermons, poetry and literature. In the South, on the contrary, fears of slave insurrections spread and conspiracy theories developed. As many Southerners believed that the Republican Party was behind the raid, Lincoln's election led to secession and war – a war that eventually did bring about the emancipation Brown had hoped to effect.[58]

Certainly, the southern conspiracy theories lacked any real basis: Lincoln had nothing to do with the raid on Harpers Ferry and thoroughly disapproved of it.[59] After four years of war, in his Second Inaugural Address delivered on 4 March 1865, he seemed to share Brown's views on sin and punishment, however, when he said:

> Fondly do we hope – fervently do we pray – that this mighty scourge of war may speedily pass away. Yet, if God wills that it continue, until all the wealth piled by the bond-man's two hundred and fifty years of unrequited toil shall be sunk, and until every drop of blood drawn with the lash, shall be paid by another drawn with the sword, as was said three thousand years ago, so still it must be said 'the judgments of the Lord are true and righteous altogether'.[60]

Just like John Brown, Lincoln could rely on his audience in the North to understand him.

4. Conclusion

By addressing biblical prophecies of history and their changing alignment with political language(s) prevalent in different political contexts at various places and points in time, this chapter has introduced Christian teleology into the intellectual endeavour pursued in this anthology. After establishing that salvation history and eschatology can be regarded as religious teleology, the argument was twofold: by addressing religious teleology and its usage in European history before and after the French Revolution, this chapter has tried to show that so-called traditional, religious teleological concepts have been fundamentally political, from the beginning. By analysing the religious and political concepts of personal biography, national and world history, which led John Brown to undertake his suicidal attempt to liberate the slaves in the southern United States, it stressed the fact that religious teleologies still played a decisive role in Europe and America in the nineteenth century and are therefore an integral part of what one usually calls modernization and modernity. Thus, the long-standing assumption that religious concepts of time are 'pre-modern', and overcome or eclipsed by the intellectual and cultural consequences of the political, industrial and scientific revolutions, needs to be reconsidered.

In this way, the chapter also incorporates concepts of time and teleology in the United States, a republic, into the standard narratives of modernity. Incorporating the United States alters these usual narratives of the history of teleological thinking and modernity in at least two respects. First, it opens up the usual Eurocentrism by including a state on the American continent in the analysis. And second, as the analysis of political eschatology's impact has focused on monarchies, so far, it broadens the perspective by showing how and in what way political eschatology can function in and for a republic. Certainly, the British colonies which founded the United States were strongly influenced by European thought and culture, so that other countries and regions of the world might serve as better examples to break up Eurocentric historical thought. Still, the important position entertained by the United States today and the tentative results produced here might justify the choice. Republics like the United States referred less to prophecies depicting the whole course of world history as a succession of mighty kingdoms; instead, they related to God's covenant with His chosen nations. In both versions, God actively intervenes in history. The degree of punishment which has to be feared is different however: when monarchies forfeit their God-given rule by misuse, it is simply passed on from one people to the next, while republics which do not live up to their covenant have to fear destruction. Accordingly, the responsibility of each member of such a republic to live up to God's laws in order to prevent this fate was – at least in theory – much higher. The difference between monarchies and republics must not be regarded as a principal one, however: by 1900, Americans had developed their own version of *translatio imperii* to the United States,[61] a theory which has prominent adherents up to today.

Notes

*   I am grateful to the editors, especially to Henning Trüper, as well as to Sabine Dworog, Thomas Etzemüller, Martin H. Geyer, Michael Hochgeschwender, Anke Klatt and Friedrich Lenger for conversations on this topic or related issues and/or this chapter. Moreover I want to thank Felix Lieb for helping me to navigate Munich's libraries. If no other source is given, the translations are mine.

1. Osborne P. Anderson, *A Voice from Harper's Ferry* [1861], Atlanta: World View Publishers, 1980, p. 69.

2. There is a large literature on John Brown. For the best historical research on his life and the raid on Harpers Ferry, see Stephen B. Oates, *To Purge This Land With Blood: A Biography of John Brown*, New York: Harper & Row, 1970; Benjamin Quarles, *Allies for Freedom* [1974], intr. William P. McFeely, Cambridge, Mass.: Da Capo Press, 2001, and Robert McGlone, *John Brown's War Against Slavery*, Cambridge: Cambridge University Press, 2009. On the trial of John Brown and his volunteers see Brian McGinty, *John Brown's Trial*, Cambridge, Mass.: Harvard University Press, 2009. For an analysis of this act of insurrectionary violence from the perspective of the history of terrorism, see my *Taten statt Worte. Acht Jahre in der Erfindung des Terrorismus*, forthcoming, Hamburg: Hamburger Edition, 2015; for the raid see ch. 2.4.

3. For John Brown's place in American history see esp. Merrill D. Peterson, *John Brown: The Legend Revisited*, Charlottesville: University of Virginia Press, 2002, and R. Blakeslee Gilpin, *John Brown Still Lives! America's Long Reckoning with Violence, Equality, and Change*, Chapel Hill: University of North Carolina Press, 2011.

4. See James M. McPherson, *Battle Cry of Freedom: The Civil War Era*, Oxford: Oxford University Press, 1988, pp. 207–13.

5. See esp. Louis A. DeCaro, *'Fire From the Midst of You': A Religious Life of John Brown*, New York: New York University Press, 2002.

6. 'Historicist' refers to histories of progress, here, as it commonly does in the English usage of the term, not to *Historismus* in its original meaning.

7. On philosophy of history and 'the secularization of its eschatological pattern' see Karl Löwith, *Meaning in History: The Theological Implications of the Philosophy of History*, Chicago: The University of Chicago Press, 1950, here p. 2. The interpretation of Jacobinism and the subsequent political movements as a 'new kind of religion' has a long history. Crucial reference points for this narrative are Alexis de Tocqueville's observations in *The Old Regime and the Revolution* and Max Weber's 1919/20 diagnosis of an *Entzauberung* ('disenchantment') of the modern world. In the 1930s, several writers and intellectuals (most importantly Eric Voegelin) began to describe Communism and National Socialism as 'substitutes for religion'. On the history of this interpretation see Michael Burleigh, *Earthly Powers: Religion and Politics in Europe from the Enlightenment to the Great War*, London: HarperCollins, 2005, here p. 4, who in his own interpretation actualizes the narrative. For the pre-modern side, see Norman Cohn, *The Pursuit of the Millennium: Revolutionary Millenarians and Mystical Anarchists of the Middle Ages* [1954], London: Paladin, 1970. For the whole narrative see Charles Taylor, *A Secular Age*, Cambridge, Mass.: Belknap Press of Harvard University Press, 2007.

8. For this aspect see esp. Reinhart Koselleck et al., 'Geschichte, Historie', in Otto Brunner et al., eds, *Geschichtliche Grundbegriffe: Historisches Lexikon zur politisch-sozialen Sprache in Deutschland*, vol. 2, Stuttgart: Ernst Klett, 1975, pp. 593–717, e.g. p. 594.

9. See John Gray, *Black Mass: Apocalyptic Religion and the Death of Utopia*, New York: Farrar, Strauss and Giroux, 2007; Martin Riesebrodt, *Die Rückkehr der Religionen. Fundamentalismus und der 'Kampf der Kulturen'*, Munich: Beck, 2000, and Jürgen Habermas, 'Faith and Knowledge', in id., *The Future of the Human Nature*, Cambridge, Mass.: Polity MIT Press, 2002, pp. 101–15.

10. See Sanjay Subrahmanyam, 'Turning the Stones Over: Sixteenth-Century Millenarianism from the Tagus to the Ganges', in *The Indian Economic and Social History Review* 40 (2003), no. 2, pp. 129–61, and Hartmut Lehmann, *Säkularisierung: Der Europäische Sonderweg in Sachen Religion*, Göttingen: Wallstein, 2004, esp. chs 1, 6 and 8. Others have elaborated on these points of critique since.

11. For the interrelatedness of personal and political experiences, expectations and acting under modern conditions see Reinhart Koselleck, '"Space of Experience" and "Horizon of Expectation" – Two Historical Categories', in id., *Futures Past: On the Semantics of Historical Time*, Cambridge, Mass.: MIT Press, 1985, pp. 267–88. For principal thoughts on the interaction between religion and politics in general see Friedrich Wilhelm Graf and Heinrich Meier, eds, *Politik und Religion: Zur Diagnose der Gegenwart*, Munich: Beck, 2013.

12. For tendencies of dechristianization, rechristianization and religious revival in the nineteenth century in Europe and the United States, see Lehmann, *Säkularisierung*, and esp. his *Säkularisierung, Dechristianisierung, Rechristianisierung im neuzeitlichen Europa: Bilanz und Perspektiven der Forschung*, Göttingen: Vandenhoeck & Ruprecht, 1997. On the adaptability of religion to modern conditions see for the American case esp. Michael Hochgeschwender, *Amerikanische Religion: Evangelikalismus, Pfingstlertum und Fundamentalismus*, Frankfurt am Main: Verlag der Weltreligionen, 2007.

13. See Lehmann, *Säkularisierung* for a similar approach to the study of religiosity in general.

14. On the importance of religious concepts of time and history for the perpetrators of terrorist acts since the end of the Cold War, see esp. Mark Juergensmeyer, *Terror in the Mind of God: The Global Rise of Religious Violence*, Berkeley: University of California Press, 2000.

15. See Norman Cohn, *Cosmos, Chaos and the World to Come: The Ancient Roots of Apocalyptic Faith*, New Haven/London: Yale University Press, 1993.

16. See Dipesh Chakrabarty, *Provincializing Europe: Postcolonial Thought and Historical Difference*, 2nd edn, Princeton and Oxford: Princeton University Press, 2008, and Carola Dietze, 'Toward a History on Equal Terms: A Discussion of *Provincializing Europe*', in *History and Theory* 47 (2008), no. 1, pp. 69–84, where I proposed a deconstruction of the concept of modernity, instead of history.

17. Oxford Dictionaries, www.oxforddictionaries.com/definition/english/eschatology and Merriam-Webster, www.merriam-webster.com/dictionary/eschatology (both accessed 22 August 2014).

18. Hans Wißmann, 'Eschatologie I. Religionsgeschichtlich', in Horst Robert Balz et al., eds, *Theologische Realenzyklopädie* 10, Berlin and New York: Walter de Gruyter, 1982, pp. 254–363, here p. 254.

19. On the history of the Bible see Bernhard Lang, *Die Bibel. Eine kritische Einführung*, Paderborn: Ferdinand Schöningh, 1990. On the prophets as 'religious politicians', see ch. 7 b and esp. Nicholas T. Wright, *Christian Origins and the Question of God*, Minneapolis: Fortress Press, 1992.

20. Authorized (King James) Version [in the following: AV], Daniel 2.31–45. The Book of Daniel is a prophecy written partly after the fact. See Hans Conzelmann and Andreas Lindemann, *Arbeitsbuch zum Neuen Testament*, 13., rev. edn, Tübingen: Mohr Siebeck, 2000, esp. § 5.4.

21. For an introduction to the exegeses of Paul's letters and the Apocalypse see Conzelmann and Lindemann, *Arbeitsbuch*, § 5.2 and 30 and § 5.4 and 40.

22. See Conzelmann and Lindemann, *Arbeitsbuch*, pp. 394–7.

23. Eusebius Hieronymus, 'Commentaria in Danielem Prophetam', in Jacques-Paul Migne, ed., *Patrologiae Cursus Completus, Series Latina* (in the following: PL), vol. 25: *Opera Omnia*, vol. 5, Paris 1884, bk I, ch. 2, col. 503f. Hieronymus was not the first to name these empires, but was the most influential.

24. Aurelius Augustinus, *The City of God Against the Pagans in seven volumes*, vol. 4, books XII–XV with an English translation by Philip Levine, London and Cambridge, Mass.:

William Heinemann and Harvard University Press, 1966, e.g. bk XVI 43, p. 202. For the respective divisions in Roman historiography see Emiel Eyben, 'Die Einteilung des menschlichen Lebens im römischen Altertum', in *Rheinisches Museum fur Philologie* 116 (1973), pp. 185–90. For a comprehensive interpretation of Augustine's views on history see Christoph Horn, 'Geschichtsdarstellung, Geschichtsphilosophie und Geschichtsbewußtsein (Buch XII 10–XVIII)', in id., ed., *Augustinus. De civitate dei*, Berlin: Akademie Verlag, 1997, pp. 171–93, who cautions against reading Augustine's historiography as too linear a philosophy of history. Augustine is also the point of reference for Catholic anti-chiliasm, which tries to go against the idea that the end of history can be expected any time soon. The discussion of this current of thought and its impact on concepts about history and teleology merits a different article, however.

25. Gregorii episcopi Turonensis. *Libri Historiarum X,* eds Bruno Krusch and Wilhelm Levison, Monumenta Germaniae Historica, Scriptorum Rerum Merovingicarum, vol. I, part 1, 2nd edn, Hannover: Impensis Bibliopolii Hahniani, 1951; Beda Venerabilis, *Bedae Opera de Temporibus*, ed. C. W. Jones, Cambridge, Mass.: The Mediaeval Academy of America, 1943, and Jacques Bénigne Bossuet, *Discours sur l'histoire universelle. Édition conforme à celle de 1700*, Paris: Firmin Didot Frères, 1842. On teleological concepts in Bede's works see Peter Darby, *Bede and the End of Time*, Burlington: Ashgate, 2012; on Gregory see Martin Heinzelmann, *Gregor von Tours (538–594), 'Zehn Bücher Geschichte': Historiographie und Gesellschaftskonzept im 6. Jahrhundert*, Darmstadt: Wissenschaftliche Buchgesellschaft, 1994, and for Bossuet see Ulrich Muhlack, *Geschichtswissenschaft im Humanismus und in der Aufklärung: Die Vorgeschichte des Historismus*, Munich: Beck, 1991, chs 2–3.

26. Christoph Cellarius, *Historia universalis: Breviter ac Perspicue Exposita, in Antiquam, et Medii Aevi ac Novam Divisa, cvm Notis Perpetuis,* 8th edn, Jena: Bielckius, 1730. The first part *Historia antiqua* was first published in 1685, the second part *Historia Medii Aevi* in 1702, and the third part *Historia Nova* on the sixteenth and seventeenth centuries in 1702. In that same year the first edition containing all three books also appeared.

27. Biblia Sacra Vulgata and AV, Dan. 2.21.

28. See Heinz Thomas, 'Translatio Imperii', in *Lexikon des Mittelalters* 8, col. 944–6, and Werner Goez, *Translatio Imperii: Ein Beitrag zur Geschichte des Geschichtsdenkens und der politischen Theorien im Mittelalter und in der frühen Neuzeit*, Tübingen: Mohr, 1958, chs 4 and 5.

29. See Thomas, 'Translatio Imperii', col. 945f. and Goez, *Translatio*, chs 7–9 and 11.

30. See Goez, *Translatio*, chs 10, 16 and 17, who focuses on the Empire and France (and also stresses the role of the reformation and Lutheran historians like Cellarius for the weakening of the concept); for Bulgaria and Russia see Edgar Hösch, 'Die Idee der Translatio Imperii im Moskauer Russland', in *Europäische Geschichte Online (EGO)*, Institut für Europäische Geschichte (IEG), Mainz, 12 March 2010. URL: http://www.ieg-ego.eu/hoesche-2010-de URN: urn: nbn:de:0159–2010102586 (accessed 15 November 2014).

31. Georg G. Iggers, *The German Conception of History: The National Tradition of Historical Thought from Herder to the Present*, Middletown, Conn.: Wesleyan University Press, 1968, p. 30.

32. Johann Gottfried von Herder, 'Auch eine Philosophie der Geschichte zur Bildung der Menschheit. Beitrag zu vielen Beiträgen des Jahrhunderts [1774]', in id., *Werke in zehn Bänden,* eds Günter Arnold et al., vol. 4: *Schriften zu Philosophie, Literatur, Kunst und Altertum 1774–1787,* eds Jürgen Brummack and Martin Bollacher, Frankfurt am Main.: Deutscher Klassiker-Verlag, 1994, pp. 9–107.

33. Löwith, *Meaning*; Georg Wilhelm Friedrich Hegel, *Werke*, eds Eva Moldenhauer, Karl Markus Michel, vol. 12: *Vorlesungen über die Philosophie der Geschichte* (1837/40), 4th edn, Frankfurt am Main.: Suhrkamp, 1995; Karl Marx, *Das Kapital, Marx-Engels-Werke (MEW)*, vols 23–5,

Berlin: Dietz, 1973. Löwith's argument has been attacked from different sides. For a concise summary of the discussion see Matthias Schloßberger, *Geschichtsphilosophie*, Berlin: Akademie Verlag, 2013, chs 8.2 and 14.2, who also comes to the conclusion that Löwith's basic idea still holds true (p. 229).

34. See Hugh Gough, *The Terror in the French Revolution*, 2nd edn, Basingstoke: Palgrave Macmillan, 2010, esp. ch. 6 iv.

35. Arthur Moeller van den Bruck, *Germany's Third Empire* [1923], authorized English edn (condensed) by Emily O. Lorimer [1934], New York: Howard Fertig, 1971, esp. ch. 8: 'The Third Empire: We must have the strength to live in antithesis.'

36. See the article 'Drittes Reich' in Cornelia Schmitz-Berning, *Vokabular des Nationalsozialismus*, Berlin and New York: Walter de Gruyter, 1998, pp. 156–60.

37. Since around the year 2000, several studies have expressly set out to include revolutions outside Europe into a global narrative of modernity. See e.g. the works of Shmuel N. Eisenstadt, *Fundamentalism, Sectarianism, and Revolution: The Jacobin Dimension of Modernity*, Cambridge and New York: Cambridge University Press, 1999 and id., *The Great Revolutions and the Civilizations of Modernity*, Leiden and Boston: Brill, 2006 as well as Jürgen Osterhammel, *Die Verwandlung der Welt: Eine Geschichte des 19. Jahrhunderts*, Munich: Beck, 2009.

38. See Johannes Calvinus, 'Praelectionum in Danielem Prophetam', in *Corpus Reformatorum*, vols 68 and 69: *Calvini Opera* [1889], vols. 40 and 41, New York, London: Johnson Reprint and Frankfurt am Main: Minerva, 1964, pp. 516–722 and 1–303. My interpretation follows Goez, *Translatio*, ch. 19, esp. pp. 371–7.

39. John Winthrop, 'A Model of Christian Charity', in *Winthrop Papers*, vol. 2, ed. Stewart Mitchell, New York: Russell & Russell, 1968, pp. 282–95, here p. 295 and Edmund P. Morgan, *The Puritan Dilemma: The Story of John Winthrop*, 3rd edn, New York: Pearson Longman, 1999, pp. 61 and 41. The parable of a 'city that is set on an hill' is part of Jesus's Sermon on the Mount (AV Matt. 5.14). The Puritan John Winthrop used this parable in 1630 in his sermon 'A Model of Christian Charity' on the ship *Arbella*. See for this and the following paragraphs on Puritan beliefs Morgan, *The Puritan Dilemma*, ch. 6; Hochgeschwender, *Amerikanische Religion*, ch. 2, and Perry Miller, *The New England Mind: The Seventeenth Century*, New York: Macmillan, 1939, Part 4.

40. As the excommunication of Anne Hutchinson following the Antinomian Controversy of 1636–8 indicates, the question of whether God recognizes and rewards good deeds was controversial among Puritans, however.

41. See Hochgeschwender, *Amerikanische Religion*, chs 3 and 4, esp. pp. 96–9. For the sceptical self-evaluation of the Puritan experiment, see p. 32.

42. See Hochgeschwender, *Amerikanische Religion*, ch. 4, esp. pp. 100–3, and Daniel Walker Howe, *What Hath God Wrought: The Transformation of America, 1815–1848*, New York: Oxford University Press, 2007, ch. 5. On the abolitionist movement see esp. James Brewer Stewart, *Holy Warriors: The Abolitionists and American Slavery*, rev. edn, New York: Hill and Wang, 1996, chs 1 and 3.

43. 'Declaration of Sentiments', in Wendell Phillips Garrison and Francis Jackson Garrison, *William Lloyd Garrison, 1805–1879: The Story of His Life*, 4 vols., New York: Century, 1885, vol. 1, pp. 408–12, here p. 412. On Garrison see Henry Mayer, *All on Fire: William Lloyd Garrison and the Abolition of Slavery*, New York: St. Martin's Press, 1998.

44. Garrison and Garrison, *William Lloyd Garrison*, here p. 408.

45. Garrison and Garrison, *William Lloyd Garrison*, here pp. 410, 409, 411 and 412.

46. Franklin B. Sanborn, *The Life and Letters of John Brown, Liberator of Kansas, and Martyr of Virginia*, Boston, Mass.: Roberts Brothers, 1885, p. 122.
47. William A. Phillips, 'Three Interviews with Old John Brown', in *John Brown, The Making of a Revolutionary: The Story of John Brown in his own Words and in the Words of those who knew him*, intr. and comm. by Louis Ruchames, New York: Grosset & Dunlap, 1969, pp. 216–26, here p. 220.
48. Garrison and Garrison, *William Lloyd Garrison*, p. 409.
49. See Stewart, *Holy Warriors*, pp. 70f. and 83–5 and esp. Leonard L. Richards, *'Gentlemen of Property and Standing': Anti-Abolition Mobs in Jacksonian America*, New York: Oxford University Press, 1970.
50. See Gerald McFarland, *A Scattered People: An American Family Moves West*, New York: Pantheon, 1985, pp. 3–17, 43–7 and 68–77; Oates, *To Purge This Land*, chs 1–3; McGlone, *John Brown's War*, chs 2.II–3.IV and generally DeCaro, *'Fire From the Midst'*. On the Western Reserve and the abolitionist activities of its inhabitants see also Howe, *What Hath God Wrought*, ch. 4. III.
51. See esp. Oates, *To Purge This Land*, pp. 15, 19, 30–3, 41–50, 53, 58 and Quarles, *Allies for Freedom*, pp. 16–19.
52. See e.g. McGlone, *John Brown's War*, ch. 3.III and DeCaro, *'Fire From the Midst'*, p. 111f.
53. See e.g. DeCaro, *'Fire From the Midst'*, e.g. pp. 139–45, 189, 239f. and 266.
54. See Oates, *To Purge This Land*, chs 9–17; McGlone, *John Brown's War*, ch. 4–6 and 9 as well as McPherson, *Battle Cry of Freedom*, p. 152f.
55. See esp. Frederick Douglass, 'Life and Times of Frederick Douglass', in id., *Autobiographies*, New York: Library of America, 1994, pp. 453–1045, p. 717f. and 759f. as the best source for Brown's plan.
56. See Oates, *To Purge This Land*, chs 16–17; DeCaro, *'Fire From the Midst'*, ch. 19f. and McGlone, *John Brown's War*, ch. 6.IV.
57. See the reconstruction and discussion of Brown's strategy in Oates, *To Purge This Land*, ch. 16; Jeffery P. Rossbach, *Ambivalent Conspirators: John Brown, the Secret Six, and a Theory of Slave Violence*, Philadelphia, PA: University of Pennsylvania Press, 1982, pp. 194 and 268f.; McGlone, *John Brown's War*, pt IV and my *Taten statt Worte*, ch. 2.3f.
58. See Oates, *To Purge This Land*, chs 20–22; DeCaro, *'Fire From the Midst'*, ch. 21; McGlone, *John Brown's War*, chs 10 and 13 and my *Taten statt Worte*, chs 2.4–2.7.
59. See e.g. his 'Speech at Elwood, Kansas, December 1 [November 30?], 1859', in id,, *Collected Works*, vol. 3, eds Roy P. Basler et al., New Brunswick, NJ: Rutgers University Press, 1953, p. 495f.
60. Abraham Lincoln, 'Second Inaugural Address', in id., *Collected Works*, eds Roy P. Basler et al., vol. 8, p. 332f., here p. 333.
61. Margaret Malamud, 'Translatio Imperii: America as the New Rome c. 1900', in Mark Bradley, eds., *Classics and Imperialism in the British Empire*, Oxford: Oxford University Press, 2010, pp. 249–83.

CHAPTER 13
'BUT WAS I REALLY PRIMED?': GERSHOM SCHOLEM'S ZIONIST PROJECT

Gabriel Piterberg

1. The argument

Gershom Scholem's (1897–1982)[1] oeuvre is voluminous, as is the literature on his life, work and politics. I make two specific and related arguments. One is that Scholem's philological-historical study of Jewish mysticism and messianism is, in fact, a Zionist theology in the Carl Schmitt sense of political theology. The other is that this Zionist theology can be helpfully interpreted under Quentin Skinner's notion of 'mythology of prolepsis'. What relates these two arguments to one another is the figure of the heretic hero. The Sabbatian and subsequently Frankist thinkers were not just the pivot of Scholem's scholarship, historical protagonists of whom he was deeply fond. In their vitae and in their viscerally indefatigable search for antinomian sources of vitality, with which to infuse Judaism, like ancient myths and return to origins, Scholem deemed them a synecdoche of the nation's *Geist* and historical destiny. Scholem, I propose, transferred this synecdoche onto himself. His rebellion against bourgeois *Deutschjudentum* – lifestyle and knowledge alike – was antinomian, as was his 'conversion' to Zionism and immigration to Palestine and the fields of study he created. In short, Scholem was a self-fashioned *heretikon*.

This categorical assertion, however, must be tempered simply because Scholem was such an intellectual giant and his personality was so complex and doubt-ridden, that one is compelled to qualify sweeping observations. Expressions of that complexity abound. Firstly, Scholem's immanent and dialectical narrative of Jewish history led to Zionism; but from the outset he doubted whether Zionism would fulfil his own expectation. Secondly, the scholarly Scholem, the Scholem of pronouncements on current affairs (both political and cultural), and the poetic (German) Scholem were not the same persona. Thirdly, Scholem, like the *heretikons* he admired, was hostile to both rabbinical Judaism and rational philosophy (he consistently called Saadia Ga'on and Maimonides to task, for instance). And yet his method and epistemology were philological-historical and, crucially, he was not a believer; he simultaneously never strayed from this method nor ceased doubting its appropriateness for the mission at hand. Many a commentator have dubbed Scholem 'a *religious* anarchist'. The adjective is utterly wrong; he was, at best, an anarchist – antinomian would have been more precise – historian of the Jewish religion. Finally, Scholem remained an Israeli patriot, averse to exile and *Deutschjudentum* (before or after the Shoah); yet, like his nemesis, Hannah Arendt, the lieu in which he felt most at home was *deutsche Kultur*.

The argument draws on my paradigmatic observation that Zionism, and subsequently the state of Israel, should be understood within the framework of comparative settler colonialism. I demonstrate this elsewhere.[2] Like other settler colonial cases, Zionism has developed from two sources: the central and east European currents of its birth, and the Middle East and Palestinian realities of its actualization. In my interpretation of Scholem I am concerned with his European – specifically Romantic German – formation, and fleetingly touch upon the settler colonial actualization, which nonetheless always looms large in the background. The neatness of the distinction between European origins and settler colonial actualization is purely analytical. The fundamental settler-national feature that inheres in Scholem's politics and scholarship is the compartmentalization of an immanently Jewish, and subsequently Zionist–Israeli, history on the one hand, and the rest of humanity's on the other. A member of the bi-nationalist Brit Shalom in the pre-state period and horrified by the post-1967 messianic explosion, Scholem was a liberal Zionist. This, however, never made him consider the Palestinian presence an intrinsic part of how his nation had been formed and what it was; in a typically liberal Zionist fashion, it always remained an extrinsic Arab problem. Analogously, Jewish history was immanently impervious to contexts. Thus, in his magisterial study of Sabbatai Zevi, the Ottoman Islamic context is barely mentioned and certainly has no explanatory force: like the Palestinians politically, the Ottoman context was understood as extrinsic – and hence immaterial – to the impermeable history of the nation. Several Ottoman historians have since shown how crucial that context was for Sabbatianism's history.[3]

Before delving into Scholem's work it is essential to chart the pertinent context in two steps. First Zionism's foundational principle is briefly presented. Then it is necessary to dwell on the not unproblematic label of 'Israeli secularity', or to explain precisely in what sense Zionist Israeli secularity is secular. This explanation is crucial for understanding not only Scholem's scholarship but also, inseparably, his politics as someone ordinarily (and correctly) identified with the Zionist Israeli liberal left.

2. Zionism

Zionism as a worldview and praxis is underlain by a foundational principle, or myth, that has three manifestations: the negation of exile, the return to the land of Israel, and the return to history. These manifestations are inextricably intertwined in the master-narrative of Zionism, the story that explains 'how we got to where we are and where we should go henceforth'. The negation of exile establishes continuity between an ancient past, in which there existed Jewish sovereignty over the land of Israel, and a present that renews it in the resettlement of Palestine. Between the two lies no more than a kind of interminable interim. Depreciation of the period of exile is shared by all Zionists, if with differing degrees of rigidity, and derives from what is, in their outlook, an incontestable presupposition: from time immemorial, the Jews constituted a territorial nation. It follows that a non-territorial existence must be abnormal, incomplete and inauthentic.

In and of itself, as a historical experience, exile is devoid of significance. Although it may have given rise to cultural achievements of moment, exile could not by definition have been a wholesome realization of the nation's *Geist*. So long as they were condemned to it, Jews – whether as individuals or communities – could lead at best a partial and transitory existence, waiting for the redemption of 'ascent' (-*aliyah*) once again to the land of Israel, the only site on which the nation's destiny could be fulfilled. Within this mythical framework, exilic Jews always lived provisionally, as potential or proto-Zionists, longing 'to return' to the land of Israel.

Here the second expression of the foundational myth complements the first. In Zionist terminology, the recovery by the people of its home promised to deliver the *normalization* of Jewish existence; and the site designated for the re-enactment of Exodus would be the territory of the biblical story, as elaborated in the Protestant culture of the eighteenth and nineteenth centuries. Zionist ideology defined this land as *empty*. This did not mean that Zionist leaders and settlers were ignorant of the presence of Arabs in Palestine, or mulishly ignored them. Israel was 'empty' in a deeper sense. For the land, too, was condemned to an exile as long as there was no Jewish sovereignty over it: it lacked any meaningful or authentic history, awaiting redemption with the return of the Jews. The best-known Zionist slogan, 'a land without a people to a people without a land', expressed a twofold denial: of the historical experience both of the Jews in exile, and of Palestine without Jewish sovereignty. Of course, since the land was not literally empty, its recovery required the establishment of a settler colonial hierarchy – sanctioned by biblical authority – of its historic custodians over such intruders as might remain after the return. Jewish settlers were to be accorded exclusive privileges deriving from the Old Testament, and Palestinian Arabs treated as part of the natural environment. The Zionist settlers were collective subjects who acted, and the native Palestinians became objects who were acted upon.

The third way in which the foundational myth is articulated, the 'return to history', reveals, more than any other, the extent to which Zionist ideology was underpinned by the emergence of Romantic nationalism and German historicism in nineteenth-century Europe. Its premise is that the natural and irreducible form of human collectivity is the nation. From the dawn of history peoples have been grouped into such units, and though they might at one time or another be undermined by internal divisions or oppressed by external forces, they are eventually bound to find political self-expression in the shape of sovereign nation-states. The nation is the autonomous historical subject par excellence, and the state is the *telos* of its march towards self-fulfilment. According to this logic, so long as they were exiles, the Jews remained a community outside history, within which all European nations dwelt. Only nations that occupy the soil of their homeland, and establish political sovereignty over it, are capable of shaping their own destiny and so of entering history by this logic. The return of the Jewish nation to the land of Israel, overcoming its docile passivity in exile, could alone allow it to rejoin the history of civilized peoples.

How to place the historiographical project of the Hebrew University's founding scholars, among whom Scholem was pivotal, within the context of the tripartite Zionist myth?[4] In the 1990s a debate took place over the term 'the Jerusalem School' of Jewish history. It revolved around the question of whether or not there was (is) a uniformly authoritative doctrine that radiated from the Institute of Jewish Studies at the Hebrew University. One of the crucial questions was whether the Jerusalem scholars created an alternative to the historical consciousness embodied in the negation of exile, given that the long period of exile was their temporal interest, or whether their project buttressed a negation-of-exile narrative. The debate is of course meaningful in itself, but for the present discussion I am less interested in the extent to which the first generation of the Jerusalem scholars (Scholem among them), and their numerous disciples, form a coherent and uniform school, or whether their diversity of approach and subject matter militates against such a categorization.[5]

The pertinent dimension for us is how that historical project relates to the foundational myth. For scholars whose vantage point is intrinsically Zionist, even those who manage a critical distance, the Jerusalem scholars' oeuvre constitutes *an alternative* to the negation of exile. In their understanding the negation of exile is synonymous with the crude – and dominant – version of it. In other words, they deem as the negation of exile only the attempts to ignore, sidestep or consign to oblivion the period of exile, and to create in its place a territorial master-narrative that proceeds from late antiquity straight to Zionism. From this perspective the Jerusalem scholars not only rejected the negation of exile but even offered an alternative; for not only did they not ignore or sidestep the period of exile, but so much of what they did was invested in that period and they did so much to illuminate it. All those within the Zionist orbit share this understanding of the negation of exile.

The scholars who are extrinsic to Zionism consider the very same corpus the most ambitious attempt to lend scientific credence to the tripartite myth of the negation of exile/return to the land of Israel/return to history in the shape of a coherently organic historical narrative.[6] Amnon Raz-Krakotzkin, a Benjamin-inspired critic of Zionism, concurs that the Jerusalem scholars' pre-modern historiography yielded an explicit divergence from the crude (and dominant) Zionist position on the negation of exile. He does not stop there, however:

> But precisely the critique contained in the historiography of 'the Middle Ages' contributed to the perfection of Zionist ideology: contrary to the radical position that utterly neglected exilic Jewish history and described it as worthless, the [Jerusalem] historians asserted that 'the Middle ages' too express Jewish nationalism, and that there is an organic unity and continuity among all expressions of the Jewish past, irrespective of time or cultural context. The purpose [of the Jerusalem school] was to underline the continuity of a consciousness of Jewish sovereignty, and thereby to ignore the perspective of Jews from various generations when they alluded to exile.[7]

What the Jerusalem scholars did, by integrating exile into a territorial narrative, was to give Zionism the most systematic consolidation for the negation of exile myth, and also for the account that leads back in time, in a teleological fashion, to the land of Israel. A scholarly narrative was crystallizing around these formerly redundant exilic centuries in the Hebrew University. Despite significant elements of diversity and even acrimony, the research and teaching of the Jerusalem scholars was underlain by a shared commitment to Zionism. And it must be recognized that overwriting the experiences of Jews in exile by retrospectively 'territorializing' these experiences and fitting them into an organic nationalist narrative is a deeper and ideologically more coherent and consistent articulation of the negation of exile than the narrative that leaps from Joshua and King David straight to David Ben-Gurion, and consigns to oblivion whatever happened in between. It is also vitally significant that from the extrinsic perspective, the presence of the Palestinians, even if they are not – or precisely because they are not – mentioned, is inextricable from the Zionist myth; for the intrinsic scholars, especially those whose position on the conflict is very dovish (including Scholem), the debate on Zionism and Jewish history is an exclusively Jewish affair, from which the Palestinians are barred.[8]

3. 'There is no God but He promised us the Land'[9]: the problem of Zionist Israeli secularity

The religious/secular division in Israel, which purportedly threatens to tear the nation apart, is conventionally misconstrued. Secularity in Israel has been inherited from secular Zionism. It is secular in the sense that it rejects in antinomian fashion rabbinical Judaism as part of the negation of exile. It is not secular in the sense that this antinomian negation of exilic Judaism is accompanied by a concomitant return to the Old Testament in a morphologically settler-Protestant way.[10] Moreover, slightly to stray from the main thrust of this essay, the religious/secular chasm, which does exist, is not a portentous sign of the nation's fragmentation; on the contrary, in a typical settler fashion, it buttresses the nation's integrity by further ossifying the settler/indigene fault-line. It forms yet another device to exclude the Palestinian citizens of the state from that nation. The labels of 'religious' and 'secular' are the preserve of Jews only. The Palestinian citizens of the very same state are neither religious nor secular within this logic; they are 'just' Arabs in the same sense that 'their' political parties are neither left nor right nor centre, but 'just' Arab parties.

In an essay tellingly entitled 'The Golem of Scholem',[11] Raz-Krakotzkin, whose view on the negation of exile was discussed earlier, addresses precisely that problem. Drawing on – but begging to differ from – his teacher Amos Funkenstein,[12] he thought-provokingly compares the *Weltanschauungs* of two seemingly unrelated – and conventionally incompatible – thinkers: Scholem and Rabbi Avraham Yizhak HaCohen Kook (1865–1935). At a young age Rabbi Kook attended the Volozhin Yeshiva, 'mother of Lithuanian yeshivas', and was identified as a prodigy. In 1904 he immigrated to Palestine, and in 1923 became the first Chief Ashkenazi Rabbi of Mandatory Palestine. Rabbi Kook was a remarkable combination of strict Halakhic authority, on the one hand, and messianic Kabbalism on the other. Four decades or so after his death, via his son Zvi-Yehudah among others, Rabbi Kook's writings became a foundational source for

Gush Emunim, the extreme right-wing movement of settlers in the Occupied Territories after 1967.

Raz-Krakotzkin is well aware of the significant differences between Rabbi Kook and Scholem and in no way suggests that they be dismissed offhandedly. What he does discern in their oeuvre is elective affinity. He insists that

> [I]n spite of the differences, the similarities between their attitudes are fundamental, and illuminate crucial aspects of Zionist consciousness. Reading them together presents us with the possibility of analyzing the interrelations between them, and of revealing the theological-messianic dimension of Zionist historical myth. It clarifies that the common distinction between 'religious' and 'secular' identities in Israel is not satisfactory, and ignores the political-theological dimension of what is considered 'secular' Zionism.[13]

Scholem and Rabbi Kook used different languages. Scholem's language was German historicism and philology, while Rabbi Kook's emanated from what was understood as the post-sixteenth-century 'Messianized' Kabbalah (i.e. the Lurianic Kabbalah developed in Safed), the subject matter of Scholem's scholarship. Nonetheless, 'They both combined German Idealism and Kabbalah, and Schelling's attitudes were a source of inspiration to both of them. Indeed, they emphasize the dialectical integration of these two cultural frameworks in Zionism.'[14]

Out of this language a common – though not identical – historical vision was conceived. It was based on the deep-seated belief that messianic mysticism imbued an ossified rabbinical Judaism with energy and vitality. It set in motion a process – simultaneously dialectical and organically immanent – whose destination was political-national redemption in the shape of sovereignty over the Promised Land. The Zionist project was the fulfilment of this project, Scholem's doubts and eventual despair notwithstanding. As Raz-Krakotzkin perceptively observes, 'They both adjusted the Jewish historical consciousness, based on the concepts of "exile" and "redemption", to the modern historical model, and described Jewish history as a Hegelian dialectical process which leads to its fulfilment in the present'.[15]

In sharing an evolutional – though dialectic rather than linear – approach to the process of messianic redemption, Scholem and Rabbi Kook concomitantly rejected apocalyptic messianism. They both regarded, in a rather similar manner, the Lurianic Kabbalah as a turning point in Jewish thought and history, in that it was a delayed response to the expulsion from Spain that released redemptive energies and rocked the foundations of the exilic world of rabbinical Judaism; at the same time both of them extolled Zionism for curbing, indeed cleansing, the apocalyptic and nihilist attributes of Sabbatianism and Frankism (the social expressions of the Lurianic Kabbalah) and 'distinguished national revival from other attributes of the messianic imagination. This distinction was crucial for the regard of Kabbalah as a national-historical myth'.[16]

What of the fact that a right-wing messianic ideology is unquestionably the dominant interpretation of Zionism in today's (2013) Israel? One may, as some of Rabbi Kook's admirers do, object that this interpretation falsifies his writings. But that this interpretation has carried the day is certain. Moreover, I concur with Raz-Krakotzkin that 'In his [Rabbi Kook's] terms, [Gush Emunim] manifests the integration of the Torah, the Land and the People into a mystic national community. This is certainly a possible reading of his writings.'[17]

And what of Scholem? After 1967 he was alarmed and became increasingly anxious about the messianic currents, whose *Sturm und Drang* Scholem was equipped to intuit better than most. Significantly his warnings against rising messianism were addressed to Zionism's representation of Jewish history, not to religion. 'In order to follow him and take this warning seriously,' Raz-Krakotzkin avers,

> it is important to understand that Scholem himself had a constitutive role in the construction and invention of the perception which made these radical interpretations possible. His intentions were certainly different, but his warnings were directed towards the attitude he himself developed and formulated. Although the right-wing settlers obviously rely on the writings of Rabbi Kook, it should be remembered that Scholem was one of those to develop that attitude, and that indeed it was embodied within the Zionist secular myth.[18]

It is perhaps not a coincidence that two of Scholem's outstanding students, Shlomo Bar-Yosef and Rivka Schatz-Uffenheimer, not only had successful careers in Israeli academia and specialized in the field of study their teacher had created, but also embraced Gush Emunim's messianic ideology and became settlers in the Occupied Territories. This does not mean that Scholem agreed with them politically. It is a clue, however, to why his post-1967 anxiety was so severe; and his disciples' path was certainly a possible emanation from his scholarly project.

4. Zionist theology

Scholem's dedication of his life to Jewish mysticism had a more deep-seated drive. In a retrospective reflection on his life's work less than a decade before his death Scholem confirmed the Romantic antinomian suspicion he shared with his Jerusalem colleagues of the adequacy of the cerebral, normative facets of Judaism as sources of energy and vitality for its survival in the past and, crucially, for its continued survival in the present. This Romantic suspicion invariably led to a search for a source of vitality that emanated from the realm of the irrational, the mythical and the non-legal:

> I was interested in the question: Does *Halakhic* Judaism have enough potency to survive? Is *Halakhah* really possible without a mystical foundation? Does it have enough vitality of its own to survive for two thousand years without degenerating? I appreciated *Halakhah* without identifying with its imperatives . . . This question was tied up with my dreams about the Kabbalah, through the notion that it might

be the Kabbalah that explains the survival of the consolidated force of *Halakhic* Judaism.[19]

This leads to the possible relationship between Scholem's project and Carl Schmitt's *Political Theology* of 1922. Schmitt has become more widely read in recent years, and has stimulated writers who do not necessarily share his, to borrow Perry Anderson's phrase, 'Intransigent Right' politics.[20] The exchange on the relevance of Schmitt's thought to the left in *New Left Review* is a very recent example.[21] However, it is little known that Schmitt informed numerous German Jewish intellectuals in the 1920s and 1930s, many of whom similarly did not share his political position. It is nevertheless recognized that Walter Benjamin was inspired by Schmitt, in particular when writing his essay on the German plays of mourning and in his 'Theses on the Concept of History'.[22] Scholem was well aware of Benjamin's fascination with Schmitt and may have become interested in his *Political Theology* through his friend.

While studying at the Hebrew University in the early 1990s Christoph Schmidt (no relation to Carl Schmitt), a scholar of modern German studies, developed an original argument on the possible connection between Scholem's scholarly project and Carl Schmitt:

> Although Leo Strauss and Walter Benjamin reacted directly to [Carl] Schmitt's provocation, the conjunction of Carl Schmitt and Gershom Scholem must appear strange at first sight. However, in the context of the epistemology of culture of those years – namely, the rediscovery of the heretic as a cultural hero who represents the critique of enlightened liberal culture – Scholem's reinvention of the Kabbalistic tradition can be interpreted as a specific strategy of political theology. Schmitt's decisionist political theology calls for the suspension of the Weimar constitution, in order to protect the state against its enemies; Scholem's Sabbatean hero Jacob Frank is the theological decisionist who calls for the suspension of Halakhic law in order to protect the Jewish people from their enemies. Schmitt turns to an authoritarian politics that legitimizes fascist dictatorship; Scholem's rediscovery of the heretic hero appears to be the condition for escaping from Schmitt's politics.[23]

I draw on Christoph Schmidt's argument in proposing that Scholem's oeuvre was nothing less than a Zionist theology. Christoph Schmidt does not elaborate on the crucial point that what made this a political theology was the fact that Scholem's narrative of Jewish history from the sixteenth century onward leads in a dialectical manner to Zionism. My proposition develops this point and explains why the dialectical march of Scholem's project to Zionism is precisely what makes it a political theology in the Carl Schmittean sense.

Let me now briefly present for the non-specialist the main subject matter of Scholem's work, as well as the schema of his dialectical narrative that inexorably leads to Zionism. In the 1650s Sabbatai Zevi, the son of a commercial agent from Izmir, an

Ottoman port-city in south-western Anatolia, and a group of his followers were busily trying to prepare Jewish communities in the eastern Mediterranean for the imminent arrival of the messianic era. In 1665, endorsed by his movement's chief ideologue, Nathan of Gaza, Sabbatai Zevi proclaimed himself Messiah. In 1666 he was arrested by the Ottoman authorities and persuaded by them to convert to Islam. However short-lived, Sabbatai Zevi's proselytizing and the movement bearing his name – Sabbatianism – spread far beyond the Ottoman eastern Mediterranean and sent shock waves throughout the Jewish world. The doctrine that was conceived in the wake of his conversion to Islam, which explained the horrifying paradox of an apostate Messiah, was in a way more important than his crowning as Messiah in the first place. Sabbatianism was succeeded by two sects in the following centuries: the Frankists in Central and Eastern Europe, and the Dönme in what is today Greece and Turkey.

What role does Sabbatianism play in Scholem's Hegelian narrative? In that narrative the transformative and de-stabilizing starting point was the expulsion of Jews from Spain in 1492. That trauma engendered the antinomian radicalization of Kabbalah, the major form of Jewish mysticism. As such Kabbalah is not inherently messianic. According to Scholem, however, the teachings of Rabbi Isaac Luria in the city of Safed in northern Palestine in the sixteenth century 'messianized' the Kabbalah as a delayed response to the expulsion's trauma. Amos Funkenstein offered an elegant double metaphor, anatomy and biography, to capture what Scholem had deemed the transformation of medieval Kabbalah by Rabbi Luria and his disciples in Safed:

> In the Lurianic myth of the contraction, self-alienation, restoration and redemption of the Godhead itself, Scholem believed he had found what constituted the most original and powerful response by the Jews, albeit belated, to the series of traumatic events prior to, during and after their expulsion from Spain (1492). The situation of the exile of the Jewish people, its alienation from its homeland, became here a symbol of the path and unfolding of the Godhead itself, as well as the final station on the cosmic itinerary . . . With the redemption of Israel, it too will be redeemed, returning to its purified original being. If medieval Kabbalah was to a certain extent an *anatomy* of God – a speculative attempt to determine and influence the interplay and counterpoint of divine forces – Lurianic Kabbalah was a *biography* of God, recounting a catastrophe in the life of the Godhead and the slow, almost automatic overcoming of that catastrophe. In this metahistorical myth, the post-exilic generation found consolation – and fuel for their eschatological hopes.[24]

The Lurianic Kabbalah saturated Sabbatianism with a brewing messianic energy, which exploded as a mass movement and continued in Frankism. This phase, the thesis in the narrative, was followed from the 1750s in Eastern Europe by its anti-thesis, namely Hasidism. Hasidism, Scholem averred, tried to heal the cul-de-sac of, especially, nihilist Frankism, by offering a cautious and a-political personal redemption, which was mystical and antinomian but not apocalyptically messianic. After the appearance of secular, enlightened Judaism in the shape of the Haskalah (the so-called Jewish Enlightenment) came the narrative's dialectical climax, the synthesis, namely Zionism. In Scholem's Hegelian dialectic, then, the messianic and nihilistic movements were the thesis, Hasidism's cautious and a-political redemption was the anti-thesis, and Zionism is the synthesis. Zionism, in Scholem's dialectical narrative, is a mass movement whose redemptive drive expresses itself in responsible political action, in a return to history and extrication from exile, but without the tendencies of the messianic and nihilistic explosions of the seventeenth and eighteenth centuries, which dangerously threatened to destroy the nation through unbelief and apostasy.

5. Scholem's Jewish history as 'mythology of prolepsis'

In a seminal essay in which he wrought havoc with the tradition of history of ideas, Quentin Skinner organized his critique along three 'mythologies', which that field of study had in the author's view ended up producing: the mythology of doctrine, the mythology of coherence and the mythology of prolepsis.[25] Skinner's mythology of prolepsis is a particularly apposite lens through which to view Scholem's complex project. An attempt to write a history of ideas may turn into a mythology of prolepsis, Skinner observes, when

> in considering what significance the argument of some classic text might be said to have for us ... no place is left for what the author himself meant to say. The characteristic result of this confusion is a type of discussion which might be labelled the mythology of prolepsis. Such confusions arise most readily, of course, when the historian is more interested – as he may legitimately be – in the retrospective significance of a given historical work or action than in its meaning for the agent himself.[26]

Crucially Skinner later adduces a synoptic comment: 'The surest symptom, in short, of this mythology of prolepsis is that the discussions which it governs are open to the crudest type of criticism that can be levelled against any teleological form of explanation: *the action has to await the future to await its meaning*.'[27]

Formally, Scholem's oeuvre is amenable to being viewed through Skinner's notion because of the historical field within which it belongs. As David Biale correctly observes: 'Scholem's history of Jewish mysticism is itself *Geistesgeschichte*: the history of the theological doctrines and speculations of a small intelligentsia.'[28] Less formally, the mythology of prolepsis is an apt description of Scholem's historiography not because it was a crude teleology, nor because the historian was deaf to the contextual voices of his past heroes. Scholem's scholarly stature was too gigantic for such trivial oversights. The *full* meaning of the Lurianic Kabbalah and its dissemination from Safed, of the messianism and apostasy of Sabbatai Zevi, of Sabbatianism and its later manifestation as Frankism, and of the Haskalah, had to await for Scholem to place himself in the authoritative and authentic position from which to reveal the full magnitude of that meaning: it had to await Scholem's becoming Zionist, his return to history and return to

Zion. That is why Skinner's observation that 'The action has to await the future to await its meaning' is so applicable to Scholem's project.

The most devastating critique of Scholem's project was levelled by Moshe Idel.[29] For the present discussion, one of the chief things Idel questions is the organic bond that Scholem identified from the late sixteenth century onwards between the experience of the mystic and the symbolic system he created, on the one hand, and the nation's history on the other. For Scholem, in other words, the historical experience of the mystic, the figure I earlier called the heretic hero, embodied the historical experience of the entire nation. The importance of this point for understanding Scholem's project is acute. Although Idel seems unaware of this, I think that the bond Scholem identified, and to which Idel objects, is basically Scholem's instinctive projection of the position and experience of the Romantic national historian (i.e. his own) onto the mystic of the early modern era. For Scholem, his own return to Zion and return to history, as well his project of making manifest the vitality that was latent in Judaism's mystic and messianic repository, embodied the nation's history and *Geist*. Similarly, the experience of the mystic and his project of making manifest the explosive force latent in the biblical myth (suppressed by rabbinical legalism and philosophical rationalism), embodied in his time the nation's history and *Geist*. This is, I believe, the full extent of the organic bond with which Idel feels ill at ease.

6. Intimate disclosures

The magnitude of Scholem's self-appointed mission was in congruity with that of his ego: it was, cautiously put, quasi-messianic. The means to achieve it was the philological descent into the abyss (I use the term for a reason that is clarified below) of the messianized Kabbalah. This mission, and the attendant doubts and melancholy, is revealingly expressed in Scholem's German verse, and the diaries and letters of his youth and early adulthood. These have come to light in the past two decades.[30] His private disclosures support my argument that in Scholem's consciousness the fate of his life and intellectual project and that of the nation were entwined, in a manner reminiscent of the early modern messianic Kabbalists he studied; or, more precisely, in the manner in which he would later interpret his protagonists.

Still in Berlin, the teenage Gerhard prepared his diary to be the recipient of his messianic mission:

> In this diary, I want to write down unadorned what I told myself clearly today and what I envisioned; I can't call it anything else ... and since this is intended solely for my own use and for my eyes only, no rude mocker may creep up to me and hear my most secret liberating thought, and I won't have to accuse myself of megalomania.[31]

The magnitude of the revelation subsequently followed. It is striking in both content and register:

[Buber] only wanted to prepare the way for the greater one after him; he sacrificed himself for the other one, his blood-comrade [*Blutsgenosse*], whom he did not know yet. He [Buber] was not the Redeemer . . . But the quiet lad in Berlin felt the seed grow from within, as he read the strange 'hero stories' of Buber and the deeds of the Baalshem in the days of the era. Among his seeking he discovered his fulfilment . . . And the young man went alone through the world and looked around for where the soul of his people waited for him. For he was deeply convinced that the soul of Judah went astray among the nations and waited in the Holy Land for the one who holds himself impudent enough to liberate her from exile and separation from her people. And he knew deep in his heart that he was the Chosen One, the one to seek and to find his people's soul. And the Dreamer – his name already marked him as the Awaited One: Scholem, the perfect one [Hebrew *shalem* – complete, perfect] prepared himself for his task and began to forge the weapons of knowledge.[32]

I agree with commentators on both diaries and poetry that one cannot dismiss expressions such as the one quoted above as youthful flights of fantasy, because he repeated them, if with more self-doubt and melancholy, and because Scholem was no ordinary teenager. Thus Michael Brenner warns that

> one would be ill-advised to dismiss such messianic pretensions as the inconsequential fantasies of a young lad who had come under Buber's influence. After all, it was Scholem who emerged as the major scholar of Jewish messianism in our century, and it was Scholem who wrote the most authoritative biography of the most important pseudo-messiah, Shabbatai Zevi. To know, as we do now, that he thought of himself as the messiah gives us a clue to his later writings, and it might explain his scholarly interests more than any other motive.[33]

Observing Scholem's instant sense of mission, Steven Wasserstrom avers that

> Fortunately for the chronicler, Scholem sprang full-born, as it were, from the head of a Jewish Zeus. He was already rhyming 'Golem' with 'Scholem'[34] (as Borges would do many years later) in verse recorded in his teenage journals. He transposed this megalomaniacal joke into various idioms, as when he told his mother he would attain the seventh level of heaven . . . or that he would master Kabbalah.[35]

Although commentary on Scholem's private verse as a corpus is beyond the scope of this essay, I should note that it evinces, as such, one of the most fundamental contradictions in his composite life. As much as he inveighed against *bürgherlisch Deutschjudentum* and mocked *Bildung*, that is precisely what he practised. His diary and intimate letters were in German, rather than Hebrew, as was his verse. The latter, one of *Bildung*'s chief garments, was, *comme il faut*, privately intended and shared only with a small group of like-minded *bürgerlich Deutschjuden*.

For this discussion two features stand out in Scholem's poems. One is the twofold oscillation, or liminal sense of existence: between imminent redemption of the nation and despair of its attainability; and, fed by the concomitant grandiose sense that nation and messianic-Self are interlaced, between assuredness and grave uncertainty of being chosen. Not infrequently oscillation leads to melancholy. The other, related, feature is the motif of the abyss. The title of a 1926 poem, 'Melancholy Redemption',[36] is emblematic of the oscillation. The first stanza bespeaks doubt, even despair: 'The light of Zion is seen no more, / the real now has won the day. / Will its still untarnished ray / attain the world's inmost core?' I would venture that Scholem made conscious use of the mystical opposition, in which the esoteric experience is the way to get at 'the world's inmost core (*Innere der Welt*)', thereby negating the exoteric interpretation, here hinted at by 'the real' (*das Wirkliche*). This negation also anticipates the poem's conclusion.

The third stanza creates the bond between Self and nation: 'Soul, you believe you are alone / and stand condemned in God's sight / for some failure on your part.' The doubt of the Self is assuaged and the despair inflicted by 'the real' is negated in the fourth and final stanza: 'Wrong! God never comes more close / than when despair bursts into shards: / in Zion's engulfing light.' It is not implausible to read 'when despair bursts into shards' as a metaphor for the spectacle of messianic dramatic appearance. It is certainly reminiscent, as we shall see later, of the way Scholem described how the messianic eruption of the seventeenth century 'exploded' the rabbinical world and momentarily brushed aside what he deemed exilic despair.

The motif of the abyss is highly significant in Scholem's verse. The abyss signified for Scholem both his mission and his doubt. In the poem 'Media In Vita' (1930/33) Scholem's sense of being on the abyss's cusp is, as always, accompanied by a sense of mission and of possibly having been chosen : 'I don't know how long I'll hold my own, / keeping watch on the edge of the abyss / in the beckoning prospect of light / sunk into such an enormous pit.' The next stanza expresses the lack of choice imposed by being chosen. By alluding to the strategy of disguise, Scholem also likens himself to a Marrano, a crucial social type for Sabbatianism in his schema (more below): 'All I know is that I am not free / to decide things for myself. / I could perhaps put on a disguise, / but the world decides everything else.' The poem is concluded with a sort of Adorno-like negative dialectic: 'The world? or rather the abyss / of nothingness in which the world appears – / the reflection of that second face / which negates me, without tears.'[37]

Is it possible to interpret more precisely what Scholem meant by abyss, or what was the abyss he visualized? The key, if there is one, may be in the poem 'Vae Victis – Or Death in the Professoriate' (circa 1937?). This poem was addressed to one of the members of the small circle of German Jews, who exchanged literary intimacy: 'To Hans Jonas, my gnostic colleague, / on the occasion of his descent / into the depths of the void / and his reascent into the far more unknown / offered in friendship / by Gerhard [note that Gershom was discarded] Scholem'.[38] I share Wasserstrom's impression that this 'is perhaps Scholem's most important poem', and that it divulges his doubts, already in the mid-1930s, about the main tool in his kit, namely historical philology.[39]

The pivot of the poem, from which emanates the published collection's title, is this stanza: 'I have brought back the blurred face / Of the fullness of time. / I was ready to leap into the abyss, / But was I really primed?'[40] I would submit that, together with the passage from the diary quoted above, this stanza is perhaps the instance which conveys most strongly Scholem's sense of being not just the heretic Kabbalist in a philologist guise, but the chosen one. Before elaborating this point, a note on the translation must be made. Where 'abyss' appears in the poem 'Media In Vita', the original German has *Nichts*. The same word, *Nichts*, appears in Scholem's dedication to Jonas; this time it is translated as 'void'. In the key stanza of 'Vae Victis' *Nichts* is absent and 'abyss' seems to be inferred, for the German says: '*Ich war zum Sprung auf den Grund bereit, / Aber habe ich ihn gemacht?*' ('I was ready to leap into the abyss, / But was I really primed?').[41] I am not suggesting that the translation is wrong but that, given the stanza's significance, the inference embedded in it should be pointed out.

Commenting on silence as 'the eeriest leitmotiv of these poems', Wasserstrom opines that this silence 'seems to be neither a failing of German nor inadequacy of Hebrew, but rather a hole in the world. Scholem called it the *abyss*.'[42] This view is not incorrect, but I think that the wider context of Scholem's oeuvre might offer a more concrete possibility. For this, one could wed 'Vae Victis' to its contemporaneous seminal essay, to which I shall later return in greater detail, 'Redemption through Sin'.[43] Principal in this remarkable undertaking is Scholem's attempt to reconstruct the doctrine that aimed to resolve, in the wake of Sabbatai Zevi's forced conversion to Islam in the mid-1660s, the paradox of an apostate Messiah.

The resolution of the paradox of an apostate messiah was crucial. Formulated according to Scholem as a new doctrine expressed in Kabbalistic discourse by Nathan of Gaza and Avraham Cardozo, it began by propounding the underlying logic that the details of how redemption would occur were unknown, and would become manifest only as the redemption unfolded; at the same time, however, everything that occurred as redemption was unfolding, according to the circular logic of envisaging redemption, that had already been alluded to in the Scriptures. Scholem remarks that this logic drew authority from no less an eminent authority than Maimonides, who on other occasions was the target of Scholem's ire as one of the chief representatives of rationalist philosophy.[44]

From this underlying logic, the doctrinal resolution of the paradox of the apostate Messiah proceeds to explain that since Adam's primordial sin the last divine sparks of holiness and good (*nitzotzot*) had been trapped within the realm of 'the hylic [a term emanating from Gnostic theology] forces of evil whose hold in the world is especially strong among the Gentiles (*kelipot*)', the realm of impurity. Redemption cannot be complete until the *nitzotzot* were salvaged from the grasp of the *kelipot* and restored to their source, prior to the primordial sin. Evil would perforce collapse when that had been achieved, for it is sustained solely by the divine sparks captured in its midst. The enormity of this task is such that only the Redeemer may accomplish it. As it entails crossing the threshold and delving into the impure domain of the *kelipot*, the Messiah must perform 'alien acts' (*ma'asim zarim*), 'of which his apostasy is the most startling'.[45] It is within the context articulated by this attempt to resolve the paradox of an apostate messiah that sayings such as 'the violation of the Torah is its fulfilment' (*bittulah shel torah zehu kiyyumah*) or 'a commandment which is fulfilled by means of a transgression' (*mitzvah ha-ba'ah ba-averah*) ought to be comprehended.

In this context too, Scholem underscored the crucial place of the Marrano state of mind:

> Underlying the novelty of Sabbatian thought more than anything else was the deeply paradoxical religious sensibility of the Marranos and their descendants, who constituted a large portion of Sephardic Jewry. Had it not been for the unique psychology of these reconverts to Judaism, the new theology [of the doctrine of apostate messianism] would never have found the fertile ground to flourish in that it did. Regardless of what the actual backgrounds of its first disseminators may have been, the Sabbatian doctrine of the Messiah was perfectly tailored to the needs of the Marranic mentality.[46]

This Scholem demonstrates through Avraham Cardozo. Cardozo, who was of Marrano origin, stated that 'It is ordained that the King Messiah don the garments of a Marrano and so go unrecognized by his fellow Jews. In a word, it is ordained that he become a Marrano like me.'[47] 'The more yawning the chasm between the inner experience of the believers and the outer reality', Scholem asserts, 'the more Marranic Sabbatianism became.' The Sabbatians' intuitive sensation was that the outwardly professed belief could not by definition be true belief; in order to be genuine, belief must be concealed and publicly denied. 'For this reason every Jew is obliged to become a Marrano.'[48]

What light is shed by this passage from 'Redemption through Sin' upon the poetry? Crucially, it suggests that Scholem's abyss, most significantly the abyss in 'Vae Victis' ('I was ready to leap into the abyss, / But was I really primed?'), was that into which the Redeemer must delve in order to salvage the *nitzotzot* (the last divine sparks of holiness and good) from their captivity within the *kelipot* (the hylic forces of evil, a term emanating from Gnostic theology), that He must cross the threshold into the domain of impurity. It was thus a specifically framed abyss. 'Redemption through Sin' further illuminates Scholem's contrasting, in the poem 'Melancholy Redemption', the mystical esoteric experience that reaches 'the world's inmost core (*Innere der Welt*)' with the exoteric interpretation, hinted at in the poem by 'the real' (*das Wirkliche*). Finally, the essay's emphasis upon 'the Marranic metality' illuminates Scholem's allusion in the poem 'Media In Vita': 'I could perhaps put on a disguise.' I would dare speculate that Scholem might have in mind Avraham Cardozo, who thought that the Messiah would have to be a Marrano like him, that He would have to don the Marrano garment.

7. The *heretikons*

I would finally like to take a closer look at two remarkable texts by Scholem, which are continuous even though three decades separate their publication. They illustrate how the combination of Zionist theology and prolepsis emerges from his research. The first text is 'Redemption through Sin', which appeared in 1937 but was written two years earlier. It was a significant summation of two decades of research and reflection on mysticism and messianism – noteworthy given that Scholem was not yet forty – and a rehearsal of the two-volume monograph on Sabbatai Zevi and the movement bearing his name that would appear two decades later. The second text is Scholem's study of the astounding life of the Frankist Moshe Dobruska.[49]

The English title 'Redemption through Sin' is not an incorrect rendering of the original, and it is understandable why the translator came up with it; but what is lost in translation is the full extent of Scholem as the virtuoso dialectician par excellence as well as his irony. The Hebrew, 'Mitzvah ha-ba'ah ba-`averah', is not successfully conveyed by the English, whose meaning is too spiritual and Christian, and insufficiently rabbinical and legalistic. *Mitzvah* is a 'do or do not do' commandment, of which there are 613 in the Halakhah, whereas redemption in Hebrew is *ge'ulah*, a term that does not appear in the title; *`averah* means transgression (implicitly of a *mitzvah*), while sin is *het'*. Concluding his explanation of how the paradox of Sabbatai Zevi as an apostate Messiah was resolved, Scholem himself intimates that 'It was at this point that a radically new content was bestowed upon the old rabbinic concept of *mitzvah ha-ba'ah ba-`averah*, literally, "a commandment which is fulfilled by means of transgression"';[50] he goes on to explain that the 'rabbinic concept' was used by two rabbis in the 1660s to define the behaviour of the Sabbatians in the wake of the Messiah's apostasy.[51]

The Hebrew title is a significant instance of Scholem's propensity for dialectic pirouettes. This seminal essay was the first pronouncement of his fundamental thesis (summarized earlier), which repeatedly emphasized the 'explosion' of rabbinical Judaism from within (and hence the argument that Jewish secularity and enlightenment were immanent rather than the result of external influence). With biting irony, Scholem chose to crown the exposition of this grand explosion and reinvigoration of Judaism with a rabbinical title that alluded both to what had been exploded (authoritative rabbinical stability) and to the explosion itself (messianic Sabbatianism, accompanied as it was by 'transgression'). This brilliant encapsulation of the text by its title is missed in the English rendering.

In the essay, Scholem promptly announces the superiority of the Zionist position in Zion, as the only location from which Jewish history can be unfolded authentically and objectively:

> It has come increasingly to be realized that a true understanding of the rise of Sabbatianism will never be possible as long as scholars continue to appraise it by inappropriate standards, whether these be the conventional beliefs of their age or the values of traditional Judaism itself. Today indeed one rarely encounters the baseless assumptions of 'charlatanry' and 'imposture' which occupy so prominent a place in earlier historical literature on the subject. On the contrary: in these times of Jewish national rebirth it is only natural that the deep though ultimately tragic yearning for national redemption to which the initial stages of Sabbatianism gave expression should meet with greater comprehension than in the past.[52]

This basic presupposition is never a matter for demonstration through evidence, but is simply stated and reiterated as a given. It is worth mentioning the epigraph of Scholem's two-volume study of Sabbatai Zevi, which is hardly noticed in commentaries on his thought. This epigraph is a citation of Wilhelm Dilthey (1833–1911), arguably one of the most important thinkers who developed German hermeneutics in the nineteenth century.[53] Scholem clearly subscribes to the hermeneutic act of recreating the psychological and historical experience of the actor from his or her own standpoint, an empathic process meant to understand – or one that presumes to understand – the actor's context and intended meaning as the actor her/himself experiences them. This hermeneutics drew on the assumption that the interpreter's position spatially and temporally enables, rather than obstructs, such an interpretation. The truthfulness of the interpretation is thus, in a sense, partial, for it fully resides neither with the interpreter nor with the subject of interpretation.

It is noteworthy that the epigraph elicited an interesting correspondence between Gershom and his older brother Reinhold, who in his youth had been a member of the Deutsche Volkspartei and was living in Australia. The relationship between the brothers was renewed in the 1970s. Reinhold noticed the epigraph just mentioned and wrote to Gershom: 'Paradox is a characteristic of truth. What *comminus opinio* has of truth is surely no more than an elementary deposit of generalizing partial understanding, related to truth even as sulphurous fumes are to lightning'. Gershom replied: 'The German quotation … (which you seem somewhat ambivalent about) … [is] in my humble opinion … an incomparable quotation, since it relates to my own opinion on the nature of truth.' Reinhold now responded: 'The epigraph did not offend me; I simply saw it as confirmation of how German your background is, when you, despite all your talmudic [sic] and Kabbalistic wisdom, used a German citation on the "partial understanding" of truth.'[54]

In Scholem's thesis, the precise point at which, in his powerful rhetoric, the abyss of nihilistic Sabbatianism became wide open was the paradox given rise to by the apostasy of the Messiah Sabbatai Zevi in 1666.

As mentioned earlier, the resolution of the paradox of an apostate messiah was crucial. It was formulated according to Scholem as a new doctrine expressed in Kabbalistic discourse by Nathan of Gaza and Avraham Cardozo. I briefly alluded to the post-apostasy doctrine in connection with Scholem's use of abyss in his verse.[55] The bottom line is that Scholem identified its gist as a revival by re-interpretation of the second century Gnostic myth on the mystery of Godhead and the God of the Old Testament. For Scholem, the doctrinal resolution to the apostate messiah paradox amounted to nothing short of a new theology: 'From bits and pieces of Scripture, from scattered paradoxes and sayings in the writings of the Kabbalah, from all the remotest corners of Jewish religious literature, an unprecedented theology of Judaism was brought into being.'[56] It is impossible to overstate the extent to which Scholem saw in this 'unprecedented theology of Judaism', and the mood that surrounded it, a fundamental transformation, and concomitantly the extent to which this argument undergirded his Zionist theology. All the components of this theology can be found in the dialogue between Scholem and his Sabbatian heroes:

the antinomian destruction of rabbinical Judaism; the negation of exile; the revival of a non-rabbinic religious belief; the insistence on the organic inclusiveness of the Jewish nation/Jewish history even – perhaps especially – in the face of something as liminal as heretic heroes and apostasy.

The 'renewed' bond between an ancient myth (the Gnostic) and the ur-text (the Hebrew Bible), without the distorting mediation of rabbinical commentary or philosophical literature, and implicitly the 'renewed' bond between the ancient myth and the land of Israel, seems to have injected with elan not only Judaism but also Scholem. From that point his negation of exile argument flows unrestrained, as does his adulation of the Sabbatian revolutionaries. The depth of Scholem's yearning for an ancient myth that would renew, reinvigorate and transform is manifest in the force of his rhetoric, in the Zionist excitement with which he negates exile and rabbinical Judaism, and in the almost visible spark in his eyes when he senses a return to the source – mythical, textual and territorial. Emphasizing the Sabbatians' fondness of paradoxes that 'reveal a dialectical daring that cannot but be respected', Scholem moves to underscore the authenticity of their Jewishness:

> Here we are given our deepest glimpse yet into the souls of these revolutionaries who regarded themselves as loyal Jews while at the same time completely overturning the traditional religious categories of Judaism. I am not of course speaking of a feeling of 'loyalty' to the Jewish religion as it was defined by rabbinical authority. For many, if not most Sabbatians, the Judaism of the rabbis, which they identified with the Judaism of exile, had come to assume an entirely dubious character. Even when they continued to live under its jurisdiction it was not out of any sense of commitment; no doubt it had been suited to its time, but in the light of the soul-shaking truth of the redemption that time had passed.[57]

Having then presented the re-interpretation of the Gnostic position, Scholem sheds any inhibition that may still linger:

> What yearnings for regeneration of faith and what disdainful negation of exile! Like true spiritual revolutionaries, with an unfeigned enthusiasm which even today cannot fail to impress the reader of [Avraham] Cardozo's books, the 'believers' unflinchingly proclaimed their belief that all during exile the Jewish people had worshipped a powerless divinity and had clung to a way of life that was fundamentally in need of reform . . . Determined to avoid a full-scale revolution within the heart of Jewry, the rabbinical traditionalists and their supporters did all they could to drive the 'believers' beyond the pale. And yet in spite of all this, one can hardly deny that a great deal that is authentically Jewish was embodied in these paradoxical individuals too, in their desire to start afresh and in their realization of the fact that negating the exile meant negating its religious and institutional forms as well and returning to the original fountainheads of the Jewish faith. This last practice – a tendency to rely on matters of belief upon the Bible and the *Aggadah*

[non-legal literature] – grew to be particularly strong among the nihilists in the movement. Here too, faith in paradox reigned supreme: the stranger the *Aggadah*, the more offensive to reason and common sense, the more likely it was to be seized upon as a symbol of that 'mystery of faith' which naturally tended to conceal itself in the most frightful and fanciful tales.[58]

Scholem identifies four forms taken by 'organized Sabbatian nihilism' from 1683 (the year of the Dönme's conversion to Islam) onward.[59] Among these forms was Frankism, and what Scholem had merely mentioned in the mid-1930s received a publication in 1970. The son of a rabbi, Jacob Frank was born in Podolia (then in Poland, now a region of Ukraine) in 1726. His travels in the Ottoman Empire in the 1740s as a merchant brought him into contact with Sabbatians, and on his return to Poland in 1755 he founded the Frankists, as an offshoot of Sabbatianism. In 1759 the Frankists underwent a spectacular mass baptism at Lvov, Poland, in the presence of members of the Polish nobility. But the Catholic Church brought charges of heresy against him, possibly prompted by the strangeness of his teaching, which resulted in his imprisonment in 1760. On emerging from prison thirteen years later, Frank assumed the role of messiah. Selecting twelve apostles, he settled at Brünn, Moravia (now Brno, Czech Republic), where he gained the patronage of Maria Theresa, Archduchess of Austria, who employed him as an apologist of Christianity to the Jews. After 1786 Frank moved to the small German town of Offenbach, where he spent the rest of his life in luxury, thanks to the donations of his followers. After his death, leadership of the sect passed to his daughter Eve Frank, but the movement was soon absorbed into the Catholic Church.

Scholem thinks that Frank 'was in all his actions a truly corrupt and degenerate individual'.[60] He is, however, unwilling to stop there, because

> in spite of all this ... we are confronted in his person with the extraordinary spectacle of a powerful and tyrannical soul living in the middle of the eighteenth century and yet immersed in a mythological world of its own making. Out of the ideas of Sabbatianism, a movement in which he was apparently raised and educated, Frank was able to weave a complete myth of religious nihilism.[61]

The most notable feature of Frank's religious myth was its striking antinomian drive. 'The Law of Moses' was utterly rejected as 'injurious and useless', the main obstacle to the re-emergence of 'the Good God'. Thirty years after his conversion to Catholicism Frank stated: 'This much I tell you: Christ ... said that he had come to redeem the world from the hands of the devil, but I have come to redeem it from all the laws and customs that have ever existed. It is my task to annihilate all this so that the Good God can reveal himself'.[62] In Scholem's schema of unfolding *Geist*s, Frankism led to the Haskalah, the so-called Jewish Enlightenment, but because of its unyielding antinomian drive Frankism would not halt there. Scholem concludes 'Redemption through Sin' by noting that the French Revolution imbued with special meaning 'Frankist subversion of the old morality and religion ... and perhaps not only in the abstract, for we know that Frank's nephews, whether as "believers" or out of some other motive, were active in high revolutionary circles in Paris and Strasbourg'.[63]

What had been hinted at in the 1930s came to fruition in the 1970s. One of Jacob Frank's nephews, whom Scholem had mentioned anonymously in 1937 in 'Redemption through Sin', became the subject of his reconstruction of a quintessential Frankist life three decades later in 'A Frankist's Career: Moshe Dobruska and His Metamorphoses'.[64] Dobruska was born in 1753 in Brünn, Moravia (now Brno), where Jacob Frank would settle in the 1760s. His father held the monopoly over sales of tobacco in the Austro-Hungarian Empire under Maria Theresa, and his mother, Scheindel Hirschl, was Jacob Frank's cousin (hence the description of Moshe and his brother Emmanuel as his nephews). She was the foremost patron of the Sabbatians in Moravia, her rabbinical detractors referring to her as 'the whore of Brünn'. Dobruska's education comprised rabbinical learning, Sabbatian Kabbalah, German letters, Latin and several European vernaculars. In 1773 he married Elke, the adopted daughter of one of the wealthiest leaders of Prague's Jewish community, Joachim Edler von Popper.

Scholem makes his point through the unfolding of Dobruska's life. Like most of his siblings, Dobruska converted to Catholicism in 1775 and became Franz Thomas Scheinfeld; his wife Elke became Wilhelmina. He moved to Vienna, where he served the Habsburgs and from 1781 to 1784 was an active member in one of the Asiatic Freemason fraternities. It was a mystically inclined fraternity, which supported Judeo-Christian interaction and which was engaged in the reading of Kabbalistic texts. In the wake of the French Revolution Dobruska/Scheinfeld began to lean leftward in both his explicit political pronouncements and the literary circles in which he moved. He was especially attracted to the Jacobin revolutionaries. In the early 1790s he left Vienna for Strasbourg, where he now became Sigmund Frey, later adding Junius, after the Roman Junius Brutus, one of the leading conspirators in the assassination of Julius Caesar. On arriving in Paris with Wilhelmina and his brother and sister, Dobruska/Scheinfeld/Frey's Jacobin tendencies intensified, and he never left home 'without wearing the carmagnole' – though the suspicion that he was a counter-revolutionary Habsburg agent never died away. His younger sister married the prominent Jacobin François Chabot. The Dobruska/Frey brothers together participated in the August 1792 onslaught on the king's Tuileries Palace, and even earned a citation from the revolutionary authorities. On 5 April 1794 Danton, Chabot and others were executed; among them, condemned to death for treason, were the brothers Frey.

Scholem concludes his account of Dobruska's life poetically:

Thus ended the overt and covert, surprising and tumultuous career of Moshe Dobruska – Franz Thomas von Scheinfeld – Junius Frey … Partially a Jew and partially an assimilated convert; partially a Kabbalist and man of the concealed and partially a man of enlightenment; partially a Jacobin and partially a spy – everything partially, but a true and complete Frankist.[65]

Ultimately then, Scholem's own self-image was that of a heretic hero at least, the chosen one at most, similar to those he studied. His own historical experience of return to an antinomian reinvigorated Judaism, which he philologically studied rather than straightforwardly believed in, to Hebrew and to Zion(ism), embodied the nation's historical experience. The meaning of Jewish history had to await these returns by Scholem as a prerequisite for its full revelation, which is why his magnificent oeuvre is best viewed as a mythology of prolepsis.

8. By way of conclusion

Towards the end of his life Scholem made some revealing comments in a conversation with the Israeli novelist Ehud Ben-Ezer. These comments, precisely because they were not made in a scholarly publication, illustrate how the three expressions of the Zionist myth – the negation of exile, the return to the land of Israel and the return to history – cohered in Scholem's consciousness. These comments also evince not only Scholem's objection to exile, but also his visceral and existential contempt for exile, and through it for humanistic universalism.

Much of the conversation was driven by Ben-Ezer's anxiety about the ethical and intellectual consequences of the Zionist project and life in Israel. When asked about the price of Zionism (for Jews, it occurs to neither interlocutor that Palestinians pay a price), Scholem erupted in a tirade:

> You ask about the price of Zionism, and the question is not *the price of Zionism but the price of exile.* Views of people like George Steiner were already heard sixty and seventy years ago ... I don't have an argument with George Steiner. He is trying to live outside of history ... If presently the spell of the Jewish intellectuals in the Diaspora is cast upon you [Ben-Ezer], I say – please go there. Live five years among them. And see the price of exile they pay. Whoever feels constrained in Israel, let him go to New York or Cambridge and find out if he feels as wonderfully there as George Steiner does. Complaints of intellectuals who do not wish to identify with any national body? ... We [the Zionists] counter-argued and retorted [against Jews who professed a humanist-universal position in Germany]: 'What is the great global thing in which you believe and of which you speak? After all no Gentile speaks this way. Only you. There is no general humanity. It exists only in your imagination' ... I have no bone to pick with a Jewish intellectual who gives precedence to his personal spiritual problems over the problem of historical *responsibility* ... If Steiner does not wish to share with us the responsibility for the state – then he is right. Let him be an exilic Jew. Perhaps one day he will be beaten on the head and will then discover that he *really* does not belong there, and that his alienation is not just an impressive and fashionable intellectual posture but also a very bitter historical reality, for which the full price must be paid ... I find it difficult to comprehend what is bothering you [Ben-Ezer]. Why is there in your question a degree of effacement before the Jewish intellectual in the Diaspora? What prevents you from leading a wholesome life?[66]

To leap into the abyss of teleology and indulge in its logic, the problem with Scholem's dialectical scheme of a Jewish history that immanently leads to secularization and ultimately Zionism, is that his protagonists belie his teleology, even within a teleological logic. Moshe Dobruska's trajectory, as Scholem himself so poetically reconstructed it, can be said to have had the 'general humanity' *telos* that Scholem so reviled. Avraham Cardozo, the Marrano formulator of the Gnostic Sabbatian doctrine that, according to Scholem, resolved for the 'believers' the paradox of the apostate messiah, even connected 'general humanity' and exile to one another. In the late 1660s Cardozo was leading a comfortable life in Tripoli in Ottoman North Africa. A physician, he had been sent there by his patron, the Duke of Tuscany, to treat the Ottoman governor Osman Pasha, and was looked after by the local grandee Receb Bey. When the Jewish judges (*dayyanim*) of Sabbatai Zevi's hometown of Izmir (Smyrna) convened to discuss the apostate messiah, they solicited testimonies from Cardozo among others. His testimony, *Epistles to the Judges of Izmir* (*Iggrot le-dayyanei Izmir*), was dated (to 1669) and published by Scholem.[67] However, in the *Epistles* Cardozo alludes to the messianic era in a way that Scholem omits to mention in 'Redemption through Sin'. Cardozo explains to the judges that his messianic belief by no means stemmed from 'my being in exile, for I experience no exile'.[68]

Cardozo explicitly objected to the notion that the messiah would bring the Jews back to the land of Israel. As David Halperin senses, 'His own image of the Messianic era is a strangely prescient foreshadowing of the Jewish political emancipation of the eighteenth and nineteenth centuries.'[69] Cardozo shared his own vision with the judges: 'When the Redeemer comes, the Jews will still be living among the Gentiles even after their salvation is accomplished. But they will not be dead men, as they had been previously. Through their redemption they will experience happiness, enjoy dignity and honor.'[70]

Not a few of Scholem's contemporaries behaved more like Dobruska and Cardozo had done, in their own context, than in the teleological role Scholem had assigned to these *heretikons*. Amidst the horrors of Nazi Europe, facing the alternatives of emigrating to either Zion or New Zion, Arendt (permanently) and Adorno (transitorily) opted for the latter. Benjamin, whose legacy Scholem did so much to both preserve and distort, committed suicide.

Notes

1. Scholem's fame and stature obviate the need for a brief CV. For this see David Biale, *Gershom Scholem, Kabbalah and Counter-History*, Cambridge, Mass.: Harvard University Press, 1979, pp. 52–9, and David Myers, *Re-Inventing the Jewish Past: European Jewish Intellectuals and the Zionist Return to History*, New York and Oxford: Oxford University Press, 1995, pp. 151–77.
2. Gabriel Piterberg, *The Returns of Zionism*, London and New York: Verso, 2008, and 'Literature of Settler Societies: Albert Camus, S. Yizhar and Amos Oz', in *Settler Colonial Studies* 1/2 (September 2011), pp. 1–49.
3. Madeline Zilfi, *The Politics of Piety*, Minneapolis and Chicago: Bibliotheca Islamica, 1988; Jane Hathaway, 'The Grand Vizier and the False Messiah', in *Journal of the American Oriental Society*

117 (Oct–Dec 1997), no. 4, pp. 665–71; Marc Baer, *The Dönme*, Stanford: Stanford University Press, 2010.

4. The best study to date on the foundation of Jewish history at the Hebrew University is David Myers, *Re-Inventing the Jewish Past: European Jewish Intellectuals and the Zionist Return to History*, New York and Oxford: Oxford University Press, 1995, especially pp. 38–74, where the early institutional history is thoroughly documented and eloquently presented.

5. Two notable loci of this debate are special issues of important journals: *Studies in Contemporary Judaism: An Annual* 10 (1994); and *History & Memory: Studies in the Representation of the Past* 7 (Spring/Summer 1995), no. 1.

6. For the most notable instance of the extrinsic perspective see Amnon Raz-Krakotzkin, 'Exile Within Sovereignty: Towards a Critique of the "Negation of Exile" in Israeli Culture' [Hebrew], 2 parts, in *Theory and Criticism* 4 (1993) and 5 (1994), pp. 23–56 and 113–32 respectively. For the most subtle, yet intrinsic, view see Myers, *Re-Inventing*, and 'Was There a "Jerusalem School"?' in *Studies in Contemporary Judaism* 10 (1994), pp. 66–92.

7. Raz-Krakotzkin, 'Exile', p. 41.

8. I should make it explicitly clear that the convergence of Raz-Krakotzkin's and my own views on this crucial matter is not coincidental, and that we developed them in close interaction at the Van Leer Institute in Jerusalem in the 1990s. See Gabriel Piterberg, 'Domestic Orientalism', in *British Journal of Middle Eastern Studies* 23 (1996), pp. 125–45, and 'The Nation and Its Raconteurs' [Hebrew], in *Theory and Criticism* 6 (Spring 1995), pp. 81–105.

9. This is the title of a brilliantly succinct essay (Hebrew) by Amnon Raz-Krakotzkin on precisely this problem in *Mitaam* 3 (September 2005), pp. 71–7.

10. I discuss this at length in Chapter 7 of *The Returns of Zionism*.

11. Amnon Raz-Krakotzkin, 'The Golem of Scholem: Messianism and Zionism in the Writings of Rabbi Avraham Isaac HaKohen Kook and Gershom Scholem', in Christoph Miething, ed., *Politik und Religion im Judentum*, Tübingen: Max Niemeyer Verlag, 1999, pp. 223–9.

12. Amos Funkenstein, 'Charisma, "Kairos" and the Messianic Dialectic', in *History & Memory* 4 (Spring–Summer 1992), no. 1, pp. 123–40, especially pp. 134–5.

13. Raz-Krakotzkin, 'Golem', p. 224.

14. Ibid., p. 226.

15. Ibid.

16. Ibid., p. 227.

17. Ibid., p. 229.

18. Ibid.

19. Biale, *Gershom Scholem*, p. 77.

20. Perry Anderson, 'The Intransigent Right', in *Spectrum*, London and New York: Verso, 2005, pp. 3–29. For more on Schmitt see Gopal Balakrishnan, *The Enemy: An Intellectual Portrait of Carl Schmitt*, London: Verso, 2000, and Mark Lilla, *The Reckless Mind*, New York: New York Review of Books, 2001, pp. 47–77.

21. See the exchange between Benno Teschke and Gopal Balakrishnan in *New Left Review* 67 (January–February 2011), 68 (March–April 2011) and 69 (May–June 2011).

22. See Lilla, *Reckless Mind*, pp. 93–4 and Michael Löwy, *Fire Alarm*, London: Verso, 2006.

23. Christoph Schmidt, 'The Political Theology of Gershom Scholem' [Hebrew], in *Theory and Criticism* 6 (Spring 1995), pp. 149–61. Schmidt was also the scientific editor of and wrote the introduction for the Hebrew translation of *Politische Theologie* (Tel Aviv: Resling, 2005).

24. Funkenstein, 'Charsima', p. 131 (emphasis in the original).
25. Quentin Skinner, 'Meaning and Understanding in the History of Ideas', in *History and Theory* 8 (1969), pp. 3–51. I quote from the reproduction in James Tulley, ed., *Meaning and Context: Quentin Skinner and his Critics*, Cambridge: Polity Press, 1988.
26. Ibid., p. 44.
27. Ibid., p. 45 (emphasis added).
28. Biale, *Gershom Scholem*, p. 127.
29. Moshe Idel, 'The History of the Kabbalah and the History of the Jews' [Hebrew], in *History and Criticism* 6 (Spring 1995), pp. 137–49. The non-Hebrew reader may consult the essay's early version in French: 'Mystique juive et histoire juive', in *Annales, Histoire, Sciences Sociales* 49 (1994), pp. 1223–40.
30. For the poetry see Gershom Scholem, *The Fullness of Time: Poems*, trans. Richard Sieburth, intr. and annotated by Steven M. Wasserstrom, Jerusalem: Ibis Editions, 2003. For bibliographic details of the diaries and letters of youth see Michael Brenner, 'From Self-Declared Messiah to Scholar Messianism: The Recently Published Diaries Present Young Gerhard Scholem in a New Light', in *Jewish Social Studies*, New Series 3 (Autumn 1996), no. 1, pp. 177–82.
31. Diary, 22 May 1915, quoted in Brenner, 'Self-Declared Messiah', p. 178. Scholem was 17 at that time.
32. Ibid.
33. Brenner, 'Self-Declared Messiah', p. 179.
34. Hence the title of Raz-Krakotzkin's article referenced earlier.
35. In Scholem, *The Fullness of Time*, pp. 14–15.
36. Ibid., pp. 68 and 69.
37. Ibid., pp. 95–7.
38. Ibid., p. 111.
39. Ibid., p. 20–1.
40. Ibid., p. 109.
41. The German is in ibid., p. 108.
42. Ibid., pp. 20 and 21 (emphasis in the original).
43. Gershom Scholem, 'Mitzvah ha-ba'ah be-'averah', in *Knesset* 2 (1937), pp. 347–92. Translated into English by Hillel Halkin as 'Redemption through Sin', in *The Messianic Idea in Judaism*, London: George Allen & Unwin, 1971, pp. 78–141. The essay was written in 1935, for which see asterisk note on p. 85 of the English translation, to which all references are made unless otherwise stated.
44. Ibid., p. 94.
45. Ibid., pp. 94–5.
46. Ibid., p. 95.
47. Ibid.
48. Ibid., pp. 110–11.
49. Gershom Scholem, 'A Frankist's Career: Moshe Dobruska and His Metamorphoses', in *Studies and Texts Concerning the History of Sabbatianism and Its Metamorphoses*, Jerusalem: Bialik Institute, 1974, pp. 141–219 [Hebrew]. Originally appeared in *Zion* 35 (1970), pp. 127–81.

50. Scholem, 'Redemption', p. 99.
51. See the asterisk note for 'Mitzvah' in Scholem, *Studies and Texts concerning the History of Sabbatianism and Its Metamorphoses* [Hebrew], Jerusalem: Bialik Institute, 1974, p. 9.
52. Ibid., p. 78.
53. The quote is: 'Paradox is a characteristic of truth. What *communis opinio* has of truth is surely no more than an elementary deposit of generalizing partial understanding, related to truth even as sulphurous fumes are to lightning.' Whereas in the Hebrew original (Tel Aviv: Am Oved, 1975) it is attributed simply to Dilthey (without even the Wilhelm), in the English translation (Princeton University Press, 1973) the attribution is 'From the correspondence of Count Yorck von Wartenburg and Wilhelm Dilthey'.
54. Correspondence quoted in Scholem, *The Fullness of Time*, pp. 28–30.
55. For a more detailed presentation see Piterberg, *Returns*, pp. 170–4.
56. Scholem, 'Redemption', pp. 96–7.
57. Ibid., pp. 103–4.
58. Ibid., p. 106.
59. Ibid., pp. 114–15.
60. Ibid., p. 126.
61. Ibid., pp. 127–8.
62. Ibid., p. 130.
63. Ibid.
64. Scholem, 'A Frankist's Career.
65. Ibid., p. 209.
66. Gershom Scholem, 'Zionism – A Dialectic of Continuity and Rebellion' [conversation with E. Ben-Ezer, Hebrew], in Avraham Shapira, ed., *Continuity and Rebellion: Gershom Scholem in Speech and Dialogue*, Tel Aviv: Am Oved, 1994, pp. 25, 26, 27 and 29 (emphasis in the original).
67. In *Studies and Texts*. The date is identified on pp. 298–303.
68. David J. Halperin, trans. and intr., *Abraham Miguel Cardozo: Selected Writings*, New York: Paulist Press, 2001, p. 48.
69. Ibid.
70. Ibid., p. 49.

CHAPTER 14
CATCHING UP WITH ONESELF: ISLAM AND THE REPRESENTATION OF HUMANITY
Faisal Devji

A global history only becomes possible once the human race emerges as its subject. All other claims to such a history are concerned only with expanding old ideas of context to the ends of the earth, so as to locate within them the ever-growing patterns of interaction and interdependence among men. But as the subject or *telos* of global history, humanity must be conceived of in its sheer materiality, the sum of living beings making up the species. Anything else, such as the figure of a humanist individual, dissolves the race into a mere category in the history of ideas. And while the species is also a figure of this kind, its elevation into the subject of history quite transforms the latter. For unlike the humanist individual, who serves either as a universal ideal or as the reality of some particular history, mankind is always self-equivalent and can neither match up to nor fall short of itself. In this way the species provides history with its first global subject, and indeed with its most sublime actor after God.

Of course humanity cannot be said to exist as an actor in any unified or self-conscious way, these criteria being themselves borrowed from the individual. And the species is for the moment deprived even of the collective agency provided by political institutions, which are still international in character. Yet it is clear that the history of mankind can no longer be confined to the doings of men and women in their multiplicity but must deal with the fate of the race as a singularity. While nineteenth-century thinkers in Europe produced a number of accounts purporting to be histories of humanity, often entailing the rise of some race or civilization to global dominance, it was in the twentieth that the species came to achieve a properly historical reality. But this only happened when the interconnections and dependencies first created by colonial expansion suddenly put the world itself at stake in moments of political or economic crisis beginning with the Great War. In diverse fields ranging from literature to medicine, but significantly not politics, the human race began to assume a historical countenance during this period, emerging as the globe's true subject during the Cold War, whose nuclear arsenals made its extinction a real possibility. It was mortality that endowed the species with a properly historical reality.

The vocabulary of mutually assured destruction and nuclear winter may have fallen into disuse after the Cold War, but humanity continues to be imagined as the globe's truest subject, if only in its negative form as a victim of pandemics or climate change. The species therefore takes on a paradoxical form in our day, as a potential actor in history, yet one whose reality cannot be discounted. For with its transformation into a statistically measurable figure, whose future we can both predict and even determine, humanity has ceased to be the abstraction and ideal it once was. As such it provides a sociological model of universality for global movements of all kinds. In this chapter I want to look at the way in which Islam comes to provide the species with its subjectivity in modern times. Beginning with the example of how those who participate in global forms of militancy attempt to speak in the name of humanity, I will go on to consider the pre-history of this claim among Muslim thinkers in nineteenth- and twentieth-century South Asia, and conclude by reflecting upon the consequences of such efforts to represent mankind. Rather than tracing the development of this extraordinary endeavour within some continuous genealogy, I will show how detached it is from any single intellectual or political position, being in this respect part of a truly universal enterprise.

1. The thief of Baghdad

Though in hiding somewhere between Pakistan and Afghanistan, one of al-Qaeda's chief spokesmen was able to answer a series of questions from friends and foes around the world in April 2008. Submitted to Ayman al-Zawahiri through the Internet and responded to in the same fashion, these queries included many expostulating with Osama bin Laden's lieutenant about the indiscriminate violence resorted to by those fighting in the name of Islam. Typical was this condemnation of militant methods:

> How do you reconcile the values of your medical training – to help people and prolong their lives – with the fact that you killed Anwar al-Sadat and that you shape the minds of bombers and suicide commandos?[1]

Zawahiri responded to his questioner in the following way:

> During my medical studies, I learned that life is Allah's miracle and his gift. Thus, one must be careful to obey him. I have learned from surgery about how to save the body by amputating failing organs and removing cancers, and how to cure illness-inducing bacteria. Medicine, when practiced as a sacrifice to Allah and to help the oppressed, will grant the soul happiness and joy, which will never be experienced by those who have twisted it into a tool for greed, robbing others and exploiting their pain for their own benefit.[2]

This justification of violence illustrates the crucial role that the language of humanity plays in the narrative of militancy. Rather than being dedicated solely to the cause of Islam, in other words, militancy stakes a claim to mankind itself as an ideal. Thus expanding upon the rhetoric of modern racism, for which threatened groups had to be purified from miscegenation and other forms of contamination by medical means, Zawahiri describes terrorism as a form of surgery whose aim is to save the human race itself from the cancers and other ailments that threaten its global body. Identified with medicine practised according to the Hippocratic oath, this vision of militancy as a form of sacrifice for the sake of mankind is opposed to humanitarianism in its conventional and commercially organized forms, which Zawahiri argues are founded upon exploitation and profit. By representing the species as an individual, or rather by making the two interchangeable, Zawahiri treats it as a potential subject, one that requires the healing touch of jihad to speak in its own name.

Militant Islam's attempt to represent humanity as a historical actor comes to the fore in Ayman al-Zawahiri's response to another question put to him over the Internet:

> Can you clear up the confusion that many Westerns [sic] have about technology – on one hand, you shun modern values, but on the other hand you accept modern Western technology such as the Internet?[3]

Hastening to brush aside any account of terrorism that would confine it to some contradiction between Muslim tradition and Western modernity, Zawahiri makes it clear that even the greatest enemies must share a common history and partake of each other's achievements as members of the same species. In other words he moves beyond the narratives of race or civilization from which the distinction of traditional and modern is often derived to focus on the human race as history's true subject:

> This question is based on two false premises. The fact that I accept or shun a certain value is not based on whether it is ancient or modern. But I am opposed to polytheism; scorning the religion; establishing relations based on material benefit and achieving sensory pleasures; lying, deceiving; acting on self-interest; alcoholism; gambling; vices; taking over other people's countries and oppressing them; stealing the riches of others; double standards; immunity against being held accountable for crimes for which others will be punished; spreading killing, abuse, destruction, and the destruction of the environment and climate merely to master the land, rob, and plunder.[4]

Let us pause here to note that apart from the ritual invocation of polytheism and blasphemy at the beginning of his response, there is nothing particularly Islamic about this assortment of crimes. Indeed Zawahiri is eager to prove that he opposes the very things that all human beings do. He then goes on to say that the West has betrayed its kinship with the rest of the species by oppressing and plundering it:

> Scientific knowledge is neither Eastern nor Western – it is the property of mankind which circulates among us equally in various times and places. The scientific progress of the West was originally based on our riches, which they are still plundering to this day. Where is our stolen share? Secondly, the West tried to cover up its crimes against us and against the rest of mankind by priding itself in its scientific supremacy. Under the cover of this progress, they have attempted to convince occupied and weaker nations that they [the West] are superior to them,

and more deserving to manage the world and to plunder its riches – and to demean other people. Neither the Muslims, nor anyone else, will be fooled by this trick any longer.[5]

Arguably the operative category of militant thinking, humanity brings Muslims and infidels together in such a way as to make possible relations of amity as well as enmity among them. I will be concerned here with the ambivalence that marks this relationship of would-be friends and foes, a quality evident in the passage from Zawahiri cited above. For at the same moment that he claims the achievements of his enemies as a properly human inheritance, bin Laden's most eminent follower also suggests that some of the credit for amassing this legacy was stolen from Muslims and needs to be recovered. In other words the relationship between Islam and its enemies is conceived as one of rivalry and theft, with Muslims having to recover their mission of representing humanity from the West's imposture. Such an intimate relationship makes teleology into a kind of racecourse where the goal's very universality allows it to be stolen by a competitor. Now this kind of reasoning possesses a history going back to the nineteenth century, when Muslim reformers sought by such apologetics to explain as well as learn from the scientific and technological dominance of Europe's colonial powers. This they did by devaluing the categories of race and civilization as sites of European privilege, and bringing humanity to the fore as history's true subject. Islam therefore represented the species by refusing to differentiate between its various components.

2. Losing Islam to the infidel

Perhaps the first and certainly the most influential Muslim thinker to forge such a link between Islam and humanity was India's Syed Ahmed Khan, a reformer of the nineteenth century whose life was dedicated to modernizing his co-religionists largely by way of inculcating Western education among them. In a monumental effort of scriptural interpretation and exegesis, Khan contended that Islam, when cleansed of superstitious accretions, was both the most natural and the most universal of religions; this in the sense of being wholly in conformity with the laws of nature and so founded for the benefit of all mankind.[6] To make this argument, however, Syed Ahmed Khan had to separate humanity from all the other forms of life with which it was traditionally associated, including angels, animals and spirits together with their respective abodes, and have it stand alone on the hard earth as the unique recipient of divine favour. Thus in his famous commentary on the Quran, this most eminent of India's Muslim modernizers had either to deny the reality of supernatural beings, or at the very least consign them to some ineffable and metaphorical place beyond the singular world of human interaction and morality. Whatever the precedents and implications of Syed Ahmed Khan's claims, therefore, which were extrapolated from the evaluation of Muhammad's mission by writers like Gibbon and Carlyle as much as from any Muslim source, it is clear that Islam's universality was predicated upon its equivalence with nineteenth-century notions of nature and therefore with the human species, both of which stood outside the doctrinal sphere with its angels and miracles to provide the criteria of religion's veracity. But this did not entail subordinating religious truth to varying conceptions of science, only insisting that it be continually engaged with the times, whose forms of knowledge regulated scriptural interpretation while keeping Islam at the centre of contemporary concerns.

Syed Ahmed Khan saw as the only miraculous aspect of the Quran its ability to keep pace with scientific change, which in his own times meant its successful interpretation within the bounds of natural law, a notion that stood apart from earlier definitions of nature as an essence (*zat*), disposition (*tabiat*) or ingrained constitution (*fitrat*). Islam's conformity with nature conceived as law had to be repeatedly demonstrated so that it might be presented as the universal religion of mankind. One consequence of naturalizing religion in this way was to generalize its doctrinal vocabulary beyond the boundaries of Islam, so that it now became possible to think even of its central concepts as being universal to humanity. Of course Muslim thinkers in the past had sought precedents and prognostications for Muhammad's revelation by linking it to religions pre-dating Islam, well beyond the monotheistic coterie this latter formed with Judaism and Christianity. While the Muslim doctrines thus discovered in Hinduism, Buddhism or Zoroastrianism might place all these religions within some universal history, there was no question about Islam representing its pinnacle. But the Victorian naturalization of religion meant that if Muslims could be said to have discovered the unity of mankind by way of Islam, or even to have developed this unity to its fullest potential, they could not claim to possess it exclusively or indeed for ever. There was always the possibility that others might be able to lay claim to Islam itself, albeit under a different name, if Muslims were to abandon their duty to represent the human race.

In fact there were many instances from the last decades of the nineteenth century of prominent Muslim figures in India warning that unbelievers had come into possession of Islam's central concepts and categories. A good example of this is provided by the century's most popular Urdu text, an epic poem on the rise and fall of Islam by Syed Ahmed Khan's disciple, Altaf Husain Hali. First published in 1879, the *Musaddas dar Madd-o Jazr-e Islam* ('the ebb and flow of Islam') sings of the virtues that brought Muslims political power in times past and put them at the forefront of the arts and sciences. Hali then catalogues the decline of India's Muslims in particular and those of the world at large in practically every department of social life, attributing their decadence to the betrayal of Islamic virtues. Chief among these was fidelity to nature, seen as providing both the form and the content of human knowledge as a set of universal laws. While Muslims might have forsaken such virtues, others, like Europe's Christians, but also the poet's Hindu neighbours, are said to have embraced them and thus moved past the Prophet's followers in representing humanity. So Hali tells his readers that the nations of the West have succeeded Muslims at the head of the species by naturalizing religion into the service of mankind:

Historical Teleologies in the Modern World

1.1: Love for God's creatures

This was the first lesson of the Book of True Guidance: 'All creatures belong to God's family'.

The beloved of the Creator of the two worlds is the one who maintains the ties of love with his creatures.

This is devotion, this is religion and faith, that man should come to the service of his fellow man in the world.

1.2: The public spirit of the peoples of the West

Those who act on the basis of this weighty utterance today flourish upon the face of the earth. They are superior to all, high and low. They are now the central axis of humanity. Those covenants of the Holy Law which we have broken have all been firmly upheld by the people of the West.[7]

In order to make the argument that Islam's role has been taken over by the Christian West, Hali had to redefine the Muslim *ummah* or community in sociological terms. No longer a juridical or theological category defined by ritual authority and political practice, the *ummah* instead became a society that could never again be contained within legal categories, and one whose global character placed Islam outside the jurisdiction of any state. While the loss of political power, therefore, was seen in the poem as a sign of decline, its restoration did not serve as a condition for Muslim greatness, which was why Hali could take colonized populations like the Hindus as models of virtue. He has this to say about Islam's loss of worldly dominion, and its as yet unsuccessful quest to find another way of representing the progress of the human race:

1.3: Address to the poet's community

Government may have drawn aside from you, but you had no monopoly over it. Who possesses a remedy against the vicissitudes of fortune? Sometimes one is an Alexander here, sometimes a Darius.

    After all, kingship is hardly divinity. What one owns today is someone else's tomorrow.

1.4: The secret of the Muslims' dominion

When God's wisdom demanded that the teaching of the Best of Scholars be set in force, And the religion of right guidance became famous in the world, He bestowed world dominion upon you, saying, 'Spread the ordinances of the Holy Law throughout the world, and bring to an end the Master's reasons for objecting to His creatures.'

1.5: Our present state

Now that government has performed its proper function, Islam has no need for it left.
But alas, oh community of the Glory of Man, humanity departed together with it.
Government was like a gilt covering upon you. As soon as it peeled off, your innate capacity emerged.
There are many nations in the world who do not possess the special quality of empire.
But nowhere can so great a calamity have come as here, where each house is overshadowed by abasement.
The partridge and the falcon, all are high up in the sky, it is only we who lack wing and pinion.[8]

A sectarian minority like the Shia, who had few pretensions to power, provided a suitably depoliticized model of Muslim society for Sunni thinkers in colonial India. After all, the great drama of Shia history had to do with the sect's military defeat and the martyrdom of its leaders, all resulting in the establishment of a political order separated from religious authority, which was now vested in a messianic future. Whatever its historical validity, this account seems to have had a certain plausibility for Hali, who very deliberately patterned his epic poem on the elegies composed and recited by the Shia for their martyred imams. So the *Musaddas* was written in the same metrical form as the ritual elegy and made use of many of its narrative devices. It was from such disparate sources that the *ummah* was put together as a new kind of historical subject, one envisioned as a global society whose reach exceeded the bounds of any state. Indeed the history of its constitution can be traced quite minutely by looking at the way in which traditional poetic genres such as elegies on the imams or laments on the ruin of cities were transformed by Hali into a narrative of Muslim decadence, where the *ummah* was for the first time defined in sociological terms as a global community.

What is important about the new Muslim community is its elegiac character. And while this mournful vision of the *ummah* is often considered the consequence of colonial dispossession, I would like to argue for a more complex reading of the trope. For the narrative of Muslim decline pioneered by Hali is related to another common in Europe at the same time. This is the story of European decadence conceived not in political or juridical terms, exemplified by the fall of kingdoms and dynasties, but in the vision of exhausted civilizations and depleted races.[9] Like the *ummah*, in other words, race and civilization are categories that may incorporate state power but continue to embody a people's greatness beyond its confines. As a consequence they have since the eighteenth century also been global categories, whose context is provided by other civilizations and races spread across the surface of the earth. From Gobineau to Spengler, the modern history of this narrative coincides with that of Europe's greatest triumphs in domains ranging from the political to the scientific, so that it becomes impossible to see its story of decadence as a reflection of some general crisis there. Of course the groups who subscribed to such accounts might well have been the losers of this history, which still tells us little about why they interpreted it in global terms. Could it be that Muslim ideas of community in the age of imperialism, as much as Christian ones of civilization and race, were attempts to imagine sociological formations at a planetary level well beyond the jurisdiction of states?

By the nineteenth century race, civilization and religious community had become categories that took for their context the human race as such, though they could only do so by dividing it into a set of comparable and competitive sociological formations. And this meant that while humanity had abandoned its earlier roles of essence, abstraction and regulative ideal to provide the demographic background for such global categories, it still did not exist as a subject in its own right. So the narrative of decline characteristic of these new formations might well represent a degree of ambivalence about their lack of political reality as much as that of the species itself. For built into the categories of race, civilization and religious community during this period was the fantasy of encompassing humanity as a whole, either by a process of assimilation or within some kind of hierarchical order. Now the *ummah* imagined by writers like Hali dispensed with race and dealt with civilization only in a minor key, these categories existing uneasily in languages like Urdu merely as new glosses for older terms like lineage (*nasl*) or pedigree (*nasab*), habitation (*tamaddun*) or refinement (*tahzib*), none of which possessed a territorial character. Indeed the Muslim community was celebrated precisely for its ethnic and cultural diversity, and therefore seen as being more natural to the species than race and civilization. But as an expression of Islam's fidelity to nature, this kind of universality surpassed the *ummah*, constituting a line of flight towards the horizon of humanity. It was only in this fleeting way that the Muslim community could represent a species still lacking subjectivity.

3. Catching up to oneself

Like some of the narratives dealing with the decadence of races or civilizations, the story of Islam's decline was predicated upon the inability of its adherents to keep pace with their own universality. In making this case, of course, Hali was invoking an old literary model, in which the fall of kingdoms was attributed to the moral corruption of their rulers, itself a consequence of worldly success. More than the ancient kingdoms that had in the past provided such cautionary tales, it was the career of Christianity that now offered Muslims a warning about the perils of victory. At times India's Muslim writers saw in Christianity's very success a premonition of failure, with its religious spirit eclipsed by Europe's material glory in much the same way they thought had happened to Islam in the days of her imperial glory. It was not the reformers of the nineteenth century, however, but a writer from the twentieth who had the most to say on this issue. Acclaimed today as the spiritual father of Pakistan, Muhammad Iqbal argued that when Christian virtues were universalized in Europe to become secular values, they ended up perverting both religious and profane life there. So he thought that the division of liberal societies into public and private realms had as its premise the metaphysical distinction of matter and spirit, which turned religion into a merely individual ideal and gave collective life over to exploitation of every kind, thus bifurcating humanity into master and slave classes, races and even continents. As Iqbal put it in a speech from 1930:

> Europe uncritically accepted the duality of spirit and matter probably from Manichaean thought. Her best thinkers are realising this initial mistake today, but her statesmen are indirectly forcing the world to accept it as an unquestionable dogma. It is, then, this mistaken separation of spiritual and temporal which has largely influenced European religious and political thought and has resulted practically in the total exclusion of Christianity from the life of European states. The result is a set of mutually ill-adjusted states dominated by interests not human but national.[10]

Taking warning from the history of Christianity, Iqbal thought that Muslims should reclaim their lost universality by purifying Islam of the corruption wrought by its worldly success, which for him included ridding it of what he called 'the stamp of Arabian imperialism'. For, like Hali before him, Iqbal was ambivalent about Islam's history of worldly success, and thought that Muslims had the opportunity of rethinking the universality of their mission in its aftermath. He had this to say about Islam's post-imperial mission in a diary entry from 1910:

> As a political force we are perhaps no longer required; but we are, I believe, still indispensable to the world as the only testimony to the absolute unity of God. Our value among the nations, then, is purely evidential.[11]

Islam's post-imperial mission, however, was not to be a quietist one, but instead an effort to represent the species against the false claims of states both colonial and national. Muslim universality, in other words, was now to be found in the idea of human solidarity alone, and set against what Iqbal saw as the factional brutalities of nation-states in particular. He thought that nationality, or indeed any other form of collective identity, had to transcend territory if it was to coexist with other forms of self-definition within the human community. Islam's post-imperial universality, then, was supposed to aim precisely at this goal, which like that of communism or liberalism had to be ideological in nature:

> With us nationality is a pure *idea*; it has no material basis. Our only rallying point is a sort of mental agreement in a certain view of the world.[12]

While Muslim states might still exist and could even be cherished, Islam's abstract universality could no longer be grounded in them, being manifested rather in the adoption of a critical attitude to all politics. It was this purely human universality that Muslims had to recover, not simply from their own history but from the virtues of others as well. The many public figures who recommended such efforts of self-recovery often did so to draw attention to the virtues of Hindus or Christians and encourage Muslims to join them in some worthy enterprise. Thus, in the days before the Great War, the influential cleric turned journalist Abul Kalam Azad, who would go on to become president of the Indian National Congress and his country's first minister of education after its independence, wrote admiringly of the efforts that Hindus struggling against oppressive Indian traditions as much as against their British rulers expended in these efforts, which he identified as a jihad truer than the archaic one professed by Muslims. In the war's aftermath, when Gandhi launched his first great movement of non-cooperation, bringing Hindus and Muslims together in an unprecedented way, the famous satirical poet Akbar Illahabadi dedicated a laudatory mock epic to him. This *Gandhinamah* not only described the Mahatma's practice of non-violent resistance as manifesting the Islamic virtue of *sabr* or fortitude, which the poet considered to be more crucial than the ideals in vogue among Muslims themselves, he also represented the holy water that pilgrims bring back in bottles from Mecca finding its freedom by being poured into the sacred waters of the Ganges.[13]

Of course generalizing Islamic virtues beyond the Muslim community was an ambivalent process, since it could serve to promote cohabitation as much as competition with unbelievers. Two of Muhammad Iqbal's poems, probably the most popular Urdu compositions of the twentieth century, provide good examples of this. Among the many imitations of Hali's epic on the *ummah*'s decline, and composed in the same metre as the *Musaddas*, this pair of laments is regularly recited on Pakistani radio and television, with the country's most celebrated performers recording their own versions of it as a rite of passage. Published in 1909 and called *Shikwah* ('complaint'), the first work accuses God of abandoning Muslims for unbelievers by showering upon them the good things of the earth and leaving the former with a merely imaginary world.[14] This dereliction was all the more unjust given that Muslims had by means of great sacrifices freed men from slavery and spread the doctrine of human equality among them. Iqbal pictures idols rejoicing at the sight of Muslims departing the world with Qurans tucked under their arms, thus providing us with one of the first posthumous descriptions of Islam, a vision standing apart from earlier apocalyptic narratives concerned with the coming of the messiah and the end of time. He even goes so far as to call God a woman dispensing favours now to her Muslim lover and now to his infidel rivals. Deploying the erotic vocabulary of the traditional lyric to great effect, Iqbal turns the stock figure of the rival for a mistress's affection into that of the strangers who would replace Muslims as God's elect and the spokesmen of their race.

A few years after the publication of this acclaimed and controversial work, Iqbal wrote the *Jawab-e Shikwah* ('complaint's answer'), in which he had God respond to the first poem, thus claiming for his composition the status of divine speech.[15] In this heavenly monologue of 1913, Muslims are blamed for abandoning their duty to represent mankind not only by taking leave of world-making activities like science and industry, but more importantly by forsaking the quest for freedom and equality to live upon past glories, described as the worship of so many idols. If infidels adopt the ways of Muslims, says the poem's divine interlocutor, then it is only right that they should receive the damsels and palaces promised to believers. But Muslim decline is finally blamed on the modern age itself, likened to a fire that feeds on traditional communities, though its flames can purify religions as well as destroy them. To find, like Abraham did in Nimrod's torments, a garden in the midst of modernity's fire, Muslims must take charge of the stylus and tablet God resigns to them and write out their own destiny, forsaking Islam's political and doctrinal inheritance if they must as long as they remained loyal to the Prophet.

Muhammad Iqbal made it clear in this poem and elsewhere that the only thing keeping Muslims true to their religion's legacy was fidelity to the Prophet, who represented the historical origins of its universality. For in the apostle's claim to be God's final messenger Iqbal saw the emergence of humanity as an actor in its own right, one cut off from the leading strings of divine guidance and put in charge of its own destiny. The founding of Islam thus signalled the coming to maturity of the human race, with the Prophet renouncing divine authority to mankind in the same way that certain European writers thought Christ had done, by putting an end to God's action in the world and marking the beginning of human history.[16] In either case the old theme of God become man is reactivated, drawn as it is from a long Christian as well as Muslim history, and Iqbal went so far as to make man into God's partner if not successor by attributing divine creativity to him. Paradoxically it was the very particularity of this origin that served as a link to Islam's lost universality, whose other virtues had all escaped the grasp of religion to be generalized across the human race. Once Islam had ceased to provide a conceptual matrix for mankind's unity, therefore, it could only represent the species by such fragmentary acts as fidelity to Muhammad.

Perhaps it is because of Islam's fragmentation as a conceptual matrix that so much Muslim writing from this period obsessively presents Muhammad as the single most important proof of Islam's universality, because unlike any of the prophets who came before, he is described in the Quran as having been sent as 'a mercy to all mankind'. Crucial here is the fact that the word *alamin* in this scriptural citation, generally translated into Urdu and English alike as 'mankind', literally means 'the worlds', and traditionally referred either to different categories of beings, such as animals, angels and spirits, or to a combination of this world and the next, and certainly not simply to all human beings on the planet. It is only by flattening out and indeed secularizing the Quran's references to multiple universes and forms of life, in other words, that Islam could be modernized as the best of religions for a humanity portrayed as standing alone in its unique habitation. This turn to the Prophet as someone who provided by his very lack of miracles and other supernatural qualities a demonstration of Islam's call to humanity, had for Syed Ahmed Khan, his associates and followers merely illustrated Islam's fidelity to nature. For Iqbal, however, who cited the work of medieval Sufis as well as contemporary philosophers like Henri Bergson in putting forward a theory of spatial and temporal multiplicity, the reference to Muhammad being practically the creator of humanity as an actor in its own right meant that history had now replaced nature as the criterion of Muslim universality. Indeed he frequently criticized the world conceived of as an external reality, claiming that Islam set itself against the particularity of what he called nature's race-making work.¹⁷ So in an open letter to Jawaharlal Nehru in 1936 he had this to say:

> The student of history knows very well that Islam was born at a time when the old principles of human unification, such as blood relationship and throne-culture, were failing. It, therefore, finds the principle of human unification not in the blood and bones but in the mind of man. Indeed its social message to mankind is: 'Deracialise yourself or perish by internecine war.' It is no exaggeration to say that Islam looks askance at nature's race-building plans and creates by means of its peculiar institutions, an outlook which would counteract the race-building forces of nature.¹⁸

History had of course been a major preoccupation among Muslim writers from the nineteenth century, and Hali devoted a whole section of his *Musaddas* to its writing, though he judged such texts by their fidelity to nature, which was supposed to provide rational and objective criteria for historians. However, for Iqbal history not only housed the origin of Islam's universality but formed the substance of its character as well, since he thought that the human race had to achieve self-consciousness by setting itself against nature. In this way the *ummah* abandoned its relations with race and civilization to join ranks with twentieth-century ideologies, which meant that Islam was now set against liberalism or communism, whose politics of class conflict was to be rendered meaningless within its universal embrace. Yet this purely ideological foundation for human unity was by that very token remarkably vulnerable to attack, with Iqbal attributing Muslim conservatism, misplaced though it might be, to a glimmering recognition among the Prophet's followers that their religion and its universal mission was based upon nothing but a set of ideas:

> Islam repudiates the race idea altogether and founds itself on the religious idea alone. Since Islam bases itself on the religious idea alone, a basis which is wholly spiritual and consequently far more ethereal than blood relationship, Muslim society is naturally much more sensitive to forces which it considers harmful to its integrity.¹⁹

The very strength of Islam's universality, therefore, was paradoxically also its weakness, necessitating what might be called a fanatical attachment to the religious idea insofar as it cannot be naturalized or taken for granted. Iqbal's view of Islam here comes close to that of Hegel, who defined that religion's modernity precisely by its attachment to an abstract idea of universality. While Hegel paired Islam with the Enlightenment in his admiring criticism of its universal ideal, in our own times such an analysis has been directed more against twentieth-century ideologies like communism, also regarded as the Enlightenment's progeny. And so it is no accident that for Iqbal communism was Islam's greatest rival because it possessed a comparably universal mission. All of which only went to show that if the history of such ideas might be claimed by Islam, only the immense effort required to instantiate them could prevent the disintegration and theft of their universality.

4. The guilt of being still alive

Once Islamic concepts and categories are universalized in the language of humanity, moving outside the field of religious doctrine and practice, the Muslim community risks sinking into a particularity from which it must constantly be rescued. Lost within the universality of mankind, this community can only reclaim greatness by being faithful to the history of its founding. Even when this fidelity is so extensive as to determine the entirety of Muslim lives, as among fundamentalists, for example, it still possesses a minimal character. For such all-encompassing forms of Islam continue to remain self-conscious minorities in the world beyond fundamentalism. But what allows loyalty to grasp at the universal is precisely its fragmentary character, whose devotion to the past is conceived as a practice of withdrawal from the inevitable partialities of the present. And the present of course belongs to democracy, where men jostle to represent the interests of the greatest number, and Islam's universality takes on a new countenance. Instead of embarking upon the futile task of representing the interests of all men, or even all Muslims, a number of thinkers following Iqbal argued that such political forms were both morally suspect and in any case appropriate to states alone. Since the species cannot be represented politically, it is only the absence and indeed the sacrifice of particular interests, and therefore of politics itself in its conventional sense, that might capture its unity. Or, to put it in Iqbal's own words:

> I am opposed to nationalism as it is understood in Europe, not because, if it is allowed to develop in India, it is likely to bring less material gain to Muslims. I am opposed to it because I see in it the germs of an atheistic materialism which I look upon as the greatest danger to modern humanity.[20]

Like Ayman al-Zawahiri's Hippocratic ideal, the kind of loyalty broached by Muhammad Iqbal is thus sacrificial in form, claiming to abandon the self-interest that defines politics by pointing to the disinterestedness of its practices. And so it is no longer the contested claim to some common interest that defines humanity, but rather its negation for a set of ideals and historical peculiarities that appear meaningless in the calculus of interests defining political representation. Islam has therefore come to represent mankind by sacrificing the very possibility of interest in the supposedly archaic demands it makes upon Muslims, for instance regarding forms of dress or comportment, whose antiquated provenance and incomprehensibility to modern minds only guarantee their impartial character. The turn to history, in other words, has little to do with the romance and nostalgia that are characteristic of nationalist approaches to the past, and is certainly not an effort to 'put the clock back', as fundamentalism's liberal critics assert. For it is precisely because the culture of Islam's origin is dead that its habits can be universalized into a kind of technical routine freed of particularity and therefore political interest. Indeed this form of Muslim devotion rejects the very idea of culture to focus on abstract and dislocated practices that make religion into something fully portable and universally convertible.[21]

Such at least was the argument put forward by the Pakistani fundamentalist Abul Ala Maududi, who supplemented the older naturalization of Islam's universality with this new faith in the resources of history. Thus he contended that the more resistant Muslim practices were to the rationality of political representation, the less likely would their misuse be in the politics of class or ethnic particularity.[22] Taking up Muhammad Iqbal's concern with the finality of prophethood, Maududi and his political party, the Jamaat-e Islami, criticized the Shia and Sufis, whose reverence for spiritual leaders coming after the Prophet was held to compromise the latter's role in barring all access to divine authority. For it was only by putting a stop to God's intervention in the present that humanity could become a historical actor, if only in the disinterested practice of what had in fact become a dead religion. Maududi's particular ire was reserved for the Ahmadis, an Indian movement founded in the nineteenth century that claimed its founder to be the recipient of divine revelation. Like Iqbal before him, who thought Ahmadi teachings about the continuity of divine grace undermined Islam's historical role in representing humanity, Maududi spearheaded a violent campaign against them in Pakistan that eventually resulted in the Ahmadis being declared non-Muslims, for in effect bringing God back to life in the revelations that he was supposed to have vouchsafed the movement's founder. After all, since Ahmadis are as rigorous about following the inherited practices of Islam as the most orthodox of Sunnis, it was not any threat they posed these devotions that was feared, so much as their perceived attack on humanity itself as a historical subject. And it was to safeguard this freedom that Maududi made neutrality and disinterest into touchstones of Islam's universality by focusing on a life lived for the sake of God alone. For these attitudes are only possible once the deity has been expelled from history and his apostles' injunctions have assumed the form of so much detritus, whose everyday functionality or beneficial consequences cannot overshadow their pointlessness as the remains of a past long gone.

If in Maududi's eyes Muslims could represent the human race by sacrificing their particular interests and living for the sake of God alone, today's militants concentrate on death in God's way as the only kind of sacrifice capable of representing humanity. Like the otherwise very different Muslim thinkers and movements I have already described, terrorist argumentation is marked by the familiarity and even intimacy with which it approaches those seen as the enemies of Islam. So al-Qaeda's foes were considered to be people of the same kind as its friends, their supposed persecution of Muslims being reciprocated by the latter in procedures of mirroring that made it difficult to tell one from the other. Instead of dehumanizing their enemies, or even condemning them to subhuman status in the name of race or civilization, militants routinely aspired to compete with such foes in virtue as well as vice, something we have seen in Zawahiri's utterances quoted above. But without defining humanity by means of a hierarchy, Osama bin Laden's acolytes were unable to establish any firm distinction between friends and enemies. So refusing to take responsibility for acts of violence, by describing these merely as responses to infidel provocation, does more than excuse such crimes. It serves to account for the dispersal of responsibility in a global arena where all are complicit in crimes against humanity, whether these are concerned with environmental degradation or genocide. Not accidentally the only act militants claimed full responsibility for was the minimal yet excessive one of martyrdom. Sacrifice therefore became the only distinctive element in al-Qaeda's rhetoric, which otherwise shared everything with its foes.

Not the common virtues and vices of men, therefore, but the claim to martyrdom was what demonstrated Islam's universality in militant circles, though even such practices of sacrifice could be stolen from Muslims and so had to be repeated in the most egregious of ways. And martyrdom was crucial because humanity cannot be represented in any positive fashion, lacking as it does a political or juridical form despite being invoked by lawyers and statesmen at every turn. As the supposed abnegation of all particularity and interest, sacrifice constituted a kind of negative embodiment of the race. It provided in fact the most appropriate manifestation of this mysterious being, which exists without having become a subject in the global arena. But such an embodiment of the species is not peculiar to Muslim terrorists, and may be found in the sacrificial practices of many who dedicate themselves to humanitarian causes, from pacifists and environmentalists to those engaged in aid and relief work. Indeed the idea of sacrificing oneself for humanity has a long and explicitly Christian history, having become common sense in the story of Jesus as a martyr not for God's sake but that of mankind. Representing as they do the most excessive forms of sacrifice, militant acts of martyrdom may be said to have placed themselves at the vanguard of all such procedures of embodiment.

The philosopher Karl Jaspers was perhaps the first to see varieties of sacrifice like martyrdom as efforts to trace the lineaments of a species that could not otherwise be represented. In a lecture of 1945 subsequently published under the title *The Question of German Guilt*, Jaspers distinguished traditional forms of guilt such as the moral, political and criminal from something he called metaphysical guilt. This last, he said, was felt by those who were innocent of wrongdoing in all its conventional senses but continued, nevertheless, to accuse themselves of living while others had died under Nazi rule. Though he took Germany as his example of a place in which metaphysical guilt had come to the fore, Jaspers was clear that fascism and the war it occasioned provided only the origins of this widespread phenomenon, which arose out of the fact that responsibility could no longer be confined to particular individuals or groups in events like the Second World War, and belonged instead to the history of mankind:

> It is only now that history has finally become world history – the global history of mankind. So our own situation can be grasped only together with the world-historical one. What has happened today has its causes in general human events and conditions, and only secondarily in special intra-national relations and the decisions of single groups of men.[23]

The problem, of course, is that humanity has no political or juridical status and thus does not exist as a subject of history. Yet it cannot be said to be a fiction either, and Jaspers tells us that metaphysical guilt is a sign of the race's otherwise invisible solidarity, betraying as it does a consciousness of shared responsibilities in the global arena brought to light by the war:

> Metaphysical guilt is the lack of absolute solidarity with the human being as such – an indelible claim beyond morally meaningful duty. This solidarity is violated by my presence at a wrong or a crime. It is not enough that I cautiously risk my life to prevent it; if it happens, and if I was there, and if I survive where the other is killed, I know from a voice within myself: I am guilty of being still alive.[24]

Going beyond all moral, legal and political determinations of responsibility, metaphysical guilt invokes the species as a potential subject of history, if only by the desire to die in its name. For dying alone provides access to its negative being. Jaspers points out that such examples of unconditioned sacrifice are to be found, and are indeed celebrated, at the level of the family or between lovers, the source of metaphysical guilt being that they are not available, or very rarely so, at a purely human level:

> That somewhere among men the unconditioned prevails – the capacity to live only together or not at all, if crimes are committed against the one or the other, or if physical living requirements have to be shared – therein consists the substance of their being. But that this does not extend to the solidarity of all men, nor to that of fellow-citizens or even of smaller groups, but remains confined to the closest human ties – therein lies this guilt of us all.[25]

By confining his analysis to the guilt of being alive, Karl Jaspers is able to deal with death in the form of desire alone, thus mitigating its Christian thematic. I would like to suggest, however, that al-Qaeda's practice of martyrdom acted upon this desire to answer the call of an invisible humanity, for which its militants were willing to kill as much as die. Osama bin Laden's rhetoric, for instance, consistently voiced a desire for global equality, in this case that between Muslims and Christians, or between the Islamic world and the West. Having accused America of hypocrisy as far as its advancement of this equality is concerned, bin Laden turned his attention to the only form in which he thought such freedom is possible: the equality of death. This was why he repeatedly emphasized the need for an equivalence of terror between the Muslim world and America, as if this were the only form in which the two might come together and even communicate one with the other. For al-Qaeda, terror was the only form in which global freedom and equality were now available. It therefore functioned as the dark side of America's own democracy, as inseparable from it as an evil twin. So in the aftermath of the 2005 Madrid bombings, bin Laden issued a statement in which he defined terrorism as an effort to universalize security as a human right, if only by refusing to accept its monopolization by the West. For equality demanded that security should be enjoyed by all or by none:

> It is well known that security is a vital necessity for every human being. We will not let you monopolize it for yourselves.[26]

In all this bin Laden did nothing more than recognize the unity of a globe in which no man can be separated from any other, each one being held responsible for his fellows, with whose suffering he must identify. Such is the humanitarian logic that characterizes global movements like environmentalism and pacifism as well. But among militants this unity was made manifest by violence, which built a bridge between enemies by demonstrating that all men are equal if in death alone. It is as if this macabre equivalence had replaced the equality that is supposed to exist between men and unite them as part of a single humanity. The militant's violence, then, ironically linked the world's people together in a web of mutual obligation and responsibility. It was this web of universal complicity, after all, that allowed American or British civilians to be killed in recompense for the killing of Muslims in Iraq.

The worldwide web of war spun by al-Qaeda existed as a kind of spectre of our global interrelatedness, one that has as yet no specific political form of its own. And the militant's obsessive demands for equal treatment within this world, even if it be only in the form of a reciprocity of violence, represented the dark side of humanity's global brotherhood, whose reality is the product of our increasingly interconnected universe. But this meant that the same web of responsibilities and obligations linking the holy war to its enemies also linked them together as a community, even as a community of brothers. For were not al-Qaeda's victims said to be merely the counterparts of innocent Muslims killed elsewhere? They were therefore in some perverse way brothers at one remove, made even more like brothers by dying alongside suicide bombers and mingling blood.

In the global perspective adopted by militant Islam, the peoples of the world are bound together in a web of mutual relations and complicities. For the moment this intimacy expresses itself in the most murderous way, though even here it represents what I have referred to as the dark side of another, more benign kind of relationship, like that of universal brotherhood. Indeed al-Qaeda's actions and rhetoric continuously invoked the spectre of a global community that has as yet no formal existence of its own. And this is what allowed its war to draw upon the forms and even the vocabulary of other global movements such as environmental and pacifist ones, all of which are concerned with the fate of humanity as a whole. In his more ironical moments, Osama bin Laden took this language of global community so far as to put al-Qaeda and its American enemy on the same side of their mutual war, saying in a 2004 video that the Bush administration's invasion of Iraq for power and profits contributed to the terror network's own aims:

> To some analysts and diplomats, it seems as if we and the White House are on the same team shooting at the United States' own goal, despite our different intentions.[27]

> It truly shows that al-Qaeda has made gains, but on the other hand it also shows that the Bush administration has likewise profited.[28]

Al-Qaeda's militants exhibited a perverse humanity by addressing their victims in the language of intimacy, reciprocity and equivalence. That this was not a merely rhetorical gesture becomes evident when we consider that such militancy, unlike all previous forms of terrorist or insurgent action, refused to set up an alternative utopia for itself, something that even anarchists are not immune to. Unlike the members of religious cults or fringe political groups, few of al-Qaeda's killers displayed signs of entering some closed ideological world, by cutting themselves off from their families or everyday life. This suggests that the Islam they sought to defend was not conceived as an ideology at all, because it did not provide a complete or alternative vision of the world into which the would-be bomber can retreat, as into a fortress. Thus bin Laden defined his own militancy merely as the obverse of the violence he attributed to the West, his refusal to claim autonomy for jihad making for a curious identity between Muslims and their enemies:

> Since we have reacted in kind, your description of us as terrorists and of our actions as terrorism necessarily means that you and your actions must be defined likewise.[29]

Apart from strictly operational agreements, there was little unity of doctrine even between Osama bin Laden and his lieutenant, Ayman al-Zawahiri, while the religion they followed possessed no established tradition, being made up of fragments snatched from differing Islamic authorities. There were at most very general patterns of thought that were neither codified nor propagated in any systematic way. Instead of being recruited to a well-defined movement, the jihad's disparate soldiers franchised al-Qaeda's expertise and brand name for a variety of equally disparate causes that existed comfortably within the structures of everyday life. Rather than offering an alternative to the world as it exists, these militants would transform it by a kind of internal convulsion, bringing forth its latent humanity by their acts of sacrifice.

Earlier movements of resistance or terror had advanced critiques of existing conditions, such as capitalism or imperialism, and offered alternatives to them. This was the case with communists and anarchists as well as nationalists and fundamentalists. Like the more pacific global movements that are its peers, al-Qaeda offered no real criticism of existing conditions (apart from inveighing against them) and possessed no alternative to take their place. Deprived of the political and ideological unity available to regional or national movements, these latter-day militants lived scattered among their enemies, whom they accuse only of heedlessness and hypocrisy. So Americans were accused of believing in the wrong religion or ideology, as of being heedless and hypocritical about the beliefs they do hold. Global movements like al-Qaeda want not an alternative to America so much as the fulfilment of America's promise of freedom for all. Indeed by dying alongside their victims, Islam's militants demonstrated that they existed in the same world as these latter, and as members of the same humanity.

For whatever the political calculations of al-Qaeda and other movements that value sacrifice, their rhetoric of dedication to the species was founded upon metaphysical guilt alone. How else did Osama bin Laden's minions justify their acts of violence if not by invoking the guilt of living while others die? These others were not the terrorist's relatives, friends or even countrymen, but unknown people in unknown lands, who by their suffering represent the race's victimization and lack of historical subjectivity. Indeed the global Muslim community serves as a kind of model of humanity insofar as it, too, possesses neither political nor juridical reality, and exists for militants only in the spectacle of its apparent victimization. Dying for Islam, as much as killing in its name, meant acknowledging the existence of Muslim solidarity around the world, and in the same moment the solidarity of the species as well. For in the end it was their unfettered hold over the language and practice of sacrifice that allowed militants to represent their own community together with the human race itself as historical subjects, both of which enjoy the curious distinction of existing without existing in the global arena that came into being after the Second World War.

Notes

1. Ayman al-Zawahiri, 'Selected questions and answers from Dr. Ayman al-Zawahiri – part 2 released on: April 17, 2008', *The Nefa Foundation*, p. 8, URL http://www.actforamericaeducation.com/downloads/All_Files_by_Type/nefazawahiri0508-2.pdf (accessed 13 March 2015).
2. Ibid.
3. Ibid., p. 7.
4. Ibid.
5. Ibid., p. 8.
6. Sayyid Ahmad Khan, *Muqaddimah-e Tafsir-e Sir Sayyid*, Patna: Khuda Bakhsh Oriental Public Library, 1995.
7. Altaf Husain Hali, *Hali's Musaddas: The Flow and Ebb of Islam*, trans. C. Shackle and J. Majeed, Delhi: Oxford University Press, 1997, p. 163.
8. Ibid., pp. 145–6.
9. Michel Foucault, *Society Must be Defended: Lectures at the College de France 1975–1976*, trans. D. Macey, New York: Picador, 2003.
10. Muhammad Iqbal, *Thoughts and Reflections of Iqbal*, Lahore: Sh. Muhammad Ashraf, 1992, pp. 163–4.
11. Muhammad Iqbal, *Stray Reflections*, Lahore: Sh. Ghulam Ali and Sons, 1961, p. 15.
12. Ibid., p. 24.
13. Akbar Illahabadi, *Gandhinamah*, Allahabad: Kitabistan, 1948.
14. Muhammad Iqbal, 'Shikwah', in *Kulliyat-e Iqbal Urdu*, Delhi: Educational Publishing House, 2001, pp. 163–9.
15. Muhammad Iqbal, 'Jawab-e Shikwah', in *Kulliyat-e Iqbal Urdu*, Delhi: Educational Publishing House, 2001, pp. 200–8.
16. Muhammad Iqbal, *The Reconstruction of Religious Thought in Islam*, New Delhi: Kitab Bhavan, 1990, p. 126.
17. Iqbal, *Thoughts and Reflections*, pp. 304–26.

18. Ibid., p. 285.
19. Ibid., pp. 248–9.
20. Ibid., pp. 196–7.
21. Olivier Roy, *Globalised Islam*, London: Hurst, 2005.
22. Sayyid Abul Ala Maududi, 'Musalmanon ka Mazi-o Hal awr Mustaqbal', in *Islami Nizam-e Zindagi*, Lahore: Islamic Publications, 1962.
23. Karl Jaspers, *The Question of German Guilt*, trans. E. B. Ashton, New York: Capricorn Books, 1961, pp. 23–4.
24. Ibid., p. 71.
25. Ibid., p. 32.
26. Bruce Lawrence, ed., *Messages to the World: The Statements of Osama Bin Laden*, London: Verso, 2005, p. 234.
27. Ibid., p. 242.
28. Ibid.
29. Ibid., p. 234.

PART VI
HISTORICAL FUTURES WITHOUT DIRECTION?

CHAPTER 15
AUTONOMY IN HISTORY: TELEOLOGY IN NINETEENTH-CENTURY EUROPEAN SOCIAL AND POLITICAL THOUGHT
Peter Wagner

The nineteenth century is the period of the rise of Europe to world domination.[1] At its dawn stood local events of supposed 'universal significance', to paraphrase Max Weber, namely the French Revolution and what came to be called the Industrial Revolution; and at its end the European governments were dividing the territory of Africa up among themselves as if no one living there had anything to say about this. It should not come as a surprise that, witnessing the transformations over this period, European thinkers were reflecting about the course of history, or more precisely, that they were embedding their reflections on philosophy, politics and economics into thoughts – in the form of assumptions, observations and/or conclusions – about the direction of history. It should not even be surprising, given the change in the global position of Europe during this period, that they saw past history as moving towards them and future history taking off from them. History had a direction, so it seemed, and it could be identified from a European angle.

The resulting phenomenon is known as the inclination towards teleology in European thought. It has long been identified, widely been criticized and denounced, but much less analysed in detail, as the editors of this volume point out in their introduction. In the strong sense of the term, namely that human social life on earth evolves towards an endpoint, a final state, towards which it is driven by some compelling dynamics or logics, teleological thinking can easily be criticized for its lack of ability to convincingly demonstrate that this is so, or why this should be so. However, every significant current of thought addresses an underlying problem, sometimes in a concealed way; and the effective criticism of untenable propositions most often does not do away with the problem that was being addressed. In this light, this chapter will search for the underlying problem rather than discussing whether particular authors or texts engage in teleological reasoning or not.

The following reflections are illustrated with the help of a very small number of sources, namely German-language texts in what we now often call social and political philosophy, more precisely key writings by Immanuel Kant, Karl Marx and Max Weber. The choice of subject area is motivated by the insight, to be detailed below, that the underlying problem is of a sociopolitical nature. More specifically, it emerges from the distinction between political and social matters that was increasingly made after the double revolution mentioned at the outset. The focus on German-language texts, in turn, invites more nuanced reflections about the contexts in which teleological thinking arises.

Historical Teleologies in the Modern World

European thought showed an inclination towards teleology during the nineteenth century, but not all European thought equally so. Finally, and following up on the preceding remark, the selection of these authors and texts, reaching across all of the 'long nineteenth century', permits reflections on differences in forms of teleology at different moments in time.[2]

1. Immanuel Kant's plan of nature: hope or despair

Immanuel Kant's *Idea for a Universal History from a Cosmopolitan Point of View* of 1784 has often been seen as proposing a teleological view of history, namely the realization of a 'plan of nature' across human history, and it is apparently easy to see why.

> Whatever concept one may hold, from a metaphysical point of view, concerning the freedom of the will, certainly its appearances, which are human actions, like every other natural event are determined by universal laws. However obscure their causes, history, which is concerned with narrating these appearances, permits us to hope that if we attend to the play of freedom of the human will in the large, we may be able to discern a regular movement in it, and that what seems complex and chaotic in the single individual may be seen from the standpoint of the human race as a whole to be a steady and progressive though slow evolution of its original endowment.[3]

These are the opening sentences of the text, and the expression of teleology could not be clearer, as it seems at first sight: there is an 'original endowment' that evolves towards fulfilling its purpose in a 'steady and progressive' way, albeit slowly. This conclusion, however, is dependent on conditions – 'if we attend to the play of human freedom in the large' – and even with the conditions fulfilled remains a hope – 'permits us to hope' – and a mere possibility – 'may be able to … may be' – to discover and recognize – 'discern … be seen' – something that otherwise is not evident at all.[4] At a closer look, thus, Kant does not claim at all that history is on a steady and progressive path; in the face of the apparent complexity and chaos he explores the conditions of possibility for identifying such a path, if any.

Let us continue that analysis, therefore, with the condition as put at the outset: 'if we attend to the play of human freedom in the large'. We need to consider the components step by step, first 'human freedom', and then its play 'in the large'. Today we are not surprised that the philosopher who defined Enlightenment as exit from self-incurred immaturity should start his reflections on history with human freedom – but maybe we should be. This assumption mirrors, true, one of Kant's core convictions. However, it also constituted his major problem, in this text and elsewhere. If human beings truly exercise their free will, there is little we can know about the outcome of this exercise. As Edmund Burke would say a few – significant – years later, in 1790: 'The effect of liberty to individuals is that they may *do* what they *please*; we ought to see what it will *please them to do*, before we risk congratulations.'[5] Kant was more audacious than his English contemporary at that moment, but he, too, was far from believing that the combination of freedom with reason would necessarily lead to a both predictable and beneficial result, as stereotypical representations of the Enlightenment have it. The key 'sociological' section of *Idea for a Universal History* (clause 4) emphasizes the ambivalent, even contradictory inclinations of human beings, termed 'unsocial sociability': to be together with other human beings and to isolate themselves from others.[6] And the following clauses are full of terms designating war, strife, greed, vanity, chaos and unruliness as a consequence of the antagonism between human beings.

To change the picture, Kant mobilizes the second part of his condition. Moving beyond the miserable detail and looking 'in the large', all the discord can be shown to have a purpose.[7] The 'resistance', namely, that human beings encounter through other human beings 'awakes all forces' in them, 'makes them overcome their laziness and … gain a rank among [their] fellow human beings'. As a result of this activity, 'the first true steps from rawness to culture' are taken; 'all talents are gradually developed; the sense of taste is formed'; and continued enlightenment can then even mark the beginning of the foundation of society as a moral whole. Thus, Kant describes the mechanism, as current analytical sociology would call it, that turns human actions into collective outcomes beyond the intention of the actors. Kant's summary of this insight takes again apparently strong teleological form: '*The means which nature employs to bring about the development of innate capacities is that of antagonism in society, in so far as this antagonism becomes in the long run the cause of a law-governed social order.*'[8] Here we have the plan of nature that avails itself of the means to realize the purpose of humankind, to bring about a desirable end-state of history.

At this point, we need to look at the architecture of Kant's reasoning to go beyond the surface of meaning. In clause 1, Kant starts out with a teleological assumption: everything in nature has a purpose. Human beings, although having the particularity of being endowed with reason, are part of nature. Therefore, human history must have a purpose. In this light, the particularity of the human condition is investigated further up to the culmination in clause 4, as detailed above. Then, however, the problems start. Clauses 5 to 7 look into the details of reaching the law-governed order, which is the end-state of history, and consider this as a 'problem' that humanity needs to solve. Kant is painfully aware of the conceptual and historical issues at stake in turning unbound freedom into rule-governed order (clause 5), both domestically (clause 6) and in inter-polity relations (clause 7). The conclusions of this exercise are found in clauses 8 and 9.

The summary heading of clause 8 states: '*The history of mankind can be seen, in the large, as the realization of Nature's secret plan to bring forth a perfectly constituted state as the only condition in which the capacities of mankind can be fully developed, and also bring forth that external relation among states which is perfectly adequate to this end.*' At the risk of being tiresome, I want to underline that 'can' neither means 'is' nor 'has to', but 'is possible', and, by implication, that this is one of several possibilities of seeing the history of humankind. As Dipesh Chakrabarty has said about Marx, Kant 'does not so much provide us with a teleology of history as with a perspectival point from which to read the archives'.⁹ The body text then tries to illustrate the grounds for this particular possibility with selected examples[10] and concludes by saying that this selection 'gives hope' that nature's ultimate purpose may at some point be fulfilled.

That this hope is the 'guiding thread' of Kant's exercise becomes even clearer in clause 9, the summary heading of which states: '*A philosophical attempt to work out a universal history according to a natural plan directed to achieving the civic union of the human race must be regarded as possible and, indeed, as contributing to this end of Nature.*' Now this way of looking at human history no longer 'is possible' but 'must be possible'. Why 'must' we embark on this project that Kant himself describes in the following sentence as 'strange and apparently silly'? What is the alternative? Kant is quite clear: the alternative is despair. To adopt his guiding thread will provide 'a consoling view of the future (which could not be reasonably hoped for without the presupposition of a natural plan)'; and without it we would be 'forced to turn our eyes from [the history of humanity] in disgust, doubting that we can ever find a perfectly rational purpose in it and hoping for that only in another world'. Thus, Kant's philosophy of history does not aim at historical truth, or even intelligibility; it aims in the first instance at consolation at the sight of the actual world.

Secondly, though, there is also practical benefit in the exercise, as indicated at the end of clause 9's summary: 'contributing to this end of Nature'. Kant does believe that a review of positive experiences in human history, as briefly given in the body text of clause 8, can enlighten collective action, or the action of rulers, in the present and thus enhance the prospect for a better future. If there is an end to human history, therefore, it is not in any plan of nature, as we would normally understand this term,[11] but it can be gathered by current 'philosophical attempts' to review human history, using the faculty of reason they are endowed with, with the objective of finding an answer to the question of living well together while accepting the other's autonomy.

Thus, the 'plan of nature' is nothing that is effective without human beings contributing to it, no external device that drives human history, the latter understood as the sum of all human actions. It is something that can be detected by a 'philosophical attempt' in history, understood as 'concerned with narrating the[se] appearances' of human actions.

The purpose of the plan of nature, thus, is something that this philosophical attempt itself needs to provide – and Kant saw himself working towards that end. Using current terminology, Kant introduces a distinction between the social and the political. The social existence of human beings is marked by their unsocial sociability, their ambivalent inclinations that they cannot overcome as singular human beings. The plan of nature, in turn, is to be read as the outline of a separate political theory that receives its guidance from reason, and not from the human inclination towards unsocial sociability itself. Rather than for substantive philosophies of history, Kant thus contributes to preparing the ground for a (rational, normative) political theory that takes its distance from the social. Starting out from the assumption of human freedom, of autonomy, and seeing the need to contain the consequences of autonomy by elaborating universal norms, his 'antagonistic' social philosophy turns towards – what we would now call – a liberal proceduralism.

2. Karl Marx's history of class struggle: socialism or barbarism

Half a century later, historical experiences suggested that this answer should be qualified. In the view of many observers, the combined effect of the political and economic transformations since the late eighteenth century had created a sociopolitical situation that, on the one side, confirmed Kant's (and in general the Enlightenment's) assumption that sociopolitical arrangements are constituted by human beings through their actions. On the other side, however, experiences with such arrangements had suggested that regularities were emerging as the outcome of human action. In the first attempt at defining his term 'in the large', Kant had indeed referred to marriages, births and deaths (!) as being subject to human freedom but nevertheless showing statistical regularities beyond the intentions of individual human beings. This is the core presupposition of the then emerging social-science mode of reasoning. In *formal* terms, it is a reasoning about social structures as the 'unintended consequences' of human action, as Robert Merton would put it much later, and as such it is already present in Kant as the distinction between what human beings want and what 'nature' makes them bring about.

Kant, though, at the time of writing, remained rather agnostic about the *substantive* (for want of a better term) outcome of the sum of human actions. His social ontology remained limited to the theorem of unsocial sociability. To resolve the problems arising from such human inclinations, he stepped out of the social realm and resorted to political institutions, and he reasoned about them in terms of conditions of possibility. Furthermore, he had no view of any temporal dynamics in the play of those human inclinations. They appear as an anthropological constant. The temporal dynamics that we find in his writings – the reason why we can refer to them as philosophy of history – is entirely related to the detection of the plan of nature, as discussed above, thus to progress on the way to a moral order of society. This would change radically in the course of the first half of the nineteenth century.

Maintaining the basic assumptions of late eighteenth-century thought, scholars became increasingly convinced that one could see and know more about the sociopolitical transformations by the mid-nineteenth century. Alexis de Tocqueville analysed the social impact of democracy, and he advanced a partial teleology when he suggested that (what we now call) democratization would not come to a halt before equal universal suffrage was reached.[12] Lorenz von Stein observed the emergence of 'social movements' in response to the economic changes related to the liberty of commerce and the rise of a market economy.[13] In both cases, the creation of specific institutional conditions for human freedom – the political vote and the economic right to buy and sell – were seen as having unleashed an unintended and unforeseen social dynamics that would need to be taken into account when considering the conditions for, to speak in Kant's terms, establishing a moral order.

The scholar who developed such a mode of thinking most forcefully at this moment, though, was Karl Marx. For Marx, the unintendedly produced structures were the capitalist mode of production with new antagonistic classes. Rather than equally free economic actors, the new sociopolitical order produced a radical divide between those who owned the means of production and those who did not. The dynamics was unleashed by market competition, as indeed foreseen and intended by classical political economy, and by class struggle, which was at the centre of Marx's political concerns.[14] Such a combination of structure and dynamics does not necessarily lead to teleological thinking. For Adam Smith, for example, freedom of commerce and division of labour would enhance the wealth of nations. There is a direction of history under this condition, but the reasoning is causal and there is no end-point. But, again, this was considerably earlier, and the experiences of the nineteenth century appeared to both require and enable stronger statements.

Having witnessed economic crises and the deterioration of the conditions of the working classes, Marx thought he was recognizing clear trends of historical change. Well acquainted with Hegel's thought (see Bo Stråth's contribution to this volume), he was also able to consider end-points of certain trends, the reaching of which would lead to a change of direction. Combining economic analysis and philosophy of history with political analysis, he elaborated his particular teleological view that foresaw movement towards the point of unsustainability of the capitalist mode of production, for reasons of both competition and class struggle, and subsequently the emergence of a new historical horizon, entirely open and to be determined by free human beings in free association.

In other words, the Kantian problem is clearly recognizable in Marx's writings. Like Kant, Marx was committed to human agency, and similarly he recognized the 'antagonism' in human social relations. For him, though, the negative consequences of this antagonism could not be overcome by an institutional design pulled from a selective reading of historical experiences. The structures and dynamics that he identified were too powerful for such a hope. But, following Kant's 'methodology', he searched through such dynamics to identify the prospect for positive change. For the relation between agency and phenomena 'in the large', this now required the situating of agency within the course of the dynamics that had been unleashed.

The tension between human agency, on the one hand, and the identification of determining structures and dynamics, on the other, is an unresolved dilemma in Marx's writings. Towards the end of the nineteenth century, it led to the peculiar political phenomenon of 'revolutionary attentism' in German social democracy, the combination of a revolutionary, that is, highly agential self-understanding with the perceived need to wait passively until history will have brought forth the revolutionary moment.[15] What I want to underline for present purposes is that this tension is never entirely absent in Marx. As close as he comes at points to embracing an exemplary teleological way of thinking, he never entirely adopts it.

In the sober analysis of *Capital*, to take one example, which as a 'critique of political economy' aims at uncovering the contradictions of a capitalist mode of production, the 'tendency of the rate of profit to fall' has often been taken as the core argument for demonstrating the inescapably self-destructive tendencies of capitalism. However, Marx adds to this analysis the enumeration of 'countervailing factors', many of which can contingently arise at any moment and lead to a transformation of capitalism – possibly both unintended and unforeseen – rather than its end.

Autonomy in History

In political pamphlets, the expression of the tension between a compelling driving force of history and the intervention of human agency can take dramatic shape. It is widely accepted that the *Communist Manifesto* of 1848, co-authored with Friedrich Engels, is a document of historical teleology in which class struggle drives history towards communism at its end-point. The fact that both the bourgeoisie, historically, and the proletariat, for the future, are hailed for their heroic actions does not change the view because the activities of both classes are effective and successful in as far as they are in harmony with the course of history. This common reading, however, overlooks the doubts that Marx and Engels, too, had about the history of humanity. At the very beginning of the pamphlet, but nevertheless mostly overlooked, we find the conjecture that class struggle may also end – indeed, sometimes ended – with the 'common ruin of the contending classes'.[16] This theme of defeat and disaster, though marginal, has never disappeared from the Marxian tradition. In 1915, Rosa Luxemburg analysed the world-historical situation after the beginning of the First World War and the vote of German social-democratic members of the *Reichstag* in favour of war loans, in terms of a stark alternative: 'either transition to socialism or regression into barbarism'.[17] Ultimately, Marx and those who followed him do not claim to know the course of history, because human beings can always act otherwise.

3. Max Weber's 'dwelling-place of steel': old ideas and new prophets

Another half-century later, European world domination was at its apex, celebrated in a series of widely attended and debated World Fairs, among them the one of 1893 in Chicago, which Max Weber had wished to attend. Weber went way beyond his usual cautious way of expressing himself when, a few decades later, he claimed 'universal significance' for cultural occurrences in the West, in these, much-quoted, terms: 'what concatenation of circumstances has led to the fact that in the Occident, and here only, cultural phenomena have appeared which – as at least *we* like to imagine – lie in a direction of development of *universal* significance and validity?'[18] Every key word of this sentence is important: Weber indeed talks about a 'direction of development of universal significance and validity'; it seems teleology could hardly be expressed more clearly. But at the beginning of his account he situates a 'concatenation of circumstances', thus something rather contingent; and these entangled circumstances do not create, initiate, generate and perpetuate the direction of development, as one might expect, but just happen to 'lie' on its path – a verb in a highly important place whose meaning here is difficult to grasp.[19] It may have been exactly the vagueness of the term that made the author select it; other verbs might have had too strong connotations. And any interpreter should get even more deeply frustrated when they start to ponder the parenthesis 'as at least we like to imagine' – 'we' must be the Westerners, but if the Westerners only imagine (fancy) the significance and validity of this direction of development, what about its *actual* significance and validity? Most readers of this passage have preferred to ignore the parenthesis.

Weber is the most important analyst of the rise of occidental rationalism. In terms of his philosophy of social science and methodology, at the same time, he is the one among the 'classical' sociologists who was least inclined to postulate laws of social change or the existence of large-scale social phenomena that determine human action. Human beings and the ways in which they give meaning to their lives and their relations to others were at the focus of his approach. His ambition was to reach an understanding of large-scale, long-term durable social phenomena ('in the large', as Kant put it) starting out from the meaningful action of human beings. *The Protestant Ethic*, with all its flaws, remains a highly instructive document for – maybe a monument to – such an attempt.

For the purpose of our reasoning here, the key observation on this text is this: Weber starts out from the way human beings – individuals whom he quotes at length, but also a group of human beings linked to each other by a common world view, a social ethics – give meaning to their lives, and then demonstrates how the actions they pursue in relation to their world-interpretation transforms the world in such a way that further work at giving meaning is neither necessary nor effective in any way: 'the spirit has escaped from the cage'.[20] Subsequently, Weber talks about the mechanical foundations of victorious capitalism and uses temporal expressions such as 'no longer' and 'finally'. This has supported the teleological interpretation of Weber's view on rationalization, as later taken up by Talcott Parsons, and the sociology of 'modernization and development'. But Weber's views have given rise to different interpretations. The comparative sociology of religions has inspired the recent research programme on 'multiple modernities', as pioneered by Shmuel Eisenstadt, suggesting a plurality of historical trajectories without convergence. And the underlying scepticism about the inhabitability of a spiritless cage is in the background of critiques of modernity, such as most significantly Theodor Adorno and Max Horkheimer's *Dialectic of the Enlightenment*.[21] This rather large variety of interpretations has been invited by Weber himself, who again inserted a parenthesis into his diagnosis of the present: 'whether finally, who knows?' And subsequently he adds an explicit rejection of teleology: 'No one knows who will live in this cage in the future, or whether at the end of this tremendous development, entirely new prophets will arise, or there will be a great rebirth of old ideas and ideals, or, if neither, mechanized petrification, embellished with a sort of convulsive self-importance.' If the range of possibilities is such, and if 'no one knows', the future could hardly be more open.

4. European modernity between teleology and contingency

We have seen that German-language contributors to social and political thought in the long nineteenth century, who are commonly associated with teleological reasoning, do indeed employ such reasoning, but they never entirely commit themselves to it. None of the three authors discussed fully suggests that a dynamics or logics is at work that drives human history towards an end-point, of which the definition has already been present at the start of such dynamics. In the end (not of history, but of their reasoning), they all clearly state that the future is uncertain. The question then is: why do they employ the teleological form of reasoning in the first place? Or in the light of our starting assumption: what is the common problem that leads authors like Kant, Marx and Weber to teleological expression if in the end they reject teleology?

This problem is human autonomy, or rather: the consequences of human autonomy. The authors we have considered, and numerous of their contemporaries, have assumed that all reasoning about, and analysis of, human social life and history has to start out from autonomy. They have done so for a variety of reasons, present to various degrees in different authors, of which I will mention the three most significant ones. In terms of normative moral philosophy, it was assumed that that autonomy *should* be the starting point. This is most clearly the case for Kant. In terms of sociohistorical analysis, it was assumed that the recent transformations had *actually* made autonomy the core principle of organization of human social life, as popular sovereignty and human rights in political terms, and as the freedom of commerce in economic terms. This is more clearly visible in mid-nineteenth-century writings, such as those by Tocqueville and Marx. And in terms of philosophy of social science, all social phenomena are *to be understood* as constituted through meaningful human action. This was Weber's point of view.

This assumption of autonomy is a problem because it makes it extremely difficult to know and understand how social life will be arranged and organized. If everyone is free to do what it pleases them to do, phenomena 'in the large' are nothing but the result of the consequences of the actions of numerous human beings. Endowed with reason, human beings give meanings to their actions; this is what makes actions, in principle, intelligible for other human beings, as Weber underlined. But we have no a priori ground to assume that the outcome of the actions of numerous free human beings is as intelligible as an individual action. And accordingly we have no ground either to assume that such an outcome is as beneficial as the intended result of an individual action would be for the actor whenever the action is successful.[22] As human beings live together with others, however, we nevertheless would like to know what the social result of the multiple exercise of autonomy is; and we would like to know in particular whether this outcome is beneficial for our lives. In other words, the commitment to autonomy introduces uncertainty and contingency. The authors we have looked at try to reduce uncertainty and contingency while maintaining the commitment to autonomy. This ambition requires them to make additional assumptions.

A few words should be devoted to the social-science mode of reasoning, as alluded to above, even though it is not as such teleological. As we have seen, Kant had already toyed with aggregate accounts as an answer to this question. Even though human beings are free, it just turns out to be the case that their actions 'in the large' show statistical regularities so that, even though not the individual actions themselves, their aggregate result is predictable. The gap between meaning-driven action, on the one hand, and the aggregate outcome of such actions in terms of large-scale social phenomena, on the other, introduces the question about the relation between the two, and the answers to this question have shaped what became known as the social sciences from the middle of the nineteenth century onwards.[23] In some versions of social science, the closure of this gap has led to social determinism, assuming that it is the position of a person in their social context that explains how they think and act, thus effectively cancelling autonomy.[24]

The assumption of socio-structural determination produces certainty, but it does so by avoiding any consideration of temporality. Coming back one more time to this example, Kant indeed seems to assume that patterns of marriage and childbirth are stable over time. However, temporality was crucial for our authors for two reasons: because sociopolitical arrangements were not the way they should be and one needed to understand the possibilities for changing them; this holds for Kant and Marx; and because the recent politico-economic transformations, related as they were to the commitment to autonomy, had unleashed a dynamics of which one needed to understand the further consequences, this holds for Marx and Weber. To these questions the standard social-science reasoning did not provide an answer: it produced certainty only under conditions of stability; under conditions of change uncertainty reigned. In this light, the inclinations to teleology can be understood as an expression to ascertain some degree of certainty under conditions of autonomy with particular regard for – desired and/or expected – social change.

5. European modernity between domination and critique

This reflection about the tension between autonomy of action and uncertainty of outcomes goes some way in understanding the resort to teleology. The tension, however, does not inevitably have to resolved in a teleological way, in particular not for those who had doubts about the direction of history. One could also have acknowledged it explicitly and accepted it as a consequence of modernity.[25] Nineteenth-century Europeans, though, have frequently adopted a teleological view, claiming to know the direction of history and putting themselves ahead of others on this course – often much more pronouncedly so than the three authors discussed above. Thus, it is worth asking why the reconciliation of freedom (autonomy) and reason (mastery) in a teleological philosophy of history seemed a so eminently plausible way of resolving this tension in the given context. The answer can be given in several steps, touching on different aspects of the issue.

First, as we have seen, the starting tension is between *personal* autonomy and *unintended collective* outcomes of such autonomy. The imaginary signification of modernity, though, was not limited to personal autonomy; it included a commitment to collective autonomy expressed as popular sovereignty or democracy. During the first half of the nineteenth century, it was often noted that the slogan of the French Revolution had been interpreted in a biased way, giving preference to individual over collective self-determination.[26] But the quest for, indeed the need for, collective self-determination had not disappeared. Kant – before and after the Revolution – aimed to detect the collective intention in the reason applied by philosophers to history, a political reason that would outweigh the play of human inclinations. Half a century later, Marx envisaged positive collective intentionality to be directly expressed by a rising universal class, the proletariat.

Another half-century later, Weber could not maintain either of these hopes when analysing history.

In general *conceptual* terms, *secondly*, the question of certainty arises with the commitment to autonomy itself. Autonomy means giving oneself one's own law. Arguably, therefore, the idea of autonomy already contains a reference to mastery, namely to establish the law that henceforth is to guide one's own actions, or in other words, to control the outcome of one's own actions. In the same move, a tension is created: once there is a law to be followed, there is a limit to autonomy, to freedom. In the first instance, the temporality of human action is at the core of the matter: we may have freely established the law to follow at one moment, but at the next moment this law turns into a constraint. Cornelius Castoriadis referred to this tension as the relation between the instituting moment of social life, giving the law, and the instituted moment, facing the law that already exists.

This relation appears dilemmatic when the self that gives the law is always exactly the same as the one that obeys the law (as Kant knew; see clause 6 of *Idea*). This is what the term autonomy suggests. In historical practice, though, these two 'entities' have been considered as standing in some separation from each other. Such separation, *thirdly*, was the *historical* way of establishing certainty under condition of autonomy. For the nineteenth century, we can single out three types of separation. First, the law can emerge from, and be implemented by, an agency that knows what human beings *should* want for their life in common rather that what they *actually* express. This agency was the more or less enlightened state that granted personal liberties but reserved the right to interfere with liberties in the name of the common good. Furthermore, it was possible to conceive of the main consequences of human autonomy as not being directed against one's fellow men, but against something or someone other. Thus, secondly, a main result of the unleashing of human autonomy was the increasing control of nature, and its exploitation, in what we have come to call the Industrial Revolution, allegedly for the good of all.[27] And, thirdly, the exercise of autonomy as domination of others found its expression in European colonialism. For our purposes it is important to underline that all three historical forms of domination – the enlightened liberal state, the Industrial Revolution and colonialism – have arisen in the context of increasing emphasis on autonomy in European politico-philosophical debate.

Across the nineteenth century, the prevailing perception was that some such combination of autonomy and domination was viable, and increasingly so. Debates about democracy, the realization of which would have moved the law-giving self closer to the law-abiding self, could be fended off and suppressed by the European elites. The progress in the industrial transformation of the world was regularly celebrated in the World Fairs. And colonial domination reached its high point with the Berlin Conference of 1884–5. Thus, the actual relation between autonomy and control, far from the dilemma that it conceptually entailed, could be seen as evolving smoothly and progressively in a 'direction of development'. It may not have had universal significance, but its global significance cannot be denied. Philosophies of history were at a loss in confirming its validity, but it was effectively validated through the power differential of the time. The increase of power and wealth of the European elites is the background against which what is discussed in terms of possibilities by Kant becomes the self-propelled dynamics of class struggle for Marx and the 'dwelling-places of steel' of 'victorious capitalism' for Weber. It was difficult to entirely rule out a pre-established direction of history.

If this was so, *fourthly*, a problem arose for those who were critical of the way history went. Kant still expressed hope, despite all evidence to the contrary, that history, well interpreted, could be made to turn the way he wanted. Weber had lost all such hope and could only resort to speculations about contingent events that might alter the course of history. In between, Marx had to face the problem in its fullest form. Committed to 'the most ruthless critique of all that which exists', he seemed to have been longing to identify a dynamics that could be denounced as driving societal development towards normatively ever more undesirable states. Critique would gain its power in proportion to the generalizability of its denunciation. To fulfil this longing, a theoretical argument had to be deployed that was applicable with a considerable degree of generality: such dynamics would need to exist across all capitalist societies and it would need to unfold over time. Teleological reasoning suited this purpose well. Such an approach, if taken to extremes, though, disarms itself in as far as it tends to present an insurmountable dynamics, in the face of which all human action is futile. That is why the turn of history needed to be introduced, the moment at which one dynamics exhausts itself and another one takes its place.[28]

6. Conclusions for the present and for a future that we do not know

The preceding reflections have tried to understand the inclination towards teleology in the context of the European nineteenth century, both in terms of the general perception of a novel situation provoked by the late-eighteenth-century transformations, marked by the commitment to autonomy, and in terms of the specific sociopolitical relations that emerged during the nineteenth century in the wake of those transformations. The last question to briefly address is: is there anything we can retrieve from these observations for the ways in which we today can and should look at the direction of history, both from the past towards our present, and from the present towards the future? Or in other words: reviewing the insights from the reflections above, to what extent do we live today in a 'teleological situation', that is, a situation that lends itself to interpret the human condition in a teleological way?

Short of a full response to this question, we can collect some elements for it. First, the tension between autonomy and certainty persists; arguably it has increased. The commitment to autonomy is more widespread; at the same time, the phenomena that exist 'in the large' appear to have increased in dimension and significance and have ever more acquired a dynamics beyond control – this is what is often meant by 'globalization'. As a consequence, a view of the world has become more widespread in which that which exists 'in the large' is nothing but the unintended aggregate of a large number of individual decisions and actions.

Secondly, namely, the ways of constructing collective agency as a response to the lack of control over the outcome of uncoordinated actions have further weakened. This statement may appear counter-intuitive at first sight. After all, has the commitment to collective self-determination, also known as democracy, not also become much more widespread in the course of the twentieth century, in particular its second half? While this is true, the meaning of democracy has been transformed in this process: rather than being based on problem-oriented communication, the giving oneself one's own law has tended to be reduced to the numerical summing up of numerous individual decisions, in elections and opinion polls. The possibility to conceptually sustain the achievement of positive collective outcomes, on the model of Kant's philosophical reason or Marx's universal class or in novel ways, seem even more remote than Weber at his time suspected.

Thirdly, there does not seem to be a situation of domination of the kind that had 'empirically' supported teleology during the nineteenth century. The hitherto last strong version of teleological thinking was the sociology of modernization and development during the 1960s. After the intense criticism of teleology during the first half of the twentieth century, this return could appear surprising. But the condition for teleological reasoning to re-emerge was again a context of domination, namely the hegemony of the United States, the site in which the teleological views of the time flourished. We may live today under the hegemony of liberal-capitalist thinking, but this thinking has much less of a specific site than the European teleological inclinations of the nineteenth century.

In a combination of the preceding three observations, fourthly, we may conclude that critique has become both more necessary and more difficult. It is more necessary because the gap between that which is collectively desirable and that which is likely to happen as the uncoordinated outcome of actions has grown very wide. But the lack of any plausible form of teleology makes critique more difficult. Earlier teleology – we call it by this name even though it often was an inclination only – could criticize a dreadful reality by drawing selectively on the past for a projection of a better future, as Kant did. Or it could identify a powerful logic of development that contains within itself the seeds of its demise and thus open the path for a different future, as Marx did. None of these avenues seems too promising in the light of our experiences.

But we do not have to resign ourselves either to the insight that we will forever live in that 'dwelling-place of steel', which is the outcome of past actions in human history. In the realm of sociopolitical matters, teleological reasoning tended to construct a conceptual opposition between human agency and collective outcomes such that the outcome of past actions escaped from the reach of future actions. This strong opposition provided the ground for teleology: if phenomena escape from the reach of agency, then they unfold according to a logic of their own towards their final destination. The contextual background for this strong opposition was domination: the divide between those who dominated and those over whom domination was exercised was of such a kind that an interruption of the dominant logic was out of reach for the dominated. Plausible as such a view may be in given situations, it is conceptually unsatisfactory. Everything constituted through human action can, in principle, be altered by human action (even though not reversed). Institutions, even those of capitalism, are nothing but sedimentations of past human action; and as such they can be submitted to a process of alteration in present and future human action.

Let me conclude by referring to Dipesh Chakrabarty's fruitful distinction between History 1, 'a past posited by Capital itself as its precondition', and History 2, 'a category charged with the function of constantly interrupting the totalizing thrusts of History 1'.[29] Even bearing in mind that these terms do not, for Chakrabarty, refer to history but are categories for interpreting history, seeing one of them as having 'totalizing' effects and the other one merely 'interrupting' those thrusts may create too much of a conceptual asymmetry between them. If, in our terms, History 1 refers to the sedimentation of past actions in the present, and History 2 to human action in the present, then History 2 can do more than 'interrupt'. It becomes the condition for History 1 continuing to exist.

I need to admit that this proposal is nothing but a new starting point. It re-opens the question as to how else we should conceive of those features that have made scholars see 'History 1' as totalizing, as many critics of current capitalism do again today. My proposal is to search for the answers in characteristics of human agency, and in particular in the problem of arriving at collective agency, rather than in postulating supra-human social phenomena that extend themselves on their own across history. But this is a proposal for orienting the search, not an answer.[30]

Notes

1. The period under consideration is the 'long nineteenth century', leading from 1789 to 1914, or, avoiding flawed precision, from the 1770s to the 1920s.
2. Work on this chapter has benefited from funding by the European Research Council for the Advanced Grant project 'Trajectories of modernity: comparing non-European and European varieties' (TRAMOD, grant no. 249438).
3. See http://www.marxists.org/reference/subject/ethics/kant/universal-history.htm (transl. Lewis White Beck); original German version at: http://gutenberg.spiegel.de/buch/3506/1 (both accessed 12 March 2015).
4. The possibility is in German expressed by the subjunctive mode, arguably leaving greater doubt than the English 'may'. In the German original, furthermore, it is 'history' that 'lets nevertheless hope of itself' and that is the grammatical subject of discernment in the remainder of the phrase. Grammatically, 'let' is a passive construction; and the subject of the phrase, 'history', is therefore not an agent, but a provider of possibility, in this case not least of 'hope'.
5. Edmund Burke, *Reflections on the Revolution in France*, 1790, at: http://www.constitution.org/eb/rev_fran.htm (accessed 12 March 2015).
6. We have analysed the text under this angle in Nathalie Karagiannis and Peter Wagner, 'Varieties of Agonism', in *Journal of Social Philosophy* 39 (2008), no. 3, pp. 323–39.
7. We will discuss later the precise meaning of 'in the large', in relation to both the distinctions between 'micro-' and 'macro-sociological' approaches, as one should say in the late twentieth century, and between conceptuality and historicity.
8. This is the first sentence of clause 4, or its summary heading, which is usually italicized. I keep the italics to underline the stylistic distinction between summary and body text, which is particularly pronounced in clauses 8 and 9 – see below.

9. Dipesh Chakrabarty, *Provincializing Europe*, Princeton: Princeton University Press, 2000, p. 63.

10. I cannot refrain from citing one example of some current relevance: 'Although, for instance, our world rulers at present have no money left over for public education and for anything that concerns what is best in the world, since all they have is already committed to future wars, they will still find it to their own interest at least not to hinder the weak and slow, independent efforts of their peoples in this work.'

11. This may be due to the fact that we are used to operating with a strong distinction between 'nature' and 'society', which Kant clearly did not. For seeing this distinction as constitutive of modernity, see Bruno Latour, *Nous n'avons jamais été modernes*, Paris: La Découverte, 1991.

12. Alexis de Tocqueville, *De la Démocratie en Amérique* (1835/1840), at: http://www.gutenberg.org/ebooks/30513 (accessed 12 March 2015).

13. Lorenz von Stein, *Die Geschichte der sozialen Bewegung in Frankreich von 1789 bis auf unsere Tage*, Leipzig, 1850.

14. We may well see market competition and class struggle as specifications of the antagonism of unsocial sociability; for such a reasoning see Karagiannis and Wagner, 'Varieties of Agonism'.

15. Dieter Groh, *Negative Integration und revolutionärer Attentismus*, Frankfurt am Main: Propyläen, 1973.

16. See Karl Marx and Friedrich Engels, *The Communist Manifesto*, 1848, ch. 1, 'Bourgeois and Proletarians', at: https://www.marxists.org/archive/marx/works/1848/communist-manifesto/ch01.htm#007; German orig. at: http://www.mlwerke.de/me/me04/me04_459.htm#Kap_I (both accessed 12 March 2015).

17. Rosa Luxemburg, *Die Krise der Sozialdemokratie*, written in 1915 and published in 1916, at: https://www.marxists.org/deutsch/archiv/luxemburg/1916/junius/teil1.htm (accessed 12 March 2015). Luxemburg credits Friedrich Engels for having termed this phrase forty years earlier, but to the best of my knowledge there is no available record of this.

18. Max Weber, 'Vorbemerkung', in *Gesammelte Aufsätze zur Religionssoziologie*, at: http://www.zeno.org/Soziologie/M/Weber,+Max/Schriften+zur+Religionssoziologie/Vorbemerkung (accessed 12 March 2015; my translation).

19. Sung Ho Kim, in the entry on Weber in the *Stanford Encyclopedia of Philosophy* (at: http://plato.stanford.edu/entries/weber/, accessed 15 March 2015), just omits a few terms in translation and puts 'came to have universal significance and validity'.

20. Max Weber, *The Protestant Ethic and the Spirit of Capitalism*, trans. Talcott Parsons, ch. V, 'Asceticism and the Spirit of Capitalism', at: https://www.marxists.org/reference/archive/weber/protestant-ethic/ch05.htm. German orig. at: http://www.zeno.org/Soziologie/M/Weber,+Max/Schriften+zur+Religionssoziologie/Die+protestantische+Ethik+und+der+Geist+des+Kapitalismus (both accessed 12 March 2015). The 'cage' is the 'iron cage', the standard but misleading translation of 'stählernes Gehäuse' ('dwelling-place of steel').

21. For some more detail on Weber's impact on twentieth-century analyses of modernity, see my *Modernity: Understanding the Present*, Cambridge: Polity, 2012, ch. 1.

22. Scholars as different as Isaiah Berlin and Cornelius Castoriadis have criticized the tendency to invoke reason itself as something that limits the range of autonomy and thus secures orderliness in social life.

23. I have discussed this issue in 'Certainty and Order, Liberty and Contingency: The Birth of Social Science as Empirical Political Philosophy', in Johan Heilbron, Lars Magnusson and Björn Wittrock, eds, *The Rise of the Social Sciences and the Formation of Modernity* (*Sociology of the Sciences Yearbook*, vol. 20), Dordrecht: Kluwer, 1998, pp. 241–63.

24. Sociologists have denied this conclusion by arguing that human beings do what they want, but that what they want is socially determined, as interiorization of social norms, for instance. This view nevertheless reduces the meaning of autonomy, which presupposes also that one *knows* what one wants, as Castoriadis put it.
25. This is so in some of the recent debates about modernity: in terms of political philosophy, see, for instance, Claude Lefort, *Essais sur le politique, xixe et xxe siècles*, Paris: Seuil, 1986; in terms of historical sociology and social theory, my *Theorizing Modernity*, London: Sage, 2001, chs 4 and 5.
26. See, for instance, William H. Sewell, Jr., *Work and Revolution in France*, Cambridge: Cambridge University Press, 1980.
27. For a discussion of the long-term consequences see Dipesh Chakrabarty, 'The Climate History: Four Theses,' in *Critical Inquiry* (Winter 2009), pp. 197–222.
28. For more detail on this point, see my *Modernity as Experience and Interpretation*, Cambridge: Polity, 2008, ch. 6.
29. Chakrabarty, *Provincializing Europe*, pp. 63 and 66.
30. For further reflections in this direction, see my *Modernity as Experience and Interpretation*, chs 6 and 7; and 'Provinz und Welt: Demokratie und Kapitalismus in Brasilien, Südafrika und Europa', in *Westend. Neue Zeitschrift für Sozialforschung* (2013), pp. 38–60.

CHAPTER 16
THE FACES OF MODERNITY: CRISIS, *KAIROS*, *CHRONOS* – KOSELLECK VERSUS HEGEL
Bo Stråth

The belief in some kind of goal-bound development is as old as the philosophical search for meaning. The teleological perspective was pronounced in the thought of Aristotle, for instance. However, with Enlightenment philosophy and with the interpretation of the French Revolution, a shift occurred towards teleology as a progressive understanding of time as opposed to the earlier cyclical ideas. The nineteenth-century belief in progress outlined potential futures in terms of expectations and hopes, but also in terms of threats. Progress signalled developments towards contested goals.

Progress was based on various imaginings of a *telos*. However, the main force came from the distinction of a past that had been different – i.e. worse – and a future that could be made different – i.e. better – by means of human action; or, from the contending nostalgic view of a past that had been better and a future that threatened to become worse. What some called progress meant regress to others. The teleological thinking, the definition of the goal in the progress or in the regress, as promise or threat, became more pronounced. Progress and its goals were thought of in more secular and less religious terms. Planning of and for progress became a nineteenth-century theme. This was the core of the term 'modernity'; the experience of a new time, which in German was called exactly that: *Neuzeit*, the new time.

The belief in the potential of human agency went in tandem with a growing belief in the development of states and societies through progressive forces intrinsic in history itself. In that sense, history became a universal category as the motor of modernity. However, as to the driving force the teleologies were ambiguous between human agency and history. At the same time universal history split up into pasts and futures, separated from the present, and into national histories supporting the new enterprise of construction of nations, i.e. histories in the plural, which each tried to identify its own past as a point of reference for the shaping of the future.

This chapter is concerned with the historical futures, the futures outlined in the past, of modern European societies. Progress means a direction towards the future, but we also know from *our* present situation and *our* experiences that the future to a considerable degree is open. We might plan for the future and give it a direction, but we do not know to what extent the plans will be realized. Moreover, there are many plans in more or less contentious relationships. We do not know *which* will be the strongest or what kinds of compromises and goal entanglements will come out of the social negotiation about shaping the future.

My focus on historical teleologies sheds light on these negotiation situations in the past over the futures. It sheds light on the *faces* of modernity, on the past constructions of the future in the plural, as opposed to the conventional understanding of modernity in sequential *phases* of path dependency. Openness of the future means two things: the absence of any direction of historical processes; i.e. no teleology, or the coexistence of a variety of competing teleologies; a plurality of beliefs in goal-bound development. The chapter aims at untangling this ambiguity.

Teleological thinking has become problematic today after the accelerating collapse of grand narratives about civilization, rationalization, modernization and, most recently, globalization, which have all dealt with progress towards some form of *telos*. There is a desire for open and contingent perspectives on historical change as opposed to causative, path dependent and goal-bound perspectives. However, it would probably be a vain enterprise to try to get fully rid of teleological thinking. We can probably not avoid thinking in terms of goals of developments. The concept has an anthropological dimension.

More precisely, the aim of this chapter is to problematize and historicize teleological thought by means of a comparison of the two philosophers of history Friedrich Hegel (1770–1831) and Reinhart Koselleck (1923–2006). This aim, in turn, is based on an interest in finding more open understandings of the future; understandings that emphasize the fragility, ambiguities and paradoxes in human planning and social organization.

Hegel is conventionally seen as a key figure on the teleological track with his emphasis on history as universal, and Koselleck as a voice for history in the plural and open towards the future. However, Hegel is not only teleology. He also helps to discern contingency and openness. Koselleck is not only openness. His concept of the pathogenesis of modern society contains a certain determinism. The argument is that there is more openness in Hegel and more path dependence in Koselleck than is generally assumed.

1. Kant laid the groundwork

The question of human progress and of whether history has a goal provoked various responses from different philosophers. A key figure in this sense was Immanuel Kant, who combined a diversity of strands of eighteenth-century thought and interpreted them in new ways. He rejected the uncritical belief in progress as espoused by the *philosophes*, finding their notion of unqualified rational and moral progress problematic. However, he nonetheless imagined a principal overall progress. In his *Critique of Judgement* (1790) he declared that teleology was indispensable for any kind of methodological knowledge, even if the principle itself remained beyond rational proof.[1]

In his essay 'Theory and Practice' (1793), Kant posed the question of whether human nature is endowed with capacities from which one can infer that the species will always advance to a better condition, so that the evil of the present and past times will be lost in the good of the future. In the third part of the essay ('Theory to Practice in International Right'), he argued against Moses Mendelssohn, who opposed the thesis of another philosopher, Gotthold Ephraim Lessing, that the human race undergoes a form of divine education. It was, according to Mendelssohn, a mere illusion to hold that the whole of mankind shall always move forward in the course of time, and thus perfect itself. Individuals might advance, but mankind as a whole moves up and down between fixed limits, and maintains a more or less consistent level of moral development through all periods of time.

Kant thought this wrong. He maintained that the human race makes continual progress in relation to the moral end of its existence. This progress, although it may sometimes be interrupted, will never be entirely broken off or stopped. His argument was based on his 'sense of duty'. Humans were not entitled to give up the guidance with which duty provided them. Already in his *Idea for a Universal History from a Cosmopolitan Point of View*, of 1784, he had maintained that there is a regular movement in the play of the freedom of the human will, and what seems complex and chaotic in the individual may be seen from the standpoint of the human race as a whole to be a steady and progressive though slow evolution of its original endowment.

Kant looked for a history with a 'definite natural plan for creatures who have no plan of their own'. In his first proposition in *Universal History* he stated that all natural capacities of a creature are destined to evolve completely to their natural end. The greatest problem for humans in their collective journey towards the perfect society was the achievement of a universal administering law of civic society among men (Fifth Thesis). Since individuals abuse their freedom with respect to other men, Kant sought a law which would limit the freedom of all. The same problem occupied Hobbes, yet his solution took a different course from that proposed by Kant. Many more were involved in the intensive discussion on contractual political philosophy. Kant was an avid reader of Rousseau on this theme, for instance.

The precondition of a perfect civic constitution was lawful external relations among states. In Kant's view nature's secret plan would bring forth the perfectly constituted state as the only condition in which the collected capacities of humankind can be fully developed (Eighth Thesis). Kant coined the term *Völkerbund*, federation of nations, where he transferred what so far had been expected as God's realm on earth into a moral and political destination. Kant hoped that a republican federation of self-organizing peoples would emerge under an accelerating velocity. This was far from the first outline of a federative supra-state plan. The new dimension was that Kant inserted it into a global organizational scheme to realize through the practice of reason. The *Völkerbund* was a concept which invested expectations in the future, transcending empirical experiences. Kant opened up the gap between experiences and expectations and made it unbridgeable. Politics based on practical reason got a direction into the future. The political task had so far been to bridge the gap. Kant indicated an alternative to the predominating Aristotelian modes of power – monarchy, aristocracy and democracy – which existed in pure, mixed or declining forms, where the experiences led to the expectation of the next stage in a circular movement. The future was not open. Kant commented on the experiences of the French Revolution, which broke up the Aristotelian mode of constitution and transformed them into a dichotomy of two exclusive alternatives: despotism or republic, whereby the alternatives got a temporal dimension from despotism to the republicanism of the future. The concept of *res publica*, the public issue, which so far had served to describe an overall category of political order, narrowed down to an exclusive goal- and future-orientated political term: republic. The connection between experiences and expectations takes on new meaning.[2]

Kant's republic was a goal destination set in advance for humankind, deduced from the practical reason. Kant used the term *Republikanismus* to describe the road to the goal. Republicanism indicated the principle of historical movement. Republic became a *telos* temporalized through the suffix -ism. Other terms followed suit in this vein during the nineteenth and twentieth centuries: liberalism, socialism, communism, parliamentarianism, fascism . . . with little or no content of experience and, as opposed to Aristotle's closed circle, opened up a new future horizon of expectation.

The development of new horizons of expectation was underpinned conceptually through the replacement of the transcendental term *profectus* with the secular term *progressus*. The goal of perfectibility got an earthly location and was temporalized. Kant was not alone in this work. Leibniz had already stated that *progressus est in infinitum prefectionis* and Rousseau's perfection theory referred to *perfectionnement* and *perfectibilité* in a process of sustained and increasing perfection, which humankind itself despite all backlashes and circumventions would plan and execute. Generation after generation updated the destination in the continued movement called progress. Kant possibly coined the German term for progress, *Fortschritt*, 'step forward', at the end of the eighteenth century, as a concept to bundle a number of new experiences during the past centuries. The universal term progress in the singular epitomized new experiences in the wake of the Copernican revolution, the technical development, the exploration of the globe and of peoples living at different levels of development, the dissolution of the corporatist world of estates and the emergence of industry and capitalism. All these experiences hinted at different rhythms and velocities of the changes, the contemporaneity of the not contemporaneous or the not contemporaneous at the same time, in the formulation of Friedrich Schlegel: 'The real problem of history is the dissimilarity of the progress between the different parts of the total human education.'[3]

The whole effort of Kant as a philosopher of history was aimed at the rejection of all objections against his thesis that the future will be different than the past and the search for arguments that confirmed the expectation of progress. He opposed the conventional opinion that things will remain as they always were, and that consequently nothing new could be predicted. The Aristotelian world view deduced prognoses about the future from the experiences of the past, like Machiavelli, when he stated that the one who wants to predict the future must look into the past, because all things on earth have had similarities with the past. A prediction which in principle expected the same was to Kant no prognosis because it contradicted his expectation that the future would be better. Experiences of the past and expectations about the future no longer corresponded in the view of Kant. The conventional pragmatic prognosis of an experience-based possible future became for Kant a long-term expectation of a new future. Experiences could not immediately resolve the task of progress. Kant invested his hope in continuously new experiences, such as the French Revolution, which would be accumulated in the future so that the teaching through tighter experiences would guarantee sustainable progress towards improvement.[4] This was an approach that Reinhart Koselleck would connect to and develop.

Kant laid the groundwork for Georg Wilhelm Friedrich Hegel, who became the key figure and the most influential propagator of a comprehensive historical philosophy in the nineteenth century. Hegel revised Kant's teleology towards the perfect society on one decisive point. His antipathy to the Kantian reticence to develop any more precise position on the end stage of historical progress became a pronounced theme in his philosophy. Kant was certainly vaguer than Hegel in this respect, but on principle he, too, seems to have believed that there is a maximal measure of collective freedom to which history at some point will arrive. Kant's imagery of perfectibility was not limitless, which he demonstrated with his remark that human beings are *krummes Holz*, a crooked piece of wood, from which 'nothing entirely straight' will be carved.[5] However, despite these reservations Kant's final goal was in many respects like the carrot that drove the horse: it remained perpetually out of reach, maybe because Kant avoided precisions. His notion of progress was of a process of infinite duration.

2. Hegel's temporary and preliminary end points

Hegel's charge was that the lack of a more precise definition of the final goal of progress consigned the advancing subject to an infinity of dissatisfaction. Without the hope of ever coming home, what was the point of setting off, he asked. Hegel introduced as we know a series of temporary end points, in which the goal towards which progress is heading, is repeatedly negated in favour of the next stage, which, in turn, is equally negated shortly after having been attained. A limit to the progress is set but is continually exceeded and replaced by a new limit, and the long-term destiny of the dialectic sequence is as vague as the view of Kant, although the temporary ends and their antithesis made the move forward less inconsolable. Change was reconciled with reiteration without any sense of an ultimate end.

In Hegel's view the dynamics of progress were essentially negative, powered by a dissatisfaction with those stages that had been reached, rather than being motivated by the idea that it was possible to arrive at the point to which the series was seen to lead. Thus it was crises that marked turning points. Hegel's turning points, or progressive epicycles, described a movement towards coming home, but the arrival had not yet taken place. Escape and new goal definitions replaced Kant's momentum of continuous approximation. Karl Marx would later radicalize Hegelian dialectics with the introduction of a notion of a final end of history.

Departing from Kant, Hegel cemented the foundation stone of a European cosmopolitan genealogy with Reason and *Weltgeschichte*, world history, as key concepts. In his wake, states and peoples, i.e. nation-states, empires or civilizations, have been seen as the entities primarily responsible for directing world history. According to Hegel, states were not eternal but, like human beings, experienced a rise, a time of prosperity and a decline. From a world historical viewpoint one particular state with its people's spirit (*Volksgeist*) in each historical moment constituted the link in the chain of world history as the carrier of Reason (*Weltgeist*).

World history was the history of peoples and their states in terms of progressiveness. The life cycles were a series of epicycles along a progressive line. Hegel provides a kind of meta-framework which continues to endure as an implicit heuristic point of reference for much of the reasoning about the world and its history. The next great figure to confirm this narrative was Karl Marx. Here too, the progression and the epicycles of rise and fall are prominent. The *topos* of such epicycles is a much older idea, however. It goes back to Polybius and earlier Greek authors. What Hegel added to the model was the progressivity of the cycles, which can be seen as a response to Kant's provocative question of whether history is permanent improvement towards a vague, undefined end.

Hegel saw the peoples of Europe and its American offshoot as the agents of history in modern time justifying colonizing projects as the development of Reason in the world. He viewed the West as the vanguard of humanity. His scheme of history repressed arguments that did not fit into his world plan. During the period in which he wrote, it was well known that sub-Saharan Africa was integrated into the world economy by means of Muslim trade routes; i.e. it was not only a passive reservoir open to the exploitation of slave merchants. Nevertheless Hegel referred to this part of Africa, *das eigentliche Afrika* – 'Africa proper', as he called it – as static and unchanging in time; unhistorical, external to universal history.[6]

The Western states were distinguished through the degree of their consciousness of freedom. The realization of freedom was the purpose of both states and world history. The undulating pattern of rise and decline of the individual cultures, and at the same time the progression towards ever higher stages of civilization for the world as a totality, moved from the East towards the West. It began with oriental despotism and proceeded via Greek democracy and Roman aristocracy towards Christian European monarchies and Napoleon's empire. According to Hegel's philosophy, this moving transmission of power constituted a series of junctions in the motion of History towards ever higher stages of freedom and the rule of reason, culminating in his hallucination in 1806 of the *Weltgeist* in the incarnation of Napoleon on a white horse in Jena.

How religious Hegel's world spirit really was is a disputed question. Hegel studied theology at the University of Tübingen, but was repelled by the bigoted atmosphere at the seminary. However, he developed lasting ties of friendship there with Hölderlin and Schelling, with whom he shared an enthusiasm for the early phase of the French Revolution and the appreciation of an undogmatic and reason-orientated Christendom, which in the philosophy of Hegel is difficult to separate from a human-orientated rationalism or atheism. The seeming opposites are entangled. In any case the world spirit was the incarnation of Reason. God was Reason in humankind.

The revolution in 1830 disturbed this world view. The revolution alerted intellectuals and conjured up apocalyptic images. The symptomatic meaning of the July revolution was that it showed that the revolutionary abyss of 1789 had only seemingly been closed and that the world was only at the beginning of a whole era of revolutions in which the masses appropriated their own political power from the stable order of the feudal and corporate estates. The world began in the wake of democratic levelling and industrialization to look very different as compared to 1806.

With indignation and horror Hegel noticed the intrusion of new splits, against which he now defended the existing order as a true longevity. In his last political writing in 1831, on the critique of the English reform bill, he characterized the will for reform as 'disobedience through the courage from below.' The political crisis in Europe was a crisis in which everything which had been valid had become problematic. He asked whether in such a politically upset time there was any scope at all for dispassionate and quiet thinking. A few days later, in November 1831, he fell sick and died. His mediating spirit did not feel at home any more in the new time and was moved towards the extremes by the next generation of philosophers, as, for instance, in the thought of Marx and Kierkegaard, who misjudged the universal equilibrium of their master as a product of a mere harmonization.[7]

3. The idealization of Hegel

Susan Buck-Morss, in *Hegel, Haiti and Universal History*, argues that the philosopher integrated the black revolution on the Caribbean slave island in his schedule for the advance of freedom through History. She is thereby above all interested in the master–slave (*Herr–Knecht*) relationships in the philosophy of Hegel rather than slavery in its more narrow meaning. In her view, the Haitian example forced Hegel to transcend his Eurocentrism.[8]

Our knowledge in retrospect is that the slave revolt did not end up in their long-term emancipation. The revolution was ultimately successful in the formal abolition of slavery in Haiti, even if there were short-lived relapses, but economic dependencies remained. Hegel could not know anything about the later developments after the revolution, of course, but the beginning of the problems was already discernible during his lifetime. The question is therefore whether his interest in Haiti was not lower than that attributed to him by Buck-Morss. More clarity on this point would in any case require a deeper investigation of to what extent the institutional failures, so obvious in retrospect, were taken note of in the contemporaneity of Hegel and how they were presented in Germany around 1800. Hegel was not only interested in the revolution as the instrument of freedom, but in freedom as manifested by statehood. The question is, in other words, whether the exciting perspective that Buck-Morss outlines is not ultimately an idealized left-Hegelianism.

One might recall what Hegel wrote about colonialism in general. It was the teleological imperative by which consciousness in the form of the superior Europeans had to appropriate the others, he argued in *Philosophy of Right*. He depicted the British colonialization of India as an inevitable stage in his process of evolution. He argued in *History of Philosophy* that the British, or rather the East India Company, were the masters of India because it was the fatal destiny of Asian empires to subject themselves to the Europeans. Like Africa, India had no history. 'The Indians have lines of kings and an enormous quantity of names, but everything is vague,' he stated.[9]

The question that Buck-Morss implicitly raises is whether we should understand Hegel as the global or the national Hegel. She argues for the global Hegel. There is undoubtedly in the debate a gap between the reading of Hegel as the theorist of the nineteenth-century state and as the theorist of world history, as the adherent of the Prussian *Rechtsstaat* or of global Christianism/humanism. Our current, or perhaps one should say recent, preoccupation with the language of 'globalization' seems to have encouraged a trend for substituting Hegel's nineteenth-century reading of progress as mediated by the state, whose statehood he derived from its legal and administrative make-up, with a more global Hegel, whose world spirit becomes the money spirit of world capitalism and the global slave emancipation its antithesis.[10] Here it may be helpful to recall that Napoleon as the incarnation of Hegel's world spirit was the son and the father of nationalism and modern nation-state building, but the source of inspiration was thereby rather the *Code Napoléon* than nationalism.

Haiti, where slaves overcame their French masters, does not seem to fit into Hegel's overall scheme for the movement of the world spirit through space and time, a story about a Western origin and destiny. In general terms, not only Africa but also Siberia and the Caribbean islands were places where, according to Hegel, the world spirit had nothing to seek, and thus Haiti was excluded by definition before the events there began to puzzle him.

Ignorance about the world outside Europe allowed Hegel to draw a borderline between in- and outsiders. At the same time, ignorance of other continents did not prevent him from lecturing about animal life in, for instance, the Amazonas. An anecdote about the comments of a student from South America on Hegel's description of a parrot from the region is illustrative. The student told Hegel that the parrots in the Amazonas were quite different from the descriptions of them the professor gave in his lectures. Hegel's well-known and unhesitating reply was that this was simply the worse for reality.[11]

The thinking behind this incident provides a bridge to the question of the place of Haiti in Hegel's universal history. Was Haiti, like the parrot, simply incompatible with the European reality, with the consequence that that reality had to be changed and Haiti integrated in such a way that the European frame became truly global? Or was Haiti the reality that did not fit with Hegel's universal history, and therefore had to be excluded from it? Hegel is enigmatic and ambiguous, although to Buck-Morss it is clear that Hegel's interpretation of the Haitian revolution triggered his master–slave reflection and led him to expand his description of the Western experience in the direction of a more universal history in the proper sense of the term. However, what *Hegel, Haiti and Universal History* promises, but fails to deliver is clear proof that Hegel at any point paid a considerable amount of attention to the Haitian revolution. This is not to downplay the fascinating perspective the work opens up.

The interesting question from the perspective of Hegel's spirit of dialectics is whether from a long-term perspective, which would also encompass the post-independence phase of exploitation in new wage-labour forms, Haiti should be seen as the victim of European slavery, or as a non-European agent of European revolutionary progress, even if in the long run the revolution stalled. On closer inspection, it must appear to be less a matter of two alternatives than a combination of both.

The history of Haiti is provocative in its sinister unfolding as a nearly continuous series of catastrophes and never-ending crisis. This might better connect it with the long-term pessimism of Reinhart Koselleck in his study of the pathogenesis of civil society (see below) than with Hegel. Having pointed at this possibility, it must also be emphasized, however, that the general problem with both Hegel and Koselleck, in an expansion of the European history beyond Europe, is their principal Eurocentrism.

Hegel never left the shores of the European continent. He was badly located to see beyond its horizon when he developed his philosophical history of the world. His idea of dialectical synthesis, the sequence of conflicts and contradictions within an overarching rational development embodied in the secular state, was a departure from theological narratives of apocalyptic time, but it held on to the Christian teleology of a divine plan, the cunning of History.[12] Hegel's argument was about the possibilities of Reason on earth, and since God was Reason, the ultimate goal was God's advent, the union of God and Man, Reason and Man. The underlying themes of freedom were arguably derived from the Apocalypse and the rest of the New Testament. Working from this interpretative framework Hegel thought that history had reached a late stage, its last stage, and that the end was near. Although he demarcated himself from church narratives about apocalyptic time the apocalyptic thought was obviously there.[13]

4. The revolutionary Hegel with openness towards the future

There was certainly also another Hegel, interested in the tensions between *Herr und Knecht*, master and slave, between the poor and the rich rabble. Here it is possible to identify in Hegel's thought a certain openness towards the future, which certainly went some way to stabilizing the relationships between the two, but which – by means of the capacity of the slaves to learn to master nature through their labour – opened up the possibility of a revolutionary overthrow of a seemingly stable order. Slave is the English translation for *Knecht*, which has a broader meaning than the connotation of slavery. On this point Karl Marx took up where Hegel left off and developed his theory on the relationships between labour subordinated to their masters as wage slaves. Nonetheless, Marx, too, soon closed down the possibility of openness and inscribed the revolution in a goal-bound teleological scheme of a similar kind to that of the source of his inspiration.

Frank Ruda, in *Hegels Pöbel*, focuses on the role of the rabble in Hegel's philosophy of right. Hegel draws attention to the rabble in his outline of the nature of the state. The problem of the rabble leads to the question of poverty and its structural anchorage in civil society. Ruda demonstrates that different kinds of rabble existed within Hegel's thought: the poor and the affluent rabble. Hegel was the first thinker to identify an inseparable connection between poverty and the *bürgerliche* production of riches. Ruda refers to a passage in *Vorlesungen zur Rechtsphilosophie*, which states that poverty will become increasingly more entrenched, as accumulated riches increase. In his lectures on the philosophy of right in 1821 and 1822 Hegel also pointed to the existence of a rich rabble. One of its most decisive characteristics was that it played off the sovereignty of its economic power against the sovereignty of the state and its institutions. The rich rabble rises, using the power its money gives it, against the right of the state.[14]

Hegel's insight was that poverty did not necessarily reduce the poor to a rabble. Humble beggars who gratefully received their alms were different from the rabble that emerged through the violation of law in an act of volition. The making of the rabble through violations of law, in turn, stood in close connection to the disproportionate concentration of wealth in the hands of a limited few. The rich rabble created the poor rabble.

Hegel was early in his attention to the social issue. The main problem in the European debate in the wake of the Vienna restoration was the connection between liberalism and nationalism and the democratic threat. What was to be called the social issue became a theme only in the 1830s. Hegel's famous society–state dichotomy, with his outline of the civil society as the mediating space between the family and the state, where each individual is his or her own end, but only in contact with others can 'attain the whole compass' of its ends, and 'therefore these others are means to the end of the particular member', focuses on the social reality and the question of solidarity between individuals and the tensions between rich and poor. 'A particular end … assumes the form of universality through this relation to other people, and it is attained in the simultaneous attainment of the welfare of others,' Hegel notes, adding that 'the whole sphere of civil Society is the territory of mediation'. He referred to the civil society as the 'external state' and a system of mutual dependencies, a 'system which interweaves the subsistence, happiness, and rights of the individuals with the subsistence, happiness, and rights of all'.[15] The discovery of social reality in the civil society of tensions, negotiations and the search for compromises and solutions, which tied the individuals to their co-citizens, contains the possibility of social protest in Hegel's philosophy. He put on the agenda what after his death was to be seen as a growing threat for social elites: the question of social cohesion. Hegel's discovery of the social question gives a dimension of the openness of the historical future in his philosophy.

5. Koselleck's crisis and pathogenesis between experiences and expectations

Hegel lived and thought in a period that preceded an imagined earthly or transcendental eschatology. The theological context permeates his thought on the apocalypse. Reinhart Koselleck, however, reflected in a period which had already witnessed the end of Western civilization twice. Hegel's future was Koselleck's past, where Koselleck's end-of-the-world scenario in the 1950s – the nuclear bomb had made the extinction of human life on earth technically possible and thinkable – did not have any theological context. Koselleck did not look forward predicting the future, but backward trying to understand how his present in the shadow of the threat of the end of the world could come about. He discerned the beginning of the pathology that ended in the twentieth-century cataclysms in the seventeenth- and eighteenth-century enlightenment project. Eschatology was progress. Others, such as Dylan Riley in *The Civic Foundations of Fascism in Europe*, put the spotlight on the nineteenth century and the failure of a Tocquevillian civil society.[16] However, both agree on the role of the civil society.

Koselleck emphasized the role of social communication and social conflict in his *Critique and Crisis: Enlightenment and the Pathogenesis of Modern Society*, with the original German as *bürgerlich* for 'modern'.[17] Koselleck referred to these processes as a form of permanent problem resolution, where social critique provokes experiences of crisis and attempts to integrate and channel the critique – or to its ignorance through the refuge in hypocrisy. He suggests that critique and responses to it promote the translation of experiences from the near past into horizons of future expectations. These dynamics are not derived from a kind of rational dialogical definition of truth but from a clash of interests, where solutions have more to do with power than with truth.

The dynamics between critique and crisis develop a positive cycle. If the critique is successful the critics are the winners of the crisis. They now often want to consolidate their new-won power and avoid new critique from new points of departure. They reject new critique by hypocrisy. The dynamics of crisis-hypocrisy turn the cycle in a negative direction. The losers may begin a self-critical reflection, as opposed to the winners' hypocrisy, and thus open up to a later sequence of critique and crisis. One might here think of Germany in 1945 and in 1968. There is a cyclical dimension in Koselleck's scenario of critique–crisis–hypocrisy/self-critique. Koselleck's own historical experiences of the Second World War, and his memory of the beginning of a foot march as a prisoner of war on 8 May 1945, impressed for ever his view on history, not least his interest in the history writing of the losers. The goal of the prisoners' march to the accompaniment of the peace bells was Auschwitz, where they would clean up after the Holocaust.

Koselleck saw the emergence of a critique of the sovereign, which developed with the early modern separation of morality and politics, as the core of modernity and the starting point of the dynamics between critique and crisis. When Enlightenment philosophy distinguished between political authority and individual moral responsibility, there emerged scope for social critique. The notion of moral responsibility as something not pertaining exclusively to the ruler made critique possible. The difference between the private and the public was established in Europe, and the imagination of the public became the discourse in which civil society and the sovereign engaged in dialogue. The initial distinction between public politics (by the monarch) and private morals was blurred, however, when the private reflection on morals expanded to critique with the like-minded against the prevailing moral authorities within secret societies, which insisted on becoming public. The long-term shift from private to public critique built up the core of civil society with the public sphere of free expressions of opinion and formulations of critique. The public sphere emerged slowly in the nineteenth century through the expansion of what had been the private sphere.

Koselleck's point is that the critique had a clear political target, although in principle it was based on the idea of a private morality separated from politics. Politics connected structures to action. Change was not brought about by inherent structures but by identifiable human action operating with or against structural forces and other human wills. Critique could be addressed to some kind of power simultaneously assumed to be responsible for the crisis and for solving it, either by reform or by stepping down and thus opening up the way for a new authority. Initially, the critique was addressed to the absolute ruler in secret societies where the borderline between private and public was not yet as fluid as it would later become. Later, when absolutism became constitutionalism, it was addressed to the political power centres in general and in public spheres in the proper sense of the term public. Critique implied the translation of past experiences into viable future horizons of expectations.

Crisis derives from the Greek word κρινειν, '*krinein*': to separate, to distinguish, to decide, to determine, to judge. It was in this sense that the Greek historian Thucydides used the term in his accounts of the Peloponnesian War and the battles on land and sea which led to the crisis in the great conflict between the Greeks and the Persians. In the same way, the Greek physician Hippocrates referred to the crises which occur in diseases at exactly the moment when the disease either increases in intensity or begins to abate. In his depiction of the plague in Athens, Thucydides relates how the crisis came after seven to nine days. More than a thousand years later, the philosophers Rousseau and Paine took up the concept in this vital and existential meaning, and transformed it. They saw crisis as an emancipating solvent of the old order. The outcome was no longer open; it had a direction. Crisis began to connote progress. From here, it was only a short step to Karl Marx's crisis theory, which described the economic depressions since 1825 as crises, an unavoidable and ultimately mortal mechanism built into the capitalist system. From Marx, the concept spilt over into neoclassical economic theory, which regarded crisis as a temporary disequilibrium in a natural state of equilibrium, where the end of each crisis was principally given. Since the equilibrium would always be re-established, this resembled Marx's formulation in the reverse. With the use of the crisis concept by neoclassical economists, the term resolutely lost its original meaning of openness towards the future and came to connote a temporary malfunction of a perfectly well-balanced economic, social and political order. In line with Koselleck, the argument here is for the use of crisis in the original sense of the term.[18]

The space between experiences and expectations is the space where politics is made. Koselleck illustrates how the gap between experiences and expectations framed politics with the experience of the execution of Charles I, which more than a century later determined the horizon of expectation of Turgot, when he urged Louis XVI to introduce reforms in order to save him from the same destiny. Turgot's warning was in vain, but a temporal connection between the past English and a future French revolution was experienced and developed into an expectation. In the medium between specific experiences and specific expectations the concrete history is brought about. Historical time is not an empty definition but an entity that changes with history. Experiences are present past and expectations present future aiming at the 'not yet' and the not experienced.[19]

Modernity, the new time, as opposed to the cyclical understanding of the relationships between experiences and expectations, could only be understood as a new time when the expectations through science and technology, and through economic and political innovations of social organization began to increase the distance to the experiences with the help of the term progress. The growing distance meant a greater openness as to the future, but at the same time a conviction that it would be a change for the better through human agency. Humans had the tools to shape the future in their hands.

Even if both categories are concepts of the present, they are not symmetric terms which complement one another. Koselleck refers to Goethe's dictum that experiences for individuals come always too late; for governments and nations they are never available. Goethe commented on a debate on to what extent we learn from history and thus suggested that we do not, an opinion that Hegel also cherished. A French diplomat who shared this view in a letter to Goethe explained it with the fact that the made experiences are concentrated in one focal point whereas the experiences to be made are extended over minutes, hours, days, years, centuries. Therefore the similar is never identical but appears in ever new constellations. Historical time contains both reiterative structures, from which we on principle *could* learn, and new dimensions, from which we have no experience and thus cannot learn from them.[20] Past and future never cover each other and expectations cannot be fully deduced from experiences. This is why history in the view of Koselleck is in the plural and open towards the future.

Experiences are not a chronological accumulation which establish continuities. They are like the glass eye of a washing machine, behind which now and then this or that piece of the wash appears. Experiences form a space in the metaphoric of Koselleck, whereas the expectations are a moving line behind which new experiences emerge. Behind the line a new future space of experiences will emerge, which cannot yet be surveyed. Koselleck illustrates this with a political joke from the Soviet Union:

> 'Communism is already visible on the horizon,' Khrushchev declared in a speech.
> Question thrown in from a listener:
> 'Comrade Khrushchev, what is that, horizon?'
> 'Look it up in a dictionary', Nikita Sergeyevich answered.
> At home the listener found the definition:
> 'Horizon, a seeming line separating sky from earth, moving away when one approaches.'[21]

The experiences of 1933 happened once and for ever, but the experiences which are derived from the events can change with time. Hopes, disappointments and new experiences, superimposed on each other, retrospectively change the experiences. They change although, once made, they always remain the same. Expectations are in this sense different. Expectations built on experiences cannot surprise when they occur. Only what was not expected can surprise. Then they result in a new experience. The breakthrough of the horizon of expectations creates new experience.

A key argument in the time philosophy of Koselleck is that modernity is accelerating time. Science and technology have stabilized since early modern time the difference between experience and expectation, as opposed to earlier Aristotelian interpretations of temporal differences where the anticipated new was a recurrence of the old. The acceleration of time accompanied the modern opening up of the gap between experiences and expectations. The time rhythms and the experience of time in the everyday life-worlds speeded up. Adam Smith had an explanation for this development. The progress of time came in his view through the time-saving in the wake of the increasing division of labour and the invention of machines. The horizon of expectations described the anticipation of a future that ever faster transformed the societies for the better.[22]

In particular, scientific and technological inventions and achievements in the name of progress, since the beginning of the sixteenth century have stretched the distance between experiences and expectations. However, Koselleck noted that this was not necessarily a perpetual movement. The realization of political outlines like republicanism, democracy or liberalism will transform the old expectations into new experiences, but these two categories are not identical. The hopes invested in the old expectations might have changed to experiences of disappointment, for instance. There is an openness towards the future on this point. This will probably at some point in the future be true also for socialism, and for communism also, if it will at all be proclaimed as introduced, Koselleck prognosticated in the mid-1970s when the influence of '1968' was still strong. He did not imagine that a new kind of liberalism would come back on the experience of the fall of communism and that around 2010 the expectations that drove the establishment of neoliberalism in the 1990s would result in new experiences of disappointment, but so far no new big expectation. The bigger the experiences of failed realization of political utopias, the warier and more open the expectations, and, at some future point, no more expectations. Koselleck indicated the possibility of the end of modernity, the *Neuzeit*, in the sense of belief in optimizing progress.[23] This was quite obviously a different understanding of the end of history than that of Francis Fukuyama in his comment on what he believed to be the final triumph of liberalism after the collapse of the Soviet empire.[24]

Koselleck wrote *Critique and Crisis* against the backdrop of the hypocrisy of the 1950s that came in the wake of the Cold War. Communism and liberalism refused to acknowledge the ontological character of the political, the fact that politics is always an arcanum of conflicts and interests in which all are striving for power. Furthermore, both argued in terms of moral and utopian ideologies aiming at mutual destruction in their pursuit of a better world and based their arguments on utmost truth claims. The hypocritical moralism of the Cold War was still visible in the War on Terror, culminating in the Iraq War in 2003 with the coalition of the willing against the axis of evil. It simply replaced the Cold War and split Europe in new ways.

After the failure of the Iraq War and the connected Afghanistan War, which began in 2001 in reaction to the 11 September terrorist attack on the USA, Koselleck's critique–crisis dynamics seems to be broken, however. No victor is visible. Hypocrisy is mobilized to explain defeat. With the perpetuation of the crisis concept in the wake of the state surrender to financial capitalism the gap between experiences and expectations seems to be overstretched. This was the gap that triggered the dynamics.

Whether one describes Koselleck's end-of-history scenario as an overstretching of the gap between experiences and expectations or as a collapse of the gap is probably just a matter of taste, but since a closing gap would recall the Aristotelian model of the cyclical relationship, where the expectations were cyclically given by the experiences, and this is definitely not the situation in which we are, overstretch is probably the better term.

His demonstration of the fragility of the democratic project, and of its proximity to utopian populism, is based on social realism with a focus on the Hegelian civil society of negotiations on coming to terms with conflicts, tensions and ambiguities, where the rich and the poor rabbles confront each other and where a certain openness towards the future is prevailing. The discovery of social reality and the references to the society–state dichotomy salvages the openness of the historical future. There is a link between Hegel and Koselleck on this point. Koselleck locates the origin of the pathology of modernity exactly in civil society. However, to label him a latter-day right-Hegelian would be to overstretch the link.

This view on civil society and the social conflicts there, which links Hegel and Koselleck, contrasts with the historical naivety of a mainstream view that takes liberal democracy for granted after it has been established, and which equally displays a particular sort of historical naivety in forgetting how seldom democracy has been put into place by democratic means. Such a view departs from the belief that we learn from history – a belief that Koselleck, as we have seen, in the vein of Goethe and Hegel rejected. In a longer historical and more global perspective since the 1870s, liberal democracy has constantly been in a highly fragile state, and the proclamation of its final triumph around 1990 ('the end of history') was premature.

Koselleck's pessimistic conception of modernity as an epoch of permanent worldwide crisis, revolution and civil war, temporarily glossed over by the hypocrisy of the victors, is based on his evaluation of the European Enlightenment as a self-destructing dialectic between *on the one side* a utopian rejection of authority through critique in the form of political moralism and *on the other side* the new authority of ideology and terror, with the French and the Russian Revolutions as cases in point, through moralist politics. The supposedly anti-authoritarian concepts of the enlightenment ('reason', 'freedom', 'liberty', 'solidarity', 'equality', 'virtue', etc.) become in the end exploited as weapons of dictatorship. This is what Koselleck described as the long-term transformation of crisis into hypocrisy and as the pathogenesis of the *bürgerliche Gesellschaft*.

The sudden but silent transformation from liberal to illiberal, from tolerant to intolerant, demonstrates how razor's edge thin the difference between such distinctions are. The same goes for other opposites in the semantics of politically potential concepts. The methodology of conceptual history focuses on such ambiguities and paradoxes where the opposites and extremes are potentially unified. Conceptual history goes hand in hand with Koselleck's philosophy of history.

Koselleck's perspective and long-term view on history has a pessimistic keynote, and ultimately this undermines its declared openness. There is a negative *telos*: the anticipation of worse things to come and a deep Heideggerian influence. In retrospect this perspective seems much more relevant than when Koselleck developed his philosophy of history during the Cold War. The end of the Cold War opened up a new and powerful horizon of universal market liberalism around the term globalization that stretched the gap between experiences and expectations and at the end overstretched it when the experiences caught up with the past expectations and became deep disappointments.

There is in Koselleck's view a subtle subtext of *post-histoire* which might be more relevant today than when he outlined it in the 1950s: modernity as a dystopian trap from which no escape seems possible. Indeed, his philosophy contains an intellectual tension, although the negative teleology and dystopian perspective is much less pronounced than in Max Weber's more imperative and definitive view on modernity as a process of inexorable disenchantment through bureaucratization. Although Koselleck emphasizes openness in principle, the empirical observations of a stretching gap between our experiences and our expectations, and the hypocrisies as the implicit outcome of critique, offer a forewarning of overstretch and the end of expectations.

The experiences accumulated over time lead to a loss of capacity to translate experiences into mobilizing future horizons of expectations under democratic conditions. Rather than triggering permanent successful critical self-reflection, critique has a tendency to become petrified into hypocrisy when the critics establish themselves as new powers, who are in turn less interested in destabilizing self-critique. There is on this point a subtle dimension of cyclical reiteration in Koselleck's view, which closes down the openness towards the future and brings him closer to the cyclical dynamics of history in the vein of Hegel.

6. Koselleck's *kairos* as an instrument to identify historical openness

In order to develop his perspective of a principle openness and contingency towards the future Koselleck deployed also another Greek term than crisis: *kairos*, which suggests an understanding of time different to that implied by *chronos*.

Ancient Greek had two terms for time: *chronos* and *kairos*. In Greek mythology Χρόνος, Chronos was the god of time, a god created out of chaos. Chronos represented the continuous flow of time independent of human, chronological and sequential time. Hegel infused *chronos* with dialectical discontinuities by means of the movement of the spirit of Reason from nation to nation, but between the ruptures the inexorable flow intangible for humans remained in his philosophy.

The second term for time was *kairos*. Καιρος referred to a fateful moment at which everything is at stake and might either be won or lost, a moment of release from the structural dictates of modernity. Such moments are not necessarily pleasant, and often they are violent and bloody. Kairos represented momentous time connected to a fateful situation of taking or leaving an opportunity, the moment in which things might develop in very different directions and everything may change or collapse. The Greek god Kairos had a tuft of hair on the front of his head, whereas the back of his head was bald. Those who tried to seize him when he had already passed did so in the void.

In (ancient) Greek kairos in fact not only refers to time but also means weather, which emphasizes the meaning of dramatic change, in the same way that time and tempest have the same origin in English and *temps* and *tempête* in French. In Italian the word *tempo* contains both meanings. Kairos is the passing instant when an opening appears which must be driven through with force if success is to be achieved.[25]

The German theologian and socialist Paul Tillich frequently discussed the distinction between chronos and kairos. Tillich programmatically proposed a historical consciousness in the sense of kairos. He also contrasted kairos with *logos*, as representing timelessness, form, law, stasis as opposed to the characteristics of kairos: change, conflict, contingency (fate) and individuality. As a theologian, Tillich transcended the particular historical situation, and its implicit social and political realities, highlighting religious and eschatological dimensions. He referred to the New Testament, where kairos means the time when God acts. However, he also referred to kairos as a historical moment of an epochal nature. He excluded nostalgic and/or prognostic understandings of time from his historical moment. *Kairoi* in plural are those crises in history, which create an opportunity for and require an existential decision from human subjects. In transcendental terms the coming of Christ is a key example. In the liberation theology of South Africa during apartheid kairos denoted 'the appointed time'. Reinhart Koselleck knew, of course, about Tillich and his circle of Christian socialists, the *Kairos-Kreis*, but whether or to what extent he was influenced is another question.[26]

In Koselleck's *Begriffsgeschichte* time as something unavoidable and inescapable is linked to kairos, to decisive moments in history provoking human action. Conceptual history is underpinned by the search for moments of kairos and their temporal structures. Kairos becomes a tool of pluralization of time in order to describe and analyse multi-layered time. However, differently to Tillich, Koselleck sees *both* the nostalgic or retrospective *and* the prognostic dimensions of the present as part of the kairos situation.[27] The future, according to Koselleck, exists only as a present future, the past only as a present past. According to this argument there can only be one time dimension, the present of human existence; past and future exist only to the extent that they are parts of this present. Only in the restricted sense of our imaginations of multi-layered time is there a place for chronos, as imaginations in the present of an unbroken flow of time, which are contradictorily linked to experiences of kairos.

However, Koselleck's argument should not be mistaken for a kind of presentism, because the present is in itself temporal and historical. Hence, the notion of a present past, a past contained in the present, corresponds to the notion of a passed present or future, *Vergangene Gegenwärte* or *Zukünfte*, presents or futures that lie behind us.[28] Analogically Koselleck refers to present and past futures, also within reach of conceptual historical analysis, which investigate complex temporal structures on the basis of the identification of moments of kairos.

Koselleck was very much motivated by a desire to undermine utopian conceptions of history as a singular, universal, progressive process, a view handed down by the Judeo-Christian tradition and formalized by the Enlightenment and its modern philosophical heirs. In pursuing this aim Koselleck drew upon the work of several forerunners such as Karl Löwith, Hans Georg Gadamer, Martin Heidegger and Carl Schmitt.[29]

Koselleck replaces chronos and the Hegelian notion of time, *Geschichte als solche*, history as such, history as a unified totality, with the notion of multi-layered time, *Zeitschichten*. The kairos situation is far from homogeneous or transparent. Koselleck's imagery of time strata focuses on the outline of different velocities of change in different spheres of social organization. Economics, politics, legislation, technological change, everyday-life practices, scientific discoveries and many other areas of change follow different time rhythms, which create tensions between them. He referred to these tensions as the contemporaneity of the non-contemporaneous, *die Gleichzeitigkeit des Ungleichzeitigen*, a term once phrased by Ernst Bloch, but Schlegel had already pronounced this human condition as we have seen. Or, as Koselleck put it, 'We have contemporaries who live in the Stone Age.' The attempts to cope with various time strata and velocities of change in moments of kairos are what make such moments so tense and contentious, so open.[30]

The identification of moments of crisis, in the original meaning of this concept, and kairos provides a means of historicizing teleologies in terms of past futures, and of destabilizing teleological perspectives in order to attune to the contingency and openness of history under a rejection of notions of societies as automatically driven by Reason or some other inherent force. Crisis and kairos are tools for an alternative historical understanding. They focus on the role of human action in terms of failure and success, responsibilities and escape from responsibilities. They undermine the belief in historical change through immanent forces in History itself.

7. Koselleck's enlightenment view

Hans Bödeker understands Koselleck's interpretation of the Enlightenment as a sequence in six steps: Enlightenment as an epoch, as critique, as secularization, as politicization, as historicization and as ideologization. The perspective of Koselleck obviously has Hobbes as the key point of reference. The enlightenment project becomes in his view a matter of breaking out of the Hobbesian straitjacket. Bödeker questions whether Koselleck's assumption of the Enlightenment as a reaction to absolutism is valid. Koselleck himself referred later, after *Kritik und Krise*, to the Enlightenment in England, Scotland, the Netherlands and Switzerland, which did not have absolutist regimes as their immediate target.

On these grounds, Bödeker questions whether the enlightenment politicization must necessarily be interpreted as radicalizing moralization without a political consciousness of responsibility, as Koselleck suggests, or if it must be revolutionary. Bödeker argues for an enlightenment which was in fact reform-orientated, inclined to cooperate with the traditional power elites in order to achieve reforms. In such an understanding, the enlightenment project of Kant is in operation. Kant developed a theory for reforms that followed certain principles. Bödeker also raises the question of whether the ancient regime did not stumble on itself rather than on the enlighteners, who did not come as revolutionaries to Versailles.[31]

The theory of Hobbes functioned in England around 1650 but not after 1688. Possibly Hobbes can be used to understand the French development with repeated revolutions followed by new ruler contracts and restoration. The Germans had an enlightenment tradition which does not really fit with Hobbes. When that tradition had narrowed down after 1848 and, in particular, after 1871, Bismarck's and Wilhelm II's authoritarian rule after all had a social dimension and there continued to be scope for a public debate on the social and on the class issue driven by conservative *Katheder* socialists as well as radical social democrats. The question is whether Koselleck exaggerated Hobbes and played down Kant.

Bödeker's questioning of a central part of Koselleck's argument undermines the subtext in *Critique and Crises* of a pessimistic teleology despite the declared openness. He does not necessarily question the critique and crisis dynamics as such, but he suggests that these dynamics might be more complex than in Koselleck's scheme.

Bödeker's critique is relevant and can be extended. Koselleck's openness of historical time seems to have a phenomenological-anthropological foundation, whereby the openness as *condition humana* becomes universalized without scope for a differentiation between imperial, colonial and post-colonial preconditions. The world in *Critique and Crisis* is the world of the Cold War, of the *Weltbürgerkrieg*, where Europe is heteronomous, *fremdbestimmt*, rather than shaped through internal–external actions and interactions with open outcomes.

Koselleck's anthropological point of departure around opposites like dead–alive, friend–enemy, above–below, superior–inferior, external–internal and before–after seems at the end to have a de-politicizing impact on the historical time. Historical time is only open within a kind of neutral space or framework for enclosed political conflicts. On the other side, Koselleck counted his key concepts, experiences and expectations to the anthropological dichotomies and no doubt Hegel's master–slave opposition (superior–inferior/above–below) also belongs to them, and in that sense they are the motor of politics rather than a de-politicized neutral space.

The problem is another: how open and how teleological is Koselleck's cyclical sequence of critique–crisis–hypocrisy of the winners/self-critic of the losers? How far from Hegel's epicycles was he other than that his cycles had a negative direction as opposed to Hegel's positive?

Koselleck was certainly neither a Hegelian nor a Weberian. Yet his moments of crisis and kairos have points in common with Hegel's antithetical turning points and Weber's *Weichensteller*, which he described in terms of a railway metaphor, in which a pointsman shunted the train onto a new track, with the effect of producing new world imageries.

There is an ambiguity in Koselleck's historical philosophy on this point, since there is an underlying thought of a social pathology as the consequence of our Hobbesian heritage, a pathology, or pathogenesis, as was the term that Koselleck used, which at the end seems to be mortal. This long-term determinism undermines the openness of the crisis concept in the same way as Weber's thought of disenchantment at the end closed down the scope of action of the *Weichensteller*.[32] Koselleck indicated the possibility of the end of modernity when experiences of disappointment caught up with the expectations invested in the design of big projects like liberalism and democracy, which were his historical examples, when the experiences of disappointment led to the investment of expectations in fascism and Nazism. His example for the future in the mid-1970s was, as we have seen, socialism and communism, of course, not the 'really existing' in the Soviet Union, but those existing in the dreams of the '1968' generation in the West.

The acceleration of time logically points to the end of teleology. However, the question must be at once whether this development will not at a certain point provoke the emergence of a new strong utopia, and at the same time if it is not the case that the prognosis of a final overstretch of the gap between experiences and expectations does not in itself contain an apocalyptic image rather than the cease of modernity.

The field which nurtured openness in history was for both Hegel and Koselleck the civil society of social conflicts and tensions, and of social work on coming to terms with them through critique, revolutions, reforms and a search for compromises. Civil society was the motor of modernity. The strife there contained the key to openness and contingency. The strife produced goals for the future organization of civil society, but, *nota bene*, goals in the plural. Hegel did not prognosticate how the conflict between the rich rabble and those poor organized as a protesting rabble would end. He only talked about the possibility of the slave through the mastery of his labour to use it as a weapon against his master. Koselleck was keen to emphasize history in the plural, which also means teleologies in the plural. Hegel did not emphasize such plurality, but he had not experienced the 150 years of past constructions of futures that lay between him and Koselleck. The openness of historical time that Koselleck, more than Hegel, leaves behind is teleologies in the plural rather than the eradication of all teleology. The openness is not total. Not least Koselleck's anthropological categories, among them experiences and expectations, set limits to the openness.

Finally, there is another aspect to the discussion of Reinhart Koselleck on this point, which provokes the question of the possible limits of his project, the possibility that his theory itself is becoming a historical category. This aspect, which links to Koselleck's argument about a possible end of modernity, deals with the potential of an end to intelligible history as a consequence of the digital revolution. This potential cannot be discussed in any depth but can only be indicated here.

Recent contributions to the debate on accelerating time argue that the digital revolution since the 1990s has speeded up to hyper-acceleration, unique in the history of humankind and making the acceleration in the wake of industrialization look comfortable. The acceleration of the circulation of commodities, persons and messages after the transition from the hippo-mobile to the steam, oil and electricity eras was enormous but nothing in comparison to the era of global electronic momentary transmission. The argument has been brought forward that the digital-based hypermodern historicity regime is leading to a radical separation between the acceleration of social life which is getting ever more intense, multiple and diverse, and the political expectation. After the old reiterative

Aristotelian, the Christian eschatological, the modern temporal teleological regimes of historicity the contours of a fourth regime take form, the a-teleological a-temporal.[33]

The growth of information and hyper-acceleration of time makes it ever more difficult to survey and translate experiences into politically viable expectations through critique. The open society becomes intransparent. Democracy becomes post-democracy. In a certain sense transparency seems to be increasing (Google, Facebook, Wikileaks, the unmasking of the National Security Agency (NSA)). The *topos* of information overload is old, widespread after the printing press revolution, but the argument is convincing that the present digital era has given the *topos* a whole new quality. A crucial question is what transparency means in the digital era. The 'reading' of hyper-increasing masses of information is ever more delegated to technical tools; algorithms, which scan the information before a selection is handed over to human scrutiny. The hybridization of the technical and the human indicates a kind of post-humanism alien to Koselleck's project. The distinction between transparency and instransparency is in crucial respects a matter of technology. We are so far only at the beginning of the exploration of the question of what the digital technology means for the question of openness in history.

These arguments for a new regime of historicity, or, better, for the collapse of the sequences of regimes of historicity, should be related to Reinhart Koselleck's statement before the digital revolution of a possible end of modernity with reference to future disappointments in the wake of a possible breakthrough of '1968'. The gap between experiences and expectations has broadened to such an extent that the relations are overstretched, whereby experiences have difficulty to generate expectations any more, and political decision-making collapses into extremely narrow presentism. There is a risk that the narrowing scope for imaginative and creative politics leads to political paralysis and inability to act. The urgent question that emerges in the wake of Koselleck's approach, and the digital revolution after him, is whether/how we can transcend the closure between political paralysis and future-orientated action.

Notes

1. Louis Dupré, 'Kant's Theory of History and Progress', in *The Review of Metaphysics* 51 (June 1998), no. 4, pp. 813–28.
2. Reinhart Koselleck, ' "Erfahrungsraum" und "Erwartungshorizont" – zwei historische Kategorien', in Reinhart Koselleck, *Vergangene Zukunft: Zur Semantik geschichtlicher Zeiten*, Frankfurt am Main: Suhrkamp, 1979, pp. 349–75, here pp. 371–2.
3. Ibid., pp. 362–3.
4. Ibid., pp. 364–5.
5. Immanuel Kant, 'Idea for a Universal History from a Cosmopolitan Point of View', Sixth Thesis, in H. S. Reiss, *Kant*, Cambridge: Cambridge University Press, 1991 [1784] (Texts in the History of Political Thought, 2nd edn), pp. 41–53.
6. Robert Bernasconi, 'Hegel at the Court of Ashanti', in Stuart Barnett, ed., *Hegel after Derrida*, London: Routledge, 1998, pp. 43, 58–60.

7. Karl Löwith, *Von Hegel zu Nietzsche: Der revolutionäre Bruch im Denken des neunzehnten Jahrhunderts*, Hamburg: Meiner, 1995 [New York, 1941], pp. 40–3.
8. Susan Buck-Morss, *Hegel, Haiti and Universal History*, Pittsburgh: University of Pittsburgh Press, 2009.
9. Georg Wilhelm Friedrich Hegel, *Werke in zwanzig Bänden. Band 19. Vorlesungen über die Geschichte der Philosophie. B. Indische Philosophie*, Frankfurt am Main: Suhrkamp, 1979, pp. 147–50. I am grateful for comments by Etienne Balibar on this point.
10. I am grateful to Thomas Hopkins for comments on this point.
11. Cord Riechelmann, review in *Frankfurter Allgemeine Sonntagszeitung*, 25 September 2011, p. 30 of Susan Buck-Morss, *Hegel, Haiti and Universal History*, and Frank Ruda, *Hegels Pöbel: Eine Untersuchung der Grundlinien der Philosophie des Rechts mit einem Vorwort von Slavoj Žižek*, Konstanz: Konstanz University Press, 2011 (Engl transl. *Hegel's Rabble: An Investigation into Hegel's Philosophy of Right [with a preface by Slavoj Žižek]*, London: Continuum, 2011).
12. Riechelmann, *Frankfurter Allgemeine Sonntagszeitung*, 25 September 2011, p. 30.
13. I am grateful to Henning Trüper for comments on this point as well as in general on earlier versions of the paper with many important observations and suggestions.
14. Ruda, *Hegels Pöbel*.
15. Georg Wilhelm Friedrich Hegel, *Gesammelte Werke. Band 14, Grundlinien der Philosophie des Rechts. 3, Anhang*, eds Klaus Grotsch and Elisabeth Weisser-Lohmann, Hamburg: Meiner, 2011 [1820], §§ 182–3.
16. Dylan J. Riley, *The Civic Foundations of Fascism in Europe: Italy, Spain, and Romania, 1870–1945*, Baltimore: Johns Hopkins University Press, 2010.
17. Reinhart Koselleck, *Critique and Crisis: Enlightenment and the Pathogenesis of Modern Society*, Cambridge, Mass.: MIT Press, 1988 [1959]. This section is based on Hagen Schulz-Forberg and Bo Stråth, *The Political History of European Integration: The Hypocrisy of Democracy-through-market*, London: Routledge, 2010.
18. Koselleck clearly saw the close etymological and semantic connection between crisis and hypocrisy. He elaborated on this connection in his theory. Hypocrisy comes from the Greek ὑπόκρισις, *hypokrisis*, which means play-acting, acting out, feigning or dissembling. The word is an amalgam of the Greek prefix *hypo-*, meaning 'under', and the verb *krinein*, just referred to, meaning to sift or decide. Thus the original meaning of hypocrisy was closely connected to the crisis concept, implying a deficiency in the ability to shift or decide. *Hypokrisis* as 'play-acting', the assumption of a counterfeiter, gives the modern word hypocrisy its negative connotation. The orator Demosthenes ridiculed his rival Aeschines, who had been a successful actor before taking up politics, as a *hypokrites* whose skill at impersonating characters on stage made him an untrustworthy politician. Hypocrisy is the act of pretending to have beliefs, opinions and qualities that one does not actually have. Hypocrisy is thus a kind of lie. Hypocrisy may come from a desire to hide from others actual motives or feelings. The German synonym *Heuchelei* comes from an old verb that means to duck, to press close against somebody, and means in a transferred sense not to show one's real intention. *Scheinheiligkeit* connotes sham, pretence or false piety, sanctimoniousness or canting, pretending to be something that one actually is not. Hypocrisy is not simply an inconsistency between speech and act. Failure or lack of courage or capacity to undertake what one wishes to do oneself or recommends to others is not hypocrisy. There is a connotation of self-care but also of self-deception and self-doubt, of glossing over, which Freud would likely have labelled repression. Without these connotations hypocrisy would simply be cynicism, or escapism from reality. Hypocrisy is a method of trying to cope with a loss of control and as such constitutes an alternative to escapism, or, perhaps, a special form of escapism.

19. Koselleck, *Vergangene Zukunft*, pp. 354–5.
20. Koselleck, *Vergangene Zukunft*, p. 355.
21. Koselleck, *Vergangene Zukunft*, p. 356. Koselleck borrowed the washing machine metaphor from Christian Meier, the historian on the ancient world.
22. Koselleck, *Vergangene Zukunft*, p. 368.
23. Koselleck, *Vergangene Zukunft*, p. 374.
24. Francis Fukuyama, *The End of History and the Last Man*, New York: Free Press, 1992. The content of this book is much more nuanced than the title suggests. The title was more a reflection of a *Zeitgeist* at the time of the collapse of the Soviet empire than of the content.
25. E. C. White, *Kaironomia: On the Will to Invent*, Ithaca: Cornell University Press, 1987.
26. Paul Tillich, ed., *Philosophie und Schicksal: Schriften zur Erkenntnislehre und Existenzphilosophie. Gesammelte Werke. Band IV*, Stuttgart: Evangelisches Verlagswerk, 1961; id., ed., *Der Widerstreit von Raum und Zeit: Schriften zur Geschichtsphilosophie. Gesammelte Werke. Bd VI*, Stuttgart: Evangelisches Verlagswerk, 1963.
27. Helge Jordheim, 'Conceptual History between Chronos and Kairos. The Case of "Empire"', in *Redescriptions: Yearbook of Political Thought and Conceptual History* 11 (2007), pp. 115–45.
28. Ibid., p. 137. See also several of the essays in Reinhart Koselleck, *Vergangene Zukunft*.
29. Niklas Olsen, *History in the Plural: An Introduction to the Work of Reinhart Koselleck*, New York: Berghahn, 2012. Cf. review of Olsen by Martin Woessner in *American Historical Review* 118 (2013), no. 1, pp. 150–1.
30. Reinhart Koselleck, 'Über die Theoriebedürftigkeit der Geschichtswissenschaft', in id., *Zeitschichten: Studien zur Historik*, Frankfurt am Main: Suhrkamp, 2000, p. 307. Cf. Bo Stråth, 'Review of Reinhart Koselleck (2000), *Zeitschichten. Studien zur Historik mit einem Beitrag von Hans-Georg Gadamer*', in *European Journal of Social Theory* 4 (2001).
31. Hans Erich Bödeker, 'Aufklärung über Aufklärung? Reinhart Kosellecks Interpretation der Aufklärung', in Carsten Dutt and Reinhard Laube, eds, *Zwischen Sprache und Geschichte: Zum Werk Reinhart Kosellecks*, Göttingen: Wallstein, 2013, pp. 128–74. I am grateful to Hans Erich Bödeker for having let me read his manuscript and for discussions on this point.
32. However, there was a tension in Weber's thought between his dystopical analysis of the bureaucratization process and his conjecture about the return of 'traditional' values or the charismatic emergence of new prophets, that is the old *Weichensteller* did not necessarily disappear.
33. Alexandre Escudier, ' "Temporalisation" et modernité politique: penser avec Reinhart Koselleck', in *Annales* 64 (2009), no. 6, pp. 269–301; Hartmut Rosa, *Beschleunigung: Die Veränderung der Zeitstruktur in der Moderne*, Frankfurt am Main: Suhrkamp, 2005; Heinz Dieter Kittsteiner, 'Einheit im Pluralismus: Wie kann Geschichtstheorie widersprüchliche Zeitvorstellungen verbinden?', in E. Schulz and W. Sonne, eds, *Kontinuität und Wandel: Geschichtsbilder in verschiedenen Fächern und Kulturen*, Zurich: vdf Hochschulverlag, 1999; Alexandre Escudier and Ingrid Holtey, 'Das Tempo des Lebens: Zeitstrukturen und Zeitwahrnehmungen', in *Trivium*, http://trivium.revues.org/4105 (accessed 13 March 2015).

INDEX

'1843 Manuscript' (Marx) 235

Abensour, Miguel 235, 242, 243–4
Abicht, Johann Heinrich 217, 218
abolitionist movement 253, 263–7
Aborigines 100
absolute justice/rights 217, 226, 239
abyss motif, in Scholem's poetry 287, 289
Académie des Sciences 83
Acts of the Apostles 135–6
Adas, Michael 29–30
Adolph Bermpohl (lifeboat) 127
Adorno, Theodor W. 91
Afghans 32–3
Africa 344
Agathon (Wieland) 50, 54–5
Ahmadis 314
Akbar, Emperor 33–4
al-Qaeda 302, 314, 316–19
Alam II, Shah 172, 178
Alliance shipwreck 121, 130
Alsberg, Paul 93, 102–7, 108
Alvarez, Alejandro 227
Amazonas 346
America *see* North America; Spanish America; United States
America emblem (Ripa) 190, 191
American Anti-Slavery Society 263, 264
Amphitrite shipwreck 121–2, 132
ancient history 17
Angostura Congress 199
animism 99
antagonistic historicities 15
antediluvians 83
anthropogenesis 97–101, 103–8
anthropology 89–113
anti-colonial movement 30
anti-slavery movement 253, 263–7
antinomian tradition 238, 275, 293
antiquarianism 10
apocalyptic time 257, 347
apostasy 291
Argentina 200–1
Aristotle 4
Augustine of Hippo (Aurelius Augustinus) 257–8
Aurangzeb 168, 175, 177, 179
Austin, John 223
Australian Aborigines 100

'autolimitation' theory 218
automaton parable 14
autonomy 217–18, 331–4
    see also free will
Azad, Abdul Kalam 310

BAAS *see* British Association for the Advancement of Science
Bacon, Francis 4
Badayuni, 'Abdul Qadir 33, 34
Baker, Richard 174
Baleswar Samvad Bahika (newspaper) 158
banditry 27
Baptist missionary narratives 143–7
Baqir Najm-i Sani, Muhammad 176
Barani, Ziauddin 176
barbarism 201
baroque tragedy 132–4
Barreda, Ignacio Mariá 194
Barros, João de 36
Barthes, Roland 160, 161
Beaumont, Élie de 78
Being and Time (Heidegger) 14, 15
Ben-Ezer, Ehud 295
Benjamin, Walter 13–15, 132–4, 282
Bermpohl, Adolph 120, 121, 134–5
'Bestimmung des Menschen' 49–70
Betrachtung über die Bestimmung des Menschen (Spalding) 52–3
Bhanja, Upendra 152
bibechana (judgement) 149, 150, 151–2
Bible 256–61, 267–8, 292–3
    Acts of the Apostles 135–6
    Book of Daniel 257–8, 260–1
    Book of Revelations 257
    Flood 72, 76, 77
    literal interpretation of 72
'Bildung' concept 55–7, 60–1, 62
bin Laden, Osama 316–19
biological reductionism 89
biology 94
Blanckenburg, Friedrich von 54
Blumenberg, Hans 89, 102, 105–6, 108, 128–9
Bluntschli, Johann Caspar 221
Bödeker, Hans Erich 356–7
Bolívar, Simón 198, 199–200, 205–6
Borkum 121
Boucher de Perthes, Jacques 83

Index

Boulogne-sur-Mer 118, 121–2
bourgeoisie 241
Brahma Dharma movement 159
Brandt, Reinhard 57
Brazil, Canudos War 26–8, 30
Brenner, Michael 286
Breton, Stanislas 238–9
Bretschneider, Karl Gottlieb 57
Breusing, Arthur 135–6
Bridgewater Treatises 72–3, 76, 77, 79–80
Britain
    Empire 168–9, 172, 345
    geological studies 71
    God's gifts 83
    libertarians 73
    lifeboat associations 122, 123, 125
British Association for the Advancement of Science (BAAS) 72, 80
Brown, John 253, 264, 265–7, 268
Büchner, Ludwig 59
Buck-Morss, Susan 345, 346
Buckland, William 72–3, 75–84
Burke, Edmund 324–5

Caister-on-Sea 122
Calvin, John 260–1, 265
Canudos War 26–8, 30
capitalism 327–9, 330
Caracas 195–6
Cardozo, Avraham 289, 296
Carr, E.H. 225
Cassese, Antonio 213
castas (free men of colour) 193–7, 202, 203
Castoriadis, Cornelius 333
catastrophism 76
Catholic anthropology 203
Catholic Church 293
Catrou, Francis 179
caudillos (warlords) 200
causa finalis, final cause 3–4, 10–11, 21, 50, 57, 94
causation 4
Cellarius, Christoph 258
Certeau, Michel de 148
César, Moreira 27
Chakrabarty, Dipesh 325, 336
Chambers, Robert 80
'character' and history 171–81
Chartists 80–1
chemistry 94
chess automaton parable 14
China, Taiping Rebellion 28–9
Christ 311
Christianity
    antinomian tradition 238
    concept of history 256–60
    and human nature 58
    Marx's analysis of 237–8
    missionary narratives 143, 144–5, 146, 147
    Puritanism 260–7
    sea rescue organizations 123, 131
    see also Bible
chronos 354, 355, 356
chronotopes 193
Cieszkowski, August 241
civil society 348, 353, 358
civilization 98–9, 157, 169–71, 197, 200–3, 221, 230, 307–8
class struggle 327–9
    see also social hierarchy/order
classical antiquity 17
coats of arms 189–93
Cohn, Norman 406
Cold War 352
collectivism 332, 335
Colombia 189–93, 198, 199
Colombian Academy of History 189–93
Colonialism
    Cuttack narratives 143–65
    Darwin, Darwinism 92, 99–101, 108
    European 29–30, 333
    Hegel on 345
    historiography 15–16, 143–65
    Indian national history 167–85
    international law and 221
    Orissa narratives 143–65
    precolonial histories 153
    resistance to 30
    sentimental histories 145–7
    settler 276–7
colour symbolism 61
Columbus, Christopher 36
communism 238, 240, 312, 329, 352
Communist Manifesto (Marx and Engels) 240, 329
Comte, Auguste 99, 246
Congregationalism 265
Conselheiro, Antônio 26–7, 31
Contest of Faculties (Kant) 8
contingent teleology 107–8
'Der Corsetten-Fritz' (Panizza) 63
cosmopolitan law 217, 218
Creoles 194–5, 198–9
crisis concept 348–54
Critique and Crisis: Enlightenment and the Pathogenesis of Modern Society (Koselleck) 349–50, 352, 357
'Critique of Hegel's Philosophy of Right' (Marx) 235–40, 242, 244
Critique of Judgment (Kant) 7, 94
Critique of Pure Reason (Kant) 216

Index

crocodiles 75
Cromwell, Oliver 38
Cuba 204–5
cultural evolution 107
cultural sciences 96
culture 96, 98–9, 107
Cunha, Euclides da 27–8, 30, 39
Cuttack, historical narratives 143–65
Cuvier, Georges 72, 74, 75

Danae (*Agathon*) 54–5
Daniel, Book of 257–8, 260–1
Danto, Arthur C. 50
Darwin, Charles 62, 92, 95, 97–8, 100–1, 107
Das, Chittranjan 169–70
Das, Harcharan 177
Dasein (being-there) 15
Declaration of the Rights of Nations 217
'Declaration of Sentiments' (Garrison) 263, 264
Degeyter, Adolphe 238
Deluge, biblical 72, 76, 77
democracy 189–211, 242–3, 333, 335, 353
demos 242, 243, 244
Descent of Man (Darwin) 92, 97, 98
'destiny' and history 171–4
digital revolution 359
Dilthey, Wilhelm 97
diluvial theory 76
Dinakrusna Dasa 152
Diponegoro, Prince 30
divine providence 83
Dobruska, Moshe 294, 296
Dr Strangelove (Kubrick, dir.) 25–6, 41
Dudley Caverns 82–3
Duhem, Pierre 134

early humans 77–8, 79, 83, 84, 104, 105
earth science 71–87
Ehrlich, Johann Nepomuk 58
end of history 257, 353
    see also eschatology; political eschatology
Engel, Manfred 56
Engels, Friedrich 329
English General Baptist Missionary Society 144
Enlightenment 6, 49–70, 349, 356
entelechy 4
Erasmus, Dediderius 36
eschatology 5, 254–6, 268
    see also political eschatology
ethnic diversity/fusion, Spanish America 189–211
Eurocentrism 16, 260, 347
Europe 16–17, 99, 123, 236–7, 255, 304, 307–9, 343–7
    Christian teleological thought 256–60
    colonialism 29–30, 333

historical writing 143, 154, 160, 174
international law 219–20
modernity 330–3
socio-political philosophy 323–38
evolution theory 62, 84, 89, 95, 97–101
exile, Jewish history 276–9, 283, 295
expectations and experiences 351, 352, 359
extermination policies, Spanish America 201
extinctions 76

Facundo: Civilization and Barbarism (Sarmiento) 200
Faizi 34
Fall of the Mughal Empire (Sarkar) 167–85
federalism 218, 341
federation of nations (*Völkerbund*) 341
Ferdinand of Aragon 35
Feuerbach, Ludwig 58–9, 61–2, 240
Fichte, Johann Gottlieb 95, 241
fictional narratives 13, 49–70
final cause, *causa finalis* 3–4, 10–11, 21, 50, 57, 94
Flood, biblical 72, 76, 77
footnotes 156–7
'Fossil Man' 79
fossil record 71, 72, 75, 79, 80
foundation myths, Zionism 276–9
France
    Declaration of the Rights of Nations 217
    'Gallic cock' 236
    Revolution 8, 238, 259, 332
    sea rescue organizations 117–18, 123–4
Frank, Jacob 293–4
Frankism 283, 293–4
'A Frankist's Career: Moshe Dobruska and His Metamorphoses' (Scholem) 294
free will 58, 324–5, 331
    see also autonomy
freedom 9
French Revolution 8, 238, 259, 332
Frey, Sigmund (Moshe Dobruska) 294
Friedmann, Wolfgang 222
fundamentalism, Islam 313–14
Funkenstein, Amos 283

Gajapatis 150
'Gallic cock' 236
Gandhi, Mahatma 137, 310
Garrison, William Lloyd 263, 265
Gehlen, Arnold 91, 102, 103
Genesis, literal interpretation of 72
Geoffroy Saint-Hilaire, Étienne 73–5, 76
geology 71–87
Geology and Mineralogy (Buckland) 76, 77, 79–80
Gerhard, Paul 62

365

Index

Germany
    as 'anachronistic' state 245
    bourgeoisie 241
    Enlightenment 49–70, 357
    metaphysical guilt 315
    philosophical anthropology 89–113
    science and teleology 93–7
    sea rescue organizations 120–1, 134–5
    social democracy 328
    Third Reich 259–60
Gibbon, Edward 150–1
globalization 226, 230, 334, 346, 354
Gnosticism 291, 292
Godlikeness 57
Goethe, Johann Wolfgang von 55–7, 351
Gómez de Avellaneda, Gertrudis 204–5
Greathead, Henry 122
Grotius, Hugo 213–14
Der grüne Heinrich (Keller) 59–62
Gudin, Théodore 119
guilt 315–16, 318–19
Gush Emunim 280, 281

Habermas, Jürgen 91–2
Haeckel, Ernst 62
Haiti 204, 345–7
Halakhah (Jewish law) 281–2, 290
Hali, Altaf Husain 305–7, 312
Halperin, David 296
Haneberg, Daniel Bonifacius 58
happiness 52, 216, 226
Harpers Ferry raid 253, 266, 267
Hartmann, Nicolai 108
Hasidism 283, 284
Hegel, Georg Wilhelm Friedrich
    civil society 358
    idealization of 345–7
    Islam 312
    Marx's critique of 235, 236–40, 242, 244
    philosophy of history 9–10, 340, 343–8, 358
    philosophy of right 347–8
    rabble concept 347–8, 358
    society–state dichotomy 348
    and teleology 95
    turning points concept 343–5
Heidegger, Martin 14, 15
Heine, Heinrich 132, 241
Heinrich (*Der grüne Heinrich*) 59–62
Helmholtz, Hermann von 95
Heraclitus 172
Herder, Johann Gottfried 259
hermeneutics 291
Hieronymus, Eusebius 257, 258, 259, 261
Hillary, William 117, 118–19, 123, 125, 126, 131
Hinduism 31, 147, 153, 310

Hippias (*Agathon*) 54, 55
historical facts 96
historical future 4, 8–9, 16, 127, 193, 214, 225, 230, 245, 262, 307, 323, 334–6, 339–42, 348–56
historical time 13–16, 133, 136, 245, 347, 351–9
historical writing 11–14, 16, 50, 124
    European 143, 154, 160, 174
'historicism' 14, 136
historicity 3–4, 10–17, 119–20, 123–8, 131–7, 194, 206, 239, 245, 358–9
historiography
    bibechana procedure 149, 150, 151–2
    and colonial/evangelical regimes 143–65
    disinterested judgement 157–8
    pastoral historiography 144–5, 147
    taula procedure 150
history
    nature of 10–13
    philosophies of 6–11, 13–16, 128, 133, 254, 259–60, 326–8, 332–3, 342, 353–4
    see also Hegel; Kant; Marx
History of Urissa: Itihasa Sarasangraha (Sutton) 143, 148–9
Hobbes, Thomas 223, 357
Holy Roman Empire 258, 259, 261
homecoming theme, novels 61
Hong Xiuquan 29
Hospitaliers Bretons 123
Hossein, Gholam 173, 174, 175
human sciences 97
humanity
    animal differences/similarities 100, 103
    evolutionary development 97–101, 103–8
    intellect 106, 107
    Islamic representation of 301–20
    nature of 6–8, 52–3, 58, 89–93, 107–8
    subject of history 301–2
    vocation of 49–70
    see also early humans
Husserl, Edmund 101

Iberian messianism 35–8
Ichthyosaurus 75
Idea for a Universal History with a Cosmopolitan Purpose (Kant) 8, 324, 341
Idel, Moshe 285
idiographic research 96
Illahabadi, Akbar 310
India
    British rule 168–9, 172, 345
    colonial historiography 143–65
    Islam 304–8
    Marathas 181
    missionary narratives 143, 144–5, 146, 147
    Mughals 33–4, 167–85

national history 167–85
nationalism 170, 171
Orissa narratives 143–65
Indians, Spanish America 201
individual rights 227
Industrial Revolution 333
information overload 359
Innocent III, Pope 259
intellect 106, 107
international law 213–34
  absolute justice/rights 217, 226, 239
  anti-teleology 223–5, 229–30
  'autolimitation' theory 218
  autonomy 217–18
  and colonialism 221
  cosmopolitan law 217, 218
  domestic law 218
  external teleologies 219–23, 229, 230
  functionalist approach 225
  globalization 226
  'harmony of interests' myth 225
  hyper-teleology 225–8, 229, 230
  'idealists' and 'realists' 214
  individual rights 227
  internal teleologies 215–19, 229, 230
  Kantian thought 216–19
  law of nations 216
  liberal reform 221
  'Oriental' cultures 221
  public opinion 224
  slavery 220
  'sociability' concept 214, 215
  sociological movement 222
  sovereignty 218, 222
  United States 223
  universal laws 217
  'unsocial sociability' principle 219
  utopianism 229
  Westphalia 'myth' 214
Iqbal, Muhammad 308–13
Iran 34, 38
Iraq War 317, 352
Irvine, William 173–6
Islam 301–20
  decline narrative 304–13
  fundamentalism 313–14
  martyrdom 315, 316
  militancy 302–4, 316–19
  natural law 305
  terrorism 302–3, 314–19
  ummah 306, 307, 308, 312
Isma'il, Shah 34
Israel
  secularization 279–81
  see also Jewish history; Zionism

Jagannatha Dasa 151–2
Jagannatha temple 147
Jamaat-e Islami 314
Jannidis, Fotis 56, 57
Jaspers, Karl 315–16
Javid Khan 177
Jawab-e Shikwah (Iqbal) 310–11
Jerusalem scholars 278–9
Jesus Christ 311
Jewish history 35, 38, 275–99
  Halakhah 281–2, 290
  Jerusalem School 278–9
  as 'mythology of prolepsis' 284–5
  see also Judaism; Zionism
João I 35–6
João III 37
John, St 257
Johnson, Lyndon B. 25
journey theme, novels 61
Judaism
  Kabbalah 238, 280–5, 291
  messianism 239–40, 275–99
  see also Jewish history
July revolution (1830) 344

Kabbalah 238, 280–5, 291
kairos 354–6
Kalapahad 151
Kant, Immanuel
  anthropology 90–1
  autonomy 331, 332
  federation of nations 341
  international law 216–19
  philosophy of history 7–10, 324–6, 327, 334, 340–3
  science 93–5, 96
  temporality 332
Kara, Viswanatha 158
Karana Kundala 155
Kaufmann, Erich 224
kavya (Oriya poetry) 151
Keene, Henry George 179
Keller, Gottfried 59–62
Kelsen, Hans 218
Khan, Syed Ahmed 304–5
Khrushchev, Nikita Sergeyevich 351
Khusrau, Amir 178
Kook, Avraham Yizhak HaCohen 279–81
Koran 304, 305, 310–11
Koselleck, Reinhart 340, 347, 348–54
Kraft und Stoff (Büchner) 59
Kubrick, Stanley 25–6
Kurze populäre Widerlegung... (brochure) 59

Lamarck, Jean-Baptiste 73–4, 75
Landes, Richard 41

Index

language
    animal/human similarities 100
    cultural evolution 107
    'linguistic palaeontology' 98
Lasson, Adolf 224
Latin America *see* Spanish America
law
    Halakhah 281–2, 290
    of nations 216, 218, 220
    natural law 215, 216, 220, 223, 226–7, 305
    rule of law 9, 213
    see also international law
Le Mercier de la Rivière, Paul-Pierre 226, 227
legalism 218
Lehmann, Hartmut 254
Leibniz, Gottfried Wilhelm 5
Leviathan (Hobbes) 223
lex parsimoniae ('nature takes the shortest way') 7
liberal democracy 353
liberal internationalism 222
life, purpose of 53
life writing 146
lifeboat associations 117–41
    foundational histories 126, 127
    heroization of lifeboatmen 125, 126
    historicity of 119–20, 123–8, 131–7
    lifeboat technology 127
    success of 129
Lincoln, Abraham 267
'linguistic palaeontology' 98
literary education 156
literature, German Enlightenment 49–70
lizards 75
Lurianic Kabbalah 283, 284
Luxemburg, Rosa 329
Lyell, Charles 84

Maclean, Derryl N. 33
Madalapanji Rajacaritra 153
Mahdawis 32–3, 34
Maimonides 288
mankind *see* humanity
Marathas 181
Marranos 289
Martens, Georg Friedrich von 220
Martí, José 205
martyrdom, Islam 315, 316
Marx, Karl
    and antinomian tradition 238
    class struggle 327–9, 347
    crisis theory 350
    philosophy of history 235–50, 334
    temporality 332
Maududi, Abdul Ala 314
'Media In Vita' (Scholem) 287, 289

Mediterranean messianism 35–8
'Melancholy Redemption' (Scholem) 287, 289
Menasseh ben Israel 38
Mendelssohn, Moses 340–1
messianism 14, 29–31, 35–8, 40–1, 235–50, 275–99, 307, 310
metaphysical guilt 315–16, 318–19
militancy, Islam 302–4, 316–19
military discipline 180
Mill, James 224
millenarianism 25–45
miscegenation 200–3
misogyny 178
missionary narratives 143, 144–5, 146, 147
modernity 17, 253–73, 330–3, 358
Moeller van den Bruck, Arthur 260
Moisset, Mr 130
'monads' 5
monarchy, monarch 26–7, 36–8, 41, 81–2, 125, 193–4, 216, 237, 241–3, 261, 268, 341
monkeys 79
monogenesis 99
Mora, Jose María Luis 206
Morais, Prudente de 26
Moretti, Franco 144
Morgenthau, Hans 225
Moros Urbina, Ricardo 189
Morse Code 131
Moses 261
Mughals 33–4, 167–85
Muhammad Jaunpuri, Sayyid 32
Muhammad, Prophet 311
mulattoes 195, 196, 198
Musaddas dar Madd-o Jazr-e Islam (Hali) 305–7, 312
Muslims *see* Islam

Najaf Khan, Mirza 180
Napoleon Bonaparte 346
Narrative of the Mission to Orissa (Sutton) 143–7
narrative schemes 13, 49–70
Nasir Khan 175
Natalia (*Wilhelm Meisters Lehrjahre*) 57
nation-states 277
National Institution for the Preservation of Life from Shipwreck 117
National Socialism 105, 260
nationalism 170, 171, 276, 313
nationality 309
nature, natural 59, 96
    human *see* humanity
    law 215, 216, 220, 223, 226–7, 305
    philosophy 3–7, 10–11, 62, 256
    sciences 96

selection *see* evolution theory
    theology 72, 80
Nautik der Alten (Breusing) 135–6
Nazis 105, 260
Nebuchadnezzar's dream 257–8
Nehru, Jawaharlal 312
Netherlands, lifeboat heroism 125
New England Puritanism 262
Nietzsche, Friedrich 106–7
nihilism 293
nomothetic research 96
North America 197
    see also Spanish America; United States
novels, German Enlightenment 54–5, 59–61, 62
nuclear weapons 25

Odisara Itihasa (Pyarimohan Acharya) 143, 154–60
'On entering Douglas Bay' (Wordsworth) 131–2
ontology 5–6, 8–13, 15, 102, 124, 133, 246, 327, 352
Oran 130, 131
organicism, organism, organic 7, 12, 72–4, 80–1,
    94–6, 239, 243, 278–80
'Oriental' cultures 221
Orissa, historical narratives 143–65
Oriya language/literature 148–9, 151–2, 156, 159
Ottomans 34–5, 38, 276

paintings, *castas* 193–5
Pakistan 314
palaeontology 72
Palestinians 276, 277, 279
Paley, William 72
Panizza, Oskar 63
pardos (mulattoes) 195, 196, 198
Parker, Geoffrey 36–7
pastoral historiography 144–5, 147
Paul, St 135–6, 257
Peace of Westphalia 214
peasant rebellions 26–9
pedagogic discourses 160
Peggs, James 144, 145, 146–7
People's Charter 81
perfectibility 16, 55, 58, 62, 127–8, 265, 342–3
'Perpetual Peace' (Kant) 217
Peru 196
phenomenology 101
Philip II 36–7
philology 10, 134–5
philosophical anthropology 89–113
Philosophie zoologique (Lamarck) 74
philosophies of history *see* Hegel; history; Kant;
    Marx
physico-theology 5–6, 72
physics 4–7, 11, 14, 94
Physiocrats 226

Pleisosaurus 75
Plessner, Helmuth 91
poetry, Oriya 151–2
politics
    animal, *zoon politikon* 6, 108
    eschatology, religion 25–45, 239, 241, 254–64,
        268
    criticisms of concept 39
    definition 25
    philosophy, European 323–38
    the political (theoretical notion) 13–14, 104, 132,
        235, 238–47, 313–14, 326, 352
    relevance in contemporary society 40–1
    shifts in 41
    theology 275, 280, 282
Portugal, messianism 28, 35–8
Pottier, Eugène 238
poverty 347–8
Prataparudra 150
predestination 261–2
prehistoric humans 77–8, 79, 83, 84, 104, 105
Primitive Culture (Tylor) 97–101
progress 339, 340–5
proletariat 237–47
prophecies, biblical 256–61, 267–8
prophet 239–41, 314, 330
prophetic movements 29–31, 39
    see also millenarianism
Prophets of Rebellion (Adas) 29–30
The Protestant Ethic (Weber) 330
Protestantism 237, 330
providentialism, Indian history 167, 168–71, 180–1
public opinion, international law 224
Pufendorf, Samuel 215, 216, 223
Puritanism 260–7
Pyarimohan Acharya 143, 154–60, 161

Qasim, Muhammad 178
Qing dynasty 29
Quesnay, François 226–7
Quran 304, 305, 310–11

rabble concept 347–8, 358
racial diversity/fusion, Spanish America 189–211
Rajwade, Viswanath Kashinath 180
Ray, Radhanatha 155
Raz-Krakotzkin, Amnon 278–81
readers of history 148–9, 152–3, 156, 157–8, 160
Realizing Utopia (Cassese) 213
Realphilologie 135
'Redemption through Sin' (Scholem) 290–3
religion 31, 40, 72, 80, 148, 236–8, 305
    teleologies 253–73
    see also Christianity; Hinduism; Islam; Judaism;
        Zoroastrianism

Index

'republican messianism' 41
Republican Party 266–7
republicanism 41, 190, 196, 243, 263, 341–2
rescue organizations *see* sea rescue organizations
Reuveni, David 37–8
Revelations, Book of 257
'revitalization movements' 29–30
revolution, Marx's philosophy of history 235–50
'revolutionary attentism' 328
Rickert, Heinrich 96
rights, absolute/individual 217, 226, 227, 239
Rijkers, Dorus 125
Ripa, Cesare 190, 191
riti (Oriya poetry) 152
RNLI *see* Royal National Lifeboat Institution
Rodríguez, Simón 196–7
Roman Empire 258–9
Roy, Rammohun 169, 170
royal 'characters' 174–5
Royal National Lifeboat Institution (RNLI) 125
Ruda, Frank 347–8
rule of law 9, 213

Sab (Gómez de Avellaneda) 204–5
Sabbatianism 283, 289, 290–3
sacred chronology 72
sacrifice 123, 127–8, 137, 310, 313–16, 318–19
Safavid dynasty 34, 38
salvation history 255–6, 268
Samper, José María 201–2, 203, 205
Sarkar, Jadunath 167–85
    'character' and history 171–81
    providentialist thinking 168–71, 180–1
Sarmiento, Domingo Faustino 200–1
saurians 75
Scelle, Georges 221–2
Scheinfeld, Franz Thomas (Moshe Dobruska) 294
Scheler, Max 90, 91
Schelling, Friedrich Wilhelm Joseph von 95
Schiller, Friedrich 56
Schlegel, Friedrich 342
Schmerling, Philippe-Charles 77–8
Schmidt, Christoph 282
Schmitt, Carl 91, 282
Schnädelbach, Herbert 95, 101–2
Scholem, Gershom 275–99
    messianism of 285–9
    poetry 286–8
Scholem, Reinhold 291
science 93–7, 352
scientific method 94
Scott, James C. 39
Scottish Enlightenment 6
SCSN *see* Société Centrale de Sauvetage des Naufragés

sea rescue organizations 117–41
    foundational histories 126, 127
    heroization of lifeboatmen 125, 126
    historicity of 124–5, 128, 133–4, 136–7
    lifeboat technology 127
    success of 129
seamen's missions 123
Sebastianism 28
Secord, James 80
secularization 5, 21, 39, 41, 80, 123, 136, 254–6, 260, 279–81, 308–9
security 316–17
Sedgwick, Adam 80
Sein und Zeit (Heidegger) 14, 15
self-determination 58
self-discipline 179–80
self-understanding 89
Sephardic Jews 38
sermons 82
Shakespeare, William 172–3
Shia Muslims 307
Shikwah (Iqbal) 310
Shipwreck with Spectator (Blumenberg) 128–9
shipwrecks
    artistic depictions 119
    metaphorical uses 128–9
    rescue organizations 117–41
Skinner, Quentin 284, 285
slavery/slaves 199, 202, 220, 264
    rebellions 204, 345
    see also abolitionist movement
Smith, Adam 10, 219
Smith, Roger 89
'sociability' concept 214, 215
social democracy 328
social determinism 332
social hierarchy/order 81–2, 83, 84
    see also class struggle
Société Centrale de Sauvetage des Naufragés (SCSN) 117–18, 119, 121
society–state dichotomy 348
socio-political philosophy, European 323–38
South America *see* Spanish America
sovereignty 218, 222, 243
Spain, messianism 36–7
Spalding, Johann Joachim 52–3, 55
Spanish America
    castas 193–5, 196, 197, 202, 203
    colonial abuses 198
    Creoles 194–5, 198, 199
    ethnic diversity/fusion 189–211
    extermination of Indians 201
    miscegenation 200–3
    mulattoes 195, 196

slavery 199, 202
social conflict 196
threats to republics 196
warlords 200
the state 277
Stein, Lorenz von 327
Steiner, George 295
storytelling 49–50, 90
Süleyman the Lawgiver 35
Sun Yat-sen 29
Sutton, Amos 143, 144–54, 161

Tagore, Rabindranath 170
Taiping Rebellion 28–9
taula (comparison) 150
technology 104, 127, 352
teleology 3–17, 39–40, 49–51, 54, 56–63, 89–90, 92–7, 99–102, 107–8, 120–1, 126–8, 136–7, 144, 147, 160, 193, 205–7, 214–15, 230, 235, 237, 245, 254–5, 284, 296, 304, 323–32, 334–5, 339–40, 354, 356–9
  anti-teleology (law) 223–5, 229–30
  crisis 62
  external teleologies (law) 219–23, 229, 230
  hyper-teleology (law) 225–8, 229, 230
  internal teleologies (law) 215–19, 229, 230
  narrative 13, 49–51, 54–6, 61, 92, 96, 126–7, 143–4, 147, 161, 202, 204–5
  project 3, 7, 11, 13, 16, 39–40, 120, 133, 149–50, 161, 193, 200, 203–4, 206–7, 225, 277–8, 284–5, 295–6, 358
  rejection of 330
  religion 253–73
Teleosaurus 75
temporality 3, 12, 14–15, 134, 193, 311, 332–3, 342, 355, 359
terrorism, Islam 302–3, 314–19
theology 5, 72, 80
Theorie des Romans (Blanckenburg) 54
'Theory and Practice' (Kant) 340
Theses on Feuerbach (Marx) 240
Third Reich 259–60
Thomas, George 177
Thousand Days' War, Colombia 189
Thucydides 350
Tillich, Paul 355
time, historical *see* historical time
Tocqueville, Alexis de 197, 327
Todorov, Tzvetan 40
tools, early human development 104, 105
Topham, Jonathan 80
totalitarianism 40
Tower Society (*Wilhelm Meisters Lehrjahre*) 56
tragedy 132–4
transcendental synthesis 246

translatio imperii (transfer of empire/imperial rule) 258, 259, 261
transmutation of species 73–5, 76, 80
Turgot, Anne-Robert-Jacques 350
Twilight of the Idols (Nietzsche) 107
Tylor, Edward Burnett 92, 97–101

ummah (Muslim community) 306, 307, 308, 312
United Nations (UN) 213, 214
United States (US)
  anti-slavery movement 253, 263–7
  international law 223
  Islamic terrorism 316, 317
  Puritanism 260–7
  Republican Party 266–7
  see also North America; Spanish America
universal laws 217
'unsocial sociability' principle 219, 325
use-inheritance 74
utilitarianism 82
Utkal Dipika (Oriya newspaper) 158
utopianism 54, 229

'Vae Victis – Or Death in the Professoriate' (Scholem) 287–8, 289
'values' problem 95–6
Vargas Llosa, Mario 27, 28
Vasconcelos, José 205
Vattel, Emerich de 216
Venezuela
  Caracas' Diocesan Synod 195
  Caracas' Royal Court 195–6
  mulattoes 198
Verelst, Harry 179
Vestiges of the Natural History of Creation (Chambers) 80
violence
  emancipation of slaves 267
  Islam 302–3, 314
  Mughal India 178
  and religious teleologies 253–73
virtue 49, 52–4, 172, 176, 196, 226, 305–6, 308–11, 314–15
vocation of man concept 49–70
Voegelin, Eric 241
Völkerbund (federation of nations) 341
Voltaire 6

War on Terror 352
Ward, Robert 220
warlords, Spanish America 200
Wasserstrom, Steven 286, 287, 288
weapons, early human development 104

371

Index

Weber, Max 329–30, 332, 334
Weltgeschichte (world history) 343–4, 346
Westphalia, Peace of 214
Whewell, William 93
Wieland, Christoph Martin 50, 54–5
Wildman, Richard 220
Wilhelm Meisters Lehrjahre (Goethe) 56–7
Windelband, Wilhelm 96, 97
Wissenschaft (science) 93–7
Wolff, Christian 3, 5
Wordsworth, William 131–2
World Fairs 329
world history (*Weltgeschichte*) 343–4, 346

Young, George 82

Zambos 203
al-Zawahiri, Ayman 302–4, 318
Zeno of Citium 128
Zevi, Sabbatai 282–3, 290, 291
Zionism 275–99
    cultural frameworks 280
    exile negation 276–9, 295
    foundation myth 276–9
    Israeli secularity 279–81
    and Jerusalem scholars 278–9
    right-wing ideology 280–1
    theology of 281–4
    see also Jewish history
zoon politikon see political animal
Zoroastrianism 31